—— 图 说 ——

中国医疗器械
注册申报法规
（第2版）

Illustrated Book of Regulations on
Medical Device Registration in China
（The second edition）

（中英文版）

本书编写组◎编写

Written by the writing group of this book

中国健康传媒集团

中国医药科技出版社

图书在版编目（CIP）数据

图说中国医疗器械注册申报法规：汉、英／国家药品监督管理局医疗器械技术审评中心编写 . — 2 版 . — 北京：中国医药科技出版社，2023.12

ISBN 978-7-5214-4164-2

Ⅰ . ①图… Ⅱ . ①国… Ⅲ . ①医疗器械—注册—申请—卫生法—中国—图解 Ⅳ . ① D922.164.04

中国国家版本馆 CIP 数据核字（2023）第 190538 号

美术编辑　　陈君杞
版式设计　　也　在

出版　**中国健康传媒集团** | 中国医药科技出版社

地址　北京市海淀区文慧园北路甲 22 号

邮编　100082

电话　发行：010-62227427　　邮购：010-62236938

网址　www.cmstp.com

规格　710×1000 mm $^{1}/_{16}$

印张　43

字数　595 千字

初版　2019 年 11 月第 1 版

版次　2023 年 12 月第 2 版

印次　2023 年 12 月第 1 次印刷

印刷　三河市万龙印装有限公司

经销　全国各地新华书店

书号　ISBN 978-7-5214-4164-2

定价　**198.00 元**

获取新书信息、投稿、为图书纠错，请扫码联系我们。

前　言

习近平总书记指出："药品安全责任重于泰山。保障药品安全是技术问题、管理工作，也是道德问题、民心工程。"在中国式现代化的新征程中，作为药品监管部门，始终以"四个最严"要求为根本遵循，立足职责、加强协同、汇聚合力，做好医疗器械安全的看门人、做好公众健康的守护者对推动医疗器械行业高质量发展至关重要。

过去五年，是我国医疗器械审评审批事业大成长、大发展、大进步的五年。五年来，我们始终坚持"以人民为中心，保护和促进公众健康"的初心使命，始终围绕"创新、质量、效率、体系、能力"五大主题，全力推进审评审批制度改革，持续优化审评审批流程，建立医疗器械审评质量管理长效机制，树立科学审评理念，持续鼓励医疗器械研发创新，形成了中国式现代化医疗器械审评体系 1.0 版。

当前，面对新时代新阶段医疗器械监管工作的新要求，面对推进中国式现代化的重大使命，面对世界百年未有之大变局带来的新挑战和新机遇，为全面推进监管体系和监管能力现代化，着力破解医疗器械产业发展面临的"卡脖子"问题，加快推动更多国产高端、临床急需医疗器械产品上市，助力国家重大区域发展战略，国家药品监督管理局医疗器械技术审评中心在上一版的基础上组织编写了本书，从注册资料方面介绍了医疗器械注册申报或备案相关法规、规章，并梳理了器审中心各类审评审批事项，进一步提高工作效率和透明度，切实增进人民群众福祉，推进健康中国建设。

本书通过图文结合的方式对注册申报流程进行了介绍，语言通俗易懂，可作为医疗器械企业科普读物。同时，医疗器械监管部门、检测机构及行业相关人员亦可阅读学习。

由于医疗器械行业涉及学科多，其涉及的新概念、新理论、新技术、新产品面广量大，本书在编写过程中得到了业界大力支持，在此要特别感谢胡玮、韩磊和高博对编撰工作提出的有益建议。本书还需在实践中得到检验，需要改进和完善之处，欢迎广大读者提出宝贵的意见和建议。

孙　磊

| Preface |

General Secretary Xi Jinping pointed out: "The responsibility for drug safety is more important than Mount Tai. Ensuring medical device safety is not only a technical issue and management work but also a moral issue and a project supported by common people." In the new journey of Chinese-style modernization, the drug regulatory departments have always fundamentally followed "the four most stringent requirements" based on responsibilities, strengthening coordination and making joint efforts to act as the gatekeeper of medical device safety and the guardian of public health, which are crucial to promoting the high-quality development of the medical device industry.

In the past five years, our country's medical device review and approval business has achieved great growth, great development, and great progress. Over the past five years, we have always adhered to the original mission of "protecting and promoting public health with the people at the center", and have always focused on the five major themes of "innovation, quality, efficiency, system, and capability" to make every effort to promote the reform of the review and approval system, continuously optimize the review and approval process, build a long-term mechanism for medical device review quality management, establish a scientific review concept, and constantly encourage the innovation of medical devices' research and development, which have formed a Chinese-style modern medical device review system version 1.0 .

At present, in the face of the new requirements of medical device supervision in the new era and stage, the major mission of promoting Chinese-style modernization, and the new challenges and new opportunities brought about by the world's major changes unseen in a century, in order to comprehensively promote the modernization of the supervision system and regulatory capability, focus on solving the "stuck neck" problem faced by the development of the medical device industry, promote the marketing of more high–quality and clinically urgent medical devices, and contribute to the development strategy of major national regions, the Center for Medical Device Evaluation (CMDE) of the National Medical Products Administration (NMPA) has organized the compilation of this book on the basis of the previous edition, introducing relevant regulations and rules on the registration application and filing of medical devices from the perspective of registration application dossiers. Besides, various evaluation and review & approval matters of CMDE have also been sorted out. With this book, it will help further improve work efficiency and transparency, and effectively improve people's well–being and advance the construction of a healthy China.

This book introduces the registration and application processes through pictures and texts. This book is easy to read and can be used as a handbook for people from the medical device enterprises, administrative supervision departments, test facilities, and other organizations related to the medical device industry.

As the medical device industry involves multiple disciplines and a wide range of new concepts, new theories, new technologies, and new products, this book has received strong support from the industry during its compilation process. Special thanks to Hu Wei, Han Lei and Gao Bo for their helpful suggestions on the compilation work. This book still needs to be tested in practice, and it may need to be adjusted, added to, deleted from, and so on as time passes. We also welcome the valuable comments and suggestions from our readers.

SUN Lei

| 目 录 |

147　第三章　注册范本示例

205　附录　医疗器械制度文件汇总

第一章　绪　论

医疗器械作为预防、诊断和治疗疾病的工具，是需要特殊管理的商品。为了使民众获得安全有效的医疗器械，我国对医疗器械的上市销售采取准入制度，申请人 / 注册人 / 备案人向我国相关监督管理部门提出注册或备案申请，获得批准后方可上市销售。对于医疗器械研发和生产企业而言，了解注册申请的要求和程序，按照相关要求准备申报资料，是产品合法上市的必经之路。

1. 医疗器械行政许可事项概述

国家药品监督管理局医疗器械技术审评中心（以下简称器审中心）作为国家药品监督管理局（以下简称国家药监局）正局级直属事业单位，主要对境内第三类和进口第二类、第三类医疗器械的注册申请开展技术审评工作，同时也承担进口第一类医疗器械备案等其他行政许可事项，共计 30 项，详情见表 1。为了使医疗器械研发、生产等相关企业准确及时地获取医疗器械注册或备案申报相关信息，本书从注册资料准备角度出发，紧紧围绕器审中心承担的各项行政事项展开详细介绍。

表 1　器审中心受理事项表

项目	分项	收费情况（万元）
境内医疗器械首次注册审批	1. 境内第三类医疗器械注册申请	15.36
	2. 境内第三类体外诊断试剂注册申请	

续表

项目	分项	收费情况（万元）
境内医疗器械变更申请	3. 境内第三类医疗器械变更备案	不收费
	4. 境内第三类医疗器械变更注册申请	5.04
	5. 境内第三类体外诊断试剂变更备案	不收费
	6. 境内第三类体外诊断试剂变更注册申请	5.04
境内第三类医疗器械延续注册审批	7. 境内第三类医疗器械延续注册申请	4.08
	8. 境内第三类体外诊断试剂延续注册申请	
进口医疗器械首次注册审批	9. 进口医疗器械注册申请	三类：30.88 二类：21.09
	10. 进口体外诊断试剂注册申请	
进口医疗器械变更申请	11. 进口医疗器械注册变更备案	不收费
	12. 进口医疗器械变更注册申请	三类：5.04 二类：4.20
	13. 进口体外诊断试剂变更备案	不收费
	14. 进口体外诊断试剂变更注册申请	三类：5.04 二类：4.20
进口医疗器械延续注册审批	15. 进口医疗器械延续注册申请	4.08
	16. 进口体外诊断试剂延续注册申请	
临床试验审批	17. 第三类高风险医疗器械临床试验审批申请	4.32
一类备案	18. 进口第一类医疗器械备案	不收费
	19. 进口第一类医疗器械变更备案	
	20. 进口第一类医疗器械取消备案	
其他事项	21. 医疗器械说明书更改告知	
	22. 医疗器械注册证/变更文件补办申请	
	23. 体外诊断试剂注册证/变更文件补办申请	
	24. 医疗器械注册证/变更文件纠错申请	

续表

项目	分项	收费情况（万元）
其他事项	25. 体外诊断试剂注册证 / 变更文件纠错申请	不收费
	26. 医疗器械注册证 / 变更文件自行注销申请	
	27. 体外诊断试剂注册证 / 变更文件自行注销申请	
	28. 自行撤回医疗器械注册 / 注册变更 / 延续注册 / 复审申请	
	29. 自行撤回体外诊断试剂注册 / 注册变更 / 延续注册 / 复审申请	
	30. 创新医疗器械特别审查申请	

2. 医疗器械注册和备案概述

医疗器械注册是药品监督管理部门根据医疗器械注册申请人的申请，依照法定程序，对其拟上市医疗器械的安全性、有效性和质量可控性研究及其结果进行系统评价，以决定是否同意其申请的过程。注册类型有首次注册、延续注册、变更注册等。器审中心依据《医疗器械监督管理条例》和国家药品监督管理部门制定的规章制度开展对注册申请事项的受理、技术审评和审批工作。注册申请人提供的申报资料是器审中心作出审评结论的依据，包含了申报产品相关技术资料、风险管理资料、临床评价资料等内容，其本质是对产品研发、生产数据资料的汇总和提炼。

医疗器械备案是指医疗器械备案人向药品监督管理部门提交备案资料存档备查的过程。

《医疗器械监督管理条例》是国家开展医疗器械监督管理的最高法，为配合条例的顺利实施，国家药品监督管理局陆续发布了《医疗器械注册与备案管理办法》《体外诊断试剂注册与备案管理办法》《医疗器械生产监督管理办法》《医疗器械经营监督管理办法》等法规，对医疗器械的研发、生产、注册、经营、使用等均作了详细的规定。就医疗器械注册事项而言，器审中心亦发布众多通知、公告、管理规定等制度文件，规范并指导申请人 / 注册人 / 备案人注册申报。

为帮助申请人 / 注册人 / 备案人更好地运用众多制度文件，本书以医疗器械注册为切入点，以注册流程为核心，对注册申报中的相关程序予以说明。

3. 信息查询

关于注册申报流程及相关信息，可在器审中心网站查询。其中，"注册申报流程简图"通过对各类注册相关文件梳理汇总，将注册申报涉及的知识分门别类，进行了从面到点、由浅入深的介绍。该流程简图框架结构分为三级：一级结构是主流程，以简洁直观的树状图形式介绍了注册申报的步骤，其中串联了相关的子流程；二级结构是子流程，以图文形式介绍了各子流程的涵盖范围、具体程序等相关信息；三级结构是相关法规文件，作为二级结构的补充和细化，链接入口分布在各个子流程页面。上述三级结构互相补充支持，层层深入，构成了医疗器械注册申报引导的"网络树"。目前，"注册申报流程简图"除主流程外，还囊括了 20 余个子流程，覆盖 160 余份现行的注册相关法规文件。

此外，对于注册申报涉及到的法规和技术性文件、审评进度等，器审中心网站也提供了相应版块供查询。

4. 参考资料

医疗器械监督管理条例（中华人民共和国国务院令第 739 号）

医疗器械注册与备案管理办法（国家市场监督管理总局令第 47 号）

体外诊断试剂注册与备案管理办法（国家市场监督管理总局令第

48 号）

关于公布医疗器械注册申报资料要求和批准证明文件格式的公告
（2021 年第 121 号）

关于公布体外诊断试剂注册申报资料要求和批准证明文件格式的公告
（2021 年第 122 号）

第二章 注册流程

1. 咨询服务

注册审评流程之 1.咨询服务

　　为了不断畅通和优化服务行政相对人／申请人／注册申请人的沟通交流渠道，帮助行政相对人／申请人／注册申请人准确理解医疗器械技术审评要求，提高注册申报资料质量，提升医疗器械注册技术审评服务功效，器审中心持续优化沟通交流资源配置，设立了多种咨询服务。

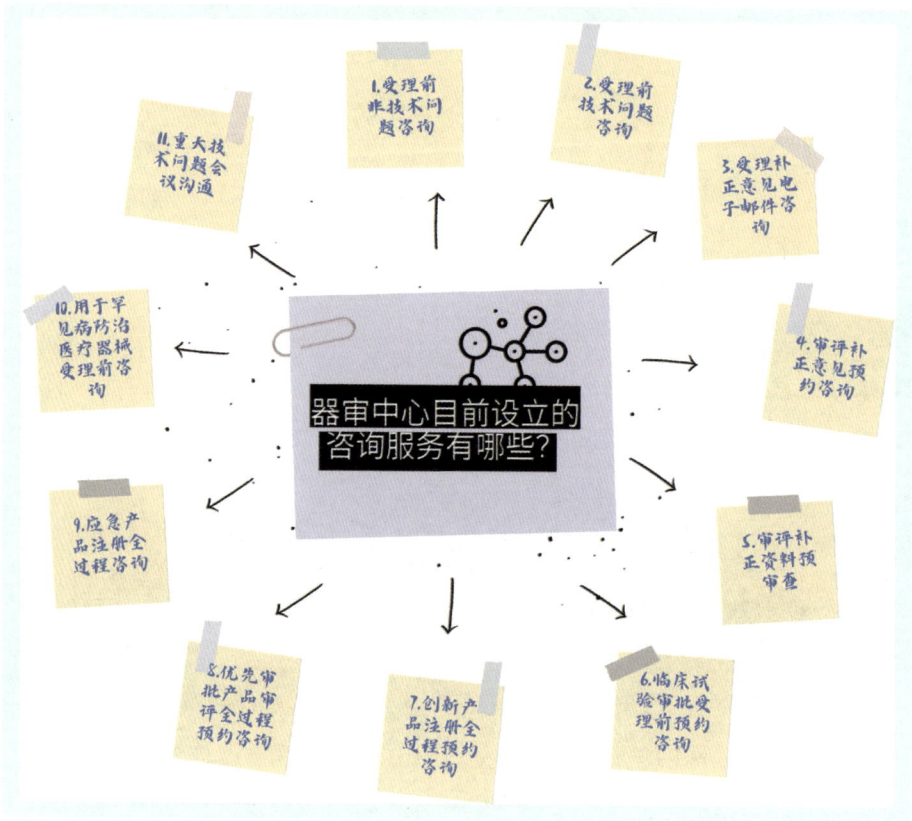

1.1 受理前非技术问题咨询

受理前非技术问题咨询主要是为了解决行政相对人在注册申报前遇到的非技术问题的咨询需求。电话咨询时间为每周三和周四全天（法定节假日除外），有咨询需求的行政相对人，可在工作时间拨打咨询电话，由受理窗口值班人员接听解答，或者在大厅现场受理时间取号现场咨询，咨询地点为国家药监局行政受理服务大厅。

1.2 受理前技术问题咨询

受理前技术问题咨询主要是为了解决行政相对人在注册申报前遇到的

技术问题的咨询需求，分为现场咨询和邮件咨询。

　　器械长三角分中心、器械大湾区分中心、海南省药品监督管理局以及部分与器审中心签署战略合作协议成立的创新工作服务站，自 2022 年 11 月 1 日起接收现场咨询，咨询时间为每周四全天（法定节假日除外），咨询的具体时段和各行政相对人咨询时间安排以各单位实际通知为准。

器审中心受理前技术问题咨询方式有哪些？

① 预约现场咨询

器审中心现场咨询时间为每周五下午13:30-16:30（法定节假日除外），咨询地点为国家药监局行政受理服务大厅。

② 邮件咨询

适用范围：除器械长三角分中心、器械大湾区分中心、海南省药品监督管理局及部分与器审中心签署战略合作协议成立的创新工作服务站以外地区，预约现场咨询未成功的单位，未预约现场咨询的单位。

邮件时间：每周一8:30-周三16:30

器审中心预约现场咨询"操作其实很简单"

通过国家药监局行政受理服务大厅网上预约受理系统预约，可以选择登录国家药品监督管理局政务服务门户网站，进入网上办事大厅；也可登录国家药监局受理和举报中心网站，点击右侧功能栏"网上预约受理"进行预约操作。

进行预约的同时应当填写并上传"医疗器械注册受理前技术问题咨询登记表"、"医疗器械注册受理前技术问题咨询信息登记表"、营业执照或法人证实扫描件。

最多填写5个咨询问题，且仅限于咨询当日对应预约端口轮值部门的职能范围。

器审中心参与单位受理前技术问题咨询方式有哪些？

1 预约现场咨询
每周一8:30至周三16:30，通过电子邮件方式预约。

2 邮件咨询
适用范围：器械长三角分中心、器械大湾区分中心、海南省药品监督管理局及部分与器审中心签署战略合作协议成立的创新工作服务站区域内境内第三类医疗器械研制机构、生产企业、进口医疗器械注册申请人在中国境内设立的持有股权的企业法人（包括独资公司、合资公司等）。

邮件时间：每周一8:30至周三16:30

1.3 受理补正意见电子邮件咨询

受理补正意见电子邮件咨询主要是为了解决医疗器械注册电子申报信息化系统（以下简称 eRPS 系统）上线后，申请人/注册申请人对于受理补正通知书所涉及问题的咨询需求，咨询时间为申请人/注册申请人接到受理补正通知书之日至下次提交注册申请之日期间的任意时间。申请人/注册申请人可将需要咨询的问题发至受理补正通知书载明的电子邮件地址，收到咨询邮件的审评员将在工作日进行回复，见"10.受理"。

什么是eRPS?

2019年5月31日，国家药品监督管理局发布了《关于实施医疗器械电子申报的公告》，为申请医疗器械注册实现了电子申报。医疗器械注册电子申报系统（以下简称eRPS）于2019年6月24日正式实施。

1.4 审评补正意见预约咨询

审评补正意见预约咨询主要是为了解决医疗器械注册审评过程中申请人／注册申请人对于补正资料通知所列问题的咨询需求，咨询时间为每周四上午 9: 00~11: 00，下午 13: 30~16: 30（法定节假日除外），咨询地点为器审中心一层业务大厅。每个符合要求的受理号最多有 3 次预约现场咨询的机会，申请人／注册申请人接到补正资料通知后，可通过 eRPS 系统预约申请。

1.5 审评补正资料预审查

审评补正资料预审查主要是为了帮助申请人／注册申请人确认准备的补充资料符合技术审评要求，提高补正资料质量和审评工作效率。适用的申请类型为境内第三类和进口第二类、第三类医疗器械产品注册、变更注册以及高风险医疗器械临床试验审批等项目。申请人／注册申请人／代理人应在补正资料时限届满 2 个月前提出预审查服务申请，线下业务将拟提交预审查的补充资料交至器审中心业务大厅后，20 个工作日内以电子邮件方式告知申请人／注册申请人／代理人预审查意见；线上业务申请提交后 20 工作日内 eRPS 系统回复，每个符合要求的注册申报事项原则上只有一次预审查服务机会，见 "13.3 补正咨询"。

1.6 临床试验审批受理前预约咨询

临床试验审批受理前预约咨询主要是为了解决需审批的医疗器械临床试验申请资料质量不高、审评补正意见较多的问题，进一步优化医疗器械临床试验审批程序。属于临床试验审批的，可以采用这种路径进行受理前预约咨询。

1.7 创新产品注册全过程预约咨询

创新产品注册预约咨询主要是为了解决创新医疗器械受理前和技术审评过程中申请人有关技术问题的咨询需求。一般性技术问题可通过咨询平台、电话、邮件等形式咨询，重大技术问题通过会议形式咨询。申请沟通交流会议的，申请人可登录 eRPS 系统提交咨询预约申请，相应部门会指定专人负责。

1.8 优先审批产品审评全过程预约咨询

优先审批产品审评预约咨询主要是为了解决同意按照《医疗器械优先审批程序》审批的境内第三类和进口第二、三类医疗器械技术审评阶段申请人的咨询需求。一般性技术问题可通过咨询平台、电话、邮件等形式咨询，重大技术问题通过会议形式咨询。申请人可登录 eRPS 系统提交咨询预约申请，相应部门会指定专人负责。

1.9 应急产品注册全过程咨询

应急产品注册咨询主要是为了解决突发公共卫生事件应急所需医疗器械受理前和技术审评过程中行政相对人 / 申请人有关技术问题的咨询需求。经国家药监局组织评估和审核确认属于进行应急审批的医疗器械后，申请人可随时与器审中心相关部门进行沟通交流。

1.10 用于罕见病防治医疗器械受理前咨询

用于罕见病防治医疗器械受理前咨询主要是为了对行政相对人拟申请的用于罕见病防治医疗器械对于指导原则的适用性以及应采取的临床评价路径进行确认，应行政相对人申请对适用指导原则注册申报项目的重大技术问题、重大安全性问题、临床试验方案等进行沟通交流，符合要求的项目，其行政相对人可在提出注册申请前，向器审中心提出咨询申请，相应部门会指定专人负责。

1.11 重大技术问题会议沟通

重大技术问题会议沟通指在注册申请受理前或技术审评阶段，器审中心可以发起关于医疗器械重大技术问题需要进行沟通的会议申请，有助于提高注册申报资料质量，提高技术审评效率，加快医疗器械上市进程。

名词解释

1.行政相对人：行政管理法律关系中与行政主体相对应的另一方当事人。

2.申请人：提出医疗器械注册申请的企业或者研制机构。

3.医疗器械注册人、备案人：取得医疗器械注册证或者办理医疗器械备案的企业或者研制机构。

4.医疗器械注册申请人：申请医疗器械注册的企业或者研制机构。

2. 产品命名及注册单元划分

注册审评流程之
2.产品命名及注册单元划分

2.1 产品命名

2.1.1 概述

医疗器械产品种类繁多、组成结构差异较大，准确、规范地为产品进行命名有助于研制、生产、流通、使用等各环节对医疗器械产品的有效识别。同时，规范医疗器械通用名称的命名也是医疗器械监管的重要基础性工作。

为重点解决医疗器械名称相对混乱、误导识别、存在夸张绝对用语等问题，2019 年 12 月 16 日，国家药监局发布了《医疗器械通用名称命名指导原则》，对在我国上市销售、使用的医疗器械产品通用名称做了进一步规范。

2.1.2 通用名称命名规则

（1）命名原则

通用名称应当合法、科学、明确、真实，并且应当使用中文，符合国家语言文字规范。

（2）内容要求和组成结构

具有相同或者相似的预期目的、共同技术的同品种医疗器械应当使用相同的通用名称。通用名称由一个核心词和一般不超过三个的特征词组成（如药物洗脱冠状动脉支架、一次性使用光学喉内窥镜等），已被广泛接受或者了解的特征词可以依据相关术语标准进行缺省，以简化产品通用名称（如眼科手术刀）。

（3）通用名称的禁止性内容

通用名称除符合《医疗器械通用名称命名规则》规定的相应要求外，不得含有"型号、规格""图形、符号等标志""人名、企业名称、注册商标或者其他类似名称""最佳、唯一、精确、速效等绝对化、排他性的词语""说明有效率、治愈率的用语"等9项禁止性要求。

此外，通用名称不得作为商标注册。

2.1.3 通用名称命名示例

以有源植入器械领域中植入式神经刺激器产品为例，可参考以下格式和内容形成命名术语表。

表 2　植入式神经刺激器命名术语表

序号	产品类别	术语类型	术语名称	术语描述
1	植入式神经刺激器	核心词	神经刺激器	通过将电脉冲施加在脑部或者神经系统的特殊部位来治疗帕金森病、控制癫痫、躯干和/或四肢的慢性顽固性疼痛或肠道控制以及排尿控制、肌张力障碍等神经调控类疾病
		特征词1——使用形式	植入式	植入人体
		特征词2——技术特点	不可充电（缺省）	电池不可充电
			可充电	电池可体外无线充电
		特征词3——使用部位	脑深部	刺激输出作用于脑深部
			脊髓	刺激输出作用于脊髓
			骶	刺激输出作用于骶神经
			迷走	刺激输出作用于迷走神经

选择典型产品，在术语表特征词和核心词项下选择适宜的术语，形成通用名称。

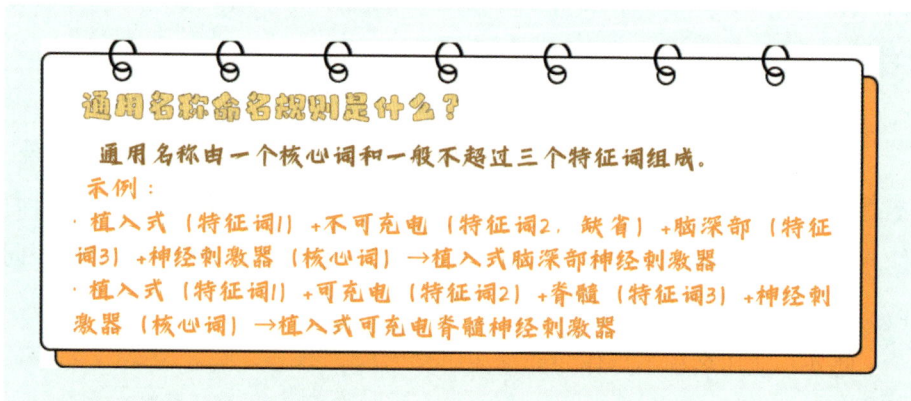

通用名称命名规则是什么？

通用名称由一个核心词和一般不超过三个特征词组成。

示例：

· 植入式（特征词1）+不可充电（特征词2，缺省）+脑深部（特征词3）+神经刺激器（核心词）→植入式脑深部神经刺激器

· 植入式（特征词1）+可充电（特征词2）+脊髓（特征词3）+神经刺激器（核心词）→植入式可充电脊髓神经刺激器

2.2 注册／备案单元划分

2.2.1 概述

医疗器械注册单元是指由技术原理、结构组成、性能指标和适用范围相同或相近的医疗器械产品组成的注册单元。申请人选择可代表本注册单元内其他产品安全性和有效性的产品进行注册检验、临床评价等安全性和有效性评估，经过医疗器械技术审评和审批后，同一注册单元产品将获得一张注册证书。

2.2.2 划分原则

医疗器械注册或者备案单元原则上以产品的技术原理、结构组成、性能指标和适用范围为划分依据。

对于体外诊断试剂产品，其注册或者备案单元应为单一试剂或者单一试剂盒，一个注册或者备案单元可以包括不同的包装规格。校准品、质控品可以与配合使用的体外诊断试剂合并申请注册，也可以单独申请注册。

注册/备案单元划分原则是什么？

医疗器械产品原则上以产品的技术原理、结构组成、性能指标和适用范围为划分依据。

体外诊断试剂产品原则上应为单一试剂或者单一试剂盒，一个注册/备案单元可以包括不同的包装规格。校准品、质控品可以与配合使用的体外诊断试剂合并申请注册，也可以单独申请注册。

可参照《医疗器械注册单元划分指导原则》（2017年第187号）。

2.3 案例解说

（1）相同材质的普通可吸收缝线与带倒刺可吸收缝线是否可以在一个注册单元内申报？

解答： 因普通可吸收缝线与带倒刺可吸收缝线的产品设计、闭合伤口的机理、性能指标等均不同，需分别开展产品性能研究、断裂强力在动物体内随时间变化的研究、临床评价等，建议划分为不同的注册单元申报注册。

（2）裸支架和药物洗脱支架能否划分为同一注册单元？

解答： 不能。涂层是药物洗脱支架重要的组成部分，对产品的安全性和有效性有重大影响，根据《医疗器械注册单元划分指导原则》无源医疗器械注册单元划分原则，含药（活性物质）与不含药（活性物质）的医疗器械宜划分为不同的注册单元。

（3）脊柱后路弹性融合固定系统产品注册单元应如何划分？

解答： 脊柱后路弹性融合固定系统用于脊柱后路融合固定，与用于融合的脊柱后路刚性内固定系统不同，应划分为不同的注册单元。产品的结构设计不同、力学性能不同，应分为不同的注册单元。产品起主要功能作用的材料不同，应划分为不同注册单元。若产品组成部件材料不同，但作为整体组配或组合使用的产品，可按同一注册单元申报。

2.4 参考资料

医疗器械通用名称命名规则（国家食品药品监督管理总局令第 19 号）

总局关于发布医疗器械注册单元划分指导原则的通告（2017 年第 187 号）

国家药监局关于发布医疗器械通用名称命名指导原则的通告（2019 年第 99 号）

3. 分类

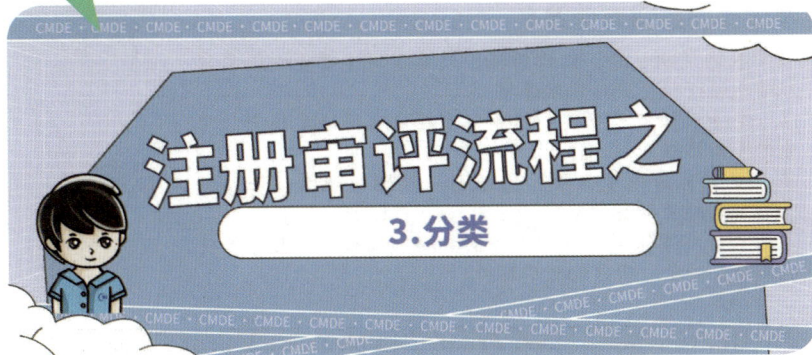

3.1 概述

医疗器械有多种分类方法，根据结构特征不同可分为无源医疗器械和有源医疗器械；根据是否接触人体，可分为接触人体器械和非接触人体器械等。国际上，部分主要国家（地区）的医疗器械监管机构为便于管理，一般根据医疗器械风险程度进行分类（表3）。医疗器械风险程度是根据医疗器械的预期目的，通过结构特征、使用形式、使用状态、是否接触人体等因素综合判定的。本书所提到的医疗器械分类主要指管理类别分类。

表3　主要国家（地区）医疗器械分类情况汇总表

安全风险　　　地区	美国	欧盟	日本	中国
低风险 ↓ 高风险	Ⅰ类	Ⅰ级	Ⅰ级	第一类
	Ⅱ类	Ⅱa级	Ⅱ级	第二类
		Ⅱb级	Ⅲ级	
	Ⅲ类	Ⅲ级	Ⅳ级	第三类

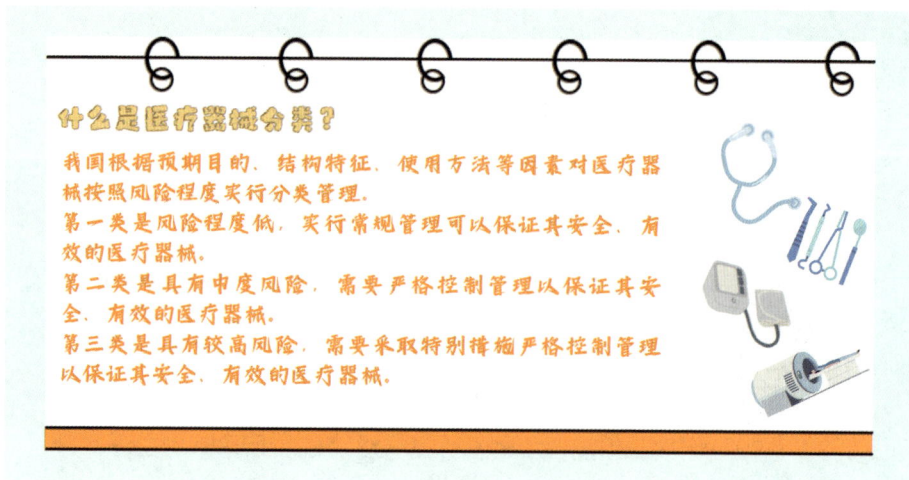

什么是医疗器械分类？

我国根据预期目的、结构特征、使用方法等因素对医疗器械按照风险程度实行分类管理。

第一类是风险程度低，实行常规管理可以保证其安全、有效的医疗器械。

第二类是具有中度风险，需要严格控制管理以保证其安全、有效的医疗器械。

第三类是具有较高风险，需要采取特别措施严格控制管理以保证其安全、有效的医疗器械。

3.2 分类规则

医疗器械分类除应根据医疗器械分类判定表进行判定外，还应遵循以下原则：

（1）如果同一医疗器械适用两个或者两个以上的分类，应当采取其中风险程度最高的分类；由多个医疗器械组成的医疗器械包，其分类应当与包内风险程度最高的医疗器械一致。

（2）可作为附件的医疗器械，其分类应当综合考虑该附件对配套主体医疗器械安全性、有效性的影响；如果附件对配套主体医疗器械有重要影响，附件的分类应不低于配套主体医疗器械的分类。

（3）监控或者影响医疗器械主要功能的医疗器械，其分类应当与被监控或者被影响的医疗器械的分类一致。

（4）以医疗器械作用为主的药械组合产品，按照第三类医疗器械管理。

（5）可被人体吸收的医疗器械，按照第三类医疗器械管理。

（6）对医疗效果有重要影响的有源接触人体器械，按照第三类医疗器械管理。

（7）医用敷料如果有以下情形，按照第三类医疗器械管理，包括：预期具有防止组织或器官粘连功能；作为人工皮肤，接触真皮深层或其以下组织受损的创面；用于慢性创面，或者可被人体全部或部分吸收。

（8）以无菌形式提供的医疗器械，其分类应不低于第二类。

（9）通过牵拉、撑开、扭转、压握、弯曲等作用方式，主动施加持续作用力于人体、可动态调整肢体固定位置的矫形器械（不包括仅具有固定、支撑作用的医疗器械，也不包括配合外科手术中进行临时矫形的医疗器械或者外科手术后或其他治疗中进行四肢矫形的医疗器械），其分类应不低于第二类。

（10）具有计量测试功能的医疗器械，其分类应不低于第二类。

（11）如果医疗器械的预期目的是明确用于某种疾病的治疗，其分类应不低于第二类。

（12）用于在内窥镜下完成夹取、切割组织或者取石等手术操作的无源可重复使用手术器械，按照第二类医疗器械管理。

3.3 分类目录

我国医疗器械（含体外诊断试剂）分类实行分类规则指导下的分类目录制，分类规则和分类目录并存，以分类目录优先。

3.3.1 医疗器械分类目录

2002 年，国务院药品监督管理部门第一次发布了《医疗器械分类目录》。此后，随着医疗器械行业发展，监管部门也不断对其进行调整和完善。对于非体外诊断试剂的医疗器械，现行《医疗器械分类目录》（以下简称《分类目录》）即是在 2017 年发布的《分类目录》版本基础上，根据《医疗器械分类规则》和《医疗器械分类目录动态调整工作程序》不断进行调整修订。

《分类目录》按技术专业和临床使用特点分为 22 个子目录，子目录由一级产品类别、二级产品类别、产品描述、预期用途、品名举例和管理类别组成。22 个子目录设置情况如下：

（1）手术类器械设置 4 个子目录，分别是：通用手术器械分设"01 有源手术器械"和"02 无源手术器械"；因分类规则中对接触神经和血管的器械有特殊要求，单独设置"03 神经和血管手术器械"；骨科手术相关器械量大面广，产品种类繁杂，单独设置"04 骨科手术器械"。

（2）有源器械为主的器械设置 8 个子目录，分别是："05 放射治疗器械""06 医用成像器械""07 医用诊察和监护器械""08 呼吸、麻醉和急救器械""09 物理治疗器械""10 输血、透析和体外循环器械""11 医疗器械消毒灭菌器械"和"12 有源植入器械"。

（3）无源器械为主的器械设置 3 个子目录，分别是："13 无源植入器械""14 注输、护理和防护器械"和"15 患者承载器械"。

（4）按照临床科室划分 3 个子目录，分别是："16 眼科器械""17 口腔科器械"和"18 妇产科、生殖和避孕器械"。

（5）"19 医用康复器械"和"20 中医器械"是根据《医疗器械监督管理条例》中对医用康复器械和中医器械两大类产品特殊管理规定而单独设置的子目录。

（6）"21 医用软件"是收录医用独立软件产品的子目录。

（7）"22 临床检验器械"子目录放置在最后，为后续体外诊断试剂修订预留空间。

3.3.2 体外诊断试剂分类

体外诊断试剂产品类别主要按照《6840 体外诊断试剂分类子目录》进行判定。《6840 体外诊断试剂分类子目录》根据体外诊断试剂的特点编制，目录结构中设置了"序号、产品类别、产品分类名称、预期用途、管理类别"等 5 个部分。此外，国家医疗器械监督管理部门还先后发布了《总局关于过敏原类、流式细胞仪配套用、免疫组化和原位杂交类体外诊断试剂产品属性及类别调整的通告》《关于调整〈6840 体外诊断试剂分类子目录

（2013 版）〉部分内容的公告》《体外诊断试剂分类规则》等文件进行补充和完善。

3.4　分类查询

申请人可进入国家药品监督管理局网站进行搜索查询，或依据《医疗器械分类规则》《体外诊断试剂分类规则》《第一类医疗器械产品目录》《医疗器械分类目录》《6840 体外诊断试剂分类子目录》、国家药品监督管理局医疗器械标准管理中心（以下简称标管中心）发布的《医疗器械产品分类界定结果汇总》，以及相关产品分类界定原则等文件判定产品类别。

3.5　申请分类界定

申请人可通过标管中心分类界定信息系统提出分类界定申请，按照分类界定程序判定管理类别。

3.6　参考资料

医疗器械分类规则（国家食品药品监督管理总局令第 15 号）

食品药品监管总局关于印发体外诊断试剂分类子目录的通知（食药监械管〔2013〕242号）

总局关于发布医疗器械分类目录的公告（2017年第104号）

总局办公厅关于规范医疗器械产品分类有关工作的通知（食药监办械管〔2017〕127号）

总局关于过敏原类、流式细胞仪配套用、免疫组化和原位杂交类体外诊断试剂产品属性及类别调整的通告（2017年第226号）

国家药监局关于调整《6840体外诊断试剂分类子目录（2013版）》部分内容的公告（2020年第112号）

国家药监局关于发布医疗器械分类目录动态调整工作程序的公告（2021年第60号）

国家药监局关于发布《体外诊断试剂分类规则》的公告（2021年第129号）

国家药监局关于发布第一类医疗器械产品目录的公告（2021年第158号）

4. 产品检验

4.1 概述

医疗器械检验是指医疗器械在生产、实验、科研、使用、维修等领域，借助于专门的仪器设备，为了及时获得被测、被控对象的信息而进行实时或非实时的定性测试和定量测量，并出具检验报告的过程。

4.2 医疗器械检验工作

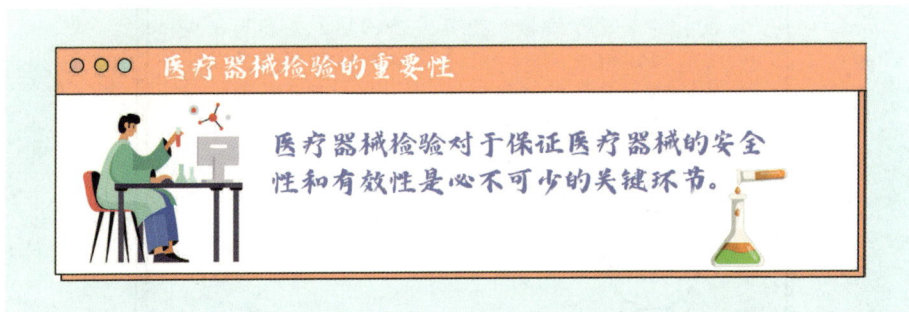

法规中规定，医疗器械注册申请人应当按照产品技术要求进行检验，并提交检验报告。检验合格的，方可开展临床试验或者申请注册。检验用产品应当能够代表申请注册产品的安全性和有效性，其生产应当符合《医疗器械生产质量管理规范》的相关要求。申请注册提交的医疗器械产品检验报告可以是医疗器械注册申请人的自检报告，也可以是委托有资质的医疗器械检验机构出具的检验报告。

注册时开展自检的，医疗器械注册申请人应当具备自检能力，并将自检工作纳入医疗器械质量管理体系，配备与产品检验要求相适应的检验设备设施，具有相应质量检验部门或者专职检验人员，严格控制检验过程，确保检验结果真实、准确、完整和可追溯，并对自检报告负主体责任。

4.3 医疗器械检验

4.3.1 检验依据

医疗器械注册申请人在产品研制过程中，基于产品技术特征，编写产品技术要求，制定用于客观判定产品有效性和安全性的性能指标。产品技术要求性能指标的制定可参考相关国家标准或行业标准，并结合具体产品

产品检验依据是什么？

医疗器械注册申请人应当依据拟申报注册产品的产品技术要求进行检验。检验方法的制定应当与相应的性能指标相适应，优先考虑采用已颁布的标准检验方法或者公认的检验方法。检验方法应当进行验证或者确认，确保检验具有可重复性和可操作性。对于体外诊断试剂产品，检验方法中还应当明确说明采用的参考品/标准品、样本制备方法、使用的试剂批次和数量、试验次数、计算方法等。

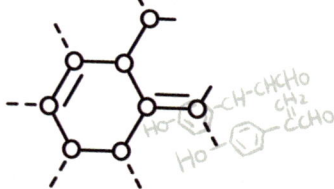

的设计特性、预期用途和质量控制水平，且不应低于产品适用的强制性国家标准或行业标准。产品技术要求应按照国家药监局发布的《医疗器械产品技术要求编写指导原则》的相关要求进行编写。医疗器械注册申请人可以随时关注国家药监局动态，参考申报产品适用的指导原则编制产品技术要求。

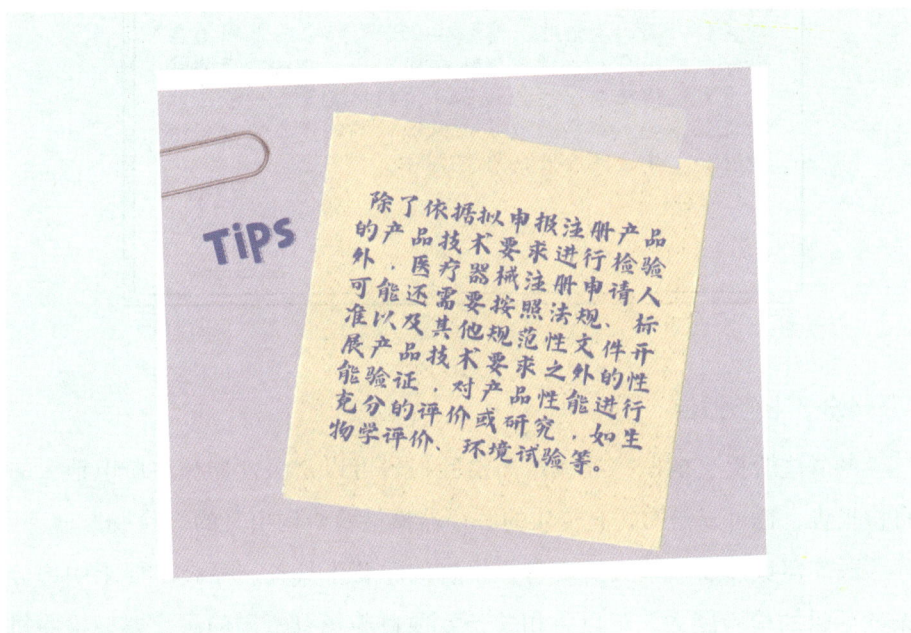

4.3.2 检验用产品

医疗器械生产企业须完成检验用产品的生产。检验用产品的数量应符合法规及产品检验批次的要求。例如，第三类体外诊断试剂应根据《体外诊断试剂注册与备案管理办法》第三十三条规定，应当提供 3 个不同生产批次的产品。

申请医疗器械委托检验的，检验用产品的数量应满足检验需要，建议医疗器械注册申请人在产品送检前咨询委托检验机构，避免检验用产品数量不足的情况。

同一注册单元的典型检验产品需要注意的事项有哪些？

医疗器械注册申请人应按照注册单元进行产品检验，对于注册单元内包含多个型号规格的产品，原则上产品技术要求应包括所有型号规格的性能指标及要求。同一注册单元内所检验的产品应能够代表本注册单元内其他产品的安全性、有效性，检验结果需要覆盖注册单元内所有产品型号规格或配置。典型检验产品需要考虑结构组成、性能指标、预期用途等，一般选取功能最齐全、结构最复杂、风险最高的产品型号规格或配置，并提供检验典型性说明。

4.3.3 检验报告

申请注册提交的医疗器械产品检验报告可以是医疗器械注册申请人的自检报告，也可以是委托有资质的医疗器械检验机构出具的检验报告。

医疗器械注册申请人提交自检报告的，若不具备产品技术要求中部分条款项目的检验能力，可以将相关条款项目委托有资质的医疗器械检验机构进行检验。有资质的医疗器械检验机构应当符合《医疗器械监督管理条例》第七十五条的相关规定。

4.4 案例解说

（1）有源产品性能检验时应用模式和配套耗材需要注意的事项有哪些？

解答： 在应用模式方面，若申报产品具有多种应用模式，建议按照典型应用模式逐项进行检验，并提供典型应用模式的选取依据。例如：是否选取最大转速/最高流量的应用模式作为典型模式；是否所有典型应用模式均进行了检验；是否不同典型应用模式之间具有一定的检验覆盖性，并选取差异项目进行了检验。

在配套耗材方面，若申报产品可以适配不同型号规格的耗材（例如：一次性使用离心泵泵头、体外循环管路等），则产品检验需要考虑申报产品配套典型耗材的所有组合情况，并分析是否需要全部进行检验。医疗器械注册申请人需要说明检验用配套耗材的典型性，以及某些组合是否仅进行了差异项目检验。

（2）有源产品 EMC 检验需要注意的事项有哪些？请举例说明。

解答： 医疗器械注册申请人需要提供 EMC 检验中产品运行模式的选取依据，并建议考虑产品报警功能。抗扰度试验中，产品基本性能相关的功能均应考虑对患者产生最不利影响的试验方式。辐射发射试验中，产品宜在最大骚扰状态下运行。

（3）关于有源产品检验情况的说明，有哪些注意事项？

解答： 医疗器械注册申请人可以提供检验情况说明和检验报告清单，描述检验报告对应的产品型号规格 / 配置和检验类型（产品性能和安规检验、EMC 检验等）。

4.5 参考资料

国家药品监督管理局关于发布《医疗器械注册自检管理规定》的公告（2021 年第 126 号）

国家药品监督管理局关于发布医疗器械产品技术要求编写指导原则的通告（2022 年第 8 号）

5. 临床评价

5.1 概述

医疗器械临床评价是指采用科学合理的方法对临床数据进行分析、评价，以确认医疗器械在其适用范围内的安全性、有效性的活动。申请人可以根据产品特征、临床风险、已有临床数据等情形，通过开展临床试验，或者通过对同品种医疗器械临床文献资料、临床数据进行分析评价，证明医疗器械的安全性、有效性。第二类、第三类医疗器械注册申报时，临床评价资料具体内容可参考《医疗器械临床评价技术指导原则》《医疗器械等同性论证技术指导原则》《决策是否开展医疗器械临床试验技术指导原则》《医疗器械注册申报临床评价报告技术指导原则》等相关指导原则。临床评价过程中收集的安全性、临床性能和/或有效性数据均应纳入分析之中，使得临床评价全面、客观。

体外诊断试剂临床试验是指在相应的临床环境中，对体外诊断试剂的临床性能进行的系统性研究。临床试验的目的在于证明体外诊断试剂能够满足预期用途要求，并确定产品的适用人群及适应证。临床试验结果为体外诊断试剂安全有效性的确认和风险受益分析提供有效的科学证据。第二类、第三类体外诊断试剂注册申报时，临床试验资料具体内容可参考《体外诊断试剂临床试验技术指导原则》等相关指导原则。临床试验过程中试验体外诊断试剂由预期使用者在预期使用环境中使用，评价产品针对目标人群获得与受试者目标状态相关的检测结果的能力。

临床评价的阶段

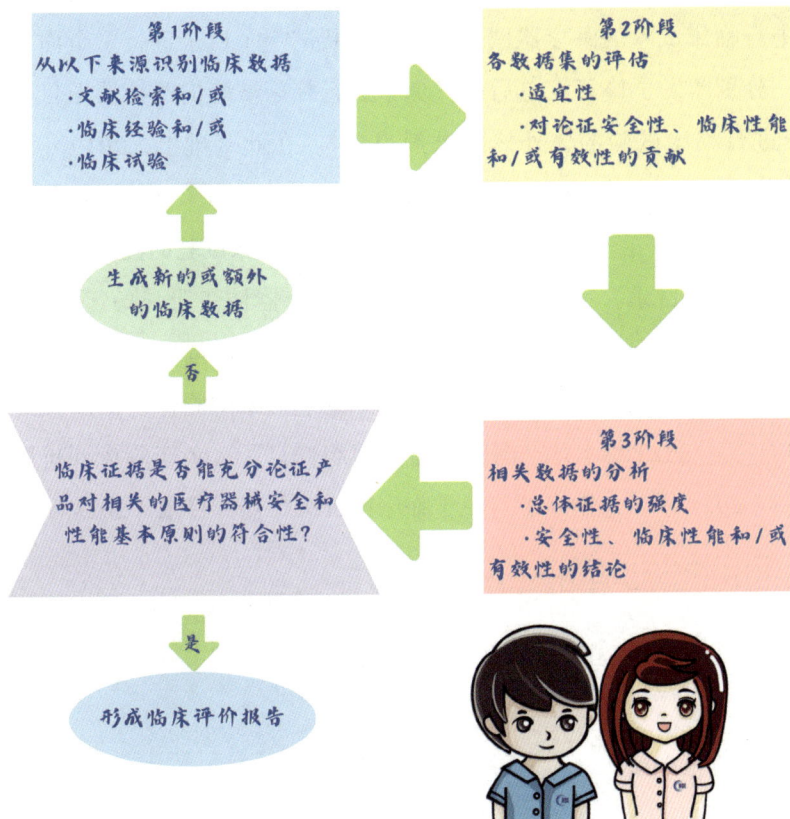

第1阶段
从以下来源识别临床数据
· 文献检索和/或
· 临床经验和/或
· 临床试验

第2阶段
各数据集的评估
· 适宜性
· 对论证安全性、临床性能和/或有效性的贡献

生成新的或额外的临床数据

否

临床证据是否能充分论证产品对相关的医疗器械安全和性能基本原则的符合性？

第3阶段
相关数据的分析
· 总体证据的强度
· 安全性、临床性能和/或有效性的结论

是

形成临床评价报告

5.2 免于进行临床评价 / 临床试验的产品

5.2.1《免于临床评价医疗器械目录》和《免于临床试验体外诊断试剂目录》简介

依据《医疗器械监督管理条例》第二十四条规定"国务院药品监督管理部门应当制定医疗器械临床评价指南。"原国家食品药品监督管理总局发布了三批免于进行临床试验目录。2018 年 9 月，国家药监局印发《关于公布新修订免于进行临床试验医疗器械目录的通告》，对前期已发布的免于进行临床试验的医疗器械（及体外诊断试剂）目录进行了全面修订和汇总，分别印发了修订汇总后的《免于进行临床试验的医疗器械目录》和《免于进行临床试验的体外诊断试剂目录》。在此基础上，2019 年 12 月，国家药监局印发《关于公布新增和修订的免于进行临床试验医疗器械目录的通告》，公布了第一批新增和修订的免于进行临床试验的医疗器械（及体外诊断试剂）目录。2021 年 9 月，根据《医疗器械注册与备案管理办法》和《体外诊断试剂注册与备案管理办法》，国家药监局组织制定了《免于临床评价医疗器械目录（2021 年）》和《免于临床试验体外诊断试剂目录（2021 年）》。2023 年 7 月，国家药监局组织修订了《免于临床评价医疗器械目录（2021 年）》，制定了《免于临床评价医疗器械目录（2023 年）》。

列入免于进行临床评价/临床试验的医疗器械目录

居然可以不做临床试验!

为了进一步规范医疗器械的注册管理工作，国家药监局组织制定了《免于进行临床试验的医疗器械目录》和《免于进行临床试验的体外诊断试剂目录》。列入此目录的医疗器械产品，可以免于进行临床试验。现行有效的为2021年发布的《免于临床评价医疗器械目录（2021版）》和《免于临床试验体外诊断试剂目录（2021版）》。

医疗器械产品注册、备案，应当进行临床评价；但是符合下列情形之一，可以免于进行临床评价：

（1）工作机理明确、设计定型，生产工艺成熟，已上市的同品种医疗器械临床应用多年且无严重不良事件记录，不改变常规用途的；

（2）其他通过非临床评价能够证明该医疗器械安全、有效的。

开展体外诊断试剂临床评价，应当进行临床试验证明体外诊断试剂的安全性、有效性。符合如下情形的，可以免于进行临床试验：

（1）反应原理明确、设计定型、生产工艺成熟，已上市的同品种体外诊断试剂临床应用多年且无严重不良事件记录，不改变常规用途的；

（2）通过进行同品种方法学比对的方式能够证明该体外诊断试剂安全、有效的。

免于进行临床试验的第二类、第三类体外诊断试剂目录由国家药品监督管理局制定、调整并公布。

免于进行临床试验的体外诊断试剂，申请人应当通过对符合预期用途的临床样本进行同品种方法学比对的方式证明产品的安全性、有效性。

注意！有些产品名称即使列入《免于临床评价医疗器械目录》中，以下情况也不能豁免

使用新材料、新技术、新活性成分、新设计或具有新作用机理、新功能的产品。

扩大或改变适用范围的产品

性能指标不满足目录中列明的标准的产品

其他《免于临床评价医疗器械目录》列明的不满足临床豁免的情况

5.2.2 需提交的资料

（1）列入《免于临床评价医疗器械目录》产品

对于列入《免于临床评价医疗器械目录》产品，注册申请人需提交申报产品相关信息与《免于临床评价医疗器械目录》所述内容的对比资料和申报产品与已获准境内注册的《免于临床评价医疗器械目录》中医疗器械的对比说明。符合条件的注册申请人应根据《列入免于临床评价医疗器械目录产品对比说明技术指导原则》的相关要求准备资料。

（2）列入《免于临床试验的体外诊断试剂目录》产品

对免于临床试验的体外诊断试剂，注册申请人应提交申报产品与《免于临床试验体外诊断试剂目录》对应项目的对比资料，该资料应能证明申报产品与《免于临床试验体外诊断试剂目录》所述的产品具有等同性。

在《免于临床评价医疗器械目录》内的产品，注册申报是需要准备哪些临床评价资料？

 申报产品相关信息与《免于临床评价医疗器械目录》所述内容的对比资料

 申报产品与《免于临床评价医疗器械目录》中已获准境内注册医疗器械的对比说明

LOOK!

请大家随时关注国家药监局官网，留意关于《免于临床评价医疗器械目录》的最新资讯。

对免于临床试验的体外诊断试剂，注册申请人可依据《免于临床试验的体外诊断试剂临床评价技术指导原则》的要求进行临床评价，也可依据《体外诊断试剂临床试验技术指导原则》的要求进行临床试验。

对免于临床试验的体外诊断试剂如何开展临床评价？

注册申请人可将待评价试剂与境内已上市产品进行比对，证明待评价试剂与已上市产品实质等同，或与参考测量程序/诊断准确度标准检测结果具有良好的一致性。此处所述实质性等同，指预期用途相同，且具有相同的安全性与有效性。

注册申请人应采用最终定型的试剂进行临床评价。进行临床评价之前，应确定产品的基本性能，通常包括适用的样本类型、特异性、精密度、检出限和/或定量限、测量区间、阳性判断值、参考区间等，以便为待评价试剂进行临床评价提供依据。

如通过临床评价无法证明待评价试剂与境内已上市产品实质等同，或与参考测量程序/诊断准确度标准检测结果具有良好的一致性，应通过临床试验的方式对申报试剂进行评价。

5.3 医疗器械临床评价主要形式

5.3.1 通过同品种医疗器械临床数据进行分析、评价

（1）等同性论证

医疗器械等同性论证是指将适用范围相同的申报产品与对比器械在技术特征和生物学特性方面进行比对，证明二者基本等同的过程。基本等同包括两种情形：

1）申报产品与对比器械具有相同的适用范围、技术特征和生物学特性；

2）申报产品与对比器械具有相同的适用范围，相似的技术特征和生物学特性；有充分的科学证据证明申报产品与对比器械具有相同的安全有效性。

（2）同品种产品的选择

根据《医疗器械临床评价技术指导原则》，当对比器械的适用范围、技术和／或生物学特性与申报产品具有广泛相似性时，可将其视为同品种医疗器械，包括等同器械和可比器械两种情形。

1）等同器械

若注册申请人按照《医疗器械等同性论证技术指导原则》相关要求，论证申报产品与对比器械具有等同性，可通过等同器械的临床数据进行临床评价。当申报产品的技术特征和生物特性与对比器械存在差异时，需提交充分的科学证据证明二者具有相同的安全有效性，从而论证其等同性。对于需要通过临床证据证明二者具有相同的安全有效性时，注册申请人可参照《医疗器械临床评价技术指导原则》第二部分第五、六、七条的要求，形成申报产品的临床证据。

2）可比器械

若注册申请人按照《医疗器械等同性论证技术指导原则》相关要求，将申报产品与对比器械进行对比，虽然不能论证二者具有等同性，但对比器械的适用范围、技术特征和／或生物学特性与申报产品具有广泛相似性，可将对比器械视为可比器械，注册申请人可使用可比器械的临床数据用于支持申报产品的部分临床评价，作为申报产品临床证据的一部分。

注册审评流程之临床评价

临床评价还有一招：同品种比对

先了解一下同品种医疗器械

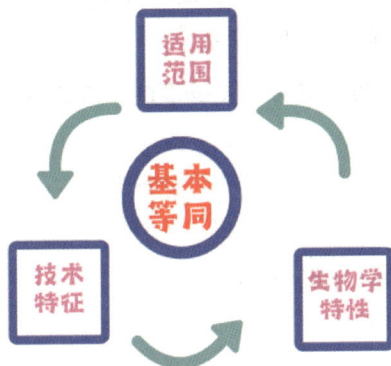

适用范围

基本等同

技术特征

生物学特性

已获准境内注册的产品

申报产品与同品种医疗器械的差异不对产品的安全性有效性产生不利影响，可视为基本等同

如何进行同品种比对？

STEP1 判定

将申报产品与同品种医疗器械进行对比，证明两者之间基本等同。

对比内容包括定性和定量数据、验证和确认结果

注册申请人应以列表形式提供对比信息，若存在不适用项目，应说明不适用理由。

对比项目

对比表

STEP2 资料收集

1.临床文献数据的收集

文献检索和筛选三步走：　要素　　方案　　报告

2.临床经验数据的收集

临床使用数据　　不良事件　　纠正措施　……

STEP3 临床数据分析与评价

1.数据的质量评价

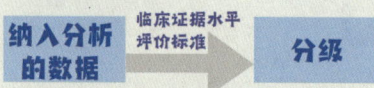

纳入分析的数据 → 临床证据水平评价标准 → 分级

2.数据的建立

数据类型　　数据质量

3.数据的统计分析

定性　　定量

4.数据评价

产品达到预期性能？

风险是否可以接受？

……

STEP4 临床评价报告

临床评价完成后需要撰写临床评价报告，在注册申请时作为临床评价资料提交。

（3）相关支持性资料的准备

等同性论证时，申报产品与对比器械进行比对时所用的数据和信息，二者存在差异时证明其具有相同的安全有效性所用的有效科学证据，均为等同性论证的支持性资料。支持性资料通常需包括准确、可靠、完整、可追溯的数据，必要时包括数据的产生过程，试验数据建议来自有良好质量控制的实验室。支持性资料可包括台架试验数据、动物试验数据、模拟试验数据、临床数据等。

5.3.2 需进行医疗器械临床试验的产品

（1）临床试验定义

医疗器械临床试验是指在符合条件的医疗器械临床试验机构中，对拟申请注册的医疗器械（含体外诊断试剂）在正常使用条件下的安全性和有效性进行确认的过程。

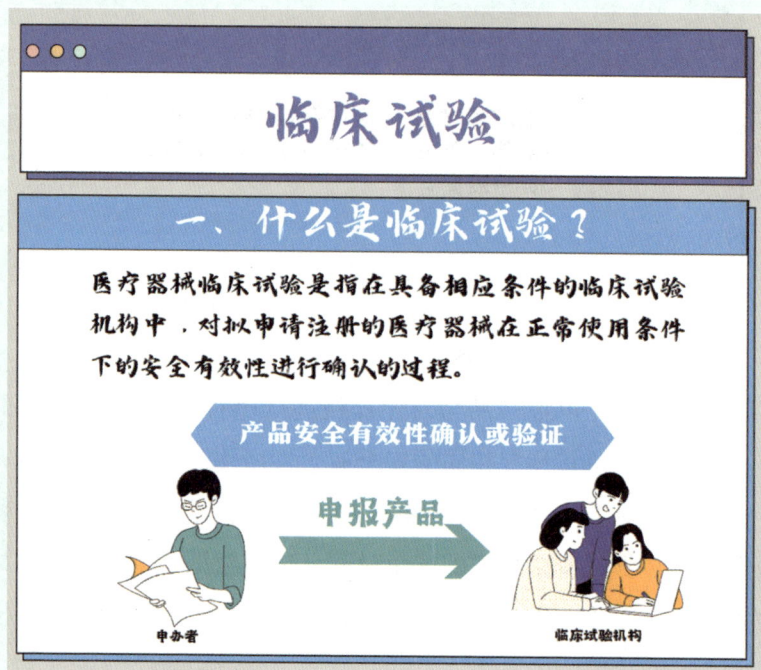

（2）临床试验前准备

1）预期的受益应当超过可能出现的损害；

2）完成试验用医疗器械临床前研究；

3）准备充足的试验用医疗器械；

4）医疗器械临床试验应当在两个或两个以上医疗器械临床试验机构中进行；

5）申办者与临床试验机构和研究者达成书面协议；

6）获得医疗器械临床试验机构伦理委员会的同意，列入需进行临床试验审批的第三类医疗器械目录的产品需获得批准；

7）申办者应向所在省、自治区、直辖市食品药品监督管理部门备案。

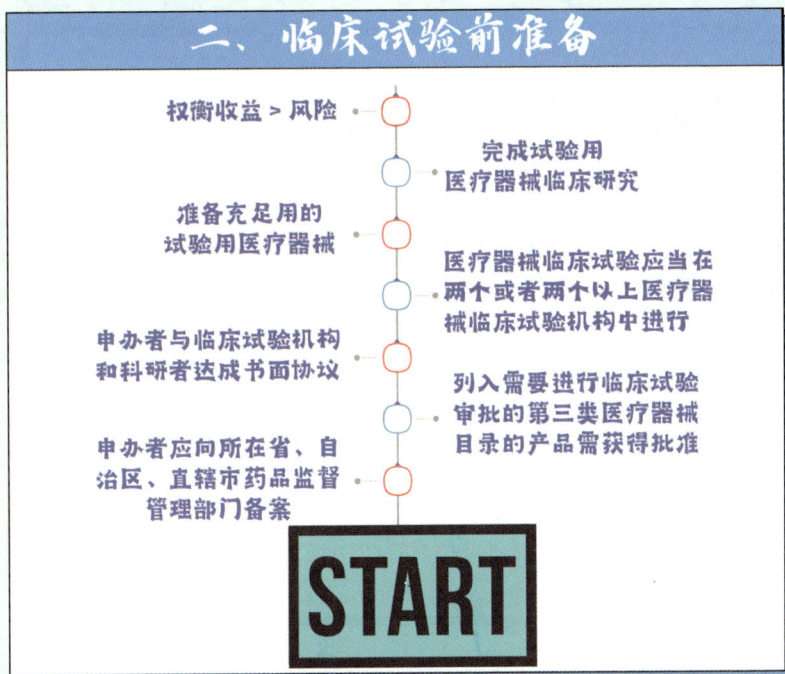

二、临床试验前准备

权衡收益 > 风险

完成试验用医疗器械临床研究

准备充足用的试验用医疗器械

医疗器械临床试验应当在两个或者两个以上医疗器械临床试验机构中进行

申办者与临床试验机构和科研者达成书面协议

列入需要进行临床试验审批的第三类医疗器械目录的产品需获得批准

申办者应向所在省、自治区、直辖市药品监督管理部门备案

START

（3）临床试验方案

1）申办者应考虑临床试验目的、医疗器械宣称及其固有特征等组织制定临床试验方案；

2）临床试验方案一般包含产品基本信息、临床试验基本信息、试验目的、风险受益分析、试验设计要素、试验设计的合理性论证、统计学考虑、实施方式（方法、内容、步骤）、临床试验终点、数据管理、对临床试验方案修正的规定、不良事件和器械缺陷定义和报告的规定、伦理学考虑等内容。

三、临床试验方案

申办者应按试验用医疗器械的类别、风险、预期用途等组织制定临床试验方案

科学、合理

临床试验方案设计时应先进行小样本可行性试验

未在境内外批准上市的新产品、安全性及性能尚未经医学证实的

医疗器械临床试验方案应包括：

- 一般信息
- 临床试验的背景资料
- 试验目的
- 试验设计
- 安全性评价方法
- 有效性评价方法

TIPS

多中心临床试验需按照同一试验方案在不同临床试验机构中同期进行

（4）临床试验数据库

临床试验应根据《医疗器械临床试验数据递交要求注册审查指导原则》的要求提交数据库。

（5）临床试验流程

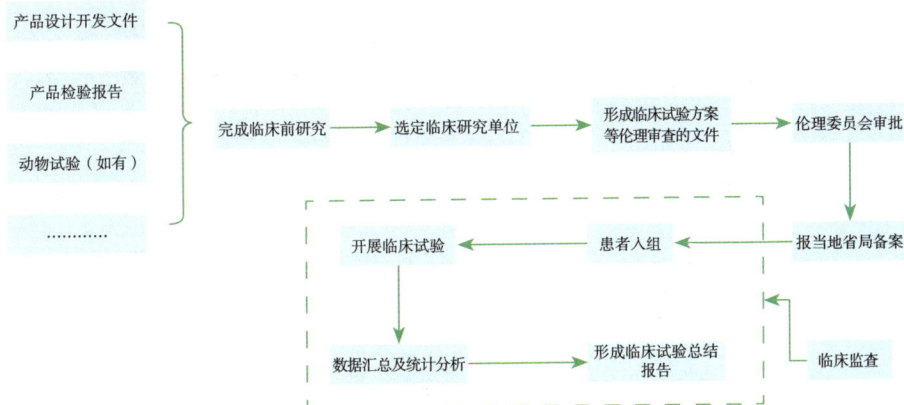

5.3.3 列入《需进行临床试验审批的第三类医疗器械目录》的产品

（1）《需进行临床试验审批的第三类医疗器械目录》（2020年修订版）简介

根据《医疗器械监督管理条例》第二十七条规定"第三类医疗器械临床试验对人体具有较高风险的，应当经国务院药品监督管理部门批准。临床试验对人体具有较高风险的第三类医疗器械目录由国务院药品监督管理部门制定、调整并公布。"为保护医疗器械临床试验受试者安全，规范临床试验审批工作，国家药品监督管理局发布了《需进行临床试验审批的第三类医疗器械目录》（表4）。该目录内的产品临床试验方案需经国家药品监督管理局审批后方可实施。

表4 需进行临床试验审批的第三类医疗器械目录（2020年修订版）

序号	产品类别	分类编码	产品描述
1	植入式心脏节律管理设备	12	植入式心脏起搏器：通常由植入式脉冲发生器和扭矩扳手组成。通过起搏电极将电脉冲施加在患者心脏的特定部位。用于治疗慢性心率失常。再同步治疗起搏器还可用于心力衰竭治疗 植入式心脏除颤器：通常由植入式脉冲发生器和扭矩扳手组成。通过检测室性心动过速和颤动，通过电极向心脏施加心律转复/除颤脉冲对其进行纠正。用于治疗快速室性心律失常。再同步治疗除颤器还可用于心力衰竭治疗
2	植入式心室辅助系统	12	通常由植入式泵体、电源部分、血管连接和控制器组成。用于为进展期难治性左心衰患者血液循环提供机械支持，用于心脏移植前或恢复心脏功能的过渡治疗和/或长期治疗。供具备心脏移植条件与术后综合护理能力的医疗机构使用，医务人员、院外护理人员以及患者须通过相应培训。抗凝治疗不耐受患者禁用
3	植入式药物输注设备	12	通常由药物灌注泵、再灌注组件和导管入口组件组成。该产品与鞘内导管配合使用，进行长期药物的输入
4	人工心脏瓣膜和血管内支架	13	人工心脏瓣膜或瓣膜修复器械：一般采用高分子材料、动物组织、金属材料、无机非金属材料制成，可含或不含表面改性物质。用于替代或修复天然心脏瓣膜 血管内支架：支架一般采用金属（包括可吸收金属材料）或高分子材料（包括可吸收高分子材料）制成，其结构一般呈网架状。支架可含或不含表面改性物质，如涂层。可含有药物成分。如用于治疗动脉粥样硬化以及各种狭窄性、阻塞性或闭塞性等血管病变
5	含活细胞的组织工程医疗产品	13/16/17	以医疗器械作用为主的含活细胞的无源植入性组织工程医疗产品
6	可吸收四肢长骨内固定植入器械	13	采用可吸收高分子材料或可吸收金属材料制成，适用于四肢长骨骨折内固定

带你了解一下临床试验审批

审批对象

《需进行临床试验审批的第三类医疗器械目录》内的产品进行临床试验均需审批。

审批机构

由国家药品监督管理部门批准。

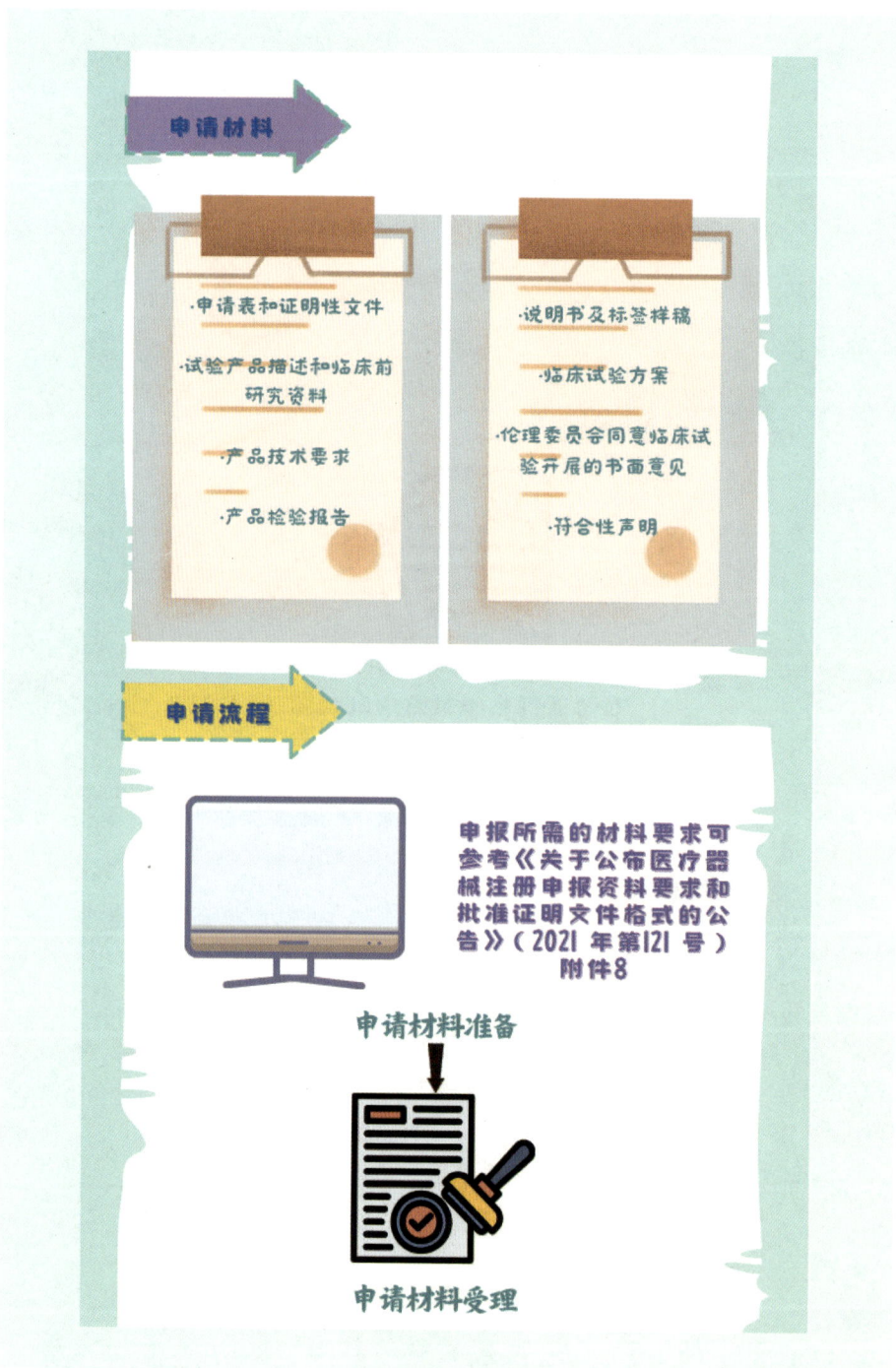

申请材料

- 申请表和证明性文件
- 试验产品描述和临床前研究资料
- 产品技术要求
- 产品检验报告

- 说明书及标签样稿
- 临床试验方案
- 伦理委员会同意临床试验开展的书面意见
- 符合性声明

申请流程

申报所需的材料要求可参考《关于公布医疗器械注册申报资料要求和批准证明文件格式的公告》（2021 年第121 号）附件8

申请材料准备

申请材料受理

申请材料受理

进入技术审评流程，60个工作日内完成技术审评工作。

一年内补回资料，收到资料后中心将于40个工作日内完成技术审评工作。

20个工作日内作出审批决定。

领取批件。

（2）其他

医疗器械临床试验审批申报资料依据《医疗器械注册申报资料要求和批准证明文件格式》准备，且受理前可申请与器审中心沟通交流，见"1.咨询服务"。

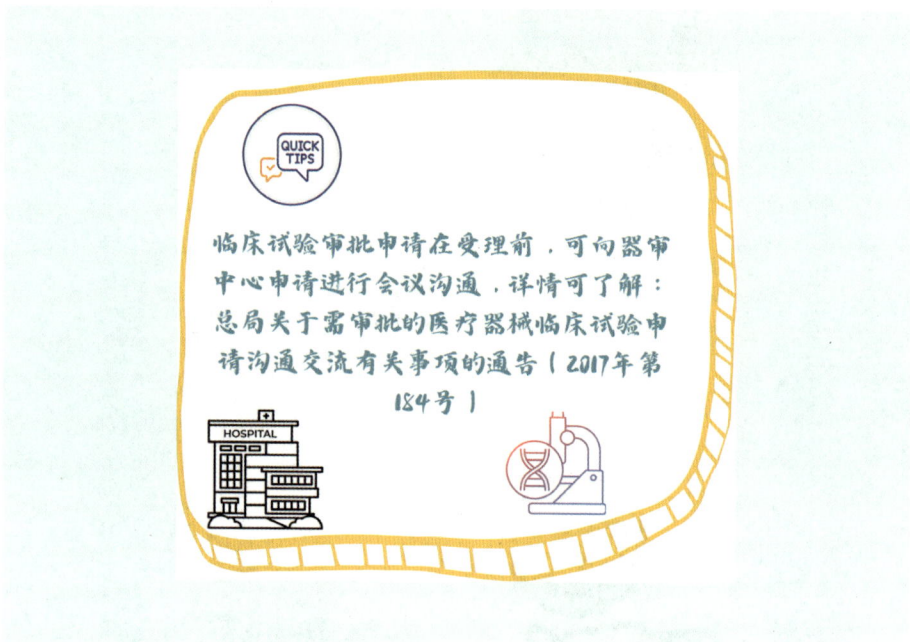

> QUICK TIPS
>
> 临床试验审批申请在受理前，可向器审中心申请进行会议沟通，详情可了解：总局关于需审批的医疗器械临床试验申请沟通交流有关事项的通告（2017年第184号）

5.4 体外诊断试剂临床试验

5.4.1 需进行医疗器械临床试验的判定

（1）列入免于临床试验体外诊断试剂目录的产品免于进行临床试验。免于进行临床试验的第二类、第三类体外诊断试剂目录由国家药品监督管理局制定、调整并公布。

（2）未列入免于临床试验体外诊断试剂目录产品的需进行临床试验。

（3）校准品、质控品单独申请注册不需要提交临床评价资料。

5.4.2 临床试验前准备

（1）预期的受益应当超过可能出现的损害；

（2）完成试验用体外诊断试剂临床前研究；

（3）准备充足的试验用体外诊断试剂；

（4）第三类体外诊断试剂临床试验应当在三个或三个以上医疗器械临床试验机构中进行；第二类产品应选择不少于两家（含两家）符合要求的临床试验机构；

（5）申办者与临床试验机构和研究者达成书面协议；

（6）获得医疗器械临床试验机构伦理委员会的同意；

（7）申办者应向所在省、自治区、直辖市食品药品监督管理部门备案。

5.4.3 临床试验方案

开展体外诊断试剂临床试验，申办者应根据试验目的，综合考虑试验体外诊断试剂的预期用途、产品特征和预期风险等，组织制定科学、合理的临床试验方案。临床试验方案经伦理委员会批准后应在临床试验全过程中严格遵循。

各临床试验机构应执行同一临床试验方案，方案中对试验设计类型、对比方法选择、受试者选择、评价指标、统计分析方法、样本量估算和质量控制要求等做出明确的规定，并根据各机构情况合理确定样本量分配计划。

5.4.4 临床试验报告

临床试验结束后应分别总结各临床试验机构的临床试验数据，出具临床试验小结，并附临床试验数据表、临床试验中所采用的其他试验方法或其他体外诊断试剂等产品的基本信息等资料，应按照《体外诊断试剂临床试验技术指导原则》的要求准备资料。

5.4.5 临床试验数据库

临床试验应根据《体外诊断试剂临床试验数据递交要求注册审查指导原则》的要求提交数据库。

5.4.6 临床试验流程

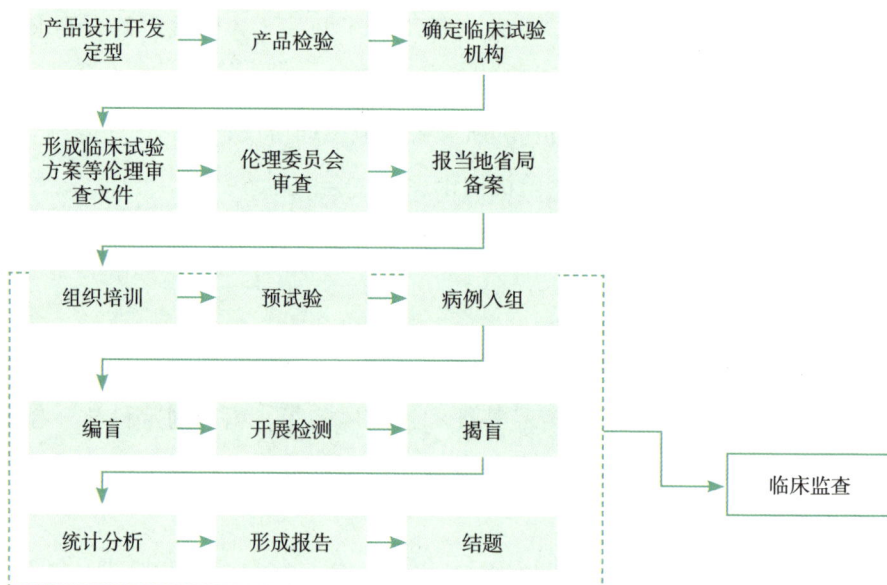

```
产品设计开发      产品检验        确定临床试验
定型                              机构


形成临床试验      伦理委员会       报当地省局
方案等伦理审      审查             备案
查文件


组织培训          预试验          病例入组


编盲             开展检测         揭盲                      临床监查


统计分析          形成报告         结题
```

5.4.7 临床试验审批申报资料

医疗器械临床试验审批申报资料依据《体外诊断试剂注册申报资料要求和批准证明文件格式》准备，且受理前可申请与器审中心沟通交流，见"1.咨询服务"。

5.5 案例解说

（1）已注册产品如未能在规定时间内申请延续注册，按照法规要求，需申请产品注册。此时，临床评价可否选择原注册产品作为同品种产品，完成临床评价？临床数据应该如何提供？

解答： 此种情形下，可选择原注册产品作为同品种产品，完成临床评价。同品种对比主要关注申报产品与原注册产品是否存在差异，如二者不存在差异，可提供该产品上市前和上市后的临床数据，包括上市后不良事件在内的临床经验数据。

（2）临床试验方案在试验过程中经多次修订，提交产品注册时，是否需提交历次试验方案、伦理委员会意见、知情同意书？

解答： 需提交最终版本的临床试验方案和知情同意书，历次变更的伦理委员会意见。最终版本的临床试验方案，应详细列明历次变更情况；如未列明，则需提交历次变更的临床试验方案。注册申请人应提供临床试验方案变更理由。

（3）如某产品的临床试验方案中包括可行性试验和确证性试验，试验结束后，是否可将可行性试验和确证性临床试验的结果合并统计？

解答： 可行性试验可初步评估产品的安全性和性能，为确证性试验设计提供信息，其与确证性临床试验的目的不同。试验结果的统计，应遵循预先规定的统计分析计划；不建议在试验结束后，将可行性试验和确证性临床试验结果合并统计。

（4）体外诊断试剂提交伦理文件应注意哪些事项？

解答： 体外诊断试剂临床试验资料中应提交临床试验执行的方案及与之对应的同意开展临床试验的伦理委员会书面意见。

由于临床试验方案的变更，可能存在多个版本号，提交申报资料时应注意以下原则：

如临床试验方案的变更发生在临床试验正式开展之前，应提交临床试验最终执行的版本号的临床试验方案，以及该版本号方案对应的伦理委员会书面意见。

如临床试验已经开始，过程中发生方案变更，应将变更前后版本的临床方案及其伦理文件一并提交，并明确说明方案变更的原因及其对已开展的临床试验的影响。

应当注意，临床试验之前应充分研究方案的科学性、合理性、可行性及合规性，制定方案并严格执行；临床试验过程中非必要原因不得随意对方案进行更改。

（5）体外诊断试剂盒说明书中的参考值涉及不同的年龄分布，应怎样进行临床试验样本选择？

解答： 临床试验设计过程中，纳入病例数除关注总体病例数、阳性和阴性病例数分布、干扰病例外，还应关注必要的病例分组、分层的需求。如试剂盒参考值在不同年龄段人群中有不同区间，在病例纳入时，应考虑不同年龄段人群的差异，分别纳入有统计学意义数量的不同年龄段人群，每个分段的人群中阳性和阴性病例比例应均衡。如参考值年龄分段较多，按照上述要求入组的总体病例数可能高于《体外诊断试剂临床试验技术指导原则》规定的最低样本量的要求。

（6）体外诊断试剂临床试验中如采用核酸序列测定、GC–MS/MS 等实验室检测参考方法作为对比方法进行比较研究，是否可以委托检验？

解答： 对于某些目前临床上尚不存在明确的临床诊断"金标准"，亦无可比的同类产品上市的体外诊断试剂，临床试验研究者应依据现有临床实践和理论基础，建立合理的方法，进行比较研究。对于部分体外诊断试剂，临床试验中采用核酸序列测定、GC–MS/MS 等实验室检测参考方法作为对比方法进行比较研究，这些方法非临床常规检测技术，需要专门的设备仪器和试验条件，且临床试验机构可能不具备相关检测条件。对于此类情况，注册申请人应尽可能选择具备相应条件的临床试验机构开展临床试验，确无检测条件的部分临床试验机构可将此部分测试委托给专门的测序机构、具备一定检测资质的实验室进行检测，并对检测结果进行认可。提交临床试验机构与受委托机构的委托证明文件，并评价对比方法的方法学研究和整体质量。

5.6 参考资料

食品药品监管总局关于发布医疗器械临床试验设计指导原则的通告（2018 年第 6 号）

食品药品监管总局关于发布接受医疗器械境外临床试验数据技术指导原则的通告（2018 年第 13 号）

国家药监局关于发布需进行临床试验审批的第三类医疗器械目录（2020 年修订版）的通告（2020 年第 61 号）

国家药监局关于发布真实世界数据用于医疗器械临床评价技术指导原则（试行）的通告（2020 年第 77 号）

国家药监局关于发布免于临床试验体外诊断试剂目录的通告（2021 年第 70 号）

国家药监局关于发布免于进行临床评价医疗器械目录的通告（2023 年第 33 号）

国家药监局关于发布体外诊断试剂临床试验技术指导原则的通告（2021 年第 72 号）

国家药监局关于发布医疗器械临床评价技术指导原则第 5 项技术指导原则的通告（2021 年第 73 号）

国家药监局关于发布免于临床试验的体外诊断试剂临床评价技术指导原则的通告（2021 年第 74 号）

国家药监局关于发布医疗器械临床试验数据递交要求第 2 项注册审查指导原则的通告（2021 年第 91 号）

国家药监局　国家卫健委关于发布《医疗器械临床试验质量管理规范》的公告（2022 年第 28 号）

6. 创新医疗器械特别审查

6.1 概述

2014年2月，原国家食品药品监督管理总局发布了《创新医疗器械特别审批程序（试行）》（食药监械管〔2014〕13号），自2014年3月1日起施行，该程序是在确保上市产品安全、有效的前提下，针对创新医疗器械设置的审批通道。2018年11月，国家药品监督管理局进行了修订，发布了《创新医疗器械特别审查程序》（以下简称本程序），自2018年12月1日起施行。

创新医疗器械特别审查是为了鼓励医疗器械的研究与创新，促进医疗器械新技术的推广和应用，推动医疗器械产业发展。

药品监督管理部门对同时符合相应条件的医疗器械按该程序实施审评审批，例如申请人应当具有产品核心技术发明专利权或者发明专利申请已由国务院专利行政部门公开，产品应当在技术上处于国际领先水平，并且具有显著的临床应用价值等。境内、境外的申请人均可按照该程序要求，提交相应的技术资料及证明性文件，提出创新医疗器械特别审查申请。经技术部门组织审查后认为符合相应条件的，可按照该程序实施审评审批。

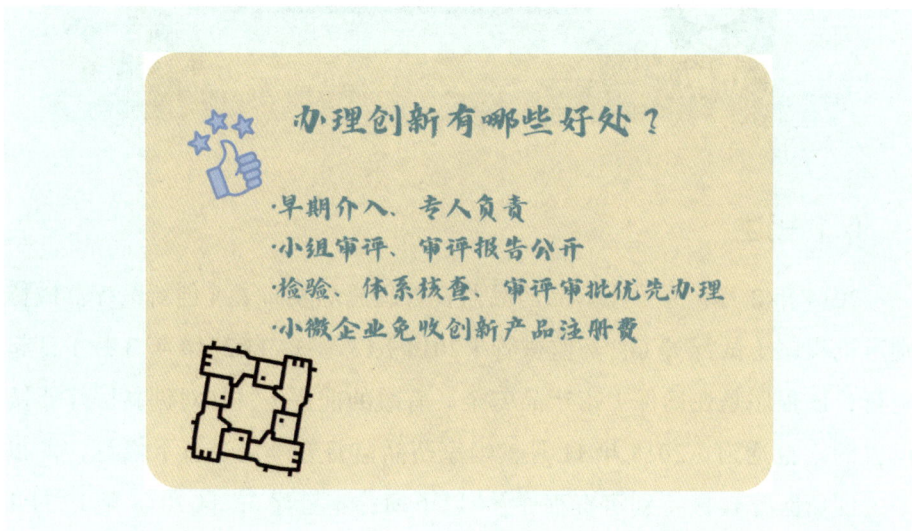

办理创新有哪些好处？

·早期介入、专人负责
·小组审评、审评报告公开
·检验、体系核查、审评审批优先办理
·小微企业免收创新产品注册费

6.2 相关定义

创新医疗器械是指符合下列情形的第二类、第三类医疗器械：

（1）申请人通过其主导的技术创新活动，在中国依法拥有产品核心技术发明专利权，或者依法通过受让取得在中国发明专利权或其使用权，创新医疗器械特别审查申请时间距专利授权公告日不超过5年；或者核心技术发明专利的申请已由国务院专利行政部门公开，并由国家知识产权局专利检索咨询中心出具检索报告，报告载明产品核心技术方案具备新颖性和创造性。

我符合条件吗？

(1)在中国依法拥有产品核心技术发明专利权，或者依法通过受让取得在中国发明专利权或其使用权，创新医疗器械特别审查申请时间距专利授权公告日不超过5年；或者核心技术发明专利的申请已由国务院专利行政部门公开，并由国家知识产权局专利检索咨询中心出具检索报告，报告载明产品核心技术方案具备新颖性和创造性。

(2)申请人已完成产品的前期研究并具有基本定型产品，研究过程真实和受控，研究数据完整和可溯源。

(3)产品主要工作原理或者作用机理为国内首创，产品性能或者安全性与同类产品比较有根本性改进，技术上处于国际领先水平，且具有显著的临床应用价值。

（2）申请人已完成产品的前期研究并具有基本定型产品，研究过程真实和受控，研究数据完整和可溯源。

（3）产品主要工作原理或者作用机理为国内首创，产品性能或者安全性与同类产品比较有根本性改进，技术上处于国际领先水平，且具有显著的临床应用价值。

6.3 申请流程

6.3.1 申请

申请人应当在医疗器械首次注册申请前，填写《创新医疗器械特别审查申请表》，并参考《创新医疗器械特别审查申报资料编写指南》，提交支持拟申报产品符合程序要求的资料。

6.3.2 初审

境内申请人应当向其所在地的省级药品监督管理部门提出创新医疗器械特别审查申请。省级药品监督管理部门对申报项目是否符合程序要求进行初审，出具初审意见。经初审不符合要求的，省级药品监督管理部门应当告知申请人；符合要求的，申请人将省级药品监督管理部门初审意见和申报资料一并报送国家药品监督管理局。

境外申请人应当向国家药品监督管理局提出创新医疗器械特别审查申请。

6.3.3 形式审查

创新医疗器械特别审查申请申报资料经形式审查后，对符合程序规定形式要求的予以受理，并给予受理编号，编排方式为：CQTS×××1×××2，其中，××××1为申请年份代码，×××2为产品流水号。

对于已受理的创新医疗器械特别审查申请，申请人可以在审查决定作出前，申请撤回创新医疗器械特别审查申请及相关资料，并说明理由。

6.3.4 审查

器审中心设立创新医疗器械审查办公室，对创新医疗器械特别审查申请进行审查。创新医疗器械审查办公室收到创新医疗器械特别审查申请后，组织专家进行审查。

创新医疗器械审查办公室收到创新医疗器械特别审查申请后，应当于60个工作日内出具审查意见（公示及异议处理时间不计算在内）。

申请资料存在以下五种情形之一的，创新医疗器械审查办公室不组织专家进行审查：

（1）申请资料虚假的；

（2）申请资料内容混乱、矛盾的；

（3）申请资料的内容与申报项目明显不符的；

（4）申请资料中产品知识产权证明文件不完整、专利权不清晰的；

（5）前次审查意见已明确指出产品主要工作原理或作用机制非国内首创，且再次申请时产品设计未发生改变的。

我应如何申报？

境内产品向当地
省局提交申请

初审，并给出
初审意见

符合要求的，申
请人将省级药品
监督管理部门初
审意见和申报资
料一并报送国家
药品监督管理
局。

经初审不符合要
求的，则通知申
请人。

DID YOU KNOW?

境外产品则直接向
国家药监局提交申
请，经形式审查
后，符合要求的将
予以受理。

6.3.5 公示

经创新医疗器械审查办公室审查，对拟进行特别审查的申请项目，在出具审查意见时一并对医疗器械管理类别进行界定，在器审中心网站将申请人、产品名称予以公示。对于公示内容有异议的，应当对相关意见研究后作出最终审查决定。

创新医疗器械审查办公室作出审查决定后，将审查结果通过器审中心网站告知申请人。

6.3.6 异议处理

任何单位和个人对拟同意按本程序进行审查产品公示存在异议的，应当在公示期内提出。异议内容仅限原申请事项及原申请资料。所提交的异议申请资料原则上应为经异议提出方签章的书面文件。

异议申请需经器审中心办公会集体研究后形成处理意见，创新审查组在形成处理意见后告知异议提出方。已有明确处理意见的，器审中心不再接受相同内容的异议申请。

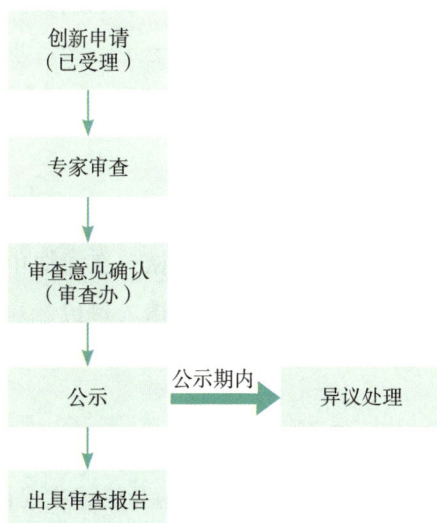

```
创新申请
（已受理）
    ↓
专家审查
    ↓
审查意见确认
（审查办）
    ↓
公示  ──公示期内──→  异议处理
    ↓
出具审查报告
```

6.4 重新申请与终止

6.4.1 重新申请

创新医疗器械临床研究工作需重大变更的，如临床试验方案修订，使用方法、规格型号、预期用途、适用范围或人群的调整等，申请人应当评估变更对医疗器械安全性、有效性和质量可控性的影响。产品主要工作原理或作用机制发生变化的创新医疗器械，应当按照本程序重新申请。

6.4.2 终止

属于下列情形之一的，国家药品监督管理局可终止本程序并告知申请人：

（1）申请人主动要求终止的；

（2）申请人未按规定的时间及要求履行相应义务的；

（3）申请人提供伪造和虚假资料的；

（4）全部核心技术发明专利申请被驳回或视为撤回的；

（5）失去产品全部核心技术发明专利专利权或者使用权的；

（6）申请产品不再作为医疗器械管理的；

（7）经专家审查会议讨论确定不宜再按照本程序管理的。

6.5 创新沟通交流

获准进入创新特别审查程序的医疗器械，在注册申请受理前以及技术审评阶段，由申请人提出，器审中心与申请人可以就注册申请事项进行沟通交流。

6.5.1 创新医疗器械沟通交流会议

创新医疗器械在注册申请受理前召开的会议，主要讨论下列问题：

（1）重大技术问题；

（2）重大安全性问题；

（3）临床试验方案；

（4）阶段性临床试验结果的总结与评价；

（5）其他需要沟通交流的问题。

创新医疗器械在技术审评阶段召开的会议，系应申请人要求，重点对补充资料通知单中内容进行的专题沟通交流。

6.5.2 创新医疗器械沟通交流申请途径

申请沟通交流会议的，申请人可登录 eRPS 系统提交咨询预约申请，相应部门会指定专人负责。

6.6 其他

（1）对于经审查同意按本程序审查的医疗器械，各级药品监督管理部门及相关技术机构，将根据各自职责和该程序规定，按照早期介入、专人负责、科学审查的原则，在标准不降低、程序不减少的前提下，对创新医疗器械予以优先办理，并加强与申请人的沟通交流。

（2）器审中心设立审查办公室对创新医疗器械特别审查申请进行审查，审查时一并对医疗器械管理类别进行界定。所申请创新医疗器械的管理属性存在疑问的，申请人应当先进行属性界定后再提出创新医疗器械特别审查申请。对于境内企业申请，如产品被界定为第二类医疗器械，相应的省级药品监督管理部门可参照本程序进行审查。

（3）审查结果告知后 5 年内，未申报注册的创新医疗器械，不再按照本程序实施审查。5 年后，申请人可重新申请创新医疗器械特别审查。

要注意的问题来了！

（1）创新医疗器械特别审查的申请必须在医疗器械产品注册申报前提交。

（2）第一类医疗器械不能申请创新医疗器械特别审查。

（3）创新医疗器械特别审查不收取申请费用。

6.7 案例解说

（1）创新医疗器械特别审查对提交的知识产权证明文件有哪些要求？

解答： 根据《创新医疗器械特别审查程序》中的有关规定：

1）申请人已获取中国发明专利权的，需提供经申请人签章的专利授权证书、权利要求书、说明书复印件和专利主管部门出具的专利登记簿副本原件。创新医疗器械特别审查申请时间距专利授权公告日不超过 5 年。

2）申请人依法通过受让取得在中国发明专利使用权的，除提交专利权人持有的专利授权证书、权利要求书、说明书、专利登记簿副本复印件外，还需提供经专利主管部门出具的《专利实施许可合同备案证明》原件。创新医疗器械特别审查申请时间距专利授权公告日不超过 5 年。

3）发明专利申请已由国务院专利行政部门公开、未获得授权的，需提供经申请人签章的发明专利已公开证明文件（如发明专利申请公布通知书、发明专利申请公布及进入实质审查阶段通知书、发明专利申请进入实质审查阶段通知书等）复印件和公布版本的权利要求书、说明书复印件。由国家知识产权局专利检索咨询中心出具检索报告，报告载明产品核心技术方案具备新颖性和创造性。发明专利申请审查过程中，权利要求书和说明书应专利审查部门要求发生修改的，需提交修改文本；专利权人发生变更的，提交专利主管部门出具的证明性文件，如手续合格通知书复印件。

（2）创新医疗器械特别审查的时限及如何查询创新申报结果？

解答： 根据《创新医疗器械特别审查程序》中的有关规定，创新医疗器械审查办公室收到创新医疗器械特别审查申请后，应当于 60 个工作日内出具审查意见（公示及异议处理时间不计算在内）。对拟进行特别审查的申请项目，应当在器审中心网站将申请人、产品名称予以公示，公示时间应当不少于 10 个工作日。对于公示内容有异议的，应当对相关意见研究后作出最终审查决定。申请人可通过登录国家药监局器审中心网站审评进度查询页面查询审查结果。

6.8 参考资料

国家药监局关于发布创新医疗器械特别审查程序的公告（2018 年第 83 号）

关于发布创新医疗器械特别审查申报资料编写指南的通告（2018 年第 127 号）

关于发布创新优先医疗器械注册技术审评沟通交流操作规范的通知（2021 年 12 月 1 日）

7. 优先审批

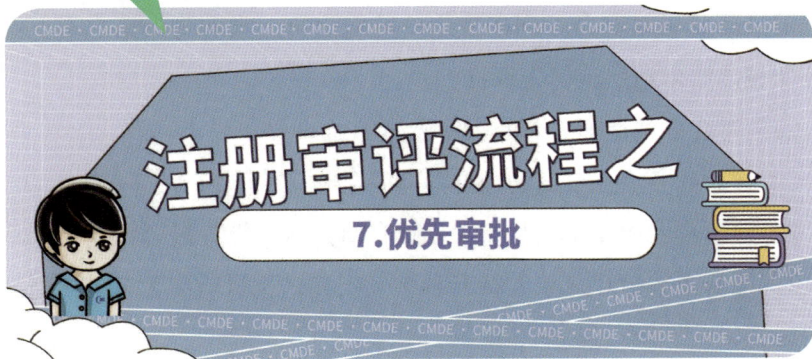

7.1 概述

2016 年 10 月，为保障医疗器械临床使用需求，原国家食品药品监督管理总局发布了《医疗器械优先审批程序》（以下简称本程序），自 2017 年 1 月 1 日起施行。

申请优先审批有哪些好处？

·审评优先排队
·体系核查优先
·审批优先
·专项交流

7.2 相关定义

国家药监局对符合下列条件之一的境内第三类和进口第二类、第三类医疗器械注册申请实施优先审批。

（1）符合下列情形之一的医疗器械：

1）诊断或者治疗罕见病，且具有明显临床优势；

2）诊断或者治疗恶性肿瘤，且具有明显临床优势；

3）诊断或者治疗老年人特有和多发疾病，且目前尚无有效诊断或者治疗手段；

4）专用于儿童，且具有明显临床优势；

5）临床急需，且在我国尚无同品种产品获准注册的医疗器械。

（2）列入国家科技重大专项或者国家重点研发计划的医疗器械。

（3）其他应当优先审批的医疗器械。

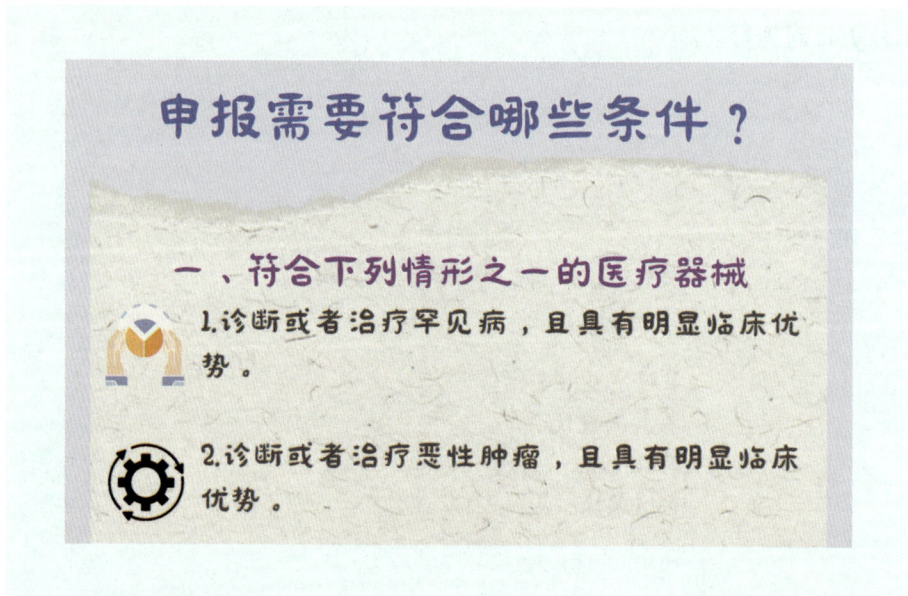

3.诊断或者治疗老年人特有和多发疾病，且目前尚无有效诊断或者治疗手段。

4.专用于儿童，且具有明显临床优势。

5.临床急需，且在我国尚无同品种产品获准注册的医疗器械。

二、列入国家科技重大专项或者国家重点研发计划的医疗器械。

三、对于其他应当优先审批的医疗器械，国家药监局根据各方面情况和意见，组织专家审查后确定是否予以优先审批。

7.3 申请流程

7.3.1 申请

对于符合医疗器械优先审批申请条件 7.2 中第（1）（2）项情形的，需要按照本程序优先审批的，申请人应当向国家药监局提出优先审批申请。对于符合医疗器械优先审批申请条件 7.2 中第（3）项情形的，由国家药监局广泛听取意见，并组织专家论证后确定。

申请人应当在提交医疗器械注册申请时一并提交《医疗器械优先审批申请表》，并参考《医疗器械优先审批申报资料编写指南（试行）》，提交支持拟申报产品符合程序要求的资料。

7.3.2 形式审查

医疗器械优先审批申请申报资料经形式审查后，对符合程序规定形式要求的予以受理。

7.3.3 审核

器审中心设立优先审批医疗器械审核办公室（以下简称优先审核办），负责优先评审批申请审核工作。

对于符合医疗器械优先审批申请条件 7.2 第（1）项情形的，器审中心优先审核办组织专家论证审核，并出具审核意见。经专家论证需要优先审批的，经优先审核办办公会确认后拟定予以优先审批。

对于符合医疗器械优先审批申请条件 7.2 第（2）项情形的，器审中心优先审核办进行审核，对申请人提交的资料进行确认，符合优先审批情形的，拟定予以优先审批。

我应如何申报？

符合申报条件第二项

提交相关证明文件

符合第一、二项的产品，在提交申报资料时，同时提交优先审批申请。

符合申报条件第一项

器审中心集中组织专家审查。

符合优先审批情形的，拟定予以优先审批。

拟定

出具审核意见，经专家论证需要优先审批的，经优先审核办办公会确认后拟定予以优先审批。

公示期内无异议的，即优先进入审评程序，并告知申请人。

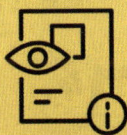

公示

列入优先审批

7.3.4 公示

拟定优先审批项目的申请人、产品名称、受理号将在器审中心网站上予以公示。公示期内无异议的，即列入优先审批，并告知申请人。

7.3.5 异议处理

任何机构或个人对拟同意按本程序进行审批产品公示存在异议的，应在规定的公示期内提出；申请人对审查结论及不同意理由存在异议的，应在收到告知后 10 个工作日内提出，异议内容仅限原申请事项及原申请资料。所提交的异议申请资料原则上应为经异议提出方签章的书面文件。

器审中心研究后对异议申请形成处理意见，并告知异议提出方。已有明确处理意见的，中心不再接受相同内容的异议申请。

7.4 优先审批沟通交流

对于列入优先审批的医疗器械，器审中心在技术审评过程中，按照相关规定积极与申请人进行沟通交流，必要时，可以安排专项交流。

申请人可登录 eRPS 系统提交咨询预约申请，相应部门会指定专人负责。

7.5 其他

（1）已经按照医疗器械应急审批程序、创新医疗器械特别审查程序进行审查的注册申请项目，不执行本程序。

（2）对公示项目有异议的，器审中心在收到异议起 10 个工作日内，对相关意见进行研究，并将研究意见告知申请人和异议提出方。

（3）器审中心经审核不予优先审批的，将不予优先审批的意见和原因告知申请人，并按常规审批程序办理。

7.6 参考资料

总局关于发布医疗器械优先审批程序的公告（2016 年第 168 号）

总局关于发布医疗器械优先审批申报资料编写指南（试行）的通告（2017 年第 28 号）

关于发布创新优先医疗器械注册技术审评沟通交流操作规范的通知（2021 年 12 月 1 日）

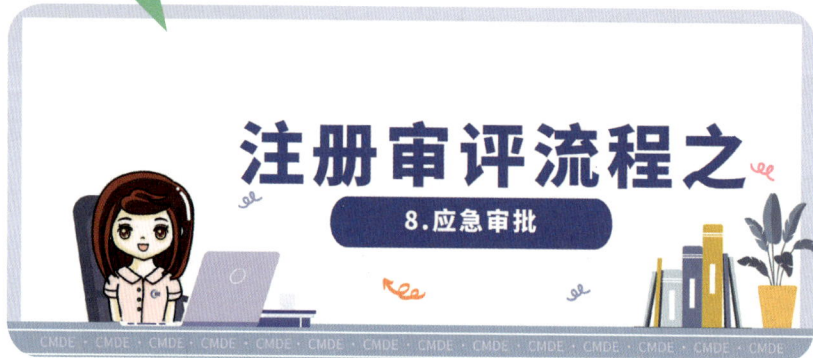

8.1 概述

2009 年 8 月，为有效预防、及时控制和消除突发公共卫生事件的危害，确保突发公共卫生事件应急所需医疗器械尽快完成审批，原国家食品药品监督管理总局发布了《关于印发医疗器械应急审批程序通知》（国食药监械〔2009〕565 号）。2021 年 12 月 29 日，国家药品监督管理局进行了修订，发布了《医疗器械应急审批程序》，自发布之日起施行。

申请医疗器械应急审批的，境内注册申请人应当将产品应急所需的情况及产品研发情况告知相应的省、自治区、直辖市药品监督管理局，省、自治区、直辖市药品监督管理局应当及时了解相关医疗器械研制情况，必要时采取早期介入的方式，对拟申报产品进行评估，并及时指导注册申请人开展相关申报工作。

医疗器械应急审批是为了有效预防、及时控制和消除突发公共卫生事件的危害，确保突发公共卫生事件应急所需医疗器械尽快完成审批。

应急审批的原则有哪些

统一指挥   早期介入   随到随审   科学审批

8.2 相关定义

国家药监局对突发公共卫生事件应急所需，且在我国境内尚无同类产品上市，或虽在我国境内已有同类产品上市，但产品供应不能满足突发公共卫生事件应急处理需要，并经国家药监局确认的境内第三类和进口第二类、第三类医疗器械的注册申请实施应急审批。

8.3 申请流程

8.3.1 申请

申请境内第三类和进口第二类、第三类医疗器械应急审批的，应当向国家药监局受理部门提交《医疗器械应急审批申请表》和产品研究综述资料及相关说明。

8.3.2 确认

国家药监局组织专家，通过会议、函审、书面征求意见等方式对申请应急审批的医疗器械和国家应急响应工作机制书面推荐的应急所需医疗器械是否符合 8.2 的要求，以及研发成熟度、生产能力等进行评估，及时对产品是否进行应急审批予以确认，并将结果通知申请人、相应技术机构、省、自治区、直辖市药品监督管理局。

8.3.3 受理前预审查

对于经国家药监局确认进行应急审批的医疗器械（以下简称应急审批医疗器械），器审中心指定专人，早期介入，按照注册申请人需求，通过适当方式开展咨询，指导注册申报资料准备，并按照医疗器械审评工作要求，对企业拟提交注册的资料按照随到随审原则开展受理前预审查。

8.3.4 受理

对于应急审批医疗器械，注册申请人应在申报表中勾选"应急审批"，器审中心于当天完成注册申请事项的签收，并按照国家药监局立卷审查要求开展立卷审查。对于缴费事宜，注册申请人可按照缴费通知书上的说明进行缴费。

8.3.5 技术审评

器审中心在应急审批医疗器械注册申请转入技术审评阶段后 10 日内完成境内和进口第三类应急审批医疗器械注册申请的技术审评；在 5 日内完成进口第二类应急审批医疗器械注册申请的技术审评。

8.4 沟通交流

经国家药监局组织评估和审核确认属于进行应急审批的医疗器械后，

申请人可随时与中心相关部门进行沟通交流。

8.5 其他

（1）对于应急审批医疗器械，附条件批准上市的，医疗器械注册证的有效期与注册证注明的附带条件的完成时限一致，原则上不超过 1 年。如注册人完成附带条件，可以在到期之日前申请办理延续注册，符合要求的给予延续注册，注册证有效期为 5 年。

（2）对于应急审批医疗器械，自确认应急审批之日起 90 日内，如注册申请人无法按照注册要求完成注册申报资料准备并获得注册申请受理，不再按照应急审批办理，原则上可以参照本程序，受理后优先审评审批。

8.6 参考资料

关于发布《医疗器械应急审批程序》的公告（2021 年第 157 号）

9. 注册和备案申报资料准备

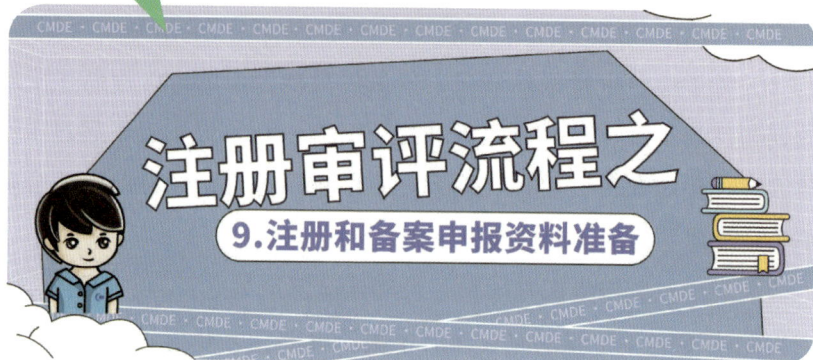

9.1 概述

医疗器械／体外诊断试剂注册是指医疗器械／体外诊断试剂注册申请人依照法定程序和要求提出医疗器械／体外诊断试剂注册申请，药品监督管理部门依据法律法规，基于科学认知，进行安全性、有效性和质量可控性等审查，决定是否同意其申请的活动。

医疗器械／体外诊断试剂备案是指医疗器械／体外诊断试剂备案人依照法定程序和要求向药品监督管理部门提交备案资料，药品监督管理部门对提交的备案资料存档备查的活动。

医疗器械/体外诊断试剂注册、备案应当遵守相关法律、法规、规章、强制性标准，遵循医疗器械/体外诊断试剂安全和性能基本原则，参照相关技术指导原则，证明注册、备案的医疗器械/体外诊断试剂安全、有效、质量可控，保证全过程信息真实、准确、完整和可追溯。

9.2 备案申请

9.2.1 备案资料的形式要求

（1）备案资料完整齐备，备案表填写完整。

（2）各项文件除关联文件外均应以中文形式提供。如关联文件为外文形式还应提供中文译本并由代理人签章。根据外文资料翻译的资料，应当同时提供原文。

（3）境内产品备案资料如无特殊说明的，应当由备案人签章。"签章"是指备案人盖公章，或者其法定代表人、负责人签名加盖备案人公章。

（4）进口产品备案资料如无特别说明，原文资料均应当由备案人签章，中文资料由代理人签章。原文资料"签章"是指备案人的法定代表人或者负责人签名，或者签名加组织机构印章；中文资料"签章"是指代理人盖公章，或者其法定代表人、负责人签名并加盖代理人公章。

（5）进口产品备案资料中由境外备案人提供的关联文件、符合性声明以及说明书、标签应当提交由备案人所在地公证机构出具的公证件。公证件可以是通过电子公证模式办理的，但应当同时提交由境外备案人出具的关于公证模式的说明文件。

（6）备案人提交纸质备案资料的，备案资料应当有所提交资料目录，包括备案资料的一级和二级标题，并以表格形式说明每项的页码。

9.2.2 备案资料要求

符合条件的备案人应按照《国家药监局关于第一类医疗器械备案有关事项的公告》的相关要求准备资料。

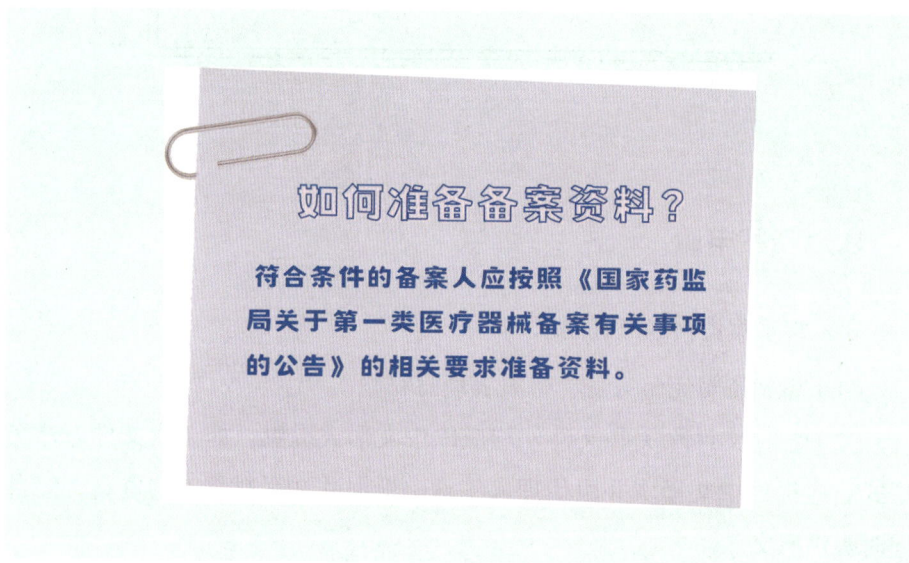

如何准备备案资料？

符合条件的备案人应按照《国家药监局关于第一类医疗器械备案有关事项的公告》的相关要求准备资料。

9.3 注册申请

9.3.1 注册资料电子申报要求

2019年5月31日，国家药品监督管理局发布了《关于实施医疗器械电子申报的公告》，为实现医疗器械注册申请了电子申报，医疗器械注册电子申报系统（eRPS 系统）于 2019 年 6 月 24 日正式实施。

施行 eRPS 系统后，各类医疗器械注册申请电子申报目录（RPS ToC）见《关于发布医疗器械注册电子申报目录（RPS ToC）文件夹结构的通告》。

申报资料一级标题	申报资料二级标题
1. 监管信息	1.1 章节目录 1.2 申请表 1.3 术语、缩写词列表 1.4 产品列表 1.5 关联文件 1.6 申报前与监管机构的联系情况和沟通记录 1.7 符合性声明
2. 综述资料	2.1 章节目录 2.2 概述 2.3 产品描述 2.4 适用范围和禁忌证 2.5 申报产品上市历史 2.6 其他需说明的内容
3. 非临床资料	3.1 章节目录 3.2 产品风险管理资料 3.3 医疗器械安全和性能基本原则清单 3.4 产品技术要求及检验报告 3.5 研究资料 3.6 非临床文献 3.7 稳定性研究 3.8 其他资料
4. 临床评价资料	4.1 章节目录 4.2 临床评价资料 4.3 其他资料
5. 产品说明书和标签样稿	5.1 章节目录 5.2 产品说明书 5.3 标签样稿 5.4 其他资料

续表

申报资料一级标题	申报资料二级标题
6. 质量管理体系文件	6.1 综述 6.2 章节目录 6.3 生产制造信息 6.4 质量管理体系程序 6.5 管理职责程序 6.6 资源管理程序 6.7 产品实现程序 6.8 质量管理体系的测量、分析和改进程序 6.9 其他质量体系程序信息 6.10 质量管理体系核查文件

注：此处以医疗器械注册申报资料要求为例

申报资料一级标题	申报资料二级标题
1. 监管信息	1.1 章节目录 1.2 申请表 1.3 术语、缩写词列表 1.4 产品列表 1.5 关联文件 1.6 申报前与监管机构的联系情况和沟通记录 1.7 符合性声明
2. 综述资料	2.1 章节目录 2.2 概述 2.3 产品描述 2.4 预期用途 2.5 申报产品上市历史 2.6 其他需说明的内容
3. 非临床资料	3.1 章节目录 3.2 产品风险管理资料 3.3 体外诊断试剂安全和性能基本原则清单 3.4 产品技术要求及检验报告 3.5 分析性能研究 3.6 稳定性研究 3.7 阳性判断值或参考区间研究 3.8 其他资料

续表

申报资料一级标题	申报资料二级标题
4. 临床评价资料	4.1 章节目录 4.2 临床评价资料
5. 产品说明书和标签样稿	5.1 章节目录 5.2 产品说明书 5.3 标签样稿 5.4 其他资料
6. 质量管理体系文件	6.1 综述 6.2 章节目录 6.3 生产制造信息 6.4 质量管理体系程序 6.5 管理职责程序 6.6 资源管理程序 6.7 产品实现程序 6.8 质量管理体系的测量、分析和改进程序 6.9 其他质量体系程序信息 6.10 质量管理体系核查文件

注：此处以体外诊断试剂注册申报资料要求为例

9.3.2 注册资料要求

符合条件的注册申请人应按照《关于公布医疗器械注册申报资料要求和批准证明文件格式的公告》中附件 5《医疗器械注册申报资料要求及说明》和《关于公布体外诊断试剂申报资料要求和批准证明文件格式的公告》中附件 4《体外诊断试剂注册申报资料要求及说明》的相关要求准备资料。

如何准备注册申报资料？

符合条件的注册申请人应按照《关于公布医疗器械注册申报资料要求和批准证明文件格式的公告》和《关于公布体外诊断试剂申报资料要求和批准证明文件格式的公告》的相关要求准备资料。

9.4 案例解说

申请表中备注栏的填写要求有哪些？

解答： 注册申请人应完整填写申请表备注内容，要求如下：注册申请人如实填写利益相关方面的专家 / 单位信息，包括并不限于理化指标检测、生物性能试验、动物试验、临床试验、合作研究者、知识产权买卖方等，并明确申请回避的专家及理由。如有涉及利益相关的专家，应明确专家参与的具体企业的名称及具体研发项目名称。备注信息不能为空，如无相关内容可填写"无"。

9.5 参考资料

关于医疗器械注册电子申报信息化系统业务办理有关事宜的通告（2019 年第 4 号）

关于发布医疗器械注册申请电子提交技术指南的通告（2019年第29号）

关于实施医疗器械电子申报的公告（2019年46号）

关于发布医疗器械注册电子申报目录文件夹结构的通告（2021年第15号）

关于公布医疗器械注册申报资料要求和批准证明文件格式的公告（2021年第121号）

关于公布体外诊断试剂注册申报资料要求和批准证明文件格式的公告（2021年第122号）

国家药监局关于第一类医疗器械备案有关事项的公告(2022年第62号)

10. 受理

10.1 概述

对第一类医疗器械实行备案管理，第二类、第三类医疗器械实行产品注册管理。申请人可根据《医疗器械监督管理条例》到相应药品监督管理部门办理。

10.1.1 备案

办理医疗器械备案时，应按照"9.注册和备案申报资料准备"要求赴相应的药品监督管理部门（以下简称药监部门）备案，对备案事项有下列不同情况：

（1）备案人提交符合《国家药监局关于第一类医疗器械备案有关事项的公告》要求的备案资料后即完成备案。对备案的医疗器械，备案部门向备案人提供备案编号（备案编号告知书），并按照规定的时间公布《第一类医疗器械备案信息表》或《第一类体外诊断试剂备案信息表》中登载的有关信息。

（2）办理医疗器械备案时，备案资料不符合要求的，相应的药监部门应告知备案人并说明理由。

（3）已备案的医疗器械，备案信息表中登载内容和备案产品技术要求发生变化时，备案人应当向原备案部门变更备案，并提交变化情况的说明及相关文件。

10.1.2 注册和注册受理

申请医疗器械注册时，申请人／注册申请人应按照"9.注册和备案申报资料准备"要求准备申报资料，并报送至相应的药监部门。申请事项属于本部门职权范围，且申报资料经立卷审查，资料齐全、符合立卷审查要求的，予以受理；申请资料不齐全或者不符合要求的，应在5日内一次告知需要补正的全部内容，逾期未告知的，自收到申请资料之日起即为受理。

办 理 流 程

网站注册

登录国家药监局行政受理服务大厅网上预约受理系统进行注册

相关操作可参考《关于启用总局行政受理服务大厅网上预约受理系统的公告》（第192号）、《关于调整行政受理服务大厅网上预约受理系统可预约时段的公告》（第220号）

预约受理

每天7：00-23：00均可登录网上预约受理系统进行预约

也可不进行网上预约，直接前往大厅取号办理

现场办理

现场叫号至窗口办理

网上预约的优先办理

tips：该内容仅针对器审中心受理的进口第二类/第三类、境内第三类注册项目~

立卷审查
（器审中心进行）

ePRS系统随机分配具备相应资质的器审中心审评人员对申报资料进行立卷审查

资料符合要求的将由器审中心正式受理，并发放"受理通知书"及"缴费通知书"

不符合要求的将发放"申请材料补正通知书"或"不予受理通知书"

NO!

10.2 申报资料提交

申报资料可通过线上和线下两种途径提交受理。

10.2.1 线上提交

申请人／注册申请人可凭数字认证证书（以下简称 CA）通过 eRPS 系统进行线上提交。eRPS 系统提供两种申报提交方式，申请人／注册申请人可使用网页版或者客户端进行登录。在通过线上途径提交申报资料前，申请人／注册申请人需先申领配套使用的 CA。

为指导申请人／注册申请人正确使用 eRPS 系统进行线上提交，国家药品监督管理局发布了《关于发布医疗器械注册申请电子提交技术指南的通告》。

10.2.2 线下提交

线下提交有两种方式，邮寄或现场递交到国家药品监督管理局行政受理服务大厅。

10.2.2.1 邮寄方式提交

申报资料邮寄至国家药品监督管理局行政受理服务大厅的，器审中心收到申报资料后将在 5 个工作日内对申报资料进行立卷审查并做出审查决定（受理、不予受理或补正材料），审查决定以邮寄方式送达申请人／注册申请人。

10.2.2.2 现场递交

申请人／注册申请人可赴国家药品监督管理局行政受理服务大厅取号排队办理业务，亦可提前在网上预约后当场递交申报资料，网上预约优先于现场取号。

申请人／注册申请人可登陆国家药品监督管理局门户网站"网上办事大厅"子网站办理网上预约。

网上预约注意事项

1 申请人需提前注册，审核通过的申请人方可办理网上预约业务。

2 一家注册企业最多可注册 10 个业务办理人，每个业务类别一个工作日只能预约一次。

3 预约成功的注册办理人须在约定时间持本人有效身份证和委托书到大厅领取预约号，办理相关业务。

4 预约成功后，申请人可在约定办理日的 4 个自然日前取消预约。未取消预约且未按预约时间前来办理业务的，视为爽约。爽约次数超过 3 次，该企业注册账户冻结 30 个自然日。期间，申请人只能通过现场取号方式办理业务。冻结期过后限制自动解除，该企业注册账户可继续使用，爽约次数重新累计。

10.3 受理缴费

经立卷审查符合要求的申报事项将由器审中心正式予以受理，并发放"受理通知书"及"缴费通知书"；不符合要求的资料将被退回，并发放"申请材料补正通知书"或"不予受理通知书"。

线下提交注册申请的，器审中心默认通过邮寄途径将纸质的行政受理文书送达申请人/注册申请人；线上提交注册申请的，申请人/注册申请人可凭 CA 登录 eRPS 系统同步查阅电子文书。

对于缴费事宜，申请人/注册申请人可按照缴费通知书上的说明进行缴费。

缴费

按照缴费通知书及时进行缴费

器审中心注册受理事项

- 境内第三类医疗器械注册申请
- 进口第二、三类医疗器械注册申请
- 进口第一类医疗器械备案
- 临床试验审批
- 其他事项

TIPS

线上或线下途径提交的电子申报资料上传成功后，转入电子申报系统签收环节，签收成功的短信通知

签收了的资料受理决定在5个工作日内作出；逾期不告知的，自收到申请资料之日起即为受理

申报事项及相应缴费标准可查询：国家食品药品监督管理总局关于发布药品、医疗器械产品注册收费标准的公告（2015年第53号）

10.4 案例解说

（1）如何有效地与受理大厅沟通受理通知书、补正通知书、备案凭证等相关纸质资料准确的快递地址及联系人信息？

解答： 受理大厅会优先以申请表其他需要说明的问题中备注的快递地址及联系人信息作为有效快递信息，如此部分无内容，则以申请表中申请人/注册人/代理人信息作为有效快递信息。为确保相关文书及时准确送达，建议准确填写注册申请表。

（2）进口医疗器械已在中国境内获得注册证，现拟由境外转移至境内生产，应如何申请注册？

解答： 依据关于实施《医疗器械注册与备案管理办法》《体外诊断试剂注册与备案管理办法》有关事项的通告（2021年第76号），境外企业在境内生产的医疗器械，应当由境内生产的企业作为注册申请人申请注册。已获得注册证的进口器械，可以参考《国家药监局关于进口医疗器械产品在中国境内企业生产有关事项的公告》（2020年104号）提交注册申报资料。

10.5 参考资料

关于发布医疗器械注册申请电子提交技术指南的通告（2019年第29号）

国家药监局关于第一类医疗器械备案有关事项的公告（2022年第62号）

11. 审评审批

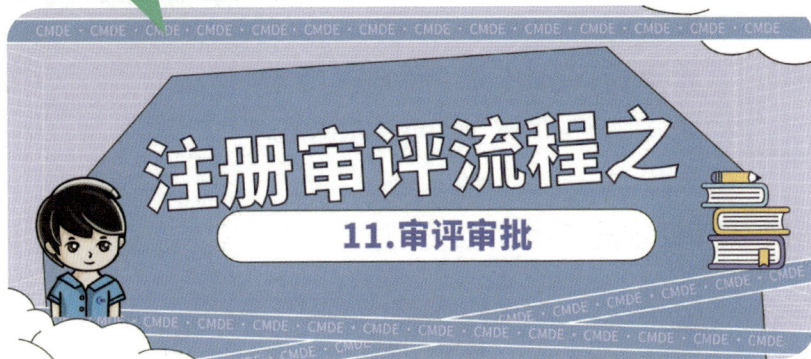

11.1 审评审批部门

医疗器械产品范围极为广泛，从简单安全的压舌板到复杂的心脏起搏器均属于医疗器械。为对医疗器械开展有效的监管，我国监管部门将医疗器械根据其风险程度分为三类，分类级别随着风险程度的增高而增大，对不同分类级别的医疗器械的监管措施也有所不同：第一类医疗器械实行备案管理；第二类、第三类医疗器械实行注册管理。

根据《医疗器械监督管理条例》，境内第一类、第二类、第三类和进口第一类、第二类、第三类医疗器械分别需向不同药品监督管理部门完成备案或注册，香港、澳门、台湾地区医疗器械的备案、注册参照进口医疗器械办理。不同类别医疗器械的备案或者注册主管部门详见表5。

表5　境内、境外医疗器械注册和备案监管归口表

产品属性		管理类型	主管部门
境内	第一类	备案	设区的市级负责药品监督管理的部门
	第二类	注册	省级药品监管部门
	第三类	注册	国家药品监督管理局

续表

产品属性	管理类型	主管部门
境外 第一类	备案	国家药品监督管理局
第二类	注册	国家药品监督管理局
第三类	注册	国家药品监督管理局

11.2 审评审批流程

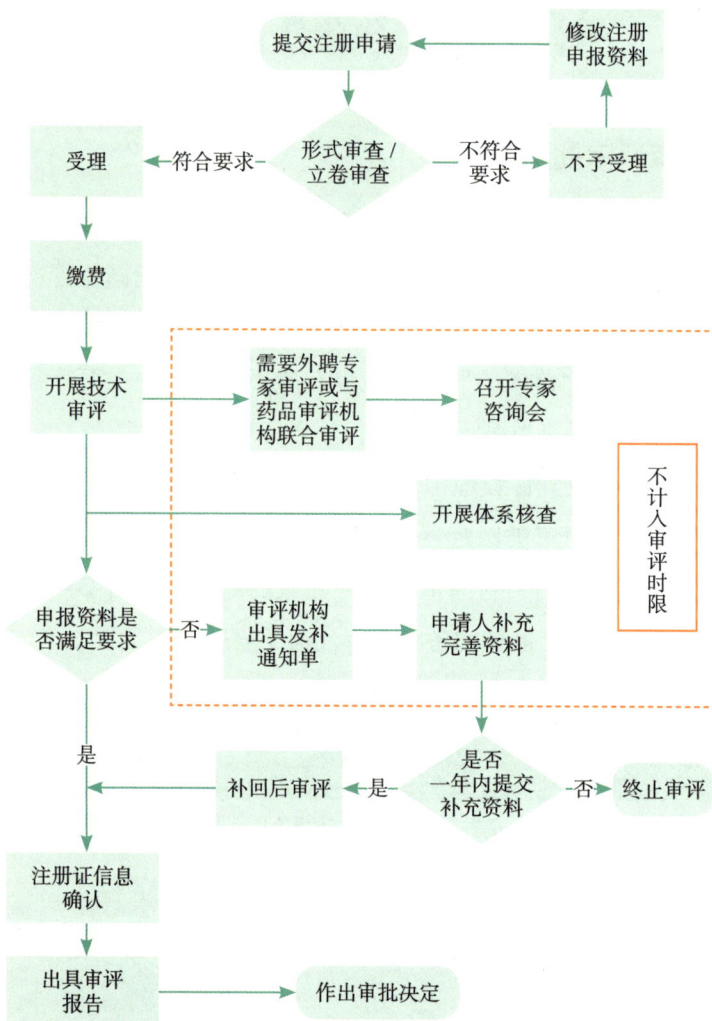

```
提交注册申请 ← 修改注册申报资料

形式审查/立卷审查 — 不符合要求 → 不予受理
          符合要求 → 受理

受理 → 缴费 → 开展技术审评

开展技术审评 → 需要外聘专家审评或与药品审评机构联合审评 → 召开专家咨询会

→ 开展体系核查

不计入审评时限

申报资料是否满足要求 — 否 → 审评机构出具发补通知单 → 申请人补充完善资料

是 ↓

申请人补充完善资料 → 是否一年内提交补充资料 — 是 → 补回后审评
                                    否 → 终止审评

注册证信息确认 → 出具审评报告 → 作出审批决定
```

11.2.1 受理

药品监督管理部门在收到备案或注册申请时，对申报资料进行受理审查，受理意见可能有以下三种情形：

（1）申请事项属于本部门职权范围，申报资料齐全、符合受理审查要求的，予以受理。

（2）申报资料不齐全或者不符合受理审查要求的，应当在5个工作日内一次告知申请人需要补正的全部内容，逾期未告知的，即为受理。

（3）申请事项不属于本部门职权范围的，告知申请人不予受理。

具体受理程序见"10.受理"。

11.2.2 缴费

器审中心受理注册申请后，注册申请人将收到受理通知书和缴费通知书，注册申请人需根据缴费通知单要求按时缴纳相关费用，见"10.3 受理缴费"。

11.2.3 技术审评

注册申请项目在受理之日起的3个工作日内转入技术审评。审评部门在60个工作日内完成第二类医疗器械注册的技术审评工作，在90个工作日内完成第三类医疗器械注册的技术审评工作；在60个工作日内完成补充资料的技术审评工作。对于医疗器械临床试验申请，技术审评时限为60个工作日，申请资料补正后的技术审评时限为40个工作日。

以下情况暂停技术审评时限计时：

（1）需要外聘专家审评、药品审评机构联合审评、召开专家咨询会的，具体要求见"14.专家咨询"。

（2）如有必要，可对注册申请人进行与产品研制、生产有关的质量管理体系核查。境内第二类、第三类医疗器械质量管理体系核查，由各省、自治区、直辖市药品监督管理部门开展。各省、自治区、直辖市药品监督管理部门应当在 30 个工作日内根据相关要求完成体系核查。进口第二类、第三类医疗器械质量管理体系核查由国家药品监督管理局质量管理体系检查技术机构开展，具体要求见"12.注册质量管理体系核查"。

（3）技术审评过程中需要注册申请人补正资料的，技术审评机构将一次告知需要补正的全部内容。注册申请人应当在收到补正通知 1 年内按照补正通知的要求一次性提供补充资料。注册申请人逾期未提交补充资料的，由技术审评机构终止技术审评，提出不予注册的建议，由药品监督管理部门核准后作出不予注册的决定。对补正资料通知内容有疑问的，申请人/注册申请人可以申请审评补正意见预约咨询，与审评人员进行沟通。具体补正资料程序见"13.补充资料"。

（4）请示国家药监局关于技术审评涉及的相关政策问题待回复意见等依据法规和相关文件可暂停审评计时的其他情形。

以下时间不计入相关工作时限：

1）申请人补充资料、核查后整改等所占用的时间；

2）因申请人原因延迟核查的时间；

3）外聘专家咨询、召开专家咨询会、药械组合产品需要与药品审评机构联合审评的时间；

4）根据规定中止审评审批程序的，中止审评审批程序期间所占用的时间；

5）质量管理体系核查所占用的时间。

11.2.4 审批

技术审评结束后 20 个工作日内由受理注册申请的药品监督管理部门作出审批决定。对于符合安全、有效、质量可控要求的产品，准予注册的，发给医疗器械注册证，经过核准的产品技术要求以附件形式发给注册申请人。对不予注册的，书面说明理由。

11.3 审评审批进度查询

NMPA

· 进入国家药品监督管理局官网

通过国家药监局官网进入
网上办事大厅登录查询

TIPS 上述方法可查询国家药品监督管理局
已受理的境内第三类、进口第二、三
类医疗器械注册申请、变更及补办申
请的办理进度。

1. 查询结果中"缴费状态"分为：已缴费、未缴费、不收费。
2. 查询结果中"办理状态"有以下情况：在审评、自行撤回、
在审批、中止审查、审查完毕—待制证、制证完毕—待发批
件、制证完毕—等待交回旧证、制证完毕—已发批件。

CMDE ⭐

- 进入器审中心官网

  点击审评进度查询，按照页面提示
  输入相应信息进行查询

- 进入eRPS系统

  通过申请人CA登录eRPS系统，在
  平台首页即可查看所有项目状态。

TIPS

通过上述途径可查询到已受理的注册申请事项审评进度，进度状态显示可能为：主审审评、处长复核、主任签发、已转器械司、已审结、已归档、已完结、补充资料、专家咨询协调实施等。

上述查询结果仅供申请人了解其已受理的医疗器械注册申请事项审评进度之用，相关信息仅供参考，并以正式通知为准，不作为任何证明途径使用。

CMDE

· 关注器审中心微信公众号

通过企业服务—产品跟踪进行查询。

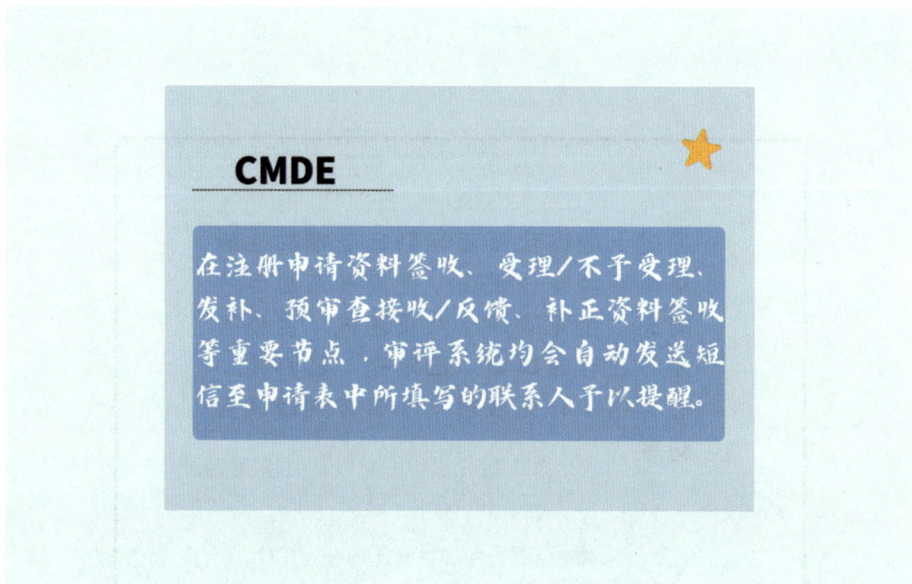

11.4 参考资料

国家食品药品监督管理总局关于调整部分医疗器械行政审批事项审批程序的决定（国家食品药品监督管理总局令第 32 号）

关于开展医疗器械注册证及其附件信息确认工作的通告（2021 年第 9 号）

国家药监局关于印发境内第三类和进口医疗器械注册审批操作规范的通知（2021 年 11 月 2 日）

国家药监局关于印发境内第二类医疗器械注册审批操作规范的通知（2021 年 11 月 2 日）

12. 注册质量管理体系核查

12.1 概述

注册申请人应当在申请注册时提交与产品研制、生产有关的质量管理体系相关资料，受理注册申请的药品监督管理部门在产品技术审评时认为有必要对质量管理体系进行核查的，应当组织开展质量管理体系核查，并可以根据需要调阅原始资料。

12.2 不同类型产品核查要求

（1）境内第三类医疗器械／体外诊断试剂质量管理体系核查，由器审中心通知注册申请人所在地的省、自治区、直辖市药品监督管理部门开展。

（2）境内第二类医疗器械／体外诊断试剂质量管理体系核查，由注册申请人所在地的省、自治区、直辖市药品监督管理部门组织开展。

（3）器审中心对进口第二类、第三类医疗器械／体外诊断试剂开展技术审评时，认为有必要进行质量管理体系核查的，通知国家药品监督管理局食品药品审核查验中心（以下简称核查中心）根据相关要求开展核查。

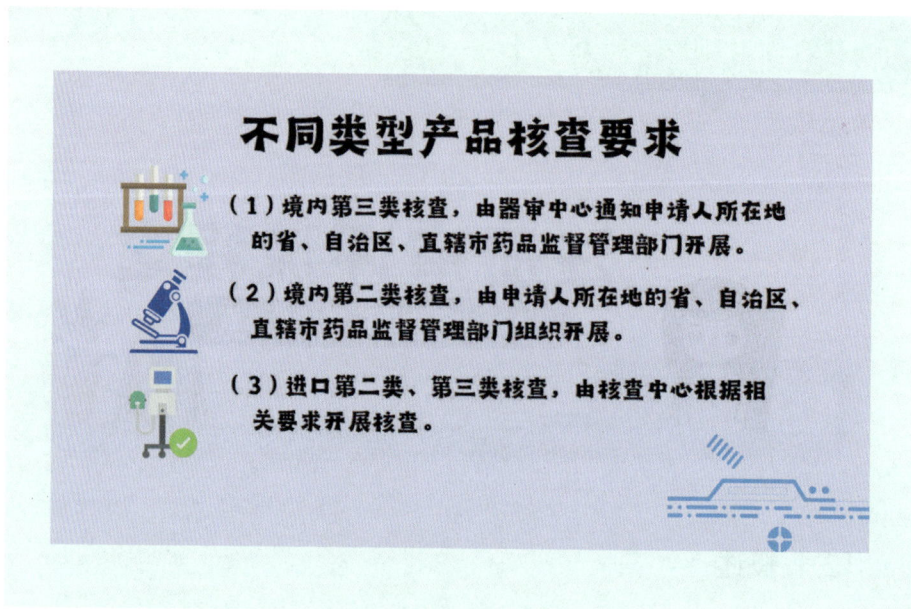

不同类型产品核查要求

（1）境内第三类核查，由器审中心通知申请人所在地的省、自治区、直辖市药品监督管理部门开展。

（2）境内第二类核查，由申请人所在地的省、自治区、直辖市药品监督管理部门组织开展。

（3）进口第二类、第三类核查，由核查中心根据相关要求开展核查。

12.3 境内第三类产品核查相关时限

（1）器审中心在医疗器械注册申请受理后 10 个工作日内，发送注册质量管理体系核查通知。

（2）省、自治区、直辖市药品监督管理部门自收到核查通知起 30 个工作日内完成质量管理体系核查工作。

（3）报告结果为"整改后复查"的，注册申请人自收到整改意见之日起 6 个月内一次性向原核查部门提交复查申请及整改报告。原核查部门自收到复查申请后 30 个工作日内完成复查。

（4）省、自治区、直辖市药品监督管理部门应当在做出"通过核查""整改后通过核查""未通过核查""整改后未通过核查"的结论 5 个工作日内，将核查结果通知发送器审中心。

12.4 境内第三类产品核查流程

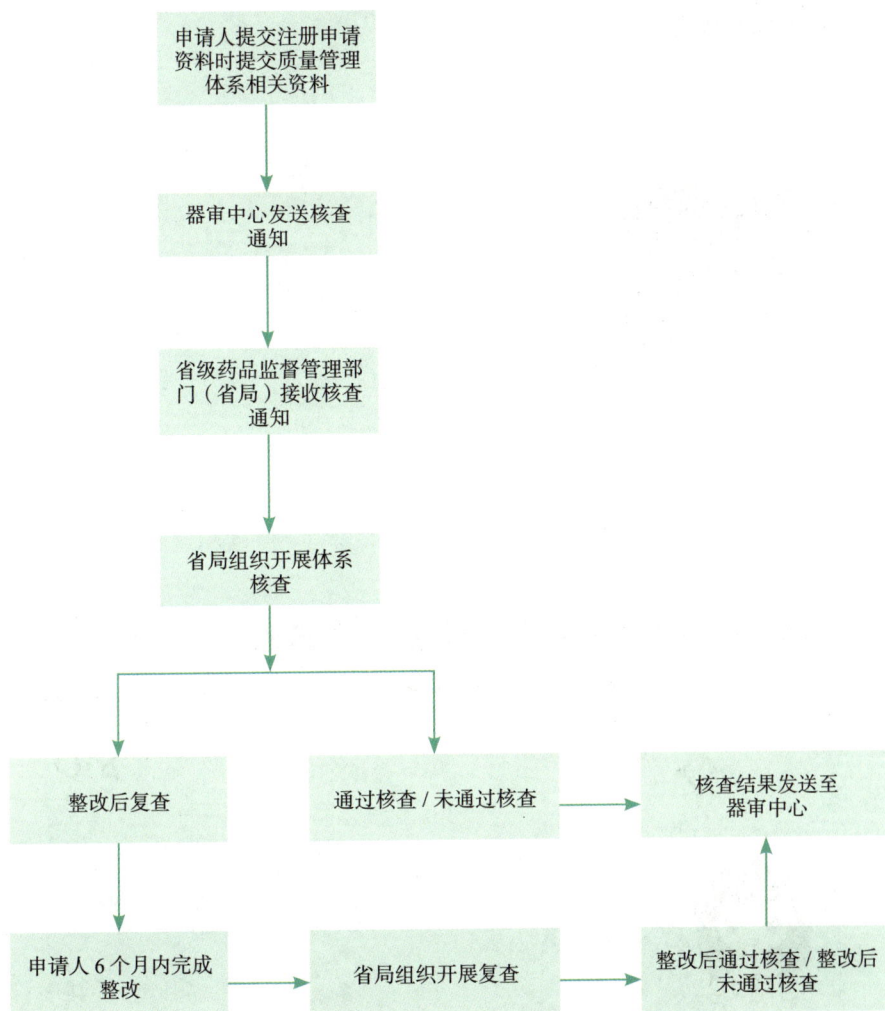

申请人提交注册申请资料时提交质量管理体系相关资料

↓

器审中心发送核查通知

↓

省级药品监督管理部门（省局）接收核查通知

↓

省局组织开展体系核查

↓

整改后复查　　　通过核查/未通过核查　→　核查结果发送至器审中心

↓

申请人6个月内完成整改　→　省局组织开展复查　→　整改后通过核查/整改后未通过核查

质量管理体系相关资料提交内容？

按照《关于公布医疗器械注册申报资料要求和批准证明文件格式的公告》中附件5《医疗器械注册申报资料要求及说明》及《关于公布体外诊断试剂注册申报资料要求和批准证明文件格式的公告》中附件4《体外诊断试剂注册申报资料要求及说明》质量管理体系相关文件内容进行提交。

变更注册申请需要提交质量管理体系相关资料？

医疗器械变更的具体原因或目的涉及产品原材料、生产工艺、适用范围、使用方法变化的，需要提交质量管理体系相关资料，应当针对变化部分进行质量管理体系核查。

体外诊断试剂变更的具体原因或目的涉及产品原材料、生产工艺变化的，需要提交质量管理体系相关资料，应当针对变化部分进行质量管理体系核查。

质量管理体系未通过核查的情况？

首次检查时，达不到"通过核查"要求的，可做出"未通过核查"核查结论；对需要复查的，未在规定期限内提交复查申请和整改报告的，以及整改复查后仍达不到"通过核查"要求的，核查结论为"整改后未通过核查"。
申请人拒绝接受质量管理体系现场检查的，核查结论为"未通过核查"。

12.5 参考资料

国家药监局综合司关于印发境内第三类医疗器械注册质量管理体系核查工作程序的通知（药监综械注〔2022〕13号）

国家药监局关于发布医疗器械注册质量管理体系核查指南的通告（2022年第50号）

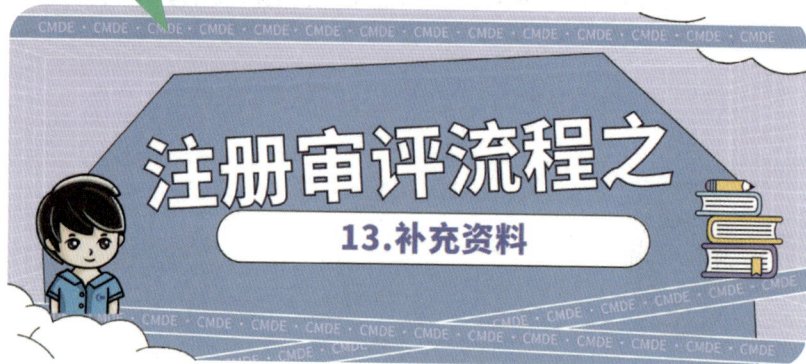

13. 补充资料

注册审评流程之

13.补充资料

13.1 定义

13.1.1 发补过程

发补过程是指在医疗器械技术审评过程中，由于注册申请人所提交的注册申报资料不能满足法规规章或相关审评要求，无法证明申报项目的安全性、有效性，审评人员以"医疗器械补正资料通知"的形式告知注册申请人提交相关补充资料的过程。

13.1.2 补回过程

补回过程是指注册申请人依据"医疗器械补正资料通知"中的要求进行客观、完整地答复，汇总形成补充资料后提交至相应审评机构的过程。

发补

当申请人提交的注册资料不能满足相关要求时，主审人会要求申请人补交所缺漏部分的资料，并以"医疗器械补正资料通知"一次性告知，俗称"发补"。

13.2 相关程序和要求

注册申请人应当在一年内按照"医疗器械补正资料通知"的要求一次提供补充资料。为保证补充资料的顺利提交，注册申请人应充分利用审评发补阶段的沟通交流途径和补正资料预审查等服务渠道与审评人员进行合理沟通。

补正资料通知

发补的载体

医疗器械补正资料通知

● 主审人将一次性告知需要补充的资料

● 以"医疗器械补正资料通知"形式寄给申请人/注册人

我该怎么做？

● 一年内一次性补回

● 书面形式一次性将资料交到器审中心

● 补充资料准备时间不计入审评时间

● 未按时补回的终止审评

13.2.1 医疗器械补正资料通知答复的原则

（1）注册申请人提交补充资料内容的基本信息应与首次提交注册申报资料保持一致，与"医疗器械补正资料通知"要求内容一一对应，分别进行阐述。

（2）注册申请人需保证提交的补充资料内容与"医疗器械补正资料通知"的要求具有相关性，并保证提交资料的真实性、有效性。

（3）注册申请人需保证提交的补充资料中用词准确，表达清晰无歧义。

（4）发补和补回过程仅针对本次注册申报时提交的信息范围，不得通过补充资料的方式变更原申请范围。

（5）注册申请人在补回过程遇到无法进行验证、确认或无法实现的补正要求，应详述理由并提供科学证据。

注册申请人应指定专人负责确认补正时限、进行预约沟通、准备补充资料等事宜，以提高补充资料的质量和效率。指定专人应当具有相应的专业知识，熟悉医疗器械注册相关法规、规章和有关审评要求。注册申请人应尽量保证补正工作的延续性，过程中不宜频繁更换指定专人。

13.2.2 医疗器械补正资料通知答复的要求

注册申请人提交相关补充资料时，应同时提交"补充资料内容说明"和针对"医疗器械补正资料通知"的具体补充资料文件。

（1）针对"补充资料内容说明"的要求

"补充资料内容说明"是针对"医疗器械补正资料通知"中所有问题的逐条说明，对补正思路和补充资料文件进行概述，阐明解答的问题，并明确各问题相关补充资料文件的名称和位置。

1）注册申请人需按"医疗器械补正资料通知"要求的内容对相应答复情况逐条说明，不重复或遗漏问题，形成"补充资料内容说明"。

2）注册申请人需列明"医疗器械补正资料通知"中提及的问题，针对如何回复补正要求进行概述，如未提交相关补充资料需进行说明论证。

资料顺序要求

1."医疗器械补正资料通知"复印件 ✓

2."补充资料内容说明" ✓

3.补充资料目录 ✓

4.具体补充内容 ✓

如何回复补正要求？

各相关条款的描述建议包括以下要素：

1 简述对补正问题的理解

2 简述应答思路或论证推理逻辑

3 补正资料的依据

4 具体包括哪些客观证据、文件、数据或信息等

5 特殊情形的说明

6 其他

　　3）"补充资料内容说明"中应明确补充资料文件名称及在"补正 RPS 目录"中的位置。

　　4）涉及产品技术要求和 / 或产品说明书更改的，注册申请人应当在"补充资料内容说明"中相应问题项下具体说明。

　　5）注册申请人如有"医疗器械补正资料通知"要求以外的其他必要补充文件，可在"补充资料内容说明"中单独描述并明确文件名称及位置。

（2）针对补充资料文件的要求

1）注册申请人需根据实际情况选择以下一种补充资料文件进行答复。

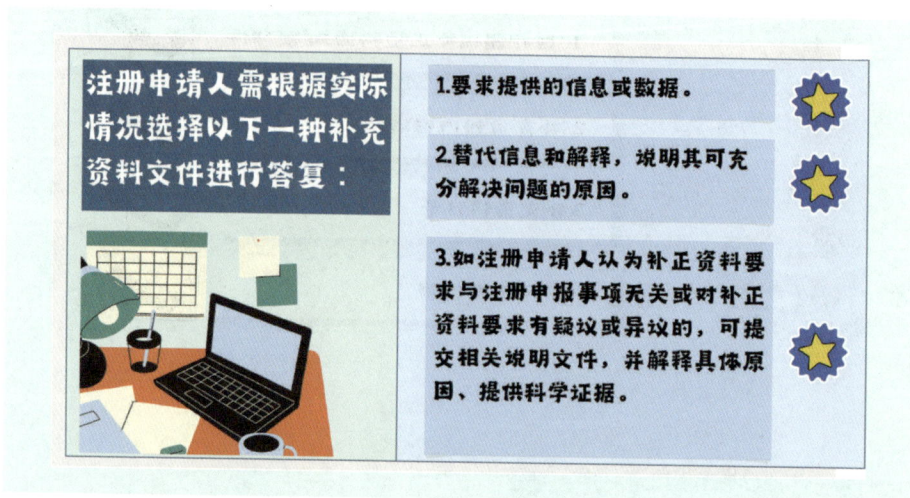

2）补充资料文件应按照"医疗器械补正资料通知"中补正资料要求的顺序逐项提交，如多条要求指向同一补充资料文件，可不必重复提交，在"补充资料内容说明"中明确即可。

3）补充资料文件的格式和签章要求与注册申报资料的要求一致。

4）如有必要，建议对某些补充资料文件中的更新信息予以特殊标注（如斜体、加粗、高亮字体、对比表等），以突出其变化内容，便于审阅。

13.3 补正咨询

13.3.1 现场咨询

注册申请人通过中心网站咨询平台预约现场咨询，按要求填写《咨询申请单》，明确具体咨询问题。每个符合要求的受理号产品申请现场咨询的机会原则上不超过3次。

审评人员接到现场咨询预约申请后，通过中心网站咨询平台对现场咨询时间进行确认，并提前3个工作日电话通知预约注册申请人，原则上在收到预约申请之日起 20 个工作日内完成现场咨询。预约注册申请人可以通过中心网站咨询平台查询预约结果，预约成功后打印《医疗器械技术审评现场咨询确认单》，一式两份，作为现场咨询凭证。

现场咨询完成后，咨询双方应在《医疗器械技术审评现场咨询确认单》上签字并各留一份。

13.3.2 网上咨询

注册申请人通过中心网站咨询平台进行网上咨询的申请，网上咨询主要用于解决相对简单、易于答复的注册咨询问题。

发补后咨询

主要针对处于发补状态的医疗器械注册项目注册申请人/注册人在补回资料前，与审评人员针对"医疗器械补正资料通知"相关内容进行沟通与答疑。咨询途径如下：

#1 现场咨询（每周四）

#2 网上咨询（20个工作日内完成答疑）

#3 共性问题解答（原则上每季度通过器审中心网站和微信公众号对外发布）

#4 补正资料预审（在补正资料届满2个月前提出资料预审的申请）

咨询前记得预约

1.登录器审中心网站，进入技术审评咨询平台，点击"一般产品咨询"（https://www.cmde.org.cn）。

2.根据《咨询平台使用说明》的指导进行操作，预约"现场咨询"或"网络咨询"。

TIPS

预约申请人可通过登录咨询平台查询预约结果

每个符合要求的受理号申请现场咨询的机会原则上不超过3次。如过期未取消预约，则现场咨询的机会减少1次。

审评人员在接到网上咨询申请后，原则上在收到申请之日起 20 个工作日内完成在线答疑。审评人员认为现场咨询方式更有利于解决注册申请人的咨询问题，可将网上咨询转为现场咨询。

13.4 预审查

补正资料预审查服务是指审评人员对拟提交的补充资料进行预审查并书面反馈注册申请人。

13.4.1 基本原则

（1）预审查服务是注册申请人与审评人员针对补充资料内容的沟通交流形式之一，并非补充资料提交前的必经程序，采取自愿原则，注册申请人自行决定是否提出预审查申请。

（2）预审查服务不能代替补充资料的正式提交，无论是否提出预审查服务申请，都应在规定时限内提交补充资料。

（3）审评人员出具的预审查意见用于指导注册申请人进一步修订完善

相关补充资料，并非对补充资料的确认依据，也与最终审评结论无关。

（4）器审中心对每个符合要求的注册申报事项原则上只提供一次预审查服务。

13.4.2 相关程序要求

注册申请人可在补正资料时限届满 2 个月前提出预审查服务申请，相关事宜见《关于提供医疗器械技术审评补正资料预审查服务的通告》。提交预审查服务的注册申请人应在取得预审查意见后，结合预审查意见作出资料完善，然后正式提交补正资料。

（1）补充资料预审查资料接收方式

1）通过 eRPS 系统线上注册申报的项目，直接在 eRPS 系统提交预审查申请；

2）线下注册申报的项目，可通过现场或邮寄方式提出预审查申请。

补正资料预审查

预审查服务是指注册申请人/代理人按照医疗器械注册补正资料通知要求完成部分或者全部补充资料后，在正式提交补充资料前，按照程序提出补充资料的预审查申请。

器审中心对每个符合要求的申报注册事项原则上只提供一次预审查服务；

预审查服务采用自愿原则，器审中心不收取费用；

注册申请人/代理人应在补正资料时限届满2个月前提出预审查服务的申请；

主审人于申请接收后20个工作日内将预审查意见告知注册申请人/代理人。

（2）补正资料预审查资料接收要求

1）按照"医疗器械补正资料通知"的时间及内容要求，按时一次性提交补充资料。

2）线下提交的补正资料预审查资料应装订成册。

3）线下提交的补正资料预审查资料首页附"医疗器械补正资料通知"及补正资料预审查申请表，如"医疗器械补正资料通知"为复印件应加盖公司公章。

4）注册申请人线下提交补正资料预审查资料每项首页应加盖公司公章，未装订成册部分应加盖骑缝章。

13.5 补充资料不予接收的情况

注册申请人线下提交的补充资料，对补充资料不齐全、不符合形式审查要求的或不属于本部门职责范围的，器审中心发补组将不予接收。

13.6 逾期处理

注册申请人逾期未提交补充资料的将终止技术审评。

（1）依据《医疗器械注册与备案管理办法》第九十二条规定和《体外诊断试剂注册与备案管理办法》第九十二条规定，技术审评过程中需要注册申请人补正资料的，技术审评机构应当一次告知需要补正的全部内容。注册申请人应当在1年内按照要求一次提供补充资料；技术审评机构应当自收到补充资料之日起60个工作日内完成技术审评。注册申请人补充资料的时间不计算在审评时限内。

（2）注册申请人逾期未提交补充资料的，由技术审评机构终止技术审评、提出不予注册的建议，由药品监督管理部门核准后作出不予注册的决定。

13.7 其他

（1）通过 eRPS 系统进行线上申报的项目，注册申请人如使用 eRPS 系统，可在"审评补正办理"界面查看"医疗器械补正资料通知"并进行答复。注册申请人提交的补充资料文件的方式应与提交申报资料的方式（线上途径或线下途径）保持一致，具体可参考 eRPS 系统的启用说明、技术指南和系统操作手册进行办理。

（2）对于小组审评、联合审评等涉及多位审评人员的情形，发补后与注册申请人进行沟通的审评人员应能够对"医疗器械补正资料通知"中所有补正资料要求进行沟通，或联合参审人员一起进行沟通。

（3）注册申请人补回的资料证明仍不足以支持判断安全有效性的，按"不予注册"的有关要求办理。

需要注意的事项

1. 注册申请人应提交《补充资料内容说明》，并按其《填表说明》要求填写。

2. 注册申请人应提交补充资料目录，顺序应与"医疗器械补正资料通知"要求一致。

3. 补充资料的准备时间不计算在技术审评时限内。

4. 对"医疗器械补正资料通知"中内容有疑问时，可以参考"发补后咨询"向审评员咨询。

13.8 参考资料

关于提供医疗器械技术审评补正资料预审查服务通告（2018 年第 8 号）

关于提供医疗器械技术审评补正资料预审查服务的补充通知（2019 年 10 月 16 日）

关于发布医疗器械注册审评补正资料要求管理规范的通告（2020 年第 1 号）

关于医疗器械注册技术审评补正意见咨询有关事宜的通告（2020 年第 24 号）

14. 专家咨询

14.1 概述

专家咨询会是指国家药品监督管理局医疗器械技术审评中心在医疗器械注册审评工作中，对需要咨询的技术问题邀请专家（以下简称专家）以会议形式进行讨论并提出意见的过程。

14.2 专家咨询流程

主审人对所负责的审评项目，经审评确认需要召开专家咨询会且符合相关要求的，主审人可提出专家咨询会申请。

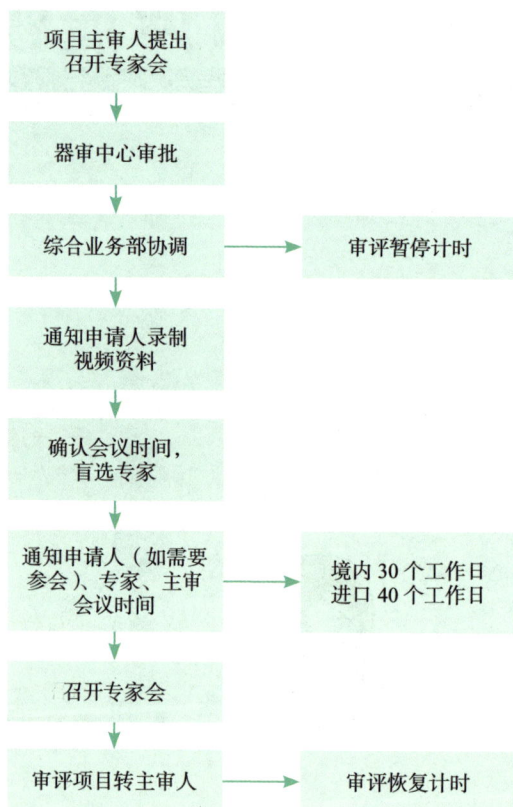

```
项目主审人提出
召开专家会
      ↓
器审中心审批
      ↓
综合业务部协调 ────→ 审评暂停计时
      ↓
通知申请人录制
视频资料
      ↓
确认会议时间，
盲选专家
      ↓
通知申请人（如需要      境内 30 个工作日
参会）、专家、主审 ───→ 进口 40 个工作日
会议时间
      ↓
召开专家会
      ↓
审评项目转主审人 ────→ 审评恢复计时
```

14.2.1 专家选取

（1）确认会议时间后，专家选取按照随机盲选原则实施，通过器审中心专家管理系统输入会议所需专业及人数，选取及确认流程全部由系统自动完成。

（2）专家选取成功后，通知相关人员会议时间及地点。

14.2.2 专家咨询会相关要求

（1）注册申请人（如需要参会）收到会议通知后应按时参会。注册申请人未能按时参会的，会议照常进行。

（2）会议主持人应当在会议开始前宣读会议议程，所有与会专家在会议开始前签署承诺书。

（3）中心工作人员不得在召开专家咨询会前泄露专家名单。

（4）注册申请人需准备有关产品设计、生产过程控制关键点、产品安全性、有效性、临床试验、着重解答本次会议所需咨询问题等情况的视频资料。如需注册申请人参会的，注册申请人需对专家及相关审评人员提出的问题进行解答，但不参与专家讨论环节。

QUICK TIPS

专家咨询意见仅作为审评过程中的参考资料，并不成为审评的最终依据。

14.3 参考资料

关于发布医疗器械技术审评中心外聘专家管理办法的通知（2020 年 2 月 20 日）

15. 延续注册

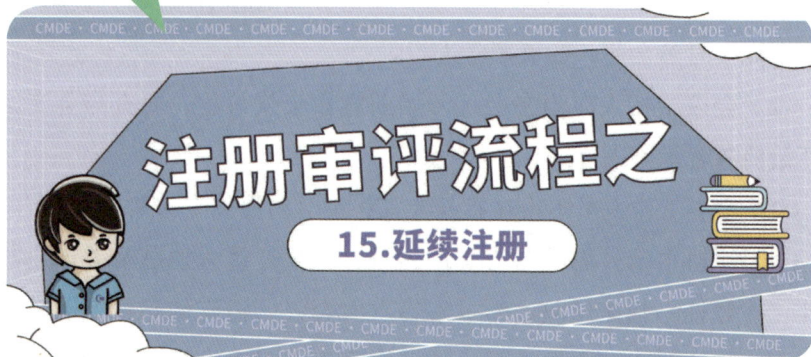

注册审评流程之
15.延续注册

15.1 概述

医疗器械注册证有效期为 5 年。有效期届满需要延续注册的，注册申请人应当在有效期届满 6 个月前向原注册部门提出延续注册的申请。

不予延续注册的情形

▼

未在规定期限内提出延续注册申请

医疗器械强制性标准已经修订，申请延续注册的医疗器械不能达到新要求

附条件批准的医疗器械，未在规定期限内完成医疗器械注册证载明事项

15.2 延续注册资料要求

符合条件的注册申请人应按照《关于公布医疗器械注册申报资料要求和批准证明文件格式的公告》中附件6《医疗器械注册申报资料要求及说明》和《关于公布体外诊断试剂申报资料要求和批准证明文件格式的公告》中附件5《体外诊断试剂延续注册申报资料要求及说明》的相关要求准备资料。

延续注册办理流程

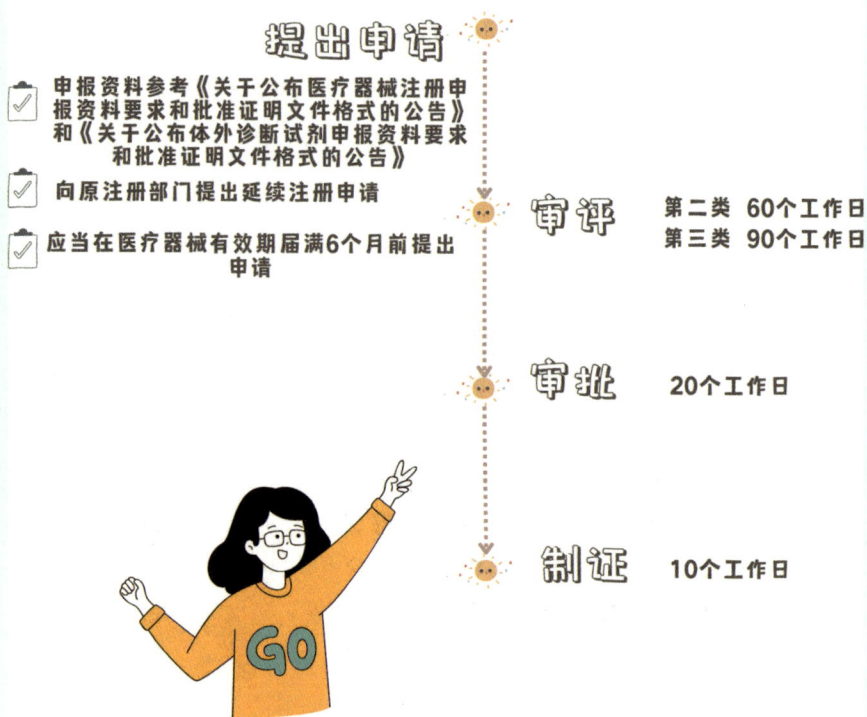

提出申请

☑ 申报资料参考《关于公布医疗器械注册申报资料要求和批准证明文件格式的公告》和《关于公布体外诊断试剂申报资料要求和批准证明文件格式的公告》

☑ 向原注册部门提出延续注册申请

☑ 应当在医疗器械有效期届满6个月前提出申请

审评　第二类　60个工作日
　　　　第三类　90个工作日

审批　20个工作日

制证　10个工作日

15.3 其他

（1）已注册产品，其管理类别由高类别调整为低类别的，医疗器械注册证在有效期内继续有效。有效期届满需要延续的，注册人应当在医疗器械注册证有效期届满6个月前，按照调整后的类别向相应的药监部门申请延续注册或者进行备案。

管理类别由低类别调整为高类别的，注册人应当按照改变后的类别向相应的药品监督管理部门申请注册。

（2）医疗器械注册证有效期为 5 年。

（3）延续注册的批准时间在原注册证有效期内的，延续注册证的注册证有效期起始日为原注册证到期次日；批准时间不在原注册证有效期内的，延续注册的注册证有效期起始日为批准延续注册的日期。

15.4 案例解说

（1）如何判断申请延续注册时间在医疗器械注册证有效期届满 6 个月前？

> **解答：** 医疗器械注册证有效期届满需要延续注册的，注册人应当在医疗器械注册证有效期届满 6 个月前申请延续注册，并按照相关要求提交申请资料。因申请资料不齐全或者不符合法定形式需要补正资料的，器审中心将在受理补正通知中注明注册人首次申请延续注册时间。注册人补正后再次申请延续注册时，应当提交受理补正通知，器审中心将根据受理补正通知中注明的注册人首次申请延续注册时间判定申请延续注册时间是否在医疗器械注册证有效期届满 6 个月前，并按照《医疗器械注册与备案管理办法》规定对申请资料进行审核。

（2）已注册产品如未能在规定时间内申请延续注册，按照法规要求，需申请产品注册。此时，临床评价可否选择原注册产品作为同品种产品，完成临床评价？临床数据应该如何提供？

> **解答：** 此种情形下，可选择原注册产品作为同品种产品，完成临床评价。同品种对比主要关注申报产品与原注册产品是否存在差异，如二者不存在差异，可提供的临床数据包括该产品上市前和上市后的临床数据，包括上市后不良事件在内的临床经验数据。

15.5 参考资料

关于公布医疗器械注册申报资料要求和批准证明文件格式的公告（2021 年第 121 号）

关于公布体外诊断试剂注册申报资料要求和批准证明文件格式的公告（2021 年第 122 号）

16. 变更注册 / 变更备案

16.1 概述

已注册的第二类、第三类医疗器械产品，其设计、原材料、生产工艺、适用范围、使用方法等发生实质性变化，有可能影响该医疗器械安全、有效的，注册申请人应当向原注册部门申请办理变更注册手续；发生其他变化的，应当按照国务院药品监督管理部门的规定备案或者报告。

什么是变更注册？

已注册的第二类、第三类医疗器械产品，其设计、原材料、生产工艺、适用范围、使用方法等发生实质性变化，有可能影响该医疗器械安全、有效的，注册申请人应当向原注册部门申请办理变更注册手续；发生其他变化的，应当按照国务院药品监督管理部门的规定备案或者报告。

16.2 变更注册 / 变更备案涉及的变更情形

16.2.1 医疗器械变更注册 / 变更备案

已注册的第二类、第三类医疗器械产品，其设计、原材料、生产工艺、适用范围、使用方法等发生实质性变化，有可能影响该医疗器械安全、有效的，注册申请人应当向原注册部门申请办理变更注册手续；发生其他变化的，应当在变化之日起 30 日内向原注册部门备案。

医疗器械变更备案情形

- 注册人名称变更
- 境内医疗器械生产地址变更
- 注册人住所变更
- 代理人住所变更
- 代理人名称变更

医疗器械变更注册情形

- 产品名称变化
- 产品技术要求变化
- 结构及组成变化
- 产品适用范围变化
- 注册证中"其他内容"变化
- 其他变化
- 进口医疗器械生产地址变化
- 型号、规格变化

注册证载明的产品名称、型号、规格、结构及组成、适用范围、产品技术要求、进口医疗器械的生产地址等，属于前款规定的需要办理变更注册的事项。注册人名称和住所、代理人名称和住所等，属于前款规定的需要备案的事项。境内医疗器械生产地址变更的，注册申请人应当在办理相应的生产许可变更后办理备案。

16.2.2 体外诊断试剂变更注册 / 变更备案

已注册的第二类、第三类体外诊断试剂产品，其设计、原材料、生产工艺、适用范围、使用方法等发生实质性变化，有可能影响该体外诊断试剂安全、有效的，注册申请人应当向原注册部门申请办理变更注册手续；发生其他变化的，应当在变化之日起 30 日内向原注册部门备案。

注册证载明的产品名称、包装规格、主要组成成分、预期用途、产品技术要求、产品说明书、进口体外诊断试剂的生产地址等，属于前款规定的需要办理变更注册的事项。注册人名称和住所、代理人名称和住所等，属于前款规定的需要备案的事项。境内体外诊断试剂生产地址变更的，注册申请人应当在办理相应的生产许可变更后办理备案。

体外诊断试剂变更备案情形

注册人名称变更　注册人住所变更　代理人名称变更　代理人住所变更　境内体外诊断试剂生产地址变更

体外诊断试剂变更注册情形

产品名称变化

包装规格变化

临床适应证变化

产品储存条件及有效期变化

产品技术要求、说明书变化

进口体外诊断试剂生产地址变化

适用的样本类型变化

适用人群变化

第三类体外诊断试剂原材料、生产工艺、反应体系变化

阴性判断值或参考区间变化

适用仪器变化

其他可能改变产品安全有效性的变化

16.3 变更注册/变更备案资料要求

符合条件的注册申请人应按照《关于公布医疗器械注册申报资料要求和批准证明文件格式的公告》中附件 7《医疗器械变更备案/变更注册申报资料要求及说明》和《关于公布体外诊断试剂申报资料要求和批准证明文件格式的公告》中附件 6《体外诊断试剂变更备案/变更注册申报资料要求及说明》的相关要求准备资料。

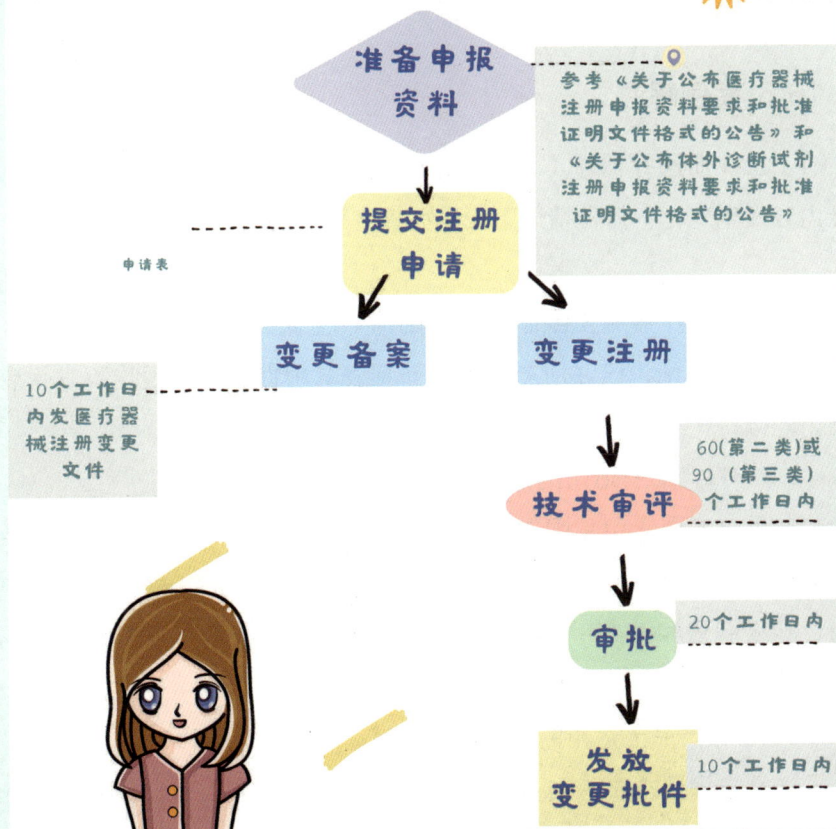

变更办理流程

准备申报资料

参考《关于公布医疗器械注册申报资料要求和批准证明文件格式的公告》和《关于公布体外诊断试剂注册申报资料要求和批准证明文件格式的公告》

提交注册申请

申请表

变更备案

变更注册

10个工作日内发医疗器械注册变更文件

技术审评

60(第二类)或90（第三类）个工作日内

审批

20个工作日内

发放变更批件

10个工作日内

16.4 其他

（1）变更事项不可与延续注册合并提出申请。

（2）医疗器械变更文件与原医疗器械注册证合并使用。有效期截止日期与原医疗器械注册证相同。

（3）取得变更文件后，注册人应当依据变更内容自行修改产品技术要求、说明书和标签。

（4）除前述变更注册和变更备案情形，发生其他变化的，注册人应当按照质量管理体系要求做好相关工作，并按照规定向药品监督管理部门报告。

16.5 案例解说

（1）已注册医疗器械（含体外诊断试剂）产品技术要求引用的强制性标准内容发生变化，何种情形下无需办理变更注册？

解答： 医疗器械（含体外诊断试剂）注册证有效期内有新的强制性标准发布实施，已注册产品的注册证及其附件载明事项均不发生变化，即符合新的强制性标准，具体包括以下两种情形：

1）申报产品有适用的强制性标准

产品技术要求引用强制性标准的形式为"直接引用强制性标准条款具体内容""标准编号"或者"标准编号+年代号"。强制性标准更新，标准编号和/或年代号发生变化，涉及产品技术要求引用的强制性标准条款内容未发生变化。

2）申报产品无适用的强制性标准

产品技术要求参考引用了某个强制性标准的条款内容，强制性标准更新，标准编号和/或年代号发生变化，涉及产品技术要求参考引用的强制性标准条款内容未发生变化；或者涉及产品技术要求参考引用的强制性标准条款内容发生变化，但产品技术要求仍参考引用更新前的强制性标准条款内容。

上述两种情形下，产品技术要求不发生变化或者仅更新引用的标准编号和/或年代号，无需办理变更注册。

（2）体外诊断设备说明书发生变化该怎么办？

> **解答：** 根据《医疗器械说明书和标签管理规定》（国家食品药品监督管理总局令第6号）第十六条规定："已注册的医疗器械发生注册变更的，注册申请人应当在取得变更文件后，依据变更文件自行修改说明书和标签。"已注册体外诊断设备的说明书，除注册证及其附件载明事项之外的其他内容发生变化，不属于变更注册范围的，应当向医疗器械注册的审批部门书面告知，并提交说明书更改情况对比说明等相关文件。

16.6 参考资料

关于公布医疗器械注册申报资料要求和批准证明文件格式的公告（2021年第121号）

关于公布体外诊断试剂注册申报资料要求和批准证明文件格式的公告（2021年第122号）

17. 说明书更改告知

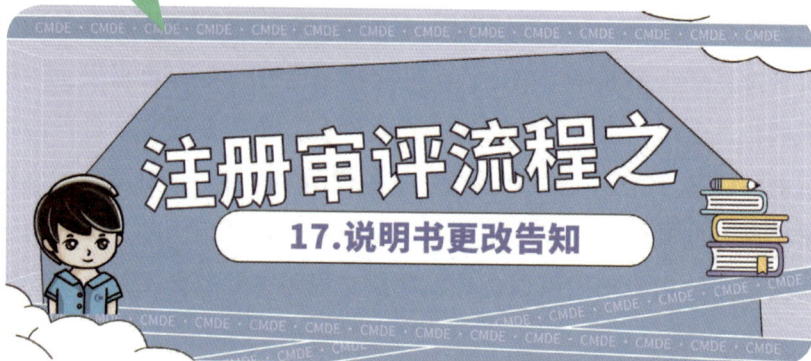

注册审评流程之
17. 说明书更改告知

说明书更改告知是指已注册医疗器械的说明书，除注册证及其附件载明事项之外的其他内容发生变化，不属于变更注册范围内的，应当向医疗器械注册的审批部门书面告知，并提交说明书更改情况对比说明等相关文件。审批部门对相关文件进行审查后，出具审查结果。

说明书更改告知需满足以下条件：

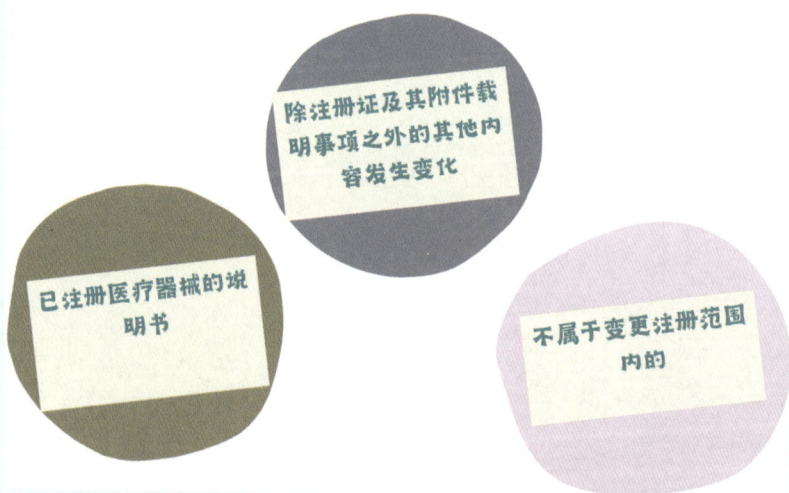

除注册证及其附件载明事项之外的其他内容发生变化

已注册医疗器械的说明书

不属于变更注册范围内的

审查结果一般分为三种

✓ 同意   ★ 部分同意   ✗ 不同意

审查结果为部分同意或不同意的，向申请人发出不予同意通知件。审批部门自收到书面告知之日起20个工作日内未发出不予同意通知件的，说明书更改生效。

17.1 申请资料要求

符合条件的行政相对人应按照《关于发布医疗器械注册证补办程序等5个相关工作程序的通告》的相关要求准备资料。

说明书更改告知申请资料要求

符合条件的行政相对人应按照《关于发布医疗器械注册证补办程序等 5 个相关工作程序的通告》的相关要求准备资料。

17.2 相关流程

注册申请人按照说明书更改告知申请资料要求向国家药监局提交申请，经受理后，医疗器械审批部门进行审查，并在 20 个工作日内出具审查结果。审查结果为部分同意或不同意的，由国家药监局向注册申请人发出不予同意通知件。审查结果为同意的，则不向注册申请人发出通知，说明书更改生效。

TIPS

- 器械注册审批进度可进入国家药品监督管理局网站"行政许可综合事项查询"板块，随时关注

- 进入国家药品监督管理局服务板块，在"送达信息"页面查看"说明书不予同意退件发布通知"

- 规定时限内未答复的视为同意

17.3 说明书更改告知的审查结果

根据《医疗器械注册与备案管理办法》《医疗器械说明书和标签管理规定》，说明书更改内容应不涉及属于变更注册的内容，如涉及，审批部门应出具不同意说明书更改的意见，并通知注册申请人按照《医疗器械注册与备案管理办法》相关规定办理。说明书更改告知材料不足以支撑更改告知事项的变更内容，审批部门应出具不同意或部分同意更改的意见，在审查意见中详细说明理由并告知申请材料存在的问题。

17.4 体外诊断试剂可以自行修改说明书的情形

（1）对于体外诊断试剂说明书"基本信息"项目中下列内容变化的，

包括体外诊断试剂的注册人或者生产企业联系方式、售后服务单位名称及联系方式、生产许可证编号或者生产备案凭证编号的变化，进口体外诊断试剂代理人联系方式变化的情况，注册人应在相关信息变化后，自行修改。其中，生产许可证编号或者生产备案凭证编号应在相应省级药品监督管理部门发放生产许可证或者生产备案凭证后再行修改。

（2）对于体外诊断试剂说明书"医疗器械注册证编号／产品技术要求编号"项目，在相应药品监督管理部门发放医疗器械注册证后，导致该项内容变化的情况，注册人应自行修改。

（3）对于体外诊断试剂说明书"标识的解释"项目，因注册人按照YY/T 0466系列标准完善体外诊断试剂说明书中相应标识的解释内容，导致该项内容变化，但不涉及其他需办理变更注册的情况，注册人应自行修改。

（4）体外诊断试剂说明书"主要组成成分"中列明，必须配套使用的医疗器械或体外诊断试剂，由于相应药品监督管理部门发放医疗器械注册证／备案凭证后，导致说明书中载明的配套使用的医疗器械或体外诊断试剂注册证编号／备案凭证编号发生变化的情况，注册人应自行修改。

17.5 参考资料

医疗器械说明书和标签管理规定（国家食品药品监督管理总局令第6号）

国家食品药品监督管理总局关于发布医疗器械注册证补办程序等5个相关工作程序的通告（2015年第91号）

18. 其他

18.1 注册证纠错

注册申请人如遇下列原因造成的错误，可提出医疗器械注册证及其附件内容纠错申请，该申请不收费：

（1）注册证、变更文件及其附件打印错误；

（2）注册证编号错误；

（3）企业填报错误；

（4）审评、审批工作中出现的其他错误。

18.1.1 申请资料准备

注册申请人在提交医疗器械注册证 / 变更文件纠错申请时应准备以下资料：

（1）由注册申请人或其代理人签章的相应申请表。

（2）医疗器械注册证及其附件的复印件。

（3）境内第三类医疗器械注册证纠错资料要求：

1）境内注册申请人应提交营业执照副本的复印件。

2）注册申请人提交的资料真实性的自我保证声明，包括所提交资料的清单以及注册申请人承担法律责任的承诺。

（4）进口第二、三类医疗器械注册证纠错资料要求：

1）注册申请人提交其在中国指定的代理人委托书、代理人承诺书及营业执照副本复印件。相应委托书应明确包括委托办理纠错事项。

如委托书为新出具的，应为原件并公证。如申报注册时已提交包含相应内容的代理人委托书，可提交代理人委托书复印件，并加盖代理人公章。

2）注册申请人提交的资料真实性的自我保证声明，包括所提交资料的清单以及注册申请人承担法律责任的承诺。真实性的自我保证声明应为原件并加盖代理人公章。

（5）具体办理人应提交注册申请人或代理人授权书及其身份证复印件。

18.1.2 办理流程

注册申请人将申请资料准备齐全后，向国家药品监督管理局行政受理服务大厅提出相关事项纠错申请，经受理大厅形式审查确认予以受理后，分为三种情况：

（1）属于注册证、变更文件及其附件打印错误，由受理大厅即时予以办理；

（2）2017年7月1日前获批的注册证、变更文件、2017年7月1日后获批的首次注册的注册证，属于注册证编号错误，按程序转器械注册司办理；

（3）2017年7月1日后获批的变更注册文件、延续注册证书提出注册证编号错误及其他情况，按程序转器审中心办理。

针对第二种情况，器械注册司经办人自接到纠错申请资料之日起，在10个工作日内提出审核意见，并交处负责人复审，处负责人在8个工作日内提出复核意见，司经办人在2个工作日内将审定意见和纠错资料转回受理大厅。针对第三种情况，器审中心自接到纠错申请资料之日起，在30个工作日内依据申请资料要求进行审核并提出意见。受理大厅应当在10个工作日内依据审定意见制作相应文件，并按照有关规定履行送达程序。同时，将相关纠错信息在国家药品监督管理局网站上及时予以公布。

2023年4月20日起,《关于调整医疗器械注册电子申报信息化系统业务范围的通告》(2023年第11号)正式实施。为配合上述文件实施,eRPS系统功能已全面升级,电子纠错申请表、电子目录将同步上线。如企业已申请CA,可自行在eRPS系统中完成医疗器械注册证纠错申请表填写、相关资料提交及受理;企业未申领CA可以线下的方式提交。

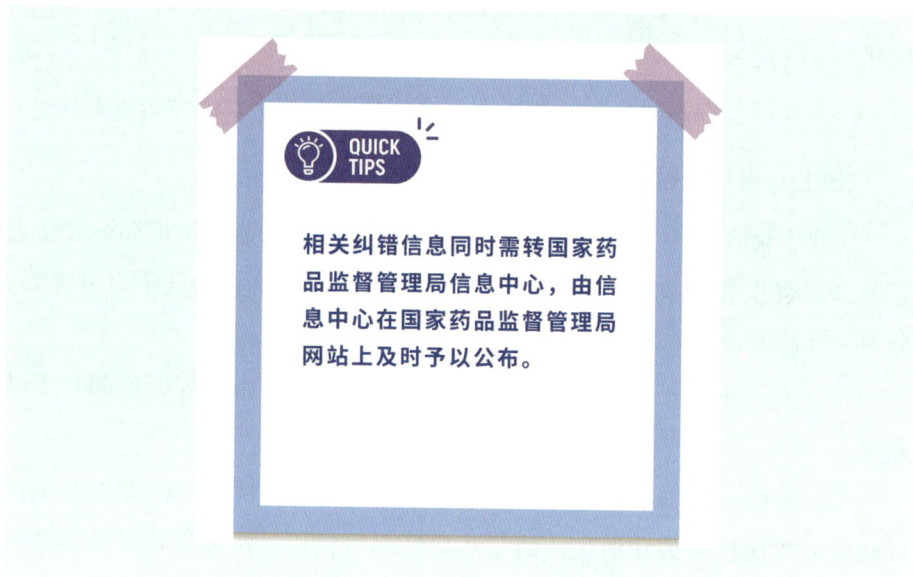

> **QUICK TIPS**
>
> 相关纠错信息同时需转国家药品监督管理局信息中心,由信息中心在国家药品监督管理局网站上及时予以公布。

18.2 自行注销注册证

注册申请人可对尚在有效期内的医疗器械注册证 / 变更文件提出自行注销申请,该申请不收费。

18.2.1 申请资料准备

注册申请人在提交自行注销注册证申请时应准备以下资料:

(1)由注册申请人签章的相应申请表。

(2)注册申请人出具的注销医疗器械注册证的原因及情况说明。

（3）医疗器械注册证及其附件原件。

（4）境内第三类医疗器械注册证注销资料要求：

1）境内注册申请人应提交营业执照副本的复印件。

2）注册申请人提交的资料真实性的自我保证声明，包括所提交资料的清单以及注册人承担法律责任的承诺。

（5）进口第二、三类医疗器械注册证注销资料要求：

1）注册申请人企业资格证明文件的原件或复印件的公证件。

2）注册申请人提交的资料真实性的自我保证声明，包括所提交资料的清单以及注册申请人承担法律责任的承诺。真实性的自我保证声明应为原件并公证。

（6）具体办理人应提交注册申请人或其代理人授权书及其身份证复印件。

18.2.2 办理流程

注册申请人将申请资料准备齐全后，向国家药品监督管理局行政受理服务大厅提出相关事项自行撤销申请，经受理大厅形式审查予以受理后，3个工作日内受理大厅将申请资料移交器械注册司。器械注册司经办人自接到资料之日起，10个工作日内核实有关情况，拟定注销公告，处负责人在5个工作日内提出复核意见，司负责人应当在5个工作日内提出审定意见，审定完成后，按照国家药品监督管理局文件发布程序报批发布。

18.3 自行撤回注册申请

已受理尚未作出行政许可决定的注册申请，申请人/注册申请人可自行撤回注册申请，该申请不收费。企业已交纳的注册费用不予退回。

18.3.1 申请资料准备

申请人/注册申请人在提交自行撤回注册证申请时应准备以下资料：

（1）由申请人/注册申请人签章的相应申请表。

（2）拟撤回的注册申请项目的受理通知书原件。

（3）具体办理人应提交申请人／注册申请人或代理人授权书及其身份证复印件。

18.3.2 办理流程

申请人／注册申请人将申请资料准备齐全后，向国家药品监督管理局行政受理服务大厅提出自行撤回注册申请，经受理大厅形式审查，予以受理后按申请事项实际审评审批状态和有关移交程序规定，将申请资料移交器审中心或器械注册司。器审中心或器械注册司核实后，终止相关注册资料审评审批。

企业如在办理其他注册相关事项，需提交已撤回医疗器械注册申请项目中已提交资料的原件，也可提交相应资料复印件，并注明原件所在申请项目的受理号，和由申请人／注册申请人签章的资料复印件与原件一致的自我保证声明。对于进口医疗器械，自我保证声明为原件并公证。

TIPS

1. 企业自行撤回注册申请事项，已缴纳的注册费不予退回。

2. 不予注册申请事项资料不可取回。

3. 终止审评申请事项资料不可取回。

相关文件：
关于发布医疗器械注册证补办程序等
5个相关工作程序的通告
（2015年第91号）

18.4 注册证补办

注册申请人可在医疗器械 / 体外诊断试剂注册证 / 变更文件有效期内，对注册证和 / 或其附件、变更文件提出补办申请，该申请不收费。

18.4.1 申请资料准备

注册申请人在提交注册证补办申请时应准备以下资料：

（1）由注册申请人或其代理人签章的相应申请表。

（2）医疗器械注册证及其附件的复印件或原注册证号。

（3）境内第三类医疗器械注册证和 / 或其附件补办资料要求。

1）注册申请人出具的补办医疗器械注册证和 / 或其附件的原因和情况说明。应包括注册人在我国省级以上公开发行的报刊上登载遗失声明的报刊原件和加盖注册申请人公章的复印件（相关遗失声明登载时间应至少在递交申请日前 1 个月）。

2）境内注册申请人应提交营业执照副本的复印件和组织机构代码证复印件。

3）注册申请人提交的资料真实性的自我保证声明，包括所提交资料的清单以及注册人承担法律责任的承诺。

（4）进口第二、三类医疗器械注册证及其附件补办资料要求：

1）注册申请人出具的补办医疗器械注册证及其附件的原因和情况说明，应包括注册人在我国省级以上公开发行的报刊上登载遗失声明的报刊原件和加盖代理人公章或注册人签章的复印件（相关遗失声明登载时间应至少在递交申请日前 1 个月）。

2）注册申请人提交其在中国指定的代理人委托书、代理人承诺书及营业执照副本复印件或者机构登记证明复印件。代理人委托书应为原件并经公证，同时应包括补办事项、产品名称、注册证编号等内容。

3）注册申请人企业资格证明文件的原件或复印件的公证件。

4）注册申请人提交的资料真实性的自我保证声明，包括所提交资料的清单以及注册申请人承担法律责任的承诺。真实性的自我保证声明应为原件并公证。

（5）具体办理人应提交注册申请人或代理人授权书及其身份证复印件。

18.4.2 办理流程

注册申请人将申请资料准备齐全后，向国家药品监督管理局行政受理服务大厅提出相关事项补办申请，经受理大厅形式审查予以受理后，按程序转器械注册司办理。器械注册司经办人自接到资料之日起，10个工作日内出具审核意见，处负责人在4个工作日内出具审定意见，反馈至受理大厅。受理大厅在10个工作日内依据相应意见制作文件，并按照有关规定履行送达程序。

补发的医疗器械注册证备注栏中载明了"××××年××月××日补发。原××××年××月××日发放的注册证作废"。

补发的医疗器械注册证备注栏中应载明"××××年××月××日补发，原××××年××月××日发放的注册证作废"

QUICK TIPS

18.5 不予注册

18.5.1 不予注册

对于已受理的注册申请，若有下列情形之一，药品监督管理部门做出不予注册的决定，并告知申请人。

（1）申请人对拟上市销售医疗器械的安全性、有效性、质量可控性进行的研究及其结果无法证明产品安全、有效、质量可控的；

（2）质量管理体系核查不通过，以及申请人拒绝接受质量管理体系现场检查的；

（3）注册申请资料虚假的；

（4）注册申请资料内容混乱、矛盾，注册申请资料内容与申请项目明显不符，不能证明产品安全、有效、质量可控的；

（5）不予注册的其他情形。

18.5.2 不通过审评结论的确认及异议处理

医疗器械注册申请审评期间，对于拟做出不通过审评结论的，包括医疗器械（含体外诊断试剂）产品注册、变更注册、延续注册项目，申请人/注册申请人可以在15日内向器审中心提出异议，异议内容仅限于原申请事项和原申请资料，异议应当自接到确认单之日起的15个工作日内提出，15个工作日内未提出异议视为同意不通过的结论和理由，申请人/注册申请人仅有一次机会对不通过的结论和理由提出异议。

对于线上申报项目，eRPS系统在固定时间将含有相应项目不通过结论和理由的《医疗器械注册技术审评不通过结论确认单》（以下简称《确认单》）推送至申请人/注册申请人并发送短信通知。申请人登录eRPS系统查看《确认单》，对不通过的结论和理由无异议的，勾选"同意"，对不通过的结论和理由有异议的，勾选"不同意"，并填写具体内容。

对于线下申报项目，申请人/注册申请人接收器审中心电子邮件后，可查看《确认单》。对不通过的结论和理由无异议的，勾选"同意"，对不通过的结论和理由有异议的，勾选"不同意"，并填写具体内容。完成确认后，申请人 / 注册申请人应通过电子邮件回复《确认单》并将经签章的纸质版《确认单》邮寄至器审中心。

对不通过的结论和理由有异议的，器审中心在收到《确认单》后对异议进行综合评估并填写《医疗器械注册技术审评不通过结论异议综合评估意见告知单》（以下简称《告知单》）。对于线上申报项目，eRPS 系统在固定时间将《告知单》推送至申请人 / 注册申请人，并发送短信通知；对于线下申报项目，器审中心通过电子邮件将《告知单》发送至申请人 / 注册申请人并电话告知申请人 / 注册申请人，申请人 / 注册申请人无需对异议评估结果再次进行确认。

维持不通过审评结论的项目，器审中心按相关规定将不予注册、不予变更、不予延续的项目转出；改变原审评结论的项目，器审中心按照相关规定对申报项目重新流转。

18.6 参考资料

国家食品药品监督管理总局关于发布医疗器械注册证补办程序等 5 个相关工作程序的通告（2015 年第 91 号）

关于调整医疗器械注册电子申报信息化系统业务范围的通告（2023 年第 11 号）

第三章 注册范本示例

本章内容仅供参考，最终解释以器审中心为准。

1. 医疗器械安全和性能基本原则清单范本

1.1 医疗器械安全和性能基本原则清单范本

表6 医疗器械安全和性能基本原则清单

条款号	要求	适用	证明符合性采用的方法	为符合性提供客观证据的文件
A	安全和性能的通用基本原则			
A1	一般原则			
A1.1	医疗器械应当实现申请人的预期性能，其设计和生产应当确保器械在预期使用条件下达到预期目的。这些器械应当是安全的并且能够实现其预期性能，与患者受益相比，其风险应当是可接受的，且不会损害医疗环境、患者安全、使用者及他人的安全和健康。	所有医疗器械	《关于公布医疗器械注册申报资料要求和批准证明文件格式的公告》《医疗器械安全和性能基本原则清单》《医疗器械产品受益–风险评估注册技术审查指导原则》……	产品风险管理资料、产品说明书、产品技术要求……

续表

条款号	要求	适用	证明符合性采用的方法	为符合性提供客观证据的文件
A1.2	申请人应当建立、实施、形成文件和维护风险管理体系，确保医疗器械安全、有效且质量可控。在医疗器械全生命周期内，风险管理是一个持续、反复的过程，需要定期进行系统性的改进更新。在开展风险管理时，申请人应当： a）建立涵盖所有医疗器械风险管理计划并形成文件； b）识别并分析涵盖所有医疗器械的相关的已知和可预见的危险（源）； c）估计和评价在预期使用和可合理预见的误使用过程中，发生的相关风险； d）依据A1.3和A1.4相关要求，消除或控制c）点所述的风险； e）评价生产和生产后阶段信息对综合风险、风险受益判定和风险可接受性的影响。上述评价应当包括先前未识别的危险（源）或危险情况，由危险情况导致的一个或多个风险对可接受性的影响，以及对先进技术水平的改变等等； f）基于对e）点所述信息影响的评价，必要时修改控制措施以符合A1.3和A1.4相关要求。	所有医疗器械	《关于公布医疗器械注册申报资料要求和批准证明文件格式的公告》、GB/T 42062……	产品风险管理资料……
A1.3	医疗器械的申请人在设计和生产过程中采取的风险控制措施，应当遵循安全原则，采用先进技术。需要降低风险时，申请人应当控制风险，确保每个危险（源）相关的剩余风险和总体剩余风险是可接受的。在选择最合适的解决方案时，申请人应当按以下优先顺序进行： a）通过安全设计和生产消除或适当降低风险； b）适用时，对无法消除的风险采取充分的防护措施，包括必要的警报； c）提供安全信息（警告/预防措施/禁忌证），适当时，向使用者提供培训。	所有医疗器械	GB/T 42062……	产品风险管理资料、产品说明书和标签……

续表

条款号	要求	适用	证明符合性采用的方法	为符合性提供客观证据的文件
A1.4	申请人应当告知使用者所有相关的剩余风险。	所有医疗器械	《医疗器械说明书和标签管理规定》、适用的标准或指导原则……	产品说明书和标签、产品风险管理资料……
A1.5	在消除或降低与使用有关的风险时，申请人应该： a）适当降低医疗器械的特性（如人体工程学/可用性）和预期使用环境（如灰尘和湿度）可能带来的风险； b）考虑预期使用者的技术知识、经验、教育背景、培训、身体状况（如适用）以及使用环境。	所有医疗器械	GB/T 42062、YY/T 9706.106、GB/T 14710、其他适用的标准或指导原则……	产品风险管理资料、产品说明书（限定使用环境以及预期使用者要求）、使用稳定性研究资料（应考虑预期使用环境最不利的情形）、可用性研究资料……
A1.6	在申请人规定的生命周期内，在正常使用、维护和校准（如适用）情况下，外力不应对医疗器械的特性和性能造成不利影响，以致损害患者、使用者及他人的健康和安全。	可重复使用医疗器械	《有源医疗器械使用期限注册技术审查指导原则》、其他适用的标准或指导原则……	使用稳定性研究资料、灭菌耐受性研究资料……
A1.7	医疗器械的设计、生产和包装，包括申请人所提供的说明和信息，应当确保在按照预期用途使用时，运输和贮存条件（例如：震动、振动、温度和湿度的波动）不会对医疗器械的特性和性能，包括完整性和清洁度，造成不利影响。申请人应能确保有效期内医疗器械的性能、安全和无菌保证水平。	所有医疗器械	《无源植入性医疗器械稳定性研究指导原则》、GB/T 14710、GB/T 4857系列标准、《医疗器械说明书和标签管理规定》、其他适用的标准或指导原则……	货架有效期研究资料、运输稳定性研究资料、产品说明书和标签……

条款号	要求	适用	证明符合性采用的方法	为符合性提供客观证据的文件
A1.8	在货架有效期内、开封后的使用期间，以及运输或送货期间，医疗器械应具有可接受的稳定性。	所有医疗器械	GB/T 14710、GB/T 4857 系列标准、YY/T 0681 系列标准、ISO 11607 系列标准、《无源植入性医疗器械稳定性研究指导原则》、其他适用的标准或指导原则……	稳定性研究资料……
A1.9	在正常使用条件下，基于当前先进技术水平，比较医疗器械性能带来的受益，所有已知的、可预见的风险以及任何不良副作用应最小化且可接受。	所有医疗器械	《关于公布医疗器械注册申报资料要求和批准证明文件格式的公告》、GB/T 42062……	产品风险管理资料……
A2	临床评价			
A2.1	基于监管要求，医疗器械可能需要进行临床评价（如适用）。所谓临床评价，就是对临床数据进行评估，确定医疗器械具有可接受的风险受益比，包括以下几种形式： a）临床试验报告 b）临床文献资料 c）临床经验数据	不属于《免于临床评价医疗器械目录》中的医疗器械	临床评价相关的指导原则……	临床评价资料……
A2.2	临床试验的实施应当符合《赫尔辛基宣言》的伦理原则。保护受试者的权利、安全和健康，作为最重要的考虑因素，其重要性超过科学和社会效益。在临床试验的每个步骤，都应理解、遵守和使用上述原则。另外，临床试验方案审批、患者知情同意等应符合相关法规要求。	需进行临床试验的医疗器械	《医疗器械临床试验质量管理规范》《关于公布医疗器械注册申报资料要求和批准证明文件格式的公告》《医疗器械临床试验设计技术指导原则》、其他适用的标准或指导原则……	临床评价资料、医疗器械临床试验审批申报资料……

续表

条款号	要求	适用	证明符合性采用的方法	为符合性提供客观证据的文件
A3	化学、物理和生物学特性			
A3.1	关于医疗器械的化学、物理和生物学特性，应当特别注意以下几点： a）所用材料和组成成分的选择，需特别考虑： – 毒性； – 生物相容性； – 易燃性； b）工艺对材料性能的影响； c）生物物理学或者建模研究结果应当事先进行验证（如适用）； d）所用材料的机械性能，如适用，应当考虑强度、延展性、断裂强度、耐磨性和抗疲劳性等属性； e）表面特性； f）器械与已规定化学和/或物理性能的符合性。	所有医疗器械（不同医疗器械适用的条款不同）	GB/T 16886 系列标准、YY/T 0758、YY/T 0345.1、YY/T 0809.4、《生物型股骨柄柄部疲劳性能评价指导原则》（如适用）、其他适用的标准或指导原则 ……	生物学特性研究资料、化学和物理性能（含机械性能）研究资料、建模研究资料、燃爆风险研究资料、产品技术要求及检验报告 ……
A3.2	基于医疗器械的预期用途，医疗器械的设计、生产和包装，应当尽可能减少污染物和残留物对使用者和患者，以及对从事医疗器械运输、贮存及其他相关人员造成的风险。特别要注意与使用者和患者暴露组织接触的时间和频次。	有污染物和残留物的医疗器械	《医疗器械产品清洗过程确认检查要点指南》、其他适用的标准或指导原则 ……	生物学特性研究资料、使用者清洁和消毒研究资料、残留毒性研究资料、包装研究资料 ……
A3.3	医疗器械的设计和生产应当适当降低析出物（包括滤沥物和/或蒸发物）、降解产物、加工残留物等造成的风险。应当特别注意致癌、致突变或有生殖毒性的泄漏物或滤沥物。	与患者直接或间接接触（体表完整皮肤接触除外）的医疗器械	GB/T 16886.16、GB/T 16886.17、GB/T 16886.18、YY/T 1550.2、GB/T 14233.1、《医疗器械已知可沥滤物测定方法验证及确认注册技术审查指导原则》《医疗器械产品清洗过程确认检查要点指南》、其他适用的标准或指导原则 ……	生物学特性研究资料、使用者清洁和消毒研究资料、残留毒性研究资料、产品技术要求中的化学性能（溶解析出物等）及检验报告 ……

续表

条款号	要求	适用	证明符合性采用的方法	为符合性提供客观证据的文件
A3.4	医疗器械的设计和生产应当考虑到医疗器械及其预期使用环境的性质，适当降低物质意外进入器械所带来的风险。	预期使用环境有其他物质的（如液体、气体等）	GB 9706.1、GB/T 42062、其他适用的标准或指导原则……	产品风险管理资料、联合使用研究资料、产品技术要求及检验报告……
A3.5	医疗器械及其生产工艺的设计应当能消除或适当降低对使用者和其他可能接触者的感染风险。设计应当： a）操作安全，易于处理； b）尽量减少医疗器械的微生物泄漏和／或使用过程中的感染风险； c）防止医疗器械或其内容物（例如：标本）的微生物污染； d）尽量减少意外风险［例如：割伤和刺伤（如针刺伤）、意外物质溅入眼睛等］。	有感染风险（患者和使用者）的医疗器械	GB/T 42062、《输注产品针刺伤防护装置要求与评价技术审查指导原则》（如适用）、其他适用的标准或指导原则……	产品风险管理资料、包装研究资料和清洁、消毒、灭菌研究资料，以及针刺伤防护装置研究资料（如适用）……
A4	灭菌和微生物污染			
A4.1	医疗器械其设计应当方便使用者对其进行安全清洁、消毒、灭菌和／重复灭菌（必要时）。	有感染风险的医疗器械	适用的标准或指导原则……	清洁、消毒、灭菌研究资料……
A4.2	具有微生物限度要求的医疗器械，其设计、生产和包装应当确保在出厂后，按照申请人规定的条件运输和贮存，符合微生物限度要求。	具有微生物限度要求的医疗器械	适用的标准或指导原则……	清洁、消毒、灭菌研究资料，以及稳定性研究资料、产品技术要求及检验报告……
A4.3	以无菌状态交付的医疗器械，其设计、生产和包装应按照适当的程序进行，以确保在出厂时无菌。在申请人规定的条件下运输和贮存的未破损无菌包装，打开前都应当保持无菌状态。应确保最终使用者可清晰地辨识包装的完整性（例如：防篡改包装）。	无菌医疗器械	GB 18278.1、GB 18279系列、GB 18280系列、YY/T 1276、YY/T 1464、GB/T 19974、YY/T 1463、其他适用的标准或指导原则……	灭菌确认报告、稳定性研究资料、包装说明……

续表

条款号	要求	适用	证明符合性采用的方法	为符合性提供客观证据的文件
A4.4	无菌医疗器械应按照经验证的方法进行加工、生产、包装和灭菌，其货架有效期应按照经验证的方法确定。	无菌医疗器械	GB 18278.1、GB 18279 系列、GB 18280 系列、YY/T 1276、YY/T 1464、GB/T 19974、YY/T 1464、其他适用的标准或指导原则……	灭菌确认报告、货架有效期研究资料、包装研究资料……
A4.5	预期无菌使用的医疗器械（申请人灭菌或使用者灭菌），均应在适当且受控的条件和设施下生产和包装。	无菌使用医疗器械	《医疗器械生产质量管理规范》附录《无菌医疗器械》、YY 0033《无菌医疗器具生产管理规范》、GB 50457《医药工业洁净厂房设计规范》、YY/T 0287、ISO 13485、其他适用的标准或指导原则……	质量体系核查报告、ISO 13485证书……
A4.6	以非无菌状态交付，且使用前灭菌的医疗器械：a）包装应尽量减少产品受到微生物污染的风险，且应适用于申请人规定的灭菌方法；b）申请人规定的灭菌方法应当经过验证。	非无菌状态交付，且使用前灭菌的医疗器械	适用的标准或指导原则……	灭菌研究资料……
A4.7	若医疗器械可以无菌和非无菌状态交付使用，应明确标识其交付状态。	可以无菌和非无菌状态交付使用的医疗器械	适用的标准或指导原则……	产品标签……

续表

条款号	要求	适用	证明符合性采用的方法	为符合性提供客观证据的文件
A5	环境和使用条件			
A5.1	如医疗器械预期与其他医疗器械或设备整合使用，应确保整合使用后的系统，包括连接系统，整体的安全性，且不影响器械本身的性能。整合使用上的限制应明确标识和/或在使用说明书中明确。对于需要使用者处理的连接，如液体、气体传输、电耦合或机械耦合等，在设计和生产过程中尽可能消除或降低所有可能的风险，包括错误连接或安全危害。	预期与其他医疗器械或设备整合使用的医疗器械	GB 9706.1、GB 9706.15、GB/T 42062、其他适用的标准或指导原则……	联合使用研究资料、产品风险管理资料、产品说明书、产品技术要求及检验报告、可用性研究资料……
A5.2	医疗器械的设计和生产应当考虑预期的使用环境和使用条件，以消除或降低下列风险： a）与物理和人体工程学/可用性的特性有关，对使用者或他人造成损伤的风险；	所有医疗器械	YY/T 9706.106、其他适用的标准或指导原则……	可用性研究资料、产品风险管理资料
	b）由于用户界面设计、人体工程学/可用性的特性以及预期使用环境导致的错误操作的风险；	所有医疗器械	YY/T 9706.106、其他适用的标准或指导原则……	可用性研究资料、产品风险管理资料……
	c）与合理可预期的外部因素或环境条件有关的风险，如磁场、外部电磁效应、静电释放、诊断和治疗带来的辐射、压力、湿度、温度和/或压力和加速度的变化；	所有医疗器械	YY 9706.102、其他适用的标准或指导原则……	电磁兼容报告、辐射安全研究资料、产品风险管理资料、稳定性研究资料……
	d）正常使用条件下与固体材料、液体和其他物质，包括气体，接触而产生的风险；	正常使用条件下与固体材料、液体和其他物质接触的医疗器械	GB 16174.2 的14.2关于植入式医疗器械与体液接触部分的要求、其他适用的标准或指导原则……	产品风险管理资料、联合使用研究资料、燃爆风险研究资料（例如富氧环境使用）、产品技术要求及检验报告……

续表

条款号	要求	适用	证明符合性采用的方法	为符合性提供客观证据的文件
A5.2	e）软件与信息技术（IT）运行环境的兼容性造成的风险；	含有软件的医疗器械	《医疗器械软件注册审查指导原则》、其他适用的标准或指导原则……	软件研究资料、产品风险管理资料、产品技术要求及检验报告、产品说明书……
	f）正常使用过程中，医疗器械非预期析出物导致的环境风险；	与患者直接或间接接触的医疗器械	GB/T 14223.2、其他适用的标准或指导原则……	产品风险管理资料、产品技术要求中溶解析出物以及检验报告、生物学特性研究资料（可沥滤物相关）……
	g）样本／样品／数据不正确识别和错误结果导致的风险，比如用于分析、测试或检测的样本容器、可拆卸部件和／或附件，其颜色和／或数字编码混淆；	需要识别样本／样品／数据的医疗器械	适用的标准或指导原则……	产品风险管理资料、可用性研究资料……
	h）与其他用于诊断、监测或治疗的医疗器械互相干扰导致的风险。	有源医疗器械	YY 9706.102、其他适用的标准或指导原则……	产品风险管理资料、电磁兼容检验报告、联合使用研究资料（例如磁共振环境安全）……
A5.3	医疗器械的设计和生产应当消除或降低在正常状态及单一故障状态下燃烧和爆炸的风险，尤其是预期用途包括暴露于易燃、易爆物质或其他可致燃物相关的器械联用。	有源医疗器械	GB 9706.1 中 11 章、其他适用的标准或指导原则……	产品风险管理资料、燃爆风险研究资料、GB 9706.1 检验报告……
A5.4	医疗器械的设计和生产应能确保调整、校准和维护过程能够安全有效的完成。	有源医疗器械	适用的标准或指导原则……	检验报告……

续表

条款号	要求	适用	证明符合性采用的方法	为符合性提供客观证据的文件
A5.4	a）对无法进行维护的医疗器械，如植入物，应尽量降低材料老化等风险；	无法进行维护的医疗器械	适用的标准或指导原则……	产品风险管理资料、稳定性研究资料……
	b）对无法进行调整和校准的医疗器械，如某些类型的温度计，应尽量降低测量或控制机制精度的损失风险。	无法进行调整和校准的医疗器械	适用的标准或指导原则……	产品风险管理资料、稳定性研究资料……
A5.5	与其他医疗器械或产品联合使用的医疗器械，其设计和生产应能保证互操作性和兼容性可靠且安全。	与其他医疗器械或产品联合使用的医疗器械	《医疗器械软件注册审查指导原则》、GB 16174.1 的 22 章、其他适用的标准或指导原则……	联合使用研究资料、互操作性研究资料、产品技术要求及检验报告
A5.6	医疗器械的设计和生产应能降低未经授权的访问风险，这种访问可能会妨碍器械正常运行，或造成安全隐患。	有访问界面的医疗器械	《医疗器械网络安全注册审查指导原则》、其他适用的标准或指导原则……	网络安全研究资料、产品技术要求及检验报告（访问控制）、产品风险管理资料、产品说明书……
A5.7	具有测量、监视或有数值显示功能的医疗器械，其设计和生产应当符合人体工程学/可用性原则，并应顾及器械预期用途、预期使用者、使用环境。	具有测量、监视或有数值显示功能的医疗器械	YY/T 9706.106、其他适用的标准或指导原则……	可用性研究资料……
A5.8	医疗器械的设计和生产应便于使用者、患者或其他人员对其以及相关废弃物的安全处置或再利用。使用说明书应明确安全处置或回收的程序和方法。	所有医疗器械	《医疗器械说明书和标签管理规定》、其他适用的标准或指导原则……	产品说明书资料
A6	对电气、机械和热风险的防护			
A6.1	医疗器械的设计和生产应具有机械相关的防护，保护使用者免于承受诸如运动阻力、不稳定性和活动部件等引起的机械风险。	具有机械风险的医疗器械	GB 9706.1 中的机械风险要求、其他适用的标准或指导原则……	GB 9706.1 检验报告、产品风险管理资料……

续表

条款号	要求	适用	证明符合性采用的方法	为符合性提供客观证据的文件
A6.2	除非振动是器械特定性能的一部分，否则医疗器械的设计和生产应当将产品振动导致的风险降到最低，应尽量采用限制振动（特别是振动源）的方法。	具有振动风险的医疗器械	GB 9706.1、其他适用的标准或指导原则 ……	GB 9706.1 检验报告、产品风险管理资料 ……
A6.3	除非噪声是器械特定性能的一部分，否则医疗器械设计和生产应将产品噪声导致的风险降到最低，应尽量采用限制噪声（特别是噪声源）的方法。	具有噪声的医疗器械	GB 9706.1、其他适用的标准或指导原则 ……	GB9706.1 检验报告、产品风险管理资料 ……
A6.4	如果医疗器械的部件在使用前或使用中需要进行连接或重新连接，其设计和生产应当降低这些部件间的连接故障风险。	医疗器械的部件在使用前或使用中需要进行连接或重新连接的	适用的标准或指导原则 ……	产品风险管理资料 ……
A6.5	医疗器械的可接触部件（不包括用于供热或既定温度设置部位）及其周围环境，在正常使用时不应存在过热风险。	有源医疗器械	GB 9706.1 中的超温要求 ……	GB 9706.1 检验报告、产品风险管理资料 ……
A7	有源医疗器械及与其连接的医疗器械			
A7.1	当有源医疗器械发生单一故障时，应当采取适当的措施消除或降低因此而产生的风险。	有源医疗器械	GB 9706.1 ……	GB 9706.1 检验报告，产品风险管理资料 ……
A7.2	患者的安全依赖于内部电源供电的医疗器械，应当具有检测供电状态的功能，并在电源容量不足时提供适当的提示或警告。	有源医疗器械	GB 9706.1 中的指示灯要求 ……	GB 9706.1 检验报告 ……
A7.3	患者的安全取决于外部电源供电状态的医疗器械，应当包括可显示任何电源故障的报警系统。	有源医疗器械	YY 9706.108、GB 9706.212、其他适用的标准或指导原则 ……	产品技术要求及检验报告 ……

续表

条款号	要求	适用	证明符合性采用的方法	为符合性提供客观证据的文件
A7.4	用于监视患者一个或多个临床指标的医疗器械，必须配备适当报警系统，在患者健康状况恶化或危及生命时，向使用者发出警报。	用于监视患者一个或多个临床指标的医疗器械	YY 9706.108、其他适用的标准或指导原则……	产品技术要求及检验报告……
A7.5	鉴于电磁干扰可能会损害正常运行的装置或设备，医疗器械的设计和生产应降低产生电磁干扰的风险。	有源医疗器械	YY 9706.102、其他适用的标准或指导原则……	电磁兼容检验报告、产品风险管理资料……
A7.6	医疗器械的设计和生产，应确保产品具有足够的抗电磁干扰能力，以确保产品的正常运行。	有源医疗器械	YY 9706.102、其他适用的标准或指导原则……	电磁兼容检验报告……
A7.7	当产品按申请人的说明进行安装和维护，在正常状态和单一故障状态时，医疗器械的设计和生产应减少使用者和他人免于遭受意外电击的风险。	有源医疗器械	GB 9706.1……	电气安全检验报告、产品风险管理资料……
A8	含有软件的医疗器械以及独立软件			
A8.1	含有电子可编程系统（内含软件组件）的医疗器械或独立软件的设计，应确保准确度、可靠性、精确度、安全和性能符合其预期用途。应采取适当措施，消除或减少单一故障导致的风险或性能降低。	含有软件的医疗器械	GB/T 20438.1、GB 16174.1 的19.3、其他适用的标准或指导原则……	产品风险管理资料、软件研究资料、产品技术要求及检验报告……
A8.2	含有软件组件的医疗器械或独立软件，应根据先进技术进行开发、生产和维护，同时应当考虑开发生存周期（如快速迭代开发、频繁更新、更新的累积效应）、风险管理（如系统、环境和数据的变化）等原则，包括信息安全（如安全地进行更新）、验证和确认（如更新管理过程）的要求。	含有软件的医疗器械	GB/T 20438 系列、GB/T 20918 等、《医疗器械软件注册审查指导原则》、其他适用的标准或指导原则……	软件研究资料、网络安全研究资料、产品风险管理资料……

续表

条款号	要求	适用	证明符合性采用的方法	为符合性提供客观证据的文件
A8.3	预期与移动计算平台整合使用的软件，其设计和开发，应当考虑平台本身（如屏幕尺寸和对比度、联通性、内存等）以及与其使用相关的外部因素（不同环境下的照明或噪声水平）。	预期与移动计算平台整合使用的软件	《移动医疗器械注册技术审查指导原则》、其他适用的标准或指导原则……	移动医疗器械研究资料……
A8.4	申请人应规定软件按照预期正常运行所必须的最低要求，如硬件、IT网络特性和IT网络安全措施，包括未经授权的访问。	含有软件的医疗器械	《医疗器械网络安全注册审查指导原则》《医疗器械软件注册审查指导原则》、其他适用的标准或指导原则……	软件研究资料、网络安全研究资料、产品风险管理资料、产品技术要求及检验报告、产品说明书……
A8.5	医疗器械的设计、生产和维护应能提供足够的网络安全水平，以防止未经授权的访问。	具有访问界面的医疗器械	《医疗器械网络安全注册审查指导原则》……	网络安全研究资料、产品风险管理资料、产品技术要求及检验报告、产品说明书……
A9	具有诊断或测量功能的医疗器械			
A9.1	具有诊断或测量（包括监测）功能的医疗器械的设计和生产，应当基于适当的科技方法，除其他性能外，还应确保相应的准确度、精密度和稳定性，以实现其预期目的。	具有诊断或测量（包括监测）功能的医疗器械	适用的标准（例如YY 9706.247）或指导原则……	稳定性研究资料、测量准确性研究资料、产品技术要求及检验报告、产品说明书、软件研究资料（算法验证与确认）……
	a）申请人应规定准确度限值（如适用）。	具有诊断或测量（包括监测）功能的医疗器械	适用的标准或指导原则……	产品技术要求及检验报告……

续表

条款号	要求	适用	证明符合性采用的方法	为符合性提供客观证据的文件
A9.1	b）为便于使用者理解和接受，数字化测量值应以标准化单位表示（如可能），推荐使用国际通用的标准计量单位，考虑到安全、使用者的熟悉程度和既往的临床实践，也可使用其他公认的计量单位。	具有诊断或测量（包括监测）功能的医疗器械	GB 9706.1 的 6.3、其他适用的标准或指导原则……	检验报告……
	c）医疗器械导示器和控制器的功能应有详细的说明，若器械通过可视化系统提供与操作、操作指示或调整参数有关的说明，该类信息应能够被使用者和患者（适用时）理解。	具有导示器和控制器的医疗器械	适用的标准或指导原则……	产品说明书、可用性研究资料……
A10	说明书和标签			
A10.1	医疗器械应附有识别该器械及其申请人所需的信息。每个医疗器械还应附有相关安全和性能信息或相关指示。这些信息可出现在器械本身、包装上或使用说明书中，或者可以通过电子手段（如网站）便捷访问，易于被预期使用者理解。	所有医疗器械	《医疗器械说明书和标签管理规定》、适用的标准或指导原则……	产品说明书和标签、可用性研究资料……
A11	辐射防护			
A11.1	医疗器械的设计、生产和包装应当考虑尽量减少使用者、他人和患者（如适用）的辐射吸收剂量，同时不影响其诊断或治疗功能。	具有辐射的医疗器械	适用的标准（例如 GB 15213）或指导原则……	产品技术要求及检验报告、辐射安全研究资料、产品说明书关于剂量的说明……
A11.2	具有辐射或潜在辐射危害的医疗器械，其操作说明应详细说明辐射的性质，对使用者、他人或患者（若适用）的防护措施，避免误用的方法，降低运输、贮存和安装的风险。	具有辐射或潜在辐射危害的医疗器械	GB 9706.1、其他适用的标准或指导原则……	辐射安全研究资料、产品检验报告、产品风险管理资料、产品说明书……

续表

条款号	要求	适用	证明符合性采用的方法	为符合性提供客观证据的文件
A11.3	若医疗器械有辐射或有潜在辐射危害，应当具备辐射泄漏声光报警功能（如可行）。	具有辐射或潜在辐射危害的医疗器械	YY 9706.108、其他适用的标准或指导原则……	产品技术要求及检验报告、产品说明书……
A11.4	医疗器械的设计和生产应降低使用者、其他人员或患者（若适用）暴露于非预期、偏离或散射辐射的风险。在可能和适当的情况下，应采取措施减少使用者、其他人员或患者（若适用）等可能受影响的人在辐射中的暴露。	具有辐射的医疗器械	适用的标准或指导原则……	产品风险管理资料、辐射安全研究、产品说明书和标签、产品技术要求及检验报告……
A11.5	具有辐射或潜在辐射危害且需要安装的医疗器械，应当在操作说明中明确有关验收和性能测试、验收标准及维护程序的信息。	具有辐射或潜在辐射危害且需要安装的医疗器械	适用的标准或指导原则……	产品说明书、辐射安全研究资料……
A11.6	若医疗器械对使用者有辐射或潜在辐射危害，其设计和生产应确保辐射剂量、几何分布、能量分布（或质量）以及其他辐射关键特性能够得到合理的控制和调整，并可在使用过程中进行监控（如适用）。上述医疗器械的设计和生产，应确保相关可变参数的重复性在可接受范围内。	具有辐射或潜在辐射危害且需要安装的医疗器械	适用的标准或指导原则……	辐射安全研究资料、产品技术要求及检验报告……
A12	对非专业用户使用风险的防护			
A12.1	对于非专业用户使用的医疗器械（如自测或近患者检测），为保证医疗器械的正常使用，其设计和生产应当考虑非专业用户的操作技能，以及因非专业用户技术和使用环境的不同对结果的影响。申请人提供的信息和说明应易于理解和使用，并可对结果做出解释。	非专业用户使用的医疗器械	YY/T 9706.106、其他适用的标准或指导原则……	产品风险管理资料、可用性研究资料、产品说明书……

续表

条款号	要求	适用	证明符合性采用的方法	为符合性提供客观证据的文件
A12.2	供非专业用户使用的医疗器械（如自测或近患者检测）的设计和生产应当： a）确保使用者可以按照使用说明书的规定安全准确的使用。当无法将与说明书相关的风险降低到适当水平时，可以通过培训来降低此类风险；	非专业用户使用的医疗器械	适用的标准或指导原则……	产品风险管理资料、可用性研究资料、产品说明书……
	b）尽可能减少非专业用户因错误操作和错误解释结果导致的风险。		GB/T 42062、其他适用的标准及指导原则……	产品风险管理资料、可用性研究资料、产品说明书……
A12.3	供非专业用户使用的医疗器械可通过以下措施方便用户： a）在使用时，可以验证器械的正常运行；	非专业用户使用的医疗器械	GB 9706.1、其他适用的标准或指导原则……	产品检验报告、产品说明书
	b）当器械不能正常运行或提供无效结果时，会发出警告。		适用的标准或指导原则……	产品说明书
A13	含有生物源材料的医疗器械			
A13.1	对于含有动植物组织、细胞或其它物质，细菌来源物质或衍生物的医疗器械，若无活性或以非活性状态交付，应当： a）组织、细胞及其衍生物应来源于已受控且符合预期用途的动物种属。动物的地理来源信息应根据相关法规要求予以保留。	含有生物源材料的医疗器械	《动物源性医疗器械注册技术审查指导原则》、YY/T 0771系列标准、其他适用的标准或指导原则……	生物安全性研究资料……
	b）动物源的组织、细胞、物质或其衍生物的采集、加工、保存、检测和处理过程，应确保患者、使用者以及其他人员（如适用）的安全。特别是病毒和其他传染性病原体，应通过经验证的先进技术消除或灭活，影响医疗器械性能的情况除外。		《动物源性医疗器械注册技术审查指导原则》、YY/T 0771系列标准、其他适用的标准或指导原则……	生物安全性研究资料、产品风险管理资料……

续表

条款号	要求	适用	证明符合性采用的方法	为符合性提供客观证据的文件
A13.2	对于监管部门而言，当医疗器械由人体来源的组织、细胞、物质或其衍生物生产时，应当采取以下措施： a）组织、细胞的捐赠、获取和检测应依据相关法规的要求进行；	含有生物源材料的医疗器械	《动物源性医疗器械注册技术审查指导原则》、其他适用的标准或指导原则……	生物安全性研究资料……
	b）为确保患者、使用者或他人的安全，应对组织、细胞或其衍生物进行加工、保存或其他处理。对于病毒和其他传染源，应通过源头控制，或在生产过程中通过经验证的先进技术消除或灭活。		《动物源性医疗器械注册技术审查指导原则》、其他适用的标准或指导原则	生物安全性研究资料、产品风险管理资料……
A13.3	当医疗器械使用A13.1、A13.2以外的生物物质（例如植物或细菌来源的材料）生产时，其加工、保存、检测和处理应确保患者、用户以及其他人员（如废弃物处置人员等）的安全。对于病毒和其他传染源，为确保安全，应通过源头控制，或在生产过程中通过经验证的先进技术消除或灭活。	含有生物源材料的医疗器械	《动物源性医疗器械注册技术审查指导原则》、其他适用的标准或指导原则……	生物安全性研究资料、产品风险管理资料……
B	适用于医疗器械的基本原则			
B1	化学、物理和生物学特性			
B1.1	根据医疗器械的预期用途，以及产品（例如某些可吸收产品）在人体的吸收、分布、代谢和排泄情况，对于医疗器械的化学、物理和生物学特性，应特别注意所用材料/物质与人体组织、细胞和体液之间的相容性。	在人体内的吸收、分布、代谢和排泄的医疗器械	适用的标准或指导原则……	物理和化学性能研究资料、生物学特性研究资料……
B1.2	医疗器械的设计和生产，应能够保证产品在预期使用中接触到其他的材料、物质和气体时，仍然能够安全使用。如果医疗器械用于配合药物使用，则该产品的设计和生产需要符合药品管理的有关规定，且具有药物相容性，同时药品和器械的性能符合其适应证和预期用途。	预期使用中接触到其他的材料、物质和气体的医疗器械	GB 16174.1的19.5，药物相容性部分可参考《药械组合医疗器械注册审查指导原则》中的相关内容、其他适用的标准或指导原则	联合使用研究资料（含药物相容性研究）……

续表

条款号	要求	适用	证明符合性采用的方法	为符合性提供客观证据的文件
B1.3	医疗器械的设计和生产，除接触完整皮肤的产品外，应当降低释放进入患者或使用者体内的颗粒，产生与颗粒尺寸和性质相关的风险。对纳米材料应给予重点关注。	可能向患者或使用者体内释放颗粒的医疗器械	《应用纳米材料的医疗器械安全性和有效性评价指导原则第一部分：体系框架》、GB 16174.1中14.2、其他适用的标准或指导原则……	生物学特性研究资料、产品风险管理资料……
B2	辐射防护			
B2.1	用于医学影像的医疗器械具有电离辐射时，其设计和生产，在保障图像和/或输出质量的同时，应尽可能降低患者、使用者和其他人员的辐射吸收剂量。	具有电离辐射的用于医学影像的医疗器械	适用的标准或指导原则……	产品风险管理资料、产品技术要求及检验报告、辐射安全研究……
B2.2	具有电离辐射的医疗器械应能够精确预估（或监测）、显示、报告和记录治疗过程中的辐射剂量。	具有电离辐射的医疗器械	适用的标准或指导原则……	产品风险管理资料、产品技术要求及检验报告、辐射安全研究……
B3	植入医疗器械的特殊要求			
B3.1	植入医疗器械的设计和生产，应当能消除或降低相关治疗风险，例如除颤器、高频手术设备的使用。	植入医疗器械	《植入式心脏起搏器注册技术审查指导原则》、GB 16174系列标准、其他适用的标准或指导原则……	产品风险管理资料、产品技术要求及检验报告……
B3.2	可编程有源植入式医疗器械的设计和生产，应保证产品在无需手术时即可准确识别。	可编程有源植入式医疗器械	适用的标准（例如 GB 16174.1中13.3）或指导原则……	产品技术要求及检验报告……

续表

条款号	要求	适用	证明符合性采用的方法	为符合性提供客观证据的文件
B4	提供能量或物质的医疗器械对患者或使用者的风险防护			
B4.1	用于给患者提供能量或物质的医疗器械，其设计和生产应能精确地设定和维持输出量，以保证患者、使用者和其他人的安全。	用于给患者提供能量或物质的医疗器械	适用的标准或指导原则 ……	产品技术要求及检验报告 ……
B4.2	若输出量不足可能导致危险，医疗器械应具有防止和/或指示"输出量不足"的功能。意外输出危险等级量的能量或物质作为较大风险，应采取适当的措施予以降低。	用于给患者提供能量或物质的医疗器械	GB9706.1、其他适用的标准或指导原则 ……	产品风险管理资料、GB 9706.1检验报告（12.4危险输出的防护） ……
B5	含有药物成分的组合产品			
B5.1	当医疗器械组成成分中含有某种物质，依据监管法规，该物质作为药用产品/药物进行管理，且该物质在体内为医疗器械提供辅助作用时，应将医疗器械和此物质作为一个整体，对其安全和性能进行验证，同时应当验证该物质的特征、安全、质量和有效性。	药械组合产品	《药械组合医疗器械注册审查指导原则》《药械组合医疗器械药物定性、定量及体外释放研究注册审查指导原则》 ……	非临床研究、临床评价、产品技术要求及检验报告 ……
说明	1. 第3列若适用，应当注明"是"。不适用应当注明"否"，并结合产品特点说明不适用的理由。 2. 第4列应当填写证明该医疗器械符合安全和性能基本原则的方法，通常可采取下列方法证明符合基本要求： （1）符合已发布的医疗器械部门规章、规范性文件。 （2）符合医疗器械相关国家标准、行业标准、国际标准。 （3）符合普遍接受的测试方法。 （4）符合企业自定的方法。 （5）与已批准上市的同类产品的比较。 （6）临床评价。 3. 证明符合性的证据包含在产品注册申报资料中，应当说明其在申报资料中的具体位置。证明符合性的证据未包含在产品注册申报资料中，应当注明该证据文件名称及其在质量管理体系文件中的编号备查。			

注：表中提及的相关法规、标准和指导原则等文件，以相关单位公布的现行有效版本为准。

1.2 体外诊断试剂安全和性能基本原则清单范本

表 7　体外诊断试剂安全和性能基本原则清单

条款号	要求	适用	证明符合性采用的方法	为符合性提供客观证据的文件
A	安全和性能的通用基本原则			
A1	一般原则			
A1.1	医疗器械应当实现申请人申报产品的预期性能，其设计和生产应当确保器械在预期使用条件下达到预期目的。这些器械应当是安全的并且能够实现其预期性能，与患者受益相比，其风险应当是可接受的，且不会损害医疗环境、患者安全、使用者及他人的安全和健康。	所有体外诊断试剂	GB/T 42062、YY/T 1441 ……	风险分析资料、产品说明书、产品技术要求、分析性能评估资料 ……
A1.2	申请人应当建立、实施、记录和维护风险管理体系，确保医疗器械安全、有效且质量可控。在医疗器械全生命周期内，风险管理是一个持续、反复的过程，需要定期进行系统性的改进更新。在开展风险管理时，申请人应当： a）建立涵盖所有医疗器械风险管理计划并形成文件； b）识别并分析涵盖所有医疗器械的相关的已知和可预见的危险（源）； c）估计和评价在预期使用和可合理预见的误使用过程中，发生的相关风险； d）依据 A1.3 和 A1.4 相关要求，消除或控制 c）点所述的风险； e）评价生产和生产后阶段信息对综合风险、风险受益判定和风险可接受性的影响。上述评价应当包括先前未识别的危险（源）或危险情况，由危险情况导致的一个或多个风险对可接受性的影响，以及对先进技术水平的改变等； f）基于对 e）点所述信息影响的评价，必要时修改控制措施以符合 A1.3 和 A1.4 相关要求。	所有体外诊断试剂	GB/T 42062 ……	风险分析资料 ……

续表

条款号	要求	适用	证明符合性采用的方法	为符合性提供客观证据的文件
A1.3	医疗器械的申请人在设计和生产过程中采取的风险控制措施，应当遵循安全原则，采用先进技术。需要降低风险时，申请人应当控制风险，确保每个危险（源）相关的剩余风险和总体剩余风险是可接受的。在选择最合适的解决方案时，申请人应当按以下优先顺序进行： a）通过安全设计和生产消除或适当降低风险； b）适用时，对无法消除的风险采取充分的防护措施，包括必要的警报； c）提供安全信息（警告/预防措施/禁忌证），适当时，向使用者提供培训。	所有体外诊断试剂	GB/T 42062、GB/T 191	风险分析资料、标签、产品说明书 ......
A1.4	申请人应当告知使用者所有相关的剩余风险。	所有体外诊断试剂	GB/T 42062、GB/T 191、	风险分析资料、标签、产品说明书 ......
A1.5	在消除或降低与使用有关的风险时，申请人应该： a）适当降低医疗器械的特性（如人体工程学/可用性）和预期使用环境（如灰尘和湿度）可能带来的风险； b）考虑预期使用者的技术知识、经验、教育背景、培训、身体状况（如适用）以及使用环境。	所有体外诊断试剂	GB/T 42062	风险分析资料 ......
A1.6	在申请人规定的生命周期内，在正常使用、维护和校准（如适用）情况下，外力不应对医疗器械的特性和性能造成不利影响，以致损害患者、使用者及他人的健康和安全。	需校准的体外诊断试剂	GB/T 42062、YY/T 1441、GB/T 21415	风险分析资料、产品说明书、产品技术要求、分析性能评估资料 ...

续表

条款号	要求	适用	证明符合性采用的方法	为符合性提供客观证据的文件
A1.7	医疗器械的设计、生产和包装，包括申请人所提供的说明和信息，应当确保在按照预期用途使用时，运输和贮存条件（例如：震动、振动、温度和湿度的波动）不会对医疗器械的特性和性能，包括完整性和清洁度，造成不利影响。申请人应能确保有效期内医疗器械的性能、安全和无菌保证水平。	所有体外诊断试剂	产品稳定性研究（实时/开封/运输稳定性研究）《医疗器械说明书和标签管理规定》……	稳定性研究资料、包装标签、产品说明书、生产工艺……
A1.8	在货架有效期内、开封后的使用期间（对于诊断试剂，包括在机稳定性），以及运输或送货期间（对于诊断试剂，包括被测样品），医疗器械应具有可接受的稳定性。	所有体外诊断试剂	产品稳定性研究（实时/开封/运输稳定性研究）……	稳定性研究资料……
A1.9	在正常使用条件下，基于当前先进技术水平，比较医器械性能带来的受益，所有已知的、可预见的风险以及任何不良副作用应最小化且可接受。	所有体外诊断试剂	GB/T 42062……	风险管理报告……
A2	临床评价			
A2.1	基于监管要求，医疗器械可能需要进行临床评价（如适用）。所谓临床评价，就是对临床数据进行评估，确定医疗器械具有可接受的风险受益比，包括以下几种形式：a）临床试验报告（诊断试剂临床性能评价报告）b）临床文献资料c）临床经验数据	非免临床目录的体外诊断试剂产品，非校准品、质控品适用	《体外诊断试剂临床试验技术指导原则》……	临床评价资料……
A2.2	临床试验的实施应当符合《赫尔辛基宣言》的伦理原则。保护受试者的权利、安全和健康，这是最重要的考虑因素，其重要性超过科学和社会效益。在临床试验的每个步骤，都应理解、遵守和使用上述原则。另外，临床试验方案审批、患者知情同意、诊断试剂剩余样本使用等应符合相关法规要求。	非免临床目录的体外诊断试剂产品，非校准品、质控品适用	《体外诊断试剂临床试验技术指导原则》……	伦理委员会批准的相关文件……

续表

条款号	要求	适用	证明符合性采用的方法	为符合性提供客观证据的文件
A3	化学、物理和生物学特性			
A3.1	关于医疗器械的化学、物理和生物学特性，应特别注意以下几点： a）所用材料和组成成分的选择，需特别考虑： – 毒性； – 生物相容性； – 易燃性； b）工艺对材料性能的影响； c）生物物理学或者建模研究结果应当事先进行验证（如适用）； d）所用材料的机械性能，如适用，应考虑强度、延展性、断裂强度、耐磨性和抗疲劳性等属性； e）表面特性； f）器械与已规定化学和/或物理性能的符合性。	所有体外诊断试剂适用a）、b）；其他条款考虑适用的体外诊断试剂	GB/T 16483、GB/T 42062 ……	综述资料、风险管理报告 ……
A3.2	基于医疗器械的预期用途，医疗器械的设计、生产和包装，应当尽可能减少污染物和残留物对使用者和患者，以及对从事医疗器械运输、贮存及其他相关人员造成的风险。特别要注意与使用者和患者暴露组织接触的时间和频次。	所有体外诊断试剂适用	GB/T 42062、《 医疗器械说明书和标签管理规定》 ……	风险管理报告、产品说明书 ……
A3.3	医疗器械的设计和生产应当适当降低析出物（包括滤沥物和/或蒸发物）、降解产物、加工残留物等造成的风险。应当特别注意致癌、致突变或有生殖毒性的泄漏物或滤沥物。	所有体外诊断试剂适用	GB/T 42062 ……	质量管理体系文件、风险管理资料 ……
A3.4	医疗器械的设计和生产应当考虑到医疗器械及其预期使用环境的性质，适当降低物质意外进入器械所带来的风险。	所有体外诊断试剂适用	GB/T 42062 ……	质量管理体系文件 风险管理资料 产品说明书 ……

续表

条款号	要求	适用	证明符合性采用的方法	为符合性提供客观证据的文件
A3.5	医疗器械及其生产工艺的设计应当能消除或适当降低对使用者和其他可能接触者的感染风险。设计应当： a）操作安全，易于处理； b）尽量减少医疗器械的微生物泄漏和 / 或使用过程中的感染风险； c）防止医疗器械或其内容物（例如：标本）的微生物污染； d）尽量减少意外风险［例如：割伤和刺伤（如针刺伤）、意外物质溅入眼睛等］。	a）c）d）所有体外诊断试剂适用； b）可能含有生物来源组分的体外诊断试剂适用	GB/T 42062 ……	生产工艺的研究资料、风险管理资料、产品说明书 ……
A4	灭菌和微生物污染			
A4.1	医疗器械其设计应当方便使用者对其进行安全清洁、消毒、灭菌和 / 或重复灭菌（必要时）。	有相关要求的体外诊断试剂适用，如传染病类	GB/T 42062 ……	风险管理资料、产品说明书 ……
A4.2	具有微生物限度要求的医疗器械，其设计、生产和包装应当确保在出厂后，按照申请人规定的条件运输和贮存，符合微生物限度要求。	有相关要求的体外诊断试剂	GB/T 42062、《医疗器械说明书和标签管理规定》 ……	质量管理体系文件、生产工艺研究资料、风险管理资料、产品说明书 ……
A4.3	以无菌状态交付的医疗器械，其设计、生产和包装应按照适当的程序进行，以确保在出厂时无菌。在申请人规定的条件下运输和贮存的未破损无菌包装，打开前都应当保持无菌状态。应确保最终使用者可清晰地辨识包装的完整性（例如：防篡改包装）。	体外诊断试剂通常为非无菌医疗器械，不适用	……	……

续表

条款号	要求	适用	证明符合性采用的方法	为符合性提供客观证据的文件
A4.4	无菌医疗器械应按照经验证的方法进行加工、生产、包装和灭菌，其货架有效期应按照经验证的方法确定。	体外诊断试剂通常为非无菌医疗器械，不适用	……	……
A4.5	预期无菌使用的医疗器械（申请人灭菌或使用者灭菌），均应在适当且受控的条件和设施下生产和包装。	体外诊断试剂通常为非无菌医疗器械，不适用	GB/T 42062 ……	……
A4.6	以非无菌状态交付，且使用前灭菌的医疗器械： a）包装应尽量减少产品受到微生物污染的风险，且应适用于申请人规定的灭菌方法； b）申请人规定的灭菌方法应当经过验证。	所有体外诊断试剂适用	GB/T 42062 ……	工艺和反应体系研究资料、风险分析资料、产品说明书 ……
A4.7	若医疗器械可以无菌和非无菌状态交付使用，应明确标识其交付状态。	不适用，通常无需标识其交付状态	……	……
A5	环境和使用条件			
A5.1	如医疗器械预期与其他医疗器械或设备整合使用，应确保整合使用后的系统，包括连接系统，整体的安全性，且不影响器械本身的性能。整合使用上的限制应明确标识和/或在使用说明书中明确。对于需要使用者处理的连接，如液体、气体传输、电耦合或机械耦合等，在设计和生产过程中尽可能消除或降低所有可能的风险，包括错误连接或安全危害。	所有体外诊断试剂适用	GB/T 42062、《医疗器械说明书和标签管理规定》 ……	风险管理资料、产品说明书 ……

续表

条款号	要求	适用	证明符合性采用的方法	为符合性提供客观证据的文件
A5.2	医疗器械的设计和生产应当考虑预期的使用环境和使用条件，以消除或降低下列风险： a）与物理和人体工程学/可用性的特性有关，对使用者或他人造成损伤的风险； b）由于用户界面设计、人体工程学/可用性的特性以及预期使用环境导致的错误操作的风险； c）与合理可预期的外部因素或环境条件有关的风险，如磁场、外部电和电磁效应、静电释放、诊断和治疗带来的辐射、压力、湿度、温度和/或压力和加速度的变化； d）正常使用条件下与固体材料、液体和其他物质，包括气体，接触而产生的风险； e）软件与信息技术（IT）运行环境的兼容性造成的风险； f）正常使用过程中，医疗器械非预期析出物导致的环境风险； g）样本/样品/数据不正确识别和错误结果导致的风险，比如用于分析、测试或检测的样本容器、可拆卸部件和/或附件，其颜色和/或数字编码混淆； h）与其他用于诊断、监测或治疗的医疗器械互相干扰导致的风险。	除了b），所有体外诊断试剂适用	GB/T 42062、《医疗器械说明书和标签管理规定》……	风险管理资料、产品说明书……
A5.3	医疗器械的设计和生产应当消除或降低在正常状态及单一故障状态下燃烧和爆炸的风险，尤其是预期用途包括暴露于易燃、易爆物质或与其他致燃物相关的器械联用。	不适用，非有源类产品	……	……

续表

条款号	要求	适用	证明符合性采用的方法	为符合性提供客观证据的文件
A5.4	医疗器械的设计和生产应能确保调整、校准和维护过程能够安全有效的完成。 a）对无法进行维护的医疗器械，如植入物，应尽量降低材料老化等风险； b）对无法进行调整和校准的医疗器械，如某些类型的温度计，应尽量降低测量或控制机制精度的损失风险。	含校准品/校准程序的体外诊断试剂适用	GB/T 42062 ……	校准品的溯源资料 主要原材料研究资料、质量管理体系文件 ……
A5.5	与其他医疗器械或产品联合使用的医疗器械的设计和生产，其互操作性和兼容性应可靠且安全。	与仪器配合使用的体外诊断试剂适用	GB/T 42062 ……	适用机型的研究资料、风险分析资料、产品说明书 ……
A5.6	医疗器械的设计和生产应能降低未经授权的访问风险，这种访问可能会妨碍器械正常运行，或造成安全隐患。	体外诊断试剂不适用	……	……
A5.7	具有测量、监视或有数值显示功能的医疗器械，考虑到预期使用环境、使用者、预期用途，其设计和生产应符合人体工程学/可用性原则。	体外诊断试剂不适用	……	……
A5.8	医疗器械的设计和生产，应便于使用者、患者或其他人员对其安全处置或再利用；应便于相关废弃物的安全处置或再利用。使用说明书应明确安全处置或回收的程序和方法。	所有体外诊断试剂	《医疗器械说明书和标签管理规定》 ……	产品说明书 ……

续表

条款号	要求	适用	证明符合性采用的方法	为符合性提供客观证据的文件
A6	具有诊断或测量功能的医疗器械			
A6.1	具有诊断或测量（包括监测）功能的医疗器械的设计和生产，应基于适当的科学和技术方法，除其他性能外，还应确保相应的准确度、精密度和稳定性，以实现其预期目的。 a）申请人应规定准确度限值（如适用）。 b）数字化测量值应以使用者理解和接受的标准化单位表示（如可能），推荐使用国际通用的标准计量单位，考虑到安全性、使用者的熟悉程度和既往的临床实践，也可使用其他公认的计量单位。 c）医疗器械导示器和控制器的功能应有详细的说明，若器械通过可视化系统提供与操作、操作指示或调整参数有关的说明，该类信息应能够被使用者和患者（适用时）理解。	所有体外诊断试剂	相应的体外诊断试剂国家标准、国家参考品或行业标准 ……	产品技术要求、检验报告 ……
A7	说明书和标签			
A7.1	医疗器械应附有识别该器械及其申请人所需的信息。每个医疗器械还应附有相关安全和性能信息或相关指示。这些信息可出现在器械本身、包装上或使用说明书中，或者可以通过电子手段（如网站）便捷访问，易于被预期使用者理解。	所有体外诊断试剂	《医疗器械说明书和标签管理规定》 ……	产品说明书、包装标签 ……
A8	对非专业用户使用风险的防护			
A8.1	对于非专业用户使用的医疗器械（如自测或近患者检测），为保证医疗器械的正常使用，其设计和生产应当考虑非专业用户的操作技能，以及因非专业用户技术和使用环境的不同对结果的影响。申请人提供的信息和说明应易于理解和使用，并可对结果做出解释。	非专业用户使用的体外诊断试剂试剂适用，如自测用试剂或近患者检测用试剂	GB/T 42062、《医疗器械说明书和标签管理规定》 ……	产品说明书、包装标签、风险分析资料 ……

续表

条款号	要求	适用	证明符合性采用的方法	为符合性提供客观证据的文件
A8.2	供非专业用户使用的医疗器械（如自测或近患者检测）的设计和生产应当： a）确保使用者可以按照使用说明书的规定安全准确的使用。当无法将与说明书相关的风险降低到适当水平时，可以通过培训来降低此类风险； b）尽可能减少非专业用户因错误操作和错误解释结果导致的风险。	非专业用户使用的体外诊断试剂试剂适用，如自测用试剂或近患者检测用试剂	GB/T 42062、《医疗器械说明书和标签管理规定》……	产品说明书、包装标签、风险分析资料……
A8.3	供非专业用户使用的医疗器械可通过以下措施方便用户： a）在使用时，可以验证器械的正常运行； b）当器械不能正常运行或提供无效结果时，会发出警告。	非专业用户使用的体外诊断试剂试剂适用，如自测用试剂或近患者检测用试剂	GB/T 42062、《医疗器械说明书和标签管理规定》……	产品说明书、包装标签、风险分析资料……
A9	含有生物源材料的医疗器械			
A9.1	对于含有动植物组织、细胞或其它物质，细菌来源物质或衍生物的医疗器械，若无活性或以非活性状态交付，应当： a）组织、细胞及其衍生物应来源于已受控且符合预期用途的动物种属。动物的地理来源信息应根据相关法规要求予以保留。 b）动物源的组织、细胞、物质或其衍生物的采集、加工、保存、检测和处理过程，应确保患者、使用者以及其他人员（如适用）的安全。特别是病毒和其他传染性病原体，应通过经验证的先进技术消除或灭活，影响医疗器械性能的情况除外。	含生物源性材料的体外诊断试剂适用	《医疗器械说明书和标签管理规定》、其他适用的标准或指导原则……	综述资料、质量体系文件、产品说明书……

续表

条款号	要求	适用	证明符合性采用的方法	为符合性提供客观证据的文件
A9.2	对于监管部门而言，当医疗器械由人体来源的组织、细胞、物质或其衍生物生产时，应当采取以下措施： a）组织、细胞的捐赠、获取和检测应依据相关法规的要求进行； b）为确保患者、使用者或他人的安全，应对组织、细胞或其衍生物进行加工、保存或其他处理。对于病毒和其他传染源，应通过源头控制，或在生产过程中通过经验证的先进技术消除或灭活。	含生物源性材料的体外诊断试剂适用	《医疗器械生产质量管理规范体外诊断试剂现场检查指导原则》《病原微生物实验室生物安全管理条例》……	质量体系文件、生产工艺……
A9.3	当医疗器械使用 A13.1、A13.2 以外的生物物质（例如植物或细菌来源的材料）生产时，其加工、保存、检测和处理应确保患者、用户以及其他人员（如废弃物处置人员等）的安全。对于病毒和其他传染源，为确保安全，应通过源头控制，或在生产过程中通过经验证的先进技术消除或灭活，以确保安全。	含生物源性材料的体外诊断试剂适用	《医疗器械生产质量管理规范体外诊断试剂现场检查指导原则》《病原微生物实验室生物安全管理条例》……	质量体系文件、生产工艺……
B	适用于 IVD 医疗器械的基本原则			
B1	化学、物理和生物特性			
B1.1	关于 IVD 医疗器械的化学、物理和生物学特性，考虑到产品的预期用途，应注意由于所用材料与待检测或测定的标本、分析物或标志物之间的物理和 / 或化学不相容性而导致分析性能受损的可能性（如生物组织、细胞、体液和微生物）。	所有体外诊断试剂	GB/T 42062、《医疗器械说明书和标签管理规定》……	产品说明书、适用的样本类型研究、风险分析资料……

续表

条款号	要求	适用	证明符合性采用的方法	为符合性提供客观证据的文件
B2	性能特性			
B2.1	IVD医疗器械应达到申请人声称的适用于预期用途的分析和临床性能指标，同时应考虑适用人群、预期使用者和使用环境。应使用合理的、经验证的、公认的技术方法，确定上述指标。 a）分析性能包括不限于， a.校准品和质控品的溯源、赋值 b.准确度（正确度和精密度） c.分析灵敏度/最低检出限 d.分析特异性 e.测量区间 f.样本稳定性 b）临床性能，如临床诊断敏感性、临床诊断特异性、阳性预测值、阴性预测值、似然比、以及正常和异常人群的阳性判断值或参考区间。 c）验证控制程序，以确保使用者按照预期用途使用IVD医疗器械，因此其结果适合预期用途。	所有体外诊断试剂	《关于公布体外诊断试剂注册申报资料要求和批准证明文件格式的公告》、相关试剂的技术审查指导原则等……	分析性能评估、临床评价……
B2.2	如果IVD医疗器械的性能取决于使用的校准品或质控品，应通过可用的参考测量程序或可提供的更高级别的参考物质，来确保这些定标液或质控品的赋值具有溯源性（当IVD医疗器械的性能依赖于校准品或质控品的使用时，应通过参考测量程序或更高级别的参考物质溯源校准品或质控品的赋值）。	含有校准品或质控品的体外诊断试剂	GB/T 21415……	校准品溯源研究、质控品定值研究……
B2.3	在可能的情况下，数字表示的数值应采用普遍接受的标准化单位，并且可被IVD医疗器械的使用者理解（数值标识应尽可能地采用标准化单位，且易于使用者理解）。	可溯源的体外诊断试剂	GB/T 21415……	产品说明书……

续表

条款号	要求	适用	证明符合性采用的方法	为符合性提供客观证据的文件
B2.4	IVD 医疗器械的性能特征应根据预期用途进行评估,包括以下内容: a)预期使用者,例如非专业人员、实验室专业人员; b)预期使用环境,例如:患者住所、急诊室、救护车、医疗中心、实验室; c)相关人群,如儿童、成人、孕妇、具有特定疾病体征和症状的个体、接受鉴别诊断的患者等。适当情况下,评估的人群应酌情代表种族、性别和遗传多样性群体,以代表产品拟上市销售地区的人群。 对于传染病,建议选择的人群具有相似的患病率。	所有体外诊断试剂	GB/T 42062、相关的技术审查指导原则 ……	风险管理、非临床研究、临床评价、质量管理体系文件 ……
说明	1. 第 3 列若适用,应当注明"是"。不适用应当注明"否",并结合产品特点说明不适用的理由。 2. 第 4 列应当填写证明该医疗器械符合安全和性能基本原则的方法,通常可采取下列方法证明符合基本要求: (1)符合已发布的医疗器械部门规章、规范性文件。 (2)符合医疗器械相关国家标准、行业标准、国际标准。 (3)符合普遍接受的测试方法。 (4)符合企业自定的方法。 (5)与已批准上市的同类产品的比较。 (6)临床评价。 3. 证明符合性的证据包含在产品注册申报资料中,应当说明其在申报资料中的具体位置。证明符合性的证据未包含在产品注册申报资料中,应当注明该证据文件名称及其在质量管理体系文件中的编号备查。			

注:表中提及的相关法规、标准和指导原则等文件,以相关单位公布的现行有效版本为准。

2. 综述资料范本

综述资料

（范本正文以医疗器械产品为例）

2.1 章节目录

应当包括本章的所有标题和小标题，注明目录中各内容的页码。

2.2 概述

依据《医疗器械分类目录》（原国家食品药品监督管理总局公告 2017 年第 104 号）和《医疗器械通用名称命名规则》（食药监械管〔2016〕35 号），产品名称为 ××××××，所属分类子目录名称为 ××××××、一级产品类别 ××，二级产品类别管理类别为 ×× 类，分类编码为 ××-××-××。

申报产品适用范围：××××××。

如适用，描述有关申报产品的背景信息概述或特别细节，如：申报产品的历史概述、历次提交的信息，与其他经批准上市产品的关系等。

2.3 产品描述

（1）器械及操作原理描述

1）无源医疗器械

描述工作原理、作用机理（如适用）、结构及组成、原材料（与使用者和/或患者直接或间接接触的材料成分；若器械中包含生物材料或衍生物，描述物质来源和原材料、预期使用目的、主要作用方式；若器械中包含活性药物成分（API）或药物，描述药物名称、预期使用目的、主要作用方式、来源）、交付状态及灭菌方式（如适用，描述灭菌实施者、灭菌方法、灭菌有效期），结构示意图和／或产品图示、使用方法及图示（如适用）以及区别于其他同类产品的特征等内容。

2）有源医疗器械

描述工作原理、作用机理（如适用）、结构及组成、主要功能及其组成部件（如关键组件和软件等）的功能、产品图示（含标识、接口、操控面板、应用部分等细节），以及区别于其他同类产品的特征等内容。含有多个组成部分的，应说明其连接或组装关系。

（2）型号／规格

具体描述申报产品的型号／规格，可通过产品标记实例进一步说明（注：应与申请表中型号／规格保持一致）。

对于存在多种型号规格的产品，应当明确各型号规格的区别。应当采用对比表或带有说明性文字的图片、图表，描述各种型号规格的结构组成（或配置）、功能、产品特征和运行模式、技术参数等内容。

（3）包装说明

1）说明所有产品组成的包装信息。对于无菌医疗器械，应当说明其无菌屏障系统的信息；对于具有微生物限度要求的医疗器械，应当说明保持其微生物限度的包装信息。说明如何确保最终使用者可清晰地辨识包装的完整性。

2）若使用者在进行灭菌前需要包装医疗器械或附件时，应当提供正确包装的信息（如材料、成分和尺寸等）。

（4）研发历程

阐述申请注册产品的研发背景和目的。如有参考的同类产品或前代产品，应当提供同类产品或前代产品的信息，并说明选择其作为研发参考的原因。

（5）与同类和／或前代产品的参考和比较

列表比较说明申报产品与同类产品和／或前代产品在工作原理、结构组成、制造材料、性能指标、作用方式（如植入、介入），以及适用范围等方面的异同。

2.4 适用范围和禁忌证

此处适用范围需与申请表中适用范围描述保持一致。列明申报产品禁忌证、预期使用环境、适用人群等。

（1）适用范围

1）应当明确申报产品可提供的治疗或诊断功能，可描述其医疗过程（如体内或体外诊断、康复治疗监测、避孕、消毒等），并写明申报产品诊断、治疗、预防、缓解或治愈的疾病或病况，将要监测的参数和其他与适用范围相关的考虑。

2）申报产品的预期用途，并描述其适用的医疗阶段（如治疗后的监测、康复等）。

3）明确目标用户及其操作或使用该产品应当具备的技能／知识／培训。

4）说明产品是一次性使用还是重复使用。

5）说明与其组合使用实现预期用途的其他产品。

（2）预期使用环境

1）该产品预期使用的地点，如医疗机构、实验室、救护车、家庭等。

2）可能影响其安全性和有效性的环境条件，如温度、湿度、压力、移动、振动、海拔等。

（3）适用人群

目标患者人群的信息（如成人、新生儿、婴儿或者儿童）或无预期治疗特定人群的声明，患者选择标准的信息，以及使用过程中需要监测的参数、考虑的因素。

如申报产品目标患者人群包含新生儿、婴儿或者儿童，应当描述预期使用申报产品治疗、诊断、预防、缓解或治愈疾病、病况的非成人特定群体。

（4）禁忌证

如适用，通过风险/受益评估后，针对某些疾病、情况或特定的人群（如儿童、老年人、孕妇及哺乳期妇女、肝肾功能不全者），认为不推荐使用该产品，应当明确说明。

2.5 申报产品上市历史

如适用，应当提交申报产品的下列资料：

（1）上市情况

截至提交注册申请前，申报产品在各国家或地区的上市批准时间、销售情况。若申报产品在不同国家或地区上市时有差异（如设计、标签、技术参数等），应当逐一描述。

（2）不良事件和召回

如适用，应当以列表形式分别对申报产品上市后发生的不良事件、召回的发生时间以及每一种情况下申请人采取的处理和解决方案，包括主动控制产品风险的措施，向医疗器械不良事件监测技术机构报告的情况，相关部门的调查处理情况等进行描述。

同时，应当对上述不良事件、召回进行分析评价，阐明不良事件、召回发生的原因并对其安全性、有效性的影响予以说明。若不良事件、召回数量大，应当根据事件类型总结每个类型涉及的数量。

（3）销售、不良事件及召回率

如适用，应当提交申报产品近五年在各国家（地区）销售数量的总结，按以下方式提供在各国家（地区）的不良事件、召回比率，并进行比率计算关键分析。

如：不良事件发生率＝不良事件数量÷销售数量×100%，召回发生率＝召回数量÷销售数量×100%。发生率可以采用每使用患者年或每使用进行计算，申请人应当描述发生率计算方法。

2.6 其他需说明的内容

列明其他需要说明的内容。

如适用，明确与申报产品联合使用实现预期用途的其他产品的详细信息。

对于已获得批准的部件或配合使用的附件，应当提供注册证编号和国家药监局官方网站公布的注册证信息。

3. 非临床资料范本

非临床资料

（范本正文以医疗器械产品为例）

3.1 章节目录

应当包括本章的所有标题和小标题，注明目录中各内容的页码。

3.2 产品风险管理资料

产品风险管理资料是对产品的风险管理过程及其评审的结果予以记录所形成的资料。应当提供下列内容，并说明对于每项已判定危害的下列各个过程的可追溯性。

（1）风险分析：包括医疗器械适用范围和与安全性有关特征的识别、危害的识别、估计每个危害处境的风险。

（2）风险评价：对于每个已识别的危害处境，评价和决定是否需要降低风险，若需要，描述如何进行相应风险控制。

（3）风险控制：描述为降低风险所执行风险控制的相关内容。

（4）任何一个或多个剩余风险的可接受性评定。

（5）与产品受益相比，综合评价产品风险可接受。

产品风险管理资料应符合 GB/T 42062《医疗器械风险管理对医疗器械的应用》。申请人需要识别和判定与产品有关的危害，估计和评价相关风险，控制风险并监测风险控制的安全性、有效性。

3.3 医疗器械安全和性能基本原则清单

申请人需要提供《医疗器械安全和性能基本原则清单》，并说明产品为了符合适用的各项要求所采用的方法，以及证明其符合性的文件。对于《医疗器械安全和性能基本原则清单》中不适用的各项要求，应当说明理由。

对于包含在产品注册申报资料中的文件，应当说明其在申报资料中的具体位置；对于未包含在产品注册申报资料中的文件，应当注明该证据文件名称及其在质量管理体系文件中的编号备查。

3.4 产品技术要求及检验报告

（1）申报产品适用标准情况

申报产品应当符合适用的强制性标准。对于强制性行业标准，若申报产品结构特征、预期用途、使用方式等与强制性标准的适用范围不一致，申请人应当提出不适用强制性标准的说明，并提供经验证的证明性资料。

上述标准均宜执行适用的国家标准、行业标准的现行有效版本，建议申请人主动跟踪相关标准的更新情况。

（2）产品技术要求

医疗器械产品技术要求需要参照《医疗器械产品技术要求编写指导原则》等规范性文件进行编制。

（3）产品检验报告

可提交以下任一形式的检验报告：

1）申请人出具的自检报告。

2）委托有资质的医疗器械检验机构出具的检验报告。

检验报告需要注明产品型号、规格或配置，样品描述应与产品技术要求的部件名称和型号等信息保持一致。

如适用，检验报告需要提供软件版本界面的真实照片或列明软件版本信息。具有用户界面的软件需要体现软件发布版本和软件完整版本，无用户界面的软件需要体现软件完整版本。

3.5 研究资料

根据申报产品适用范围和技术特征，提供非临床研究综述，逐项描述所开展的研究，概述研究方法和研究结论。根据非临床研究综述，提供相应的研究资料，各项研究可通过文献研究、实验室研究、模型研究等方式开展，一般应当包含研究方案、研究报告。采用建模研究的，应当提供产品建模研究资料。

（1）化学和物理性能研究

申请人需要提供产品性能研究资料，以及产品技术要求的编制说明，列表说明产品性能指标条款，逐项解释条款来源和制定依据。有源医疗器械需要说明适用的标准或方法，解释引用或采用的理由。关于适用标准中的不适用条款，需要提供必要的说明。申请人可以结合综述资料中描述的产品应用模式、运行模式、产品配置等，提供相应的测试验证资料。申报产品需要重点关注技术缺陷、故障、误操作等相关的不良事件。

1）应当提供产品化学/材料表征、物理和/或机械性能指标的确定依据、设计输入来源以及临床意义，所采用的标准或方法、采用的原因及理论基础。

2）燃爆风险

对于暴露于易燃、易爆物质或与其他可燃物、致燃物联合使用的医疗器械，应当提供燃爆风险研究资料，证明在正常状态及单一故障状态下，燃爆风险可接受。

3）联合使用

如申报产品预期与其他医疗器械、药品、非医疗器械产品联合使用实现同一预期用途，应当提供证明联合使用安全有效的研究资料，包括互联基本信息（连接类型、接口、协议、最低性能）、联合使用风险及控制措施、联合使用上的限制，兼容性研究等。

联合药物使用的，应当提供药物相容性研究资料，证明药品和器械联合使用的性能符合其适应证和预期用途。

4）量效关系和能量安全

对于向患者提供能量或物质治疗的医疗器械，应当提供量效关系和能量安全性研究资料，提供证明治疗参数设置的安全性、有效性、合理性，以及除预期靶组织外，能量不会对正常组织造成不可接受的伤害的研究资料。

（2）电气系统安全性研究

应当提供电气安全性、机械和环境保护以及电磁兼容性的研究资料，说明适用的标准以及开展的研究。

应列明需要符合的标准，例如：GB 9706.1，YY 9706.102 等。

（3）辐射安全研究

对于具有辐射或潜在辐射危害（包括电离辐射和非电离辐射）的产品，应当提供辐射安全的研究资料，包括：

1）说明符合的辐射安全通用及专用标准，对于标准中的不适用条款应详细说明理由；

2）说明辐射的类型并提供辐射安全验证资料，应确保辐射能量、辐射分布以及其他辐射关键特性能够得到合理的控制和调整，并可在使用过程中进行预估、监控（如适用）；

3）提供减少使用者、他人和患者在运输、贮存、安装、使用中辐射吸收剂量的防护措施，避免误用的方法。对于需要安装的产品，应当明确有关验收和性能测试、验收标准及维护程序的信息。

（4）软件研究

1）软件

含有软件组件的产品和独立软件，应当提供软件的研究资料，包括基本信息、实现过程、核心功能、结论等内容，详尽程度取决于软件安全性级别（严重、中等、轻微）。其中，基本信息包括软件标识、安全性级别、结构功能、物理拓扑、运行环境、注册历史，实现过程包括开发概况、风险管理、需求规范、生存周期、验证与确认、可追溯性分析、缺陷管理、更新历史，明确核心功能、核心算法、预期用途的对应关系。

申请人可以依据《医疗器械软件注册审查指导原则》，明确申报产品的软件安全性级别，并提供相应级别的软件研究资料。软件研究报告需要覆盖全部软件组件，并建议关联综述资料描述的产品功能。

申请人应参考说明书列明软件核心功能的相关信息。必要时，可以提供专题研究资料，针对某个核心算法进行详述。

2）网络安全

具备电子数据交换、远程控制或用户访问功能的独立软件和含有软件组件的产品，应当提供网络安全研究资料，包括基本信息、实现过程、漏洞评估、结论等内容，详尽程度取决于软件安全性级别。其中，基本信息包括软件信息、数据架构、网络安全能力、网络安全补丁、安全软件，实现过程包括风险管理、需求规范、验证与确认、可追溯性分析、更新维护计划，漏洞评估明确已知漏洞相关信息。

申请人可以参照《医疗器械网络安全注册审查指导原则》提供网络安全研究资料。

3）现成软件

产品若使用现成软件，应当根据现成软件的类型、使用方式等情况提供相应软件研究资料和网络安全研究资料。

4）人工智能

产品若采用深度学习等人工智能技术实现预期功能与用途，应当提供算法研究资料，包括算法基本信息、数据收集、算法训练、算法性能评估等内容。

申请人可以参照《人工智能医疗器械注册审查指导原则》提供人工智能研究资料。

5）互操作性

产品若通过电子接口与其他医疗器械或非医疗器械交换并使用信息，应当提供互操作性研究资料，包括基本信息、需求规范、风险管理、验证与确认、维护计划等内容。

6）其他

产品若采用移动计算、云计算、虚拟现实等信息通信技术实现预期功能与用途，应当提供相应技术研究资料，包括基本信息、需求规范、风险管理、验证与确认、维护计划等内容。

（5）生物学特性研究

对于与患者直接或间接接触的器械，应当进行生物学评价。生物学评价资料应当包括：

1）描述产品所用材料及与人体接触性质，设计和生产过程中可能引入的污染物和残留物，设计和生产过程中可能产生的析出物（包括滤沥物和/或蒸发物）、降解产物、加工残留物，与医疗器械直接接触的包装材料等相关信息。

2）描述申报产品的物理和/或化学信息并考虑材料表征（如适用），如器械的物理作用可能产生生物学风险，应当进行评价。

3）生物学评价的策略、依据和方法。

4）已有数据和结果的评价。

5）选择或豁免生物学试验的理由和论证。

6）完成生物学评价所需的其他数据。

若医疗器械材料可能释放颗粒进入患者和使用者体内，从而产生与颗粒尺寸和性质相关风险，如纳米材料，对所有包含、产生或由其组成的医疗器械，应当提供相关生物学风险研究资料。

若根据申报产品预期用途，其会被人体吸收、代谢，如可吸收产品，应当提供所用材料/物质与人体组织、细胞和体液之间相容性的研究资料。

有源医疗器械可以依据 GB16886.1《医疗器械生物学评价第 1 部分：

风险管理过程中的评价与试验》的方法，开展生物学评价研究。

（6）生物源材料的安全性研究

对于含有同种异体材料、动物源性材料或生物活性物质等具有生物安全风险的产品，应当提供相应生物安全性研究资料。

生物安全性研究资料应当包括：

1）相应材料或物质的情况，组织、细胞和材料的获取、加工、保存、测试和处理过程。

2）阐述来源，并说明生产过程中灭活和去除病毒和/或传染性因子的工艺过程，提供有效性验证数据或相关资料。

3）说明降低免疫原性物质的方法和/或工艺过程，提供质量控制指标与验证性实验数据或相关资料。

4）支持生物源材料安全性的其他资料。

（7）清洁、消毒、灭菌研究

1）生产企业灭菌：应当明确灭菌工艺（方法和参数）和无菌保证水平（SAL），并提供灭菌验证及确认的相关研究资料。

2）使用者灭菌：应当明确推荐的灭菌工艺（方法和参数）、所推荐灭菌工艺的确定依据以及验证的相关研究资料；对可耐受两次或多次灭菌的产品，应当提供产品所推荐灭菌工艺耐受性的研究资料。

3）使用者清洁和消毒：应当明确推荐的清洗和消毒工艺（方法和参数）、工艺的确定依据以及验证的相关研究资料。申请人宜结合综述资料，说明推荐的消毒周期、消毒方式、消毒剂的型号和供应商等。若适用，建议说明不同的消毒剂的消毒效果，提供相关研究资料。

4）残留毒性：若产品经灭菌或消毒后可能产生残留物质，应当对灭菌或消毒后的产品进行残留毒性的研究，明确残留物信息及采取的处理方法，并提供相关研究资料。

5）以非无菌状态交付，且使用前需灭菌的医疗器械，应当提供证明包装能减少产品受到微生物污染的风险，且适用于生产企业规定灭菌方法的研究资料。

（8）动物试验研究

为避免开展不必要的动物试验，医疗器械是否开展动物试验研究应当进行科学决策，并提供论证／说明资料。经决策需通过动物试验研究验证／确认产品风险控制措施有效性的，应当提供动物试验研究资料，研究资料应当包括试验目的、实验动物信息、受试器械和对照信息、动物数量、评价指标和试验结果、动物试验设计要素的确定依据等内容。

（9）证明产品安全性、有效性的其他研究资料。

3.6 非临床文献

提供与申报产品相关的已发表的非临床研究（如尸体研究、生物力学研究等）文献／书目列表，并提供相关内容的复印件（外文应同时提供翻译件）。如未检索到与申报产品相关的非临床文献／书目，应当提供相关的声明。

3.7 稳定性研究

（1）货架有效期

如适用，应当提供货架有效期和包装研究资料，证明在货架有效期内，在生产企业规定的运输贮存条件下，产品可保持性能功能满足使用要求，具有微生物限度要求的产品还应当符合微生物限度要求，以无菌状态交付的产品还应保持无菌状态。

（2）使用稳定性

如适用，应当提供使用稳定性／可靠性研究资料，证明在生产企业规定的使用期限／使用次数内，在正常使用、维护和校准（如适用）情况下，产品的性能功能满足使用要求。

申请人可以依据《有源医疗器械使用期限注册技术审查指导原则》，提供产品使用期限的研究资料。申请人应考虑在正常条件和不利条件下对产品进行分析。

（3）运输稳定性

应当提供运输稳定性和包装研究资料，证明在生产企业规定的运输条件下，运输过程中的环境条件（例如：震动、振动、温度和湿度的波动）不会对医疗器械的特性和性能，包括完整性和清洁度，造成不利影响。

申请人可以参考 GB/T 14710 等相关标准进行研究。

3.8 其他资料

免于进行临床评价的第二类、第三类医疗器械，申请人应当按照《列入免于进行临床评价医疗器械目录产品对比说明技术指导原则》，从基本原理、结构组成、性能、安全性、适用范围等方面，证明产品的安全有效性。

对于一次性使用的医疗器械，还应当提供证明其无法重复使用的支持性资料。

申请人可以依据产品特征，进一步提供其他研究资料。例如：关于综述资料中描述的产品关键技术和重要功能，可以提供专题研究资料，详述其工作原理、实现方式、应用场景、预期用途、临床价值和标准工作流程，以及验证标准、测试规范、测试设备等。

4. 医疗器械产品技术要求范本

产品技术要求的内容一般包括产品名称，型号、规格及其划分说明（必要时），性能指标，检验方法，术语（如适用）及附录（如适用）。

申请人应参照《医疗器械产品技术要求编写指导原则》编写医疗器械产品技术要求。

4.1 医疗器械产品技术要求编号

产品技术要求编号为相应产品的注册证号（备案号）。拟注册（备案）的产品技术要求编号可留空。

4.2 产品名称

产品技术要求中的产品名称应使用中文，并与申请注册或备案的产品名称相一致。

4.3 型号、规格及其划分说明

产品技术要求中应明确产品型号、规格。对同一注册单元中存在多种型号、规格的产品，应明确不同型号、规格的划分说明（推荐采用图示和/或表格的方式），表述文本较多的内容可以在附录中列明。

对包含软件的产品，应明确软件发布版本和软件完整版本命名规则，示例如下：

× 软件信息

软件型号规格：（明确软件的型号/规格，无需体现软件发布版本）

软件发布版本：［明确软件发布版本，若软件模块（含医用中间件）单独进行版本控制亦需提供其发布版本］

软件版本命名规则：X.Y.Z.B

明确软件完整版本全部字段的位数、范围、含义，若软件模块（含医用中间件）单独进行版本控制亦需提供其版本命名规则，并明确与软件版本命名规则的关系。软件和软件模块的版本命名规则均需与质量管理体系保持一致。

4.4 性能指标

（1）产品技术要求中的性能指标是指可进行客观判定的成品的功能性、安全性指标。对产品安全有效性不产生实质性影响的项目可不在技术要求性能指标处列明。例如，部分引流导管产品主要关注其畅通性，产品需要能有效连接吸引装置及使用端，并保证连接牢固，导管的直径、长度等信息必要时可作为产品描述性信息在技术要求附录体现，而不作为产品性能指标。其他如产品工程图等则不需要在技术要求中列明。但某些产品的尺寸信息会对其安全有效性产生重要影响，宜在技术要求性能指标中规定，例如血管支架产品的长度、外径，骨科植入物的尺寸公差等。

（2）技术要求中性能指标的制定可参考相关国家标准／行业标准并结合具体产品的设计特性、预期用途且应当符合产品适用的强制性国家标准／行业标准。如产品结构特征、预期用途、使用方式等与强制性标准的适用范围不一致，注册人／备案人应当提出不适用强制性标准的说明，并提供相关资料。

（3）产品技术要求中的性能指标应明确具体要求，不应以"见随附资料""按供货合同"等形式提供。

检验项目	标准要求	试验方法
外观	1. 设备外表面应光洁、无裂纹	目测
	2.……	……
	3.……	……
尺寸	1. 产品附件尺寸应符合表 1 的要求。	用通用量具检验
	2.……	……
产品性能	1. 测量范围……	型式检验
	2. 测量精度……	型式检验
	3. 机械性能……	型式检验
	4. 软件功能……	型式检验
	……	
电气安全	应符合 GB 9706.1–2020、……的要求。	型式检验
	……	
电磁兼容	应符合 YY 9706.102–2021、……的要求。	型式检验
	……	

4.5 性能指标要求

根据《医疗器械注册与备案管理办法》《体外诊断试剂注册与备案管理办法》等文件规定，技术要求中的性能指标是指可进行客观判定的成品的功能性、安全性指标。

可进行客观判定的指标通常是指可量化或可客观描述的指标。例如，该指标可直接通过一个确定的且可验证其特性值的试验方法进行检验，并直接获得数据结果。例如，血液透析器产品重要功能是对目标物质的清除，该功能实现的效果可直接通过测量被清除目标物质的剩余量获得验证，因此宜在技术要求规定，以表征其主要功能性；血管内导管产品要求其在使用过程中必须保持无泄漏，因此技术要求中宜规定产品无泄漏的性能要求，并给出客观、科学的试验方法，保证在规定条件下产品无泄漏；输液泵重要的功能性指标是输液流速和对应的精确度，技术要求中宜规定上述指标，同时应按照规定的方法进行验证以保证产品在临床中有效应用；影像型超声诊断设备成像分辨力是图像质量的重要技术指标，技术要求中宜规定该指标，并给出客观、科学的试验方法，以保证产品性能满足其宣称的功能性要求。

以下内容不建议在技术要求性能指标中规定：

（1）研究性及评价性内容

研究性内容一般是为了研究产品特点而开展的试验、分析的组合，通常为在产品设计开发阶段为了确定产品某一特定属性而开展的验证性活动。例如，医疗器械货架有效期是指保证医疗器械终产品正常发挥预期功能的期限，产品设计开发阶段需完成产品货架有效期研究。对于无源医疗器械产品而言，有效期研究需设定老化试验条件，例如温度、湿度等，进行老化试验，并根据设定好的老化条件及老化后的产品性能、包装性能等数据计算并确定其货架有效期。对于有源医疗器械而言，可以对该产品进行使用状态列举，完整分析出临床使用的情况，直接进行产品的老化试验研究；

也可以将产品（系统）分解为不同子系统／部件进行评价，应详细分析分解关系，在此基础上通过不同的分解方式（如将产品分为关键部件及非关键部件等）确定产品的使用期限。除此之外，其他研究性内容还包括灭菌验证研究、疲劳研究、体外降解研究、人因验证研究、可靠性验证研究、磁共振兼容研究等。

评价性内容一般是指对产品所规定目标的适宜性、充分性和／或有效性的评价。这种评价既可采用多个试验组合进行综合评价，也可以采用其他方式（如历史数据、已上市产品信息等）进行评定。例如，生物相容性研究（包括材料介导热原）一般认为属于评价性项目，可以采用多个生物学试验组合进行综合评价，也可以采用历史数据、已上市产品信息等多种数据，利用比对方式进行评价，还可以采用化学分析的方法结合毒理学数据进行判定。再如，医用电器环境要求是评价产品在各种工作环境和模拟贮存、运输环境下的适应性，一般认为属于稳定性评价项目。可以制定不同的气候环境条件和机械环境条件来进行试验，或通过对关键部件的试验来评价整机的情况，也可以通过已上市同类产品比对方式进行判断。

其他评价性项目还包括病毒灭活效果评价、免疫原性评价等内容。

（2）非成品相关内容

技术要求规定的是成品相关性能，原材料、半成品性能指标及特征一般不建议在技术要求中体现。例如，某些原材料的力学性能、化学性能等。

4.6 检验方法

检验方法是用于验证产品是否符合规定要求的方法，检验方法的制定应与相应的性能指标相适应。应优先考虑采用适用的已建立标准方法的检验方法，必要时，应当进行方法学验证，以确保检验方法的可重现性和可操作性。

通常情况下，检验方法宜包括试验步骤和结果的表述（如计算方法等）。必要时，还可增加试验原理、样品的制备和保存、仪器等确保结果可重现的所有条件、步骤等内容。

对于体外诊断试剂类产品，检验方法中还应明确说明采用的参考品 / 标准品、样本制备方法、试验次数、计算方法。

4.7 附录

对于第三类体外诊断试剂类产品，产品技术要求中应以附录形式明确主要原材料、生产工艺要求。

对于医疗器械产品，必要时可在附录中更为详尽地注明某些描述性特性内容，如产品灭菌或非灭菌供货状态、产品有效期、主要原材料、生产工艺、产品主要安全特征、关键的技术规格、关键部件信息、磁共振兼容性等。

4.8 格式要求

医疗器械产品技术要求格式见附件。

附

医疗器械产品技术要求格式

医疗器械产品技术要求编号:（宋体小四号，加粗）

产品名称（宋体小二号，加粗）

1. 产品型号 / 规格及其划分说明（宋体小四号，加粗）（如适用）

1.1 ……（宋体小四号）

1.1.1 ……

……

2. 性能指标（宋体小四号，加粗）

2.1 ……（宋体小四号）

2.1.1 ……

……

3. 检验方法（宋体小四号，加粗）

3.1 ……（宋体小四号）

3.1.1 ……

……

4. 术语（宋体小四号，加粗）（如适用）

4.1 ……（宋体小四号）

4.2 ……

……

（分页）

附录 A ……（宋体小四号，加粗）（如适用）

A1. ……（宋体小四号）

A1.1 ……

注：

1. 涉及西文字体内容可采用 Times New Roman 字体。

2. 不要添加封面、注册人名称及标志、落款等未规定内容。

3. 页码可采用 x（第 x 页）/y(总页码) 的形式，如 1/9。

5. 符合性声明范本

5.1 医疗器械符合性声明范本

申请人应当声明下列内容：

（1）申报产品符合《医疗器械注册与备案管理办法》和相关法规的

要求。

（2）申报产品符合《医疗器械分类规则》有关分类的要求。

（3）申报产品符合现行国家标准、行业标准，并提供符合标准的清单。

（4）保证所提交资料的真实性（境内产品由申请人出具，进口产品由申请人和代理人分别出具）。

5.2 体外诊断试剂符合性声明范本

申请人应当声明下列内容：

（1）申报产品符合《体外诊断试剂注册与备案管理办法》和相关法规的要求。

（2）申报产品符合《体外诊断试剂分类规则》《体外诊断试剂分类子目录》有关分类的要求。

（3）申报产品符合现行国家标准、行业标准，并提供符合标准的清单。

（4）申报产品符合国家标准品的清单。

（5）保证所提交资料的真实性（境内产品由申请人出具，进口产品由申请人和代理人分别出具）。

6. 代理人委托书范本

境外注册人×××××× / 备案人××××××指定中国境内的企业法人××××××公司作为代理人，办理相关医疗器械 / 体外诊断试剂注册 / 备案事项。代理人应当依法协助注册人 / 备案人履行下列义务：

（1）建立与产品相适应的质量管理体系并保持有效运行；

（2）制定上市后研究和风险管控计划并保证有效实施；

（3）依法开展不良事件监测和再评价；

（4）建立并执行产品追溯和召回制度；

（5）国务院药品监督管理部门规定的其他义务。

7. 体外诊断试剂说明书范本

7.1 体外诊断试剂说明书格式

××××××（产品通用名称）说明书

【产品名称】××××××

【包装规格】××××××

【预期用途】××××××

【检验原理】××××××

【主要组成成分】××××××

【储存条件及有效期】××××××

【适用仪器】××××××

【样本要求】××××××

【检验方法】××××××

【阳性判断值或者参考区间】××××××

【检验结果的解释】××××××

【检验方法的局限性】××××××

【产品性能指标】××××××

【注意事项】××××××

【标识的解释】××××××

【参考资料】××××××

【基本信息】××××××

【医疗器械注册证编号 / 产品技术要求编号】（或者【医疗器械备案凭证编号 / 产品技术要求编号】）××××××

【说明书核准及修改日期】××××××

以上项目如对于某些产品不适用，说明书中可以缺省。

7.2 各项内容撰写的说明

产品说明书内容原则上应全部使用中文进行表述；如含有国际通用或行业内普遍认可的英文缩写，可用括号在中文后标明；对于确实无适当中文表述的词语，可使用相应英文或其缩写表示。

【产品名称】

（1）通用名称

通用名称应当按照《体外诊断试剂注册管理办法》（国家食品药品监督管理总局令第5号）规定的命名原则进行命名，可适当参考相关"分类目录"和/或国家标准及行业标准。

除特殊用途产品可在通用名称中注明样本类型外，其余产品的通用名称中均不应当出现样本类型、定性/定量等内容。

（2）英文名称

【包装规格】注明可测试的样本数或装量，如××测试/盒、××人份/盒、××mL，除国际通用计量单位外，其余内容均应采用中文进行表述。如产品有不同组分，可以写明组分名称。如有货号，可增加货号信息。

【预期用途】第一段内容详细说明产品的预期用途，如定性或定量检测、自测、确认等，样本类型和被测物等，具体表述形式根据产品特点做适当调整。若样本来源于特殊受试人群，如孕妇、新生儿等，应当予以注明。第二段内容说明与预期用途相关的临床适应症及背景情况，说明相关的临床或实验室诊断方法等。

【检验原理】详细说明检验原理、方法，必要时可采用图示方法描述。

【主要组成成分】

（1）对于产品中包含的试剂组分

1）说明名称、数量及在反应体系中的比例或浓度，如果对于正确的操作很重要，应提供其生物学来源、活性及其他特性。

2）对于多组分试剂盒，明确说明不同批号试剂盒中各组分是否可以互换。

3）如盒中包含耗材，应列明耗材名称、数量等信息。如塑料滴管、封板膜、自封袋等。

（2）对于产品中不包含，但对该试验必需的试剂组分，说明书中应列出此类试剂的名称、纯度，提供稀释或混合方法及其他相关信息。

（3）对于校准品和质控品

1）说明主要组成成分及其生物学来源。

2）注明校准品的定值及其溯源性。

3）注明质控品的靶值范围。如靶值范围为批特异，可注明批特异，并附单独的靶值单。

【储存条件及有效期】

（1）说明产品的储存条件，如2~8℃、-18℃以下、避免／禁止冷冻等。其他影响稳定性的条件，如光线、湿度等也必须说明。如果打开包装后产品或组分的稳定性不同于原包装产品，则打开包装后产品或组分的储存条件也必须注明。

（2）有效期：说明在储存条件下的有效期。如果打开包装后产品或组分的稳定性不同于原包装产品，打开包装后产品或组分的有效期也必须注明。

（3）如试剂盒各组分的稳定性不一致，则应对各组分的储存条件和有效期分别进行描述。

【适用仪器】说明可适用的仪器及型号，并提供与仪器有关的信息以便用户能够正确选择使用。

【样本要求】应在以下几方面进行说明：

（1）适用的样本类型。

（2）在样本收集过程中的特别注意事项。

（3）为保证样本各组分稳定所必需的抗凝剂或保护剂等。

（4）已知的干扰物。

（5）能够保证样本稳定的储存、处理和运输方法。

【检验方法】为保证试验的正确进行，应在以下几方面对试验的每一步进行详细说明：

（1）试剂配制：各试剂组分的稀释、混合及其他必要的程序。

（2）必须满足的试验条件：如 pH、温度、每一步试验所需的时间、波长、最终反应产物的稳定性等。试验过程中必须注意的事项。

（3）校准程序（如果需要）：校准品的准备和使用，校准曲线的绘制方法。

（4）质量控制程序：质控品的使用、质量控制方法。

（5）试验结果的计算或读取，包括对每个系数及对每个计算步骤的解释。如果可能，应举例说明。

【阳性判断值或者参考区间】说明阳性判断值或者参考区间，并简要说明阳性判断值或者参考区间的确定方法。

【检验结果的解释】说明可能对试验结果产生影响的因素；说明在何种情况下需要进行确认试验。

【检验方法的局限性】说明该检验方法的局限性。

【产品性能指标】说明该产品的主要性能指标。

【注意事项】注明必要的注意事项，如本品仅用于体外诊断等。如该产品含有人源或动物源性物质，应给出具有潜在感染性的警告。

【标识的解释】如有图形或符号，请解释其代表的意义。

【参考资料】注明引用的参考资料。

【基本信息】

（1）境内体外诊断试剂

1）注册人（或者备案人）与生产企业为同一企业的，按以下格式标注基本信息：

注册人（或者备案人）/生产企业名称

住所

联系方式

售后服务单位名称

联系方式

生产地址

生产许可证编号或者生产备案凭证编号

2）委托生产的按照以下格式标注基本信息：

注册人（或者备案人）名称

住所

联系方式

售后服务单位名称

联系方式

受托企业的名称

住所

生产地址

生产许可证编号或者生产备案凭证编号

（2）进口体外诊断试剂

按照以下格式标注基本信息：

注册人（或者备案人）/生产企业名称

住所

生产地址

联系方式

售后服务单位名称

联系方式

代理人的名称

住所

联系方式

【医疗器械注册证编号/产品技术要求编号】(或者【医疗器械备案凭证编号/产品技术要求编号】)注明该产品的注册证编号或者备案凭证编号。

【说明书核准日期及修改日期】注明该产品说明书的核准日期。如曾进行过说明书的变更申请,还应该同时注明说明书的修改日期。

附录　医疗器械制度文件汇总

医疗器械监督管理条例

（中华人民共和国国务院令第 739 号）

第一章　总　则

第一条　为了保证医疗器械的安全、有效，保障人体健康和生命安全，促进医疗器械产业发展，制定本条例。

第二条　在中华人民共和国境内从事医疗器械的研制、生产、经营、使用活动及其监督管理，适用本条例。

第三条　国务院药品监督管理部门负责全国医疗器械监督管理工作。

国务院有关部门在各自的职责范围内负责与医疗器械有关的监督管理工作。

第四条　县级以上地方人民政府应当加强对本行政区域的医疗器械监督管理工作的领导，组织协调本行政区域内的医疗器械监督管理工作以及突发事件应对工作，加强医疗器械监督管理能力建设，为医疗器械安全工作提供保障。

县级以上地方人民政府负责药品监督管理的部门负责本行政区域的医疗器械监督管理工作。县级以上地方人民政府有关部门在各自的职责范围内负责与医疗器械有关的监督管理工作。

第五条　医疗器械监督管理遵循风险管理、全程管控、科学监管、社会共治的原则。

第六条　国家对医疗器械按照风险程度实行分类管理。

第一类是风险程度低，实行常规管理可以保证其安全、有效的医疗器械。

第二类是具有中度风险，需要严格控制管理以保证其安全、有效的医疗器械。

第三类是具有较高风险，需要采取特别措施严格控制管理以保证其安全、有效的医疗器械。

评价医疗器械风险程度，应当考虑医疗器械的预期目的、结构特征、使用方法等因素。

国务院药品监督管理部门负责制定医疗器械的分类规则和分类目录，并根据医疗器械生产、经营、使用情况，及时对医疗器械的风险变化进行分析、评价，对分类规则和分类目录进行调整。制定、调整分类规则和分类目录，应当充分听取医疗器械注册人、备案人、生产经营企业以及使用单位、行业组织的意见，并参考国际医疗器械分类实践。医疗器械分类规则和分类目录应当向社会公布。

第七条 医疗器械产品应当符合医疗器械强制性国家标准；尚无强制性国家标准的，应当符合医疗器械强制性行业标准。

第八条 国家制定医疗器械产业规划和政策，将医疗器械创新纳入发展重点，对创新医疗器械予以优先审评审批，支持创新医疗器械临床推广和使用，推动医疗器械产业高质量发展。国务院药品监督管理部门应当配合国务院有关部门，贯彻实施国家医疗器械产业规划和引导政策。

第九条 国家完善医疗器械创新体系，支持医疗器械的基础研究和应用研究，促进医疗器械新技术的推广和应用，在科技立项、融资、信贷、招标采购、医疗保险等方面予以支持。支持企业设立或者联合组建研制机构，鼓励企业与高等学校、科研院所、医疗机构等合作开展医疗器械的研究与创新，加强医疗器械知识产权保护，提高医疗器械自主创新能力。

第十条 国家加强医疗器械监督管理信息化建设，提高在线政务服务水平，为医疗器械行政许可、备案等提供便利。

第十一条　医疗器械行业组织应当加强行业自律，推进诚信体系建设，督促企业依法开展生产经营活动，引导企业诚实守信。

第十二条　对在医疗器械的研究与创新方面做出突出贡献的单位和个人，按照国家有关规定给予表彰奖励。

第二章　医疗器械产品注册与备案

第十三条　第一类医疗器械实行产品备案管理，第二类、第三类医疗器械实行产品注册管理。

医疗器械注册人、备案人应当加强医疗器械全生命周期质量管理，对研制、生产、经营、使用全过程中医疗器械的安全性、有效性依法承担责任。

第十四条　第一类医疗器械产品备案和申请第二类、第三类医疗器械产品注册，应当提交下列资料：

（一）产品风险分析资料；

（二）产品技术要求；

（三）产品检验报告；

（四）临床评价资料；

（五）产品说明书以及标签样稿；

（六）与产品研制、生产有关的质量管理体系文件；

（七）证明产品安全、有效所需的其他资料。

产品检验报告应当符合国务院药品监督管理部门的要求，可以是医疗器械注册申请人、备案人的自检报告，也可以是委托有资质的医疗器械检验机构出具的检验报告。

符合本条例第二十四条规定的免于进行临床评价情形的，可以免于提交临床评价资料。

医疗器械注册申请人、备案人应当确保提交的资料合法、真实、准确、完整和可追溯。

第十五条 第一类医疗器械产品备案，由备案人向所在地设区的市级人民政府负责药品监督管理的部门提交备案资料。

向我国境内出口第一类医疗器械的境外备案人，由其指定的我国境内企业法人向国务院药品监督管理部门提交备案资料和备案人所在国（地区）主管部门准许该医疗器械上市销售的证明文件。未在境外上市的创新医疗器械，可以不提交备案人所在国（地区）主管部门准许该医疗器械上市销售的证明文件。

备案人向负责药品监督管理的部门提交符合本条例规定的备案资料后即完成备案。负责药品监督管理的部门应当自收到备案资料之日起5个工作日内，通过国务院药品监督管理部门在线政务服务平台向社会公布备案有关信息。

备案资料载明的事项发生变化的，应当向原备案部门变更备案。

第十六条 申请第二类医疗器械产品注册，注册申请人应当向所在地省、自治区、直辖市人民政府药品监督管理部门提交注册申请资料。申请第三类医疗器械产品注册，注册申请人应当向国务院药品监督管理部门提交注册申请资料。

向我国境内出口第二类、第三类医疗器械的境外注册申请人，由其指定的我国境内企业法人向国务院药品监督管理部门提交注册申请资料和注册申请人所在国（地区）主管部门准许该医疗器械上市销售的证明文件。未在境外上市的创新医疗器械，可以不提交注册申请人所在国（地区）主管部门准许该医疗器械上市销售的证明文件。

国务院药品监督管理部门应当对医疗器械注册审查程序和要求作出规定，并加强对省、自治区、直辖市人民政府药品监督管理部门注册审查工作的监督指导。

第十七条 受理注册申请的药品监督管理部门应当对医疗器械的安全性、有效性以及注册申请人保证医疗器械安全、有效的质量管理能力等进行审查。

受理注册申请的药品监督管理部门应当自受理注册申请之日起 3 个工作日内将注册申请资料转交技术审评机构。技术审评机构应当在完成技术审评后,将审评意见提交受理注册申请的药品监督管理部门作为审批的依据。

受理注册申请的药品监督管理部门在组织对医疗器械的技术审评时认为有必要对质量管理体系进行核查的,应当组织开展质量管理体系核查。

第十八条 受理注册申请的药品监督管理部门应当自收到审评意见之日起 20 个工作日内作出决定。对符合条件的,准予注册并发给医疗器械注册证;对不符合条件的,不予注册并书面说明理由。

受理注册申请的药品监督管理部门应当自医疗器械准予注册之日起 5 个工作日内,通过国务院药品监督管理部门在线政务服务平台向社会公布注册有关信息。

第十九条 对用于治疗罕见疾病、严重危及生命且尚无有效治疗手段的疾病和应对公共卫生事件等急需的医疗器械,受理注册申请的药品监督管理部门可以作出附条件批准决定,并在医疗器械注册证中载明相关事项。

出现特别重大突发公共卫生事件或者其他严重威胁公众健康的紧急事件,国务院卫生主管部门根据预防、控制事件的需要提出紧急使用医疗器械的建议,经国务院药品监督管理部门组织论证同意后可以在一定范围和期限内紧急使用。

第二十条 医疗器械注册人、备案人应当履行下列义务:

(一)建立与产品相适应的质量管理体系并保持有效运行;

(二)制定上市后研究和风险管控计划并保证有效实施;

(三)依法开展不良事件监测和再评价;

(四)建立并执行产品追溯和召回制度;

(五)国务院药品监督管理部门规定的其他义务。

境外医疗器械注册人、备案人指定的我国境内企业法人应当协助注册人、备案人履行前款规定的义务。

第二十一条 已注册的第二类、第三类医疗器械产品，其设计、原材料、生产工艺、适用范围、使用方法等发生实质性变化，有可能影响该医疗器械安全、有效的，注册人应当向原注册部门申请办理变更注册手续；发生其他变化的，应当按照国务院药品监督管理部门的规定备案或者报告。

第二十二条 医疗器械注册证有效期为 5 年。有效期届满需要延续注册的，应当在有效期届满 6 个月前向原注册部门提出延续注册的申请。

除有本条第三款规定情形外，接到延续注册申请的药品监督管理部门应当在医疗器械注册证有效期届满前作出准予延续的决定。逾期未作决定的，视为准予延续。

有下列情形之一的，不予延续注册：

（一）未在规定期限内提出延续注册申请；

（二）医疗器械强制性标准已经修订，申请延续注册的医疗器械不能达到新要求；

（三）附条件批准的医疗器械，未在规定期限内完成医疗器械注册证载明事项。

第二十三条 对新研制的尚未列入分类目录的医疗器械，申请人可以依照本条例有关第三类医疗器械产品注册的规定直接申请产品注册，也可以依据分类规则判断产品类别并向国务院药品监督管理部门申请类别确认后依照本条例的规定申请产品注册或者进行产品备案。

直接申请第三类医疗器械产品注册的，国务院药品监督管理部门应当按照风险程度确定类别，对准予注册的医疗器械及时纳入分类目录。申请类别确认的，国务院药品监督管理部门应当自受理申请之日起 20 个工作日内对该医疗器械的类别进行判定并告知申请人。

第二十四条 医疗器械产品注册、备案，应当进行临床评价；但是符合下列情形之一，可以免于进行临床评价：

（一）工作机理明确、设计定型，生产工艺成熟，已上市的同品种医疗器械临床应用多年且无严重不良事件记录，不改变常规用途的；

（二）其他通过非临床评价能够证明该医疗器械安全、有效的。

国务院药品监督管理部门应当制定医疗器械临床评价指南。

第二十五条　进行医疗器械临床评价，可以根据产品特征、临床风险、已有临床数据等情形，通过开展临床试验，或者通过对同品种医疗器械临床文献资料、临床数据进行分析评价，证明医疗器械安全、有效。

按照国务院药品监督管理部门的规定，进行医疗器械临床评价时，已有临床文献资料、临床数据不足以确认产品安全、有效的医疗器械，应当开展临床试验。

第二十六条　开展医疗器械临床试验，应当按照医疗器械临床试验质量管理规范的要求，在具备相应条件的临床试验机构进行，并向临床试验申办者所在地省、自治区、直辖市人民政府药品监督管理部门备案。接受临床试验备案的药品监督管理部门应当将备案情况通报临床试验机构所在地同级药品监督管理部门和卫生主管部门。

医疗器械临床试验机构实行备案管理。医疗器械临床试验机构应当具备的条件以及备案管理办法和临床试验质量管理规范，由国务院药品监督管理部门会同国务院卫生主管部门制定并公布。

国家支持医疗机构开展临床试验，将临床试验条件和能力评价纳入医疗机构等级评审，鼓励医疗机构开展创新医疗器械临床试验。

第二十七条　第三类医疗器械临床试验对人体具有较高风险的，应当经国务院药品监督管理部门批准。国务院药品监督管理部门审批临床试验，应当对拟承担医疗器械临床试验的机构的设备、专业人员等条件，该医疗器械的风险程度，临床试验实施方案，临床受益与风险对比分析报告等进行综合分析，并自受理申请之日起 60 个工作日内作出决定并通知临床试验申办者。逾期未通知的，视为同意。准予开展临床试验的，应当通报临床试验机构所在地省、自治区、直辖市人民政府药品监督管理部门和卫生主管部门。

临床试验对人体具有较高风险的第三类医疗器械目录由国务院药品监

督管理部门制定、调整并公布。

第二十八条 开展医疗器械临床试验，应当按照规定进行伦理审查，向受试者告知试验目的、用途和可能产生的风险等详细情况，获得受试者的书面知情同意；受试者为无民事行为能力人或者限制民事行为能力人的，应当依法获得其监护人的书面知情同意。

开展临床试验，不得以任何形式向受试者收取与临床试验有关的费用。

第二十九条 对正在开展临床试验的用于治疗严重危及生命且尚无有效治疗手段的疾病的医疗器械，经医学观察可能使患者获益，经伦理审查、知情同意后，可以在开展医疗器械临床试验的机构内免费用于其他病情相同的患者，其安全性数据可以用于医疗器械注册申请。

第三章 医疗器械生产

第三十条 从事医疗器械生产活动，应当具备下列条件：

（一）有与生产的医疗器械相适应的生产场地、环境条件、生产设备以及专业技术人员；

（二）有能对生产的医疗器械进行质量检验的机构或者专职检验人员以及检验设备；

（三）有保证医疗器械质量的管理制度；

（四）有与生产的医疗器械相适应的售后服务能力；

（五）符合产品研制、生产工艺文件规定的要求。

第三十一条 从事第一类医疗器械生产的，应当向所在地设区的市级人民政府负责药品监督管理的部门备案，在提交符合本条例第三十条规定条件的有关资料后即完成备案。

医疗器械备案人自行生产第一类医疗器械的，可以在依照本条例第十五条规定进行产品备案时一并提交符合本条例第三十条规定条件的有关资料，即完成生产备案。

第三十二条 从事第二类、第三类医疗器械生产的，应当向所在地省、自治区、直辖市人民政府药品监督管理部门申请生产许可并提交其符合本条例第三十条规定条件的有关资料以及所生产医疗器械的注册证。

受理生产许可申请的药品监督管理部门应当对申请资料进行审核，按照国务院药品监督管理部门制定的医疗器械生产质量管理规范的要求进行核查，并自受理申请之日起20个工作日内作出决定。对符合规定条件的，准予许可并发给医疗器械生产许可证；对不符合规定条件的，不予许可并书面说明理由。

医疗器械生产许可证有效期为5年。有效期届满需要延续的，依照有关行政许可的法律规定办理延续手续。

第三十三条　医疗器械生产质量管理规范应当对医疗器械的设计开发、生产设备条件、原材料采购、生产过程控制、产品放行、企业的机构设置和人员配备等影响医疗器械安全、有效的事项作出明确规定。

第三十四条　医疗器械注册人、备案人可以自行生产医疗器械，也可以委托符合本条例规定、具备相应条件的企业生产医疗器械。

委托生产医疗器械的，医疗器械注册人、备案人应当对所委托生产的医疗器械质量负责，并加强对受托生产企业生产行为的管理，保证其按照法定要求进行生产。医疗器械注册人、备案人应当与受托生产企业签订委托协议，明确双方权利、义务和责任。受托生产企业应当依照法律法规、医疗器械生产质量管理规范、强制性标准、产品技术要求和委托协议组织生产，对生产行为负责，并接受委托方的监督。

具有高风险的植入性医疗器械不得委托生产，具体目录由国务院药品监督管理部门制定、调整并公布。

第三十五条　医疗器械注册人、备案人、受托生产企业应当按照医疗器械生产质量管理规范，建立健全与所生产医疗器械相适应的质量管理体系并保证其有效运行；严格按照经注册或者备案的产品技术要求组织生产，保证出厂的医疗器械符合强制性标准以及经注册或者备案的产品技术要求。

医疗器械注册人、备案人、受托生产企业应当定期对质量管理体系的运行情况进行自查，并按照国务院药品监督管理部门的规定提交自查报告。

第三十六条 医疗器械的生产条件发生变化，不再符合医疗器械质量管理体系要求的，医疗器械注册人、备案人、受托生产企业应当立即采取整改措施；可能影响医疗器械安全、有效的，应当立即停止生产活动，并向原生产许可或者生产备案部门报告。

第三十七条 医疗器械应当使用通用名称。通用名称应当符合国务院药品监督管理部门制定的医疗器械命名规则。

第三十八条 国家根据医疗器械产品类别，分步实施医疗器械唯一标识制度，实现医疗器械可追溯，具体办法由国务院药品监督管理部门会同国务院有关部门制定。

第三十九条 医疗器械应当有说明书、标签。说明书、标签的内容应当与经注册或者备案的相关内容一致，确保真实、准确。

医疗器械的说明书、标签应当标明下列事项：

（一）通用名称、型号、规格；

（二）医疗器械注册人、备案人、受托生产企业的名称、地址以及联系方式；

（三）生产日期，使用期限或者失效日期；

（四）产品性能、主要结构、适用范围；

（五）禁忌、注意事项以及其他需要警示或者提示的内容；

（六）安装和使用说明或者图示；

（七）维护和保养方法，特殊运输、贮存的条件、方法；

（八）产品技术要求规定应当标明的其他内容。

第二类、第三类医疗器械还应当标明医疗器械注册证编号。

由消费者个人自行使用的医疗器械还应当具有安全使用的特别说明。

第四章 医疗器械经营与使用

第四十条 从事医疗器械经营活动，应当有与经营规模和经营范围相适应的经营场所和贮存条件，以及与经营的医疗器械相适应的质量管理制度和质量管理机构或者人员。

第四十一条　从事第二类医疗器械经营的，由经营企业向所在地设区的市级人民政府负责药品监督管理的部门备案并提交符合本条例第四十条规定条件的有关资料。

按照国务院药品监督管理部门的规定，对产品安全性、有效性不受流通过程影响的第二类医疗器械，可以免于经营备案。

第四十二条　从事第三类医疗器械经营的，经营企业应当向所在地设区的市级人民政府负责药品监督管理的部门申请经营许可并提交符合本条例第四十条规定条件的有关资料。

受理经营许可申请的负责药品监督管理的部门应当对申请资料进行审查，必要时组织核查，并自受理申请之日起20个工作日内作出决定。对符合规定条件的，准予许可并发给医疗器械经营许可证；对不符合规定条件的，不予许可并书面说明理由。

医疗器械经营许可证有效期为5年。有效期届满需要延续的，依照有关行政许可的法律规定办理延续手续。

第四十三条　医疗器械注册人、备案人经营其注册、备案的医疗器械，无需办理医疗器械经营许可或者备案，但应当符合本条例规定的经营条件。

第四十四条　从事医疗器械经营，应当依照法律法规和国务院药品监督管理部门制定的医疗器械经营质量管理规范的要求，建立健全与所经营医疗器械相适应的质量管理体系并保证其有效运行。

第四十五条　医疗器械经营企业、使用单位应当从具备合法资质的医疗器械注册人、备案人、生产经营企业购进医疗器械。购进医疗器械时，应当查验供货者的资质和医疗器械的合格证明文件，建立进货查验记录制度。从事第二类、第三类医疗器械批发业务以及第三类医疗器械零售业务的经营企业，还应当建立销售记录制度。

记录事项包括：

（一）医疗器械的名称、型号、规格、数量；

（二）医疗器械的生产批号、使用期限或者失效日期、销售日期；

（三）医疗器械注册人、备案人和受托生产企业的名称；

（四）供货者或者购货者的名称、地址以及联系方式；

（五）相关许可证明文件编号等。

进货查验记录和销售记录应当真实、准确、完整和可追溯，并按照国务院药品监督管理部门规定的期限予以保存。国家鼓励采用先进技术手段进行记录。

第四十六条 从事医疗器械网络销售的，应当是医疗器械注册人、备案人或者医疗器械经营企业。从事医疗器械网络销售的经营者，应当将从事医疗器械网络销售的相关信息告知所在地设区的市级人民政府负责药品监督管理的部门，经营第一类医疗器械和本条例第四十一条第二款规定的第二类医疗器械的除外。

为医疗器械网络交易提供服务的电子商务平台经营者应当对入网医疗器械经营者进行实名登记，审查其经营许可、备案情况和所经营医疗器械产品注册、备案情况，并对其经营行为进行管理。电子商务平台经营者发现入网医疗器械经营者有违反本条例规定行为的，应当及时制止并立即报告医疗器械经营者所在地设区的市级人民政府负责药品监督管理的部门；发现严重违法行为的，应当立即停止提供网络交易平台服务。

第四十七条 运输、贮存医疗器械，应当符合医疗器械说明书和标签标示的要求；对温度、湿度等环境条件有特殊要求的，应当采取相应措施，保证医疗器械的安全、有效。

第四十八条 医疗器械使用单位应当有与在用医疗器械品种、数量相适应的贮存场所和条件。医疗器械使用单位应当加强对工作人员的技术培训，按照产品说明书、技术操作规范等要求使用医疗器械。

医疗器械使用单位配置大型医用设备，应当符合国务院卫生主管部门制定的大型医用设备配置规划，与其功能定位、临床服务需求相适应，具有相应的技术条件、配套设施和具备相应资质、能力的专业技术人员，并经省级以上人民政府卫生主管部门批准，取得大型医用设备配置许可证。

大型医用设备配置管理办法由国务院卫生主管部门会同国务院有关部门制定。大型医用设备目录由国务院卫生主管部门商国务院有关部门提出，报国务院批准后执行。

第四十九条　医疗器械使用单位对重复使用的医疗器械，应当按照国务院卫生主管部门制定的消毒和管理的规定进行处理。

一次性使用的医疗器械不得重复使用，对使用过的应当按照国家有关规定销毁并记录。一次性使用的医疗器械目录由国务院药品监督管理部门会同国务院卫生主管部门制定、调整并公布。列入一次性使用的医疗器械目录，应当具有充足的无法重复使用的证据理由。重复使用可以保证安全、有效的医疗器械，不列入一次性使用的医疗器械目录。对因设计、生产工艺、消毒灭菌技术等改进后重复使用可以保证安全、有效的医疗器械，应当调整出一次性使用的医疗器械目录，允许重复使用。

第五十条　医疗器械使用单位对需要定期检查、检验、校准、保养、维护的医疗器械，应当按照产品说明书的要求进行检查、检验、校准、保养、维护并予以记录，及时进行分析、评估，确保医疗器械处于良好状态，保障使用质量；对使用期限长的大型医疗器械，应当逐台建立使用档案，记录其使用、维护、转让、实际使用时间等事项。记录保存期限不得少于医疗器械规定使用期限终止后 5 年。

第五十一条　医疗器械使用单位应当妥善保存购入第三类医疗器械的原始资料，并确保信息具有可追溯性。

使用大型医疗器械以及植入和介入类医疗器械的，应当将医疗器械的名称、关键性技术参数等信息以及与使用质量安全密切相关的必要信息记载到病历等相关记录中。

第五十二条　发现使用的医疗器械存在安全隐患的，医疗器械使用单位应当立即停止使用，并通知医疗器械注册人、备案人或者其他负责产品质量的机构进行检修；经检修仍不能达到使用安全标准的医疗器械，不得继续使用。

第五十三条 对国内尚无同品种产品上市的体外诊断试剂，符合条件的医疗机构根据本单位的临床需要，可以自行研制，在执业医师指导下在本单位内使用。具体管理办法由国务院药品监督管理部门会同国务院卫生主管部门制定。

第五十四条 负责药品监督管理的部门和卫生主管部门依据各自职责，分别对使用环节的医疗器械质量和医疗器械使用行为进行监督管理。

第五十五条 医疗器械经营企业、使用单位不得经营、使用未依法注册或者备案、无合格证明文件以及过期、失效、淘汰的医疗器械。

第五十六条 医疗器械使用单位之间转让在用医疗器械，转让方应当确保所转让的医疗器械安全、有效，不得转让过期、失效、淘汰以及检验不合格的医疗器械。

第五十七条 进口的医疗器械应当是依照本条例第二章的规定已注册或者已备案的医疗器械。

进口的医疗器械应当有中文说明书、中文标签。说明书、标签应当符合本条例规定以及相关强制性标准的要求，并在说明书中载明医疗器械的原产地以及境外医疗器械注册人、备案人指定的我国境内企业法人的名称、地址、联系方式。没有中文说明书、中文标签或者说明书、标签不符合本条规定的，不得进口。

医疗机构因临床急需进口少量第二类、第三类医疗器械的，经国务院药品监督管理部门或者国务院授权的省、自治区、直辖市人民政府批准，可以进口。进口的医疗器械应当在指定医疗机构内用于特定医疗目的。

禁止进口过期、失效、淘汰等已使用过的医疗器械。

第五十八条 出入境检验检疫机构依法对进口的医疗器械实施检验；检验不合格的，不得进口。

国务院药品监督管理部门应当及时向国家出入境检验检疫部门通报进口医疗器械的注册和备案情况。进口口岸所在地出入境检验检疫机构应当及时向所在地设区的市级人民政府负责药品监督管理的部门通报进口医疗器械的通关情况。

第五十九条　出口医疗器械的企业应当保证其出口的医疗器械符合进口国（地区）的要求。

第六十条　医疗器械广告的内容应当真实合法，以经负责药品监督管理的部门注册或者备案的医疗器械说明书为准，不得含有虚假、夸大、误导性的内容。

发布医疗器械广告，应当在发布前由省、自治区、直辖市人民政府确定的广告审查机关对广告内容进行审查，并取得医疗器械广告批准文号；未经审查，不得发布。

省级以上人民政府药品监督管理部门责令暂停生产、进口、经营和使用的医疗器械，在暂停期间不得发布涉及该医疗器械的广告。

医疗器械广告的审查办法由国务院市场监督管理部门制定。

第五章　不良事件的处理与医疗器械的召回

第六十一条　国家建立医疗器械不良事件监测制度，对医疗器械不良事件及时进行收集、分析、评价、控制。

第六十二条　医疗器械注册人、备案人应当建立医疗器械不良事件监测体系，配备与其产品相适应的不良事件监测机构和人员，对其产品主动开展不良事件监测，并按照国务院药品监督管理部门的规定，向医疗器械不良事件监测技术机构报告调查、分析、评价、产品风险控制等情况。

医疗器械生产经营企业、使用单位应当协助医疗器械注册人、备案人对所生产经营或者使用的医疗器械开展不良事件监测；发现医疗器械不良事件或者可疑不良事件，应当按照国务院药品监督管理部门的规定，向医疗器械不良事件监测技术机构报告。

其他单位和个人发现医疗器械不良事件或者可疑不良事件，有权向负责药品监督管理的部门或者医疗器械不良事件监测技术机构报告。

第六十三条 国务院药品监督管理部门应当加强医疗器械不良事件监测信息网络建设。

医疗器械不良事件监测技术机构应当加强医疗器械不良事件信息监测，主动收集不良事件信息；发现不良事件或者接到不良事件报告的，应当及时进行核实，必要时进行调查、分析、评估，向负责药品监督管理的部门和卫生主管部门报告并提出处理建议。

医疗器械不良事件监测技术机构应当公布联系方式，方便医疗器械注册人、备案人、生产经营企业、使用单位等报告医疗器械不良事件。

第六十四条 负责药品监督管理的部门应当根据医疗器械不良事件评估结果及时采取发布警示信息以及责令暂停生产、进口、经营和使用等控制措施。

省级以上人民政府药品监督管理部门应当会同同级卫生主管部门和相关部门组织对引起突发、群发的严重伤害或者死亡的医疗器械不良事件及时进行调查和处理，并组织对同类医疗器械加强监测。

负责药品监督管理的部门应当及时向同级卫生主管部门通报医疗器械使用单位的不良事件监测有关情况。

第六十五条 医疗器械注册人、备案人、生产经营企业、使用单位应当对医疗器械不良事件监测技术机构、负责药品监督管理的部门、卫生主管部门开展的医疗器械不良事件调查予以配合。

第六十六条 有下列情形之一的，医疗器械注册人、备案人应当主动开展已上市医疗器械再评价：

（一）根据科学研究的发展，对医疗器械的安全、有效有认识上的改变；

（二）医疗器械不良事件监测、评估结果表明医疗器械可能存在缺陷；

（三）国务院药品监督管理部门规定的其他情形。

医疗器械注册人、备案人应当根据再评价结果，采取相应控制措施，对已上市医疗器械进行改进，并按照规定进行注册变更或者备案变更。再评价结果表明已上市医疗器械不能保证安全、有效的，医疗器械注册人、备案人应当主动申请注销医疗器械注册证或者取消备案；医疗器械注册人、备案人未申请注销医疗器械注册证或者取消备案的，由负责药品监督管理的部门注销医疗器械注册证或者取消备案。

省级以上人民政府药品监督管理部门根据医疗器械不良事件监测、评估等情况，对已上市医疗器械开展再评价。再评价结果表明已上市医疗器械不能保证安全、有效的，应当注销医疗器械注册证或者取消备案。

负责药品监督管理的部门应当向社会及时公布注销医疗器械注册证和取消备案情况。被注销医疗器械注册证或者取消备案的医疗器械不得继续生产、进口、经营、使用。

第六十七条 医疗器械注册人、备案人发现生产的医疗器械不符合强制性标准、经注册或者备案的产品技术要求，或者存在其他缺陷的，应当立即停止生产，通知相关经营企业、使用单位和消费者停止经营和使用，召回已经上市销售的医疗器械，采取补救、销毁等措施，记录相关情况，发布相关信息，并将医疗器械召回和处理情况向负责药品监督管理的部门和卫生主管部门报告。

医疗器械受托生产企业、经营企业发现生产、经营的医疗器械存在前款规定情形的，应当立即停止生产、经营，通知医疗器械注册人、备案人，并记录停止生产、经营和通知情况。医疗器械注册人、备案人认为属于依照前款规定需要召回的医疗器械，应当立即召回。

医疗器械注册人、备案人、受托生产企业、经营企业未依照本条规定实施召回或者停止生产、经营的，负责药品监督管理的部门可以责令其召回或者停止生产、经营。

第六章　监督检查

第六十八条　国家建立职业化专业化检查员制度，加强对医疗器械的监督检查。

第六十九条　负责药品监督管理的部门应当对医疗器械的研制、生产、经营活动以及使用环节的医疗器械质量加强监督检查，并对下列事项进行重点监督检查：

（一）是否按照经注册或者备案的产品技术要求组织生产；

（二）质量管理体系是否保持有效运行；

（三）生产经营条件是否持续符合法定要求。

必要时，负责药品监督管理的部门可以对为医疗器械研制、生产、经营、使用等活动提供产品或者服务的其他相关单位和个人进行延伸检查。

第七十条　负责药品监督管理的部门在监督检查中有下列职权：

（一）进入现场实施检查、抽取样品；

（二）查阅、复制、查封、扣押有关合同、票据、账簿以及其他有关资料；

（三）查封、扣押不符合法定要求的医疗器械，违法使用的零配件、原材料以及用于违法生产经营医疗器械的工具、设备；

（四）查封违反本条例规定从事医疗器械生产经营活动的场所。

进行监督检查，应当出示执法证件，保守被检查单位的商业秘密。

有关单位和个人应当对监督检查予以配合，提供相关文件和资料，不得隐瞒、拒绝、阻挠。

第七十一条　卫生主管部门应当对医疗机构的医疗器械使用行为加强监督检查。实施监督检查时，可以进入医疗机构，查阅、复制有关档案、记录以及其他有关资料。

第七十二条　医疗器械生产经营过程中存在产品质量安全隐患，未及时采取措施消除的，负责药品监督管理的部门可以采取告诫、责任约谈、责令限期整改等措施。

对人体造成伤害或者有证据证明可能危害人体健康的医疗器械，负责药品监督管理的部门可以采取责令暂停生产、进口、经营、使用的紧急控制措施，并发布安全警示信息。

第七十三条　负责药品监督管理的部门应当加强对医疗器械注册人、备案人、生产经营企业和使用单位生产、经营、使用的医疗器械的抽查检验。抽查检验不得收取检验费和其他任何费用，所需费用纳入本级政府预算。省级以上人民政府药品监督管理部门应当根据抽查检验结论及时发布医疗器械质量公告。

卫生主管部门应当对大型医用设备的使用状况进行监督和评估；发现违规使用以及与大型医用设备相关的过度检查、过度治疗等情形的，应当立即纠正，依法予以处理。

第七十四条　负责药品监督管理的部门未及时发现医疗器械安全系统性风险，未及时消除监督管理区域内医疗器械安全隐患的，本级人民政府或者上级人民政府负责药品监督管理的部门应当对其主要负责人进行约谈。

地方人民政府未履行医疗器械安全职责，未及时消除区域性重大医疗器械安全隐患的，上级人民政府或者上级人民政府负责药品监督管理的部门应当对其主要负责人进行约谈。

被约谈的部门和地方人民政府应当立即采取措施，对医疗器械监督管理工作进行整改。

第七十五条　医疗器械检验机构资质认定工作按照国家有关规定实行统一管理。经国务院认证认可监督管理部门会同国务院药品监督管理部门认定的检验机构，方可对医疗器械实施检验。

负责药品监督管理的部门在执法工作中需要对医疗器械进行检验的，应当委托有资质的医疗器械检验机构进行，并支付相关费用。

当事人对检验结论有异议的，可以自收到检验结论之日起 7 个工作日内向实施抽样检验的部门或者其上一级负责药品监督管理的部门提出复检申请，由受理复检申请的部门在复检机构名录中随机确定复检机构进行复检。承担复检工作的医疗器械检验机构应当在国务院药品监督管理部门规定的时间内作出复检结论。复检结论为最终检验结论。复检机构与初检机构不得为同一机构；相关检验项目只有一家有资质的检验机构的，复检时应当变更承办部门或者人员。复检机构名录由国务院药品监督管理部门公布。

第七十六条　对可能存在有害物质或者擅自改变医疗器械设计、原材料和生产工艺并存在安全隐患的医疗器械，按照医疗器械国家标准、行业标准规定的检验项目和检验方法无法检验的，医疗器械检验机构可以使用国务院药品监督管理部门批准的补充检验项目和检验方法进行检验；使用补充检验项目、检验方法得出的检验结论，可以作为负责药品监督管理的部门认定医疗器械质量的依据。

第七十七条　市场监督管理部门应当依照有关广告管理的法律、行政法规的规定，对医疗器械广告进行监督检查，查处违法行为。

第七十八条　负责药品监督管理的部门应当通过国务院药品监督管理部门在线政务服务平台依法及时公布医疗器械许可、备案、抽查检验、违法行为查处等日常监督管理信息。但是，不得泄露当事人的商业秘密。

负责药品监督管理的部门建立医疗器械注册人、备案人、生产经营企业、使用单位信用档案，对有不良信用记录的增加监督检查频次，依法加强失信惩戒。

第七十九条　负责药品监督管理的部门等部门应当公布本单位的联系方式，接受咨询、投诉、举报。负责药品监督管理的部门等部门接到与医疗器械监督管理有关的咨询，应当及时答复；接到投诉、举报，应当及时核实、处理、答复。对咨询、投诉、举报情况及其答复、核实、处理情况，应当予以记录、保存。

有关医疗器械研制、生产、经营、使用行为的举报经调查属实的，负责药品监督管理的部门等部门对举报人应当给予奖励。有关部门应当为举报人保密。

第八十条　国务院药品监督管理部门制定、调整、修改本条例规定的目录以及与医疗器械监督管理有关的规范，应当公开征求意见；采取听证会、论证会等形式，听取专家、医疗器械注册人、备案人、生产经营企业、使用单位、消费者、行业协会以及相关组织等方面的意见。

第七章　法律责任

第八十一条　有下列情形之一的，由负责药品监督管理的部门没收违法所得、违法生产经营的医疗器械和用于违法生产经营的工具、设备、原材料等物品；违法生产经营的医疗器械货值金额不足 1 万元的，并处 5 万元以上 15 万元以下罚款；货值金额 1 万元以上的，并处货值金额 15 倍以上 30 倍以下罚款；情节严重的，责令停产停业，10 年内不受理相关责任人以及单位提出的医疗器械许可申请，对违法单位的法定代表人、主要负责人、直接负责的主管人员和其他责任人员，没收违法行为发生期间自本单位所获收入，并处所获收入 30% 以上 3 倍以下罚款，终身禁止其从事医疗器械生产经营活动：

（一）生产、经营未取得医疗器械注册证的第二类、第三类医疗器械；

（二）未经许可从事第二类、第三类医疗器械生产活动；

（三）未经许可从事第三类医疗器械经营活动。

有前款第一项情形、情节严重的，由原发证部门吊销医疗器械生产许可证或者医疗器械经营许可证。

第八十二条　未经许可擅自配置使用大型医用设备的，由县级以上人民政府卫生主管部门责令停止使用，给予警告，没收违法所得；违法所得不足 1 万元的，并处 5 万元以上 10 万元以下罚款；违法所得 1 万元以上的，并处违法所得 10 倍以上 30 倍以下罚款；情节严重的，5 年内不受理相关责任人以及单位提出的大型医用设备配置许可申请，对违法单位的法定代表人、主要负责人、直接负责的主管人员和其他责任人员，没收违法行为发生期间自本单位所获收入，并处所获收入 30% 以上 3 倍以下罚款，依法给予处分。

第八十三条　在申请医疗器械行政许可时提供虚假资料或者采取其他欺骗手段的，不予行政许可，已经取得行政许可的，由作出行政许可决定的部门撤销行政许可，没收违法所得、违法生产经营使用的医疗器械，10 年内不受理相关责任人以及单位提出的医疗器械许可申请；违法生产经营使用的医疗器械货值金额不足 1 万元的，并处 5 万元以上 15 万元以下罚款；货值金额 1 万元以上的，并处货值金额 15 倍以上 30 倍以下罚款；情节严重的，责令停产停业，对违法单位的法定代表人、主要负责人、直接负责的主管人员和其他责任人员，没收违法行为发生期间自本单位所获收入，并处所获收入 30% 以上 3 倍以下罚款，终身禁止其从事医疗器械生产经营活动。

伪造、变造、买卖、出租、出借相关医疗器械许可证件的，由原发证部门予以收缴或者吊销，没收违法所得；违法所得不足 1 万元的，并处 5 万元以上 10 万元以下罚款；违法所得 1 万元以上的，并处违法所得 10 倍以上 20 倍以下罚款；构成违反治安管理行为的，由公安机关依法予以治安管理处罚。

第八十四条　有下列情形之一的，由负责药品监督管理的部门向社会公告单位和产品名称，责令限期改正；逾期不改正的，没收违法所得、违法生产经营的医疗器械；违法生产经营的医疗器械货值金额不足 1 万元的，并处 1 万元以上 5 万元以下罚款；货值金额 1 万元以上的，并处货值金额 5 倍以上 20 倍以下罚款；情节严重的，对违法单位的法定代表人、主要负责人、直接负责的主管人员和其他责任人员，没收违法行为发生期间自本单位所获收入，并处所获收入 30% 以上 2 倍以下罚款，5 年内禁止其从事医疗器械生产经营活动：

（一）生产、经营未经备案的第一类医疗器械；

（二）未经备案从事第一类医疗器械生产；

（三）经营第二类医疗器械，应当备案但未备案；

（四）已经备案的资料不符合要求。

第八十五条 备案时提供虚假资料的，由负责药品监督管理的部门向社会公告备案单位和产品名称，没收违法所得、违法生产经营的医疗器械；违法生产经营的医疗器械货值金额不足 1 万元的，并处 2 万元以上 5 万元以下罚款；货值金额 1 万元以上的，并处货值金额 5 倍以上 20 倍以下罚款；情节严重的，责令停产停业，对违法单位的法定代表人、主要负责人、直接负责的主管人员和其他责任人员，没收违法行为发生期间自本单位所获收入，并处所获收入 30% 以上 3 倍以下罚款，10 年内禁止其从事医疗器械生产经营活动。

第八十六条 有下列情形之一的，由负责药品监督管理的部门责令改正，没收违法生产经营使用的医疗器械；违法生产经营使用的医疗器械货值金额不足 1 万元的，并处 2 万元以上 5 万元以下罚款；货值金额 1 万元以上的，并处货值金额 5 倍以上 20 倍以下罚款；情节严重的，责令停产停业，直至由原发证部门吊销医疗器械注册证、医疗器械生产许可证、医疗器械经营许可证，对违法单位的法定代表人、主要负责人、直接负责的主管人员和其他责任人员，没收违法行为发生期间自本单位所获收入，并处所获收入 30% 以上 3 倍以下罚款，10 年内禁止其从事医疗器械生产经营活动：

（一）生产、经营、使用不符合强制性标准或者不符合经注册或者备案的产品技术要求的医疗器械；

（二）未按照经注册或者备案的产品技术要求组织生产，或者未依照本条例规定建立质量管理体系并保持有效运行，影响产品安全、有效；

（三）经营、使用无合格证明文件、过期、失效、淘汰的医疗器械，或者使用未依法注册的医疗器械；

（四）在负责药品监督管理的部门责令召回后仍拒不召回，或者在负责药品监督管理的部门责令停止或者暂停生产、进口、经营后，仍拒不停止生产、进口、经营医疗器械；

（五）委托不具备本条例规定条件的企业生产医疗器械，或者未对受托生产企业的生产行为进行管理；

（六）进口过期、失效、淘汰等已使用过的医疗器械。

第八十七条 医疗器械经营企业、使用单位履行了本条例规定的进货查验等义务，有充分证据证明其不知道所经营、使用的医疗器械为本条例第八十一条第一款第一项、第八十四条第一项、第八十六条第一项和第三项规定情形的医疗器械，并能如实说明其进货来源的，收缴其经营、使用的不符合法定要求的医疗器械，可以免除行政处罚。

第八十八条 有下列情形之一的，由负责药品监督管理的部门责令改正，处1万元以上5万元以下罚款；拒不改正的，处5万元以上10万元以下罚款；情节严重的，责令停产停业，直至由原发证部门吊销医疗器械生产许可证、医疗器械经营许可证，对违法单位的法定代表人、主要负责人、直接负责的主管人员和其他责任人员，没收违法行为发生期间自本单位所获收入，并处所获收入30%以上2倍以下罚款，5年内禁止其从事医疗器械生产经营活动：

（一）生产条件发生变化、不再符合医疗器械质量管理体系要求，未依照本条例规定整改、停止生产、报告；

（二）生产、经营说明书、标签不符合本条例规定的医疗器械；

（三）未按照医疗器械说明书和标签标示要求运输、贮存医疗器械；

（四）转让过期、失效、淘汰或者检验不合格的在用医疗器械。

第八十九条 有下列情形之一的，由负责药品监督管理的部门和卫生主管部门依据各自职责责令改正，给予警告；拒不改正的，处1万元以上10万元以下罚款；情节严重的，责令停产停业，直至由原发证部门吊销医疗器械注册证、医疗器械生产许可证、医疗器械经营许可证，对违法单位的法定代表人、主要负责人、直接负责的主管人员和其他责任人员处1万元以上3万元以下罚款：

（一）未按照要求提交质量管理体系自查报告；

（二）从不具备合法资质的供货者购进医疗器械；

（三）医疗器械经营企业、使用单位未依照本条例规定建立并执行医疗器械进货查验记录制度；

（四）从事第二类、第三类医疗器械批发业务以及第三类医疗器械零售业务的经营企业未依照本条例规定建立并执行销售记录制度；

（五）医疗器械注册人、备案人、生产经营企业、使用单位未依照本条例规定开展医疗器械不良事件监测，未按照要求报告不良事件，或者对医疗器械不良事件监测技术机构、负责药品监督管理的部门、卫生主管部门开展的不良事件调查不予配合；

（六）医疗器械注册人、备案人未按照规定制定上市后研究和风险管控计划并保证有效实施；

（七）医疗器械注册人、备案人未按照规定建立并执行产品追溯制度；

（八）医疗器械注册人、备案人、经营企业从事医疗器械网络销售未按照规定告知负责药品监督管理的部门；

（九）对需要定期检查、检验、校准、保养、维护的医疗器械，医疗器械使用单位未按照产品说明书要求进行检查、检验、校准、保养、维护并予以记录，及时进行分析、评估，确保医疗器械处于良好状态；

（十）医疗器械使用单位未妥善保存购入第三类医疗器械的原始资料。

第九十条 有下列情形之一的，由县级以上人民政府卫生主管部门责令改正，给予警告；拒不改正的，处 5 万元以上 10 万元以下罚款；情节严重的，处 10 万元以上 30 万元以下罚款，责令暂停相关医疗器械使用活动，直至由原发证部门吊销执业许可证，依法责令相关责任人员暂停 6 个月以上 1 年以下执业活动，直至由原发证部门吊销相关人员执业证书，对违法单位的法定代表人、主要负责人、直接负责的主管人员和其他责任人员，没收违法行为发生期间自本单位所获收入，并处所获收入 30% 以上 3 倍以下罚款，依法给予处分：

（一）对重复使用的医疗器械，医疗器械使用单位未按照消毒和管理的规定进行处理；

（二）医疗器械使用单位重复使用一次性使用的医疗器械，或者未按照规定销毁使用过的一次性使用的医疗器械；

（三）医疗器械使用单位未按照规定将大型医疗器械以及植入和介入类医疗器械的信息记载到病历等相关记录中；

（四）医疗器械使用单位发现使用的医疗器械存在安全隐患未立即停止使用、通知检修，或者继续使用经检修仍不能达到使用安全标准的医疗器械；

（五）医疗器械使用单位违规使用大型医用设备，不能保障医疗质量安全。

第九十一条 违反进出口商品检验相关法律、行政法规进口医疗器械的，由出入境检验检疫机构依法处理。

第九十二条 为医疗器械网络交易提供服务的电子商务平台经营者违反本条例规定，未履行对入网医疗器械经营者进行实名登记，审查许可、注册、备案情况，制止并报告违法行为，停止提供网络交易平台服务等管理义务的，由负责药品监督管理的部门依照《中华人民共和国电子商务法》的规定给予处罚。

第九十三条 未进行医疗器械临床试验机构备案开展临床试验的，由负责药品监督管理的部门责令停止临床试验并改正；拒不改正的，该临床试验数据不得用于产品注册、备案，处5万元以上10万元以下罚款，并向社会公告；造成严重后果的，5年内禁止其开展相关专业医疗器械临床试验，并处10万元以上30万元以下罚款，由卫生主管部门对违法单位的法定代表人、主要负责人、直接负责的主管人员和其他责任人员，没收违法行为发生期间自本单位所获收入，并处所获收入30%以上3倍以下罚款，依法给予处分。

临床试验申办者开展临床试验未经备案的，由负责药品监督管理的部门责令停止临床试验，对临床试验申办者处 5 万元以上 10 万元以下罚款，并向社会公告；造成严重后果的，处 10 万元以上 30 万元以下罚款。该临床试验数据不得用于产品注册、备案，5 年内不受理相关责任人以及单位提出的医疗器械注册申请。

临床试验申办者未经批准开展对人体具有较高风险的第三类医疗器械临床试验的，由负责药品监督管理的部门责令立即停止临床试验，对临床试验申办者处 10 万元以上 30 万元以下罚款，并向社会公告；造成严重后果的，处 30 万元以上 100 万元以下罚款。该临床试验数据不得用于产品注册，10 年内不受理相关责任人以及单位提出的医疗器械临床试验和注册申请，对违法单位的法定代表人、主要负责人、直接负责的主管人员和其他责任人员，没收违法行为发生期间自本单位所获收入，并处所获收入 30% 以上 3 倍以下罚款。

第九十四条　医疗器械临床试验机构开展医疗器械临床试验未遵守临床试验质量管理规范的，由负责药品监督管理的部门责令改正或者立即停止临床试验，处 5 万元以上 10 万元以下罚款；造成严重后果的，5 年内禁止其开展相关专业医疗器械临床试验，由卫生主管部门对违法单位的法定代表人、主要负责人、直接负责的主管人员和其他责任人员，没收违法行为发生期间自本单位所获收入，并处所获收入 30% 以上 3 倍以下罚款，依法给予处分。

第九十五条　医疗器械临床试验机构出具虚假报告的，由负责药品监督管理的部门处 10 万元以上 30 万元以下罚款；有违法所得的，没收违法所得；10 年内禁止其开展相关专业医疗器械临床试验；由卫生主管部门对违法单位的法定代表人、主要负责人、直接负责的主管人员和其他责任人员，没收违法行为发生期间自本单位所获收入，并处所获收入 30% 以上 3 倍以下罚款，依法给予处分。

第九十六条　医疗器械检验机构出具虚假检验报告的，由授予其资质的主管部门撤销检验资质，10 年内不受理相关责任人以及单位提出的资质认定申请，并处 10 万元以上 30 万元以下罚款；有违法所得的，没收违法所得；对违法单位的法定代表人、主要负责人、直接负责的主管人员和其他责任人员，没收违法行为发生期间自本单位所获收入，并处所获收入 30% 以上 3 倍以下罚款，依法给予处分；受到开除处分的，10 年内禁止其从事医疗器械检验工作。

第九十七条　违反本条例有关医疗器械广告管理规定的，依照《中华人民共和国广告法》的规定给予处罚。

第九十八条　境外医疗器械注册人、备案人指定的我国境内企业法人未依照本条例规定履行相关义务的，由省、自治区、直辖市人民政府药品监督管理部门责令改正，给予警告，并处 5 万元以上 10 万元以下罚款；情节严重的，处 10 万元以上 50 万元以下罚款，5 年内禁止其法定代表人、主要负责人、直接负责的主管人员和其他责任人员从事医疗器械生产经营活动。

境外医疗器械注册人、备案人拒不履行依据本条例作出的行政处罚决定的，10 年内禁止其医疗器械进口。

第九十九条　医疗器械研制、生产、经营单位和检验机构违反本条例规定使用禁止从事医疗器械生产经营活动、检验工作的人员的，由负责药品监督管理的部门责令改正，给予警告；拒不改正的，责令停产停业直至吊销许可证件。

第一百条　医疗器械技术审评机构、医疗器械不良事件监测技术机构未依照本条例规定履行职责，致使审评、监测工作出现重大失误的，由负责药品监督管理的部门责令改正，通报批评，给予警告；造成严重后果的，对违法单位的法定代表人、主要负责人、直接负责的主管人员和其他责任人员，依法给予处分。

第一百零一条　负责药品监督管理的部门或者其他有关部门工作人员违反本条例规定，滥用职权、玩忽职守、徇私舞弊的，依法给予处分。

第一百零二条　违反本条例规定，构成犯罪的，依法追究刑事责任；

造成人身、财产或者其他损害的，依法承担赔偿责任。

第八章　附　则

第一百零三条　本条例下列用语的含义：

医疗器械，是指直接或者间接用于人体的仪器、设备、器具、体外诊断试剂及校准物、材料以及其他类似或者相关的物品，包括所需要的计算机软件；其效用主要通过物理等方式获得，不是通过药理学、免疫学或者代谢的方式获得，或者虽然有这些方式参与但是只起辅助作用；其目的是：

（一）疾病的诊断、预防、监护、治疗或者缓解；

（二）损伤的诊断、监护、治疗、缓解或者功能补偿；

（三）生理结构或者生理过程的检验、替代、调节或者支持；

（四）生命的支持或者维持；

（五）妊娠控制；

（六）通过对来自人体的样本进行检查，为医疗或者诊断目的提供信息。

医疗器械注册人、备案人，是指取得医疗器械注册证或者办理医疗器械备案的企业或者研制机构。

医疗器械使用单位，是指使用医疗器械为他人提供医疗等技术服务的机构，包括医疗机构、计划生育技术服务机构、血站、单采血浆站、康复辅助器具适配机构等。

大型医用设备，是指使用技术复杂、资金投入量大、运行成本高、对医疗费用影响大且纳入目录管理的大型医疗器械。

第一百零四条　医疗器械产品注册可以收取费用。具体收费项目、标准分别由国务院财政、价格主管部门按照国家有关规定制定。

第一百零五条　医疗卫生机构为应对突发公共卫生事件而研制的医疗器械的管理办法，由国务院药品监督管理部门会同国务院卫生主管部门制定。

从事非营利的避孕医疗器械的存储、调拨和供应，应当遵守国务院卫生主管部门会同国务院药品监督管理部门制定的管理办法。

中医医疗器械的技术指导原则，由国务院药品监督管理部门会同国务院中医药管理部门制定。

第一百零六条 军队医疗器械使用的监督管理，依照本条例和军队有关规定执行。

第一百零七条 本条例自 2021 年 6 月 1 日起施行。

医疗器械注册与备案管理办法

（国家市场监督管理总局令第 47 号）

第一章 总 则

第一条 为了规范医疗器械注册与备案行为，保证医疗器械的安全、有效和质量可控，根据《医疗器械监督管理条例》，制定本办法。

第二条 在中华人民共和国境内从事医疗器械注册、备案及其监督管理活动，适用本办法。

第三条 医疗器械注册是指医疗器械注册申请人（以下简称申请人）依照法定程序和要求提出医疗器械注册申请，药品监督管理部门依据法律法规，基于科学认知，进行安全性、有效性和质量可控性等审查，决定是否同意其申请的活动。

医疗器械备案是指医疗器械备案人（以下简称备案人）依照法定程序和要求向药品监督管理部门提交备案资料，药品监督管理部门对提交的备案资料存档备查的活动。

第四条 国家药品监督管理局主管全国医疗器械注册与备案管理工作，负责建立医疗器械注册与备案管理工作体系和制度，依法组织境内第三类和进口第二类、第三类医疗器械审评审批，进口第一类医疗器械备案以及相关监督管理工作，对地方医疗器械注册与备案工作进行监督指导。

第五条 国家药品监督管理局医疗器械技术审评中心（以下简称国家局器械审评中心）负责需进行临床试验审批的医疗器械临床试验申请以及境内第三类和进口第二类、第三类医疗器械产品注册申请、变更注册申请、延续注册申请等的技术审评工作。

国家药品监督管理局医疗器械标准管理中心、中国食品药品检定研究院、国家药品监督管理局食品药品审核查验中心（以下简称国家局审核查验中心）、国家药品监督管理局药品评价中心、国家药品监督管理局行政事项受理服务和投诉举报中心、国家药品监督管理局信息中心等其他专业技术机构，依职责承担实施医疗器械监督管理所需的医疗器械标准管理、分类界定、检验、核查、监测与评价、制证送达以及相应的信息化建设与管理等相关工作。

第六条 省、自治区、直辖市药品监督管理部门负责本行政区域内以下医疗器械注册相关管理工作：

（一）境内第二类医疗器械注册审评审批；

（二）境内第二类、第三类医疗器械质量管理体系核查；

（三）依法组织医疗器械临床试验机构以及临床试验的监督管理；

（四）对设区的市级负责药品监督管理的部门境内第一类医疗器械备案的监督指导。

省、自治区、直辖市药品监督管理部门设置或者指定的医疗器械专业技术机构，承担实施医疗器械监督管理所需的技术审评、检验、核查、监测与评价等工作。

设区的市级负责药品监督管理的部门负责境内第一类医疗器械产品备案管理工作。

第七条 医疗器械注册与备案管理遵循依法、科学、公开、公平、公正的原则。

第八条 第一类医疗器械实行产品备案管理。第二类、第三类医疗器械实行产品注册管理。

境内第一类医疗器械备案，备案人向设区的市级负责药品监督管理的部门提交备案资料。

境内第二类医疗器械由省、自治区、直辖市药品监督管理部门审查，批准后发给医疗器械注册证。

境内第三类医疗器械由国家药品监督管理局审查，批准后发给医疗器械注册证。

进口第一类医疗器械备案，备案人向国家药品监督管理局提交备案资料。

进口第二类、第三类医疗器械由国家药品监督管理局审查，批准后发给医疗器械注册证。

第九条　医疗器械注册人、备案人应当加强医疗器械全生命周期质量管理，对研制、生产、经营、使用全过程中的医疗器械的安全性、有效性和质量可控性依法承担责任。

第十条　国家药品监督管理局对临床急需医疗器械实行优先审批，对创新医疗器械实行特别审批，鼓励医疗器械的研究与创新，推动医疗器械产业高质量发展。

第十一条　国家药品监督管理局依法建立健全医疗器械标准、技术指导原则等体系，规范医疗器械技术审评和质量管理体系核查，指导和服务医疗器械研发和注册申请。

第十二条　药品监督管理部门依法及时公开医疗器械注册、备案相关信息，申请人可以查询审批进度和结果，公众可以查阅审批结果。

未经申请人同意，药品监督管理部门、专业技术机构及其工作人员、参与评审的专家等人员不得披露申请人或者备案人提交的商业秘密、未披露信息或者保密商务信息，法律另有规定或者涉及国家安全、重大社会公共利益的除外。

第二章　基本要求

第十三条　医疗器械注册、备案应当遵守相关法律、法规、规章、强制性标准，遵循医疗器械安全和性能基本原则，参照相关技术指导原则，证明注册、备案的医疗器械安全、有效、质量可控，保证全过程信息真实、准确、完整和可追溯。

第十四条　申请人、备案人应当为能够承担相应法律责任的企业或者研制机构。

境外申请人、备案人应当指定中国境内的企业法人作为代理人，办理相关医疗器械注册、备案事项。代理人应当依法协助注册人、备案人履行《医疗器械监督管理条例》第二十条第一款规定的义务，并协助境外注册人、备案人落实相应法律责任。

第十五条 申请人、备案人应当建立与产品相适应的质量管理体系，并保持有效运行。

第十六条 办理医疗器械注册、备案事项的人员应当具有相应的专业知识，熟悉医疗器械注册、备案管理的法律、法规、规章和注册管理相关规定。

第十七条 申请注册或者进行备案，应当按照国家药品监督管理局有关注册、备案的要求提交相关资料，申请人、备案人对资料的真实性负责。

注册、备案资料应当使用中文。根据外文资料翻译的，应当同时提供原文。引用未公开发表的文献资料时，应当提供资料权利人许可使用的文件。

第十八条 申请进口医疗器械注册、办理进口医疗器械备案，应当提交申请人、备案人注册地或者生产地所在国家（地区）主管部门准许该医疗器械上市销售的证明文件。

申请人、备案人注册地或者生产地所在国家（地区）未将该产品作为医疗器械管理的，申请人、备案人需提供相关文件，包括注册地或者生产地所在国家（地区）准许该产品上市销售的证明文件。

未在申请人、备案人注册地或者生产地所在国家（地区）上市的创新医疗器械，不需提交相关文件。

第十九条 医疗器械应当符合适用的强制性标准。产品结构特征、预期用途、使用方式等与强制性标准的适用范围不一致的，申请人、备案人应当提出不适用强制性标准的说明，并提供相关资料。

没有强制性标准的，鼓励申请人、备案人采用推荐性标准。

第二十条 医疗器械注册、备案工作应当遵循医疗器械分类规则和分类目录的有关要求。

第二十一条 药品监督管理部门持续推进审评审批制度改革，加强医疗器械监管科学研究，建立以技术审评为主导，核查、检验、监测与评价等为支撑的医疗器械注册管理技术体系，优化审评审批流程，提高审评审批能力，提升审评审批质量和效率。

第二十二条 医疗器械专业技术机构建立健全沟通交流制度，明确沟通交流的形式和内容，根据工作需要组织与申请人进行沟通交流。

第二十三条 医疗器械专业技术机构根据工作需要建立专家咨询制度，在审评、核查、检验等过程中就重大问题听取专家意见，充分发挥专家的技术支撑作用。

第三章 医疗器械注册

第一节 产品研制

第二十四条 医疗器械研制应当遵循风险管理原则，考虑现有公认技术水平，确保产品所有已知和可预见的风险以及非预期影响最小化并可接受，保证产品在正常使用中受益大于风险。

第二十五条 从事医疗器械产品研制实验活动，应当符合我国相关法律、法规和强制性标准等的要求。

第二十六条 申请人、备案人应当编制申请注册或者进行备案医疗器械的产品技术要求。

产品技术要求主要包括医疗器械成品的可进行客观判定的功能性、安全性指标和检测方法。

医疗器械应当符合经注册或者备案的产品技术要求。

第二十七条 申请人、备案人应当编制申请注册或者进行备案医疗器械的产品说明书和标签。

产品说明书和标签应当符合《医疗器械监督管理条例》第三十九条要

求以及相关规定。

第二十八条　医疗器械研制，应当根据产品适用范围和技术特征开展医疗器械非临床研究。

非临床研究包括产品化学和物理性能研究，电气安全研究，辐射安全研究，软件研究，生物学特性研究，生物源材料安全性研究，消毒、灭菌工艺研究，动物试验研究，稳定性研究等。

申请注册或者进行备案，应当提交研制活动中产生的非临床证据，包括非临床研究报告综述、研究方案和研究报告。

第二十九条　医疗器械非临床研究过程中确定的功能性、安全性指标及方法应当与产品预期使用条件、目的相适应，研究样品应当具有代表性和典型性。必要时，应当进行方法学验证、统计学分析。

第三十条　申请注册或者进行备案，应当按照产品技术要求进行检验，并提交检验报告。检验合格的，方可开展临床试验或者申请注册、进行备案。

第三十一条　检验用产品应当能够代表申请注册或者进行备案产品的安全性和有效性，其生产应当符合医疗器械生产质量管理规范的相关要求。

第三十二条　申请注册或者进行备案提交的医疗器械产品检验报告可以是申请人、备案人的自检报告，也可以是委托有资质的医疗器械检验机构出具的检验报告。

第二节　临床评价

第三十三条　除本办法第三十四条规定情形外，医疗器械产品注册、备案，应当进行临床评价。

医疗器械临床评价是指采用科学合理的方法对临床数据进行分析、评价，以确认医疗器械在其适用范围内的安全性、有效性的活动。

申请医疗器械注册，应当提交临床评价资料。

第三十四条　有下列情形之一的，可以免于进行临床评价：

（一）工作机理明确、设计定型，生产工艺成熟，已上市的同品种医疗器械临床应用多年且无严重不良事件记录，不改变常规用途的；

（二）其他通过非临床评价能够证明该医疗器械安全、有效的。

免于进行临床评价的，可以免于提交临床评价资料。

免于进行临床评价的医疗器械目录由国家药品监督管理局制定、调整并公布。

第三十五条 开展医疗器械临床评价，可以根据产品特征、临床风险、已有临床数据等情形，通过开展临床试验，或者通过对同品种医疗器械临床文献资料、临床数据进行分析评价，证明医疗器械的安全性、有效性。

按照国家药品监督管理局的规定，进行医疗器械临床评价时，已有临床文献资料、临床数据不足以确认产品安全、有效的医疗器械，应当开展临床试验。

国家药品监督管理局制定医疗器械临床评价指南，明确通过同品种医疗器械临床文献资料、临床数据进行临床评价的要求，需要开展临床试验的情形，临床评价报告的撰写要求等。

第三十六条 通过同品种医疗器械临床文献资料、临床数据进行临床评价的，临床评价资料包括申请注册产品与同品种医疗器械的对比，同品种医疗器械临床数据的分析评价，申请注册产品与同品种产品存在差异时的科学证据以及评价结论等内容。

通过临床试验开展临床评价的，临床评价资料包括临床试验方案、伦理委员会意见、知情同意书、临床试验报告等。

第三十七条 开展医疗器械临床试验，应当按照医疗器械临床试验质量管理规范的要求，在具备相应条件并按照规定备案的医疗器械临床试验机构内进行。临床试验开始前，临床试验申办者应当向所在地省、自治区、直辖市药品监督管理部门进行临床试验备案。临床试验医疗器械的生产应当符合医疗器械生产质量管理规范的相关要求。

第三十八条 第三类医疗器械进行临床试验对人体具有较高风险的，应当经国家药品监督管理局批准。

临床试验审批是指国家药品监督管理局根据申请人的申请，对拟开展临床试验的医疗器械的风险程度、临床试验方案、临床受益与风险对比分析报告等进行综合分析，以决定是否同意开展临床试验的过程。

需进行临床试验审批的第三类医疗器械目录由国家药品监督管理局制定、调整并公布。需进行临床试验审批的第三类医疗器械临床试验应在符合要求的三级甲等医疗机构开展。

第三十九条 需进行医疗器械临床试验审批的，申请人应当按照相关要求提交综述资料、研究资料、临床资料、产品说明书和标签样稿等申请资料。

第四十条 国家局器械审评中心对受理的临床试验申请进行审评。对临床试验申请应当自受理申请之日 60 日内作出是否同意的决定，并通过国家局器械审评中心网站通知申请人。逾期未通知的，视为同意。

第四十一条 审评过程中需要申请人补正资料的，国家局器械审评中心应当一次告知需要补正的全部内容。申请人应当在收到补正通知 1 年内，按照补正通知的要求一次提供补充资料。国家局器械审评中心收到补充资料后，按照规定的时限完成技术审评。

申请人对补正通知内容有异议的，可以向国家局器械审评中心提出书面意见，说明理由并提供相应的技术支持资料。

申请人逾期未提交补充资料的，终止技术审评，作出不予批准的决定。

第四十二条 对于医疗器械临床试验期间出现的临床试验医疗器械相关严重不良事件，或者其他严重安全性风险信息，临床试验申办者应当按照相关要求，分别向所在地和临床试验机构所在地省、自治区、直辖市药品监督管理部门报告，并采取风险控制措施。未采取风险控制措施的，省、自治区、直辖市药品监督管理部门依法责令申办者采取相应的风险控制措施。

第四十三条 医疗器械临床试验中出现大范围临床试验医疗器械相关严重不良事件，或者其他重大安全性问题时，申办者应当暂停或者终止医疗器械临床试验，分别向所在地和临床试验机构所在地省、自治区、直辖市药品监督管理部门报告。未暂停或者终止的，省、自治区、直辖市药品监督管理部门依法责令申办者采取相应的风险控制措施。

第四十四条　已批准开展的临床试验，有下列情形之一的，国家药品监督管理局可以责令申请人终止已开展的医疗器械临床试验：

（一）临床试验申请资料虚假的；

（二）已有最新研究证实原批准的临床试验伦理性和科学性存在问题的；

（三）其他应当终止的情形。

第四十五条　医疗器械临床试验应当在批准后 3 年内实施；医疗器械临床试验申请自批准之日起，3 年内未有受试者签署知情同意书的，该医疗器械临床试验许可自行失效。仍需进行临床试验的，应当重新申请。

第四十六条　对正在开展临床试验的用于治疗严重危及生命且尚无有效治疗手段的疾病的医疗器械，经医学观察可能使患者获益，经伦理审查、知情同意后，可以在开展医疗器械临床试验的机构内免费用于其他病情相同的患者，其安全性数据可以用于医疗器械注册申请。

第三节　注册体系核查

第四十七条　申请人应当在申请注册时提交与产品研制、生产有关的质量管理体系相关资料，受理注册申请的药品监督管理部门在产品技术审评时认为有必要对质量管理体系进行核查的，应当组织开展质量管理体系核查，并可以根据需要调阅原始资料。

第四十八条　境内第三类医疗器械质量管理体系核查，由国家局器械审评中心通知申请人所在地的省、自治区、直辖市药品监督管理部门开展。

境内第二类医疗器械质量管理体系核查，由申请人所在地的省、自治区、直辖市药品监督管理部门组织开展。

第四十九条　省、自治区、直辖市药品监督管理部门按照医疗器械生产质量管理规范的要求开展质量管理体系核查，重点对申请人是否按照医疗器械生产质量管理规范的要求建立与产品相适应的质量管理体系，以及与产品研制、生产有关的设计开发、生产管理、质量控制等内容进行核查。

在核查过程中，应当同时对检验用产品和临床试验产品的真实性进行核查，重点查阅设计开发过程相关记录，以及检验用产品和临床试验产品生产过程的相关记录。

提交自检报告的，应当对申请人、备案人或者受托机构研制过程中的检验能力、检验结果等进行重点核查。

第五十条　省、自治区、直辖市药品监督管理部门可以通过资料审查或者现场检查的方式开展质量管理体系核查。根据申请人的具体情况、监督检查情况、本次申请注册产品与既往已通过核查产品生产条件及工艺对比情况等，确定是否现场检查以及检查内容，避免重复检查。

第五十一条　国家局器械审评中心对进口第二类、第三类医疗器械开展技术审评时，认为有必要进行质量管理体系核查的，通知国家局审核查验中心根据相关要求开展核查。

第四节　产品注册

第五十二条　申请人应当在完成支持医疗器械注册的安全性、有效性研究，做好接受质量管理体系核查的准备后，提出医疗器械注册申请，并按照相关要求，通过在线注册申请等途径向药品监督管理部门提交下列注册申请资料：

（一）产品风险分析资料；

（二）产品技术要求；

（三）产品检验报告；

（四）临床评价资料；

（五）产品说明书以及标签样稿；

（六）与产品研制、生产有关的质量管理体系文件；

（七）证明产品安全、有效所需的其他资料。

第五十三条　药品监督管理部门收到申请后对申请资料进行审核，并根据下列情况分别作出处理：

（一）申请事项属于本行政机关职权范围，申请资料齐全、符合形式审核要求的，予以受理；

（二）申请资料存在可以当场更正的错误的，应当允许申请人当场更正；

（三）申请资料不齐全或者不符合法定形式的，应当当场或者在5日内一次告知申请人需要补正的全部内容，逾期不告知的，自收到申请资料之日起即为受理；

（四）申请事项依法不属于本行政机关职权范围的，应当即时作出不予受理的决定，并告知申请人向有关行政机关申请。

药品监督管理部门受理或者不予受理医疗器械注册申请，应当出具加盖本行政机关专用印章和注明日期的受理或者不予受理的通知书。

医疗器械注册申请受理后，需要申请人缴纳费用的，申请人应当按规定缴纳费用。申请人未在规定期限内缴纳费用的，视为申请人主动撤回申请，药品监督管理部门终止其注册程序。

第五十四条　技术审评过程中需要申请人补正资料的，技术审评机构应当一次告知需要补正的全部内容。申请人应当在收到补正通知1年内，按照补正通知要求一次提供补充资料；技术审评机构收到补充资料后，在规定的时限内完成技术审评。

申请人对补正通知内容有异议的，可以向相应的技术审评机构提出书面意见，说明理由并提供相应的技术支持资料。

申请人逾期未提交补充资料的，终止技术审评，药品监督管理部门作出不予注册的决定。

第五十五条　对于已受理的注册申请，申请人可以在行政许可决定作出前，向受理该申请的药品监督管理部门申请撤回注册申请及相关资料，并说明理由。同意撤回申请的，药品监督管理部门终止其注册程序。

审评、核查、审批过程中发现涉嫌存在隐瞒真实情况或者提供虚假信息等违法行为的，依法处理，申请人不得撤回医疗器械注册申请。

第五十六条　对于已受理的注册申请，有证据表明注册申请资料可能虚假的，药品监督管理部门可以中止审评审批。经核实后，根据核实结论继续审查或者作出不予注册的决定。

第五十七条　医疗器械注册申请审评期间，对于拟作出不通过的审评结论的，技术审评机构应当告知申请人不通过的理由，申请人可以在15日内向技术审评机构提出异议，异议内容仅限于原申请事项和原申请资料。技术审评机构结合申请人的异议意见进行综合评估并反馈申请人。异议处理时间不计入审评时限。

第五十八条　受理注册申请的药品监督管理部门应当在技术审评结束后，作出是否批准的决定。对符合安全、有效、质量可控要求的，准予注册，发给医疗器械注册证，经过核准的产品技术要求以附件形式发给申请人。对不予注册的，应当书面说明理由，并同时告知申请人享有依法申请行政复议或者提起行政诉讼的权利。

医疗器械注册证有效期为5年。

第五十九条　对于已受理的注册申请，有下列情形之一的，药品监督管理部门作出不予注册的决定，并告知申请人：

（一）申请人对拟上市销售医疗器械的安全性、有效性、质量可控性进行的研究及其结果无法证明产品安全、有效、质量可控的；

（二）质量管理体系核查不通过，以及申请人拒绝接受质量管理体系现场检查的；

（三）注册申请资料虚假的；

（四）注册申请资料内容混乱、矛盾，注册申请资料内容与申请项目明显不符，不能证明产品安全、有效、质量可控的；

（五）不予注册的其他情形。

第六十条　法律、法规、规章规定实施行政许可应当听证的事项，或者药品监督管理部门认为需要听证的其他涉及公共利益的重大行政许可事项，药品监督管理部门应当向社会公告，并举行听证。医疗器械注册申请直接涉及申请人与他人之间重大利益关系的，药品监督管理部门在作出行政许可决定前，应当告知申请人、利害关系人享有要求听证的权利。

第六十一条　对用于治疗罕见疾病、严重危及生命且尚无有效治疗手段的疾病和应对公共卫生事件等急需的医疗器械，药品监督管理部门可以作出附条件批准决定，并在医疗器械注册证中载明有效期、上市后需要继续完成的研究工作及完成时限等相关事项。

第六十二条　对附条件批准的医疗器械，注册人应当在医疗器械上市后收集受益和风险相关数据，持续对产品的受益和风险开展监测与评估，采取有效措施主动管控风险，并在规定期限内按照要求完成研究并提交相关资料。

第六十三条　对附条件批准的医疗器械，注册人逾期未按照要求完成研究或者不能证明其受益大于风险的，注册人应当及时申请办理医疗器械注册证注销手续，药品监督管理部门可以依法注销医疗器械注册证。

第六十四条　对新研制的尚未列入分类目录的医疗器械，申请人可以直接申请第三类医疗器械产品注册，也可以依据分类规则判断产品类别并向国家药品监督管理局申请类别确认后，申请产品注册或者进行产品备案。

直接申请第三类医疗器械注册的，国家药品监督管理局按照风险程度确定类别。境内医疗器械确定为第二类或者第一类的，应当告知申请人向相应的药品监督管理部门申请注册或者进行备案。

第六十五条　已注册的医疗器械，其管理类别由高类别调整为低类别的，医疗器械注册证在有效期内继续有效。有效期届满需要延续的，应当在医疗器械注册证有效期届满 6 个月前，按照调整后的类别向相应的药品监督管理部门申请延续注册或者进行备案。

医疗器械管理类别由低类别调整为高类别的，注册人应当按照改变后的类别向相应的药品监督管理部门申请注册。国家药品监督管理局在管理类别调整通知中应当对完成调整的时限作出规定。

第六十六条 医疗器械注册证及其附件遗失、损毁的，注册人应当向原发证机关申请补发，原发证机关核实后予以补发。

第六十七条 注册申请审查过程中及批准后发生专利权纠纷的，应当按照有关法律、法规的规定处理。

第四章 特殊注册程序

第一节 创新产品注册程序

第六十八条 符合下列要求的医疗器械，申请人可以申请适用创新产品注册程序：

（一）申请人通过其主导的技术创新活动，在中国依法拥有产品核心技术发明专利权，或者依法通过受让取得在中国发明专利权或其使用权，且申请适用创新产品注册程序的时间在专利授权公告日起5年内；或者核心技术发明专利的申请已由国务院专利行政部门公开，并由国家知识产权局专利检索咨询中心出具检索报告，载明产品核心技术方案具备新颖性和创造性；

（二）申请人已完成产品的前期研究并具有基本定型产品，研究过程真实和受控，研究数据完整和可溯源；

（三）产品主要工作原理或者作用机理为国内首创，产品性能或者安全性与同类产品比较有根本性改进，技术上处于国际领先水平，且具有显著的临床应用价值。

第六十九条 申请适用创新产品注册程序的，申请人应当在产品基本定型后，向国家药品监督管理局提出创新医疗器械审查申请。国家药品监督管理局组织专家进行审查，符合要求的，纳入创新产品注册程序。

第七十条 对于适用创新产品注册程序的医疗器械注册申请，国家药品监督管理局以及承担相关技术工作的机构，根据各自职责指定专人负责，及时沟通，提供指导。

纳入创新产品注册程序的医疗器械，国家局器械审评中心可以与申请人在注册申请受理前以及技术审评过程中就产品研制中的重大技术问题、重大安全性问题、临床试验方案、阶段性临床试验结果的总结与评价等问题沟通交流。

第七十一条 纳入创新产品注册程序的医疗器械，申请人主动要求终止或者国家药品监督管理局发现不再符合创新产品注册程序要求的，国家药品监督管理局终止相关产品的创新产品注册程序并告知申请人。

第七十二条 纳入创新产品注册程序的医疗器械，申请人在规定期限内未提出注册申请的，不再适用创新产品注册程序。

第二节 优先注册程序

第七十三条 满足下列情形之一的医疗器械，可以申请适用优先注册程序：

（一）诊断或者治疗罕见病、恶性肿瘤且具有明显临床优势，诊断或者治疗老年人特有和多发疾病且目前尚无有效诊断或者治疗手段，专用于儿童且具有明显临床优势，或者临床急需且在我国尚无同品种产品获准注册的医疗器械；

（二）列入国家科技重大专项或者国家重点研发计划的医疗器械；

（三）国家药品监督管理局规定的其他可以适用优先注册程序的医疗器械。

第七十四条 申请适用优先注册程序的，申请人应当在提出医疗器械注册申请时，向国家药品监督管理局提出适用优先注册程序的申请。属于第七十三条第一项情形的，由国家药品监督管理局组织专家进行审核，符合的，纳入优先注册程序；属于第七十三条第二项情形的，由国家局器械审评中心进行审核，符合的，纳入优先注册程序；属于第七十三条第三项情形的，由国家药品监督管理局广泛听取意见，并组织专家论证后确定是否纳入优先注册程序。

第七十五条 对纳入优先注册程序的医疗器械注册申请，国家药品监督管理局优先进行审评审批，省、自治区、直辖市药品监督管理部门优先安排医疗器械注册质量管理体系核查。

国家局器械审评中心在对纳入优先注册程序的医疗器械产品开展技术审评过程中，应当按照相关规定积极与申请人进行沟通交流，必要时，可以安排专项交流。

第三节 应急注册程序

第七十六条 国家药品监督管理局可以依法对突发公共卫生事件应急所需且在我国境内尚无同类产品上市，或者虽在我国境内已有同类产品上市但产品供应不能满足突发公共卫生事件应急处理需要的医疗器械实施应急注册。

第七十七条 申请适用应急注册程序的，申请人应当向国家药品监督管理局提出应急注册申请。符合条件的，纳入应急注册程序。

第七十八条 对实施应急注册的医疗器械注册申请，国家药品监督管理局按照统一指挥、早期介入、随到随审、科学审批的要求办理，并行开展医疗器械产品检验、体系核查、技术审评等工作。

第五章 变更注册与延续注册

第一节 变更注册

第七十九条 注册人应当主动开展医疗器械上市后研究，对医疗器械的安全性、有效性和质量可控性进行进一步确认，加强对已上市医疗器械的持续管理。

已注册的第二类、第三类医疗器械产品，其设计、原材料、生产工艺、适用范围、使用方法等发生实质性变化，有可能影响该医疗器械安全、有效的，注册人应当向原注册部门申请办理变更注册手续；发生其他变化的，应当在变化之日起30日内向原注册部门备案。

注册证载明的产品名称、型号、规格、结构及组成、适用范围、产品技术要求、进口医疗器械的生产地址等，属于前款规定的需要办理变更注册的事项。注册人名称和住所、代理人名称和住所等，属于前款规定的需要备案的事项。境内医疗器械生产地址变更的，注册人应当在办理相应的生产许可变更后办理备案。

发生其他变化的，注册人应当按照质量管理体系要求做好相关工作，并按照规定向药品监督管理部门报告。

第八十条　对于变更注册申请，技术审评机构应当重点针对变化部分进行审评，对变化后产品是否安全、有效、质量可控形成审评意见。

在对变更注册申请进行技术审评时，认为有必要对质量管理体系进行核查的，药品监督管理部门应当组织开展质量管理体系核查。

第八十一条　医疗器械变更注册文件与原医疗器械注册证合并使用，有效期截止日期与原医疗器械注册证相同。

第二节　延续注册

第八十二条　医疗器械注册证有效期届满需要延续注册的，注册人应当在医疗器械注册证有效期届满 6 个月前，向原注册部门申请延续注册，并按照相关要求提交申请资料。

除有本办法第八十三条规定情形外，接到延续注册申请的药品监督管理部门应当在医疗器械注册证有效期届满前作出准予延续的决定。逾期未作决定的，视为准予延续。

第八十三条　有下列情形之一的，不予延续注册：

（一）未在规定期限内提出延续注册申请；

（二）新的医疗器械强制性标准发布实施，申请延续注册的医疗器械不能达到新要求；

（三）附条件批准的医疗器械，未在规定期限内完成医疗器械注册证载明事项。

第八十四条　延续注册的批准时间在原注册证有效期内的，延续注册的注册证有效期起始日为原注册证到期日次日；批准时间不在原注册证有效期内的，延续注册的注册证有效期起始日为批准延续注册的日期。

第八十五条　医疗器械变更注册申请、延续注册申请的受理与审批程序，本章未作规定的，适用本办法第三章的相关规定。

第六章　医疗器械备案

第八十六条　第一类医疗器械生产前，应当进行产品备案。

第八十七条　进行医疗器械备案，备案人应当按照《医疗器械监督管理条例》的规定向药品监督管理部门提交备案资料，获取备案编号。

第八十八条　已备案的医疗器械，备案信息表中登载内容及备案的产品技术要求发生变化的，备案人应当向原备案部门变更备案，并提交变化情况的说明以及相关文件。药品监督管理部门应当将变更情况登载于备案信息中。

第八十九条　已备案的医疗器械管理类别调整为第二类或者第三类医疗器械的，应当按照本办法规定申请注册。

第七章　工作时限

第九十条　本办法所规定的时限是医疗器械注册的受理、技术审评、核查、审批等工作的最长时间。特殊注册程序相关工作时限，按特殊注册程序相关规定执行。

国家局器械审评中心等专业技术机构应当明确本单位工作程序和时限，并向社会公布。

第九十一条　药品监督管理部门收到医疗器械注册申请及临床试验申请后，应当自受理之日起 3 日内将申请资料转交技术审评机构。临床试验申请的受理要求适用于本办法第五十三条规定。

第九十二条　医疗器械注册技术审评时限，按照以下规定执行：

（一）医疗器械临床试验申请的技术审评时限为 60 日，申请资料补正后的技术审评时限为 40 日；

（二）第二类医疗器械注册申请、变更注册申请、延续注册申请的技术审评时限为 60 日，申请资料补正后的技术审评时限为 60 日；

（三）第三类医疗器械注册申请、变更注册申请、延续注册申请的技术审评时限为 90 日，申请资料补正后的技术审评时限为 60 日。

第九十三条　境内第三类医疗器械质量管理体系核查时限，按照以下规定执行：

（一）国家局器械审评中心应当在医疗器械注册申请受理后 10 日内通知相关省、自治区、直辖市药品监督管理部门启动核查；

（二）省、自治区、直辖市药品监督管理部门原则上在接到核查通知后 30 日内完成核查，并将核查情况、核查结果等相关材料反馈至国家局器械审评中心。

第九十四条　受理注册申请的药品监督管理部门应当自收到审评意见之日起 20 日内作出决定。

第九十五条　药品监督管理部门应当自作出医疗器械注册审批决定之日起 10 日内颁发、送达有关行政许可证件。

第九十六条　因产品特性以及技术审评、核查等工作遇到特殊情况确需延长时限的，延长时限不得超过原时限的二分之一，经医疗器械技术审评、核查等相关技术机构负责人批准后，由延长时限的技术机构书面告知申请人，并通知其他相关技术机构。

第九十七条　原发证机关应当自收到医疗器械注册证补办申请之日起 20 日内予以补发。

第九十八条　以下时间不计入相关工作时限：

（一）申请人补充资料、核查后整改等所占用的时间；

（二）因申请人原因延迟核查的时间；

（三）外聘专家咨询、召开专家咨询会、药械组合产品需要与药品审评机构联合审评的时间；

（四）根据规定中止审评审批程序的，中止审评审批程序期间所占用的时间；

（五）质量管理体系核查所占用的时间。

第九十九条　本办法规定的时限以工作日计算。

第八章 监督管理

第一百条 药品监督管理部门应当加强对医疗器械研制活动的监督检查，必要时可以对为医疗器械研制提供产品或者服务的单位和个人进行延伸检查，有关单位和个人应当予以配合，提供相关文件和资料，不得拒绝、隐瞒、阻挠。

第一百零一条 国家药品监督管理局建立并分步实施医疗器械唯一标识制度，申请人、备案人应当按照相关规定提交唯一标识相关信息，保证数据真实、准确、可溯源。

第一百零二条 国家药品监督管理局应当及时将代理人信息通报代理人所在地省、自治区、直辖市药品监督管理部门。省、自治区、直辖市药品监督管理部门对本行政区域内的代理人组织开展日常监督管理。

第一百零三条 省、自治区、直辖市药品监督管理部门根据医疗器械临床试验机构备案情况，组织对本行政区域内已经备案的临床试验机构开展备案后监督检查。对于新备案的医疗器械临床试验机构，应当在备案后60日内开展监督检查。

省、自治区、直辖市药品监督管理部门应当组织对本行政区域内医疗器械临床试验机构遵守医疗器械临床试验质量管理规范的情况进行日常监督检查，监督其持续符合规定要求。国家药品监督管理局根据需要对医疗器械临床试验机构进行监督检查。

第一百零四条 药品监督管理部门认为有必要的，可以对临床试验的真实性、准确性、完整性、规范性和可追溯性进行现场检查。

第一百零五条 承担第一类医疗器械产品备案工作的药品监督管理部门在备案后监督中，发现备案资料不规范的，应当责令备案人限期改正。

第一百零六条 药品监督管理部门未及时发现本行政区域内医疗器械注册管理系统性、区域性风险，或者未及时消除本行政区域内医疗器械注册管理系统性、区域性隐患的，上级药品监督管理部门可以对下级药品监督管理部门主要负责人进行约谈。

第九章　法律责任

第一百零七条　违反本办法第七十九条的规定，未按照要求对发生变化进行备案的，责令限期改正；逾期不改正的，处1万元以上3万元以下罚款。

第一百零八条　开展医疗器械临床试验未遵守临床试验质量管理规范的，依照《医疗器械监督管理条例》第九十四条予以处罚。

第一百零九条　医疗器械技术审评机构未依照本办法规定履行职责，致使审评工作出现重大失误的，由负责药品监督管理的部门责令改正，通报批评，给予警告；造成严重后果的，对违法单位的法定代表人、主要负责人、直接负责的主管人员和其他责任人员，依法给予处分。

第一百一十条　负责药品监督管理的部门工作人员违反规定，滥用职权、玩忽职守、徇私舞弊的，依法给予处分。

第十章　附　则

第一百一十一条　医疗器械注册或者备案单元原则上以产品的技术原理、结构组成、性能指标和适用范围为划分依据。

第一百一十二条　获准注册的医疗器械，是指与该医疗器械注册证及附件限定内容一致且在医疗器械注册证有效期内生产的医疗器械。

第一百一十三条　医疗器械注册证中"结构及组成"栏内所载明的组合部件，以更换耗材、售后服务、维修等为目的，用于原注册产品的，可以单独销售。

第一百一十四条　申请人在申请医疗器械产品注册、变更注册、临床试验审批中可以经医疗器械主文档所有者授权，引用经登记的医疗器械主文档。医疗器械主文档登记相关工作程序另行规定。

第一百一十五条　医疗器械注册证格式由国家药品监督管理局统一

制定。

注册证编号的编排方式为：

×1 械注 ×2×××3×4××5×××6。其中：

×1 为注册审批部门所在地的简称：

境内第三类医疗器械、进口第二类、第三类医疗器械为"国"字；

境内第二类医疗器械为注册审批部门所在地省、自治区、直辖市简称；

×2 为注册形式：

"准"字适用于境内医疗器械；

"进"字适用于进口医疗器械；

"许"字适用于香港、澳门、台湾地区的医疗器械；

×××3 为首次注册年份；

×4 为产品管理类别；

××5 为产品分类编码；

×××6 为首次注册流水号。

延续注册的，×××3 和 ×××6 数字不变。产品管理类别调整的，应当重新编号。

第一百一十六条 第一类医疗器械备案编号的编排方式为：

×1 械备 ×××2×××3。其中：

×1 为备案部门所在地的简称：

进口第一类医疗器械为"国"字；

境内第一类医疗器械为备案部门所在地省、自治区、直辖市简称加所在地设区的市级行政区域的简称（无相应设区的市级行政区域时，仅为省、自治区、直辖市的简称）；

×××2 为备案年份；

×××3 为备案流水号。

第一百一十七条 药品监督管理部门制作的医疗器械注册证、变更注册文件电子文件与纸质文件具有同等法律效力。

第一百一十八条　根据工作需要，国家药品监督管理局可以依法委托省、自治区、直辖市药品监督管理部门或者技术机构、社会组织承担有关的具体工作。

第一百一十九条　省、自治区、直辖市药品监督管理部门可以参照本办法第四章规定制定本行政区域内第二类医疗器械特殊注册程序，并报国家药品监督管理局备案。

第一百二十条　医疗器械产品注册收费项目、收费标准按照国务院财政、价格主管部门的有关规定执行。

第一百二十一条　按照医疗器械管理的体外诊断试剂的注册与备案，适用《体外诊断试剂注册与备案管理办法》。

第一百二十二条　定制式医疗器械监督管理的有关规定，由国家药品监督管理局另行制定。

药械组合产品注册管理的有关规定，由国家药品监督管理局另行制定。

医疗器械紧急使用的有关规定，由国家药品监督管理局会同有关部门另行制定。

第一百二十三条　香港、澳门、台湾地区医疗器械的注册、备案，参照进口医疗器械办理。

第一百二十四条　本办法自 2021 年 10 月 1 日起施行。2014 年 7 月 30 日原国家食品药品监督管理总局令第 4 号公布的《医疗器械注册管理办法》同时废止。

体外诊断试剂注册与备案管理办法

（国家市场监督管理总局令第 48 号）

第一章 总 则

第一条 为了规范体外诊断试剂注册与备案行为，保证体外诊断试剂的安全、有效和质量可控，根据《医疗器械监督管理条例》，制定本办法。

第二条 在中华人民共和国境内开展体外诊断试剂注册、备案及其监督管理活动，适用本办法。

第三条 本办法所称体外诊断试剂，是指按医疗器械管理的体外诊断试剂，包括在疾病的预测、预防、诊断、治疗监测、预后观察和健康状态评价的过程中，用于人体样本体外检测的试剂、试剂盒、校准品、质控品等产品，可以单独使用，也可以与仪器、器具、设备或者系统组合使用。

按照药品管理的用于血源筛查的体外诊断试剂、采用放射性核素标记的体外诊断试剂不属于本办法管理范围。

第四条 体外诊断试剂注册是指体外诊断试剂注册申请人（以下简称申请人）依照法定程序和要求提出体外诊断试剂注册申请，药品监督管理部门依据法律法规，基于科学认知，进行安全性、有效性和质量可控性等审查，决定是否同意其申请的活动。

体外诊断试剂备案是指体外诊断试剂备案人（以下简称备案人）依照法定程序和要求向药品监督管理部门提交备案资料，药品监督管理部门对提交的备案资料存档备查的活动。

第五条 国家药品监督管理局主管全国体外诊断试剂注册与备案管理工作，负责建立体外诊断试剂注册与备案管理工作体系，依法组织境内第三类和进口第二类、第三类体外诊断试剂审评审批，进口第一类体外诊断试剂备案以及相关监督管理工作，对地方体外诊断试剂注册与备案工作进行监督指导。

第六条 国家药品监督管理局医疗器械技术审评中心（以下简称国家局器械审评中心）负责境内第三类和进口第二类、三类体外诊断试剂产品注册申请、变更注册申请、延续注册申请等的技术审评工作。

国家药品监督管理局医疗器械标准管理中心、中国食品药品检定研究院、国家药品监督管理局食品药品审核查验中心（以下简称国家局审核查验中心）、国家药品监督管理局药品评价中心、国家药品监督管理局行政事项受理服务和投诉举报中心、国家药品监督管理局信息中心等其他专业技术机构，依职责承担实施体外诊断试剂监督管理所需的体外诊断试剂标准管理、分类界定、检验、核查、监测与评价、制证送达以及相应的信息化建设与管理等相关工作。

第七条 省、自治区、直辖市药品监督管理部门负责本行政区域内以下体外诊断试剂注册相关管理工作：

（一）境内第二类体外诊断试剂注册审评审批；

（二）境内第二类、第三类体外诊断试剂质量管理体系核查；

（三）依法组织医疗器械临床试验机构以及临床试验的监督管理；

（四）对设区的市级负责药品监督管理的部门境内第一类体外诊断试剂备案的监督指导。

省、自治区、直辖市药品监督管理部门设置或者指定的医疗器械专业技术机构，承担实施体外诊断试剂监督管理所需的技术审评、检验、核查、监测与评价等工作。

设区的市级负责药品监督管理的部门负责境内第一类体外诊断试剂产品备案管理工作。

第八条 体外诊断试剂注册与备案遵循依法、科学、公开、公平、公正的原则。

第九条 第一类体外诊断试剂实行产品备案管理。第二类、第三类体外诊断试剂实行产品注册管理。

境内第一类体外诊断试剂备案，备案人向设区的市级负责药品监督管理的部门提交备案资料。

境内第二类体外诊断试剂由省、自治区、直辖市药品监督管理部门审查，批准后发给医疗器械注册证。

境内第三类体外诊断试剂由国家药品监督管理局审查，批准后发给医疗器械注册证。

进口第一类体外诊断试剂备案，备案人向国家药品监督管理局提交备案资料。

进口第二类、第三类体外诊断试剂由国家药品监督管理局审查，批准后发给医疗器械注册证。

第十条 体外诊断试剂注册人、备案人应当加强体外诊断试剂全生命周期质量管理，对研制、生产、经营、使用全过程中的体外诊断试剂的安全性、有效性和质量可控性依法承担责任。

第十一条 国家药品监督管理局对临床急需体外诊断试剂实行优先审批，对创新体外诊断试剂实行特别审批。鼓励体外诊断试剂的研究与创新，推动医疗器械产业高质量发展。

第十二条 国家药品监督管理局依法建立健全体外诊断试剂标准、技术指导原则等体系，规范体外诊断试剂技术审评和质量管理体系核查，指导和服务体外诊断试剂研发和注册申请。

第十三条 药品监督管理部门依法及时公开体外诊断试剂注册、备案相关信息，申请人可以查询审批进度和结果，公众可以查阅审批结果。

未经申请人同意，药品监督管理部门、专业技术机构及其工作人员、参与评审的专家等人员不得披露申请人或者备案人提交的商业秘密、未披露信息或者保密商务信息，法律另有规定或者涉及国家安全、重大社会公共利益的除外。

第二章　基本要求

第十四条　体外诊断试剂注册、备案，应当遵守相关法律、法规、规章、强制性标准，遵循体外诊断试剂安全和性能基本原则，参照相关技术指导原则，证明注册、备案的体外诊断试剂安全、有效、质量可控，保证信息真实、准确、完整和可追溯。

第十五条　申请人、备案人应当为能够承担相应法律责任的企业或者研制机构。

境外申请人、备案人应当指定中国境内的企业法人作为代理人，办理相关体外诊断试剂注册、备案事项。代理人应当依法协助注册人、备案人履行《医疗器械监督管理条例》第二十条第一款规定的义务，并协助境外注册人、备案人落实相应法律责任。

第十六条　申请人、备案人应当建立与产品研制、生产有关的质量管理体系，并保持有效运行。

第十七条　办理体外诊断试剂注册、备案事项的人员应当具有相关专业知识，熟悉体外诊断试剂注册、备案管理的法律、法规、规章和注册管理相关规定。

第十八条　申请注册或者进行备案，应当按照国家药品监督管理局有关注册、备案的要求提交相关资料，申请人、备案人对资料的真实性负责。

注册、备案资料应当使用中文。根据外文资料翻译的，应当同时提供原文。引用未公开发表的文献资料时，应当提供资料权利人许可使用的文件。

第十九条　申请进口体外诊断试剂注册、办理进口体外诊断试剂备案，应当提交申请人、备案人注册地或者生产地所在国家（地区）主管部门准许上市销售的证明文件。

申请人、备案人注册地或者生产地所在国家（地区）未将该产品作为医疗器械管理的，申请人、备案人需提供相关文件，包括注册地或者生产地所在国家（地区）准许该产品上市销售的证明文件。

未在申请人、备案人注册地或者生产地所在国家（地区）上市的按照创新产品注册程序审批的体外诊断试剂，不需提交相关文件。

第二十条 体外诊断试剂应当符合适用的强制性标准。产品结构特征、技术原理、预期用途、使用方式等与强制性标准的适用范围不一致的，申请人、备案人应当提出不适用强制性标准的说明，并提供相关资料。

没有强制性标准的，鼓励申请人、备案人采用推荐性标准。

第二十一条 体外诊断试剂注册、备案工作应当遵循体外诊断试剂分类规则和分类目录的有关要求。

第二十二条 药品监督管理部门持续推进审评审批制度改革，加强监管科学研究，建立以技术审评为主导，核查、检验、监测与评价等为支撑的体外诊断试剂注册管理技术体系，优化审评审批流程，提高审评审批能力，提升审评审批质量和效率。

第二十三条 医疗器械专业技术机构建立健全沟通交流制度，明确沟通交流的形式和内容，根据工作需要组织与申请人进行沟通交流。

第二十四条 医疗器械专业技术机构根据工作需要建立专家咨询制度，在审评、核查、检验等过程中就重大问题听取专家意见，充分发挥专家的技术支撑作用。

第三章 体外诊断试剂注册

第一节 产品研制

第二十五条 体外诊断试剂研制应当遵循风险管理原则，考虑现有公认技术水平，确保产品所有已知和可预见的风险以及非预期影响最小化并可接受，保证产品在正常使用中受益大于风险。

第二十六条 从事体外诊断试剂产品研制实验活动，应当符合我国相关法律、法规和强制性标准等的要求。

第二十七条 申请人、备案人应当编制申请注册或者进行备案体外诊断试剂的产品技术要求。

产品技术要求主要包括体外诊断试剂成品的可进行客观判定的功能性、安全性指标和检测方法。

第三类体外诊断试剂的产品技术要求中应当以附录形式明确主要原材料以及生产工艺要求。

体外诊断试剂应当符合经注册或者备案的产品技术要求。

第二十八条　申请人、备案人应当编制申请注册或者进行备案体外诊断试剂的产品说明书和标签。

产品说明书和标签应当符合《医疗器械监督管理条例》第三十九条要求以及相关规定。

第二十九条　体外诊断试剂研制，应当根据产品预期用途和技术特征开展体外诊断试剂非临床研究。

非临床研究指在实验室条件下对体外诊断试剂进行的试验或者评价，包括主要原材料的选择及制备、产品生产工艺、产品分析性能、阳性判断值或者参考区间、产品稳定性等的研究。

申请注册或者进行备案，应当提交研制活动中产生的非临床证据。

第三十条　体外诊断试剂非临床研究过程中确定的功能性、安全性指标及方法应当与产品预期使用条件、目的相适应，研究样品应当具有代表性和典型性。必要时，应当进行方法学验证、统计学分析。

第三十一条　申请注册或者进行备案，应当按照产品技术要求进行检验，并提交检验报告。检验合格的，方可开展临床试验或者申请注册、进行备案。

第三十二条　同一注册申请包括不同包装规格时，可以只进行一种包装规格产品的检验，检验用产品应当能够代表申请注册或者进行备案产品的安全性和有效性，其生产应当符合医疗器械生产质量管理规范的相关要求。

第三十三条　申请注册或者进行备案提交的检验报告可以是申请人、

备案人的自检报告，也可以是委托有资质的医疗器械检验机构出具的检验报告。

第三类体外诊断试剂应当提供 3 个不同生产批次产品的检验报告。

第三十四条 对于有适用的国家标准品的，应当使用国家标准品对试剂进行检验。中国食品药品检定研究院负责组织国家标准品的制备和标定工作。

第二节 临床评价

第三十五条 体外诊断试剂临床评价是指采用科学合理的方法对临床数据进行分析、评价，对产品是否满足使用要求或者预期用途进行确认，以证明体外诊断试剂的安全性、有效性的过程。

第三十六条 体外诊断试剂临床试验是指在相应的临床环境中，对体外诊断试剂的临床性能进行的系统性研究。

国家药品监督管理局制定体外诊断试剂临床试验指南，明确开展临床试验的要求、临床试验报告的撰写要求等。

第三十七条 开展体外诊断试剂临床评价，应当进行临床试验证明体外诊断试剂的安全性、有效性。

符合如下情形的，可以免于进行临床试验：

（一）反应原理明确、设计定型、生产工艺成熟，已上市的同品种体外诊断试剂临床应用多年且无严重不良事件记录，不改变常规用途的；

（二）通过进行同品种方法学比对的方式能够证明该体外诊断试剂安全、有效的。

免于进行临床试验的第二类、第三类体外诊断试剂目录由国家药品监督管理局制定、调整并公布。

第三十八条 免于进行临床试验的体外诊断试剂，申请人应当通过对符合预期用途的临床样本进行同品种方法学比对的方式证明产品的安全性、有效性。

国家药品监督管理局制定免于进行临床试验的体外诊断试剂临床评价

相关指南。

第三十九条　体外诊断试剂临床评价资料是指申请人进行临床评价所形成的文件。

开展临床试验的，临床试验资料包括临床试验方案、伦理委员会意见、知情同意书、临床试验报告以及相关数据等。

列入免于进行临床试验目录的体外诊断试剂，临床评价资料包括与同类已上市产品的对比分析、方法学比对数据、相关文献数据分析和经验数据分析等。

第四十条　同一注册申请包括不同包装规格时，可以只采用一种包装规格的产品进行临床评价，临床评价用产品应当代表申请注册或者进行备案产品的安全性和有效性。

校准品、质控品单独申请注册不需要提交临床评价资料。

第四十一条　开展体外诊断试剂临床试验，应当按照医疗器械临床试验质量管理规范的要求，在具备相应条件并按照规定备案的医疗器械临床试验机构内进行。临床试验开始前，临床试验申办者应当向所在地省、自治区、直辖市药品监督管理部门进行临床试验备案。临床试验体外诊断试剂的生产应当符合医疗器械生产质量管理规范的相关要求。

第四十二条　对于体外诊断试剂临床试验期间出现的临床试验体外诊断试剂相关严重不良事件，或者其他严重安全性风险信息，临床试验申办者应当按照相关要求，分别向所在地和临床试验机构所在地省、自治区、直辖市药品监督管理部门报告，并采取风险控制措施。未采取风险控制措施的，省、自治区、直辖市药品监督管理部门依法责令申办者采取相应的风险控制措施。

第四十三条　体外诊断试剂临床试验中出现大范围临床试验体外诊断试剂相关严重不良事件，或者其他重大安全性问题时，申办者应当暂停或者终止体外诊断试剂临床试验，分别向所在地和临床试验机构所在地省、自治区、直辖市药品监督管理部门报告。未暂停或者终止的，省、自治区、直辖市药品监督管理部门依法责令申办者采取相应的风险控制措施。

第四十四条 对预期供消费者个人自行使用的体外诊断试剂开展临床评价时，申请人还应当进行无医学背景的消费者对产品说明书认知能力的评价。

第四十五条 对正在开展临床试验的用于诊断严重危及生命且尚无有效诊断手段的疾病的体外诊断试剂，经医学观察可能使患者获益，经伦理审查、知情同意后，可以在开展体外诊断试剂的临床试验的机构内免费用于其他病情相同的患者，其安全性数据可以用于体外诊断试剂注册申请。

第三节 注册体系核查

第四十六条 申请人应当在申请注册时提交与产品研制、生产有关的质量管理体系相关资料，受理注册申请的药品监督管理部门在产品技术审评时认为有必要对质量管理体系进行核查的，应当组织开展质量管理体系核查，并可以根据需要调阅原始资料。

第四十七条 境内第三类体外诊断试剂质量管理体系核查，由国家局器械审评中心通知申请人所在地的省、自治区、直辖市药品监督管理部门开展。

境内第二类体外诊断试剂质量管理体系核查，由申请人所在地省、自治区、直辖市药品监督管理部门组织开展。

第四十八条 省、自治区、直辖市药品监督管理部门按照医疗器械生产质量管理规范的要求开展质量管理体系核查，重点对申请人是否按照医疗器械生产质量管理规范的要求建立与产品相适应的质量管理体系，以及与产品研制、生产有关的设计开发、生产管理、质量控制等内容进行核查。

在核查过程中，应当同时对检验用产品和临床试验产品的真实性进行核查，重点查阅设计开发过程相关记录，以及检验用产品和临床试验产品生产过程的相关记录。

提交自检报告的，应当对申请人、备案人或者受托机构研制过程中的检验能力、检验结果等进行重点核查。

第四十九条　省、自治区、直辖市药品监督管理部门可以通过资料审查或者现场检查的方式开展质量管理体系核查。根据申请人的具体情况、监督检查情况、本次申请注册产品与既往已通过核查产品生产条件及工艺对比情况等，确定是否现场检查以及检查内容，避免重复检查。

第五十条　国家局器械审评中心对进口第二类、第三类体外诊断试剂开展技术审评时，认为有必要进行质量管理体系核查的，通知国家局审核查验中心根据相关要求开展核查。

第四节　产品注册

第五十一条　申请人应当在完成支持体外诊断试剂注册的安全性、有效性研究，做好接受质量管理体系核查的准备后，提出体外诊断试剂注册申请，并按照相关要求，通过在线注册申请等途径向药品监督管理部门提交下列注册申请资料：

（一）产品风险分析资料；

（二）产品技术要求；

（三）产品检验报告；

（四）临床评价资料；

（五）产品说明书以及标签样稿；

（六）与产品研制、生产有关的质量管理体系文件；

（七）证明产品安全、有效所需的其他资料。

第五十二条　药品监督管理部门收到申请后对申请资料进行审核，并根据下列情况分别作出处理：

（一）申请事项属于本行政机关职权范围，申请资料齐全、符合形式审核要求的，予以受理；

（二）申请资料存在可以当场更正的错误的，应当允许申请人当场更正；

（三）申请资料不齐全或者不符合法定形式的，应当当场或者在 5 日内一次告知申请人需要补正的全部内容，逾期不告知的，自收到申请资料之日起即为受理；

（四）申请事项依法不属于本行政机关职权范围的，应当即时作出不予受理的决定，并告知申请人向有关行政机关申请。

药品监督管理部门受理或者不予受理体外诊断试剂注册申请，应当出具加盖本行政机关专用印章和注明日期的受理或者不予受理的通知书。

体外诊断试剂注册申请受理后，需要申请人缴纳费用的，申请人应当按规定缴纳费用。申请人未在规定期限内缴纳费用的，视为申请人主动撤回申请，药品监督管理部门终止其注册程序。

第五十三条 技术审评过程中需要申请人补正资料的，技术审评机构应当一次告知需要补正的全部内容。申请人应当在收到补正通知1年内，按照补正通知要求一次提供补充资料；技术审评机构收到补充资料后，在规定的时限内完成技术审评。

申请人对补正通知内容有异议的，可以向相应的技术审评机构提出书面意见，说明理由并提供相应的技术支持资料。

申请人逾期未提交补充资料的，终止技术审评，药品监督管理部门作出不予注册的决定。

第五十四条 对于已受理的注册申请，申请人可以在行政许可决定作出前，向受理该申请的药品监督管理部门申请撤回注册申请及相关资料，并说明理由。同意撤回申请的，药品监督管理部门终止其注册程序。

审评、核查、审批过程中发现涉嫌存在隐瞒真实情况或者提供虚假信息等违法行为的，依法处理，申请人不得撤回注册申请。

第五十五条 对于已受理的注册申请，有证据表明注册申请资料可能虚假的，药品监督管理部门可以中止审评审批。经核实后，根据核实结论继续审查或者作出不予注册的决定。

第五十六条 体外诊断试剂注册申请审评期间，对于拟作出不通过的审评结论的，技术审评机构应当告知申请人不通过的理由，申请人可以在15日内向技术审评机构提出异议，异议内容仅限于原申请事项和原申请资料。技术审评机构结合申请人的异议意见进行综合评估并反馈申请人。异议处理时间不计入审评时限。

第五十七条　受理注册申请的药品监督管理部门应当在技术审评结束后，作出是否批准的决定。对符合安全、有效、质量可控要求的，准予注册，发给医疗器械注册证，经过核准的产品技术要求和产品说明书以附件形式发给申请人。对不予注册的，应当书面说明理由，并同时告知申请人享有依法申请行政复议或者提起行政诉讼的权利。

医疗器械注册证有效期为 5 年。

第五十八条　对于已受理的注册申请，有下列情形之一的，药品监督管理部门作出不予注册的决定，并告知申请人：

（一）申请人对拟上市销售体外诊断试剂的安全性、有效性、质量可控性进行的研究及其结果无法证明产品安全、有效、质量可控的；

（二）质量管理体系核查不通过，以及申请人拒绝接受质量管理体系现场检查的；

（三）注册申请资料虚假的；

（四）注册申请资料内容混乱、矛盾，注册申请资料内容与申请项目明显不符，不能证明产品安全、有效、质量可控的；

（五）不予注册的其他情形。

第五十九条　法律、法规、规章规定实施行政许可应当听证的事项，或者药品监督管理部门认为需要听证的其他涉及公共利益的重大行政许可事项，药品监督管理部门应当向社会公告，并举行听证。医疗器械注册申请直接涉及申请人与他人之间重大利益关系的，药品监督管理部门在作出行政许可决定前，应当告知申请人、利害关系人享有要求听证的权利。

第六十条　对用于罕见疾病、严重危及生命且尚无有效诊断手段的疾病和应对公共卫生事件等急需的体外诊断试剂，药品监督管理部门可以作出附条件批准决定，并在医疗器械注册证中载明有效期、上市后需要继续完成的研究工作及完成时限等相关事项。

第六十一条　对附条件批准的体外诊断试剂，注册人应当在体外诊断试剂上市后收集受益和风险相关数据，持续对产品的受益和风险开展监测与评估，采取有效措施主动管控风险，并在规定期限内按照要求完成研究并提交相关资料。

第六十二条　对附条件批准的体外诊断试剂，注册人逾期未按照要求完成研究或者不能证明其受益大于风险的，注册人应当及时申请办理医疗器械注册证注销手续，药品监督管理部门可以依法注销医疗器械注册证。

第六十三条　对新研制的尚未列入体外诊断试剂分类目录的体外诊断试剂，申请人可以直接申请第三类体外诊断试剂产品注册，也可以依据分类规则判断产品类别并向国家药品监督管理局申请类别确认后，申请产品注册或者进行产品备案。

直接申请第三类体外诊断试剂注册的，国家药品监督管理局按照风险程度确定类别。境内体外诊断试剂确定为第二类或者第一类的，应当告知申请人向相应的药品监督管理部门申请注册或者进行备案。

第六十四条　已注册的体外诊断试剂，其管理类别由高类别调整为低类别的，医疗器械注册证在有效期内继续有效。有效期届满需要延续的，注册人应当在医疗器械注册证有效期届满6个月前，按照调整后的类别向相应的药品监督管理部门申请延续注册或者进行备案。

体外诊断试剂管理类别由低类别调整为高类别的，注册人应当按照改变后的类别向相应的药品监督管理部门申请注册。国家药品监督管理局在管理类别调整通知中应当对完成调整的时限作出规定。

第六十五条　医疗器械注册证及其附件遗失、损毁的，注册人应当向原发证机关申请补发，原发证机关核实后予以补发。

第六十六条　注册申请审查过程中及批准后发生专利权纠纷的，应当按照有关法律、法规的规定处理。

第四章　特殊注册程序

第一节　创新产品注册程序

第六十七条　符合下列要求的体外诊断试剂，申请人可以申请适用创新产品注册程序：

（一）申请人通过其主导的技术创新活动，在中国依法拥有产品核心技术发明专利权，或者依法通过受让取得在中国发明专利权或其使用权，且申请适用创新产品注册程序的时间在专利授权公告日起 5 年内；或者核心技术发明专利的申请已由国务院专利行政部门公开，并由国家知识产权局专利检索咨询中心出具检索报告，载明产品核心技术方案具备新颖性和创造性；

（二）申请人已完成产品的前期研究并具有基本定型产品，研究过程真实和受控，研究数据完整和可溯源；

（三）产品主要工作原理或者作用机理为国内首创，产品性能或者安全性与同类产品比较有根本性改进，技术上处于国际领先水平，且具有显著的临床应用价值。

第六十八条　申请适用创新产品注册程序的，申请人应当在产品基本定型后，向国家药品监督管理局提出创新医疗器械审查申请。国家药品监督管理局组织专家进行审查，符合要求的，纳入创新产品注册程序。

第六十九条　对于适用创新产品注册程序的体外诊断试剂注册申请，国家药品监督管理局以及承担相关技术工作的机构，根据各自职责指定专人负责，及时沟通，提供指导。

纳入创新产品注册程序的体外诊断试剂，国家局器械审评中心可与申请人在注册申请受理前以及技术审评过程中就产品研制中的重大技术问题、重大安全性问题、临床试验方案、阶段性临床试验结果的总结与评价等问题沟通交流。

第七十条　纳入创新产品注册程序的体外诊断试剂，申请人主动要求终止或者国家药品监督管理局发现不再符合创新产品注册程序要求的，国家药品监督管理局可终止相关产品的创新产品注册程序并告知申请人。

第七十一条 纳入创新产品注册程序的体外诊断试剂，申请人在规定期限内未提出注册申请的，不再适用创新产品注册程序。

第二节　优先注册程序

第七十二条 满足下列情形之一的体外诊断试剂，可以申请适用优先注册程序：

（一）诊断罕见病、恶性肿瘤，且具有明显临床优势，诊断老年人特有和多发疾病且目前尚无有效诊断手段，专用于儿童且具有明显临床优势，或者临床急需且在我国尚无同品种产品获准注册的医疗器械；

（二）列入国家科技重大专项或者国家重点研发计划的医疗器械；

（三）国家药品监督管理局规定的其他可以适用优先注册程序的医疗器械。

第七十三条 申请适用优先注册程序的，申请人应当在提出体外诊断试剂注册申请时，向国家药品监督管理局提出适用优先注册程序的申请。属于第七十二条第一项情形的，由国家药品监督管理局组织专家进行审核，符合的，纳入优先注册程序；属于第七十二条第二项情形的，由国家局器械审评中心进行审核，符合的，纳入优先注册程序；属于第七十二条第三项情形的，由国家药品监督管理局广泛听取意见，并组织专家论证后确定是否纳入优先注册程序。

第七十四条 对纳入优先注册程序的体外诊断试剂注册申请，国家药品监督管理局优先进行审评审批，省、自治区、直辖市药品监督管理部门优先安排注册质量管理体系核查。

国家局器械审评中心在对纳入优先注册程序的医疗器械产品开展技术审评过程中，应当按照相关规定积极与申请人进行沟通交流，必要时，可以安排专项交流。

第三节　应急注册程序

第七十五条 国家药品监督管理局可以依法对突发公共卫生事件应急

所需且在我国境内尚无同类产品上市，或者虽在我国境内已有同类产品上市但产品供应不能满足突发公共卫生事件应急处理需要的体外诊断试剂实施应急注册。

第七十六条　申请适用应急注册程序的，申请人应当向国家药品监督管理局提出应急注册申请。符合条件的，纳入应急注册程序。

第七十七条　对实施应急注册的体外诊断试剂注册申请，国家药品监督管理局按照统一指挥、早期介入、随到随审、科学审批的要求办理，并行开展体外诊断试剂产品检验、体系核查、技术审评等工作。

第五章　变更注册与延续注册

第一节　变更注册

第七十八条　注册人应当主动开展体外诊断试剂上市后研究，对体外诊断试剂的安全性、有效性和质量可控性进行进一步确认，加强对已上市体外诊断试剂的持续管理。

已注册的第二类、第三类体外诊断试剂产品，其设计、原材料、生产工艺、适用范围、使用方法等发生实质性变化，有可能影响该体外诊断试剂安全、有效的，注册人应当向原注册部门申请办理变更注册手续；发生其他变化的，应当在变化之日起 30 日内向原注册部门备案。

注册证载明的产品名称、包装规格、主要组成成分、预期用途、产品技术要求、产品说明书、进口体外诊断试剂的生产地址等，属于前款规定的需要办理变更注册的事项。注册人名称和住所、代理人名称和住所等，属于前款规定的需要备案的事项。境内体外诊断试剂生产地址变更的，注册人应当在办理相应的生产许可变更后办理备案。

发生其他变化的，注册人应当按照质量管理体系要求做好相关工作，并按照规定向药品监督管理部门报告。

第七十九条　已注册的第二类、第三类体外诊断试剂，产品的核心技术原理等发生实质性改变，或者发生其他重大改变、对产品安全有效性产生重大影响，实质上构成新的产品的，不属于本章规定的变更申请事项，应当按照注册申请的规定办理。

第八十条 对于变更注册申请，技术审评机构应当重点针对变化部分进行审评，对变化后产品是否安全、有效、质量可控形成审评意见。

在对变更注册申请进行技术审评时，认为有必要对质量管理体系进行核查的，药品监督管理部门应当组织开展质量管理体系核查。

第八十一条 医疗器械变更注册文件与原医疗器械注册证合并使用，有效期截止日期与原医疗器械注册证相同。

第二节 延续注册

第八十二条 医疗器械注册证有效期届满需要延续注册的，注册人应当在医疗器械注册证有效期届满6个月前，向原注册部门申请延续注册，并按照相关要求提交申请资料。

除有本办法第八十三条规定情形外，接到延续注册申请的药品监督管理部门应当在医疗器械注册证有效期届满前作出准予延续的决定。逾期未作决定的，视为准予延续。

第八十三条 有下列情形之一的，不予延续注册：

（一）未在规定期限内提出延续注册申请；

（二）新的体外诊断试剂强制性标准或者国家标准品发布实施，申请延续注册的体外诊断试剂不能达到新要求；

（三）附条件批准的体外诊断试剂，未在规定期限内完成医疗器械注册证载明事项。

第八十四条 延续注册的批准时间在原注册证有效期内的，延续注册的注册证有效期起始日为原注册证到期日次日；批准时间不在原注册证有效期内的，延续注册的注册证有效期起始日为批准延续注册的日期。

第八十五条 体外诊断试剂变更注册申请、延续注册申请的受理与审批程序，本章未作规定的，适用本办法第三章的相关规定。

第六章　体外诊断试剂备案

第八十六条　第一类体外诊断试剂生产前，应当进行产品备案。

第八十七条　进行体外诊断试剂备案，备案人应当按照《医疗器械监督管理条例》的规定向药品监督管理部门提交备案资料，获取备案编号。

第八十八条　已备案的体外诊断试剂，备案信息表中登载内容及备案的产品技术要求发生变化的，备案人应当向原备案部门变更备案，并提交变化情况的说明以及相关文件。药品监督管理部门应当将变更情况登载于备案信息中。

第八十九条　已备案的体外诊断试剂管理类别调整为第二类或者第三类体外诊断试剂的，应当按照本办法规定申请注册。

第七章　工作时限

第九十条　本办法所规定的时限是体外诊断试剂注册的受理、技术审评、核查、审批等工作的最长时间。特殊注册程序相关工作时限，按特殊注册程序相关规定执行。

国家局器械审评中心等专业技术机构应当明确本单位工作程序和时限，并向社会公布。

第九十一条　药品监督管理部门收到体外诊断试剂注册申请后，应当自受理之日起 3 日内将申请资料转交技术审评机构。

第九十二条　体外诊断试剂注册技术审评时限，按照以下规定执行：

（一）第二类体外诊断试剂注册申请、变更注册申请、延续注册申请的技术审评时限为 60 日，申请资料补正后的技术审评时限为 60 日；

（二）第三类体外诊断试剂注册申请、变更注册申请、延续注册申请的技术审评时限为 90 日，申请资料补正后的技术审评时限为 60 日。

第九十三条　境内第三类体外诊断试剂质量管理体系核查时限，按照以下规定执行：

（一）国家局器械审评中心应当在体外诊断试剂注册申请受理后 10 日内通知相关省、自治区、直辖市药品监督管理部门启动核查；

（二）省、自治区、直辖市药品监督管理部门原则上在接到核查通知后 30 日内完成核查，并将核查情况、核查结果等相关材料反馈至国家局器械审评中心。

第九十四条　受理注册申请的药品监督管理部门应当自收到审评意见之日起 20 日内作出决定。

第九十五条　药品监督管理部门应当自作出体外诊断试剂注册审批决定之日起 10 日内颁发、送达有关行政许可证件。

第九十六条　因产品特性以及技术审评、核查等工作遇到特殊情况确需延长时限的，延长时限不得超过原时限的二分之一，经医疗器械技术审评、核查等相关技术机构负责人批准后，由延长时限的技术机构书面告知申请人，并通知其他相关技术机构。

第九十七条　原发证机关应当自收到医疗器械注册证补办申请之日起 20 日内予以补发。

第九十八条　以下时间不计入相关工作时限：

（一）申请人补充资料、核查后整改等所占用的时间；

（二）因申请人原因延迟核查的时间；

（三）外聘专家咨询、召开专家咨询会、需要与药品审评机构联合审评的时间；

（四）根据规定中止审评审批程序的，中止审评审批程序期间所占用的时间；

（五）质量管理体系核查所占用的时间。

第九十九条　本办法规定的时限以工作日计算。

第八章　监督管理

第一百条　药品监督管理部门应当加强体外诊断试剂研制活动的监督

检查，必要时可以对为体外诊断试剂研制提供产品或者服务的单位和个人进行延伸检查，有关单位和个人应当予以配合，提供相关文件和资料，不得拒绝、隐瞒、阻挠。

第一百零一条 国家药品监督管理局建立并分步实施医疗器械唯一标识制度，申请人、备案人应当按照相关规定提交唯一标识相关信息，保证数据真实、准确、可溯源。

第一百零二条 国家药品监督管理局应当及时将代理人信息通报代理人所在地省、自治区、直辖市药品监督管理部门。省、自治区、直辖市药品监督管理部门对本行政区域内的代理人组织开展日常监督管理。

第一百零三条 省、自治区、直辖市药品监督管理部门根据医疗器械临床试验机构备案情况，组织对本行政区域内已经备案的临床试验机构开展备案后监督检查。对于新备案的医疗器械临床试验机构，应当在备案后60日内开展监督检查。

省、自治区、直辖市药品监督管理部门应当组织对本行政区域内医疗器械临床试验机构遵守医疗器械临床试验质量管理规范的情况进行日常监督检查，监督其持续符合规定要求。国家药品监督管理局根据需要对医疗器械临床试验机构进行监督检查。

第一百零四条 药品监督管理部门认为有必要的，可以对临床试验的真实性、准确性、完整性、规范性和可追溯性进行现场检查。

第一百零五条 承担第一类体外诊断试剂产品备案工作的药品监督管理部门在备案后监督中，发现备案资料不规范的，应当责令备案人限期改正。

第一百零六条 药品监督管理部门未及时发现本行政区域内体外诊断试剂注册管理系统性、区域性风险，或者未及时消除本行政区域内体外诊断试剂注册管理系统性、区域性隐患的，上级药品监督管理部门可以对下级药品监督管理部门主要负责人进行约谈。

第九章 法律责任

第一百零七条 违反本办法第七十八条的规定，未按照要求对发生变化进行备案的，责令限期改正；逾期不改正的，处 1 万元以上 3 万元以下罚款。

第一百零八条 开展体外诊断试剂临床试验未遵守临床试验质量管理规范的，依照《医疗器械监督管理条例》第九十四条予以处罚。

第一百零九条 医疗器械技术审评机构未依照本办法规定履行职责，致使审评工作出现重大失误的，由负责药品监督管理的部门责令改正，通报批评，给予警告；造成严重后果的，对违法单位的法定代表人、主要负责人、直接负责的主管人员和其他责任人员，依法给予处分。

第一百一十条 负责药品监督管理的部门工作人员违反规定，滥用职权、玩忽职守、徇私舞弊的，依法给予处分。

第十章 附 则

第一百一十一条 体外诊断试剂的命名应当遵循以下原则：

体外诊断试剂的产品名称一般由三部分组成。第一部分：被测物质的名称；第二部分：用途，如测定试剂盒、质控品等；第三部分：方法或者原理，如磁微粒化学发光免疫分析法、荧光 PCR 法、荧光原位杂交法等，本部分应当在括号中列出。

如果被测物组分较多或者有其他特殊情况，可以采用与产品相关的适应症名称或者其他替代名称。

第一类产品和校准品、质控品，依据其预期用途进行命名。

第一百一十二条 体外诊断试剂的注册或者备案单元应为单一试剂或者单一试剂盒，一个注册或者备案单元可以包括不同的包装规格。

校准品、质控品可以与配合使用的体外诊断试剂合并申请注册，也可以单独申请注册。

第一百一十三条 获准注册的体外诊断试剂，是指与该医疗器械注册证及附件限定内容一致且在医疗器械注册证有效期内生产的体外诊断试剂。

第一百一十四条 医疗器械注册证中"主要组成成分"栏内所载明的独立试剂组分，用于原注册产品的，可以单独销售。

第一百一十五条 申请人在申请体外诊断试剂产品注册、变更注册中可以经医疗器械主文档所有者授权，引用经登记的医疗器械主文档。医疗器械主文档由其所有者或代理机构办理登记，相关工作程序另行规定。

第一百一十六条 医疗器械注册证格式由国家药品监督管理局统一制定。

注册证编号的编排方式为：

$\times 1$ 械注 $\times 2 \times \times \times 3 \times 4 \times \times 5 \times \times \times 6$。其中：

$\times 1$ 为注册审批部门所在地的简称：

境内第三类体外诊断试剂、进口第二类、第三类体外诊断试剂为"国"字；

境内第二类体外诊断试剂为注册审批部门所在地省、自治区、直辖市简称；

$\times 2$ 为注册形式：

"准"字适用于境内体外诊断试剂；

"进"字适用于进口体外诊断试剂；

"许"字适用于香港、澳门、台湾地区的体外诊断试剂；

$\times \times \times 3$ 为首次注册年份；

$\times 4$ 为产品管理类别；

$\times \times 5$ 为产品分类编码；

$\times \times \times 6$ 为首次注册流水号。

延续注册的，$\times \times \times 3$ 和 $\times \times \times 6$ 数字不变。产品管理类别调整的，应当重新编号。

第一百一十七条 第一类医疗器械备案编号的编排方式为：

$\times 1$ 械备 $\times \times \times 2 \times \times \times 3$。

其中：

$\times 1$ 为备案部门所在地的简称：

进口第一类体外诊断试剂为"国"字；

境内第一类体外诊断试剂为备案部门所在地省、自治区、直辖市简称加所在地设区的市级行政区域的简称（无相应设区的市级行政区域时，仅为省、自治区、直辖市的简称）；

×××2为备案年份；

×××3为备案流水号。

第一百一十八条 药品监督管理部门制作的医疗器械注册证、变更注册文件电子文件与纸质文件具有同等法律效力。

第一百一十九条 根据工作需要，国家药品监督管理局可以依法委托省、自治区、直辖市药品监督管理部门或者技术机构、社会组织承担有关的具体工作。

第一百二十条 省、自治区、直辖市药品监督管理部门可以参照本办法第四章规定制定本行政区域内第二类体外诊断试剂特殊注册程序，并报国家药品监督管理局备案。

第一百二十一条 体外诊断试剂产品注册收费项目、收费标准按照国务院财政、价格主管部门的有关规定执行。

第一百二十二条 体外诊断试剂紧急使用的有关规定，由国家药品监督管理局会同有关部门另行制定。

第一百二十三条 国内尚无同品种产品上市，医疗机构根据本单位的临床需要自行研制，在执业医师指导下在本单位内使用的体外诊断试剂，相关管理规定由国家药品监督管理局会同有关部门另行制定。

第一百二十四条 香港、澳门、台湾地区体外诊断试剂的注册、备案，参照进口体外诊断试剂办理。

第一百二十五条 本办法自2021年10月1日起施行。2014年7月30日原国家食品药品监督管理总局令第5号公布的《体外诊断试剂注册管理办法》同时废止。

Contents

469 Chapter III Registration Templates

555 Attachment Summary of Medical Device System Documents

Chapter I Introduction

As a tool for the prevention, diagnosis, and treatment of diseases, medical devices are commodities that require special management. To enable the public to obtain safe and effective medical devices, China implements a market access system for medical devices. Before marketing a medical device in China, the applicant/registration applicant/filing applicant shall apply for approval of registration or filing from the relevant regulatory authorities. For the developers and manufacturers of medical devices, understanding and following the requirements and procedures for the preparation of application dossiers is the only way to market their products legally in China.

1. Overview of Administrative Licensing of Medical Devices

The Center for Medical Device Evaluation of the National Medical Products Administration (hereinafter referred to as CMDE), as a bureau–level public institution directly under the National Medical Products Administration (hereinafter referred to as NMPA), mainly conducts the technical evaluation for the registration application of domestic Class Ⅲ medical devices and imported Class Ⅱ and Class Ⅲ medical devices, and undertakes a total of 30 administrative licensing matters, such as filing of imported Class Ⅰ medical devices, please refer to Table 1 for details. To provide the developers and manufacturers of medical devices with accurate and timely information on relevant provisions for medical device filing or registration application, this book, starting from the preparation of registration dossiers, illustrates in detail all the administrative licensing–related matters handled by CMDE.

Table 1 Items Responsible by CMDE

Item	Sub-item	Charging (10,000 CNY)
Initial registration of domestic medical devices	1. Registration application of domestic Class Ⅲ medical devices	15.36
	2. Registration application of domestic Class Ⅲ IVD reagents	
Change application of domestic medical devices	3. Filing of the change of domestic Class Ⅲ medical devices	Free of charge
	4. Change application of registration of domestic Class Ⅲ medical devices	5.04
	5. Filing of the change of domestic Class Ⅲ IVD reagents	Free of charge
	6. Change registration of domestic Class Ⅲ IVD reagents	5.04
Review of renewal registration of domestic Class Ⅲ medical devices	7. Application for renewal registration of domestic Class Ⅲ medical devices	4.08
	8. Application for renewal registration of domestic Class Ⅲ IVD reagents	
Initial registration of imported medical devices	9. Registration application of imported medical devices	Class Ⅲ : 30.88 Class Ⅱ : 21.09
	10. Registration application of imported IVD reagents	
Change application of imported medical devices	11. Filing of the change registration of imported medical devices	Free of charge
	12. Change application of registration of imported medical devices	Class Ⅲ : 5.04 Class Ⅱ : 4.20
	13. Filing of the change of imported IVD reagents	Free of charge
	14. Change application of registration of imported IVD reagents	Class Ⅲ : 5.04 Class Ⅱ : 4.20

Continued

Item	Sub-item	Charging (10,000 CNY)
Review of renewal registration of imported medical devices	15. Application for renewal registration of imported medical devices	4.08
	16. Application for renewal registration of imported IVD reagents	
Review of clinical trial	17. Application for the review and approval of clinical trial of Class Ⅲ high−risk medical devices	4.32
Filing of Class Ⅰ devices	18. Filing of imported Class Ⅰ medical devices	Free of charge
	19. Filing of the change of imported Class Ⅰ medical devices	
	20. Cancellation of the filing of imported Class Ⅰ medical devices	
Other items	21. Change notification of IFU of medical device	
	22. Application for the post−register of medical device registration certificate/change documents	
	23. Application for the post−register of IVD reagent registration certificate/change documents	
	24. Application for the correction of medical device registration certificate/change documents	
	25. Application for the correction of IVD reagent registration certificate/change documents	
	26. Application for the voluntary cancellation of medical device registration certificate/change documents	
	27. Application for the voluntary cancellation of IVD reagent registration certificate/change documents	
	28. Application for the voluntary revocation of medical device registration/change registration/renewal registration/ re−review	
	29. Application for the voluntary revocation of IVD reagent registration/change registration/renewal registration/re−review	Free of charge
	30. Application for the special review of innovative medical devices	

2. Overview of Medical Device Filing and Registration

Medical device registration is a legal process in which the medical products administration conducts a systematic evaluation on the study results of the safety, effectiveness and quality controllability of a medical device under application to determine whether or not the medical device can be marketed. The registration types include initial registration, renewal registration, and change registration. CMDE conducts the acceptance, technical evaluation, and approval of the registration application in accordance with the *Regulations for the Supervision and Administration of Medical Devices* and the rules and regulations formulated by NMPA. The conclusions made by CMDE will be based on the evaluation results of the registration application dossiers submitted by the applicants, including the technical data, risk management data, and clinical evaluation data of the proposed product. In other words, the registration application dossiers are the summary and refining of the proposed product's R&D and production data.

Medical device filing is a process in which the applicant submits the required dossiers to the medical products administration for filing a medical device.

The *Regulations for the Supervision and Administration of Medical Devices* is the supreme law to implement the supervision and administration of medical devices in China. To complement, NMPA has successively issued the *Measures for the Administration of Registration and Filing of Medical Devices*, the *Measures for the Administration of Registration and Filing of In Vitro Diagnostic Reagents*, the *Measures for the Supervision and Administration of Medical Device Production*, the *Measures for the Supervision and Administration of Medical Device Operation*, and other relevant regulations to specify the provisions on the R&D, manufacturing, registration, operation, and use of medical devices. For medical device registration, CMDE has also issued many system documents such as notices, announcements, and administrative provisions to regulate and guide the applicant/registration applicant/filing applicant in the registration application.

To help the applicant/registration applicant/filing applicant to better follow these laws and regulations, this book, starting with the registration aspect and focusing on the processes, specifically illustrates the processes from application to submission.

3. Information Query

For the registration processes and related information, please view the website of CMDE. The "Flow chart of registration" summarizes and classifies these registration-related documents according to their types, and illustrates each and every aspect of the registration-related information in an easy-to-understand way. The flow chart can be divided into three levels: the first level includes the main processes, which briefly and vividly illustrate the steps of registration using a tree diagram and hyperlink to all the relevant sub-processes; the second level includes sub-processes that illustrate the scope of each sub-process, specific procedures, and other relevant information; the third level contains regulation documents that are used as the supplement and refinement of the second level documents. Each sub-process page contains clickable links. The above three levels of documents are crossly accessible as a "tree network" that links the procedures throughout the medical device registration. At present, in addition to the main process, the "Flow chart of registration" also includes more than 20 sub-processes, covering more than

160 current registration–related regulatory documents.

There is also quick access to relevant regulatory and technical documents involved in the registration application and to the evaluation progress in the corresponding section on the website of CMDE.

4. References

Regulations for the Supervision and Administration of Medical Devices (Decree No.739 of the State Council of the People's Republic of China)

Measures for the Administration of Registration and Filing of Medical Devices (Decree No.47 of the State Administration for Market Regulation)

Measures for the Administration of Registration and Filing of In Vitro Diagnostic Reagents (Decree No.48 of the State Administration for Market Regulation)

Announcement on Issuing the Requirements for Registration Application Dossiers of Medical Devices and Formats of Approval Documents (No. 121, 2021)

Announcement on Issuing the Requirements for Registration Application Dossiers of In Vitro Diagnostic Reagents and Formats of Approval Documents (No. 122, 2021)

Chapter II Registration Processes

1. Consultation Services

Technical Review Process

1.Consultation Services

In order to continuously smooth and optimize communication channels with the administrative counterpart/applicant/registration applicant, help the administrative counterpart/applicant/registration applicant accurately understand the technical evaluation requirements of medical devices, improve the quality of registration application dossiers, and increase the technical evaluation service efficiency for the registration of medical devices, CMDE has been continuously optimizing the allocation of communication resources and has set up multiple consultation services.

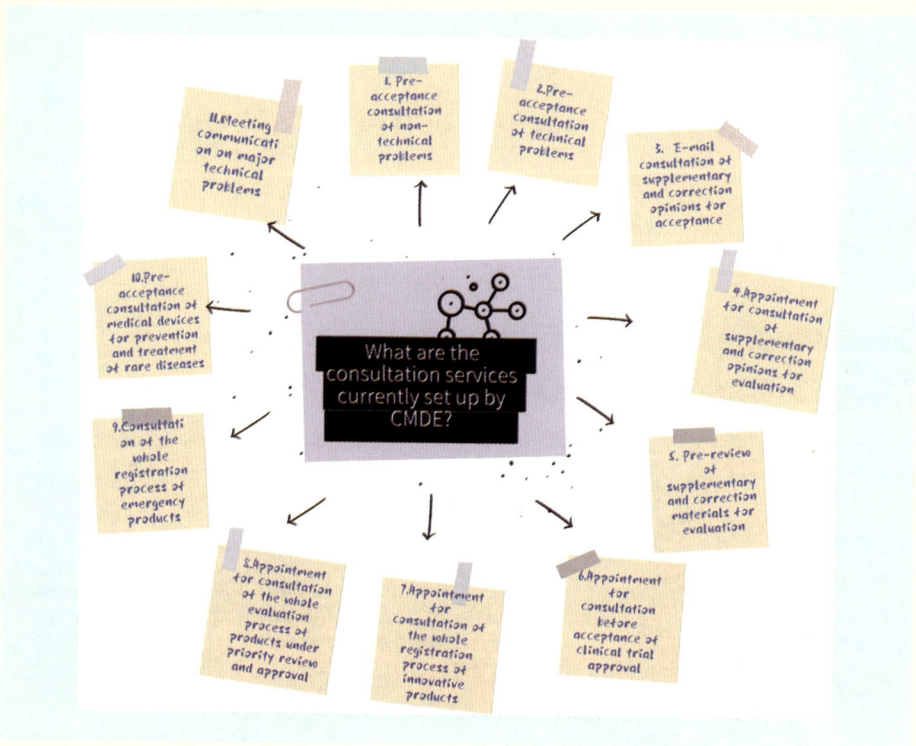

1.1 Consultation of pre-acceptance non-technical problems

Pre-acceptance consultation of non-technical problems is mainly to solve the consultation needs of administrative counterparts for non-technical problems before registration application. Telephone consultations are available all day every Wednesday and Thursday (except for legal holidays). The administrative counterpart who has consultation needs can call the hotline during office hours, and the operator on duty at the reception window will answer the call and give a reply, or he/she can take a number for on-site consultation during on-site reception hours at the reception hall (consultation place: Administrative Reception Service Hall of NMPA).

1.2 Pre-acceptance consultation of technical problems

Pre–acceptance consultation of technical problems is mainly to solve the consultation needs of administrative counterparts for technical problems before registration application. On–site consultation and e–mail consultation are available.

The Yangtze River Delta Center for Medical Device Evaluation and Inspection, the GBA Center for Medical Device Evaluation and Inspection, Hainan Medical Products Administration and other innovation service stations that established after signing strategic cooperation agreements with CMDE, started to accept on–site consultation on November 1, 2022. The on–site consultation is available all day every Thursday (except for legal holidays). The specific consultation time range and consultation time arrangement for each administrative counterpart shall be subject to the actual notice issued by each institution.

What are the methods of the pre–acceptance consultation of technical problems of CMDE?

① **Make a reservation for on-site consultation**

On–site consultations of CMDE are available from 13:30 to 16:30 every Friday afternoon (except for legal holidays) (consultation place: Administrative Acceptance Service Hall of NMPA).

② **E-mail consultation**

Scope of application: Institutions that fail to or do not make a reservation for on-site consultation beyond the Yangtze River Delta Center for Medical Device Evaluation and Inspection, the GBA Center for Medical Device Evaluation and Inspection, Hainan Medical Products Administration and other innovation service stations that established after signing strategic cooperation agreements with CMDE.

E-mail consultation hours: From 8:30 every Monday to 16:30 every Wednesday

Appointment for On-site Consultation of CMDE ("The operation is very simple as a matter of fact")

When you make a reservation via the Online Appointment Acceptance System of NMPA at the Administrative Acceptance Service Hall, you can select to log in to the service portal website of NMPA for government affairs and enter the Online Service Hall, or you can also log in to the website of the Center for Administrative Services and Complaints & Reports and click on the function bar "Online Appointment Acceptance" on the right to make a reservation.

When you make a reservation, you should fill in and upload the "Registration Form for Consultation of Technical Problems before Acceptance of Medical Device Registration", "Information Registration Form for Consultation of Technical Problems before Acceptance of Medical Device Registration", and a scanned copy of Business License or Legal Person Certificate.

You are allowed to fill in 5 consultation questions at most, which are limited to the functional scope of the department on duty at the corresponding reservation port on the very day of consultation.

What are the methods of the pre-acceptance consultation of technical problems by each participating institution of CMDE?

1 Make a reservation for on-site consultation

A reservation can be made for on-site consultation from 8:30 every Monday to 16:30 every Wednesday via e-mail.

2 E-mail consultation

Scope of application: Domestic class III medical device developers and manufacturers and enterprise legal personsl including wholly-owned companies and joint ventures) established by imported medical device registration applications in China within the Yangtze River Delta Center for Medical Device Evaluation and Inspection, the GBA Center for Medical Device Evaluation and Inspection, Hainan Medical Products Administration and other innovation service stations that established after signing strategic cooperation agreements with CMDE.

E-mail consultation hours: From 8:30 every Monday to 16:30 every Wednesday

1.3 E-mail consultation of supplementary and correction opinions for acceptance

The e-mail consultation of supplementary and correction opinions for acceptance is mainly to solve the consultation needs of applicants/ registration applicants on the issues involved in the notice of supplementary and correction materials for acceptance after the electronic Regulated Product Submission system (hereinafter referred to as the eRPS system) for medical devices is launched. The consultation is available at any time from the date when the applicant/registration applicant receives the notice of supplementary and correction materials for acceptance to the date when the next registration application is submitted. The applicant/registration applicant can send consultation questions to the e-mail address stated in the notice of supplementary and correction materials for acceptance, and the reviewer who receives the consultation e-mail will give a reply on working days, as shown in "10. Acceptance."

> ## What is the eRPS system?
>
> On May 31, 2019, NMPA issued the **Announcement on Implementing Electronic Regulated Product Submission (eRPS) for Medical Devices.** In order to realize the electronic application for medical device registration, the electronic Regulated Product Submission (eRPS) system (hereinafter referred to as the eRPS system) was officially implemented on June 24, 2019.

1.4 Appointment for consultation of supplementary and correction opinions for evaluation

The reservation for a consultation of supplementary and correction opinions for evaluation is mainly to solve the consultation needs of applicants/registration applicants for the problems listed in the notice of supplementary and correction materials during the registration and evaluation of medical devices. Consultation hours: 9:00–11:00 a.m. and 13:30–16:30 p.m. on every Thursday (except for legal holidays) (consultation place: Business Hall, Floor

1, CMDE). At most three reservations for on-site consultation can be made with each eligible acceptance number. The applicant/registration applicant can make a reservation via the eRPS system after receiving the notice of supplementary and correction materials.

1.5 Pre-review of supplementary and correction materials for evaluation

The pre-review of supplementary and correction materials for evaluation is mainly to facilitate the applicant/registration applicant to confirm that the prepared supplementary materials meet the requirements of technical evaluation and improve the quality of supplementary and correction materials and the efficiency of evaluation. Applicable application types: Product registration and change registration of domestic Class III and imported Class II / III medical devices, and approval for clinical trials of high-risk medical devices. The applicant/registration applicant/agent shall submit a pre-review application two months before the time-limit for supplementary and correction materials expires. Regarding offline business, after the supplementary and correction materials are submitted to the Business Hall of CMDE for pre-review, the pre-review opinions will be sent to the applicant/registration applicant/agent via e-mail within 20 working days. Regarding online business, the eRPS system will give a reply within 20 working days after the application is submitted. In principle, the pre-review service will only be provided once for each eligible registration application matter, as shown in "13.3 Consultation of Supplementary and Correction Materials."

1.6 Appointment for consultation before acceptance of clinical trial approval

The reservation for a consultation before the acceptance of clinical trial approval is mainly to solve the problems of low-quality application dossiers for medical device clinical trials to be approved and more opinions on supplementary and correction materials and to further optimize procedures for the approval of medical device clinical trials. For matters regarding clinical trial approval, a reservation can be made through this communication pathway for pre-acceptance consultation.

1.7 Appointment for consultation of the whole registration process of innovative products

The reservation for a consultation of the registration of innovative products is mainly to solve the applicant's consultation needs on technical issues before the acceptance and during the technical evaluation of innovative medical devices. General technical problems can be consulted via the consultation platform, hotline, or e-mail, while major technical problems should be consulted via meetings. The applicant who applies for a communication meeting can log in to the eRPS system to submit an application for a consultation reservation, and the corresponding department will designate a special person to handle it.

1.8 Appointment for consultation of the whole evaluation process of products under priority review and approval

The reservation for a consultation of the evaluation of products under priority review and approval is mainly to solve the consultation needs of applicants who are at the technical evaluation stage of domestic Class III and imported Class II / III medical devices and agree with the approval according to the *Priority Review and Approval Procedure for Medical Device*. General technical problems can be consulted via the consultation platform, hotline, or e-mail, while major technical problems should be consulted via meetings. The applicant can log in to the eRPS system to submit an application for a consultation reservation, and the corresponding department will designate a special person to handle it.

1.9 Consultation of the whole registration process of emergency products

The consultation of the registration of emergency products is mainly to solve the consultation needs of administrative counterparts/applicants on technical issues before the acceptance of medical devices urgently needed for public health emergencies and during their technical evaluation. The applicant can communicate with relevant departments of CMDE at any time after the product is assessed and verified by NMPA as a medical device for emergency review and approval.

1.10 Pre-acceptance consultation of medical devices for prevention and treatment of rare diseases

The pre-acceptance consultation of medical devices for the prevention and treatment of rare diseases is mainly to confirm the applicability of medical devices for the prevention and treatment of rare diseases that the administrative counterpart intends to apply to the guidelines and to confirm the clinical evaluation pathway that should be adopted. At the application of the administrative counterpart, communication will be conducted on the major technical problems, major safety problems, clinical trial protocols, etc. of the registration application projects applicable to the guidelines. For eligible projects, the administrative counterpart can apply for a consultation with CMDE before applying for a registration, and the corresponding departments will designate a special person to handle it.

1.11 Meeting communication on major technical problems

The meeting communication on major technical problems means that CMDE can initiate an application for a communication meeting on major technical problems of medical devices before the acceptance of the registration application or at the technical evaluation stage. This will be conducive to improving the quality of registration application dossiers, increasing the technical evaluation efficiency, and accelerating the marketing of medical devices.

Glossary

1. Administrative counterpart: The other party corresponding to the administrative subject in the legal relationship of administrative management.

2. Applicant: An enterprise or research institution that applies for the registration of medical devices.

3. Medical device registration applicant and filing applicant refer to the enterprises or research institutions that have obtained the medical device registration certificate or applied for filing of medical devices.

4. Medical device registration applicant: An enterprise or research institution that applies for the registration of medical devices.

2. Product Naming and Registration Unit Division

2.1 Product Naming

2.1.1 Overview

Due to the wide variety of medical device products and great differences in composition and structure, accurate and standardized naming of products is conducive to the effective identification of medical device products in each process such as development, production, distribution and use. In the meantime, standardized naming of the generic name of the medical device also lays the essential groundwork for medical device supervision.

In order to focus on solving the problems of relatively confused medical device names that are misleading with exaggerated and absolute wording, on December 16, 2019, NMPA issued the *Guidelines for the Nomenclature of Generic Names of Medical Devices*, which further standardizes the generic names of medical devices marketed and used in China.

2.1.2 Naming Rules for Generic Names

(1) Nomenclature

Generic names shall be legal, scientific, clear and authentic. They shall be named in Chinese, and in conformity with the norms of the standard spoken and written Chinese language.

(2) Content Requirements and Composition and Structure

The same variety of medical devices with the same or similar intended purposes and common technologies shall use the same generic names. The generic name consists of a core word and generally not more than three feature words (such as drug-eluting coronary stent, and disposable optical laryngeal endoscope). The feature words that have been widely accepted or understood can be defaulted according to the relevant terminological standards, so as to simplify the generic name of the product (such as ophthalmic scalpel).

(3) Prohibited Content in Generic Name

In addition to meeting the corresponding requirements specified in the *Naming Rules for the Generic Names of Medical Devices,* the generic name shall not contain 9 prohibited content, such as "model/specification", "figures, symbols and other marks", "person name, enterprise name, registered trademark or other similar names", "optimal, unique, accurate, rapid-acting and other absolute and exclusive words", "expressions indicating effective rate and cure rate".

In addition, the generic name may not be registered as a trademark.

2.1.3 Naming Example of Generic Name

Taking the implantable neural stimulator products in the field of active implantable devices as an example, the nomenclature can be formed by reference to the following formats and contents:

Table 2 Nomenclature of Implantable Neural Stimulator

No.	Product Category	Term Type	Term	Term Description
1	Implantable Neural Stimulator	Core Word	Neural Stimulator	Used to apply electric pulse at special site of brain and nervous system to treat parkinsonism, control epilepsy, chronic intractable pain of trunk and/or limb or intestinal tract control as well as such control of neuroregulatory disorders as urination and myodystony.
		Feature Word 1–Application Methods	Implantable	Implanted in the human body.
1	Implantable Neural Stimulator	Feature Word 2–Technical Features	Non–rechargeable (defaulted)	The battery is non–rechargeable.
			Rechargeable	The battery can be charged wirelessly in vitro.
		Feature Word 3–Application Sites	Deep Brain	The stimulation output acts on the deep part of the brain.
			Spinal	The stimulation output acts on the spinal cord.
			Sacral	The stimulation output acts on the sacral nerve.
			Vagus	The stimulation output acts on the vagus.

Select typical products, select appropriate terms under the feature words and core words of the nomenclature, and form the generic name.

What are the naming rules for generic names?

The generic names are composed of one core word and no more than three feature words generally.

E.g. : Implantable (feature word I) + non-rechargeable (feature word 2, defaulted) + deep brain (feature word 3) + neural stimulator (core word) → implantable deep brain neural stimulator.

Implantable (feature word I) + rechargeable (feature word 2) + spinal (feature word 3) + neural stimulator (core word) → implantable rechargeable spinal neural stimulator.

2.2 Registration/Filing Unit Division

2.2.1 Overview

The registration unit of the medical device refers to the registration unit composed of medical device products with the same or similar technical principles, structure and composition, performance indicators and scope of application. The applicant shall select the products that can represent the safety and effectiveness of other products in the same registration unit for registration type testing, clinical evaluation and other safety and effectiveness assessments. After the technical review and approval of medical devices, a registration certificate will be obtained for the products in the same registration unit.

2.2.2 Division Principles

Medical device registration/filing unit shall, in principle, be classified on the basis of product technical principles, structure and composition, performance indicators and scope of application.

Registration unit or filing unit for IVD reagents shall be single reagent or single kit, and each registration unit or filing unit may include different packaging specifications. Calibrators and quality controls may apply for registration separately or in conjunction with matching IVD reagents in conjunct use.

What is the principle for the division of registration/filing units?

In principle, medical device products shall be divided according to the technical principle, structure and composition, performance indicators and scope of application of the product.

In principle, the IVD reagents shall be single reagent or single kit, and each registration unit or filing unit may include different packaging specifications. Calibrators and quality controls may apply for registration separately or in conjunction with matching IVD reagents in conjunct use.

Refer to the *Guidelines for the Division of Registration Units of Medical Devices* (No.187, 2017).

2.3 Case Interpretation

(1) Whether the registration of common absorbable suture and barbed absorbable suture made of the same material can be applied for in the same registration unit?

Interpretation: Since there are differences in product design, mechanisms for wound closure, performance indicators, etc., between common absorbable sutures and barbed absorbable sutures, it is necessary to carry out product performance study, study on the change of breaking force in animals over time, clinical evaluation, etc. respectively. It is recommended to divide them into different registration units for registration application.

(2) Whether the bare stent and drug–eluting stent can be divided into the same registration unit?

Interpretation: No. The coating is an important component of the drug–eluting stent, which has a significant impact on the safety and effectiveness of the product. According to the principles for the division of registration units of passive medical devices specified in the *Guidelines for the Division of Registration Units of Medical Devices*, medical devices containing drugs (active substances) and those without drugs (active substances) should be divided into different registration units.

(3) How to divide the registration units of the posterior spinal elastic fusion fixation system?

Interpretation: The posterior spinal elastic fusion fixation system is used for posterior spinal fusion fixation, which is different from the posterior spinal rigid internal fixation system used for fusion. Therefore, they shall be divided into different registration units. Products with different structural designs and mechanical properties shall be divided into different registration units. Products with different materials that play a major functional role shall be divided into different registration units. If the materials of components of the product are different, but the product is used as a whole or in combination, which can be divided into the same registration unit for application.

2.4 References

Naming Rules for the Generic Names of Medical Devices (CFDA No.19)

CFDA Announcement on the Issuance of the Guideline for the Division of Registration Units of Medical Devices (No. 187, 2017)

NMPA Announcement on the Issuance of the Guidance for the Nomenclature of the Generic Names of Medical Devices (No.99, 2019)

3. Classification

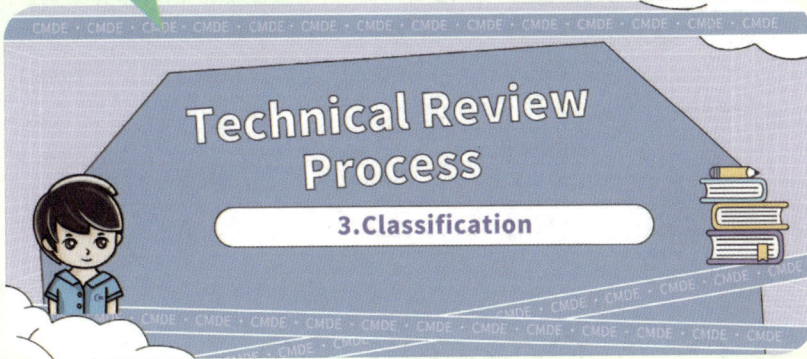

3.1 Overview

Medical devices are classified in a variety of ways, for example, they can be divided into passive and active medical devices according to different structural features; body–contact and non–body–contact medical devices according to the contact way with human body. Internationally, for ease of supervision, however, the regulatory authorities in some major countries (regions) generally perform classification according to the risk level of medical devices (as shown in Table 3). The risk degree of a medical device shall be determined comprehensively according to the intended purpose, structural characteristics, pattern of use, status of use as well as whether the device is body contacting. The medical device classification stated herein mainly refers to the management category classification.

Table 3 Summary for Classification of Medical Devices in Major Countries (Regions)

Security Risk \ Region	USA	EU	Japan	China
Low Risk ↓ High Risk	Class I	Class I	Class I	Class I
	Class II	Class II a	Class II	Class II
		Class II b	Class III	
	Class III	Class III	Class IV	Class III

What is the medical device classification?

In China, medical devices are subject to classification management according to the degree of risk based on such factors as intended purpose, structural characteristics and usage.

Class I medical devices are those with lower risks for which safety and effectiveness can be guaranteed through routine administration.

Class II medical devices are of moderate risks and require strict control and administration to ensure their safety and effectiveness.

Class III medical devices are those with higher risks for which special measures and strict control are required to guaantee their safety and effectiveness.

3.2 Classification Rules

In addition to classification decision per the decision table of medical devices classification, the medical devices classification shall follow the following rules:

(1) If the same medical device falls in two or more classifications, from which the highest risk level shall be adopted; for the kit composed of multiple medical devices, of which classification shall be consistent with the medical devices of the highest risk level.

(2) For the medical devices served as accessories, of which classification shall give overall considerations on the effect of the accessory on the safety and efficacy of the matched main medical device; if that accessory exerts important impact on the matched main medical device, the level of classification of the accessory shall not be lower than that of the compatible medical device.

(3) For those that monitor or affect the main functions of another medical device, their classification shall be consistent with that of the medical device being monitored or affected.

(4) The drug–device combined products oriented in the action of medical devices are subject to supervision of Class III medical devices.

(5) The medical devices that can be absorbed by the human body are subject to the management of Class III medical devices.

(6) The active devices coming into contact with human body that can significantly affect the efficacy are subject to the management of Class III medical devices.

(7) The medical dressings, if any following situations, are subject to the management of Class III medical devices, including: intended to prevent tissue or organ adhesion; as artificial skin in contact with the deep dermis or the wound surface of the tissue below it; for chronic wound surface, or completely or partially absorbed by human body.

(8) For the medical devices supplied sterile, of which classification shall not be lower than Class II .

(9) For the orthopedic instruments that actively exert sustained force to human body and that can dynamically adjust the permanent position of an amine body in mode of action such as traction, distraction, torsion, gripping and bending (excluding the medical devices only for fixation and supporting,

and those used for temporary correction in orthopaedic surgery or those for limb correction either after an orthopaedic surgery or in other treatments), of which classification shall be no less than Class Ⅱ.

(10) For the medical devices with measuring test function, of which classification shall be no less than Class Ⅱ.

(11) If the medical devices are intended to determine the treatment of certain disease, of which classification shall be not less than Class Ⅱ.

(12) The passive, reusable surgical devices that are intended for surgical operations such as completing clamping, cutting tissues or removing calculus under an endoscope are subject to the management of Class Ⅱ medical devices.

3.3 Classification Catalogue

The classification of medical devices (including in vitro diagnostic reagents) in China applies the classification catalog system under the guidance of classification rules. The classification rules and classification catalog coexist, with the latter taking precedence.

3.3.1 Classification Catalogue for Medical Devices

The *Classification Catalogue for Medical Devices* was firstly issued by the medical products administration under the State Council in 2002. Since then, with the development of the medical device industry, regulatory authorities have also continued to adjust and improve it. For medical devices other than IVD reagents, the current *Classification Catalogue for Medical Devices* (hereinafter referred to as the *Classification Catalogue*) is continuously adjusted and revised according to the *Rules for the Classification of Medical Devices* and the *Working Procedures for Dynamic Adjustment of Classification Catalogue for Medical Devices* based on the version of *Classification Catalogue* issued in 2017.

The *Classification Catalogue*, according to the technology specialty and clinical application characteristics, is divided into 22 sub-catalogs, each of which consists of Class I product category, Class II product category, product description, intended use, product name example and management classification. The 22 sub-catalogs are as follows:

(1) Four sub-catalogs are set for surgical devices: "01 Active Surgical Devices" and "02 Passive Surgical Devices" for general surgical devices; "03 Nerve and Vascular Surgical Devices" is separately set due to the special requirements in the Rules for Classification for the devices in immediate contact with nerves and vessels; "04 Orthopedic Surgical Devices" was separately set for the devices related to orthopedic surgery due to great quantity and wide coverage as well as great diversity.

(2) Eight sub-catalogs are set for active devices: "05 Radiation Therapy Device", "06 Medical Imaging Device", "07 Medical Examination and Monitoring Device", "08 Respiratory, Anesthesia and First Aid Device", "09 Physical Therapy Device", "10 Blood Transfusion, Dialysis and Extracorporeal Circulation Devices", "11 Medical Device Disinfection and Sterilization Device" and "12 Active Implant Devices".

(3) Three sub-catalogs are set for passive devices: "13 Passive Implant Devices", "14 Infusion, Nursing and Protective Device" and "15 Patient Carrying Devices".

(4) Three sub-catalogs are set according to the clinical settings: "16 Ophthalmic Devices", "17 Stomatological Devices" and "18 Obstetrics and Gynecology, Assisted Reproductive and Contraceptive Devices".

(5) "19 Medical Rehabilitation Device" and "20 TCM Device", both

of which require the particular administrative provisions specified by the *Regulations for the Supervision and Administration of Medical Devices*.

(6) "21 Medical Software", which covers all the independent medical software products.

(7) "22 Clinical Testing Devices" is the last sub–catalog, offering a space for further revision of IVD reagents.

3.3.2 Classification of IVD Reagents

The category of IVD reagent products is, in the main, determined according to the *6840 Classification Sub-catalogue of IVD Reagents*. The *6840 Classification Sub-catalogue of IVD Reagents* is compiled according to the characteristics of IVD reagents, and "serial number, product category, product category name, intended use and management category" are set in the catalogue schema. In addition, the National Medical Products Administration have successively issued the CFDA *Announcement on Allergen, Flow Cytometer for Matching, Immunohistochemical and In Situ Hybridization IVD Reagent Product Properties and Category Adjustment, Announcement on Partial Content Adjustment of 6840 In Vitro Diagnostic Reagent Classification Sub-catalogue* (2013 Edition), *Classification Rules for In Vitro Diagnostic Reagents* and other documents for supplement and perfection.

3.4 Classification Inquiry

The applicant can enter the official website of NMPA for search queries, or determine the product category according to the *Rules for the Classification of Medical Devices, Rules for the Classification of In Vitro Diagnostic Reagents, Catalogue of Class* I *Medical Device Products, Classification Catalogue for Medical Devices, 6840 Classification Sub-catalogue of IVD*

Reagents, Summary of Classification Definition Results of Medical Device Products issued by Center for Medical Device Standardization Administration NMPA (hereinafter referred to as the CMDSA), guidelines for classification definition of relevant products and other documents.

3.5 Application for Classification Definition

The applicant may submit an application for classification definition through the classification definition information system of the CMDSA, and determine the management category according to the classification definition procedures.

How to make classification?

You can refer to *Notice of General Office of CFDA on Regulating the Work Related to Classification of Medical Devices* (CFDA No.127, 2017).

1 Search online

Enter NMPA website
——
click medical device title bar——
click Medical Device Search——
click Classification Catalogue for Medical Devices

2 Search documents

Input *Rules for the Classification of Medical Devices* and click search, or download *Classification Catalogue for Medical Devices* and search in it.

3 Classification Definition

Domestic products submit an application to the local provincial administration, and the imported product submits an application to Standardization Administration (directly log on to the Standardization Administration website to search and submit)

3.6 References

Rules for the Classification of Medical Devices (CFDA Decree No.15)

CFDA Notice on Releasing of Classification Sub-catalogue of IVD Reagents (CFDA No. 242, 2013)

CFDA Announcement on Classification Catalogue for Medical Devices (No.104, 2017)

Notice of General Office of CFDA on Regulating the Work Related to Classification of Medical Devices (CFDA No.127, 2017)

CFDA Announcement on Allergen, Flow Cytometer for Matching, Immunohistochemical and In Situ Hybridization IVD Reagent Product Properties and Category Adjustment (No.226, 2017)

NMPA Announcement on Partial Content Adjustment of 6840 In Vitro Diagnostic Reagent Classification Sub-catalogue (2013 Edition) (No.112, 2020)

NMPA Announcement on the Working Procedures for Dynamic Adjustment of the Classification Catalogue for Medical Devices (No.60, 2021)

NMPA Announcement on Issuing the Classification Rules for In Vitro Diagnostic Reagents (No.129, 2021)

NMPA Announcement on Issuing the Catalogue of Class I Medical Devices (No.158, 2021)

4. Product Test

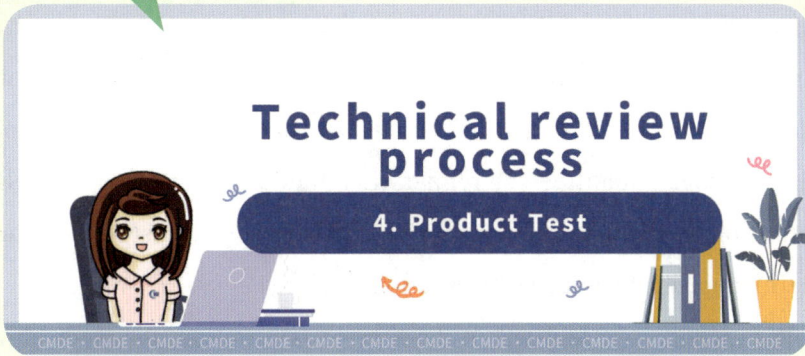

4.1 Overview

Medical device test refers to the process in which the medical device, in the stages such as manufacturing, experiment, scientific research, usage and maintenance, is qualitatively tested or quantitatively measured real–time or non–real–time for purpose of timely access to the information on object under test and control with a report be issued.

4.2 Medical Device Test

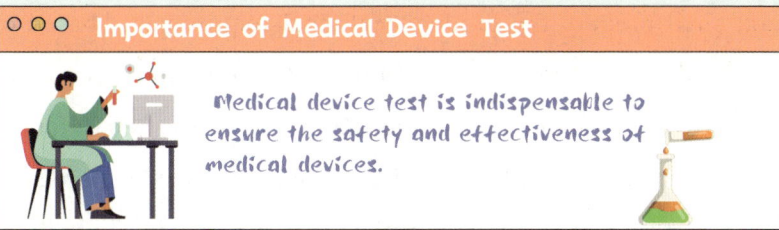

According to the regulations, medical device registration applicants shall conduct the test in accordance with the product technical requirements and submit the test report. Clinical trials can be carried out or registration can be applied only after the test result is qualified. The tested products shall be able to represent the safety and effectiveness of the products under the application for registration, and their production shall meet the relevant requirements of the *Good Manufacturing Practice for Medical Devices*. The test report of medical device submitted for registration application may be the self–test report of the medical device registration applicant, or the test report issued by a qualified medical device test institution entrusted.

For carrying out self–test at the time of registration, the medical device registration applicant shall have self–test capacity, include self–test in the medical device quality management system, be equipped with test equipment and facilities that meet the product test requirements, have corresponding quality test departments or full–time test personnel, conduct the test with strict process control to ensure that the test results are authentic, accurate, complete and traceable, and bear principal responsibilities for the self–test report.

4.3 Medical Device Test

4.3.1 Test Basis

In the process of product development, the medical device registration applicant shall prepare the product technical requirements based on the product technical characteristics, and formulate the performance indicators that can be used to objectively judge the effectiveness and safety of the product. The performance indicators of the product technical requirements can refer to the relevant national or industrial standards, combining with the design characteristics, intended use and quality control level of the product concerned, which shall not be lower than the applicable mandatory national or industrial standards. Product technical requirements shall be prepared according to the *Guidelines for the Preparation of Product Technical Requirements of Medical Devices* issued by the NMPA. Medical device registration applicants may pay attention to the dynamic of NMPA at any time and formulate the product technical requirements by reference to the applicable guidelines for the proposed product.

○ ○ ○ **What is the test basis for the product?**

Medical device registration applicants shall conduct the test according to the product technical requirements of the product to be applied for registration. The formulation of test methods shall be compatible with the corresponding performance indicators. Priority shall be given to the issued standard test methods or recognized test methods. The test methods shall be verified or validated to ensure the test repeatability and operability.

For in vitro diagnostic reagent products, the test method shall also specify the reference materials/standard materials used, sample preparation method, batch and quantity of reagent used, number of tests, and calculation method.

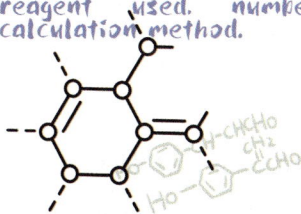

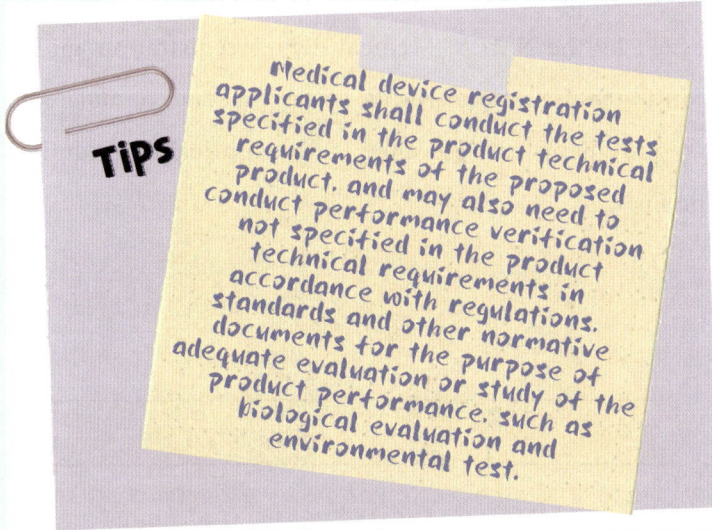

TiPS

Medical device registration applicants shall conduct the tests specified in the product technical requirements of the proposed product, and may also need to conduct performance verification not specified in the product technical requirements in accordance with regulations, standards and other normative documents for the purpose of adequate evaluation or study of the product performance, such as biological evaluation and environmental test.

4.3.2 Test Product

Medical device manufacturers shall complete the production of the test product. The quantity of the test product shall comply with the requirements of regulations as well as the requirements for the test batch of the product. For example, as for Class Ⅲ IVD reagents, three different production batches of the product shall be provided according to Article 33 of the *Measures for the Administration of Registration and Filing of In Vitro Diagnostic Reagents*.

For the application for the entrusted test of medical devices, the quantity of the test product shall meet the test needs. It is recommended that the medical device registration applicant consult the entrusted test institution before the product is submitted for testing, so as to avoid the insufficient quantity of the test product.

What matters shall be paid attention to for typical test products in the same registration unit?

The medical device registration applicant shall conduct the product test according to the registration unit. When a registration unit contains products with multiple models and specifications, in principle, the product technical requirements shall include the performance indicators and requirements of all models and specifications, and the products tested in the same registration unit shall be able to represent the safety and effectiveness of other products in this registration unit. Moreover, test results shall cover the models and specifications or configurations of all the products in this registration unit. Structure and composition, performance indicators, and intended use shall be considered for typical test products. Generally, the model, specification or configuration of the product with the most complete function, the most complex structure and the highest risk shall be selected, and the typical test description shall be provided.

4.3.3 Test Report

The test report of medical device submitted for registration application may be the self-test report of the medical device registration applicant, or the test report issued by a qualified medical device test institution entrusted.

If a medical device registration applicant submits the self-test report but does not have the test capability for terms in product technical requirements in partial, the relevant items are allowed to be entrusted to a qualified medical device test institution for test. Qualified medical device test institutions shall comply with relevant provisions in Article 75 of the *Regulations for the Supervision and Administration of Medical Devices*.

4.4 Case Interpretation

(1) What matters shall be paid attention to for the application mode and supporting consumables during the performance inspection of active products?

Interpretation: In terms of the application mode, if the proposed product has multiple application modes, it is recommended to conduct the test item by item according to the typical application mode, and provide the basis for selecting the typical application mode. For example, whether the application mode of the maximum speed/maximum flow is selected as a typical mode for test; whether all typical application models have been tested; whether there is a certain test coverage among typical application modes, and different items are selected for test.

If the proposed product can be adapted to the consumables of different models/specifications (e.g., single–use centrifugal pump head, extracorporeal circulation pipes, etc.), it is necessary to consider all combinations of typical supporting consumables of the proposed product for the product test and analyze whether tests are required for all of them. The medical device registration applicant shall state the typicality of the supporting consumables used for test and whether some combinations have only been tested for different items.

(2) Please give examples of matters that shall be paid attention to during the EMC test of active products.

Interpretation: The medical device registration applicant shall provide the basis for selecting the product operation mode in EMC test, and it is recommended to consider the product alarm function. In the immunity test, all product functions related to basic performance shall consider the test mode which may generate the most adverse impact on patients. In radiation emission tests, the product is advised to be operated under the maximum disturbance state.

(3) What are the matters that shall be paid attention to for the instructions on the testing of active products?

Interpretation: The medical device registration applicant may provide the description on the test condition and the list of test reports to describe the product model and specification/configuration and test type corresponding to the test report (such as product performance test, production compliance test, and EMC test).

4.5 References

NMPA Announcement on Issuing the Regulations on the Administration of Registration Self-testing of Medical Devices (No.126, 2021)

NMPA Announcement on Issuing the Guidelines for the Preparation of Product Technical Requirements of Medical Devices (No.8, 2022)

5. Clinical Evaluation

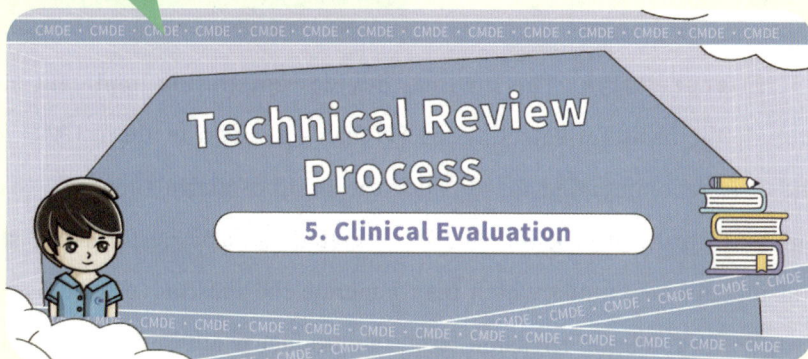

Technical Review Process
5. Clinical Evaluation

5.1 Overview

Clinical evaluation of medical device refers to an activity that analyzes and evaluates the clinical data by using scientific and reasonable methods to confirm the safety and effectiveness of the medical device within its scope of application. The applicant is feasible to prove the safety and effectiveness of the medical device by carrying out the clinical trial, or by performing analysis and evaluation on the clinical literature data and/or clinical data of predicate medical devices according to the product characteristics, clinical risks and the existing clinical data. The registration of Class II and Class III medical devices can refer to the *Technical Guidelines for Clinical Evaluation of Medical Devices*, *Technical Guidelines for Equivalence Demonstration of Medical Devices*, *Technical Guidelines for Deciding Whether to Carry out Clinical Trials of Medical Devices*, *Technical Guidelines for Clinical Evaluation Report of Registration Application of Medical Devices* and other relevant guidelines for the specific contents of clinical evaluation data. The safety, clinical performance and/or effectiveness data collected throughout the clinical evaluation shall be included in analysis, so as to get a comprehensive and objective clinical evaluation.

Stage of Clinical Evaluation

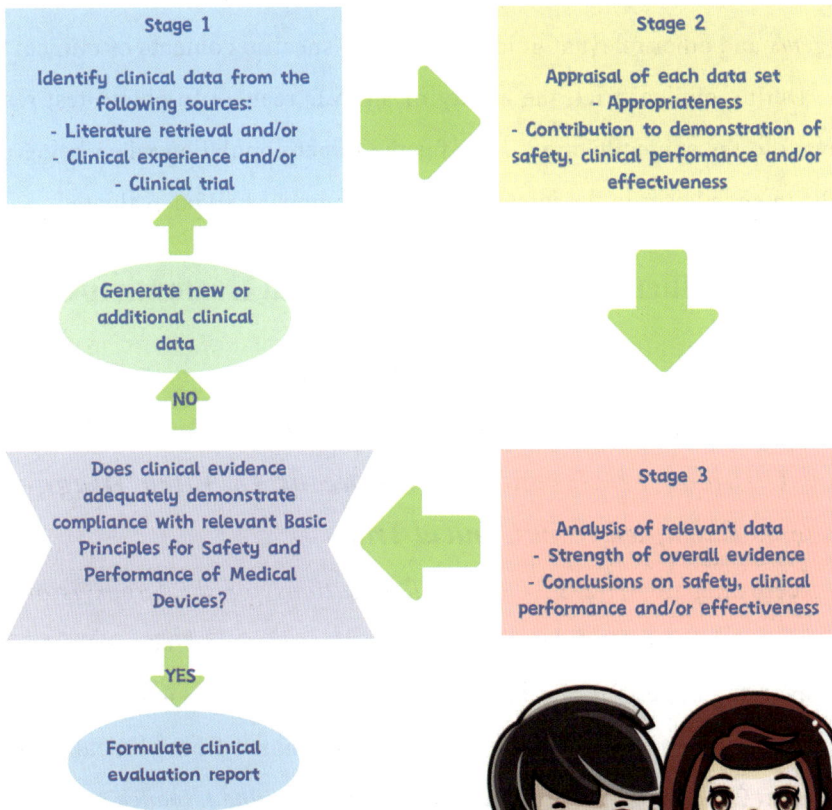

Stage 1

Identify clinical data from the following sources:
- Literature retrieval and/or
- Clinical experience and/or
- Clinical trial

Stage 2

Appraisal of each data set
- Appropriateness
- Contribution to demonstration of safety, clinical performance and/or effectiveness

Generate new or additional clinical data

NO

Does clinical evidence adequately demonstrate compliance with relevant Basic Principles for Safety and Performance of Medical Devices?

Stage 3

Analysis of relevant data
- Strength of overall evidence
- Conclusions on safety, clinical performance and/or effectiveness

YES

Formulate clinical evaluation report

IVD reagent clinical trial refers to systematic study of clinical performance of IVD reagents in corresponding clinical environment. The purpose of clinical trial is to prove that the IVD reagent can satisfy its intended use and to define target population and indications of the product. The result of clinical trial provides effective scientific evidence for the confirmation of safety and effectiveness of IVD reagents and risk–benefit analysis. The registration of Class II and Class III in vitro diagnostic reagents can refer to the *Technical Guidelines for Clinical Trials of In Vitro Diagnostic Reagents* and other relevant guidelines for the specific contents of clinical trial data. During clinical trial, the ability of an IVD reagent to obtain test results relevant to the subject's target state for the target population when being used by the intended user in the intended use environment will be evaluated.

5.2 Product Exempted from Clinical Evaluation/Clinical Trials

5.2.1 Introduction to *Catalogue of Medical Devices Exempted from Clinical Trials* and *Catalogue of In Vitro Diagnostic Reagents Exempted from Clinical Trials*

According to Article 24 of the *Regulations for the Supervision and Administration of Medical Devices* stipulating that "The NMPA shall formulate guidelines for clinical evaluation of medical devices.", the former CFDA issued the catalogue of three batches exempted from clinical trials. In September 2018, NMPA issued the *Announcement on the Issuance of the Newly Revised Catalogue of Medical Devices Exempted from Clinical Trials*, which comprehensively revised and summarized the previously published *Catalogue of Medical Devices Exempted from Clinical Trials* and *Catalogue of In Vitro Diagnostic Reagents Exempted from Clinical Trials*. Consequently, the revised and summarized *Catalogue of Medical Devices Exempted from Clinical Trials* and *Catalogue of In Vitro Diagnostic Reagents Exempted from Clinical Trials* were issued respectively. On this basis, in December 2019, the NMPA issued the *Announcement on the Issuance of the Catalogue of Newly Added and Revised Medical Devices Exempted from Clinical Trials*, and announced the *Catalogue of the First Batch of Newly Added and Revised Medical Devices (and IVD Reagents) Exempted from Clinical Trials*. In September 2021, according to the *Measures for the Administration of Registration and Filing of Medical Devices* and *Measures for the Administration of Registration and Filing of In Vitro Diagnostic Reagents*, NMPA organized to formulate the *Catalogue of Medical Devices Exempted from Clinical Evaluation* (2021 Edition) and the *Catalogue of In Vitro Diagnostic Reagents Exempted from Clinical Trials* (2021 Edition). In July 2023, NMPA Organized to revise the *Catalogue of Medical Devices Exempted from Clinical Evaluation* (2021 Edition), and formulate the *Catalogue of Medical Devices Exempted from Clinical Evaluation* (2023 Edition).

Catalogue of Medical Devices Exempted from Clinical Evaluation/Clinical Trials

Some medical devices can be exempted from clinical trials!

In order to further standardize the registration management of medical devices, NMPA has organized the formulation of the *Catalogue of Medical Devices Exempted from Clinical Trials* and the *Catalogue of In Vitro Diagnostic Reagents Exempted from Clinical Trials*. Medical devices listed in the Catalogue can be exempted from clinical trials. Current valid catalogues are *Catalogue of Medical Devices Exempted from Clinical Evaluation (2021 Edition)* and *Catalogue of In-vitro Diagnostic Reagents Exempted from Clinical Trials (2021 Edition)* issued in 2021.

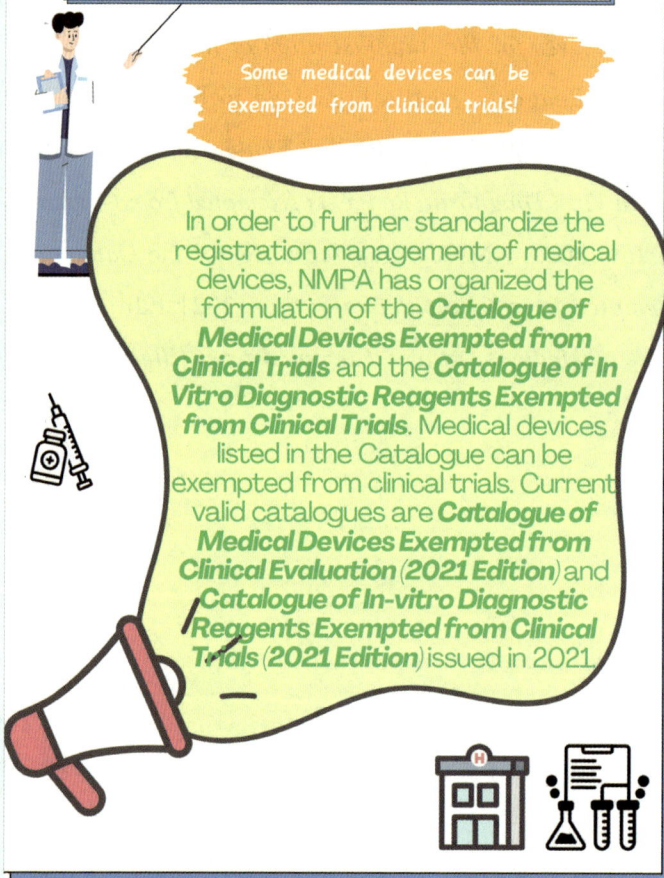

To apply for registration and filing of medical devices, clinical evaluation shall be conducted; however, in any of the following circumstances, the clinical evaluation could be exempted:

(1) The medical device to be registered or filed has clear working mechanism, finalized design and mature production process; the predicate medical devices which have been marketed have been in clinical use for many years and no severe adverse events associated with these devices and the conventional uses of medical device have not been changed;

(2) The safety and effectiveness of the medical device to be registered or filed can be proved through non-clinical evaluation.

When conducting clinical evaluation of IVD reagents, clinical trials shall be carried out to prove the safety and effectiveness of IVD reagents. In any of the following circumstances, the clinical trial could be exempted:

(1) The IVD reagent to be registered or filed has clear reaction mechanism, finalized design and mature production process; the predicate IVD reagents which have been marketed have been in clinical use for many years and no severe adverse events have been associated with these reagents and the conventional uses of predicate IVD reagents have not been changed;

(2) The safety and effectiveness of the IVD reagents to be registered or filed can be proved through methodological comparison study on predicate IVD reagents.

The Catalogue of Class II and Class III IVD Reagents Exempted from Clinical Trials shall be formulated, adjusted and issued by NMPA.

For IVD reagents exempted from clinical trials, the applicant shall prove the safety and effectiveness of the proposed products by comparing the clinical samples that meet the intended use through methodological comparison study on predicate IVD reagents.

Note! Products, in case for the following conditions, cannot be exempted even when their names are in the Catalogue:

Involving new materials, new technologies, new active ingredients, new design or products with new operation principles or new functions

Expanding or changing the application scope of the products

Performance indicators that failed to meet the standards listed in the catalogue

Other scenarios that do not meet clinical evaluation exemption requirements listed in *Catalogue of Medical Devices Exempted from Clinical Evaluation*

5.2.2 Data to be Submitted

(1) Products Listed in the *Catalogue of Medical Devices Exempted from Clinical Evaluation*

For the products listed in the *Catalogue of Medical Devices Exempted from Clinical Evaluation*, the registration applicant shall submit the comparison data of relevant information of the proposed product and the contents described in the *Catalogue of Medical Devices Exempted from Clinical Trials* and the explanation on the comparison between the proposed product and the medical devices in the *Catalogue of Medical Devices Exempted from Clinical Evaluation* that have been approved for registration in China. Eligible registration applicants shall prepare the dossiers in accordance with the relevant requirements of the *Technical Guidelines for Comparative Instructions of Products Listed in the Catalogue of Medical Devices Exempted from Clinical Evaluation*.

For the products listed in the **Catalogue of Medical Devices Exempted from Clinical Evaluation**, which clinical evaluation data shall be prepared upon applying for registration?

Comparison data of relevant information of the proposed product and the contents described in the **Catalogue of Medical Devices Exempted from Clinical Trials.**

Explanation on the comparison between the proposed product and the medical devices in the **Catalogue of Medical Devices Exempted from Clinical Evaluation** that have been approved for registration in China.

LOOK!

Please pay attention to the NMPA website for latest news about the **Catalogue of Medical Devices Exempted from Clinical Trials.**

(2) IVD Reagents Listed in the *Catalogue of In Vitro Diagnostic Reagents Exempted from Clinical Trials*

For IVD reagents exempted from clinical trials, the registration applicants shall submit the comparison data between the proposed product to corresponding item in the *Catalogue of In Vitro Diagnostic Reagents Exempted from Clinical Trials*, which should be able to prove the equivalence between the proposed product and the product(s) described in the *Catalogue of In Vitro Diagnostic Reagents Exempted from Clinical Trials*.

For IVD reagents exempted from clinical trials, the registration applicant may conduct the clinical evaluation in accordance with the *Technical Guidelines for Clinical Evaluation of In Vitro Diagnostic Reagents Exempted from Clinical Trials*, and may also conduct the clinical trials in accordance with the *Technical Guidelines for Clinical Trials of In Vitro Diagnostic Reagents*.

How to conduct the clinical evaluation on IVD reagents exempted from clinical trials?

The registration applicants may compare the investigational reagent with the product already marketed in China to prove that the investigational reagent is substantially equivalent to the marketed product, or well consistent with the test results of reference measurement procedure/criteria for diagnostic accuracy. Substantial equivalence mentioned herein refers to that the intended use is the same, and the safety and effectiveness are the same.

The applicant shall use finalized reagents for clinical evaluation. Prior to the clinical evaluations, the applicant shall determine basic performance of the product, generally including applicable sample type, specificity, precision, limit of detection and/or limit of quantitation, measurement interval, cut-off value or reference interval, so as to provide the basis for clinical evaluation of the investigational reagent.

If the clinical evaluation cannot prove that the investigational reagent is substantially equivalent to the product already marketed in China, or well consistent with the test results of reference measurement procedure/criteria for diagnostic accuracy, the application reagent shall be evaluated by means of clinical trial.

5.3 Primary Types of Clinical Evaluation of Medical Devices

5.3.1 Analysis and Evaluation Based on the Clinical Data of the Predicate Medical Device

(1) Equivalence Demonstration

The demonstration of equivalence of medical devices refers to the process of comparing proposed product with the comparative device in terms of technical characteristics and biological characteristics, so as to prove that the two are essentially equivalent. The essential equivalence includes two situations:

1) The proposed product has the same scope of application, technical characteristics and biological characteristics as the predicate device.

2) The proposed product has the same scope of application, similar technical characteristics and biological characteristics as the comparative device; there is sufficient scientific evidence to prove that the proposed product has the same safety and effectiveness as the predicate device.

(2) Selection of Predicate Product

According to the *Technical Guidance for Clinical Evaluation of Medical Devices*, when a comparative device is broadly similar to the proposed product in terms of the scope of application, and technical and/or biological characteristics, it can be regarded as predicate medical device, including equivalent device and comparable device.

1) Equivalent device

If registration applicants demonstrate the equivalence between the proposed product and comparable device in accordance with the relevant requirements of the *Technical Guidance for the Demonstration of Equivalence of Medical Devices*, the clinical evaluation can be conducted based on the clinical data of the equivalent device. When technical and biological characteristics of the proposed product are different from those of the comparable device, sufficient scientific evidences shall be submitted to prove the same safety and effectiveness between the two, and thus demonstrate their equivalence. Where clinical evidence is needed to prove the same safety and effectiveness between the two, the registration applicants can form the clinical evidences of the equivalence between the proposed product and the comparable device according to the requirements of Articles 5, 6 and 7 of Part 2 in the *Technical Guidance for Clinical Evaluation of Medical Devices*.

2) Comparable device

If registration applicants compare the proposed product with the comparative device in accordance with the relevant requirements in the *Technical Guidance for the Demonstration of Equivalence of Medical Devices*, which cannot demonstrate the equivalence of the two, but demonstrate that the scope of application, technical characteristics and/or biological characteristics of the comparative device are broadly similar to those of the proposed product, the comparative device can be regarded as a comparable device, and registration applicants may use clinical data from the comparable device to support partial clinical evaluation of the proposed product as part of the clinical evidences for the proposed product.

Technical Review Process of Clinical Evaluation

Clinical Evaluation Pathway of Comparison with Predicate Device

Know about Predicate Device

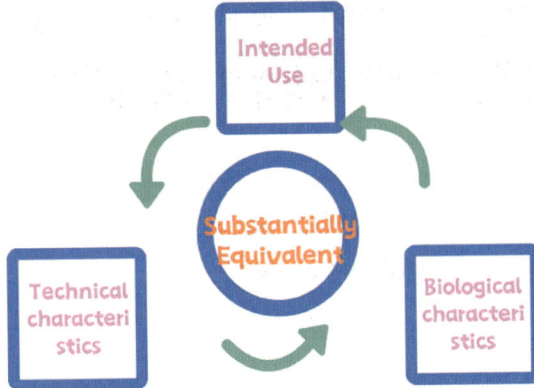

Intended Use

Substantially Equivalent

Technical characteristics

Biological characteristics

Products that have been approved in China

The difference between the proposed product and the predicate device does not adversely affect the safety and effectiveness of the product, it can be regarded as substantially equivalent

How to conduct comparison with predicate device?

STEP1 Determination

Compare the proposed product with the predicate device to prove that both are basically equivalent.

Comparison item

The comparison contents include qualitative and quantitative data, as well as verification and validation results.

Comparison table

The registration applicant shall provide comparison information in the form of a list and explain the reasons for inapplicability if there are any inapplicable items.

STEP2 Data Collection

1.Data collection of clinical literature

Three steps for literature search and screening:

2.Data collection of clinical experience

Element   Report   Protocol

Clinical use data   Adverse event   Corrective action   ....

STEP3 Clinical Data Analysis and Evaluation

1.Data quality evaluation

Data included in the analysis   →   Evaluation criteria for clinical evidence level   Grades

2.Establishment of data

Data type   Data quality

3.Statistic analysis of data

Qualitative   Quantitative

4.Data evaluation

? Can the product achieve its intended performance?

Is the risk acceptable?

......

STEP4 Clinical Evaluation Report

After the clinical evaluation is completed, a clinical evaluation report needs to be written, and submitted as the clinical evaluation data during the application for registration.

(3) Preparation of Relevant Supporting Data

In the equivalence demonstration, the data and information used in the comparison between proposed product and the comparative device, and the valid scientific evidence used to prove that proposed product and the comparative device have the same safety and effectiveness when there are difference between them are all the supporting data for the equivalence demonstration. Supporting data shall usually include accurate, reliable, complete and traceable data, and shall include the process of data generation if necessary. It's suggested that the test data come from the laboratory with good quality control. Supporting data may include bench test data, animal test data, simulation test data, clinical data, etc..

5.3.2 Products that Require Clinical Trials

(1) Definition of clinical trials

Medical Device Clinical Trial refers to the validation conducted by an institution with corresponding qualification, in which the safety and effectiveness of a medical device (including IVD reagent) to be registered is investigated under its normal service condition.

Clinical Trials

I. What is the Clinical Trial ?

Medical Device Clinical Trial refers to the validation conducted by an institution with corresponding qualification, in which the safety and effectiveness of a medical device (including IVD reagent) to be registered is investigated under its normal service condition.

Validation of the safety and effectiveness of a medical device (including IVD reagent)

Proposed Product

Sponsor

Institution

(2) Preparations prior to clinical trials

1) The expected benefits shall outweigh the potential risks;

2) Complete pre-clinical study on investigational medical devices;

3) Prepare sufficient investigational medical devices;

4) Medical device clinical trials shall be conducted in two or more clinical trial institutions;

5) The sponsor reaches a written agreement with clinical trial institutions and investigator;

6) The clinical trial shall be approved by the Ethics Committee of clinical trial institutions, and for products listed in the Catalogue of Class III Medical Devices Requiring Approval of Clinical Trials shall be approved;

7) The sponsor shall file with medical product administration under provinces, autonomous regions and municipalities.

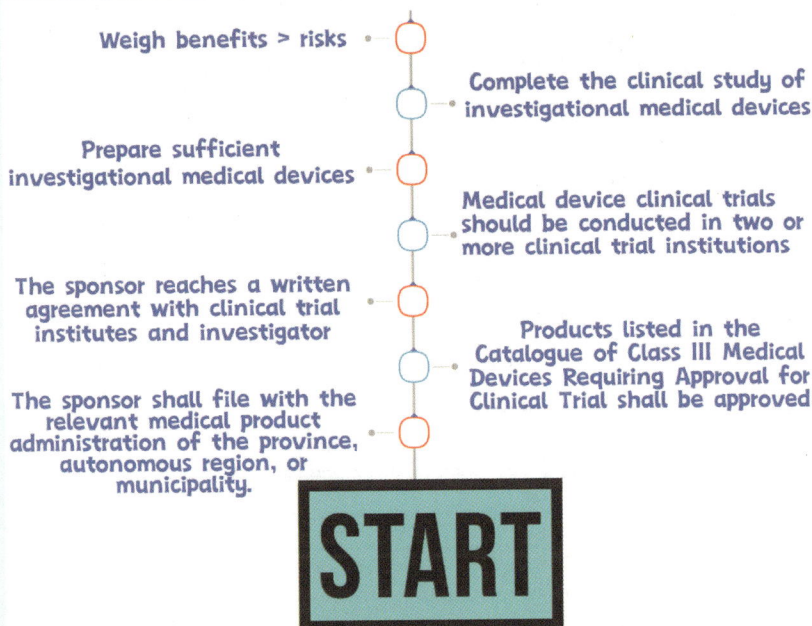

2. Preparations prior to Clinical Trials

Weigh benefits > risks

Complete the clinical study of investigational medical devices

Prepare sufficient investigational medical devices

Medical device clinical trials should be conducted in two or more clinical trial institutions

The sponsor reaches a written agreement with clinical trial institutes and investigator

Products listed in the Catalogue of Class III Medical Devices Requiring Approval for Clinical Trial shall be approved

The sponsor shall file with the relevant medical product administration of the province, autonomous region, or municipality.

START

(3) Clinical trial protocol

1) The sponsor shall organize the formulation of the clinical trial protocol in consideration of the purpose of the clinical trial, the claims of the medical device and its inherent characteristics;

2) Clinical trial protocol generally includes basic information of product, basic information of clinical trial, purpose of trial, risk benefit analysis, elements of trial design, rationality demonstration of trial design, statistical consideration, implementation mode (method, content and steps), end point of clinical trial, data management, the regulation of revision of clinical trial

protocol, definition and report of adverse events and device defects, ethical considerations, etc..

3.Clinical Trial Protocol

The sponsor shall formulate clinical trial protocol according to the category, risk, intended use and other elements of investigational medical devices

Scientific and reasonable

A small sample feasibility test shall be performed first before the design of the clinical trial protocol

New products that have not been approved for marketing at home and abroad, and whose safety and performance have not been medically demonstrated

The clinical trial protocol of medical devices shall include:

- General information
- Background information of clinical trial
- Trial purpose
- Trial purpose
- Safety evaluation methods
- Effectiveness evaluation methods
- ⋯⋯⋯

TIPS

The multicenter clinical trial shall be conducted in different clinical trial institutions at the same time according to the same clinical trial protocol

(4) Clinical Trial Database

For clinical trials, database shall be submitted according to *Guidelines for Registration Review of Submission Requirements of Clinical Trial Data for Medical Devices*.

(5) Clinical trial process

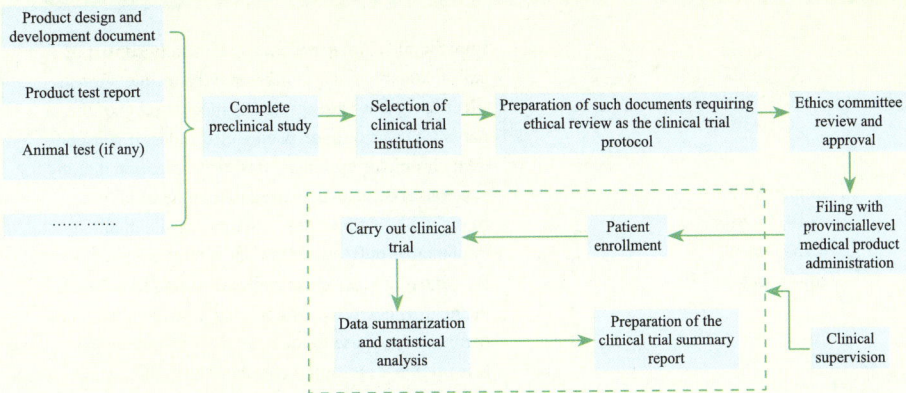

5.3.3 Products listed in Catalogue of Class III Medical Devices Requiring Approval for Clinical Trials

(1) Introduction to *Catalogue of Class III Medical Devices Requiring Approval for Clinical Trials* (2020 Revision)

In accordance with the Article 27 of the *Regulations for the Supervision and Administration of Medical Devices*: The clinical trial of Class III medical devices with higher risk to human body shall be subject to the approval by NMPA. The Catalogue of Class III medical devices whose clinical trials pose higher risks to human body shall be formulated, adjusted and published by NMPA. To protect the safety of subjects participating in medical device clinical trials and standardize the clinical trial approval, NMPA issued the *Catalogue of Class III Medical Devices Requiring Approval for Clinical Trials*

(Table 4). The clinical trial protocol of products listed in the Catalogue can be implemented only after it is approved by NMPA.

Table 4 Catalogue of Class III Medical Devices Requiring Approval of Clinical Trials (Revision 2020)

No.	Product Category	Classification Code	Product Description
1	Implantable cardiac rhythm management equipment	12	Implantable cardiac pacemakers: usually consist of an implantable pulse generator and a torque wrench. Electrical pulses are applied to specific parts of the patient's heart through pacing electrodes. It is used to treat chronic arrhythmias. Resynchronization therapy pacemakers can also be used to treat heart failure. Implantable defibrillators: usually consist of an implantable pulse generator and a torque wrench. By detecting ventricular tachycardia and fibrillation, the heart is corrected by applying a cardioversion / defibrillation pulse to the heart through electrodes. It is used to treat rapid ventricular arrhythmias. Resynchronization therapy defibrillator can also be used for heart failure treatment.
2	Implantable ventricular assistant system	12	It usually consists of an implanted pump body, a power supply part, a vascular connection, and a controller. It is used to provide mechanical support for the blood circulation of patients with advanced refractory left heart failure as well as transitional treatment and/or long-term treatment before heart transplantation or restoration of heart function. It is used by medical institutions with heart transplantation conditions and comprehensive postoperative care capabilities. Medical staff, out-of-hospital nursing staff and patients must pass corresponding training. It is contraindicated in patients with intolerance to anticoagulant therapy.
3	Implantable drug infusion equipment	12	It usually consists of a drug infusion pump, a reperfusion component and a catheter-portal component. This product is used in conjunction with an intra-sheath catheter for long-term drug infusion.

Continued

No.	Product Category	Classification Code	Product Description
4	Cardiac valve prosthesis and endovascular stent	13	Cardiac valve prosthesis or valve repair device: The product is generally made from polymer materials, animal tissues, metal materials, and inorganic non–metal materials. It may or may not contain surface modification substances. It is used to replace or repair natural cardiac valves. Endovascular stents: Stents are generally made of metal (including absorbable metal materials) or polymer materials (including absorbable polymer materials), and their structures are generally grid–shaped. The stent may contain or not contain surface modification substances, such as coating. It may contain pharmaceutical ingredients, such as for treating atherosclerosis and various vascular diseases such as stenosis, obstruction or occlusion.
5	Tissue engineered medical products containing viable cells	13/16/17	Passive implantable tissue engineered medical products containing viable cells mainly used as medical devices.
6	Absorbable internal fixation devices in limb long bone	13	It is made of absorbable macromolecule material or absorbable metal material, applicable for internal fracture fixation of limb long bone.

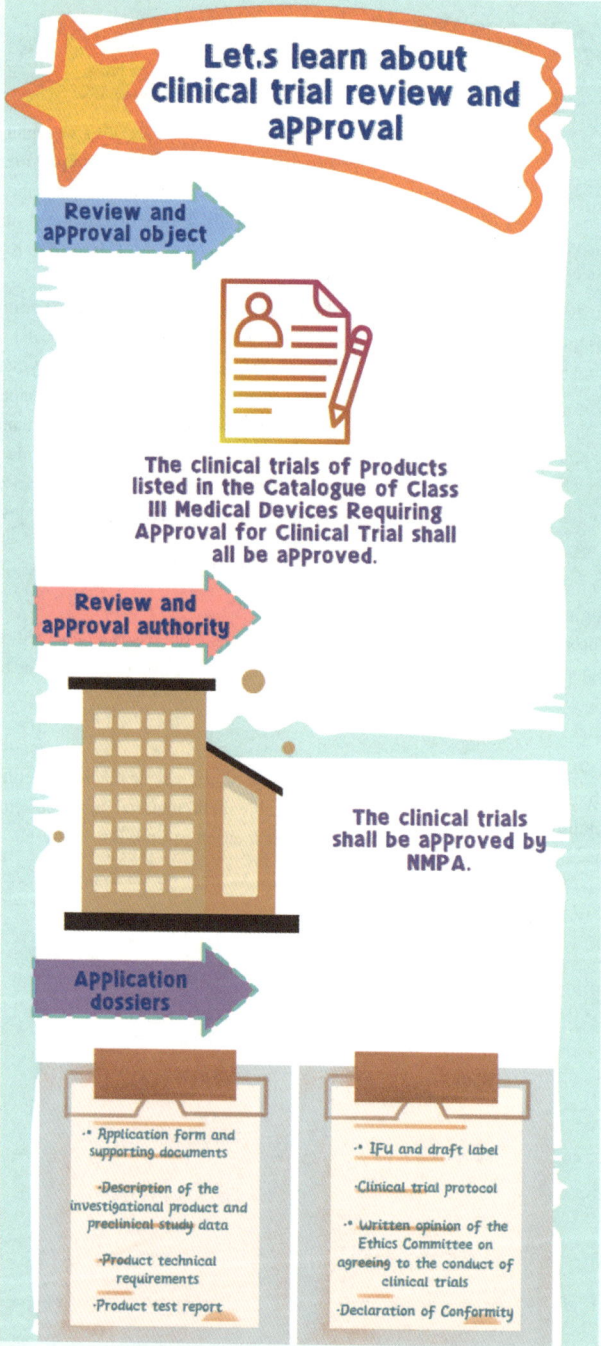

Let.s learn about clinical trial review and approval

Review and approval object

The clinical trials of products listed in the Catalogue of Class III Medical Devices Requiring Approval for Clinical Trial shall all be approved.

Review and approval authority

The clinical trials shall be approved by NMPA.

Application dossiers

- Application form and supporting documents
- Description of the investigational product and preclinical study data
- Product technical requirements
- Product test report

- IFU and draft label
- Clinical trial protocol
- Written opinion of the Ethics Committee on agreeing to the conduct of clinical trials
- Declaration of Conformity

Application Process

For the application dossiers requirements, please refer to Attachment 8 of the *Announcement on Issuing the Requirements for Registration Application Dossiers of Medical Devices and Formats of Approval Documents* (No.121, 2021)

Preparation of application dossiers

Acceptance of application dossiers

After entry into the technical review process, the technical review will be completed within 60 working days.

Relevant dossiers shall be supplemented within one year and CMDE will complete the supplementary materials technical review within 40 working days upon receipt of these dossiers.

The decision on review and approval will be made within 20 working days.

Obtain the approval letter.

(2) Others

The application dossiers for the review and approval of medical device clinical trials shall be prepared in accordance with the *Requirements for Registration Application Dossiers of Medical Devices and Formats of Approval Documents*, and communication with CMDE can be applied prior to acceptance. See 1. Consultation Services.

QUICK TIPS

Before the clinical trials application, meeting communication with CMDE can be applied before acceptance. Refer to **Notice of the CFDA on Matters Related to the Clinical Trial Applications for Medical Devices Subject to Approval** (No.184 in 2017) for details.

5.4 Clinical Trials of IVD Reagents

5.4.1 Determination of Requiring Clinical Trials of Medical Devices

(1) The products listed in the *Catalogue of In Vitro Diagnostic Reagents Exempted from Clinical Trials* shall be exempted from clinical trials. The *Catalogue of Class II and Class III IVD Reagents Exempted from Clinical Trials* shall be formulated, adjusted and issued by NMPA.

(2) The products not listed in the *Catalogue of In Vitro Diagnostic Reagents Exempted from Clinical Trials* shall conduct clinical trials.

(3) When the registration of calibrator and quality control is applied separately, it is not necessary to submit the clinical evaluation data.

5.4.2 Preparations Prior to Clinical Trials

(1) The expected benefits shall outweigh the potential harms;

(2) Complete pre–clinical study on investigational IVD reagents;

(3) Prepare sufficient investigational IVD reagents;

(4) Clinical trials of Class III IVD reagents shall be conducted in three or more medical device clinical trial institutions; no less than 2 (inclusive) eligible clinical trial institutions shall be selected for Class II products.

(5) The sponsor reaches a written agreement with clinical trial institutions and investigator;

(6) The clinical trial shall be approved by the Ethics Committee of clinical trial institutions of medical devices;

(7) The sponsor shall file with food and drug administration under provinces, autonomous regions and municipalities directly under the central government.

5.4.3 Clinical Trial Protocol

When carrying out clinical trials of IVD reagents, the sponsor shall not only comprehensively consider the intended use, product characteristics, expected risks, etc. of the investigational IVD reagents according to the clinical trial purpose, but also organize the formulation of a scientific and reasonable clinical trial protocol. The clinical trial protocol shall be strictly followed throughout the clinical trials after being approved by the Ethics Committee.

All clinical trial institutions shall implement the same clinical trial protocol which clearly specifies the type of trial design, selection of comparison methods, selection of subjects, evaluation indicators, statistical analysis methods, sample size estimation and quality control requirements, etc. and shall reasonably determine a sample size allocation plan according to the actual situation of each clinical trial institution.

5.4.4 Clinical Trial Report

After the completion of the clinical trial, the investigators of each clinical trial institution shall summarize their own clinical trial data, issue a summary of the clinical trial, and attach the clinical trial data sheet, basic information of other trial methods or other IVD reagents used in clinical trials. The data shall be prepared in accordance with the *Technical Guidelines for Clinical Trials of In Vitro Diagnostic Reagents*.

5.4.5 Clinical Trial Database

For clinical trials, the database shall be submitted in accordance with the requirements of the *Guidelines for Registration Review of Requirements for Submission of Clinical Trial Data of In Vitro Diagnostic Reagents*.

5.4.6 Clinical Trial Process

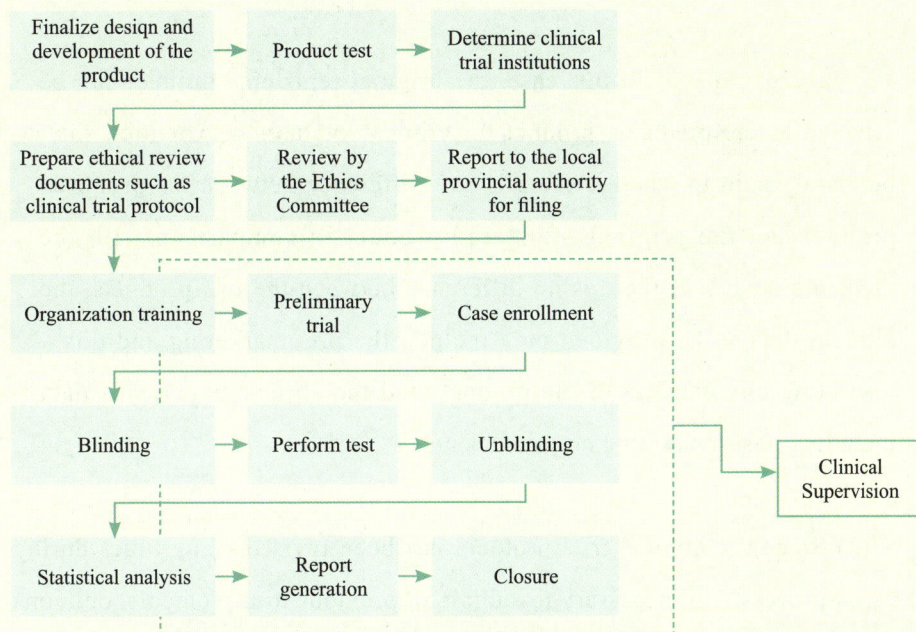

```
┌──────────────────┐      ┌──────────────┐      ┌──────────────────┐
│ Finalize desiqn and │ → │ Product test │ → │ Determine clinical │
│ development of the  │    │              │    │ trial institutions │
│ product             │    │              │    │                    │
└──────────────────┘      └──────────────┘      └──────────────────┘
        ↓
┌──────────────────┐      ┌──────────────┐      ┌──────────────────┐
│ Prepare ethical review │ → │ Review by   │ → │ Report to the local │
│ documents such as      │    │ the Ethics  │    │ provincial authority │
│ clinical trial protocol│    │ Committee   │    │ for filing          │
└──────────────────┘      └──────────────┘      └──────────────────┘
        ↓
┌──────────────────┐      ┌──────────────┐      ┌──────────────────┐
│ Organization training │ → │ Preliminary │ → │ Case enrollment │
│                       │    │ trial       │    │                 │
└──────────────────┘      └──────────────┘      └──────────────────┘
        ↓
┌──────────────────┐      ┌──────────────┐      ┌──────────────────┐      ┌──────────────┐
│ Blinding         │ → │ Perform test │ → │ Unblinding      │ → │ Clinical     │
│                  │    │              │    │                 │    │ Supervision  │
└──────────────────┘      └──────────────┘      └──────────────────┘      └──────────────┘
        ↓
┌──────────────────┐      ┌──────────────┐      ┌──────────────────┐
│ Statistical analysis │ → │ Report      │ → │ Closure         │
│                      │    │ generation  │    │                 │
└──────────────────┘      └──────────────┘      └──────────────────┘
```

5.4.7 Registration Application Dossiers for the Review and Approval of Clinical Trials

The registration application dossiers for the review and approval of medical device clinical trials shall be prepared in accordance with the *Requirements for Registration Application Dossiers of Medical Devices and Formats of Approval Documents,* and communication with CMDE can be applied prior to acceptance. See "1.Consultation Services".

5.5 Case Interpretation

(1) In case of failure in applying for renewal registration within the specified time for a registered product, application for registration of the product shall be made according to regulatory requirements. In this case, can

the original registered product be selected as the predicate product for clinical evaluation? How shall clinical data be provided?

Interpretation: In this case, the original registered product can be selected as the predicate product for clinical evaluation. Attention shall be mainly paid to whether there is any difference between the proposed product and the original registered product in comparison with the predicate device. If there is no difference between the two products, the clinical data to be provided may include the pre-marketing and post-marketing clinical data of the product, and the clinical experience data including post-marketing adverse events.

(2) Since the clinical trial protocol has been revised many times during the trial process, is it necessary to submit all previous trial protocols, opinions of the ethics committee and informed consent forms when submitting the clinical trial protocol for product registration?

Interpretation: The final version of the clinical trial protocol and informed consent form as well as opinions of ethics committee on all previous changes shall be submitted. All previous changes shall be listed in detail in the final version of the clinical trial protocol; if not, all previously changed clinical trial protocols shall be submitted. The registration applicant shall provide reasons for changing the clinical trial protocol.

(3) If the clinical trial protocol of a product includes feasibility trial and confirmatory trial, can the results of feasibility trial and confirmatory clinical

trial be combined for statistics after the trial?

Interpretation: Feasibility trial can make an initial assessment of product safety and performance to provide information for confirmatory trial design, and is different from confirmatory clinical trial in terms of purpose. The statistics of test results shall follow the prescribed statistical analysis plan; it is not recommended to combine the results of feasibility trial and confirmatory clinical trial for statistics after the trial.

(4) What matters shall be paid attention to during the submission of ethical documents for IVD reagents?

Interpretation: In the clinical trial data of IVD reagents, the protocol according to which the clinical trial is conducted and the corresponding written comments of the Ethics Committee approving to conduct the clinical trial shall be submitted.

Due to the change of the clinical trial protocol, there may be multiple version numbers. The following principles shall be noted in the submission of registration application dossiers:

If the change of the clinical trial protocol occurs before the formal implementation of the clinical trial, the clinical trial protocol with the version number according to which the clinical trial is finally implemented and the written comments of the Ethics Committee corresponding to the protocol with this version number shall be submitted.

If the clinical trial is ongoing and there is a change of the protocol during the trial process, the clinical protocol versions before and after the change and their ethical documents shall be submitted together, and the reasons for the protocol change and its impact on the ongoing clinical trial shall be clearly stated.

It shall be noted that the scientificity, rationality, feasibility and compliance of the protocol shall be fully studied before the clinical trial, and the protocol shall be formulated and strictly implemented; the protocol shall not be changed at will for unnecessary reasons during the clinical trial.

(5) The reference values in the instructions for use of an IVD kit may involve different age distributions, how to select clinical trial samples?

Interpretation: Throughout the clinical trial design, in addition to the total number of cases, distribution of positive and negative cases and interference cases, the included cases shall also meet the requirements for necessary case grouping and stratification. If the reference value of the kit varies in different age groups, the differences from different age groups shall be taken into account when cases are included, and statistically significant numbers of different age groups shall be included separately. The proportion of positive and negative cases in each age group shall be balanced. If there are many age segments of reference values, the total number of cases enrolled according to the above requirements may be larger than the minimum sample size in accordance with the specifications of *Technical Guidelines for Clinical Trials of In Vitro Diagnostic Reagents*.

(6) If laboratory testing reference methods such as nucleotide sequencing and GC–MS/MS are used as control methods in IVD reagent clinical trials for

a comparative study, can such tests be entrusted?

Interpretation: For some IVD reagents that have no definite clinically diagnostic "Gold Standard", and no comparable predicate IVD reagents, the clinical trial investigators shall establish reasonable methods based on existing clinical practices and theoretical basis for a comparative study. For some IVD reagents, clinical trials use laboratory testing reference methods such as nucleotide sequencing and GC–MS/MS as comparative methods for a comparative study, these methods are not routine clinical testing techniques, requiring specialized equipment, instruments and test conditions, and clinical trial institutions may not be qualified with relevant testing conditions. For such cases, the registration applicants shall select the clinical trial institutions with corresponding conditions to develop the clinical trials as far as possible, and some without testing conditions can entrust this test to a special sequencing institution or a qualified test laboratory, and then approve the test results. Submit the commissioned certificate of clinical trial institution and entrusted institution, and evaluate the methodological study and overall quality of the comparative method.

5.6 References

CFDA Announcement on Guidelines for Medical Device Clinical Trial Design (No.6, 2018)

CFDA Announcement on Technical Guidelines for Accepting Overseas Clinical Trial Data of Medical Devices (No.13, 2018)

NMPA Announcement on the Issuance of the Catalogue of Class III

Medical Devices Requiring Approval for Clinical Trials (2020 Revision) (No. 61, 2020)

NMPA Announcement on the Issuance of the Technical Guidelines for Application of Real-World Data in Clinical Evaluation of Medical Devices (Trial) (No. 77, 2020)

NMPA Announcement on the Issuance of the Catalogue of In Vitro Diagnostic Reagents Exempted from Clinical Trials (No.70, 2021)

NMPA Announcement on the Issuance of the Catalogue of Medical Devices Exempted from Clinical Trials (No.33, 2023)

NMPA Announcement on the Issuance of the Technical Guidelines for Clinical Trials of In Vitro Diagnostic Reagents (No.72, 2021)

NMPA Announcement on 5 terms Technical Guidelines for Clinical Evaluation of Medical Devices and Others (No.73, 2021)

NMPA Announcement on Technical Guidelines for Clinical Evaluation of In Vitro Diagnostic Reagents Exempted from Clinical Trials (No.74, 2021)

NMPA Announcement on 2 terms Guidelines for Registration Review of Submission Requirements of Clinical Trial Data for Medical Devices and Others (No.91, 2021)

NMPA, National Health and Family Planning Commission of the People's Republic of China (NHFPC) Notice on Good Clinical Practice for Medical Devices (No. 28, 2022)

6. Special Review of Innovative Medical Devices

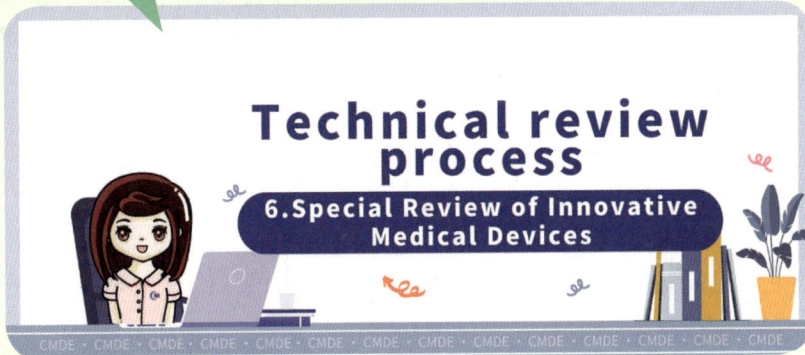

6.1 Overview

In February 2014, the former CFDA issued *Special Review and Approval Procedure for Innovative Medical Devices (Interim)* (CFDA No.13, 2014), which was implemented from March 1, 2014. This Procedure is a review and approval approach set for innovative medical device (IMD) on the premise of ensuring the safety and effectiveness of marketed products. In November 2018, NMPA revised it and issued the *Special Review Procedure for Innovative Medical Devices* (hereinafter referred to as the Procedure), which was implemented on December 1st, 2018.

Medical administration authority shall conduct review and approval of medical devices that meet the corresponding conditions at the same time according to this procedure. For example, the applicants should have the patent right for invention of the product core technology, or the patent application has been published by the Administrative Department for Patent under the State Council, the products are international leading ones with significant clinical application value. In accordance with the requirements of the Procedure, both domestic and overseas applicants can submit applicable technical data and supporting documents, and apply for special review of IMD; if they comply with corresponding conditions after reviewed by Technical Section, evaluation, review & approval may be implemented according to this Procedure.

Special review of IMD is to encourage the research and innovation on medical devices, facilitate promotion and application of new technologies in medical devices and accelerate development of medical device industry.

What are the benefits of applying for the special review of innovative medical devices?

·More quickly accepted and handled by designated staff
·Team review, publish the review report.
·Giving priority to type testing, system verification, evaluation, and review& approval
·Free of registration fee of innovative products for small and micro enterprises

6.2 Relevant Definitions

The IMDs are Classes II and III medical devices that comply with the following situations:

(1) Through their predominant technological innovation activities, the applicants legally own the patent right for the product core technology invention in China, or obtain patent for invention in China or their rights to

Am I qualified?

(1) The applicants legally own the patent right for the product core technology invention in China, or obtain patent for invention in China or their rights to use through legal transfer. The application duration for special review of IMD shall not exceed 5 years from the announcement of patent licensing; or, the application for patent right for core technology invention has been made public by Administrative Department for Patent under the State Council, and a search report is issued by Patent Search and Consultation Center of SIPO, in which states that the product core technology protocol is of novelty and creativity.

(2) The applicants have finalized the preliminary study of the product, with basically finalized products, and the study process is authentic and controlled, and the study data is complete and traceable.

(3) The primary working principle or mechanism of action of the product is pioneering in China, the product performance or safety has radical improvements compared with predicate products, with internationally-advanced technology and significant clinical application value.

use through legal transfer. The application duration for special review of IMD shall not exceed 5 years from the announcement of patent licensing; or, the application for patent right for core technology invention has been published by Administrative Department for Patent under the State Council, and a search report is issued by Patent Search and Consultation Center of State Intellectual Property Office (SIPO), in which states that the product core technology protocol is of novelty and creativity.

(2) The applicants have finalized the preliminary research of the product, with basically finalized products, and the study process is authentic and controlled, and the study data is complete and traceable.

(3) The primary working principle or mechanism of action of the product is pioneering in China, the product performance or safety has radical improvements compared with predicate products, with internationally-advanced technology and significant clinical application value.

6.3 Application Process

6.3.1 Application

Prior to application for the initial registration of medical devices, the applicants shall fill in the *Application Form for Special Review of Innovative Medical Devices*, and refer to the *Guidance for the Preparation of Application Dossiers for Special Review of Innovative Medical Devices*, and submit information supporting that the proposed product complies with requirements of Procedure.

6.3.2 Preliminary Review

Domestic applicants should submit an application for special review of innovative medical devices to provincial medical products administration in the place where he/she is located. The provincial medical products administration shall conduct the preliminary review on whether the application projects meet the procedural requirements and issue preliminary review opinions. For those which cannot comply with relevant requirements upon preliminary review, the provincial medical products administration shall notify the applicant; for those which comply with relevant requirements, the applicant shall submit the preliminary review opinions of the provincial medical products administration and the registration application dossiers to NMPA.

Overseas applicants should submit an application for special review of innovative medical devices to NMPA.

6.3.3 Formal Review

After the formal review of the registration submission dossiers for special review of innovative medical devices, those that meet the format requirements stipulated in the Procedure will be accepted and given an acceptance number. The arrangement of the acceptance number is as follows: CQTS $\times \times \times \times 1 \times \times \times 2$, in which $\times \times \times \times 1$ is the codo of the year of application, and $\times \times \times 2$ is the product serial number.

For an application for special review of innovative medical devices that has been accepted, an applicant may apply for withdrawing the application for special review of innovative medical devices and relevant dossiers before a review and approval decision is made and specify the reasons.

6.3.4 Review

CMDE has established an Office of Innovative Medical Device Review (OIMDR) to review the special review applications for innovative medical devices. After receiving an application for special review of innovative medical devices, the OIMDR shall organize experts to review the application.

After receiving an application for special review for IMD, OIMDR shall issue the review opinions within 60 working days (publicity and objection handling period not included).

In any of the following five circumstances, the OIMDR will not organize experts to review the application:

(1) False application dossiers;
(2) Confused and contradictory contents of registration application dossiers;
(3) Significantly unconformable contents of registration application dossiers to proposed projects;
(4) Incomplete documentary evidences of product intelligence property in registration application dossiers and unclear patent right;
(5) The previous review has clearly pointed out that the primary working principle or mechanism of action of the product is not domestically pioneering, and the product design remains unchanged at reapplication.

6.3.5 Publicity

For the application projects intended for special review, after review by the OIMDR, the OIMDR will define the management category of medical devices and publicize the applicants and product names via the CMDE's official website. If any objection to the content that is publicized, the OIMDR shall make the final review decision after the study of relevant opinions.

After making the review decision, the OIMDR shall notify the applicant of the review results through the website of the CMDE.

6.3.6 Objection Handling

Any organization and individual who has objections to the publicity of the review of the product in accordance with the Procedure shall put forward such objections during the publicity period. The objection contents are only limited to the original application items and the original registration application dossiers. In principle, the application materials for objections submitted shall be written documents signed and sealed by the opposition.

The objection application shall be subject to collective study by the Office Meeting of CMDE to form handling opinions, and the innovative review group shall inform the opposition after forming handling opinions. Where there are clear handling opinions, CMDE will no longer accept the objection application for the same content.

How to apply?

Domestic products shall submit an application to the local provincial administration

Preliminary review, issue preliminary review opinions

If it can meet relevant requirements, the applicant shall submit the preliminary review opinions of the provincial medical products administration and the registration application dossiers to NMPA.

If it cannot meet relevant requirements, notify the applicant.

DID YOU KNOW?

Applications for imported products are submitted directly to the NMPA and accepted if they meet the requirements.

Innovation application
(Accepted)

↓

Expert review

↓

Confirmation of
review opinions
(OIMDR)

↓

Publicity → During publicity period → Objection handling

↓

Issue review report

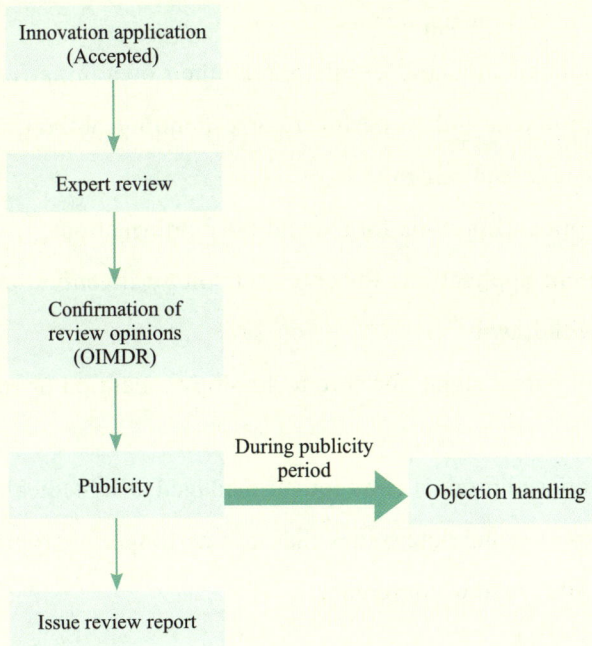

6.4 Reapplication and Termination

6.4.1 Reapplication

If that clinical study on IMD needs substantial changes, such as clinical trial protocol revision, method of application, specifications and models, intended use and scope of application or adjustment of target population, the applicants shall evaluate the impact of changes on the safety, effectiveness, and quality controllability of medical devices. If any change in the main working principle or mechanism of action of an innovative medical device, the application shall be submitted again in accordance with the present Procedure.

6.4.2 Termination

Under any of the following situations, the NMPA may terminate the procedure and inform the applicants:

(1) The applicants request termination on their own initiatives;

(2) The applicants fail to perform corresponding obligations within the prescribed time and requirements;

(3) The applicants provide forged and false information;

(4) All patent applications for core technology invention are rejected or deemed to be withdrawn;

(5) Lose all patent rights for core technology invention or rights to use of products;

(6) The proposed product is no longer managed as a medical device;

(7) The expert group determines that it is no longer appropriate to follow this procedure after review conference.

6.5 Innovation Communication

For IMDs that have been approved to enter the special review procedure, the applicants shall submit application before the registration application is accepted, or during the technical review process, CMDE and the applicants can communicate about the registration application matters.

6.5.1 Communication Conference on IMD

The conference before the application for IMD is accepted mainly covers the following topics:

(1) Major technical issues;

(2) Major safety issues;

(3) Clinical trial protocol;

(4) Summary and evaluation of stage clinical trial results;

(5) Other issues in need of communication.

The conferences held in the technical review stage of IMD are requested by the applicants, focused on the special communication on contents of *Deficiency Letter*.

6.5.2 Approach to Communication Application for IMD

The applicant who applies for a communication meeting can log in to the eRPS system to submit an application for a consultation appointment, and the corresponding department will designate a special person to handle it.

6.6 Others

(1) For the innovative medical devices that are approved in accordance with the Procedure through evaluation, the medical products administration at all levels and technical organizations concerned, according to their responsibilities and provisions of the Procedure, will provide priority to process the IMD and strengthen the communication with the applicants according to the principles of early intervention, dedicated staff and scientific review, under the premise that standards and procedures are not reduced.

(2) CMDE sets up the OIMDR to review the special review application for IMD and determine the management category of medical devices upon reviewing. If the management attributes of the applied IMD are questionable, the applicants shall first define the attributes and then submit the application for special review of IMD. For domestic enterprise applications, if the products are rated as Class II medical devices, the corresponding provincial medical products administration may follow this Procedure for review.

Here are things to be noted!

(1) The application for special review for IMD must be submitted before registration application of medical devices.
(2) Class I medical devices cannot be applied for special review for IMD.
(3) No application fee for special review for IMD.

(3) If IMD doesn't apply registration within 5 years after the notification of review results, such IMD shall not be reviewed according to the Procedure. After 5 years, the applicant can apply for special review of IMD again.

6.7 Case Interpretation

(1) What are the requirements for supporting documents of product intelligence property submitted in special review for IMD?

Interpretation: According to the relevant provisions in the *Special Review Procedure for Innovative Medical Devices*:

1) Where the applicant has obtained the patent right for invention of China, he/she shall provide the copy of the patent authorization certificate, claims, and specification signed and sealed by the applicant and the original copy of the patent register issued by the competent patent authority. The time for the special review of IMD shall not exceed five years from the patent publication date.

2) Where the applicant obtains the right to use the invention patent in China through transfer according to law, in addition to submitting the copy of the patent authorization certificate, claims, specification and copy of the patent register held by the patentee, the applicant shall also provide the original copy of the Filing Certificate of the Patent Licensing Contract issued by the patent authority. The time for the special review of IMD shall not exceed five years from the patent publication date.

3) Where an application for an invention patent has been disclosed by the patent administration department under the State Council and has not been licensed, it is necessary to provide the copies of supporting documents of the disclosure of the invention patent signed and sealed by the applicant (such as the notice of publication of the application for an invention patent, the notice of publication of the application for an invention patent and entry into the substantive review stage, the notice of entry into the substantive review stage of the application for an invention patent, etc.) and copies of the published version of the claims and specification. The search report is issued by Patent Search and Consultation Center of State Intellectual Property Office (SIPO), in which states that the product core technology protocol is of novelty and

creativity. In the course of reviewing an invention patent application, where the claim or the specification has been revised at the request of the competent patent review authority, the modified text shall be submitted. Where the patentee is changed, the supporting documents such as the copy of the notification of conformity with required procedures issued by the competent patent authority shall be submitted.

(2) What's the time limit for special review for IMD and how to inquire the innovation application results?

Interpretation: According to the relevant provisions in the *Special Review Procedure for Innovative Medical Devices,* after receiving an application for special review for IMD, OIMDR shall issue the review opinions within 60 working days (publicity and objection handling period not included). The OIMDR shall publicize the applicant and product name of an application project to be subject to special review on the website of the CMDE for no less than 10 working days. If any objection to the content that is publicized, the OIMDR shall make the final review decision after the study of relevant opinions. Applicants may inquire the review results by logging in the review progress query page on the website of CMDE.

6.8 References

NMPA Announcement on Issuing the Special Review Procedure for Innovative Medical Device (No. 83, 2018)

Announcement on Issuing the Guidance for the Preparation of Application

Dossiers for Special Review of Innovative Medical Devices (No.127, 2018)

Notice on Issuing the Operating Specification for the Communication for Technical Evaluation for the Registration of Innovative and Priority Medical Devices (December 1, 2021)

7. Priority Review and Approval

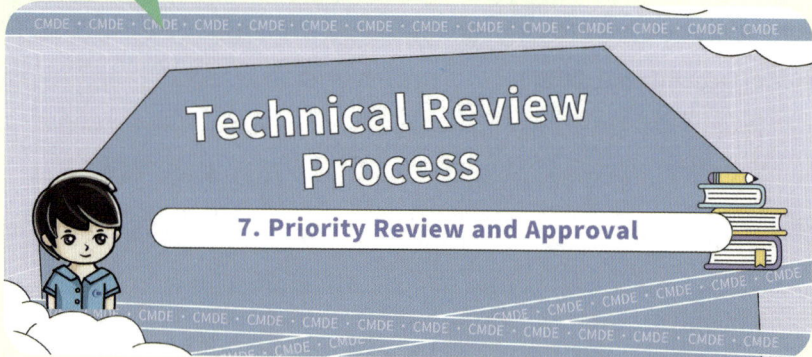

Technical Review Process

7. Priority Review and Approval

7.1 Overview

In October 2016, in order to ensure the clinical use needs of medical devices, the former CFDA issued the *Priority Review and Approval Procedure for Medical Devices* (hereinafter referred to as the Procedure), which was implemented on January 1, 2017.

What are the benefits of applying for priority review and approval?

·Getting priority on the waiting list for evaluation

·Getting priority for quality management system audit

·Getting priority for review and approval

·Getting special communication

7.2 Relevant Definitions

NMPA implements the priority review and approval policy for the registration of domestic Class III medical devices and imported Classes II and III medical devices which meet one of the following conditions.

(1) The medical devices which meet one of the following conditions:

1) The medical devices for diagnosis or treatment of rare diseases and with obvious clinical advantages;

2) The medical devices for diagnosis or treatment of malignant tumors and with obvious clinical advantages;

3) The medical devices for diagnosis or treatment of diseases which are endemic to and prevalent in the elderly and against which the existent diagnosis or treatment approaches have been ineffective;

4) The medical devices specific to children and with obvious clinical advantages;

5) The medical devices which are in urgent clinical need and there are no predicate products approved for registration in China.

(2) Medical devices under the national major scientific and technological projects or the national key research and development programs.

(3) Other medical devices that shall be subject to priority review and approval.

Conditions for application

1. The medical devices which meet one of the following conditions:

(1) The medical devices for diagnosis or treatment of rare diseases and with obvious clinical advantages;

(2) The medical devices for diagnosis or treatment of malignant tumors and with obvious clinical advantages;

(3) The medical devices for diagnosis or treatment of diseases which are endemic to and prevalent in the elderly and against which the existent diagnosis or treatment approaches have been ineffective;

(4) The medical devices specific to children and with obvious clinical advantages;

(5) The medical devices which are in urgent clinical need and there are no predicate products approved for registration in China.

2.Medical devices under the national major scientific and technological projects or the national key research and development programs.

3.Other medical devices that shall be subject to priority review and approval. According to the situation and opinions of various parties, NMPA organizes experts to review and decide whether to give priority review and approval.

7.3 Application Process

7.3.1 Application

For a medical device meeting the priority review and approval conditions described in (1) and (2) of 7.2 which shall be subject to priority review and approval according to the Procedure, the applicant shall submit an application for priority review and approval to NMPA. For a medical device meeting the priority review and approval conditions described in (3) of 7.2, NMPA will organize experts for assessment and then make a decision through broad–based consultation.

The applicant shall submit the *Application Form of Medical Device*

Priority Review and Approval together with the application for medical device registration, and submit the materials by reference to the *Guidance for Compilation of Application Dossiers of Priority Review and Approval Procedure for Medical Devices (Trial)*, in support of the procedural compliance of the applied products.

7.3.2 Formal Review

After formal review, application dossiers for priority review and approval of medical devices that meet the formal requirements specified in the Procedure shall be accepted.

7.3.3 Review

The Review Office of Medical Device Priority Review and Approval (hereinafter referred to as Priority Review Office) of CMDE is in charge of the review of priority evaluation, review & approval applications.

For a medical device meeting the priority review and approval application conditions described in (1) of 7.2, the Priority Review Office will organize experts for assessment and review and issue the review opinions. If it is proved by experts that priority review and approval is needed, it is proposed to give priority review and approval after confirmed by the Review Office.

For a medical device meeting the priority review and approval conditions described in (2) of 7.2, the Priority Review Office will review the applicant's submission and propose to approve the priority application if such application meets the requirements.

How to submit ?

If it conforms to the second item, submit the supporting documents

If the first and second items are met, the application form for priority review and approval shall be submitted at the same time as the registration submission

If it conforms to the first item, the Priority Review Office will organize experts for assessment and review

Those who meet the requirements are temporarily considered to be given priority for review and approval

Draw up

Issue the review opinions. If it is proved by experts that priority review and approval is needed, it shall be confirmed by the Review Office of priority review and approval

If there is no objection within the publicity period, it will enter the priority review and approval procedure, and CMDE will inform the applicant.

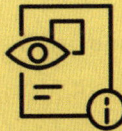

Publicity

Be included in the priority review and approval list

7.3.4 Publicity

The application proposed to be granted with priority review and approval, including the applicant name, product name and acceptance number will be publicized on CMDE's official website. If no objection is raised in the period of publicity, priority review and approval will be listed and the applicant will be notified.

7.3.5 Objection Handling

Any institution or individual who has any objection to the publicity of the product to be reviewed and approved in accordance with the Procedure shall put forward the objection within the specified publicity period; if the applicant has any objection to the review conclusion and the reasons for disapproval, it shall raise the objection within 10 working days upon receipt of the notification. The content of the objection is only limited to the original application items and original registration application dossiers. In principle, the application materials for objections submitted shall be written documents signed and sealed by the opposition.

After research, CMDE will formulate handling opinions on the application for objection and inform the opposition. Where there are clear handling opinions, CMDE will no longer accept the objection application for the same content.

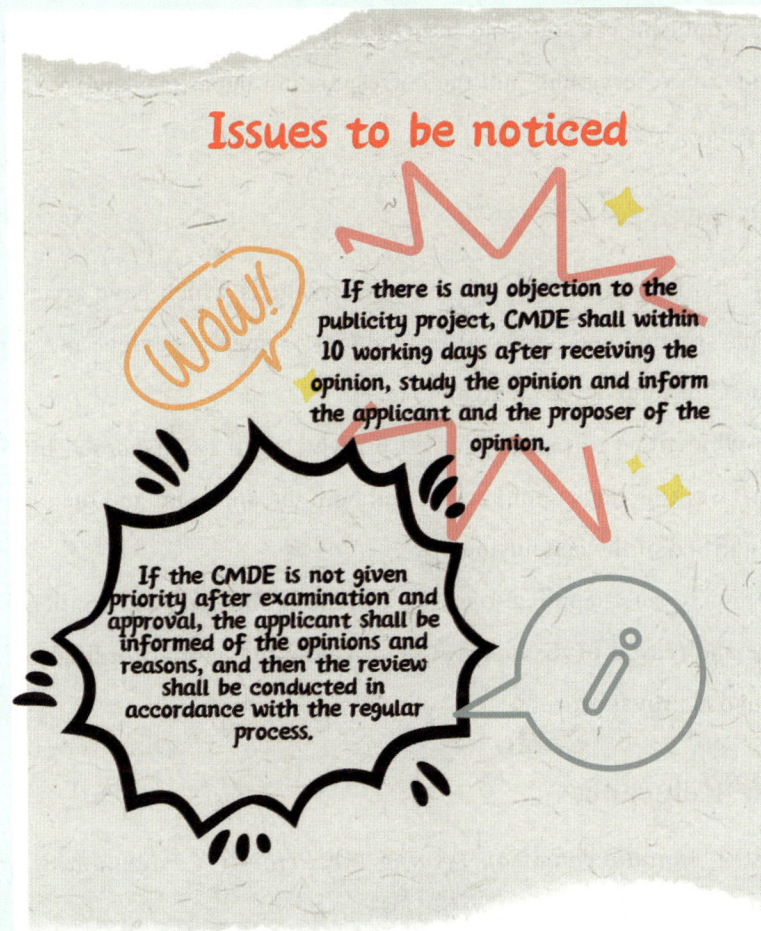

7.4 Priority Review and Approval Communication

For the medical devices approved for priority review and approval, the CMDE will proactively communicate with the applicant in the course of technical evaluation as required, and may arrange special communication as necessary.

The applicant can log in to the eRPS system to submit an application for a consultation reservation, and the corresponding department will designate a special person to handle it.

7.5 Others

(1) This Procedure does not apply to products which have gone through emergency review and approval procedures or special review and approval procedures for innovative medical devices.

(2) Objections to the publicized projects shall be discussed by CMDE within 10 working days upon receipt and both the applicant and the opposition will be notified of the conclusions.

(3) For rejected applications, the CMDE shall notify the applicant of its opinions and reason of disapproval, and handle the case according to regular review and approval procedures.

7.6 References

CFDA Announcement on Issuing the Priority Review and Approval Procedure for Medical Devices (No.168, 2016)

CFDA Announcement on the Issuance of the Guidance for Compilation of Application Dossiers of Priority Review and Approval Procedure for Medical Devices (Trial) (No. 28, 2017)

Notice on Issuing the Operating Specification for the Communication for Technical Evaluation for the Registration of Innovative and Priority Medical Devices (December 1, 2021)

8. Emergency Review and Approval

Technical review process

8.Emergency Review and Approval

8.1 Overview

In August 2009, in order to effectively prevent, timely control and eliminate the hazards of public health emergencies and ensure that the medical devices required for public health emergencies are reviewed and approved

Emergency Review and Approval for Medical Devices is to effectively prevent, timely control and eliminate the hazards of public health emergencies, and ensure that medical devices required for public health emergencies are approved as soon as possible.

as soon as possible, the former CFDA issued the *Notice on Printing and Issuing the Emergency Review and Approval Procedure for Medical Devices* (CFDA No.565, 2009). On December 29, 2021, the National Medical Products Administration revised and issued the *Emergency Review and Approval Procedure for Medical Devices*, which shall come into force as of the date of issuance.

When applying for emergency review and approval of medical devices, the domestic registration applicant shall inform the medical products administration of the corresponding province, autonomous region or municipality directly under the central government of the information of product required for emergency and product R&D. The medical products administration of provinces, autonomous regions and municipalities directly under the central government shall timely understand the development of relevant medical devices, take early intervention when necessary, evaluate the products to be proposed, and timely guide the registration applicant to carry out relevant application work.

What are the Principles for Emergency Review and Approval?

| Unified command | early intervention | on-demand review | scientific review and approval |

8.2 Relevant Definitions

The registration for domestic Class Ⅲ and imported Class Ⅱ and Class Ⅲ medical devices confirmed by the NMPA, which meet the emergency needs of public health emergencies, for which at present there are no similar products on the market in China, or although similar products have been on the market in China, the product supply cannot meet the emergency treatment needs of public health emergencies, shall be subject to emergency review and approval.

8.3 Application Process

8.3.1 Application

To apply for the emergency review and approval of domestic Class III and imported Class II and Class III medical devices, the *Application Form for Emergency Review and Approval of Medical Devices*, product research summary data and relevant instructions shall be submitted to the Acceptance Department of the NMPA.

8.3.2 Validation

The NMPA shall organize experts to assess whether the medical devices proposed for emergency review and approval and the medical devices required for emergency recommended in writing by the national emergency response working mechanism meet the requirements of 8.2, as well as the R&D maturity and production capacity, through meetings, letter review and written solicitation of opinions, and timely confirm whether the products are subject to emergency review and approval, and notify the applicant, the corresponding technical institutions and the medical products administration of provinces, autonomous regions and municipalities directly under the central government of the results.

8.3.3 Pre-review before Acceptance

For medical devices that have been confirmed by the NMPA for emergency review and approval (hereinafter referred to as medical devices subject to emergency review and approval), CMDE designates a dedicated person to intervene early, conduct consultation through appropriate methods according to the needs of the registration applicant, guide the preparation of registration application dossiers, and carry out pre-review before acceptance of the dossiers to be submitted for registration by the enterprise based on the principle of review in no time according to the requirements of medical device evaluation.

8.3.4 Acceptance

For medical devices subject to emergency review and approval, registration applicants shall tick "emergency review and approval" in the application form, CMDE shall sign for the registration application items on the same day and carry out the filing review in accordance with the requirements of the NMPA. For payment matters, the registration applicant can pay the fee according to the instructions on the payment notice.

8.3.5 Technical Evaluation

CMDE shall complete the technical evaluation on the registration application of domestic and imported Class III medical devices subject to emergency review and approval within 10 days after the registration application of emergency review and approval medical devices is transferred to the technical evaluation stage; the technical evaluation for registration application of imported Class II medical devices for emergency review and approval shall be completed within 5 days.

8.4 Communication

The applicant may communicate with relevant departments of the CMDE at any time after assessment and review by the NMPA to confirm that the medical device is subject to emergency review and approval.

8.5 Others

(1) For medical devices subject to emergency review and approval that are approved to go to the market with conditions, the validity period of the Medical Device Registration Certificate shall be consistent with the completion time limit in the additional conditions specified in the registration certificate, in principle, shall not exceed 1 year. If the registrant completes the additional conditions, he/she may apply for renewal registration before the expiry date. If the registration is qualified, the renewal registration will be approved and the registration certificate shall be valid for 5 years.

(2) For medical devices subject to emergency review and approval, if the registration applicant fails to complete the preparation of registration application dossiers and obtain the acceptance of registration application according to the registration requirements within 90 working days after the emergency review and approval is confirmed, the registration applicant will not be handled in accordance with the emergency review and approval. In principle, the applicant can refer to the Procedure for Priority Review and Approval of Medical Devices, and the evaluation and review & approval will be given priority after acceptance.

8.6 Reference

Announcement on Issuing the Emergency Review and Approval Procedure for Medical Devices (No.157, 2021)

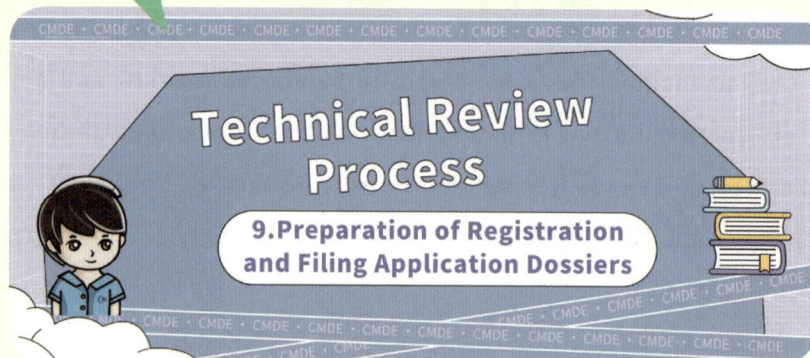

9. Preparation of Registration and Filing Application Dossiers

Technical Review Process

9. Preparation of Registration and Filing Application Dossiers

9.1 Overview

Medical device/IVD reagent registration refers to the activity that the registration applicant of medical device/IVD reagent submits an application for medical device/IVD reagent registration in accordance with the legal procedures and relevant requirements, and the medical products administration reviews the safety, effectiveness and quality controllability based on laws and regulations as well as the scientific cognition, and decide whether or not to approve such an application.

Medical device/IVD reagent filing refers to the activity that the filing applicant of medical device/IVD reagent submits the filing dossiers to the medical products administration in accordance with the legal procedures and relevant requirements, and the medical products administration files such submitted filing dossiers for future reference.

> Medical device/IVD reagent registration and filing shall comply with relevant laws, regulations, rules, and mandatory standards, follow the basic principles of medical device/IVD reagent safety and performance, and refer to relevant technical guidelines to prove that the registered and filing medical devices/IVD reagents are safe, effective, and controllable in quality, and ensure that the information in the whole process is true, accurate, complete and traceable.

9.2 Filing Application

9.2.1 Formal Requirements for Filing Dossiers

(1) Filing dossiers shall be complete, with the filing form well completed.

(2) All the documents other than the associated documents must be provided in Chinese. For the associated documents in foreign languages, a Chinese version shall be provided and signed and sealed by the agent. With regard to the application dossiers translated from foreign languages, the originals shall be provided.

(3) For a product made in China, the filing applicant shall affix its signature and seal thereon in case there are no special indications. "Signature and Seal" means that the filing applicant affixes the official seal or its legal

representative or person–in–charge affixes his/her signature and official seal.

(4) Unless otherwise specifically indicated, the originals of filing dossiers for imported products shall be sealed and signed by the filing applicant, while the dossier of Chinese version shall be sealed and signed by the agent. The "signature and seal" for originals of filing dossiers shall mean that the legal representative or person–in–charge of the filing applicant affixes his/her signature, or signature and official seal; with regard to the dossiers of Chinese version, the "signature and seal" shall mean that the agent affixes its official seal, or its legal representative or person–in–charge affixes his/her signature and official seal.

(5) For the associated documents, declaration of conformity, IFU and label in the filing dossiers of imported products provided by the overseas filing applicant, notarized documents issued by a notary authority at the location of the filing applicant shall be provided. The notarized documents can be obtained in manner of electronic notarization, but the explanatory documents on the notarization mode issued by the overseas filing applicant shall be submitted at the same time.

(6) Where the filing applicant submitted the hard copy of filing dossiers, a catalogue of filing dossiers submitted is required and shall contain the headings of Levels 1 and 2. In addition, a list must be attached to describe the specific page of each dossier.

9.2.2 Requirements for Filing Dossiers

Eligible filing applicants shall prepare the dossiers in accordance with the relevant requirements of the *Announcement of the National Medical Products Administration on the Matters Related to the Filing of Class I Medical Devices*.

> **How to prepare the filing dossiers?**
>
> Eligible filers shall prepare the dossiers in accordance with the relevant requirements of the *Announcement of the National Medical Products Administration on the Matters Related to the Filing of Class I Medical Devices*.

9.3 Registration Application

9.3.1 Requirements for Electronic Application of Registration Dossiers

On May 31, 2019, NMPA issued the *Announcement on Implementing Electronic Regulated Product Submission (eRPS) for Medical Devices*. In order to realize the electronic application for medical device registration, the eRPS system was officially implemented on June 24, 2019.

After implementing the eRPS system, see the *Announcement on Issuing the eRPS ToC Folder Structure for Medical Device Registration* for the RPS ToC for various medical device registration applications.

Level 1 heading of registration dossiers	Level 2 heading of registration dossiers
1. Regulatory Information	1.1 Chapter Table of Contents 1.2 Application Form 1.3 List of Terms/Acronyms 1.4 Product List 1.5 Associated Documents 1.6 Records of Contacts and Communications with Regulatory Authorities before Application 1.7 Declaration of Conformity
2. Summary Data	2.1 Chapter Table of Contents 2.2 Overview 2.3 Product Description 2.4 Scope of Application and Contraindications 2.5 Marketing History of the Proposed Product 2.6 Other Contents that Need to be Explained
3. Non–Clinical Data	3.1 Chapter Table of Contents 3.2 Risk Management Data of Product 3.3 General Principles Checklist for the Safety and Performance of Medical Devices 3.4 Product Technical Requirements and Test Report 3.5 Study Data 3.6 Non–clinical Bibliography 3.7 Stability Study 3.8 Other Data
4. Clinical Evaluation Data	4.1 Chapter Table of Contents 4.2 Clinical Evaluation Data 4.3 Other Data
5. Draft Label and Instructions for Use	5.1 Chapter Table of Contents 5.2 Instructions for Use 5.2 Draft Label 5.3 Other Data
6. Quality Management System Documents	6.1 Overview 6.2 Chapter Table of Contents 6.3 Manufacturing information 6.4 Quality Management System Procedure 6.4 Management Responsibility Procedure 6.5 Resource Management Procedure 6.7 Product Realization Procedure 6.8 Measurement, Analysis and Improvement Procedure for the Quality Management System 6.9 Information of Other Procedures of the Quality System 6.10 Quality Management System Verification Documents

Note: The requirements for registration application dossiers of medical devices are taken as an example here.

Level 1 heading of registration dossiers	Level 2 heading of registration dossiers
1. Regulatory Information	1.1 Chapter Table of Contents 1.2 Application Form 1.3 List of Terms/Acronyms 1.4 Product List 1.5 Associated Documents 1.6 Records of Contacts and Communications with Regulatory Authorities before Application 1.7 Declaration of Conformity
2. Summary Data	2.1 Chapter Table of Contents 2.2 Overview 2.3 Product Description 2.4 Intended Use 2.5 Marketing History of the Proposed Product 2.6 Other Contents that Need to be Explained
3. Non–Clinical Data	3.1 Chapter Table of Contents 3.2 Risk Management Data of Product 3.3 Basic Principles Checklist for the Safety and Performance of In Vitro Diagnostic Reagents 3.4 Product Technical Requirements and Test Report 3.5 Analytical Performance Study 3.6 Stability Study 3.7 Study on Cut–off Value or Reference Interval 3.8 Other Data
4. Clinical Evaluation Data	4.1 Chapter Table of Contents 4.2 Clinical Evaluation Data
5. Draft Label and Instructions for Use	5.1 Chapter Table of Contents 5.2 Instructions for Use 5.2 Draft Label 5.3 Other Data
6. Quality Management System Documents	6.1 Overview 6.2 Chapter Table of Contents 6.3 Manufacturing information 6.4 Quality Management System Procedure 6.4 Management Responsibility Procedure 6.5 Resource Management Procedure 6.7 Product Realization Procedure 6.8 Measurement, Analysis and Improvement Procedure for the Quality Management System 6.9 Information of Other Procedures of the Quality System 6.10 Quality Management System Verification Documents

Note: The requirements for registration application dossiers of IVD reagents are taken as an example here.

9.3.2 Requirements for Registration Dossiers

Eligible registration applicants should prepare dossiers in accordance with the relevant requirements of Attachment 5 *Requirements and Instructions for Registration Application Dossiers of Medical Devices* in the *Announcement on Issuing the Requirements for Registration Application Dossiers of Medical Devices and Formats of Approval Documents* and Attachment 4 *Requirements and Instructions for Registration Application Dossiers of In Vitro Diagnostic Reagents* in the *Announcement on Issuing the Requirements for Registration Application Dossiers of In Vitro Diagnostic Reagents and Formats of Approval Documents*.

HOW TO PREPARE THE REGISTRATION APPLICATION DOSSIERS?

Eligible registration applicants shall prepare the dossiers in accordance with the relevant requirements of the **Announcement on Issuing the Requirements for Registration Application Dossiers of Medical Devices and Formats of Approval Documents** and the **Announcement on Issuing the Requirements for Registration Application Dossiers of In Vitro Diagnostic Reagents and Formats of Approval Documents**.

9.4 Case Interpretation

What are the requirements for filling in the remark column in the application form?

Interpretation: The registration applicant shall complete the remarks of the application form, and the requirements are as follows: The applicant shall accurately write the expert/entity information of the stakeholders, including but not limited to physical and chemical indicator test, biological performance test, animal experiment, clinical trial, co-investigator, intellectual property buyer and seller, and shall clarify the experts to be avoided and the reasons therefore. If there are experts which are stakeholders, the name of the specific enterprise in which the experts participate and the name of the specific R&D project shall be specified. The remarks shall not be empty. If there is no relevant content, please fill in "None".

9.5 References

Announcement on the Issues Related to the Service Operation of Electronic Regulated Product Submission (eRPS) System (No.4, 2019)

Announcement on Issuing the Technical Guidelines for Electronic Submission of Medical Device Registration Application (No. 29, 2019)

Announcement on Implementing Electronic Regulated Product Submission (eRPS) for Medical Devices (No.46, 2019)

Announcement on Issuing the eRPS ToC Folder Structure for Medical Device Registration (No.15, 2021)

Announcement on Issuing the Requirements for Registration Application Dossiers of Medical Devices and Formats of Approval Documents (No. 121, 2021)

Announcement on Issuing the Requirements for Registration Application Dossiers of In Vitro Diagnostic Reagents and Formats of Approval Documents (No.122, 2021)

NMPA Announcement on the Matters Related to the Filing of Class I Medical Devices (No.62, 2022)

10. Acceptance

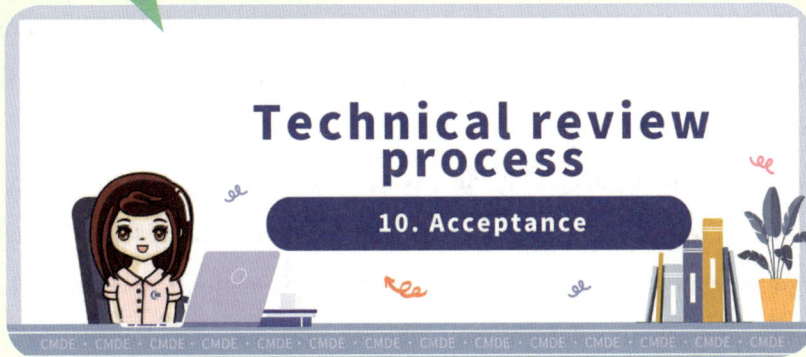

Technical review process

10. Acceptance

10.1 Overview

Class Ⅰ medical devices are subject to filing administration, while Class Ⅱ and Ⅲ medical devices are subject to registration administration. The applicant may handle the procedures with the corresponding medical regulatory authorities in accordance with the *Regulations for the Supervision and Administration of Medical Devices*.

10.1.1 Filing

With regard to medical device filing, the applicant shall go through filing with the medical products administration according to the requirements under "9. Preparation of Registration and Filing Application Dossiers". Different filing matters are specified as follows:

(1) The filing applicant will complete the filing after submitting the filing dossiers that comply with the requirements of the *NMPA Announcement on the Matters Related to the Filing of Class I Medical Devices*. For a medical device to be filed, the filing authority shall provide the filing number (Notification of Filing Number) and disclose relevant information set forth in the Filing

Information Form for Class Ⅰ Medical Devices or the Filing Information Form for Class Ⅰ In Vitro Diagnostic Reagents within the specified time limit.

(2) When handling the filing of medical devices, if the filing dossiers cannot meet the requirements, the corresponding medical products administration shall inform the filing applicant and explain the reasons.

(3) For a filed medical device, where the contents set forth in the filing information form and the product technical requirements filed are changed, the filing applicant shall apply for change filing information to the original filing authority and submit a description of the changes and related documents.

10.1.2　Registration and Acceptance of registration

When applying for medical device registration, the applicant/registration applicant shall prepare the application dossiers according to the requirements of "9. Preparation of Registration and Filing Application Dossiers" and submit them to the corresponding medical products administration. If the application items fall within the authority of the department and the application dossiers are complete and meet the requirements for filing review upon filing review, the application dossiers will be accepted; if the application dossiers are incomplete or do not meet the requirements, all the contents to be supplemented and corrected shall be informed once within 5 days; if they are not informed, the application shall be deemed as being accepted from the date the application dossiers are received.

When and Where?

Time

Working Day (9:
00- 11 : 00 a.m. 13:00 -
4:30 p.m.)
Closed on Wednesday
and Friday afternoon

Site

Administrative
hand service hall

What are needed to take

✓ Registration application dossier (hard copies and U-key)

✓ Original and photocopy of the identity certificate of the staff

✓ The power of attorney of the applicant (consistent with the unit with the seal and seal of the application form) for the matters done by the entrusted personnel

For more information on the template of "power of attorney", see "*Notice on handling Administrative license acceptance and approval to receive and submit Power of Attorney* (No. 232, 2019)"

Procedures

Register in Website

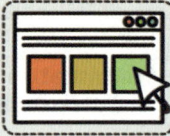

Log in to NMPA's online reservation system to register.

Refer to the **Announcement on Starting Online Reservation System of Administrative Service Hall of the National Medical Products Administration** (No.192) and the **Announcement on Adjusting the Reservation Period of Online Reservation System of Administrative Service Hall of the National Medical Products Administration** (No.220) for relevant operation.

Reservation for Acceptance

You can log in to the online reservation acceptance system from 7 a.m. to 11:00 p.m. every day to make on-line reservation, or

Come directly to the Administrative Service Hall of NMPA.

On-site handling

Go to the window for on-site handling by queuing.

Priority handling for the online reservation.

tips : The following illustration contents are only applicable to the registration items of imported Class II/Class III medical devices and domestic Class III medical devices accepted by CMDE.

Filing review (By CMDE)

The eRPS system randomly assigns qualified CMDE reviewers to filing review the application dossier.

The CMDE will give formal examination on the application items meeting the requirements upon filing review and issue the "Notice of Acceptance" and "Bill of Payment";

otherwise, those not meeting the requirements will be returned together with a "Notice of Supplement and Correction of Application Dossiers" or "Notice of Rejection".

NO!

10.2 Submission of Application Dossiers

The application dossiers can be subject to online and offline submission.

10.2.1 Online Submission

The applicant/registration applicant may submit the application dossiers online through the eRPS system with a Certificate Authority (hereinafter referred to as CA). The eRPS system provides two ways of application submission. The applicant/registration applicant can log in to the system using the web version or the client. Before submitting the application dossiers online, the applicant/registration applicant shall apply for the supporting CA.

To guide the applicant/registration registrant to use the eRPS system for online submission correctly, NMPA issued the *Announcement on Issuing the Technical Guidelines for Electronic Submission of Medical Device Registration Application.*

10.2.2 Offline Submission

There are two ways of offline submission: by post or on–site submission to the Administrative Service Hall of NMPA.

10.2.2.1 Submission by Post

The application dossiers may be posted to the Administrative Service Hall of NMPA. The CMDE shall, within five working days upon receipt, conduct filing review on the application dossiers to decide whether or not to accept the application or request the application to submit the supplementary and correction materials. The review conclusions will be delivered to the applicant/ registration applicant by post.

10.2.2.2 On-site Submission

The applicant/registration applicant can go directly to the Administrative

Service Hall of NMPA with or without an online reservation, and take a waiting list number for their on–site submission. Priority is given to those with an on–line reservation.

The applicant/registration applicant can log in to the sub–website of the "Online Service Hall" of the portal website of NMPA for on–line reservation.

Precautions for on-line reservation

①	②	③	④
Applicants shall sign up in advance. Approved applicants are accessible to on-line reservation service.	An applicant enterprise can sign up at most for 10 registration agents dealing with their registration matters. Each agent can make only one reservation on one service type each working day.	The agent with a reservation registered shall take his/her valid identity certificate and power of attorney and go to the Administrative Service Hall to take the reservation number for their business handling.	A registered reservation can be canceled four natural days before the reserved date. Failure to show up for a scheduled reservation without canceling is considered as a no-show. The applicants whose no-show times is higher than three will have their on-line reservation account frozen for 30 days, during which the applicant can only apply for business handling on-site at the service hall. The frozen account will be unlocked automatically 30 days later, the enterprise registration account can continue to be used, and the times of no-show will be recounted.

10.3 Payment for Service Fees

The CMDE will give formal examination on the application items meeting the requirements upon filing review and issue the "Notice of Acceptance" and "Bill of Payment"; otherwise, those not meeting the requirements will be returned together with a "Notice of Supplement and Correction of Application Dossiers" or "Notice of Rejection".

Where the registration application is submitted offline, the CMDE shall deliver the paper administrative acceptance document to the applicant/

registration applicant by post by default; if the registration application is submitted online, the applicant/registration applicant can log in to the eRPS system with CA to simultaneously consult the electronic document.

For the matters involving payment, the applicant/registration applicant shall pay for the service fees according to the instructions on the Bill of Payment.

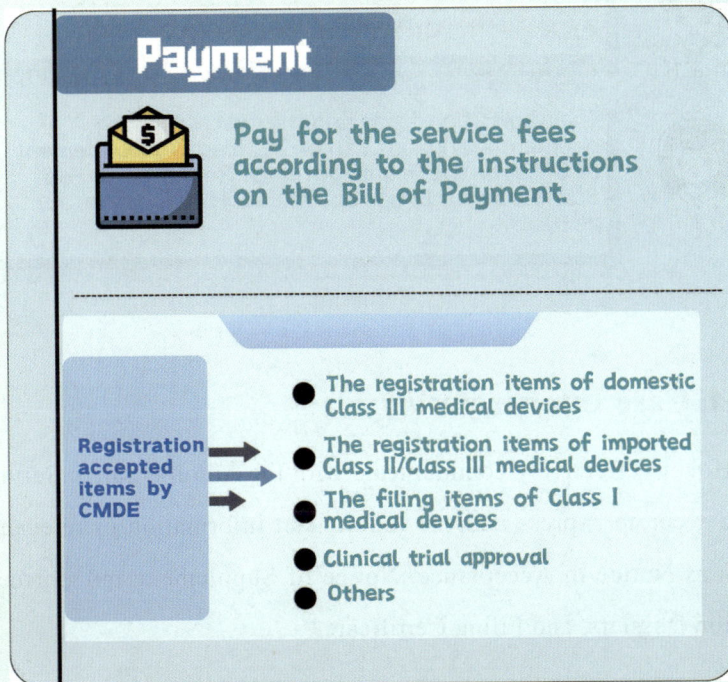

Payment

Pay for the service fees according to the instructions on the Bill of Payment.

Registration accepted items by CMDE

- The registration items of domestic Class III medical devices
- The registration items of imported Class II/Class III medical devices
- The filing items of Class I medical devices
- Clinical trial approval
- Others

TIPS

After the registration dossier submitted online or on-site are uploaded successfully, the registration dossier will be transferred to the receiving link of the eRPS system to sign the successful SMS notification.

The decision on the registration dossier will be made within 5 working days: if they are not informed, the application shall be deemed as being accepted from the date the application dossiers are received

The application items and the corresponding payment standards can be inquired: *Announcement of CFDA on the Promulgation of Registration Fee Standards for Drugs and Medical Devices* (No. 53, 2015)

10.4 Case Interpretation

(1) How to effectively communicate with the Administrative Service Hall about the accurate express address and contact information of relevant paper data such as Notice of Acceptance, Notice of Supplement and Correction of Application Dossiers, and Filing Certificate?

Interpretation: The Administrative Service Hall will give priority to the express address and contact information noted in "Other Questions to Describe" in the application form as the effective express information. If there is no content in this part, the information of the applicant/registrant/agent in the application form will be used as the effective express information. In order to ensure the timely and accurate delivery of relevant documents, it is recommended to accurately fill in the registration application form.

(2) How to apply for registration of imported medical devices that have obtained the registration certificate within the territory of China and for which the production is to be transferred from overseas to China?

Interpretation: According to the *Announcement of National Medical Products Administration on Matters Concerning the Implementation of the Measures for the Administration of Registration and Filing of Medical Devices* and the *Measures for the Administration of Registration and Filing of In Vitro Diagnostic Reagents* (No.76, 2021), the registration of medical devices manufactured in China by overseas enterprises shall be applied for by domestic manufacturers as registration applicants. For imported medical devices for which the registration certificate has been obtained, the registration application dossiers can be submitted by reference to the *Announcement of National Medical Products Administration on Matters Concerning the Production of Imported Medical Devices in Domestic Enterprises in China* (No.104, 2020).

10.5 References

Announcement on Issuing the Technical Guidelines for Electronic Submission of Medical Device Registration Application (No. 29, 2019)

NMPA Announcement on the Matters Related to the Filing of Class I Medical Devices (No.62, 2022)

11. Review and Approval

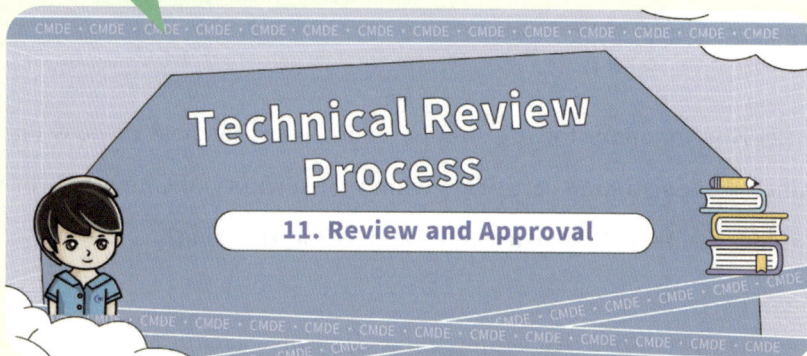

Technical Review Process
11. Review and Approval

11.1 Review and Approval Authority

Medical device covers a wide variety of products, ranging from simple tongue depressors to complicated cardiac pacemakers. To effectively regulate medical devices, the regulatory authorities in China divide medical devices into three classes according to risks. The classes will increase along with the increase of risks. The regulatory measures are different along with classification categories: Class I medical devices shall be subject to the product filing administration, and Class II and Class III medical devices shall be subject to the product registration administration.

In accordance with the *Regulations for the Supervision and Administration of Medical Devices*, the domestic medical devices of Classes I , II and III and the imported medical devices of Classes I , II and III shall be subject to the filing or registration application with different medical products administration. The filing and registration of medical devices made in Hong Kong, Macao and Taiwan shall be subject to the procedures as imported medical devices. See Table 5 for the competent authorities of filing or registration for medical devices at different classification categories.

Table 5 Table of Centralized Supervision and Registration/Filing of Medical Devices at Home and abroad

Product attribute		Type of management	Competent authority
Domestic	Class I	Filing	Municipal–level medical products administration within the district
	Class II	Registration	Provincial–level medical products administration
	Class III	Registration	National Medical Products Administration
Overseas	Class I	Filing	National Medical Products Administration
	Class II	Registration	National Medical Products Administration
	Class III	Registration	National Medical Products Administration

11.2 Review and Approval Process

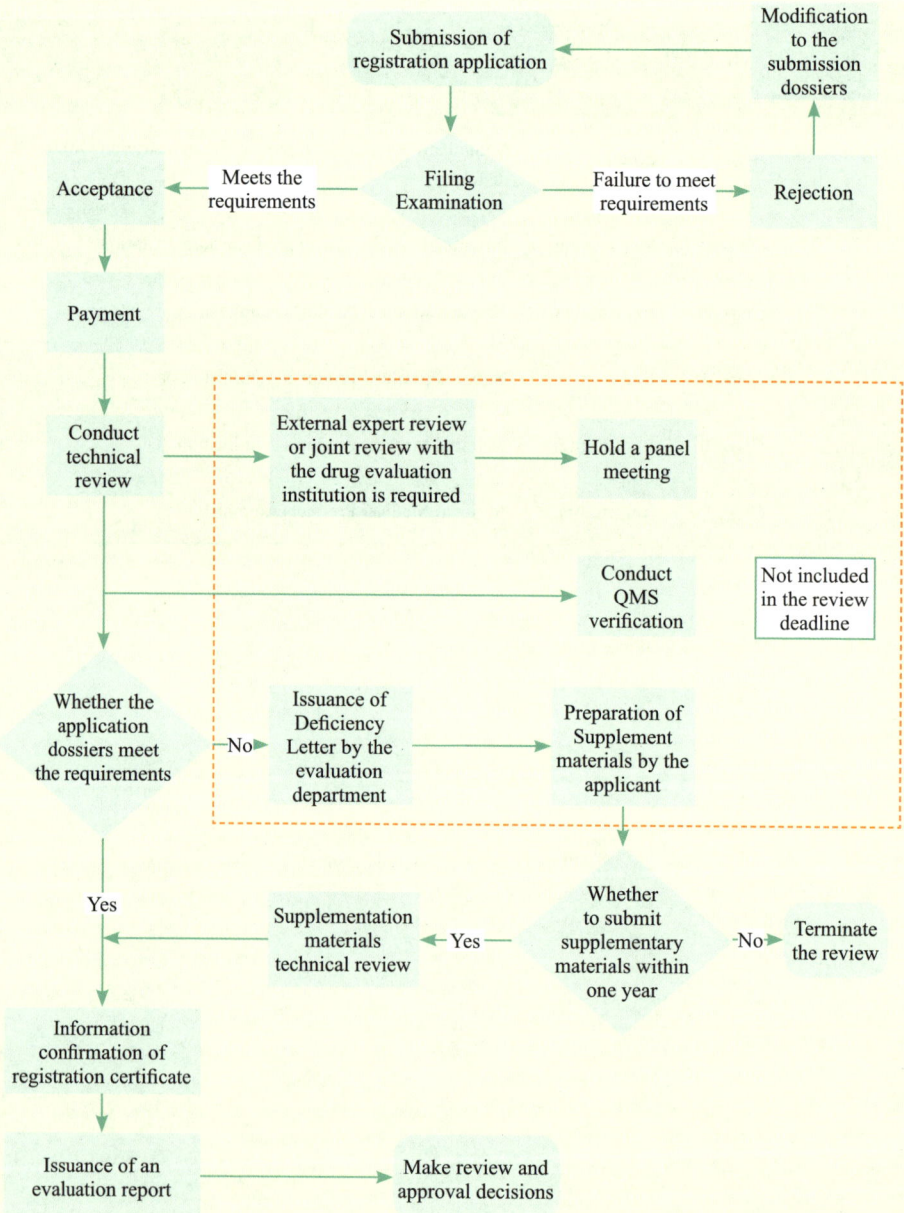

```
                                          Submission of  ◄───────  Modification
                                          registration              to the
                                          application               submission
                                                                    dossiers
                                              │                         ▲
                                              ▼                         │
Acceptance ◄── Meets the ──── Filing ──── Failure to meet ──► Rejection
               requirements   Examination  requirements
    │
    ▼
Payment
    │
    ▼
Conduct          External expert review
technical   ───► or joint review with   ───► Hold a panel
review           the drug evaluation          meeting
                 institution is required

                                          Conduct         Not included
                          ──────────────► QMS             in the review
                                          verification    deadline

    │
    ▼
Whether the      Issuance of              Preparation of
application      Deficiency               Supplement
dossiers meet ◄─No─ Letter by the    ───► materials by the
the requirements    evaluation             applicant
                    department

    │                                         │
  Yes                                         ▼
    │            Supplementation          Whether
    │            materials        ◄─Yes─  to submit      ─No─► Terminate
    │◄────────── technical review          supplementary        the review
    │                                      materials within
    ▼                                      one year
Information
confirmation of
registration certificate
    │
    ▼
Issuance of an   ────────────────► Make review and
evaluation report                  approval decisions
```

11.2.1 Acceptance

When receiving the filing or registration application, the medical product administration shall conduct filing examination on the application dossiers, and the acceptance opinions may involve the following three circumstances:

(1) For the application subjects that are within the authority scope of the authority with complete application dossiers and in conformity with the acceptance review, the application shall be accepted.

(2) If the application dossiers are incomplete or do not meet the acceptance review requirements, the medical product administration will notify, within five working days, the applicant of all the materials to be supplemented and corrected; if no additional information is required within five working days, the dossiers are considered accepted.

(3) Application matters not corresponding to the responsibilities of the authority where the application is made will be rejected.

See "10. Acceptance" for specific acceptance procedures.

11.2.2 Payment

After a registration application is accepted, the CMDE will issue a Notice of Acceptance and a Bill of Payment to the applicant, who shall pay relevant expenses on schedule according to the Bill of Payment upon receipt. See "10.3 Payment for Service Fees".

11.2.3 Technical Review

The registration application projects shall be transferred to technical review department within 3 working days from the date of acceptance. The technical review department will complete technical review within the specified time frame: 60 working days for registration of Class II medical devices, 90 working days for registration of Class Ⅲ medical devices and 60 working days for supplementary materials. The time frame for technical review of medical device clinical trial application is 60 working days, and the time frame for technical review after supplementary materials submission is 40 working days.

Technical review timing will cease in any of the following circumstances:

(1) An expert consultation meeting shall be convened when it is necessary to conduct external expert review and joint review of drug evaluation departments. See the detailed requirements in "14. Expert Consultation".

(2) When it is necessary to conduct the quality management system verification on research, development and production of products for registration applicants, the medical products administration under provinces, autonomous regions and municipalities directly under the central government shall be responsible for quality management system verification of domestic medical devices of Classes Ⅱ and Ⅲ. The quality management system verification shall be completed within 30 working days by the medical products administration under provinces, autonomous regions and municipalities directly under the central government according to relevant requirements. The technical departments of quality management system verification under NMPA is in charge of quality management system verification of Classes Ⅱ and Ⅲ imported medical devices. See the detailed requirements in "12. Verification of Registration Quality Management System".

(3) Where the technical review department requires the applicant to supplement application dossiers during technical review, it shall notify the applicant at one time of all content that needs to be supplemented. The registration applicant shall, within one year after receiving the Deficiency Letter, provide supplementary materials one-off in accordance with

the Deficiency Letter. Where a registration applicant fails to submit the supplementary materials within the specified time limit, the technical review department may terminate the technical review, make suggestions on rejection of registration application, and the medical product administration will make decision that the registration application is rejected after review. If there is any doubt about the content of the Deficiency Letter, the applicant/registration applicant can apply for an appointment to consult the supplementary and correction opinions and communicate with the reviewer. See "13. Supplementary Materials" for the specific procedures for supplementary materials.

(4) Request instructions from the NMPA on relevant policy issues involved in the technical review, pending comments, etc., and other circumstances in which the review timing can be suspended according to regulations and relevant documents.

The following time is not included in the relevant working time limit:

1) The time taken by the applicant for supplementary materials and rectification after verification;

2) Time for delaying the verification due to the applicant;

3) The time when external expert consultation is needed, the expert consultation meeting is held, and the drug–device combination products need to be jointly reviewed with the drug review agency;

4) If the review and approval procedures are suspended in accordance with regulations, the time taken during the suspension of the review and approval procedures;

5) The time taken for quality management system verification.

11.2.4 Approval

The medical product administration shall decide whether to approve the application within 20 working days after the end of technical review. For those products meeting the requirements of safety, effectiveness and quality control, the registration shall be approved, and the Medical Device Registration Certificate will be issued, and the approved product technical requirements shall be sent to the registration applicant in the form of attachment. For the products that are not approved for registration, the reasons shall be given in written form.

11.3 Query of Review and Approval Progress

NMPA

- **Go to the Official Website of the NMPA**

  Log into the Official Website of the NMPA to enter the Online Service Hall for query

TIPS Through the methods above, you can query the application status of the new product registration, change registration and reissue application of domestic Class III medical devices, imported Class II medical devices and Class III medical devices that have been accepted by the National Medical Products Administration.

1. The "Payment Status" in the query results is divided into: Paid, Unpaid, No charge.

2. There are the following circumstances for the "Registration Status" in the query results: Under technical review, Voluntary revocation, Under approval, Suspension of the review, Review completed - certificate to be issued, Certificate making completed - approvals to be issued, Certificate making completed - the old certificate to be returned, Certificate making completed - approvals having been issued.

CMDE

• Enter the Official Website of the CMDE

Click on Review Progress Query and follow the prompt on the page to enter the appropriate information for query

• Enter the eRPS system

The status of all projects can be viewed on the platform home page by logging into the eRPS system via the applicant's CA.

TIPS

The evaluation progress of the accepted registration application can be queried through the above channels. The progress status may be as follows: Under review by the chief reviewer, Under division chief review, Director issuance, Transferred to the Department of Medical Device Regulation, Evaluation completed, Filed, Completed, Under supplementary materials preparation, Coordination of panel meeting, etc.

The above query results are only for the applicant to understand the evaluation progress of accepted medical device registration application matters. The relevant information is for reference only, and the formal notice shall prevail. The query results shall not be used as any proof.

CMDE
· **Follow the WeChat Official Account of the CMDE**

Query via Corporate Services – Product Registration Status Tracking.

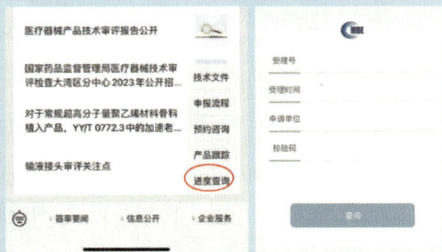

CMDE

The evaluation system will automatically send an SMS to the contact persons who filled in the application form to remind them of important matters such as the receipt of application dossiers, acceptance/rejection, notification of supplementary and correction materials, receipt of pre-review/feedback and receipt of supplementary and correction materials.

11.4 References

CFDA's Decision on Adjusting Certain Procedures for Administrative Review and Approval of Medical Devices (CFDA Decree No. 32)

Announcement on the Information Confirmation of Registration Certificate for Medical Devices and the Attachments thereof (No. 9, 2021)

NMPA Notice on Issuing the Operation Specifications for the Review and Approval of Registration of Domestic Class III and Imported Medical Devices (November 2, 2021)

NMPA Notice on Issuing the Operation Specifications for the Review and Approval of Registration of Domestic Class II Medical Devices (November 2, 2021)

12. Verification of Registration Quality Management System

Technical review process

12. Verification of Registration Quality Management System

12.1 Overview

The registration applicant shall submit quality management system materials related to product R&D or production at the time of registration. When a medical products administration accepting the registration considers that it is necessary to verify the quality management system (QMS) during technical evaluation, the medical products administration shall organize the verification on the quality management system and may refer to the original data as needed.

12.2 Verification Requirements for Different Types of Products

(1) The verification of the quality management system of domestic Class Ⅲ medical device or IVD reagens shall be conducted by medical products administration of the provinces, autonomous regions, and municipalities directly under the Central Government where registration

applicants are located after notified by the CMDE.

(2) The verification of the quality management system for domestic Class II medical devices or IVD reagents shall be organized and conducted by medical products administration of the provinces, autonomous regions, and municipalities directly under the Central Government where registration applicants are located.

(3) When conducting the technical evaluation on imported Class II and Class III medical devices or IVD reagents, if CMDE deems it necessary to verify the quality management system, it shall notify the Center for Food and Drug Inspection (CFDI) of NMPA to conduct verification according to relevant requirements.

Verification Requirements for Different Types of Products

(1) CMDE shall notify medical regulatory authorities of the provinces, autonomous regions, or municipalities directly under the Central Government where applicants are located to conduct the verification of domestic Class III products.

(2) Medical regulatory authorities of the provinces, autonomous regions, or municipalities directly under the Central Government where applicants are located shall organize and conduct the verification of domestic Class II products.

(3) CFDI shall conduct the verification of imported Class II and Class III products according to relevant requirements.

12.3 Relevant Time Limit for Verification of Domestic Class III Products

(1) CMDE shall issue the notice on the verification of the registration

quality management system within 10 working days after the acceptance of the application for medical device registration.

(2) The medical products administration of the provinces, autonomous regions or municipalities directly under the Central Government shall complete the quality management system verification within 30 working days upon receipt of the verification notice.

(3) If the verification result is reported as re-verification after rectification, the registration applicant shall submit a re-verification application and rectification report to the original verification department at one time within 6 months from the date of receiving the rectification opinion. The original verification department shall complete the re-verification within 30 working days after receiving the application for re-verification.

(4) The medical products administration of the provinces, autonomous regions or municipalities directly under the Central Government shall send the notice on the verification result to the CMDE within 5 working days after making the conclusions of "pass", "pass after rectification", "fail" and "fail to pass after rectification".

12.4 Verification Process of Domestic Class III Products

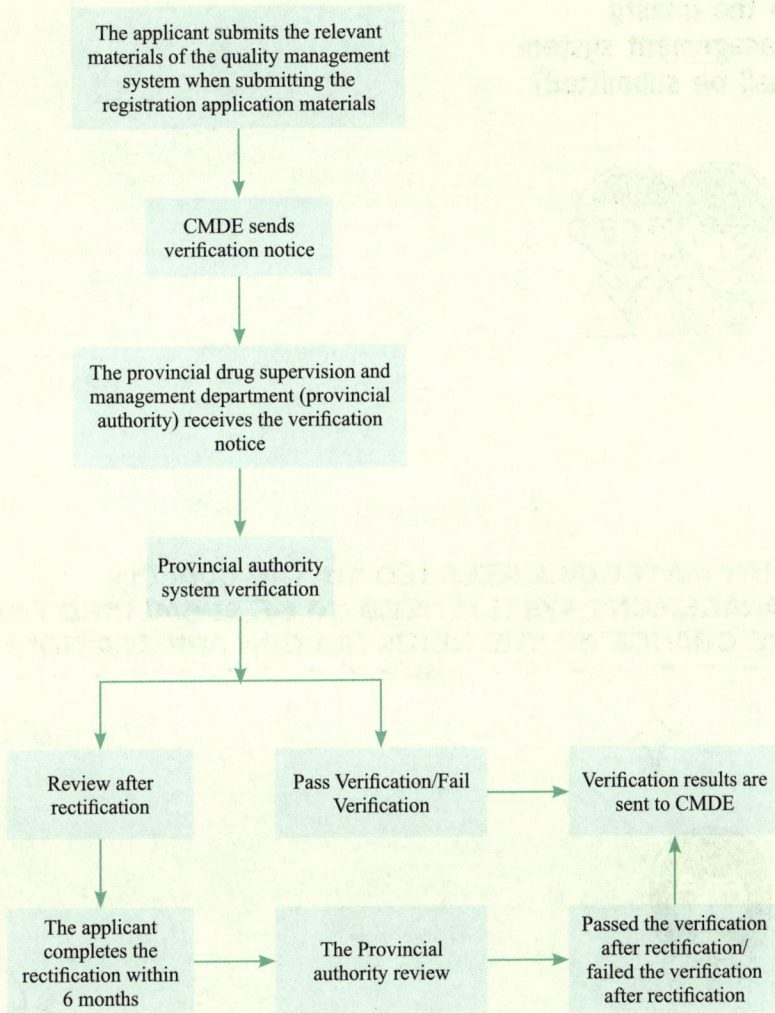

```
┌─────────────────────────────────┐
│ The applicant submits the relevant │
│ materials of the quality management │
│ system when submitting the        │
│ registration application materials │
└─────────────────────────────────┘
                │
                ▼
        ┌──────────────────┐
        │ CMDE sends       │
        │ verification notice │
        └──────────────────┘
                │
                ▼
┌─────────────────────────────────┐
│ The provincial drug supervision and │
│ management department (provincial │
│ authority) receives the verification │
│ notice                            │
└─────────────────────────────────┘
                │
                ▼
        ┌──────────────────┐
        │ Provincial authority │
        │ system verification │
        └──────────────────┘
```

| Review after rectification | Pass Verification/Fail Verification | → | Verification results are sent to CMDE |

| The applicant completes the rectification within 6 months | → | The Provincial authority review | → | Passed the verification after rectification/ failed the verification after rectification |

What materials related to the quality management system shall be submitted?

The documents shall be submitted in accordance with the contents related to quality management system documents described in the relevant requirements of *Attachment 5 Requirements and Instructions for Registration Application Dossiers of Medical Devices* in the *Announcement on Issuing the Requirements for Registration Application Dossiers of Medical Devices and Formats of Approval Documents* and *Attachment 4 Requirements and Instructions for Application Dossiers of In Vitro Diagnostic Reagents* in the *Announcement on Issuing the Requirements for Application Dossiers of In Vitro Diagnostic Reagents and Formats of Approval Documents.*

WHAT MATERIALS RELATED TO THE QUALITY MANAGEMENT SYSTEM NEED TO BE SUBMITTED FOR THE CHANGE OF THE REGISTRATION APPLICATION?

If the specific reasons or purposes for the change of medical devices involve changes in the raw materials, production process, scope of application, and usage method, materials related to the quality management system shall be submitted, and the audit of the quality management system shall be conducted on the changed parts.

If the specific reasons or purposes for the change of IVD reagents involve changes in the raw materials and production process, materials related to the quality management system shall be submitted, and the audit of the quality management system shall be conducted on the changed parts.

WHAT ARE THE SCENARIOS WHERE THE QUALITY MANAGEMENT SYSTEM FAILS TO PASS THE AUDIT?

IN THE INITIAL INSPECTION, IF THE REQUIREMENTS OF "VERIFICATION PASSED" CANNOT BE MET, THE VERIFICATION CONCLUSION SHALL BE RECORDED AS "VERIFICATION FAILED". FOR THE SCENARIOS WHERE RE-VERIFICATION IS REQUIRED, IF THE RE-VERIFICATION APPLICATION AND RECTIFICATION REPORT ARE NOT SUBMITTED WITHIN THE SPECIFIED TIME LIMIT AND THE REQUIREMENTS OF "VERIFICATION PASSED" STILL CANNOT BE MET AFTER RECTIFICATION AND RE-VERIFICATION, THE VERIFICATION CONCLUSION SHALL BE RECORDED AS "VERIFICATION FAILED AFTER RECTIFICATION". IF THE APPLICANT REFUSES TO ACCEPT THE ON-SITE INSPECTION OF THE QUALITY MANAGEMENT SYSTEM, THE VERIFICATION CONCLUSION SHALL BE RECORDED AS "VERIFICATION FAILED".

12.5 References

Notice of the Department of Comprehensive Affairs, Planning, and Finance Affairs of NMPA on Issuing the Working Procedures for Verification of Registration Quality Management System of Domestic Class III Medical Devices (NMPA No.13, 2022)

NMPA Announcement on Issuing Guidelines for the Inspection of Quality Management System for Medical Device Registration (No. 50, 2022)

13. Supplementary Materials

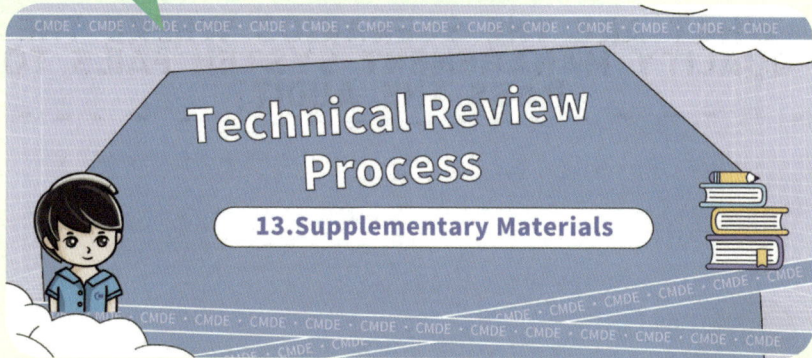

Technical Review Process

13.Supplementary Materials

13.1 Definition

13.1.1 Process of Issuing Deficiency Letter

The process of issuing Deficiency Letter refers to the process in which the reviewers develop and issue a Deficiency Letter of Medical Devices to

Issuance of Deficiency Letter

When the registration application dossiers submitted by the registration applicant do not meet the relevant requirements, CMDE reviewer will ask the registration applicant to submit the Supplementary Materials, and issues the "Deficiency Letter" to one-time notification.

the registration applicant to require supplementary materials because the registration application dossiers submitted by the registration applicant do not meet the regulations and rules or the relevant evaluation requirements, fail to prove the safety and effectiveness of the proposed product.

13.1.2 Process of Submitting Supplementary and Correction Materials

The process of submitting supplementary and correction materials herein refers to the process in which the materials required are objectively and fully explained, summarized with reference to the requirements of the Deficiency Letter of Medical Devices, and then submitted by the registration applicant to the responsible evaluation authority.

13.2 Relevant Procedures and Requirements

The registration applicant shall submit the supplementary materials within a year in accordance with the requirements of the Deficiency Letter of Medical Devices. In order to ensure the smooth submission of supplementary materials, the registration applicant shall make full use of the communication and exchange approaches at the stages of evaluation and issuing Deficiency Letter, and the pre–review of supplementary materials and other service channels to communicate reasonably with the reviewers.

13.2.1 Principles for Reply to the Deficiency Letter of Medical Devices

(1) The basic contents of the supplementary materials submitted by the registration applicant shall be consistent with that of the registration dossiers submitted for the first time, in one–to–one correspondence with the required contents of Deficiency Letter of Medical Devices, and shall be described

Deficiency Letter

The carrier of deficiency letter

What should I do?

Deficiency Letter

- One-time notification for deficiency letter by CMDE reviewer
- Issues the "Deficiency Letter" and send it to the registration applicant

- Submit the Supplementary Materials within one year
- Submit the information to CMDE in official form at one time
- The time for the preparation of Supplementary Materials shall not be included in the time limit for review.
- Termination of the review process for failure to submit Supplementary Materials on time

separately.

(2) The registration applicant shall ensure that the supplementary materials to be submitted are authentic and valid, and are relevant to the requirements of Deficiency Letter of Medical Devices.

(3) The registration applicant shall ensure that the contents regarding the supplementary materials to be submitted are grammatically correct and readable without ambiguity.

(4) The processes of issuing Deficiency Letter and submitting Supplementary and Correction Materials shall be only relevant to the scope of materials submitted during the registration application, and change to the scope of original application shall not be made through supplementary materials.

(5) In case of requirements for supplementary and correction materials for which the registration applicant is unable to verify, confirm or implement, the registration applicant shall give detailed reasons and provide scientific evidence.

The registration applicant shall designate a dedicated person to confirm the time frame for supplementary and correction, communication appointment, preparation of supplementary materials and other relevant matters, so as to improve the quality and efficiency of supplementary. The dedicated person shall have corresponding specialized knowledge and be familiar with the laws, rules, regulations related to medical device registration as well as relevant technical evaluation requirements. The registration applicant shall ensure the continuity of the supplementary and correction, and shall not change the dedicated person frequently during the process.

13.2.2 Requirements for Reply to the Deficiency Letter of Medical Devices

When the registration applicant submits relevant supplementary materials, it is necessary to simultaneously submit the "Description on the Content of Supplementary Materials" and specific supplementary documents for "Deficiency Letter of Medical Devices".

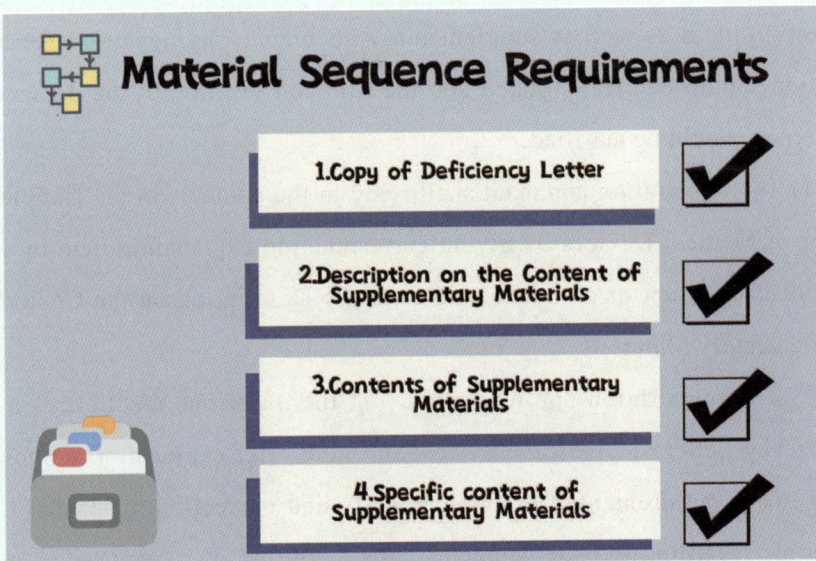

How to reply to the requirements for supplementary and correction materials?

It is recommended that the description of each relevant clause include the following elements:	1 Brief description of the understanding to the questions mentioned in Deficiency Letter of Medical Devices	2 Brief description of the reply idea or demonstrative inference	3 Basis for supplementary and correction materials
	4 Objective evidences, documents, data or information, etc. specifically included	5 Description of special circumstances	6 Others

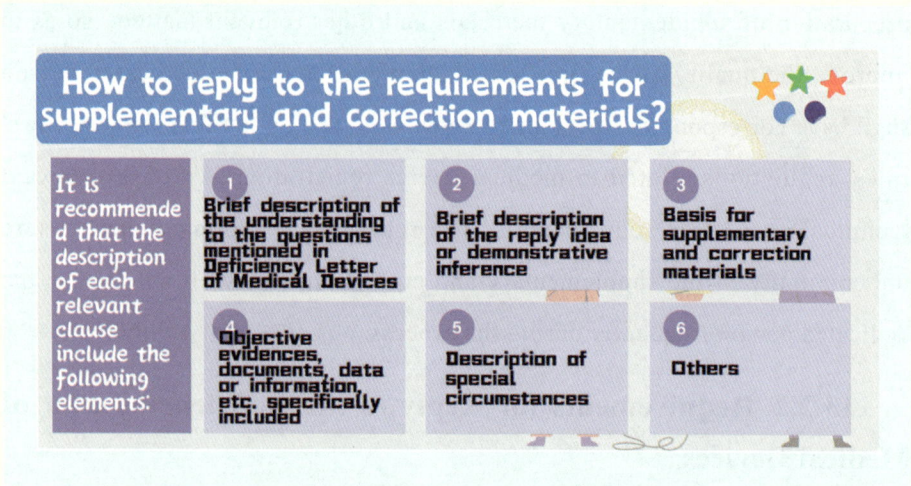

(1) Requirements for the "Description on the Content of Supplementary Materials"

The Description on the Content of Supplementary Materials is to give explanation for the questions item by item that are listed in the Deficiency Letter of Medical Devices, summarize the concepts of supplementary and correction ideas as well as supplementary documents; explanations for each question should be clearly stated and the title and location of the documents concerned should be clarified.

1) The registration applicant shall reply to the contents in the Deficiency Letter of Medical Devices by giving corresponding explanation item by item without duplication or omission, and form the Description on the Content of Supplementary Materials.

2) The registration applicant shall list the questions mentioned in the Deficiency Letter of Medical Devices, and give brief explanation on how to reply to the requirements for supplementary and correction materials. If no materials regarding the supplementary are submitted, it is required to make explanation.

3) The Description on the Content of Supplementary Materials shall clarify the title of the supplementary documents and the document location in the RPS ToC of Supplementary and Correction Materials.

4) In case of any change in product technical requirements and/or product IFU, the registration applicant shall make a specific statement in the Description on the Content of Supplementary Materials.

5) If the registration applicant has other necessary documents to be submitted regarding the Deficiency Letter of Medical Devices, the file name and location can be separately described in the Description on the Content of Supplementary Materials.

(2) Requirements for supplementary documents

1) The registration applicant shall reply according to one of the followings supplementary documents based on their actual situation.

The registration applicant shall reply according to one of the following supplementary documents based on their actual situation:

1. Information or data required.

2. Alternative information and explanation on why the information provided addresses the issue.

3. If the registration applicant believes that the requirements for supplementary materials are irrelevant to the registration matters or be in doubt or dissent regarding the supplementary materials, they can submit relevant statement document to explain the reasons and provide scientific evidence.

2) Supplementary documents shall be submitted item by item according to the order specified in the Deficiency Letter of Medical Devices. If one supplementary document covers more than one requirement, there is no need

for repeat submission but should be stated clearly in the Description on the Content of Supplementary Materials.

3) The format and seal & signature of the supplementary document shall be consistent with those of the application dossiers.

4) If necessary, it is recommended that the updated information of supplementary documents is highlighted (such as italics, bold, highlight, contrast sheets, etc.) show the changes to facilitate review.

13.3 Consultation of Supplementary and Correction Materials

13.3.1 On-site Consultation

Registration applicants can make an appointment for on-site consultation through the Consultation Platform on the CMDE website, and fill out the *Application Form of Consultation* according to relevant requirements so as to specify the concrete questions. For each product acceptance number in line with the requirements, the applicant may have access to on-site consultation services for 3 times at most in principle.

Upon receiving an appointment for on-site consultation, the reviewer shall verify the on-site consultation time through the Consulting Platform on the website of CMDE, and notify the registration applicant by telephone 3 working days in advance. The reviewer shall in principle complete the on-site consultation within 20 working days upon the receipt of the consultation appointment. The appointment applicant may query the appointment result through the Consulting Platform on the CMDE's website. After successful appointment, the applicant shall print the Confirmation Letter on Technical Review On-site Consultation for Medical

Devices (in duplicate), which shall be regarded as the vouchers of on–site consultation.

Upon the completion of on–site consultation, both parties to consultation shall sign the Confirmation Letter on Technical Review On–site Consultation for Medical Devices and hold one copy each.

13.3.2 Online Consultation

The registration applicants may apply for online consultation through the Consulting Platform on the CMDE's website. Online consultation is mainly intended to solve the registration consultation problems that are relatively simple and easily answered.

After receiving an application for online consultation, the reviewer shall in principle complete the online Q&A services within 20 working days as from the date of receipt. If reviewers consider that the on–site consultation is more conducive to solving consultation questions of registration applicants, they may transfer online consultation to on–site consultation.

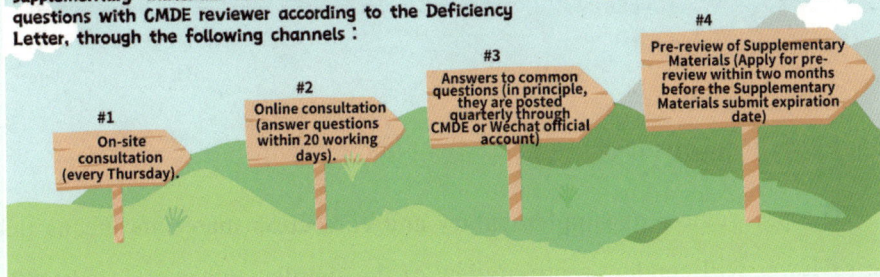

Consultation after Issuing Deficiency Letter of Medical Devices

Registration applicant that has not yet submitted supplementary materials will communicate and answer questions with CMDE reviewer according to the Deficiency Letter, through the following channels :

#1 On-site consultation (every Thursday).

#2 Online consultation (answer questions within 20 working days).

#3 Answers to common questions (in principle, they are posted quarterly through CMDE or Wechat official account)

#4 Pre-review of Supplementary Materials (Apply for pre-review within two months before the Supplementary Materials submit expiration date)

Remember to make an appointment before the consultation

1.Log on to the CMDE website, enter the technical review consultation platform, and click "General Product consultation" (http://www.cmde.org.cn)

2.Operate according to the instructions of the Consulting platform, and make an appointment for "on-site consultation" or "network consultation".

TIPS

The consultation platform can query the reservation results.

In principle, there are no more than 3 opportunities for on-site consultation for each application that meets the requirements. If the appointment is not cancelled after the expiration date, the opportunity for on-site consultation will be reduced once.

TIPS

Supplementary Materials Sequence

Have a question about Deficiency Letter

Description on the Content of Supplementary Materials, Contents of Supplementary Materials, and Specific content of Supplementary Materials should be in the same order as Deficiency Letter

If you have any questions about Deficiency Letter, you can consult the relevant reviewer. For more information, please see "Consultation after Issuing Deficiency Letter of Medical Devices ".

13.4 Pre-review

The pre-review of supplementary and correction materials means that the reviewer will conduct a pre-review of the supplementary materials to be submitted and make written feedback to the registration applicant.

Pre-review of Supplementary and Correction Materials

Pre-review service refers to registration applicant submitted in accordance with the procedure after the applicant has completed some or all of the information in accordance with the requirements of Deficiency Letter and before formally submitting the Supplementary Materials.

In principle. CMDE only provides one pre-review service for each registration submission that meets the requirements.	Pre-review services are voluntary and CMDE is free of charge.	Apply for pre-review within two months before the Supplementary Materials submit expiration date.	The reviewer shall inform the registration applicant of the pre-review opinion within 20 working days after the application is accepted.

13.4.1 Basic Principles

(1) Pre-review services are one of the forms of communication between the registration applicant and the reviewer regarding the contents of the supplementary materials and are not a necessary procedure prior to the submission of supplementary materials. In respect of pre-view services, the principle of voluntariness is observed, that is, the registration applicant decides whether to apply for a pre-review or not.

(2) Pre-review services cannot replace the formal submission of supplementary materials. Whether or not a pre-review service application is made, supplementary materials shall be submitted within the prescribed time frame.

(3) The pre-review opinion issued by the reviewer shall be used to guide the registration applicant to further revise and improve relevant supplementary

materials and shall not be regarded as the basis for the confirmation of the supplementary materials, nor as the final review conclusion.

(4) In principle, the CMDE only provides one-time pre-review service for each eligible registration application.

13.4.2 Relevant Procedures and Requirements

The registration applicant can make an application for pre-review service 2 months prior to the expiration of the timeframe for supplementary and correction materials. See details in the *Announcement on Providing Pre-review Services of Supplementary and Correction Materials for Technical Evaluation of Medical Devices*. The registration applicant submitting the pre-review service shall, after obtaining the pre-review comments, improve the materials in combination with the pre-review comments before the formal submission of supplementary materials.

(1) Way of receiving supplementary materials for pre-review

1) For projects applied for registration online via the eRPS system, the pre-review application can be directly submitted via the eRPS system;

2) For projects applied for registration offline, the pre-review application can be submitted on the spot or by mail.

(2) Requirements of receiving supplementary materials for pre-review

1) Supplementary materials shall be submitted on schedule at one time according to the time and content required by the *Deficiency Letter*.

2) The supplementary and correction materials submitted offline for pre-review shall be bound into a volume.

3) The *Deficiency Letter* and the Application Form for Pre-review of Supplementary and Correction Materials shall be attached to the first page of supplementary and correction materials submitted offline for pre-review, in

which the photocopy of the *Deficiency Letter* shall be stamped with the official seal.

4) The home page of each item of supplementary and correction materials submitted offline for pre-review shall be stamped with the official seal, and cross-page seals shall be stamped on the parts not bound into a volume.

13.5 Circumstances for Rejection of Supplementary Materials

With regard to the supplementary materials submitted by a registration applicant offline, the Deficiency Team of CMDE will reject such data if they are incomplete, do not comply with review requirements, or fall outside the scope of responsibilities of the department.

13.6 Overdue Handling

If the registration applicant fails to submit supplementary materials within the due time, the technical evaluation shall be terminated.

(1) According to Article 92 of the *Measures for the Administration of Registration and Filing of Medical Devices* and Article 92 of the *Measures for the Administration of Registration and Filing of In Vitro Diagnostic Reagents*, if the registration applicant needs to submit supplementary and correction materials during technical evaluation, the technical evaluation authority shall inform the registration applicant of all the supplementary and correction contents at one time. The registration applicant shall submit all necessary supplementary once within a year according to the relevant requirements; the technical evaluation institution shall complete the technical evaluation within 60 working days since the date of accepting the supplementary materials. The supplementation time for materials will not be counted in the time frame for

evaluation.

(2) Where a registration applicant fails to submit the supplementary data within the specified time limit, the technical evaluation institution may terminate the technical evaluation, make suggestions on rejection of registration, and the medical products administration will make decision that the registration is rejected after review.

13.7 Others

(1) For registration applied through eRPS system, if the registration applicant uses the eRPS system, they can view the Deficiency Letter of Medical Devices in the interface of "Handling of Supplementary and Correction Materials for Evaluation" and make response. The registration applicant shall make sure that the submission mode of the supplementary materials is consistent with that of the application dossiers (online or offline). For details, refer to the use instructions, technical guidelines and operation manual of the eRPS system.

(2) Where the process, such as group evaluation and joint evaluation, in which multiple reviewers are involved, the reviewers should be able to independently or jointly discuss with the applicant with regard to the matters in the Deficiency Letter of Medical Devices issued to the applicant.

(3) If the supplementary materials submitted by the registration applicant is still not sufficient to demonstrate the safety and effectiveness, the application for registration will be "rejected".

Notes

1. The registration applicant shall submit the Description on the Content of Supplementary Materials, and fill it out according to the requirements of the Filling Instructions.

2. The registration applicant shall submit a catalogue of supplementary materials, and the material sequence shall be consistent with the requirements of the Deficiency Letter.

3. The time for preparing supplementary materials shall not be calculated in the time limit for technical evaluation.

4. In case of any questions about the contents of the Deficiency Letter, please consult the reviewer by reference to the "Consultation after Deficiency Letter".

13.8 References

Announcement on the Provision of Pre-review Services for Supplementary and Correction Materials of Medical Devices Technical Evaluation (No. 8, 2018)

Supplementary Notice on Providing Pre-review Services of Supplementary and Correction Materials for Technical Evaluation of Medical Devices (October 16, 2019)

Announcement on the Issuance of Management Specifications for Requirements to Supplementary and Correction Materials of Medical Devices Technical Evaluation (No. 1, 2020)

Announcement on Matters Concerning Consultation of Supplementary and Correction Comments for Registration Technical Evaluation of Medical Devices (No.24, 2020)

14. Expert Consultation

Technical review process

14. Expert Consultation

Expert Consultation meeting

What situations call for an expert consultation?

The process of convening experts in the form of meetings to discuss and provide opinions on technical issues that need consultation during the medical device registration review by CMDE.

Projects that pass innovative review, priority approval or emergence approval

Application for clinical trial approval

First application for predicate medical devices

Decided after researched by CMDE technical committee

14.1 Overview

Expert consultation meeting refers to the process in which the CMDE will invite consultancy experts (hereinafter referred to as Experts) to discuss the technical problems to be consulted and offer opinions during its review work for medical device registration.

14.2 Expert Consultation Process

If the review project under the charge of a Chief Reviewer requires an expert consultation meeting and meets relevant requirements, the Chief Reviewer can submit an application for an expert consultation meeting.

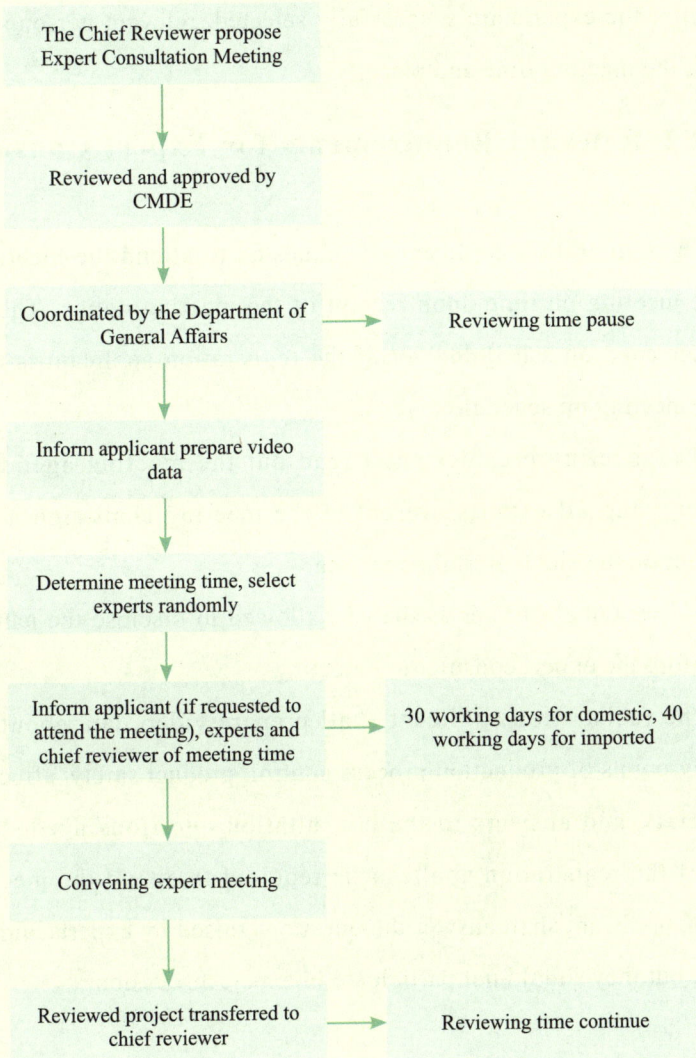

```
┌─────────────────────────────┐
│ The Chief Reviewer propose  │
│ Expert Consultation Meeting │
└─────────────────────────────┘
              │
              ▼
┌─────────────────────────────┐
│ Reviewed and approved by    │
│ CMDE                        │
└─────────────────────────────┘
              │
              ▼
┌─────────────────────────────┐          ┌─────────────────────────────┐
│ Coordinated by the Department│ ──────▶ │ Reviewing time pause        │
│ of General Affairs          │          └─────────────────────────────┘
└─────────────────────────────┘
              │
              ▼
┌─────────────────────────────┐
│ Inform applicant prepare    │
│ video data                  │
└─────────────────────────────┘
              │
              ▼
┌─────────────────────────────┐
│ Determine meeting time,     │
│ select experts randomly     │
└─────────────────────────────┘
              │
              ▼
┌─────────────────────────────┐          ┌─────────────────────────────┐
│ Inform applicant (if        │ ──────▶ │ 30 working days for domestic,│
│ requested to attend the     │          │ 40 working days for imported │
│ meeting), experts and       │          └─────────────────────────────┘
│ chief reviewer of meeting   │
│ time                        │
└─────────────────────────────┘
              │
              ▼
┌─────────────────────────────┐
│ Convening expert meeting    │
└─────────────────────────────┘
              │
              ▼
┌─────────────────────────────┐          ┌─────────────────────────────┐
│ Reviewed project transferred│ ──────▶ │ Reviewing time continue     │
│ to chief reviewer           │          └─────────────────────────────┘
└─────────────────────────────┘
```

14.2.1 Expert Selection

(1) After the meeting time is confirmed, experts will be selected in a random and blind manner. After the specialty and number of experts are entered into the expert management system of CMDE, the system will automatically complete the selection and verification.

(2) After the experts are successfully selected, relevant personnel will be notified of the meeting time and place.

14.2.2 Relevant Requirements for Expert Consultation Meeting

(1) The registration applicant (if requested to attend the meeting) shall attend the meeting on time upon receipt of the meeting notice. The meeting will be convened on schedule even if the registration applicant is unable to attend the meeting on schedule.

(2) The meeting presider shall read out the meeting agenda before the meeting, and all experts present at the meeting shall sign a letter of commitment on the site before the meeting.

(3) No personnel of CMDE shall be allowed to disclose the name list of experts before the expert consultation meeting.

(4) The registration applicant shall prepare video data about product design, key points of production process control, product safety, effectiveness, clinical trials, and answers to the consultation questions needed for this meeting. If the registration applicant is required to attend the meeting, the registration applicant shall answer the questions raised by experts and relevant reviewers, but they should not participate in expert discussion.

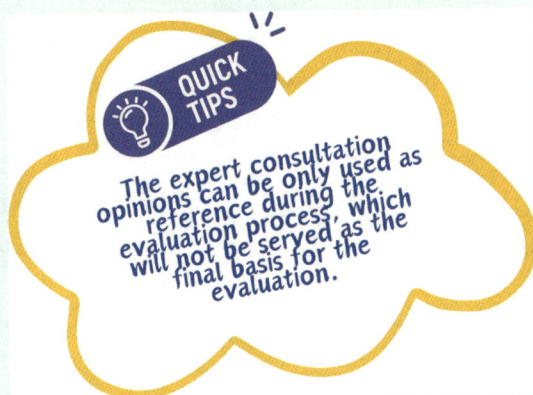

QUICK TIPS

The expert consultation opinions can be only used as reference during the evaluation process, which will not be served as the final basis for the evaluation.

14.3 References

Notice on Issuing the Measures for the Administration of External Experts of the Center for Medical Device Evaluation (February 20, 2020)

15. Renewal Registration

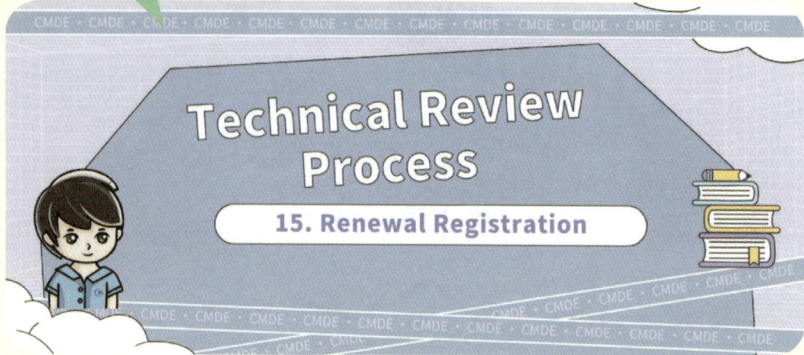

Technical Review Process
15. Renewal Registration

15.1 Overview

The valid term of Medical Device Registration Certificate is 5 years. In the case of the expiration of the Medical Device Registration Certificate which needs to be renewed, the registration applicant shall apply to the original registration department for renewal registration within 6 months before the expiration of the validity period.

The renewal registration shall not be approved in any of the following circumstances

The registrant fails to apply for renewal registration within the prescribed time limit.

As the mandatory standards for medical devices have been revised, the medical devices for renewal registration fail to meet the new requirements.

For the medical device with conditional approval, the items specified in the medical device registration certificate are not completed within the specified time limit.

15.2 Requirements for Renewal Registration Dossiers

Eligible registration applicants shall prepare the dossiers in accordance with the relevant requirements of Attachment 6 *Requirements and Instructions for Registration Application Dossiers of Medical Devices* in the *Announcement on Issuing the Requirements for Registration Application Dossiers of Medical Devices and Formats of Approval Documents* and Attachment 5 *Requirements and Instructions for the Registration Application Dossiers for the Renewal Registration of In Vitro Diagnostic Reagents* in the *Announcement on Issuing the Requirements for Registration Application Dossiers of Medical Devices and Formats of Approval Documents*.

How to prepare dossiers for renewal registration?

▼

Eligible registration applicants shall prepare the dossiers in accordance with the relevant requirements of the **Announcement on Issuing the Requirements for Registration Application Dossiers of Medical Devices and Formats of Approval Documents** and the **Announcement on Issuing the Requirements for Registration Application Dossiers of In Vitro Diagnostic Reagents and Formats of Approval Documents**.

Process for renewal registration

Submit an application

For application dossiers, please refer to the **Announcement on Issuing the Requirements for Registration Application Dossiers of Medical Devices and Formats of Approval Documents** and the **Announcement on Issuing the Requirements for Registration Application Dossiers of In Vitro Diagnostic Reagents and Formats of Approval Documents**

The registration applicant shall apply to the original registration department

Renewal registration application within 6 months before the expiration of the validity period.

Evaluation — For Class II: 60 Working Days / For Class III: 90 Working Days

Review and approval — 20 Working Days

Print and issue the registration certificate — 10 Working Days

15.3 Others

(1) For registered products of which the management category is adjusted from a higher class to a lower class, the medical devices registration certificate shall continue to be valid within the period of validity. Where the validity period expires and renewal registration is needed, the registrant shall apply for renewal registration or filing as per the adjusted category to the corresponding medical products administration 6 months prior to the expiration of the validity period of Medical Device Registration Certificate.

For registered products of which the management category is adjusted from a lower class to a higher class, the registrant shall submit registration application based on the adjusted category to the corresponding medical products administration.

(2) The valid period of the Medical Device Registration Certificate is 5 years.

(3) If the approval time of renewal registration is within the validity period of the original registration certificate, the starting date of the validity period of the renewal registration certificate shall be the next day after the expiration date of the original registration certificate; If the approval time is not within the validity period of the original registration certificate, the starting date of the validity period of the renewal registration certificate shall be the date when the renewal registration is approved.

15.4 Case Interpretation

(1) How to determine whether the application for renewal registration is 6 months before the expiration of the registration certificate for medical device?

Interpretation: If the medical device registration certificate needs to be renewed upon expiry, the registrant shall apply for renewal registration 6 months before the expiry together with the application dossiers in accordance with the relevant requirements. If supplementary and correction materials are required due to incomplete application dossiers or incompliance with legal form, CMDE shall indicate the time for the registrant to apply for renewal registration for the first time in the notice of supplementary and correction materials for acceptance. The registrant shall submit the notice of supplementary and correction materials for acceptance when re-applying for renewal registration after supplementing and correcting the materials, and the CMDE will determine whether the time for application for renewal registration is 6 months prior to the expiration of the medical device registration certificate according to the time for the first application for renewal registration indicated in the notice of supplementary and correction materials for acceptance, and review the application dossiers according to the *Measures for the Administration of Registration and Filing of Medical Devices*.

(2) In case of failure in applying for renewal registration within the specified time for a registered product, application for registration of the product shall be made according to regulatory requirements. In this case, can the original registered product be selected as the predicate product for clinical evaluation? How shall clinical data be provided?

Interpretation: In this case, the original registered product can be selected as the predicate product for clinical evaluation. Attention shall be mainly paid to whether there is any difference between the proposed product and the original registered product in comparison with the predicate device. If there is no difference between the two products, the clinical data to be provided may include the pre-marketing and post-marketing clinical data of the product, and the clinical experience data including post-marketing adverse events.

15.5 References

Announcement on Issuing the Requirements for Registration Application Dossiers of Medical Devices and Formats of Approval Documents (No. 121, 2021)

Announcement on Issuing the Requirements for Registration Application Dossiers of In Vitro Diagnostic Reagents and Formats of Approval Documents (No. 122, 2021)

16. Change Registration/Change Filing

Technical review process
16.Change Registration/Change Filing

16.1 Overview

If substantial changes in the design, raw materials, production process, scope of application, methods of application and other factors have happened to the registered Class II and Class III medical devices, so that the safety and

What does change registration mean?

Where there is any substantial change in the design, raw materials, manufacturing process, scope of application and method of use of Class II and Class III medical devices that have been registered, which may affect the safety and effectiveness of the medical devices, the registrant shall apply to the original registration authority for the change registration procedures; other changes shall be filed or reported in accordance with the provisions of the medical products administration directly under the State Council.

effectiveness of the medical devices may be affected, the registration applicant shall apply to the original registration authority for change registration. If other changes have happened, the changes shall be filed or reported as required by NMPA.

16.2 Changes Involved in Change Registration/ Change Filing

16.2.1 Change Registration/Change Filing of Medical Devices

If substantial changes in the design, raw materials, production process, scope of application, methods of application and other factors have happened to the registered Class II and Class III medical devices, so that the safety and effectiveness of the medical devices may be affected, the registration applicant shall apply to the original registration authority for change registration. If other changes have happened, the changes shall be filed with the original registration authority with 30 days from the date of change.

Product name, model, specification, structure and composition, scope of application, product technical requirements, production address of imported medical devices, etc. indicated on the Registration Certificate belong to the items that are subject to change registration as stipulated in the preceding paragraph. If the name, domicile address of registrant, or the name and domicile address of the agent changes, the item is subject to change registration as stipulated in the preceding paragraph. If the production address of domestic medical devices is changed, the registration applicant shall apply for the filing after completing the corresponding production licensing change.

Change Filing of Medical Devices

- Change in the name of the registrant
- Change in the domicile address of the registrant
- Change in the domicile address of the agent
- Change in the domestic production address of medical devices
- change in the name of the agent

Change Registration of Medical Devices

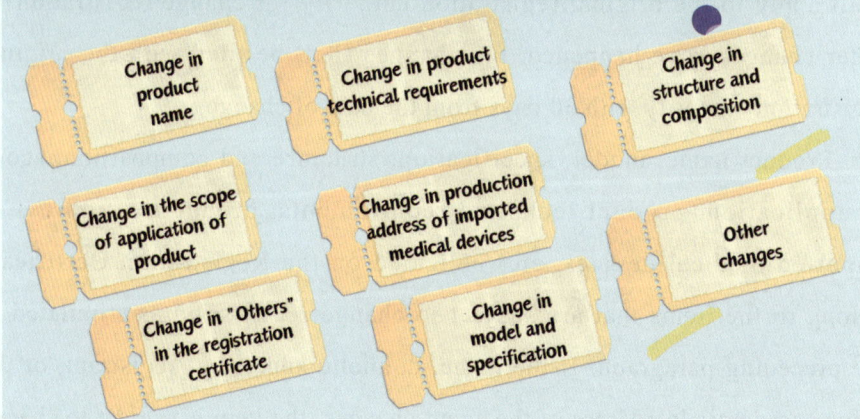

- Change in product name
- Change in product technical requirements
- Change in structure and composition
- Change in the scope of application of product
- Change in production address of imported medical devices
- Other changes
- Change in "Others" in the registration certificate
- Change in model and specification

16.2.2 Change Registration/Change Filing of IVD Reagents

If substantial changes in the design, raw materials, production process, scope of application, methods of application and other factors have happened to the registered Class II and Class III IVD reagents, so that the safety and effectiveness of the IVD reagents may be affected, the registration applicant shall apply to the original registration authority for change registration. If other changes have happened, the changes shall be filed with the original registration authority with 30 days from the date of change.

Product name, packaging specification, main components, intended use, product technical requirements, product IFU, production address of imported IVD reagents, etc. indicated on the Registration Certificate belong to the items that are subject to change registration as stipulated in the preceding paragraph. If the name, domicile address of registrant, or the name and domicile address of the agent changes, the item is subject to change registration as stipulated in the preceding paragraph. If the production address of domestic IVD reagents is changed, the registration applicant shall apply for the filing after completing the corresponding production licensing change.

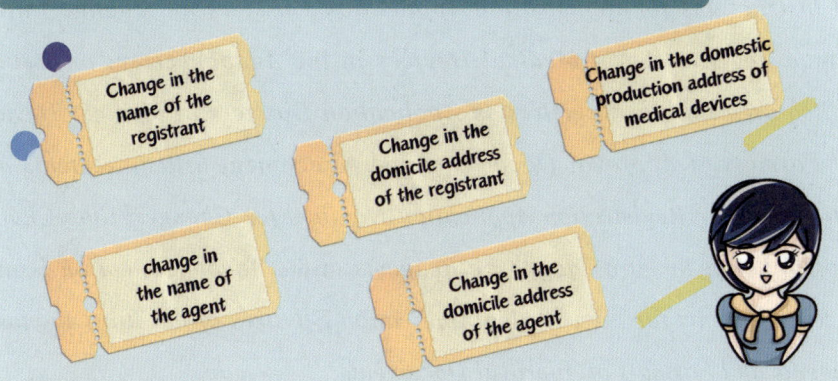

Change Filing of IVD Reagents

- Change in the name of the registrant
- change in the name of the agent
- Change in the domicile address of the registrant
- Change in the domicile address of the agent
- Change in the domestic production address of medical devices

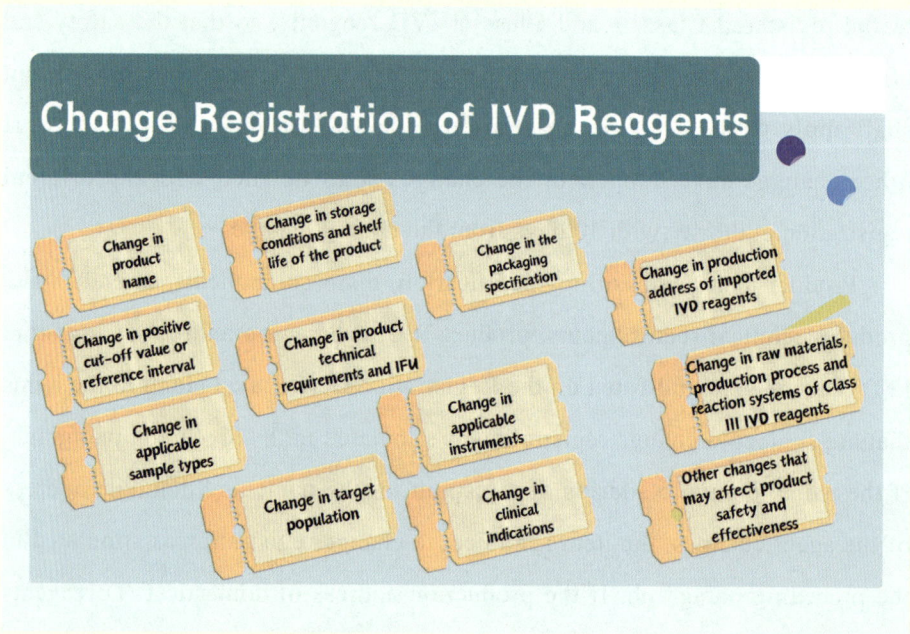

Change Registration of IVD Reagents

- Change in product name
- Change in storage conditions and shelf life of the product
- Change in the packaging specification
- Change in production address of imported IVD reagents
- Change in positive cut-off value or reference interval
- Change in product technical requirements and IFU
- Change in raw materials, production process and reaction systems of Class III IVD reagents
- Change in applicable sample types
- Change in applicable instruments
- Change in target population
- Change in clinical indications
- Other changes that may affect product safety and effectiveness

16.3 Dossier Requirements for Change Registration/ Change Filing

Registration applicants who meet the conditions should prepare dossiers in accordance with the relevant requirements of Attachment 7 *Requirements and Instructions for Registration Application Dossiers for Change Filing/ Change Registration of Medical Devices* in the *Announcement on Issuing the Requirements for Registration Application Dossiers of Medical Devices and Formats of Approval Documents* and Attachment 6 *Requirements and Instructions for Registration Application Dossiers for Change Filing/Change Registration of In Vitro Diagnostic Reagents* in the *Announcement on Issuing the Requirements for Registration Application Dossiers of In Vitro Diagnostic Reagents and Formats of Approval Documents*.

Process for Change Registration

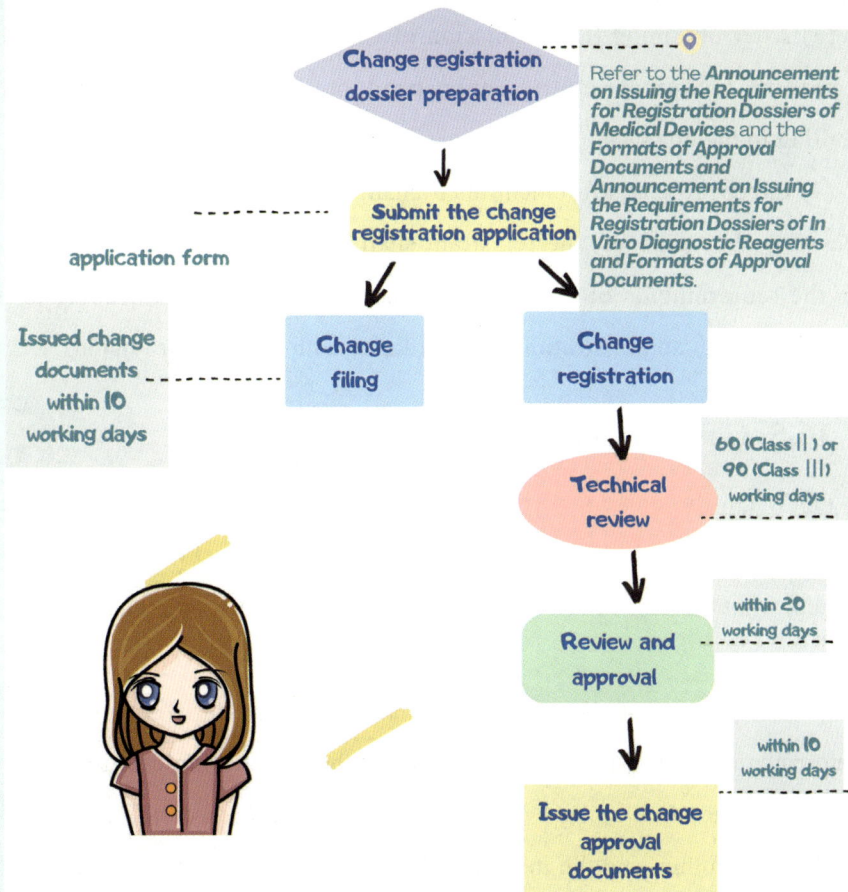

Change registration dossier preparation

Refer to the *Announcement on Issuing the Requirements for Registration Dossiers of Medical Devices* and the *Formats of Approval Documents* and *Announcement on Issuing the Requirements for Registration Dossiers of In Vitro Diagnostic Reagents and Formats of Approval Documents.*

application form

Submit the change registration application

Issued change documents within 10 working days

Change filing

Change registration

60 (Class II) or 90 (Class III) working days

Technical review

within 20 working days

Review and approval

within 10 working days

Issue the change approval documents

16.4 Others

(1) The registrant shall not submit a pooled application for change matters

and renewal registration.

(2) The medical device change document shall be used in conjunction with the original Medical Device Registration Certificate. The expiration date of the shelf life shall be the same as that stated in the original Medical Device Registration Certificate.

(3) After obtaining the Permission of Change, the registrant shall revise the product technical requirements, product IFU and labels voluntarily according to the changes.

(4) Except for the aforementioned change registration and change filing, in case of other changes, the registrant shall do relevant work in accordance with the requirements of the quality management system and report to the medical products administration in accordance with relevant provisions.

16.5 Case Interpretation

(1) When the content of the mandatory standard cited by the technical requirements of registered medical devices (including IVD reagents) has changed, what circumstances do not need to apply for change registration?

Interpretation: Where a new mandatory standard is issued and implemented within the validity period of the registration certificate for medical device (including IVD reagent), the registration certificate of the registered product and the items indicated in its attachments meet the new mandatory standard without any change, which specifically includes the following two circumstances:

1) There is(are) applicable mandatory standard(s) for the proposed product

In the Product Technical Requirements (PTR), a mandatory standard is cited in the form of "direct citing the specific clause in the mandatory standard", "standard number" or "standard number + year number". In case of the update of the mandatory standard, the standard number and/or year number is changed, but the clause of the mandatory standard cited in the PTR is not changed.

2) There is(are) no applicable mandatory standard(s) for the proposed product

In case of the update of the mandatory standard, the standard number and/or year number is changed, but the clause of the mandatory standard cited in the PTR is not changed; or there is a change in the clause of the mandatory standard cited in the PTR, but the PTR still cites the clause of the mandatory standard before such update.

In the above two cases, the PTR will not be changed or only the cited standard number and/or year number are updated, and no change registration is required.

(2) What if the IFU of IVD equipment changes?

Interpretation: In accordance with Article 16 of the *Provisions for the Instructions for Use and Labels of Medical Devices* (Decree No.6), "If the change registration is involved in a registered medical device, the registration applicant shall modify the IFU and labels according to the change documents after obtaining them." Regarding the IFU of registered IVD equipment, if there are changes in the contents other than the items stated in the Medical Device Registration Certificate and its attachments and they do not fall within the scope of change registration, the registration applicant shall inform the review and approval authority for medical device registration in writing, and submit relevant documents such as a change comparison of the IFU.

16.6 References

Announcement on Issuing the Requirements for Registration Application Dossiers of Medical Devices and Formats of Approval Documents (No. 121, 2021)

Announcement on Issuing the Requirements for Registration Application Dossiers of In Vitro Diagnostic Reagents and Formats of Approval Documents (No. 122, 2021)

17. IFU Filing Notification

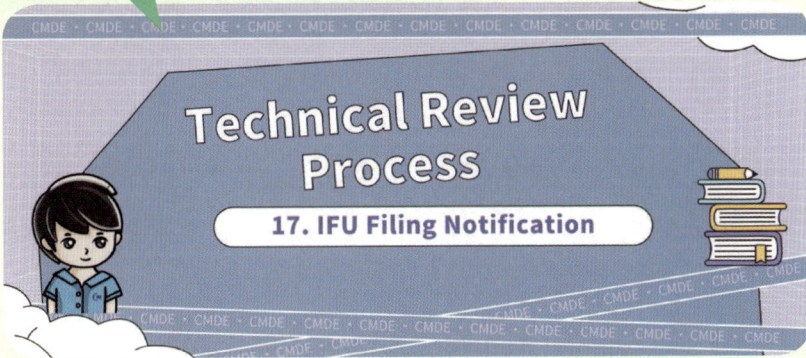

Technical Review Process

17. IFU Filing Notification

The IFU Filing Notification is indicated the registered medical device IFU which changes in other contents other than those specified in the registration certificates and its attachments and not within the scope of change registration, the registration applicant shall apply the written notice and submit relevant documents such as a change comparison of the IFU to the Medical Device

The following conditions shall be met for the IFU Filing Notification :

Changes in other contents other than those specified in the registration certificates and its attachments

Registered Medical Device IFU

The changes that not within the scope of change registration

The review results are generally divided into three types

If the review result is "partial approval" or "rejected", a rejected notification shall be issued to the applicant. IFU Filing takes effects if the approval authority does not send a formal rejection notice within 20 working days from the date of receipt of the written notification by the applicant

Approval

partial approval

rejected

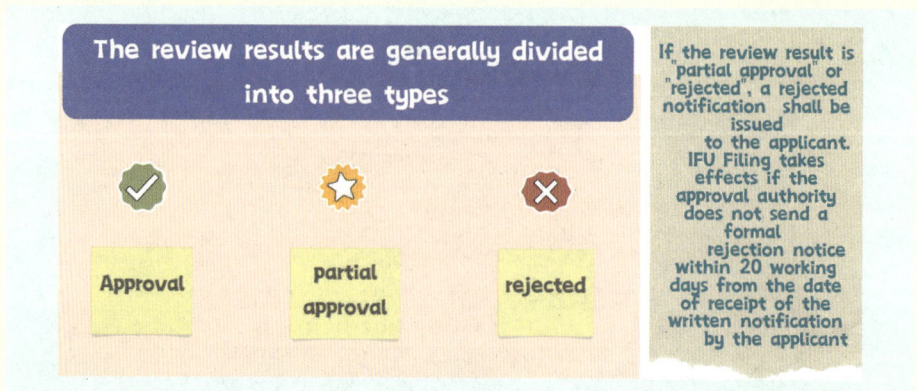

Registration and Approval Authority. After reviewing relevant documents, the approval authority shall issue the reviewing results.

17.1 Requirements for Application Dossiers

The eligible administrative counterpart shall prepare dossiers in accordance with the relevant requirements of the *Announcement on Issuing Five Relevant Working Procedures Including the Procedures for Reissuance of Medical Device Registration Certificate*.

Requirements for Application Dossiers

The eligible administrative counterpart shall prepare dossiers in accordance with the relevant requirements of the *Announcement on Issuing Five Relevant Working Procedures Including the Procedures for Reissuance of Medical Device Registration Certificate*.

17.2 Relevant Processes

The registration applicant shall submit application dossiers to NMPA in accordance with the requirements of IFU filing notification. After acceptance, the medical device approval authority shall conduct a review and issue the review results within 20 working days. If the review result is "partial approval" or "rejected", NMPA shall issue a rejected notification to the registration applicant. If the review result is "approval", no notification shall be issued to the registration applicant, and the IFU changes shall take effect.

TIPS

The medical device registered approval status can be timely followed up from the NMPA website "Administrative Licensing Comprehensive Matters Query" module

Check the "IFU Filing Rejection Notification" on the "Delivery Information" page in the service section from the NMPA website

Approved if there is no reply within the specified timeline

17.3 Review Result of IFU Filing Notification

In accordance with the *Measures for the Administration of Registration and Filing of Medical Devices* and the *Provisions for the Instructions for Use and Labels of Medical Devices*, the IFU contents changes shall not involve the contents that related to change of registration. If so, the approval authority shall issue rejected suggestion for the IFU filing and notify the registration applicant to follow the relevant provisions of the *Measures for the Administration of Registration and Filing of Medical Devices*. If the IFU filing dossiers are insufficient to support the change items, the approval authority shall issue rejected or partial approval, detailed explain the reasons and inform application dossiers problems in the review suggestions.

17.4 Individually modified the IVD Reagent IFU

(1) In case of any changes in the following content under the item "General Information" in the IVD Reagent IFU, including the contact information of the IVD reagent registrant or manufacturer, name and contact information of aftersales service agency, production permit number or production filing certificate number, as well as the contact information of the agent of imported IVD reagents, the registrant shall modify relevant information individually after the change. Specifically, the production permit number or production filing certificate number shall be modified after the provincial food and drug administration have issued the production permit or production filing certificate.

(2) With regard to the item "Medical Device Registration Certificate No./ Product Technical Requirement No." in the IVD Reagent IFU, the registrant shall make modifications individually if such content is changed after the

food and drug administration has issued the Medical Device Registration Certificate.

(3) With regard to the item "Interpretation of Identification" in the IVD Reagent IFU, the registrant shall make modifications individually if such content is changed after it has improved the interpretation of corresponding identifications in the IVD Reagent IFU according to the YY/T 0466 series standards, but such case shall not involve other situations requiring change registration.

(4) With regard to the medical devices or IVD reagents that should be used as a set, as indicated in the item "Main Components" in the IVD Reagent IFU, the registrant shall make modifications individually if the Registration Certificate No. or filling certificate No. of such medical devices or IVD reagents is changed after the medical product administration has issued the Medical Device Registration Certificate/Filing Certificate.

17.5 References

Provisions for the Instructions for Use and Labels of Medical Devices (CFDA Decree No. 6)

CFDA Announcement on Issuing Five Relevant Working Procedures Including the Procedures for Reissuance of Medical Device Registration Certificate (No.91, 2015)

18. Others

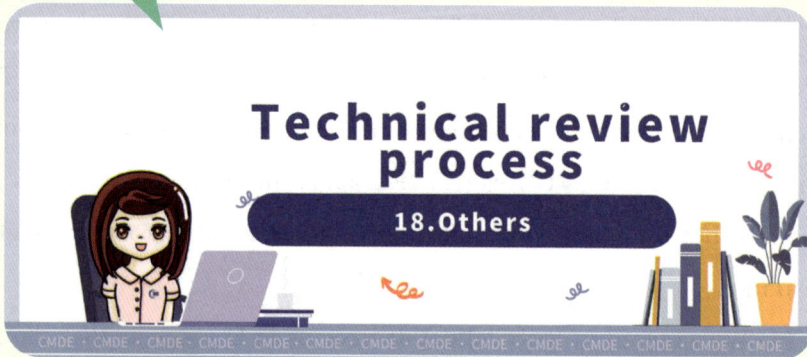

18.1 Correction of Registration Certificate

In case of the following corrigendum to the certificate, a registration applicant may, free of charge, apply for the content error correction of the Medical Device Registration Certificate and its attachments:

(1)Printing error of registration certificate or change registration document and its attachments;

(2)Error of Registration Certificate No.;

(3)Filing information error of the enterprise;

(4)Other errors in the work of evaluation, review, and approval.

18.1.1 Preparation for Application Dossiers

The registration applicant shall prepare the following materials upon submitting the application for error correction of the Medical Device Registration Certificate/change documents:

(1) The corresponding application form with the signature and seal of the registration applicant or its agent.

(2) Photocopies of the Medical Device Registration Certificate and its attachments.

(3) Requirements for error correction materials of the registration certificate for Class III domestic medical devices:

1) The domestic registration applicant shall submit a photocopy of its Business License (duplicate).

2) The self-guarantee statement on the authenticity of the materials submitted by the registration applicant shall include a list of submitted materials and the registration applicant's commitments on undertaking legal responsibilities.

(4) Requirements for error correction materials of registration certificate for Class II and III imported medical devices:

1) The registration applicant shall submit the Letter of Authorization with regard to the agent designated by it in China, the Letter of Commitment of the agent, and a photocopy of the agent's Business License (duplicate). The Letter of Authorization shall expressly include the entrusted error correction matters.

If the Letter of Authorization is newly issued, it shall be original and notarized. Where the Letter of Authorization containing the corresponding content for the agent has been submitted upon the registration, the agent may submit the photocopy of such Letter of Authorization which is stamped with the official seal of the agent.

2) The self-guarantee statement on the authenticity of the materials submitted by the registration applicant shall include a list of submitted materials and the registration applicant's commitments on undertaking legal responsibilities. The self-guarantee statement for the authenticity shall be original and affixed with the agent's official seal.

(5) The agent shall submit the Letter of Authorization of the registration

applicant or the agent and his/her identity card photocopy.

18.1.2 Handling Process

After preparing all application dossiers, the registration applicant shall apply to the Administrative Acceptance Service Hall of NMPA for error correction of relevant matters. After the Acceptance Hall accepts the application through formal examination, there will be the following three circumstances:

(1) The Acceptance Hall will immediately handle the matters with regard to the printing error of the registration certificate, and the change document and its attachments;

(2) If the errors of the registration certificate approved before July 1, 2017, the change document, and the registration certificate approved after July 1, 2017 for initial registration belong to those in terms of registration certificate number, relevant matters shall be transferred to the Department of Medical Device Registration for handling according to relevant procedures;

(3) The error of the registration certificate number and other situations in the change registration documents and renewal registration certificate approved after July 1, 2017 shall be transferred to CMDE for handling according to relevant procedures.

With regard to circumstance (2), the staff of the Department of Medical Device Registration shall offer examination opinions within 10 working days upon receipt of the application dossiers for error correction and submit them to the person in charge of CMDE for review. The person in charge of CMDE shall offer examination opinions within 8 working days, and the staff of the Department of Medical Device Registration shall transfer the review opinions and dossiers for error correction back to the Acceptance Hall within 2 working days. With regard to circumstance (3), CMDE shall review the application dossiers according to relevant requirements and offer opinions within 30 working days upon receipt of the application dossiers for error correction. The Acceptance Hall shall prepare relevant documents according to the review opinions within 10 working days and perform service procedures as required. Meanwhile, relevant information on error correction shall be released on the website of NMPA in a timely manner.

On April 20, 2023, the *Announcement on Adjusting the Service Scope of the Electronic Regulated Product Submission (eRPS) System* (No.11, 2023) was officially implemented. In order to cooperate with the implementation of the above documents, the functions of the eRPS system have been upgraded in an all-around way. In addition, the electronic application form for error correction and electronic catalogue will be launched simultaneously. If an enterprise has applied for CA, it can complete the filling of the application form for error correction of the Medical Device Registration Certificate, and the submission and acceptance of relevant materials via the eRPS system. If the enterprise has not applied for CA, it can submit relevant materials offline.

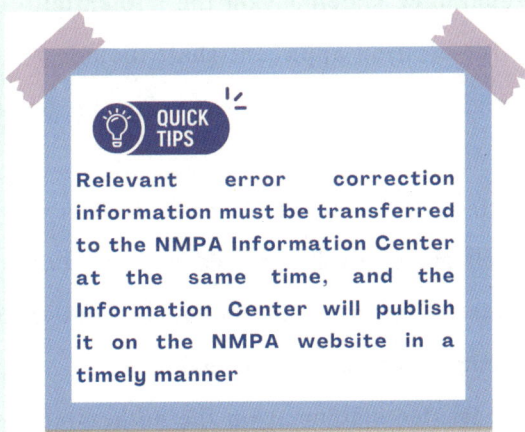

QUICK TIPS

Relevant error correction information must be transferred to the NMPA Information Center at the same time, and the Information Center will publish it on the NMPA website in a timely manner

18.2 Initiative Cancellation of Registration Certificate

A registration applicant may, free of charge, initiatively apply for cancellation of the Medical Device Registration Certificate/change document which is still within its validity period.

18.2.1 Preparation of Application Dossiers

A registration applicant shall prepare the following materials upon applying for initiative cancellation of the registration certificate:

(1) The application form with the signature and seal of the applicant.

(2) Reason for cancellation of the Medical Device Registration Certificate and letter of presentation issued by the registration applicant.

(3) The originals of the Medical Device Registration Certificate and its attachments.

(4) The material requirements for cancellation of registration certificate for Class III domestic medical devices:

1) The domestic registration applicant shall submit a photocopy of its Business License (duplicate).

2) The self–guarantee statement on the authenticity of the materials submitted by the registration applicant shall include a list of submitted materials and the registration applicant's commitments on undertaking legal responsibilities.

(5) The material requirements for cancellation of the registration certificate for Class II and Class III imported medical devices:

1) The originals or notarized photocopies of enterprise qualification certification documents of the registration applicant.

2) The self–guarantee statement on the authenticity of the materials

submitted by the registration applicant shall include a list of submitted materials and the registration applicant's commitments on undertaking legal responsibilities. The self–guarantee statement for the authenticity shall be the notarized original photocopy.

(6) The agent shall submit the Letter of Authorization of the registration applicant or the agent and his/her identity card photocopy.

18.2.2 Handling Process

After preparing all application dossiers, the registration applicant shall apply to the Administrative Acceptance Service Hall of NMPA for initiative cancellation of relevant matters. The Acceptance Hall shall transfer the application dossiers to the Department of Medical Device Registration within 3 working days after it accepts the application through formal examination. The staff of the Department of Medical Device Registration shall verify relevant information and draw up the announcement on cancellation within 10 working days upon the receipt of application dossiers and the person in charge of CMDE shall offer his/her re–review opinions within 5 working days. The person in charge of the Department shall conclude his/her validation opinions within 5 working days and submit it for release according to the document release procedures of NMPA.

18.3 Initiative Revocation of Registration Application

An applicant/registration applicant may, free of charge, initiatively withdraw the registration application which has been accepted but an administrative licensing decision has not been made. The registration fees paid by enterprises will not be refunded.

18.3.1 Preparation for Application Dossiers

An applicant/registration applicant shall prepare the following materials upon applying for initiative revocation of application for registration certificate:

(1) The corresponding application form with the signature and seal of the applicant/registration applicant.

(2) The original of Notice Letter of Acceptance on the registration application matters to be revoked.

(3) The agent shall submit the Letter of Authorization of the applicant/registration applicant or the agent and his/her identity card photocopy.

18.3.2 Handling Process

After preparing all application dossiers, the applicant/registration applicant shall apply to the Administrative Acceptance Service Hall of NMPA for initiative revocation of the registration application. The Acceptance Hall shall transfer the application dossiers to CMDE or the Department of Medical Device Registration after it accepts the application through formal examination according to the actual evaluation and review & approval status of the application matters as well as relevant transfer procedures. CMDE or the Department of Medical Device Registration shall terminate the evaluation and review & approval of relevant registration dossiers after information verification.

To handle other relevant matters of registration, an enterprise shall submit the originals of the submitted materials in the revoked application items of medical device registration. The enterprise may also submit the photocopies of relevant materials on which the acceptance number of the application item in the original shall be indicated, and the self–guarantee statement in proof of the consistency between the photocopies signed and sealed by the applicant/ registration applicant and the originals. For imported medical devices, the self-guarantee statement shall be a notarized original copy.

> **TIPS**
>
> 1.The enterprise withdraws the application on its own, the registration fees paid by enterprises will not be refunded.
> 2.Initiative Revocation of Registration Certificate materials will not be refunded.
> 3.Initiative Cancellation of Registration Certificate materials will not be refunded.
>
> *CFDA Announcement on Issuing Five Relevant Working Procedures Including the Procedures for Reissuance of Medical Device Registration Certificate (No.91,2015)*

18.4 Re-issuance of Registration Certificate

A registration applicant may, free of charge, apply for re-issuance of the registration certificate and/or its attachments and change documents within the validity period of the Medical Device/IVD Reagent Registration Certificate/ change documents.

18.4.1 Preparation of Application Dossiers

A registration applicant shall prepare the following materials upon applying for re-issuance of the registration certificate:

(1) The corresponding application form with the signature and seal of the registration applicant or its agent.

(2) Photocopies of Medical Device Registration Certificate and its attachments, or original registration certificate number.

(3) The material requirements for re-issuance of the registration certification of Class III domestic medical devices and/or its attachments.

1) Reason for re-issuance of Medical Device Registration Certificate and/or its attachments and letter of presentation issued by the registration applicant. The materials shall include the original of China's provincial newspapers where the registrant issued the Announcement of Loss and the photocopy with the official seal of the registration applicant (the publication time of the Announcement of Loss shall be at least one month ahead of the submission date of application).

2) A domestic registration applicant shall submit photocopies of the Business License (duplicate) and the Organization Code Certificate.

3) The self-guarantee statement on the authenticity of the materials submitted by the registration applicant shall include a list of submitted materials and the registrant's commitments on undertaking legal responsibilities.

(4) The material requirements for re-issuance of the registration certificate of Class II and Class III imported medical devices and attachments thereof:

1) Reason for re-issuance of Medical Device Registration Certificate and

its attachments and letter of presentation issued by the registration applicant. The materials shall include the original of China's provincial newspapers where the registrant issued the Announcement of Loss and the photocopy with the official seal of the agent or the signature and seal of the registrant (the publication time of the Announcement of Loss shall be at least one month ahead of the submission date of application).

2) A registration applicant shall submit the Letter of Authorization with regard to the agent designated by it in China, the Letter of Commitment by and a photocopy of Business License (duplicate) or the Company Registration Certificate of such agent. The Letter of Authorization for the agent shall be the notarized original, and include such content as re–issuance matters, product name, registration certificate No. and so forth.

3) The originals or notarized photocopies of enterprise qualification certification documents of the registration applicant.

4) The self–guarantee statement on the authenticity of the materials submitted by the registration applicant shall include a list of submitted materials and the registration applicant's commitments on undertaking legal responsibilities. The self–guarantee statement for the authenticity shall be the notarized original photocopy.

(5) The agent shall submit the Letter of Authorization of the registration applicant or the agent and his/her identity card photocopy.

18.4.2 Handling Process

After preparing all application dossiers, the registration applicant shall apply to the Administrative Acceptance Service Hall of NMPA for the re–issuance of relevant matters. The Acceptance Hall shall transfer the application dossiers to the Department of Medical Device Registration for handling after it accepts the application through formal examination. The staff of the Department of Medical Device Registration shall offer examination opinions within 10 working days upon receipt of the application dossiers, and the person in charge of CMDE shall give his/her opinions of approval within 4 working days and report to the Acceptance Hall. The Acceptance Hall shall prepare relevant documents according to corresponding opinions within 10 working days and perform service procedures as required.

For the re-issued Medical Device Registration Certificate, the column "Remark" will indicate "the Certificate is re-issued on YYYY-MM-DD, and the original Certificate issued YYYY-MM-DD has been abolished".

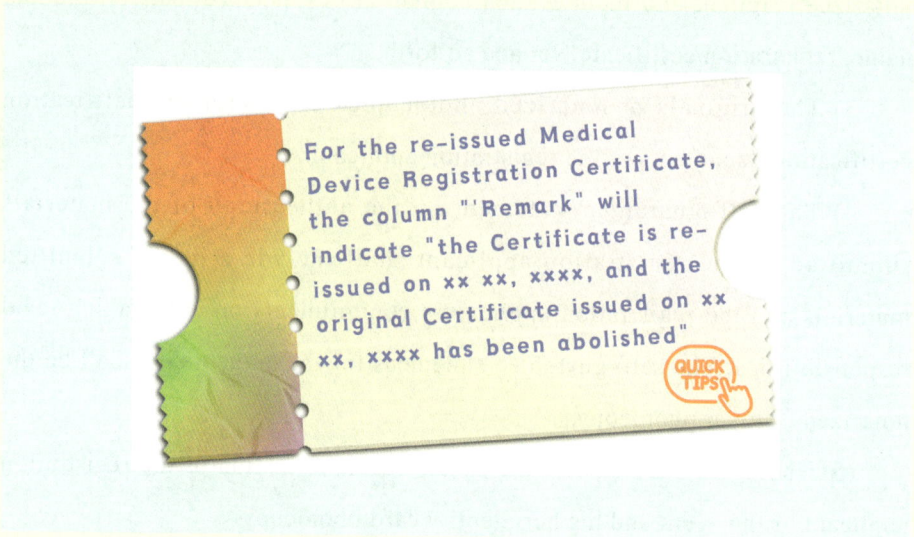

For the re-issued Medical Device Registration Certificate, the column "'Remark" will indicate "the Certificate is re-issued on xx xx, xxxx, and the original Certificate issued on xx xx, xxxx has been abolished"

QUICK TIPS

18.5 Rejected Registration

18.5.1 Rejected Registration

For the registration application that has been accepted, the medical regulatory authority shall decide to deny the registration in one of the following circumstances, and notify the applicant.

(1) The applicant cannot, through research and its findings, prove the safety, effectiveness, and quality controllability of the product to be marketed;

(2) The quality management systems fail to pass the verification, and the applicant refuses to accept the on-site inspection of the quality management systems;

(3) The registration dossiers are fake and false;

(4) The contents of the registration dossiers are confusing, contradictory, or obviously inconsistent with the application items, and the product cannot be proved to be safe, effective and controllable in quality;

(5) Other situations not allowed for registration.

18.5.2 Confirmation of the Conclusion "Evaluation Failed" and Objection Handling

During the registration evaluation of medical devices, the applicant/ registration applicant may raise objections related to the registration, change registration, and renewal registration of medical devices (including IVD reagents) to CMDE within 15 days. The contents of the objections are limited to the original application items and original registration dossiers. The objections shall be raised within 15 working days after the *Confirmation Sheet* is received. Failure to raise objections within 15 working days shall be deemed as agreement with the conclusion "evaluation failed" and the corresponding reasons.

For projects applied online, the eRPS system will send the *Confirmation Sheet of the Conclusion "Evaluation Failed" for Registration Evaluation of Medical Devices* (hereinafter referred to as the *Confirmation Sheet*) including the conclusion "evaluation failed" and the corresponding reasons for relevant projects to the applicant/registration applicant at a fixed time, with a notice of text message sent. The applicant can log in to the eRPS system to check the *Confirmation Sheet*. In case of no objection to the conclusion "evaluation failed" and the corresponding reasons, please tick "Agree". In case of any objections to the conclusion "evaluation failed" and the corresponding reasons, please tick "Disagree" and fill in the specific contents.

For projects applied offline, the applicant/registration applicant can check the *Confirmation Sheet* after receiving the e-mail sent by CMDE. In case of no objection to the conclusion "evaluation failed" and the corresponding reasons, please tick "Agree". In case of any objections to the conclusion "evaluation failed" and the corresponding reasons, please tick "Disagree" and fill in the specific contents. After the confirmation is completed, the applicant/ registration applicant shall reply to the *Confirmation Sheet* via e-mail and mail the signed and sealed written version to CMDE.

For any objections to the conclusion "evaluation failed" and the corresponding reasons, CMDE shall conduct a comprehensive assessment after receiving the *Confirmation Sheet* and fill in the *Notice Sheet of Comprehensive Assessment Opinions on Objections to the Conclusion "Evaluation Failed" for Registration Evaluation of Medical Devices* (hereinafter referred to as the *Notice Sheet*). For projects applied online, the eRPS system will send the *Notice Sheet* to the applicant/registration applicant at a fixed time and send a notice of text message at the same time. For projects applied offline, CMDE will send the *Notice Sheet* to the applicant/registration applicant via e-mail and informs the applicant/registration applicant by telephone at the same time. The applicant/registration applicant will not need to re-confirm the objection assessment results.

With regard to projects for which the conclusion "evaluation failed" is upheld, CMDE will transfer out the projects with the conclusion recorded as "rejected registration" "rejected change", or "rejected renewal" according to relevant provisions. With regard to projects for which the original evaluation conclusions are changed, CMDE will re–circulate them according to relevant provisions.

18.6 References

CFDA Announcement on Issuing Five Relevant Working Procedures Including the Procedures for Reissuance of Medical Device Registration Certificate (No.91, 2015)

Announcement on Adjusting the Service Scope of the Electronic Regulated Product Submission (eRPS) System (No.11, 2023)

Chapter III Registration Templates

This chapter is for reference only. The CMDE reserves the right for final explanation.

1. Template for the Essential Principles Checklist for Safety and Performance of Medical Devices

1.1 Template for the Essential Principles Checklist for Safety and Performance of Medical Devices

Table 6 Essential Principles Checklist for Safety and Performance of Medical Devices

Clause No.	Requirements	Applicable	Standards used to prove conformity	Documents providing the objective evidence for conformity
A	General essential principles for safety and performance			
A1	General principles			
A1.1	Medical devices shall achieve the performance intended by applicants, and their design and production shall ensure that the devices can achieve the intended purpose under the intended conditions of use. With safety and intended performance, the risks brought by medical devices shall be acceptable when weighed against its benefit, without compromising the medical environment, safety of patients, as well as the safety and health of users and others.	All medical devices	*Announcement on Issuing the Requirements for Registration Application Dossiers of Medical Devices and Formats of Approval Documents, Essential Principles Checklist for Safety and Performance of Medical Devices,* and *Guidelines for Technical Review of the Registration of Medical Devices Under Benefit-Risk Assessment* ...	Product risk management data, IFU, and product technical requirements ...

Continued

Clause No.	Requirements	Applicable	Standards used to prove conformity	Documents providing the objective evidence for conformity
A1.2	The applicant shall be able to establish, implement, document and maintain a risk management system to ensure the safety, performance and quality controllability of medical devices. In the whole life cycle of medical devices, risk management is a continuous and repeated process, which requires regular and systematic improvement and update. In carrying out risk management, the applicant shall: a) Establish and document a risk management plan covering all medical devices; b) Identify and analyze all known and foreseeable hazards related to all medical devices; c) Estimate and evaluate the relevant risks during the expected use and reasonably foreseeable misuse; d) Eliminate or control the risks described in Item c) in accordance with the relevant requirements of A1.3 and A1.4; e) Evaluate the impact of production and post–production information on comprehensive risk, risk–benefit determination and risk acceptability. The evaluation described above shall include previously unidentified hazards or hazardous situations, the impact of one or more risks resulting from hazardous situations on acceptability, and changes in the level of advanced technology. f) Modify the control measures as necessary to meet the relevant requirements of A1.3 and A1.4 based on the impact evaluation of the information in Item e).	All medical devices	*Announcement on Issuing the Requirements for Registration Application Dossiers of Medical Devices and Formats of Approval Documents* and GB/ T 42062 …	Risk management data of the product …

Continued

Clause No.	Requirements	Applicable	Standards used to prove conformity	Documents providing the objective evidence for conformity
A1.3	The risk control measures adopted by the applicant of medical devices in the process of design and production shall follow the principle of safety and adopt advanced technology. When risk reduction is required, the applicant should control risks so that the residual risk associated with each hazard as well as the overall residual risk is judged acceptable. In selecting the most appropriate solutions, applicant should, in the following order of priority: a) Eliminate or appropriately reduce risks through safety design and production; b) Take adequate protective measures against risks that can not be eliminated, including necessary alarms, if applicable; c) Provide safety information (warnings/precautions/contraindications), and offer training to users as appropriate.	All medical devices	GB/T 42062	Product risk management data, IFU, and labels ...
A1.4	The applicant should inform users of any relevant residual risks.	All medical devices	*Provisions for Instructions and Labels of Medical Devices* and applicable standards or guidelines ...	IFU, labels, and product risk management data ...

Continued

Clause No.	Requirements	Applicable	Standards used to prove conformity	Documents providing the objective evidence for conformity
A1.5	To eliminate or reduce the risks associated with use, the applicants should: a) Appropriately reduce risks associated with the characteristics of medical devices (e.g. ergonomics/availability) and the intended use environment (e.g. dust and humidity); b) Take into account the technical know–how, experience, educational background, training, physical condition (if applicable) and use environment of intended users.	All medical devices	GB/T 42062, YY/T 9706.106, GB/T 14710, and other applicable standards or guidelines ...	Product risk management data, IFU (requirements of defining use environment and expected user, etc.), use stability study data (the most unfavorable situation of the expected use environment shall be considered, etc.), usability study data ...
A1.6	During the life cycle prescribed by the applicant, any external force, in the case of normal use, maintenance and calibration (if applicable), shall not adversely affect the characteristics and performance of the medical device to the detriment of the health and safety of the patients, users and others.	Reusable medical devices	*Guidelines for Technical Review of Registration of Service Life of Active Medical Devices*, and other applicable standards or guidelines ...	Study data on use stability and study data on sterilization tolerance ...
A1.7	The design, production and packaging of the medical device, including instructions and information provided by the applicant, shall ensure that the transport and storage conditions (e.g. shaking, vibration, temperature and humidity fluctuations) will not adversely affect the characteristics and performance of the medical device, including its integrity and cleanliness, when used for the intended use. Applicants shall be able to ensure the performance, safety and sterility assurance level of medical devices within the shelf life.	All medical devices	*Guidelines for Stability Study of Passive Implantable Medical Devices*, GB/T 14710, GB/T 4857 series, *Provisions for Instructions and Labels of Medical Devices*, other applicable standards or guidelines ...	Study data on shelf life, study data on transport stability, IFU, and labels ...

Continued

Clause No.	Requirements	Applicable	Standards used to prove conformity	Documents providing the objective evidence for conformity
A1.8	Medical devices shall have acceptable stability during the shelf life, after being unpackaged for use and during transportation or delivery.	All medical devices	GB/T 14710, GB/T 4857 series, YY/T 0681 series, ISO 11607 series, *Guidelines for Stability Study of Passive Implantable Medical Devices*, other applicable standards or guidelines ...	Stability study data ...
A1.9	Under normal use conditions, all known and foreseeable risks and any adverse side effects shall be minimized and acceptable compared to the performance benefits of medical devices, based on the state of the art.	All medical devices	*Announcement on Issuing the Requirements for Registration Application Dossiers of Medical Devices and Formats of Approval Documents* and GB/T 42062 ...	Risk management data of the product ...
A2	Clinical evaluation			
A2.1	Based on regulatory requirements, medical devices may be subject to clinical evaluation (if applicable). The clinical evaluation is designed to evaluate the clinical data and determine the acceptable risk–benefit ratio of medical devices, including the following forms: a) Clinical trial report b) Clinical literature c) Clinical experience data	Medical devices not listed in the *Catalogue of Medical Devices Exempted from Clinical Evaluation*	Relevant guidelines for clinical evaluation ...	Clinical evaluation data ...

Continued

Clause No.	Requirements	Applicable	Standards used to prove conformity	Documents providing the objective evidence for conformity
A2.2	Clinical trials should be conducted in accordance with the ethical principles of the *Declaration of Helsinki*. The protection of subjects' rights, safety and health, as the most important consideration, is more important than the scientific and social benefits. The above principles shall be understood, followed and used at each step of the clinical trial. In addition, the review and approval of clinical trial protocol, informed consent of patients, etc., shall meet the relevant regulatory requirements.	Medical devices subject to clinical trials	*Good Clinical Practice for Medical Devices*, *Announcement on Issuing the Requirements for Registration Application Dossiers of Medical Devices and Formats of Approval Documents*, *Technical Guidelines for Clinical Trial Design of Medical Devices*, and other applicable standards or guidelines …	Clinical evaluation data and application dossiers for approval of medical device clinical trials …
A3	Chemical, physical and biological properties			
A3.1	With regard to the chemical, physical and biological properties of medical devices, special attention shall be paid to the following aspects: a) Selection of materials and components used, especially: – Toxicity; – Biocompatibility; – Flammability; b) Impact of the process on material properties; c) Biophysical or modeling research results shall be verified in advance (if applicable); d) Mechanical properties of the materials used, such as strength, ductility, fracture resistance, abrasive resistance and fatigue resistance, if applicable; e) Surface properties; f) Compliance of the device with specified chemical and/ or physical properties.	All medical devices (different terms apply to different medical devices)	GB/T 16886 series, YY/T 0758, YY/T 0345.1, YY/T 0809.4, *Guidelines for Fatigue Performance Evaluation of Biological Femoral Stem* (if applicable), other applicable standards or guidelines …	Study data on biological properties, study data on chemical and physical properties (including mechanical properties), modeling study data, ignition and explosion risk study data, product technical requirements, and test reports …

Continued

Clause No.	Requirements	Applicable	Standards used to prove conformity	Documents providing the objective evidence for conformity
A3.2	Medical devices should be designed, manufactured and packaged in such a way as to minimize the risk posed by contaminants and residues to users and patients, taking account of the intended use of the medical device, and to the persons involved in the transport, storage and use of the medical device. Special attention shall be paid to the time and frequency of contact with the exposed tissues of users and patients.	Medical devices with contamin-ants and residues	*Guidance on Key Inspection Points for Cleaning Process Validation of Medical Devices*, and other applicable standards or guidelines ...	Study data on biological properties, study data on cleaning and disinfection by users, study data on residual toxicity, and study data on packaging ...
A3.3	Medical devices shall be designed and manufactured to appropriately reduce the risk of precipitation (including leaching and/or evaporation), degradation products, and processing residues, etc. Special attention shall be paid to leaking or leaching of substances that are carcinogenic, mutagenic or reproductively toxic.	Medical devices that come into direct or indirect contact with patients (except for intact skin contact)	GB/T 16886.16, GB/T 16886.17, GB/T 16886.18, YY/T 1550.2, GB/T 14233.1, *Guidelines for Registration Technical Review of Verification and Validation of Determination Methods for Known Leachables in Medical Devices*, *Guidance on Key Inspection Points for Cleaning Process Validation of Medical Devices*, and other applicable standards or guidelines ...	Study data on biological properties, study data on cleaning and disinfection by users, study data on residual toxicity, chemical properties (dissolved precipitates, etc.) in product technical requirements, and test reports ...
A3.4	The nature of the medical devices and their intended use environment shall be considered in the design and production of medical devices, to appropriately reduce the risk resulting from accidental entry of substances into the device.	Medical devices whose intended use environment contains other substances (e.g. liquids and gases)	GB 9706.1, GB/T 42062, and other applicable standards or guidelines ...	Product risk management data, study data on combined use, product technical requirements, and test reports ...

Continued

Clause No.	Requirements	Applicable	Standards used to prove conformity	Documents providing the objective evidence for conformity
A3.5	Medical devices and their manufacturing processes shall be designed to eliminate or appropriately reduce the risk of infection to users and other potential contacts. The design should: a) Safe and easy to handle; b) Minimize the risk of microbial leakage from medical devices and/or infection during the use of medical devices; c) Prevent microbial contamination of medical devices or their contents (e.g., specimens); d) Minimize the risk of accidents [e.g., cuts and stabs (e.g., needle stick injuries), accidental spillage into the eyes, etc.].	Medical devices with risk of infection (patient and user)	GB/T 42062, *Guidelines for Technical Review of Requirements and Evaluation of Needle Stick Protective Devices for Infusion Products*, other applicable standards or guidelines ...	Product risk management data, study data on packaging, study data on cleaning, disinfection, and sterilization, and study data on needle stick protective devices (if applicable) ...
A4	Sterilization and microbial contamination			
A4.1	Medical devices shall be designed to facilitate safe cleaning, disinfection, sterilization and/or re–sterilization (if necessary) by the user.	Medical devices with risk of infection	Applicable standards or guidelines ...	Study data on cleaning, disinfection, and sterilization ...
A4.2	Medical devices with microbial limits shall be designed, manufactured and packaged to ensure that they are transported and stored under the conditions specified by the applicant and meet the requirements for microbial limits after they leave the factory.	Medical devices with microbial limits	Applicable standards or guidelines ...	Study data on cleaning, disinfection, and sterilization, study data on stability, product technical requirements, and test reports ...

Continued

Clause No.	Requirements	Applicable	Standards used to prove conformity	Documents providing the objective evidence for conformity
A4.3	Medical devices provided in sterile shall be designed, manufactured and packaged in accordance with appropriate procedures to ensure that they are sterile upon delivery. Undamaged sterile package transported and stored under conditions specified by applicant should remain sterile until opened. The integrity of package shall be clearly identifiable by the end user (e.g. tamper-proof packaging).	Sterile medical device	GB 18278.1, GB 18279 series, GB 18280 series, YY/T 1276, YY/T 1464, GB/T 19974, YY/T 1463, other applicable standards or guidelines ...	Sterilization validation reports, study data on stability, and packaging instructions ...
A4.4	Sterile medical devices shall be processed, manufactured, packaged and sterilized according to the verified methods, and their shelf life shall be determined by validated methods.	Sterile medical device	GB 18278.1, GB 18279 series, GB 18280 series, YY/T 1276, YY/T 1464, GB/T 19974, YY/T 1464, other applicable standards or guidelines ...	Sterilization validation reports, study data on shelf life, and study data on packaging ...
A4.5	Medical devices intended for sterile use (sterilization by applicant or user) shall be manufactured and packaged under appropriate and controlled conditions and facilities.	Medical devices for sterile use	*Good Manufacturing Practice for Medical Devices - Appendix: Sterile Medical Devices*, YY 0033 *Good manufacture practice for sterile medical devices*, GB 50457 *Code for design of pharmaceutical industry clean room*, YY/T 0287, ISO 13485, and other applicable standards or guidelines ...	Quality system audit report, ISO 13485 Certificate ...

Continued

Clause No.	Requirements	Applicable	Standards used to prove conformity	Documents providing the objective evidence for conformity
A4.6	Medical devices provided in non–sterile condition and sterilized before use shall be: a) Packaging should minimize the risk of microbial contamination for the product and be applicable to the sterilization method specified by the applicant; b) The sterilization method specified by the applicant should be validated .	Medical devices provided in non–sterile condition and sterilized before use	Applicable standards or guidelines ...	Study data on sterilization ...
A4.7	The delivery status shall be clearly marked if the medical device can be delivered in sterile and non–sterile condition.	Medical devices that can be delivered for use in sterile and non–sterile states	Applicable standards or guidelines ...	Product label ...
A5	Environment and conditions of use			
A5.1	If the medical device is expected to be used in combination with other medical devices or equipment, the integrated system, including the connection system, shall be ensured for overall safety and shall not affect the performance of the device. Restrictions on integrated use shall be indicated on the label and/ or specified in the IFU. For connections to be completed by the user, such as liquid, gas transmission, electrical or mechanical coupling, all possible risks, including faulty connections or safety hazards, shall be eliminated or minimized as far as possible in the design and manufacturing procedures.	Medical devices intended to be used in combination with other medical devices or equipment	GB 9706.1, GB 9706.15, GB/ T 42062, and other applicable standards or guidelines ...	Study data on combined use, product risk management data, IFU, product technical requirements, test reports, and study data on usability ...

Continued

Clause No.	Requirements	Applicable	Standards used to prove conformity	Documents providing the objective evidence for conformity
A5.2	The intended use environment and conditions shall be considered in the design and production of medical devices to eliminate or reduce the following risks: a) Risk of injury to users or others related to physical and ergonomic/availability characteristics;	All medical devices	YY/T 9706.106 and other applicable standards or guidelines ...	Study data on usability and product risk management data ...
	b) Risk of incorrect operation due to user interface design, ergonomic/availability characteristics and the intended use environment;	All medical devices	YY/T 9706.106 and other applicable standards or guidelines ...	Study data on usability and product risk management data ...
	c) Risks related to reasonably foreseeable external factors or environmental conditions, such as magnetic field, external electromagnetic effect, electrostatic discharge, radiation caused by diagnosis and treatment, as well as changes in pressure, humidity, temperature and/or pressure and acceleration;	All medical devices	YY 9706.102 and other applicable standards or guidelines ...	Electromagnetic compatibility reports, study data on radiation safety, product risk management data, and study data on stability ...
	d) Risks arising from contact with solid materials, liquids and other substances, including gases, under normal use conditions;	Medical devices that come into contact with solid materials, liquids and other substances under normal use conditions	14.2 of GB 16174.2 on the requirements of implantable medical devices in contact with body fluids, other applicable standards or guidelines ...	Product risk management data, study data of combined use, study data of risk of ignition and explosion (such as use in oxygen rich environment), product technical requirements and test reports ...

Continued

Clause No.	Requirements	Applicable	Standards used to prove conformity	Documents providing the objective evidence for conformity
A5.2	e) Risks caused by the compatibility of software and information technology (IT) operating environment;	Medical devices with software	*Guidelines for Registration Review of Medical Device Software*, and other applicable standards or guidelines ...	Study data on software, product risk management data, product technical requirements, test reports, and IFU ...
	f) Environmental risks caused by unexpected precipitates of medical devices during normal use;	Medical devices that come into direct or indirect contact with patients	GB/T 14223.2, other applicable standards or guidelines ...	Product risk management data, dissolved precipitates in product technical requirements, test reports, and study data on biological properties (related to leachables) ...
	g) Risks caused by incorrect identification and wrong results of specimens/samples/data, such as confused color and/or digital code of sample containers, detachable parts and/or accessories used for analysis, test or detection;	Medical devices requiring identification of specimen/ samples/data	Applicable standards or guidelines ...	Product risk management data and study data on usability ...
	h) Risks caused by interference with other medical devices used for diagnosis, monitoring or treatment.	Active medical devices	YY 9706.102 and other applicable standards or guidelines ...	Product risk management data, electromagnetic compatibility test reports, and study data on combined use (such as magnetic resonance environmental safety) ...

Continued

Clause No.	Requirements	Applicable	Standards used to prove conformity	Documents providing the objective evidence for conformity
A5.3	Medical devices shall be designed and manufactured to eliminate or reduce the risk of ignition and explosion under normal condition and single fault condition, especially the intended use, including combined use exposure to flammable, explosive substances or other combustibles.	Active medical devices	Clause 11 of GB 9706.1 and other applicable standards or guidelines ...	Product risk management data, study data on ignition and explosion risks, and GB 9706.1 test reports ...
A5.4	Medical devices shall be designed and manufactured to ensure that the adjustment, calibration and maintenance process can be completed in a safely and effectively way.	Active medical devices	Applicable standards or guidelines ...	Test report ...
	a) For medical devices that can not be maintained, such as implants, the risk of material aging shall be minimized;	Medical devices that cannot be maintained	Applicable standards or guidelines ...	Product risk management data and study data on stability ...
	b) For medical devices that can not be adjusted and calibrated, such as some types of thermometers, the risk of accuracy loss of measurement or control mechanism shall be minimized.	Medical devices that cannot be adjusted and calibrated	Applicable standards or guidelines ...	Product risk management data and study data on stability ...
A5.5	For medical devices used in combination with other medical devices or products, their design and production shall ensure interoperability, compatibility, reliability and safety.	Medical devices used in combination with other medical devices or products	Guidelines for Registration Review of Medical Device Software, Clause 22 of GB 16174.1, and other applicable standards or guidelines ...	Study data on combined use, study data on interoperability, product technical requirements, and test reports ...

Continued

Clause No.	Requirements	Applicable	Standards used to prove conformity	Documents providing the objective evidence for conformity
A5.6	Medical devices shall be designed and manufactured to reduce the risk of unauthorized access, which may hinder the normal operation of the device or cause potential safety hazards.	Medical devices with access interface	*Guidelines for Registration Review of Medical Device Cybersecurity*, and other applicable standards or guidelines …	Study data on cybersecurity, product technical requirements, test reports (access control), product risk management data, and IFU …
A5.7	The design and production of medical devices with measurement, monitoring or numerical display functions shall conform to the principles of ergonomics/availability and take into account the intended use, intended users and service environment of the devices.	Medical devices with measuring, monitoring or numerical display functions	YY/T 9706.106 and other applicable standards or guidelines …	Study data on usability …
A5.8	Medical devices shall be designed and manufactured to facilitate the safe disposal or reuse of them and related wastes by users, patients or others. The IFU shall specify the procedures and methods for safe disposal or recycling	All medical devices	*Provisions for Instructions and Labels of Medical Devices*, and other applicable standards or guidelines …	IFU …
A6	Protection against electrical, mechanical and thermal risks			
A6.1	Medical devices shall be designed and manufactured with mechanical protection to protect users from mechanical risks caused by motion resistance, instability and moving parts.	Medical devices with mechanical risks	Mechanical risk requirements and other applicable standards or guidelines under GB 9706.1 …	GB 9706.1 test reports and product risk management data …

Continued

Clause No.	Requirements	Applicable	Standards used to prove conformity	Documents providing the objective evidence for conformity
A6.2	Medical devices shall be designed and manufactured to minimize the risk caused by product vibration, and the measures of limiting vibration (especially vibration source) shall be adopted as far as possible, unless vibration is a part of the specific performance of the device.	Medical devices with risk of vibration	GB 9706.1, other applicable standards or guidelines ...	GB 9706.1 test reports and product risk management data ...
A6.3	Medical devices shall be designed and manufactured to minimize the risk caused by product noise, and the measures of limiting noise (especially noise source) shall be adopted as far as possible, unless noise is a part of the specific performance of the device.	Medical devices with noise	GB 9706.1, other applicable standards or guidelines ...	GB 9706.1 test reports, and product risk management data ...
A6.4	If it is required to connect or reconnect some parts of medical devices before or during use, the medical devices shall be designed and manufactured in such a way to minimize the risks of connection error.	If it is required to connect or reconnect some parts of medical devices before or during use	Applicable standards or guidelines ...	Risk management data of the product ...
A6.5	The accessible parts of medical devices (excluding the parts used for heating or the set temperature) and their surrounding environment shall be free from the risk of overheating during normal use.	Active medical devices	Overtemperature requirements in GB 9706.1 ...	GB 9706.1 test reports and product risk management data ...

Continued

Clause No.	Requirements	Applicable	Standards used to prove conformity	Documents providing the objective evidence for conformity
A7	Active medical devices and medical devices connected with them			
A7.1	In case of single fault condition occurs in the active medical device, appropriate measures shall be taken to eliminate or reduce the resulting risks.	Active medical devices	GB 9706.1	GB 9706.1 test reports and product risk management data ...
A7.2	Medical devices that depend on internal power supply for patient safety shall have the function of detecting the power supply status, and give appropriate prompt or warning when the power capacity is insufficient.	Active medical devices	Indicator requirements in GB 9706.1 ...	GB 9706.1 test reports ...
A7.3	For devices where the safety of patients depends on an external power supply power failure, the device must be fitted with an alarm system that indicates whether a power failure has occurred.	Active medical devices	YY 9706.108, GB 9706.212, and other applicable standards or guidelines ...	Technical requirements and test reports ...
A7.4	The medical devices intended for monitoring one or more clinical indicators of patients shall be equipped with an appropriate alarm system for alarming when the patients' life and health are seriously deteriorated or in a critical condition.	The medical devices intended for monitoring one or more clinical indicators	YY 9706.108, other applicable standards or guidelines ...	Technical requirements and test reports ...
A7.5	For devices or equipment whose normal operation may be damaged by electromagnetic interference, the risk of electromagnetic interference shall be reduced in design and production of medical devices.	Active medical devices	YY 9706.102 and other applicable standards or guidelines ...	Electromagnetic compatibility test reports and product risk management data ...

Continued

Clause No.	Requirements	Applicable	Standards used to prove conformity	Documents providing the objective evidence for conformity
A7.6	Medical devices shall be designed and manufactured to ensure sufficient anti–electromagnetic interference ability for normal operation.	Active medical devices	YY 9706.102 and other applicable standards or guidelines ...	Electromagnetic compatibility test reports ...
A7.7	Medical device shall be designed and manufactured to reduce the risk of users and others from accidental electric shock in normal and single fault conditions, when the product is installed and maintained in accordance with the instructions of the applicant.	Active medical devices	GB 9706.1	Electrical safety test reports and product risk management data ...
A8	Medical devices with software and SaMD			
A8.1	The medical devices with electronic programmable system (containing SiMD) or SaMD shall be designed to ensure that the accuracy, reliability, precision, safety and performance meet its intended use. Appropriate measures shall be taken to eliminate or reduce the risk or performance degradation caused by single fault.	Medical devices with software	GB/T 20438.1, Subclause 19.3 of GB 16174.1, other applicable standards or guidelines ...	Product risk management data, study data on software, product technical requirements, and test reports ...
A8.2	The SiMD or SaMD shall be developed, produced and maintained by advanced technology, and the development life cycle (such as rapid iterative development, frequent updates, cumulative effect of updates), risk management (such as changes in system, environment and data) and other principles shall be considered, including the requirements for information security (such as safe updating), verification and confirmation (such as management process updating).	Medical devices with software	GB/T 20438 series, GB/T 20918, etc., *Guidelines for Registration Review of Medical Device Software*, and other applicable standards or guidelines ...	Study data on software, study data on cybersecurity, and product risk management data ...

Continued

Clause No.	Requirements	Applicable	Standards used to prove conformity	Documents providing the objective evidence for conformity
A8.3	The software expected to be integrated with the mobile computing platform shall be designed and developed considering the platform itself (such as screen size and contrast, connectivity, memory, etc.) and the external factors related to its use (lighting or noise level in different environments).	Software intended for integration with mobile computing platforms	*Guidelines for Registration Technical Review of Mobile Medical Devices,* and other applicable standards or guidelines ...	Study data on mobile medical devices ...
A8.4	The applicant shall specify the minimum requirements necessary for the normal operation of the software as expected, such as hardware, IT network features and IT cybersecurity measures, including unauthorized access.	Medical devices with software	*Guidelines for Registration Review of Medical Device Cybersecurity, Guidelines for Registration Review of Medical Device Software,* other applicable standards or guidelines ...	Study data on software, study data on cybersecurity, product risk management data, product technical requirements, test reports, and IFU ...
A8.5	The medical devices shall be designed, produced and maintained to provide sufficient cybersecurity to prevent unauthorized access.	Medical devices with access interface	*Guidelines for Registration Review of Medical Device Cybersecurity* ...	Study data on cybersecurity, product risk management data, product technical requirements, test reports, and IFU ...
A9	Medical device with diagnostic or measuring function			
A9.1	The medical devices with the function of diagnosis or measuring function (including monitoring) shall be designed and produced based on appropriate scientific and technological methods. In addition to other performance, the corresponding accuracy, precision and stability shall also be guaranteed to achieve its intended purpose.	Medical device with diagnostic or measuring (including monitoring) functions	Applicable standards (e.g., YY 9706.247) or guidelines ...	Stability study data, study data on measurement accuracy, product technical requirements, test reports, IFU, software study data (algorithm verification and validation) ...

Continued

Clause No.	Requirements	Applicable	Standards used to prove conformity	Documents providing the objective evidence for conformity
A9.1	a) Applicants should specify the limit of accuracy (if applicable).	Medical device with diagnostic or measuring (including monitoring) functions	Applicable standards or guidelines ...	Technical requirements and test reports ...
	b) In order to facilitate the user to understand and accept, the digitized measured values shall be expressed in standardized unit (if possible), and the international standard measurement units are recommended. Considering the safety, user's familiarity and previous clinical practice, other recognized measurement units can also be used.	Medical device with diagnostic or measuring (including monitoring) functions	Subclause 6.3 of GB 9706.1, other applicable standards or guidelines ...	Test report ...
	c) The functions of the medical device indicator and controller shall be described in detail. If the device provides descriptions related to operation, operation instruction or adjustment parameters through the visualization system, such information shall be easily understood by the user and the patient (when applicable).	Medical device with indicator and controller	Applicable standards or guidelines ...	IFU and study data on usability ...

Continued

Clause No.	Requirements	Applicable	Standards used to prove conformity	Documents providing the objective evidence for conformity
A10	IFU and labels			
A10.1	Medical devices shall be accompanied with the information needed to identify the device and its applicant. Each medical device shall also be accompanied with relevant safety and performance information or relevant instructions. Such information can appear in the device itself, on the package or in the IFU, or can be easily accessed by electronic means (such as website) and easily understood by the intended user.	All medical devices	*Provisions for Instructions and Labels of Medical Devices* and applicable standards or guidelines ...	IFU, labels, and study data on usability ...
A11	Radiation protection			
A11.1	The medical devices shall be designed, manufactured and packaged to minimize the radiation absorbed dose of users, other people and patients (if applicable), without affecting its diagnosis or treatment functions.	Medical devices with radiation	Applicable standards (e.g., GB 15213) or guidelines ...	Product technical requirements, test reports, study data on radiation safety, and instructions for dosage in IFU ...
A11.2	The IFU of medical devices with radiation or potential radiation hazards shall specify the nature of radiation, protective measures for users, other people or patients (if applicable), methods of avoiding misuse, and reducing the risk during transportation, storage and installation.	Medical devices with radiation or potential radiation hazards	GB 9706.1, other applicable standards or guidelines ...	Study data on radiation safety, product test reports, product risk management data, and IFU ...

Continued

Clause No.	Requirements	Applicable	Standards used to prove conformity	Documents providing the objective evidence for conformity
A11.3	If the medical device has radiation or potential radiation hazards, it shall have the sound and light alarm function for radiation leakage (if feasible).	Medical devices with radiation or potential radiation hazards	YY 9706.108, other applicable standards or guidelines ...	Product technical requirements, test reports, and IFU ...
A11.4	The medical devices shall be designed and produced to reduce the risk of users, other people or patients (if applicable) being exposed to unexpected, deviating or scattered radiation. Where possible and appropriate, measures shall be taken to reduce exposure to radiation for users, other people, or patients (if applicable) who may be affected.	Medical devices with radiation	Applicable standards or guidelines ...	Product risk management data, study data on radiation safety, IFU, and labels, product technical requirements and test reports ...
A11.5	The IFU of medical devices that have radiation or potential radiation hazards and need to be installed shall provide information on acceptance and performance test, acceptance standards and maintenance procedures.	Medical devices with radiation or potential radiation hazards that require installation	Applicable standards or guidelines ...	IFU and study data on radiation safety ...
A11.6	If the medical device has radiation or potential radiation hazard to users, such medical device shall be designed and manufactured to ensure that the radiation dose, geometric distribution, energy distribution (or quality) and other key radiation characteristics can be reasonably controlled and adjusted, and can be monitored during use (if applicable). The design and production of the above medical devices shall ensure that the repeatability of the relevant variable parameters is within acceptable range.	Medical devices with radiation or potential radiation hazards that require installation	Applicable standards or guidelines ...	Study data on radiation safety, product technical requirements, and test reports ...

Continued

Clause No.	Requirements	Applicable	Standards used to prove conformity	Documents providing the objective evidence for conformity
A12	Protection against risk on non–professional user operation			
A12.1	For medical devices used by non–professional users (such as self–test or near–patient test), in order to ensure the normal use of medical devices, the design and production of medical devices shall consider the operating skills of non–professional users, and the impact on the results due to the non–professional user's technology and different use environment. The information and instructions provided by the applicant shall be easy to understand and use, and explain the results.	Medical devices used by non–professional users	YY/T 9706.106 and other applicable standards or guidelines ...	Product risk management data, study data on usability, and IFU ...
A12.2	Medical devices used by non–professional users (such as self–test or near–patient test) should be designed and manufactured in such a way as to: a) Ensure that the users can use it safely and accurately in accordance with the IFU. When the risks related to the instructions cannot be reduced to an appropriate level, such risks can be reduced through training;	Medical devices used by non–professional users	Applicable standards or guidelines ...	Product risk management data, study data on usability, and IFU ...
	b) Minimize the non–professional users' risks caused by incorrect operation and interpretation of results.	Medical devices used by non–professional users	GB/T 42062 and other applicable standards and guidelines ...	Product risk management data, study data on usability, and IFU ...

Continued

Clause No.	Requirements	Applicable	Standards used to prove conformity	Documents providing the objective evidence for conformity
A12.3	The medical devices used by non–professional users can facilitate users through the following measures: a) Verify whether the device operates normally during operation;	Medical devices used by non–professional users	GB 9706.1, other applicable standards or guidelines ...	Product test reports and IFU ...
	b) Give alarm when the device fails to operate normally or provides invalid results.	Medical devices used by non–professional users	Applicable standards or guidelines ...	IFU ...
A13	Medical devices containing biological materials			
A13.1	For medical devices containing animal or plant tissues, cells or other substances, bacterial–derived substances or derivatives, if inactive or delivered in inactive state, the following requirements shall be satisfied: a) Tissues, cells and their derivatives shall be derived from animal species that are controlled and suitable for their intended use. Information on geographical origin of animals shall be retained in accordance with the requirements of relevant laws and regulations.	Medical devices containing biological materials	*Guidelines for Registration Technical Review of Medical Device Utilizing Animal Tissues and Their Derivatives*, YY/T 0771 series, and other applicable standards or guidelines ...	Study data on biosafety ...
	b) The tissues, cells, substances or derivatives of animal origin shall be collected, processed, stored, tested and treated to ensure the safety of patients, users and other person (if applicable). In particular, viruses and other infectious pathogens shall be eliminated or inactivated by proven advanced technology, provided that the performance of medical devices shall not be affected.	Medical devices containing biological materials	*Guidelines for Registration Technical Review of Medical Device Utilizing Animal Tissues and Their Derivatives*, YY/T 0771 series, and other applicable standards or guidelines ...	Study data on biosafety and product risk management data ...

Continued

Clause No.	Requirements	Applicable	Standards used to prove conformity	Documents providing the objective evidence for conformity
A13.2	When the medical devices are produced from tissues, cells, substances or derivatives of human origin, the regulatory authority shall take the following measures: a) Donation, acquisition and test of tissues and cells shall be performed in accordance with the requirements of relevant laws and regulations;	Medical devices containing biological materials	*Guidelines for Registration Technical Review of Medical Device Utilizing Animal Tissues and Their Derivatives*, and other applicable standards or guidelines ...	Study data on biosafety ...
	b) To ensure the safety of patients, users or other people, tissues, cells or their derivatives shall be processed, preserved or otherwise handled. Viruses and other sources of infection shall be eliminated or inactivated through source control or through verified advanced technology during production.	Medical devices containing biological materials	*Guidelines for Registration Technical Review of Medical Device Utilizing Animal Tissues and Their Derivatives*, and other applicable standards or guidelines	Study data on biosafety and product risk management data ...
A13.3	When the medical devices are produced from biological substances other than those specified in A13.1 and A13.2 (such as plant or bacterial materials), its processing, storage, testing and treatment process shall be implemented to ensure the safety of patients, users or other people (such as waste disposal personnel, etc.). In order to ensure safety, viruses and other sources of infection shall be eliminated or inactivated through source control or through verified advanced technology during production.	Medical devices containing biological materials	*Guidelines for Registration Technical Review of Medical Device Utilizing Animal Tissues and Their Derivatives*, and other applicable standards or guidelines ...	Study data on biosafety and product risk management data ...

Continued

Clause No.	Requirements	Applicable	Standards used to prove conformity	Documents providing the objective evidence for conformity
B	Essential principles applicable to medical devices			
B1	Chemical, physical and biological properties			
B1.1	In accordance with the intended use of the medical device and the absorption, distribution, metabolism and excretion of products (such as some absorbable products) in the human body, special attention shall be paid to the compatibility of used materials/substances with human tissues, cells and body fluids for chemical, physical and biological characteristics of medical devices.	Medical devices for absorption, distribution, metabolism, and excretion in the human body	Applicable standards or guidelines …	Study data on physical and chemical properties, and study data on biological properties …
B1.2	The medical devices shall be designed and manufactured to ensure that the products can still be used safely when it comes into contact with other materials, substances and gases during intended use. If the medical devices are used in combination with drugs, such products shall be designed and produced in accordance with the relevant regulations on drug management and have drug compatibility, and the performance of drugs and devices shall be consistent with its indications and intended use.	Medical devices intended for use in contact with other materials, substances and gases	Subclause 19.5 of GB 16174.1, the drug compatibility part can refer to the relevant contents in the *Guidelines for Registration Review of Drug-Device Combination Medical Devices*, other applicable standards or guidelines …	Study data on combined use (including drug compatibility study) …
B1.3	The medical devices shall be designed and manufactured to appropriately reduce particles released into the patients' or users' bodies and risks related to particle size and properties except for the products that contact intact skin. Special attention shall be paid to nanomaterials.	Medical devices that may release particles into the patient or user	*Guidelines for Safety and Effectiveness Evaluation of Medical Devices Using Nanomaterials Part 1: System Framework*, Subclause 14.2 of GB 16174.1, and other applicable standards or guidelines …	Study data on biological properties and product risk management data …

Continued

Clause No.	Requirements	Applicable	Standards used to prove conformity	Documents providing the objective evidence for conformity
B2	Radiation protection			
B2.1	When the medical devices used for medical imaging have ionizing radiation, they shall be designed and manufactured to ensure the image and/or output quality while minimizing the radiation absorbed dose of patients, users and other persons.	Medical devices for medical imaging with ionizing radiation	Applicable standards or guidelines ...	Product risk management data, product technical requirements, test reports, and study data on radiation safety ...
B2.2	Medical devices with ionizing radiation shall be designed to accurately estimate (or monitor), display, report, and record the radiation dose during treatment.	Medical devices with ionizing radiation	Applicable standards or guidelines ...	Product risk management data, product technical requirements, test reports, and study data on radiation safety ...
B3	Special requirements for implantable medical devices			
B3.1	The implantable medical devices shall be designed and manufactured to eliminate or reduce the relevant treatment risks, such as the use of defibrillators and HF surgical equipment.	Implantable medical devices	*Guidelines for Technical Review of Registration of Implantable Cardiac Pacemaker*, GB 16174 series, other applicable standards or guidelines ...	Product risk management data, product technical requirements, and test reports ...
B3.2	The programmable active implantable medical devices shall be designed and manufactured to ensure that the product can be accurately identified without the need for surgery.	Programmable active implantable medical devices	Applicable standards (such as Subclause 13.3 of GB 16174.1) or guidelines ...	Technical requirements and test reports ...

Continued

Clause No.	Requirements	Applicable	Standards used to prove conformity	Documents providing the objective evidence for conformity
B4	Risk protection for patients or users of medical devices that provide energy or substances			
B4.1	The medical devices used to provide energy or substances to patients shall be designed and manufactured to accurately set and maintain output to ensure the safety of patients, users and other people.	Medical devices used to provide energy or substances to patients	Applicable standards or guidelines ...	Technical requirements and test reports ...
B4.2	If insufficient output may lead to risks, medical devices shall have methods to prevent and/or indicate "insufficient output". The appropriate measures shall be taken to reduce accidental output of dangerous level of energy or substance as a greater risk.	Medical devices used to provide energy or substances to patients	GB 9706.1, other applicable standards or guidelines ...	Product risk management data and GB 9706.1 test reports (12.4 Protection of hazardous output) ...
B5	A combination product containing drug ingredients			
B5.1	When the components of medical devices contain some kind of substances, such substance shall be managed as medicinal product/ drug in accordance with the supervision laws and regulations, and when such substance plays a helpful role for the medical device in the body, the medical device and the substance shall be taken as a whole to verify its safety and performance and verify the characteristics, safety, quality and effectiveness of the substance at the same time.	Drug–device combination products	*Guidelines for Registration Review of Drug-Device Combination Medical Devices, Guidelines for Registration Review of Qualitative, Quantitative and In Vitro Release Studies of Drugs in Drug-Device Combination Medical Devices* ...	Non–clinical study, clinical evaluation, product technical requirements, and test reports ...

Continued

Clause No.	Requirements	Applicable	Standards used to prove conformity	Documents providing the objective evidence for conformity
Description	1. If Column 3 is applicable, please indicate "Yes". If not applicable, indicate "No" and state relevant reasons regarding the product characteristics. 2. The methods for proving that this medical device complies with the essential principles for safety and performance shall be filled into the fourth column, and the following methods may be generally adopted to prove that this medical device complies with the essential requirements: (1) Compliance with published regulations and normative documents of medical devices. (2) Compliance with relevant national standards, industry standards, and international standards for medical devices. (3) Compliance with the test methods commonly accepted in the industry. (4) Compliance with the methods stipulated by the manufacturer. (5) Comparison with similar products approved to be marketed. (6) Clinical evaluation. 3. If the evidence provided for conformity is included in the product registration dossiers, its specific position in the application dossiers shall be stated. For the evidence provided for conformity is not included in the product registration application dossiers, their file names and numbers in the quality management system should be noted for inspection.			

Note: Relevant laws, regulations, standards, and guidelines mentioned in the table shall be subject to the currently valid versions published by relevant institutions.

1.2 Template for the Essential Principles Checklist for Safety and Performance of In Vitro Diagnostic Reagents

Table 7 Essential Principles Checklist for Safety and Performance of In Vitro Diagnostic Reagents

Clause No.	Requirements	Applicable	Standards used to prove conformity	Documents providing the objective evidence for conformity
A	General essential principles for safety and performance			
A1	General principles			
A1.1	Medical devices shall achieve the intended performance of the product proposed by the applicant and shall be designed and manufactured in such a way that, during intended conditions of use, they are suitable for their intended purpose. With safety and intended performance, the risks brought by medical devices shall be acceptable compared to its benefit, without compromising the medical environment, safety of patients, as well as the health and safety of users and others.	All IVD reagents	GB/T 42062, YY/T 1441	Risk analysis data, IFU, product technical requirements, and analytical performance evaluation data ...
A1.2	The applicant shall be able to establish, implement, record and maintain a risk management system to ensure the safety, effectiveness and quality controllability of medical devices. In the whole life cycle of medical devices, risk management is a continuous and repeated process, which requires regular and systematic improvement and update. In carrying out risk management, the applicant shall:	All IVD reagents	GB/T 42062	Risk analysis data ...

Continued

Clause No.	Requirements	Applicable	Standards used to prove conformity	Documents providing the objective evidence for conformity
A1.2	a) Establish and document a risk management plan covering all medical devices; b) Identify and analyze all known and foreseeable hazards related to all medical devices; c) Estimate and evaluate the relevant risks during the expected use and reasonably foreseeable misuse; d) Eliminate or control the risks described in Item c) in accordance with the relevant requirements of A1.3 and A1.4; e) Evaluate the impact of production and post–production information on comprehensive risk, risk–benefit determination and risk acceptability. The evaluation described above shall include previously unidentified hazards or hazardous situations, the impact of one or more risks resulting from hazardous situations on acceptability, and changes in the level of advanced technology. f) Modify the control measures as necessary to meet the relevant requirements of A1.3 and A1.4 based on the impact evaluation of the information in Item e).			

Continued

Clause No.	Requirements	Applicable	Standards used to prove conformity	Documents providing the objective evidence for conformity
A1.3	The risk control measures adopted by the applicant of medical devices in the process of design and production shall follow the principle of safety and adopt advanced technology. When risk reduction is required, the applicant should control risks so that the residual risk associated with each hazard as well as the overall residual risk is judged acceptable. In selecting the most appropriate solutions, applicant should, in the following order of priority: a) Eliminate or appropriately reduce risks through safety design and production; b) Take adequate protective measures against risks that cannot be eliminated, including necessary alarms, if applicable; c) Provide safety information (warnings/precautions/ contraindications), and offer training to users as appropriate.	All IVD reagents	GB/T 42062, GB/T 191	Risk analysis data, label and IFU of product ...
A1.4	The applicant should inform users of any relevant residual risks.	All IVD reagents	GB/T 42062, GB/T 191, ...	Risk analysis data, label and IFU of product ...
A1.5	To eliminate or reduce the risks associated with use, the applicants should: a) Appropriately reduce risks associated with the characteristics of medical devices (e.g., ergonomics/ availability) and the intended use environment (e.g., dust and humidity); b) Considering the technical know-how, experience, educational background, training, physical condition (if applicable) and use environment of intended users.	All IVD reagents	GB/T 42062	Risk analysis data ...

Continued

Clause No.	Requirements	Applicable	Standards used to prove conformity	Documents providing the objective evidence for conformity
A1.6	During the life cycle prescribed by the applicant, any external force, in the case of normal use, maintenance and calibration (if applicable), shall not adversely affect the characteristics and performance of the medical device to the detriment of the health and safety of the patients, users and others.	IVD reagents requiring calibration	GB/T 42062, YY/T 1441, GB/T 21415	Risk analysis data, IFU, product technical requirements, and analytical performance evaluation data ...
A1.7	The design, production and packaging of the medical device, including instructions and information provided by the applicant, shall ensure that the transport and storage conditions (e.g., shaking, vibration, temperature and humidity fluctuations) will not adversely affect the characteristics and performance of the medical device, including its integrity and cleanliness, when used for the intended use. Applicants shall be able to ensure the performance, safety and sterility assurance level of medical devices within the shelf life.	All IVD reagents	Product stability study (real–time/unsealing/ transport stability study) Provisions for the Instructions for Use and Labels of Medical Devices	Stability study data, package labels, product IFU and manufacturing processes .....
A1.8	Medical devices shall be of acceptable stability during shelf life, during use after opening (including the onboard stability, for diagnostic reagents), and during transportation or delivery (including tested samples, for diagnostic reagents).	All IVD reagents	Product stability study (real–time/unsealing/ transport stability study)	Stability study data .....

Continued

Clause No.	Requirements	Applicable	Standards used to prove conformity	Documents providing the objective evidence for conformity
A1.9	Under normal use conditions, all known and foreseeable risks and any adverse side effects shall be minimized and acceptable compared to the performance benefits of medical devices, based on the state of the art.	All IVD reagents	GB/T 42062	Risk management report .....
A2	Clinical evaluation			
A2.1	Based on regulatory requirements, medical devices may be subject to clinical evaluation (if applicable). The clinical evaluation is designed to evaluate the clinical data and determine the acceptable risk–benefit ratio of medical devices, including the following forms: a) Clinical trial report (clinical performance evaluation report of diagnostic reagents) b) Clinical literature c) Clinical experience data	IVD reagent products not listed in the *Catalogue of In Vitro Diagnostic Reagents Exempted from Clinical Trials*, non–calibrators and quality controls	Technical Guidelines for Clinical Trials of In Vitro Diagnostic Reagents	Clinical evaluation data .....
A2.2	Clinical trials should be conducted in accordance with the ethical principles of the *Declaration of Helsinki*. The protection of subjects' rights, safety and health, as the most important consideration, is more important than the scientific and social benefits. The above principles shall be understood, followed and used at each step of the clinical trial. In addition, the approval of clinical trial protocol, informed consent of patients, and the use of the remaining samples of diagnostic reagents shall meet the relevant regulatory requirements.	IVD reagent products not listed in the *Catalogue of In Vitro Diagnostic Reagents Exempted from Clinical Trials*, non–calibrators and quality controls	Technical Guidelines for Clinical Trials of In Vitro Diagnostic Reagents	Relevant Documents Approved by the Ethics Committee .....

Continued

Clause No.	Requirements	Applicable	Standards used to prove conformity	Documents providing the objective evidence for conformity
A3	Chemical, physical and biological properties			
A3.1	With regard to the chemical, physical and biological properties of medical devices, special attention shall be paid to the following aspects: a) Selection of materials and components used, especially: – Toxicity; – Biocompatibility; – Flammability; b) Impact of the process on material properties; c) Biophysical or modeling research results shall be verified in advance (if applicable); d) Mechanical properties of the materials used, such as strength, ductility, breaking strength, abrasive resistance and fatigue resistance, if applicable; e) Surface properties; f) Compliance of the device with specified chemical and/or physical properties.	a) and b) are applicable to all IVD reagents; other clauses are applicable to certain IVD reagents as appropriate	GB/T 16483, GB/T 42062	Summary data, and risk management report ...
A3.2	Medical devices should be designed, manufactured and packaged in such a way as to minimize the risk posed by contaminants and residues to users and patients, taking account of the intended use of the medical device, and to the persons involved in the transport, storage and use of the medical device. Special attention shall be paid to the time and frequency of contact with the exposed tissues of users and patients.	All IVD reagents applicable	GB/T 42062, and *Provisions for the Instructions for Use and Labels of Medical Devices*	Risk management report, and product IFU .....

Continued

Clause No.	Requirements	Applicable	Standards used to prove conformity	Documents providing the objective evidence for conformity
A3.3	Medical devices shall be designed and produced to appropriately reduce the risk of precipitation (including leachate and/or evaporant), degradation products, and processing residues, etc. Special attention shall be paid to leaks or leachates that are carcinogenic, mutagenic or reproductively toxic.	All IVD reagents applicable	GB/T 42062	Quality management system document and risk management data .....
A3.4	The nature of the medical devices and their intended use environment shall be considered in the design and production of medical devices, to appropriately reduce the risk resulting from accidental entry of substances into the device.	All IVD reagents applicable	GB/T 42062	Quality management system documents Risk management data IFU .....
A3.5	Medical devices and their manufacturing processes shall be designed to eliminate or appropriately reduce the risk of infection to users and other potential contacts. The design should: a) Safe and easy to handle; b) Minimize the risk of microbial leakage from medical devices and/or infection during the use of medical devices; c) Prevent microbial contamination of medical devices or their contents (e.g., specimens); d) Minimize the risk of accidents [e.g., cuts and stabs (e.g., pricking wound), accidental spillage into the eyes, etc.].	a) c) and d) are applicable to all IVD reagents; b) is applicable to IVD reagents that may contain components of biological origin	GB/T 42062	Study data of manufacturing processes, risk management data, and product IFU .....

Continued

Clause No.	Requirements	Applicable	Standards used to prove conformity	Documents providing the objective evidence for conformity
A4	Sterilization and microbial contamination			
A4.1	Medical devices shall be designed to facilitate safe cleaning, disinfection, sterilization and/or re–sterilization (if necessary) by the user.	Applicable to IVD reagents with relevant require–ments, such as infectious diseases	GB/T 42062	Risk management data and product IFU .....
A4.2	Medical devices with microbial limits shall be designed, produced and packaged to ensure that they are transported and stored under the conditions specified by the applicant and meet the requirements for microbial limits after they leave the factory.	IVD reagents with relevant require–ments	GB/T 42062, and *Provisions for the Instructions for Use and Labels of Medical Devices*	Quality management system documents, study data of manufacturing processes, risk management data, and product IFU .....
A4.3	Medical devices provided in sterile shall be designed, manufactured and packaged in accordance with appropriate procedures to ensure that they are sterile upon delivery. Undamaged sterile package transported and stored under conditions specified by applicant should remain sterile until opened. The integrity of package shall be clearly identifiable by the end user (e.g., tamper–proof packaging).	Not applicable, because IVD reagents are usually non–sterile medical devices	.....	.....

Continued

Clause No.	Requirements	Applicable	Standards used to prove conformity	Documents providing the objective evidence for conformity
A4.4	Sterile medical devices shall be processed, manufactured, packaged and sterilized according to the verified methods, and their shelf life shall be determined by verified methods.	Not applicable, because IVD reagents are usually non-sterile medical devices	.....	.....
A4.5	Medical devices intended for sterile use (sterilization by applicant or user) shall be manufactured and packaged under appropriate and controlled conditions and facilities.	Not applicable, because IVD reagents are usually non-sterile medical devices	GB/T 42062	.....
A4.6	Medical devices provided in non–sterile condition and sterilized before use shall be: a) Packaging should minimize the risk of microbial contamination for the product and be applicable to the sterilization method specified by the applicant; b) The sterilization method specified by the applicant should be verified.	All IVD reagents applicable	GB/T 42062	Study data of process and reaction system, risk analysis data, and product IFU .....
A4.7	The delivery status shall be clearly marked if the medical device can be delivered in sterile and non–sterile condition.	Not applicable, typically not required to identify the delivery status	.....	.....

Continued

Clause No.	Requirements	Applicable	Standards used to prove conformity	Documents providing the objective evidence for conformity
A5	Environment and service conditions			
A5.1	If the medical device is expected to be used in combination with other medical devices or equipment, the integrated system, including the connection system, shall be ensured for overall safety and shall not affect the performance of the device. Restrictions on integrated use shall be clearly identified and/or specified in the IFU. For connections to be completed by the user, such as liquid, gas transmission, electrical or mechanical coupling, all possible risks, including faulty connections or safety hazards, shall be eliminated or minimized as far as possible in the design and manufacturing procedures.	All IVD reagents applicable	GB/T 42062, and *Provisions for the Instructions for Use and Labels of Medical Devices*	Risk management data and product IFU .....
A5.2	The intended use environment and conditions shall be considered in the design and production of medical devices to eliminate or reduce the following risks: a) Risk of injury to users or others related to physical and ergonomic/availability characteristics; b) Risk of incorrect operation due to user interface design, ergonomic/availability characteristics and the intended use environment;	Applicable to all IVD reagents, except for b)	GB/T 42062, and *Provisions for the Instructions for Use and Labels of Medical Devices*	Risk management data and product IFU .....

Continued

Clause No.	Requirements	Applicable	Standards used to prove conformity	Documents providing the objective evidence for conformity
A5.2	c) Risks related to reasonably foreseeable external factors or environmental conditions, such as magnetic field, external electrical and electromagnetic effect, electrostatic discharge, radiation caused by diagnosis and treatment, as well as changes in pressure, humidity, temperature and/or pressure and acceleration; d) Risks arising from contact with solid materials, liquids and other substances, including gases, under normal use conditions; e) Risks caused by the compatibility of software and information technology (IT) operating environment; f) Environmental risks caused by unexpected precipitates of medical devices during normal use; g) Risks caused by incorrect identification and wrong results of specimens/samples/data, such as confused color and/or digital code of sample containers, detachable parts and/or accessories used for analysis, test or detection; h) Risks caused by interference with other medical devices used for diagnosis, monitoring or treatment.	Applicable to all IVD reagents, except for b)	GB/T 42062, and *Provisions for the Instructions for Use and Labels of Medical Devices*	Risk management data and product IFU .....

Continued

Clause No.	Requirements	Applicable	Standards used to prove conformity	Documents providing the objective evidence for conformity
A5.3	Medical devices shall be designed and manufactured to eliminate or reduce the risk of combustion and explosion under normal condition and single fault condition, especially the intended use, including combined use exposure to flammable, explosive substances or other combustibles.	Not applicable, non–active products	.....	.....
A5.4	Medical devices shall be designed and manufactured to ensure that the adjustment, calibration and maintenance process can be completed in a safely and effectively way. a) For medical devices that cannot be maintained, such as implants, the risk of material aging shall be minimized; b) For medical devices that cannot be adjusted and calibrated, such as some types of thermometers, the risk of accuracy loss of measurement or control mechanism shall be minimized.	IVD reagents containing calibrators/ calibration procedures applicable	GB/T 42062	Traceability data of calibrators Study data of main raw materials and quality management system documents .....
A5.5	Medical devices that are intended to be operated together with other medical devices or products shall be designed and manufactured in such a way that the interoperability and compatibility are reliable and safe.	Applicable to IVD reagents used in combination with instruments	GB/T 42062	Study data, risk analysis data, and IFU of applicable models .....
A5.6	Medical devices shall be designed and manufactured to reduce the risk of unauthorized access, which may hinder the normal operation of the device or cause potential safety hazards.	Not applicable to IVD reagents	.....	.....

Continued

Clause No.	Requirements	Applicable	Standards used to prove conformity	Documents providing the objective evidence for conformity
A5.7	Any medical device with the function of measurement, monitoring or value display shall be designed and manufactured in line with ergonomic/usability principles, taking account of the intended environmental conditions, users and intended use of the medical devices.	Not applicable to IVD reagents	.....	.....
A5.8	Medical devices shall be designed and manufactured to facilitate the safe disposal or reuse of them by users, patients or other personnel; and facilitate the safe disposal or reuse of the relevant waste. The IFU shall specify the procedures and methods for safe disposal or recovery.	All IVD reagents	Provisions for the Instructions for Use and Labels of Medical Devices	IFU .....
A6	Medical device with diagnostic or measuring function			
A6.1	The medical devices with the function of diagnosis or measurement (including monitoring) shall be designed and manufactured based on appropriate scientific and technological methods. In addition to other performance, the corresponding accuracy, precision and stability shall also be guaranteed to achieve its intended purpose. a) Applicants should specify the limit of accuracy (if applicable).	All IVD reagents	Corresponding national standards, national reference materials or industry standards for IVD reagents	Product technical requirements and test report .....

Continued

Clause No.	Requirements	Applicable	Standards used to prove conformity	Documents providing the objective evidence for conformity
A6.1	b) Digital measurements shall be expressed (where possible) in standardized units understood and accepted by the user. The use of internationally accepted standard units of measurement is recommended and other recognized units of measurement may be used for safety, user familiarity and established clinical practice. c) The functions of the medical device indicator and controller shall be described in detail. If the device provides descriptions related to operation, operation instruction or adjustment parameters through the visualization system, such information shall be easily understood by the user and the patient (when applicable).	All IVD reagents	Corresponding national standards, national reference materials or industry standards for IVD reagents	Product technical requirements and test report .....
A7	IFU and labels			
A7.1	Medical devices shall be accompanied with the information needed to identify the device and its applicant. Each medical device shall also be accompanied with relevant safety and performance information or relevant instructions. Such information can appear in the device itself, on the package or in the IFU, or can be easily accessed by electronic means (such as website) and easily understood by the intended user.	All IVD reagents	Provisions for the Instructions for Use and Labels of Medical Devices	Product IFU and package label .....

Continued

Clause No.	Requirements	Applicable	Standards used to prove conformity	Documents providing the objective evidence for conformity
A8	Protection against risk on non–professional user operation			
A8.1	For medical devices used by non–professional users (such as self–test or near–patient test), in order to ensure the normal use of medical devices, the design and production of medical devices shall consider the operating skills of non–professional users, and the impact on the results due to the non–professional user's technology and different use environment. The information and instructions provided by the applicant shall be easy to understand and use, and explain the results.	Applicable to IVD reagents used by non–professional users, such as reagents for self–testing or reagents for near–patient testing	GB/T 42062, and *Provisions for the Instructions for Use and Labels of Medical Devices*	Product IFU, package label and risk analysis data .....
A8.2	Medical devices used by non–professional users (such as self–test or near–patient test) should be designed and manufactured in such a way as to: a) Ensure that the users can use it safely and accurately in accordance with the IFU. When the risks related to the instructions cannot be reduced to an appropriate level, such risks can be reduced through training; b) Minimize the non–professional users' risks caused by incorrect operation and interpretation of results.	Applicable to IVD reagents used by non–professional users, such as reagents for self–testing or reagents for near–patient testing	GB/T 42062, and *Provisions for the Instructions for Use and Labels of Medical Devices*	Product IFU, package label and risk analysis data .....

Continued

Clause No.	Requirements	Applicable	Standards used to prove conformity	Documents providing the objective evidence for conformity
A8.3	The medical devices used by non–professional users can facilitate users through the following measures: a) Verify whether the device operates normally during operation; b) Give alarm when the device fails to operate normally or provides invalid results.	Applicable to IVD reagents used by non–professional users, such as reagents for self–testing or reagents for near–patient testing	GB/T 42062, and *Provisions for the Instructions for Use and Labels of Medical Devices*	Product IFU, package label and risk analysis data .....
A9	Medical devices containing biological materials			
A9.1	For medical devices containing animal or plant tissues, cells or other substances, bacterial–derived substances or derivatives, if inactive or delivered in inactive state, the following requirements shall be satisfied: a) Tissues, cells and their derivatives shall be derived from animal species that are controlled and suitable for their intended use. Information on geographical origin of animals shall be retained in accordance with the requirements of relevant laws and regulations. b) The tissues, cells, substances or derivatives of animal origin shall be collected, processed, stored, tested and treated to ensure the safety of patients, users and other person (if applicable). In particular, viruses and other infectious pathogens shall be eliminated or inactivated by proven advanced technology, provided that the performance of medical devices shall not be affected.	Applicable to IVD reagents containing materials of biological origin	*Provisions for the Instructions for Use and Labels of Medical Devices*, and other applicable standards or guidelines	Summary data, quality system documents, and product IFU .....

Continued

Clause No.	Requirements	Applicable	Standards used to prove conformity	Documents providing the objective evidence for conformity
A9.2	When the medical devices are produced from tissues, cells, substances or derivatives of human origin, the regulatory authority shall take the following measures: a) Donation, acquisition and test of tissues and cells shall be performed in accordance with the requirements of relevant laws and regulations; b) To ensure the safety of patients, users or other people, tissues, cells or their derivatives shall be processed, preserved or otherwise handled. Viruses and other sources of infection shall be eliminated or inactivated through source control or through verified advanced technology during production.	Applicable to IVD reagents containing materials of biological origin	*Guidelines for On-site Inspection of the Implementation of Good Manufacturing Practice for Medical Devices for In Vitro Diagnostic Reagents*, and *Regulations for the Biosafety Management of Pathogenic Microorganism Laboratories*	Quality system documents, and manufacturing processes .....
A9.3	When the medical devices are produced from biological substances other than those specified in A13.1 and A13.2 (such as plant or bacterial materials), its processing, storage, testing and treatment process shall be implemented to ensure the safety of patients, users or other people (such as waste disposal personnel, etc.). In order to ensure safety, viruses and other sources of infection shall be eliminated or inactivated through source control or through proven advanced technology during production.	Applicable to IVD reagents containing materials of biological origin	*Guidelines for On-site Inspection of the Implementation of Good Manufacturing Practice for Medical Devices for In Vitro Diagnostic Reagents*, and *Regulations for the Biosafety Management of Pathogenic Microorganism Laboratories*	Quality system documents, and manufacturing processes .....

Continued

Clause No.	Requirements	Applicable	Standards used to prove conformity	Documents providing the objective evidence for conformity
B	Essential principles applicable to IVD medical devices			
B1	Chemical, physical and biological properties			
B1.1	With regards to chemical, physical, and biological properties for IVD medical devices, considering the intended use of the product, attention should be paid to the possibility of impairment of analytical performance due to physical and/or chemical incompatibility between the materials used and the specimens, analyte or marker to be detected and measured (such as biological tissues, cells, body fluids and micro–organisms).	All IVD reagents	GB/T 42062, and *Provisions for the Instructions for Use and Labels of Medical Devices*	Product IFU, applicable sample type study and risk analysis data .....
B2	Performance characteristics			
B2.1	IVD medical devices shall achieve the analytical and clinical performance indicators, as stated by the applicant that are applicable to the intended use, considering the target population, the intended user, and the use environment. Reasonable, verified and accepted technical methods shall be used to determine the above indicators. a) Analytical performance includes, but is not limited to, a. Traceability and value assignment of calibrators and quality controls b. Accuracy (correctness and precision)	All IVD reagents	*Announcement on Issuing the Requirements for Registration Application Dossiers of In Vitro Diagnostic Reagents and Formats of Approval Documents*, guidelines for technical review of relevant reagents, etc.	Analytical performance assessment, and clinical evaluation .....

Continued

Clause No.	Requirements	Applicable	Standards used to prove conformity	Documents providing the objective evidence for conformity
B2.1	c. Analytical sensitivity/ minimum limit of detection d. Analysis specificity e. Measurement interval f. Sample stability b) Clinical performance, such as clinical diagnostic sensitivity, clinical diagnostic specificity, positive predictive value, negative predictive value, likelihood ratio, and positive cut–off value or reference interval for normal and abnormal population. c) Verification control procedure, which ensures that users use the IVD medical devices according to the intended use and that the results are therefore suitable for the intended use.	All IVD reagents	*Announcement on Issuing the Requirements for Registration Application Dossiers of In Vitro Diagnostic Reagents and Formats of Approval Documents*, guidelines for technical review of relevant reagents, etc.	Analytical performance assessment, and clinical evaluation .....
B2.2	Where the performance of an IVD medical device depends on the calibrators or quality controls used, the available reference measurement procedures or the higher–level reference materials that can be provided should be used to ensure that the value assignment of these calibration solution or quality controls are traceable. (Where the performance of an IVD medical device depends on the use of the calibrators or quality controls, reference measurement procedures or higher level reference substances should be used to trace the value assignment of the calibrators or quality controls.)	IVD reagents containing calibrators or quality controls	GB/T 21415	Traceability study of calibrators and value assignment study of quality controls .....

Continued

Clause No.	Requirements	Applicable	Standards used to prove conformity	Documents providing the objective evidence for conformity
B2.3	Where possible, numerical representations of values should be in standardized units generally accepted and understandable to the users of IVD medical devices. (The numerical identification shall be in standardized units as far as possible and easy for users to understand.)	Traceable IVD reagents	GB/T 21415	IFU .....
B2.4	The performance characteristics of an IVD medical device should be evaluated against its intended use, including the following: a) Intended users, such as non–professionals, laboratory professionals; b) Intended operating environment, such as: patient residence, emergency room, ambulance, medical center, laboratory; c) Relevant populations, such as children, adults, pregnant women, individuals with specific disease signs and symptoms, patients receiving differential diagnosis, etc. Where appropriate, the population evaluated should be representative of the population, gender, and population of genetic diversity, as appropriate, to represent the population in which the product is intended to be marketed. For infectious diseases, it is recommended that the selected population have similar prevalence rates.	All IVD reagents	GB/T 42062, and relevant technical review guidelines	Risk management, non–clinical studies, clinical evaluation, and quality management system documents .....

Continued

Clause No.	Requirements	Applicable	Standards used to prove conformity	Documents providing the objective evidence for conformity
Description	1. If Column 3 is applicable, please indicate "Yes". If not applicable, indicate "No" and state relevant reasons regarding the product characteristics. 2. The methods for proving that this medical device complies with the essential principles for safety and performance shall be filled into the fourth column, and the following methods may be generally adopted to prove that this medical device complies with the essential requirements: (1) Compliance with published regulations and normative documents of medical devices. (2) Compliance with relevant national standards, industry standards, and international standards for medical devices. (3) Compliance with the test methods commonly accepted in the industry. (4) Compliance with the methods stipulated by the manufacturer. (5) Comparison with similar products approved to be marketed. (6) Clinical evaluation. 3. If the evidence provided for conformity is included in the product registration dossiers, its specific position in the application dossiers shall be stated. For the evidence provided for conformity is not included in the product registration application dossiers, their file names and numbers in the quality management system should be noted for inspection.			

Note: Relevant laws, regulations, standards, and guidelines mentioned in the table shall be subject to the currently valid versions published by relevant institutions.

2. Template for Summary Data

Summary Data

(The main text of the template takes medical device products as an example)

2.1 Chapter Table of Contents

All headings and subheadings of this chapter should be included, with the page number of each item in the table of contents.

2.2 Overview

According to the *Classification Catalogue for Medical Devices*

(Announcement No.104 of the former China Food and Drug Administration in 2017) and the *Rules for the Nomenclature of Generic Names of Medical Devices* (SYJXG〔2016〕No.35), the product name is ××××××, the classification sub-catalogue name is ××××××, the primary product category is XX, the management category of the secondary product category is ××, and the classification code is ××-××-××.

Scope of application of the proposed product: ××××××.

Where applicable, describe the overview of background information or specific details of the proposed product, such as, history overview of the proposed product, information of previous submissions, and its relationship with other products approved to be marketed.

2.3 Product Description

(1) Description of the device and its principle of operation

1) Passive medical devices

Describe the principle of operation, mechanism of action (if applicable), structure and composition, raw materials (Describe the components of materials in direct or indirect contact with users and/or patients; describe the source and raw material, the reason for its intended use, and the main mode of action of the substances if a device contains biomaterials or derivatives; describe the substance name, reason for intended use, main mode of action, and source if a device contains an active pharmaceutical ingredient (API) or drug), delivery status and method of sterilization (if applicable, describe the sterilizer, method of sterilization, and validity period of sterilization), structural schematic diagram and/or product drawings, methods of use and graphical representation (if applicable), and features that distinguish the product from other similar products.

2) Active medical devices

Describe the principle of operation, mechanism of action (if applicable), structure and composition, main functions and the functions of their components (e.g., key components and software), product drawings (including details of identification, interface, control panel, applied part, etc.), and features that distinguish the product from other similar products. If the product comprises more than one component, the connection or assembly relationship among them shall be described.

(2) Model/specification

Provide a specific description of the model/specification of proposed product. Provide further description via product marking example (note: maintain consistent with the model/specification in application form).

For the products with multiple models and specifications, the differences of each model and specification should be made clear. The structure and composition (or configuration), functions, features, operating modes and technical parameters of each model and specification should be described using comparison table or pictures/diagrams with supporting text.

(3) Packaging description

1) Describe the packaging information of all product components. For sterile medical devices, information on the sterile barrier system should be described; for medical devices with requirements for microbial limit, information on the package to maintain the microbial limit should be described. Describe how to ensure that the final user can clearly identify the package integrity.

2) If a user needs to package the medical device or accessories prior to sterilization, the user should provide the correct packaging information (e.g., material, composition and size).

(4) R&D history

The R&D background and purpose of the proposed product shall be elaborated. If there is any similar product or predecessor product for reference, the information of the similar product or the predecessor product shall be provided, and the reasons for selecting them as reference for R&D shall be stated.

(5) Reference and comparison with similar and/or predecessor products

Differences and similarities between the proposed product and similar products and/or predecessor products with respect to operating principle, structure and composition, manufacturing material, performance indicator, mode of action (e.g., implantation, intervention), scope of application and others shall be compared in a tabular form.

2.4 Scope of Application and Contraindications

The scope of application here shall be consistent with the description of scope of application in application form. Applicant shall list the contraindications, intended use environment, target population, etc. of the proposed product.

(1) Scope of application

1) The treatment or diagnosis function that can be provided by the proposed product should be clarified, describing the medical procedures (e.g., in vivo or in vitro diagnosis, monitoring of rehabilitation treatment, contraception, sterilization, etc.), and specifying the disease or the patient's condition that can be diagnosed, treated, prevented, alleviated or cured by the proposed product as well as the parameters to be monitored and other considerations related to the scope of application.

2) Intended use of the proposed product, and the medical stage in which

it is applicable (e.g., post–treatment monitoring, rehabilitation, etc.) shall be described.

3) Identify the target users and the skills/knowledge/training required for their operation or use of the product.

4) Indicate whether the product is disposable or reusable.

5) Other products used in combination with the product to achieve the intended use shall be stated.

(2) Expected use environment

1) The locations where the product is intended to be used should be specified, such as medical institutions, laboratories, ambulances, homes, etc..

2) Environmental conditions that may affect its safety and effectiveness, such as temperature, humidity, pressure, movement, vibration, altitude, etc..

(3) Target population

Information of target patient populations (e.g., adults, newborns, infants or children) or the statement of unanticipated treatment specific population, information of patient selection standards as well as parameters needed to be monitored and factors to be considered during use.

If the target patient populations of the proposed product include newborns, infants or children, the non–adult specific population intended to use the proposed product in treatment, diagnosis, prevention, relief or curing of diseases and conditions shall be described.

(4) Contraindications

Where applicable, if the product is not recommended for certain diseases, conditions or specific populations (e.g., children, the elderly, pregnant and lactating women, people with liver and kidney dysfunction) after a risk/benefit assessment, a clear statement should be made.

2.5 Marketing History of the Proposed Product

If applicable, the following information shall be submitted for the proposed products:

(1) Marketing information

The marketing approval date and sales of the proposed product in each country or region before the submission of the registration application have been submitted. If there are differences (e.g., design, label, technical parameters) in the proposed product when it is marketed in different countries or regions, such differences shall be described one by one.

(2) Adverse events and recalls

If applicable, the post-marketing adverse events and the recall time of the proposed products as well as approaches and solutions adopted by the applicant in each case, including the measures taken to actively control the product risks, the report made to the medical device adverse event monitoring technical institutions, and the investigation and handling of relevant departments have been described in a tabular form.

At the same time, the above-mentioned adverse events and recalls shall be analyzed and evaluated, the causes of adverse events and recalls shall be clarified, and their impact on safety and effectiveness shall be explained. If the adverse events and recalls are in great amount, the number involved for each type shall be summarized according to the event type.

(3) Sales, adverse events, and recall ratio

Where applicable, a summary of the sales quantity of the proposed product in each country (region) in the last five years should be submitted, the ratio of adverse events and recalls in each country (region) should be provided in the following manner, and ratio calculation and key analysis should be carried out.

For example, Incidence of Adverse Events = Number of Adverse Events ÷ Sales Quantity × 100%; Recall Incidence = Recall Quantity ÷ Sales Quantity × 100%. The incidence can be calculated per patient year or per use, and the applicant shall describe the calculation method of incidence.

2.6 Other Contents that Need to be Explained

Other contents need to be explained.

The details of other products used in combination with the proposed product to achieve the intended use shall be specified, if applicable.

For approved components or accessories used in combination, the registration certificate number and the registration certificate information published on the official website of the NMPA should be provided.

3. Template for Non-clinical Data

Non-clinical data

(The main text of the template takes medical device products as an example)

3.1 Chapter Table of Contents

All headings and subheadings of this chapter should be included, with the page number of each item in the table of contents.

3.2 Risk Management Data of Product

The risk management data of a product is defined as data formed by recording the risk management process of product as well as the review results. The following contents should be provided with the statement that the traceability for each of following processes for which the hazards have been determined.

(1) Risk analysis: including identification of scope of application of medical device and safety–related characteristics, identification of hazards, and estimation of risk of each hazardous situation.

(2) Risk evaluation: evaluate and determine whether the risk needs to be reduced for each identified hazardous situation, and, if so, describe the corresponding risk controls.

(3) Risk control: describe the contents related to risk control implemented to reduce risks.

(4) The acceptability evaluation of any one or several residual risks.

(5) Comparing with the product benefits, the product risks are acceptable in comprehensive evaluation.

Product risk management data shall comply with GB/T 42062 *Medical devices - Application of risk management to medical devices*. The applicant shall identify and determine hazards related to the product, estimate and evaluate relevant risks, control the risks, and monitor the safety and effectiveness of risk control.

3.3 List of General Principles for the Safety and Performance of Medical Devices

The applicant shall provide the *List of Essential Principles for the Safety and Performance of Medical Devices*, explain the methods used to comply with the applicable requirements, and document the proof of compliance. Reasons shall be given if any of the requirements in the *List of Essential Principles for the Safety and Performance of Medical Devices* is not applicable.

For documents included in the product registration application dossiers, the specific position in the application dossiers should be stated; for documents not included in the product registration application dossiers, the name of evidence file and the document number in the quality management system documents should be stated for future reference.

3.4 Product Technical Requirements and Test Report

(1) Applicability of the proposed product to the standards

The proposed product shall comply with applicable compulsory standards. If the structural features, intended use, use methods, etc. of the proposed product is not within the scope of the compulsory standards, the applicant shall explain that the compulsory standards are not applicable and provide verified certification data.

The above standards shall be in the current effective versions of applicable national standards and industry standards. It is suggested that the applicant take the initiative to track the update of relevant standards.

(2) Product technical requirements

Product technical requirements of medical device shall comply with the requirements of *Guidelines for the Preparation of Product Technical Requirements of Medical Devices* and other normative documents.

(3) Product test report

Test report can be submitted in any of the following forms:

1) Self–test report issued by the applicant.

2) The test report issued by a qualified medical device test institution entrusted.

The test report shall include the product model, specification or configuration, and the sample description shall be consistent with the name and model of the parts described in the product technical requirements.

If applicable, the test report shall provide real photos of the software version interface or list software version information. The software with a user interface shall reflect the software release version and the full software version, and the software without a user interface shall reflect the full software version.

3.5 Study Data

Based on the scope of application and technical characteristics of the proposed product, the applicant shall provide a non-clinical study overview to describe the studies conducted item by item and outline the study methods and conclusions. Corresponding study data shall be provided according to the non-clinical study overview. Each study can be carried out through literature study, laboratory study, model study, etc., which shall generally include study protocol and study report. Where modeling study is used, product modeling study data should be provided.

(1) Study on chemical and physical properties

The applicant shall provide the product performance study data and preparation description on the product technical requirements, list the clauses on product performance indicators, and explain the source of clauses and the formulation basis item by item. For active medical devices, the applicable standards or methods shall be explained, and the reasons for citation or adoption shall be explained. Necessary explanation on the inapplicable clauses in the applicable standards shall be given. The applicant can provide the corresponding test and verification data taking account of the product application mode, operation mode and product configuration described in the summary data. As for the proposed product, it is necessary to focus on technical defects, product failures, mis–operation and other related adverse events.

Study data on chemical and physical properties shall include the following information.

1) The basis for the determination of the chemical/material characterization, physical and/or mechanical properties of the product, the source of design input and its clinical significance, the standards or methods used, the reasons for adoption, and the theoretical basis shall be provided.

2) Ignition and explosion risk

For medical devices exposed to flammable and explosive substances or used in combination with other flammables and inflammable substances, study data on the risk of ignition and explosion should be provided to prove that the risk of ignition and explosion is acceptable under normal condition and single fault condition.

3) Combined use

If the proposed product is intended to be used in combination with other medical devices, drugs, and non–medical device products, study data demonstrating the safety and effectiveness of the combined use shall be provided, including basic information of interconnection (type of connection, interface, protocol, and minimum performance), risks in the combined use and the control measures thereof, restrictions on the combined use, compatibility studies, etc.

If the product is used in combination with drugs, the study data of drug compatibility shall be provided to prove that the performance of the drug and device meets its indications and intended use.

4) Dose−effect relationship and energy safety

For medical devices that provide patients with energy or substance treatment, data on the dose−effect relationship and energy safety studies should be provided, and the study data on the safety, effectiveness. rationality of the setting of therapeutic parameters, and the energy that causes no unacceptable harm to normal tissues other than the intended target tissues should be provided.

(2) Study on electrical system safety

The study data on electrical safety, mechanical and environmental protection, and electromagnetic compatibility shall be provided. In addition, the applicable standards and the studies conducted shall also be described.

The standards to be met shall be listed, for example: GB 9706.1, YY 9706.102, etc..

(3) Study on radiation safety

Study data on radiation safety shall be provided for the products with radiation or potential radiation hazards (such as ionizing radiation and non−ionizing radiation), including:

1) Describe the general and special standards for radiation safety, and elaborate on the reasons for inapplicable clauses in the standards;

2) Describe the types of radiation, provide radiation safety verification data, and ensure that radiation energy, radiation distribution and other key characteristics of radiation can be reasonably controlled, adjusted, estimated, and monitored during use (if applicable);

3) Provide protective measures to reduce the absorbed radiation dose of users, patients and others and ways to avoid misuse during transportation, storage, installation and use. For products requiring installation, the information about the acceptance and performance test, acceptance criteria and

maintenance procedures shall be clarified.

(4) Software study

1) Software

For products and SaMD containing SiMD, study data on the software shall be provided, including basic information, software development process, core functions, conclusions, etc., and the degree of detail depends on the safety classification (severe, moderate, and mild) of the software. Among them, basic information includes software identification, safety level, structure and function, physical topology, running environment, and registration history, and software development process includes the development overview, risk management, requirements specification, life cycle, verification and validation, traceability analysis, defect management, and update history. The corresponding relationship among core functions, core algorithms and intended use shall be made clear.

Applicants can clearly define the software safety classification of the proposed product and provide corresponding software study data in accordance with the *Guidelines for Registration Review of Medical Device Software*. The software study report shall cover all SiMD and is suggested to be associated with the product functions described in the summary data.

The applicant should refer to the IFU to list the relevant information about the core functions of the software. If necessary, special study data can be provided to explain a certain core algorithm in detail.

2) Cybersecurity

For SaMD and SiMD provided with electronic data interchange, remote control or user access, their study data on cybersecurity should be provided, including basic information, software development process, vulnerability assessment, conclusion and other contents, and the degree of detail depends on the safety classification of the software. Among them, basic information includes software information, data architecture, cybersecurity capabilities, cybersecurity patches, security software, the software development processes include the risk management, requirements specifications, verification and validation, traceability analysis, and update maintenance plans, and the vulnerability assessment should clarify the relevant information of the known vulnerability.

The applicants can provide cybersecurity study data according to the Guidelines for Registration Review of Medical Device Cybersecurity.

3) Off-the-shelf software

If a product uses off-the-shelf software, the study data on corresponding software and cybersecurity should be provided according to the type and usage mode of the off-the-shelf software.

4) Artificial intelligence

If a product adopts artificial intelligence technologies such as deep learning to achieve the intended functions and uses, the study data on the algorithm should be provided, including basic algorithm information, data collection, algorithm training, algorithm performance evaluation, and other contents.

Applicants can refer to the *Guidelines for Registration Review of Artificial Intelligence Medical Devices* to provide artificial intelligence study data.

5) Interoperability

If a product exchanges information with other medical devices and non-medical devices and uses such information through electronic interfaces, the study data on interoperability should be provided, including basic information, requirements specification, risk management, verification and validation, maintenance plan, etc..

6) Others

If a product adopts mobile computing, cloud computing, virtual reality and other information and communication technologies to achieve the intended functions and uses, the corresponding technical study data should be provided, including basic information, requirements specifications, risk management, verification and validation, maintenance plans, etc..

(5) Study on biological characteristics

Devices in direct or indirect contact with the patient should be subject to biological evaluation. The data on biological evaluation should include:

1) Whether the materials used in the product and the nature of the contact with the human body, pollutants and residues that may be introduced during the process of design and production, precipitates (including leachable and/or evaporant) that may be produced during the process of design and production, degradation products, processing residues, and packaging materials in direct or indirect contact with medical devices and related information have been described.

2) Describe the physical and/or chemical information of the proposed product with the consideration of the material characterization (if applicable). The physical effects of the device that may pose a biological risk should be evaluated.

3) Strategies, basis, and methods for biological evaluation.

4) Evaluation of existing data and results.

5) Reasons and demonstration for selection or exemption from biological test.

6) Other data required to complete the biological evaluation.

If the materials of a medical device may release particles into the body of the patient and user, and thus create risks related to particle size and properties, such as nanomaterials, the study data on relevant biological risks shall be provided for all medical devices that contain, produce, or are composed of them.

If the materials will be absorbed and metabolized by the human body according to the intended use of the proposed product, such as absorbable products, the study data on the compatibility of the materials/substances used with human tissues, cells and body fluids should be provided.

For active medical devices, biological evaluation research can be conducted according to the method of GB/T 16886.1 *Biological Evaluation of Medical Devices - Part 1: Evaluation and Testing within a Risk Management Process*.

(6) Safety study of biological materials

For the products with biosafety risks which contain allogenic materials, materials utilizing animal tissues and their derivatives or bioactive substances, the relevant biosafety study data should be provided.

Biosafety study data should include:

1) The information of corresponding materials or substances, and the acquisition, processing, preservation, testing and handling of tissues, cells and materials.

2) Describe the source, explain the technological process used to inactivate and remove the virus and/or infectious agents during the manufacturing process and provide the effectiveness verification data or related data.

3) The methods and/or technological process to reduce material with immunogenicity and quality control indicators and confirmatory test data or related data.

4) Other data supporting the safety of biological materials.

(7) Cleaning, disinfection and sterilization study

1) Sterilization by manufacturers: The sterilization process (methods and parameters) and sterility assurance level (SAL) shall be defined, and the relevant study data on the verification and validation of sterilization shall be provided.

2) Sterilization by users: The recommended sterilization process (methods and parameters), the basis for the determination of the recommended sterilization process and the relevant study data for verification should be clarified. For products that can withstand two or more sterilizations, study data on the tolerance of the recommended sterilization process for the product shall be provided.

3) Cleaning and disinfection by users: the recommended cleaning and disinfection process (methods and parameters), the basis for determination of the process and the relevant study data on verification shall be clearly defined. The applicant shall specify the recommended disinfection cycle, disinfection method, disinfectant model and supplier taking account of the summary data. Where applicable, it is recommended to explain the disinfection effect of different disinfectants and provide relevant study data.

4) Residual toxicity: If the product may produce residual substances after sterilization or disinfection, the study on residual toxicity of the sterilized or disinfected product shall be conducted, the residual information and treatment methods adopted shall be defined, and the relevant study data shall be provided.

5) For medical devices that are delivered in a non–sterile state and need to be sterilized before use, the study data that proves that the packaging can reduce the risk of microbial contamination to the product and is applicable to

the sterilization method prescribed by the manufacturer shall be provided.

(8) Animal test study

In order to avoid unnecessary animal tests, a scientific decision should be made on whether to carry out animal tests for medical devices, and demonstrative/explanatory data should be provided. Where an animal test needs to be conducted to verify/validate the effectiveness of product risk control measures through decision, the study data of the animal test should be provided, including the test objective, information of the animals for the test, information of the investigational device and the control, the number of animals, evaluation indicators and the test results, basis for the determination of design elements of the animal test, etc..

(9) Other study data proving the safety and effectiveness of the product.

3.6 Non-clinical Bibliography

The list of published non-clinical study (such as cadaver study, biomechanical study, etc.) literatures/bibliographies related to the proposed product shall be provided, including the copies of relevant contents (translations shall also be provided for them in foreign languages). If no non-clinical literature/bibliography related to the proposed product is retrieved, whether relevant statements have been provided.

3.7 Stability Study

(1) Shelf life

Where applicable, the study data on shelf life and package should be provided to demonstrate that the product can maintain performance and function to meet the requirements of use under the transportation and storage conditions specified by the manufacturer during shelf life. Products with microbiological limits shall also comply with microbiological requirements, and products delivered in a sterile state shall keep sterile.

(2) Stability in use

Where applicable, study data on stability/reliability in use shall be provided to prove that the performance and function of the product can meet the requirements in the use under normal use, maintenance and calibration (if applicable) and within the service life/number of uses specified by the manufacturer.

The applicant may provide the study data of product's service life shall be provided in accordance with the requirements of the *Guidelines for Technical Review of Service Life Registration of Active Medical Devices*. The applicant shall consider the analysis on the product under both normal and adverse conditions.

(3) Transport stability

The study data on transport stability and packaging should be provided to demonstrate that environmental conditions during transportation (e.g., shaking, vibration, and fluctuation in temperature and humidity) cause no adverse effect on the features and performance of the medical device, including its integrity and cleanliness, under the transportation conditions specified by the manufacturer.

Applicants can refer to relevant standards such as GB/T 14710 for study.

3.8 Other Data

For Class II and Class III medical devices exempted from clinical evaluation, the applicant shall prove the safety and effectiveness of the product from the perspectives of basic principle, structure and composition, performance, safety, scope of application, etc. in accordance with the

Technical Guidelines for Comparative Instructions of Products Listed in the Catalogue of Medical Devices Exempted from Clinical Evaluation.

For single–use medical devices, supporting data proving that they cannot be reused should also be provided.

The applicant may further provide other study data based on the product characteristics. For example, special study data can be provided for the key technologies and important functions of the product described in the overview data to specify the principle of operation, implementation method, application scenario, intended use, clinical value and standard workflow, as well as validation criteria, test specifications and test equipment.

4. Template for Product Technical Requirements

The contents of the product technical requirements generally include product name, models & specifications and division description (if necessary), performance indicators, test methods, terminologies (if applicable) and appendices (if applicable).

Applicants shall refer to the *Guidelines for the Preparation of Product Technical Requirements of Medical Devices* to compile product technical requirements of medical devices.

4.1 Number of Product Technical Requirements for Medical Devices

Number of Medical Device Product technical requirements is the registration number (or filing number) of the corresponding product. For products to be registered (filed), the number of the product technical requirements shall be left blank.

4.2 Product Name

The product name described in the product technical requirements shall be in Chinese and consistent with that applied for registration or filing.

4.3 Models, Specifications and Division Description

Product models and specifications shall be clarified in the product technical requirements. If the product has multiple models and specifications in the same registration unit, the description on the division of different models and specifications shall be clarified (diagrams and/or tables recommended). The contents with more description text shall be listed in an appendix.

If the product contains software, the naming rules for the release version and complete version of the software shall be clarified, example shown below.

× software information

Software model/specification: (specify the model/specification of the software, and there is no need to reflect the software release version)

Release version of the software: [Clarify the software release version, and if the software module (including medical middleware) is under separate version control, the release version must also be provided]

Software Version Nomenclature: X.Y.Z.B

Specify the number of digits, ranges, and meanings of all fields in the integral version of the software. If the version control is separately conducted for the software module (including medical middleware), its version nomenclature shall also be provided, and clarify the relationship with software version nomenclature. The version nomenclature for software and software modules shall be consistent with the quality management system.

4.4 Performance Indicator

(1) The performance indicators in the product technical requirements refer to the functional and safety indicators of the finished products that can be objectively determined. The items without substantial impact on the safety and effectiveness of the product shall not be listed as performance indicators in the product technical requirements. For example, patency is the main concern of some drainage catheters. The catheter needs to be able to effectively and firmly connect a suction device with the user end, whereas such information as the diameter, length, etc. of the catheter shall not be listed as performance indicators but only reflected in the appendix of the product technical requirements as descriptive information when necessary. Other information such as product engineering drawings, etc., shall not be listed in the product technical requirements. However, the dimension information of some products may have a significant impact on their safety and effectiveness, which shall be specified as performance indicators in the product technical requirements, such as the length and outer diameter of vascular stents, the dimensional tolerance of orthopedic implants, etc..

(2) The performance indicators in the product technical requirements shall be formulated according to relevant national/industry standards in combination with the design features and intended uses of specific products, which shall also conform to the mandatory national/industry standards applicable to them. If the structural features, intended uses, use methods, etc. of the products are inconsistent with the scope of application specified in the mandatory standards, registrants/filing applicants shall explain that the mandatory standards are not applicable and provide relevant data.

(3) Specific requirements of the performance indicators shall be clarified

in the product technical requirements, which shall not be described like that "see the accompanying document", "subject to the supply contract", etc..

Test item	Standards requirements	Test methods
Appearance	1. The external surface of the equipment shall be clean and free from cracks	Visual inspection
	2. ...	...
	3. ...	...
Dimensions	1. The dimensions of product accessories shall comply with the requirements of Table 6.	Inspect with a universal measuring tool
	2. ...	...
Product performance	1. Measuring range...	Type testing
	2. Measuring accuracy...	Type testing
	3. Mechanical properties...	Type testing
	4. Software function...	Type testing
	...	
Electrical safety	It shall comply with the requirements of GB 9706.1–2020, etc.	Type testing
	...	
Electromagnetic compatibility	It shall comply with the requirements of YY 9706.102–2021, etc.	Type testing
	...	

4.5 Performance Indicators Requirements

In accordance with such documents as the *Measures for the Administration of Registration and Filing of Medical Devices*, the *Measures for the Administration of Registration and Filing of In Vitro Diagnostic Reagents*, etc., the performance indicators described in the product technical requirements shall be functional and safety indicators of finished products that can be objectively identified.

The indicators that can be objectively identified generally refer to those capable of being quantified or objectively described. For example, the indicator can be directly tested by a certain test method of which the characteristic value can be verified, and the data results can be directly obtained. For example, the important function of a hemodialyzer is to remove target substances, the effect of which can be directly verified through the measurement of the residual amount of the removed target substances. Therefore, it shall be specified in the product technical requirements to characterize the main function of the hemodialyzer. An intravascular catheter is required to have zero leakage during use, which shall be specified in the product technical requirements. Moreover, objective and scientific test methods shall also be provided to ensure that the intravascular catheter is free from leakage under specified circumstances. The important functional indicators of an infusion pump include its infusion flow rate and corresponding accuracy, which shall be specified in the product technical requirements. At the same time, verification shall be carried out according to the specified methods to ensure the effective clinical application of the infusion pump. The imaging resolution of imaging ultrasonic diagnostic equipment is the important technical indicator related to image quality, which shall be specified in the product technical requirements. Moreover, objective and scientific test methods shall also be provided to ensure that the product performance indeed meets the claimed functional requirements.

It is not recommended to specify the following contents in the performance indicators of the product technical requirements:

(1) Research and evaluation content

Research content is generally refer to the combination of tests and analysis carried out to study the product characteristics, specifically the verification activities carried out to determine a specific product attribute at the product design and development stage. For example, the shelf life of a medical device refers to the period during which the end product of the medical device can normally play its intended functions. The shelf life of the product shall be studied at the product design and development stage. Such aging test conditions as temperature, humidity, etc. shall be set to carry out aging tests and study the shelf life of passive medical devices. Then the shelf life shall be calculated and determined according to the set aging conditions and such data as the product performance, packaging performance, etc. after aging. The use states of an active medical device can be enumerated to fully analyze its clinical use and directly perform the aging test study. Besides, the product (system) can also be decomposed into different subsystems/components for evaluation, during which the decomposition relationship shall be analyzed in detail. On this basis, the shelf life of the product shall be determined by different decomposition methods (for example, the product is decomposed into critical components and non-critical components, etc.). In addition, other research contents also include sterilization verification study, fatigue study, in vitro degradation study, human factor verification study, reliability verification study, magnetic resonance compatibility study, etc..

Evaluation contents generally refer to the evaluation of the suitability, adequacy and/or effectiveness of the product on the basis of its specified objectives. The above can be comprehensively evaluated according to multiple test combinations or evaluated by other methods (such as on the basis of historical data, information of products that have been marketed, etc.). For example, the biocompatibility study (including material mediated pyrogens) is generally deemed as an evaluation item, which can be comprehensively evaluated according to the combination of multiple biological tests or evaluated by the comparison method on the basis of historical data, information of products that have been marketed, etc. In addition, it can also be determined according to chemical analysis and toxicological data. For another example, environmental requirements for medical electrical equipment are used to evaluate the adaptability of the products in various working environments and simulated storage and transportation environments, which are generally deemed as stability evaluation items. Different climatic and mechanical environmental conditions shall be established for tests, or critical components shall be tested to evaluate the condition of the whole equipment. In addition, it can also be assessed through the comparison with similar products that have been marketed.

Other evaluation items also include the virus inactivation effect, immunogenicity, etc..

(2) Content related to non-finished products

The product technical requirements stipulate the relevant performance of finished products, and the performance indicators and characteristics of raw materials, semi-finished products are generally not recommended to be reflected in the product technical requirements. For example, the mechanical properties and chemical properties of certain raw materials.

4.6 Test Methods

Test methods are used to validate whether the product conforms to the specified requirements, which shall be formulated according to the corresponding performance indicators. Priority shall be given to the applicable test methods with established criteria. When necessary, methodological verification shall be carried out to ensure their reproducibility and operability.

Generally, the test steps and results (such as calculation methods, etc.) of the test methods shall be described. When necessary, all conditions and steps to ensure the reproducibility of the test results can also be added, such as the test principle, sample preparation and preservation, test instruments, etc..

For in vitro diagnostic reagent products, the test method should also specify the reference materials/standard materials used, sample preparation method, number of tests, and calculation method.

4.7 Appendix

The requirements for main raw materials and production processes of Class III in vitro diagnostic reagents shall be clarified in an appendix of the product technical requirements.

When necessary, some descriptive characteristics of medical devices shall be indicated in an appendix in detail, such as the sterilized or non-sterilized state of supply, shelf life, main raw materials, manufacturing process, main safety characteristics, key technical specifications, information of key components, magnetic resonance compatibility, etc..

4.8 Format Requirements

See the attachment for the format of product technical requirements for medical devices.

Attachment

Format of Product Technical Requirements for Medical Devices

Number of product technical requirements for medical devices: (Song typeface, 12pt, bold)

Product name (Song typeface, 18pt, bold)

1. Product model/specification and division description (Song typeface, 12pt, bold) (if applicable)

1.1 ··· (Song typeface, 12pt)

1.1.1 ...

...

2. Performance indicators (Song typeface, 12pt, bold)

2.1 ··· (Song typeface, 12pt)

2.1.1 ...

...

3. Test method (Song typeface, 12pt, bold)

3.1 ··· (Song typeface, 12pt)

3.1.1 ...

...

4. Terminology (Song typeface, 12pt, bold) (if applicable)

4.1 ··· (Song typeface, 12pt)

4.2 ...

...

(Paging)

Appendix A ... (Song typeface, 12pt, bold) (if applicable)

A1. ... (Song typeface, 12pt)

A1.1 ...

Note:

1. Times New Roman font may be used for content in western font.

2. Do not add such unspecified contents as a cover page, registrant's name and logo, signature, etc..

3. The page number can be described as x (page x)/y (total page number), such as 1/9.

5. Template for Statement of Conformity

5.1 Template for Statement of Conformity for Medical Devices

Applicants shall make statement on the following contents:

(1) The proposed product complies with relevant requirements of the *Measures for the Administration of Registration and Filing of Medical Devices* and other relevant regulations.

(2) The proposed product complies with requirements related to the classification in the *Rules for the Classification of Medical Devices*.

(3) The proposed product conforms to the current national standards and industry standards. Also, a list of applicable standards conforming to shall be provided.

(4) The authenticity of the dossiers submitted (domestic product dossiers are issued by the applicant, and imported product dossiers are issued by the applicant and the agent respectively) is guaranteed.

5.2 Template for Statement of Conformity for In Vitro Diagnostic Reagents

Applicants shall make statement on the following contents:

(1) The proposed product complies with relevant requirements of the *Measures for the Administration of Registration and Filing of In Vitro Diagnostic Reagents* and other relevant regulations.

(2) The proposed product complies with the requirements related to the classification in the *Classification Rules for In Vitro Diagnostic Reagents* and *Classification Sub-catalogue of In Vitro Diagnostic Reagents*.

(3) The proposed product conforms to the current national standards and industry standards. Also, a list of applicable standards conforming to shall be provided.

(4) The list of applicable national standard materials that the proposed product conforms to.

(5) The authenticity of the dossiers submitted (domestic product dossiers are issued by the applicant, and imported product dossiers are issued by the applicant and the agent respectively) is guaranteed.

6. Template for Letter of Authorization

The overseas registration applicant ×××××× /filing applicant ×××××× designates ×××××× Company, as the local agent in China, to represent with regards to medical devices/in vitro diagnostic reagents registration/filing affairs. The local agent shall assist the registrant/ filing applicant to fulfill the obligations specified below and implement the corresponding legal responsibilities:

(1) To establish a quality management system suitable for the products and maintain its effective operation;

(2) To formulate plans for post–marketing study and risk control plan and ensure its effective implementation thereof;

(3) To carry out adverse event monitoring and re–evaluation according to law;

(4) To establish and implement product traceability and recall systems;

(5) Other obligations specified by the medical product administration under the State Council.

7. Template for Instructions for Use for In Vitro Diagnostic Reagents

7.1 Format of Instructions for Use for In Vitro Diagnostic Reagents

Instructions for Use of × × × × × × (Product Generic Name)

【Product Name】× × × × × ×

【Packaging Specification】× × × × × ×

【Intended Use】× × × × × ×

【Test Principle】× × × × × ×

【Main Components】× × × × × ×

【Storage Conditions and Shelf Life】× × × × × ×

【Applicable Instrument】× × × × × ×

【Sample Requirements】× × × × × ×

【Test Method】× × × × × ×

【Cut–off Value or Reference Interval】× × × × × ×

【 Interpretation of Test Results 】× × × × × ×

【 Limitation of Test Method 】× × × × × ×

【 Product Performance Indicators 】× × × × × ×

【 Precautions 】× × × × × ×

【 Explanation of Identification 】× × × × × ×

【 References 】× × × × × ×

【 Basic Information 】× × × × × ×

【 Medical Device Registration Certificate No./Product Technical Requirements No. 】(or【 Medical Device Filing Certificate No./Product Technical Requirements No. 】) × × × × × ×

【 Date of Approval and Modification of Instructions for Use 】× × × × × ×

If not applicable to some products, the above items can be omitted in the IFU.

7.2 Description on the Preparation of Each Item

In principle, the contents of the IFU shall be illustrated in Chinese. If internationally general or intra–industrially accepted English abbreviations are contained, they shall be indicated in parentheses after the Chinese. For words that cannot be expressed appropriately in Chinese, they can be expressed with corresponding English or its abbreviation.

【 Product Name 】

(1) Generic name

The generic names should be named according to the naming principle stipulated in the *Provisions for In Vitro Diagnostic Reagent Registration* (Decree No.5 of NMPA), with appropriate reference to relevant "Classification Catalog" and/or national standards and industry standards.

Except that sample types can be indicated in the generic name of products with special use, sample types and qualitative/quantitative contents shall not be indicated in the generic name of other products.

(2) English name

【Packaging Specification】Indicate the number of samples or filling that can be tested, such as × × test/kit, × × person/kit, × × mL. In addition to the international general measurement unit, other contents shall be expressed in Chinese. For products with different components, the names of these components should be specified. For products with article number, the information about the article number should be added.

【Intended Use】The first paragraph shall describe in detail the intended use, such as qualitative or quantitative detection, self-test, confirmation, sample type and substance to be tested and shall be adjusted appropriately according to product characteristics. If the samples are derived from special subject populations, such as pregnant women and neonates, they shall be indicated. The second paragraph describes the clinical indications and background related to intended use, and relevant clinical or laboratory diagnostic methods shall be explained.

【Test Principle】The test principle and method shall be described in detail, and graphical representation method may be used if necessary.

【Main Components】

(1) For reagent components included in the product

1) Indicate the name, quantity and the proportion or concentration in the reaction system. If necessary, the biological source, activity and other features shall be described.

2) For multi-component kit, it shall be clearly stated whether the components in different batch of kits can be interchanged.

3) If the kit contains consumables, indicate the name, quantity and other information of the consumables. Such as plastic droppers, sealing films and zip lock bags.

(2) For components not included in the product but necessary for the test, the name and purity of such reagents shall be listed, and dilution or mixing methods and other relevant information shall be provided in the IFU.

(3) For calibrators and quality controls

1) Indicate the main components and the biological source.

2) Indicate the value assignment of calibrator and its traceability.

3) Indicate the target value range of quality controls. If the target value range is specific to the batch, "batch specificity" should be indicated, and a separate list of target value should be attached.

【Storage Conditions and Shelf Life】

(1) Describe the storage conditions of the product: 2 – 8℃, below –18℃, or to avoid/prohibit freezing and so on. The other conditions affect the stability shall also be indicated, including light, humidity, etc. If the stability of the product or its components after opening differs from that of the original package, then the storage condition after the opening of the package shall also be indicated.

(2) Shelf life: Describe the shelf life under the storage conditions. If the stability of the product or ingredient after opening differs from that of the original package, then the shelf life after the opening of the package shall also be indicated.

(3) If the stability of each component in the kit is inconsistent, the storage conditions and shelf life of each component should be described separately.

【Applicable Instrument】Indicate the applicable instruments and model, and provide information related to the instrument so that the user can choose and use it correctly.

【Sample Requirements】The following aspects shall be explained:

(1) Applicable sample types.

(2) Special precautions during sample collection process.

(3) Anticoagulants or protective agent necessary to ensure the stability of each component of sample.

(4) Known interfering substances.

(5) The storage, handling and transportation methods which can guarantee the stability of the samples.

【Test Method】In order to ensure the proper progress of the test, the following aspects shall be described in detail:

(1) Reagent preparation: the dilution, mixing and other necessary procedures for all reagent component.

(2) Test conditions must be met: such as the pH, temperature, the time required for each step of the test, wavelength, and stability of the final reaction products. Matters that must be paid attention to during the test.

(3) Calibration procedures (if necessary): the preparation and usage of the calibrator, and method to draw the calibration curves.

(4) Quality control procedures: The use of the quality controls and quality control methods.

(5) The calculation or reading of the test results, including the explanation of each factor and each calculation step. If possible, examples shall be provided.

【Cut-off Value or Reference Interval】Indicate the cut-off value or reference interval, and briefly explain the method for determining the cut-off value or reference interval.

【Interpretations of Test Results】Indicate the factors that may affect the test results and under what circumstances the confirmation tests are required.

【 Limitation of Test Method 】Indicate the limitations of the test method.

【 Product Performance Indicators 】 Indicate the main performance indicators of the product.

【 Precautions 】 Indicate the necessary precautions, e.g., this product is only used for in vitro diagnosis. If the product contains any human substance or substance utilizing animal tissues and their derivatives, a warning of potential infectivity shall be given.

【 Explanation of Identification 】 If the identification is represented by graphics or symbols, the corresponding meaning shall be interpreted.

【 References 】Indicate the references cited.

【 Basic Information 】

(1) Domestic in vitro diagnostic reagents

1) If the registrant (or filing applicant) and the manufacturer are the same, basic information shall be indicated upon the following format:

Name of registrant (or filing applicant)/manufacturer

Domicile

Contact information

Name of after-sale service unit

Contact information

Production address

Production License No. or Production Filing Certificate No.

2) If the product is under contract production, basic information shall be indicated upon the following format:

Name of registrant (or filing applicant)

Domicile

Contact information

Name of after-sale service unit

Contact information

Name of trustee

Domicile

Production address

Production License No. or Production Filing Certificate No.

(2) Imported in vitro diagnostic reagents

Basic information shall be indicated upon the following format:

Name of registrant (or filing applicant)/manufacturer

Domicile

Production address

Contact information

Name of after-sale service unit

Contact information

Name of agent

Domicile

Contact information

【Medical Device Registration Certificate No./Product Technical Requirements No.】or【Medical Device Filing Certificate No./Product Technical Requirements No.】Indicate the Registration Certificate No. or Filing Certificate No. of the product.

【Date of Approval and Modification of the IFU】Indicate the date of approval of the IFU. If any modification application for the IFU was submitted, then the modification date shall be indicated.

Regulations for the Supervision and Administration of Medical Devices

(Decree No.739 of the State Council of the People's Republic of China)

(Published by Decree No. 276 of the State Council of the People's Republic of China on January 4, 2000, revised and adopted on 39th Executive Meeting of the State Council on February 12, 2014, and amended based on the *Decisions on the Amendment of the Regulations for the Supervision and Administration of Medical Devices by the State Council* on May 4, 2017, revised and adopted on 119th Executive Meeting of the State Council on December 21, 2020)

Chapter I General Provisions

Article 1 The Regulations is hereby formulated with a view to ensuring the safety and effectiveness of medical devices, protecting human health and life safety and promoting the development of the medical device industry.

Article 2 All activities in the research and development, production, operation, use, supervision and administration of medical devices within the territory of the People's Republic of China shall comply with the Regulations.

Article 3 NMPA is responsible for supervision and administration of medical devices nationwide.

The relevant authorities under the State Council are responsible for supervision and administration related to medical devices in their own duty scope.

Article 4 The local people's governments at or above the county level shall strengthen their leadership over the supervision and administration of medical devices within their respective administrative regions, organize and coordinate the supervision and administration of medical devices and the response to emergencies within their respective administrative regions, strengthen the capacity-building of supervision and administration of medical devices, and provide work guarantee for the safety of medical devices.

The local medical product administrations at the county level and above are responsible for supervision and administration of medical devices within their respective administrative areas. The relevant authorities under the local People's Government at county level and above are responsible for supervision and administration of medical devices in their own duty scope.

Article 5 The supervision and administration of medical devices shall follow the principles of risk management, whole-process control, scientific supervision, and social co-governance.

Article 6 The State shall classify and administer medical devices on the basis of risk level.

Class I Medical Devices are those for which risk is low, and safety and effectiveness can be ensured through routine administration.

Class II Medical Devices are those for which risk is medium, and strict controls are required to ensure their safety and effectiveness.

Class III Medical Devices are those for which risk is high, and strict regulations with special measures are required to ensure their safety and effectiveness.

The intended use, structural characteristics, method of application and other factors shall be considered when evaluate the risk level of medical devices.

NMPA is responsible for stipulating the Rules for the Classification of Medical Devices and Classification Catalogue for Medical Devices, timely analyzing and evaluating the risk changes of medical device in accordance with the production, operation and use, and adjusting the the classification rules and classification catalogue. To stipulate and adjust the Rules for the Classification of Medical Devices and Classification Catalogue for Medical Devices, opinions from medical device registrants, filing applicants, production and operation enterprises, user units, and industry organizations shall be listened, and international classification experience shall be referenced. Rules for the Classification of Medical Devices and Classification Catalogue for Medical Devices shall be promulgated to the public.

Article 7 Medical devices shall comply with the mandatory national standards. In case of absence of mandatory national standards, mandatory industrial standards shall be complied with.

Article 8 The State shall formulate plans and policies for the medical device industry to include medical device innovation as a development priority, prioritize review and approval for innovative medical devices, and support the clinical promotion and use of innovative medical devices, so as to promote the high-quality development of medical device industry. NMPA shall coordinate with relevant authorities under the State Council in the implementation of industry planning and guidance policies of medical devices.

Article 9 The State shall improve the innovation system of medical devices, support the basic and applied research of medical devices, promote the popularization and application of new technologies of medical devices, and provide support in scientific and technological project approval, financing, credit, bidding and procurement, medical insurance and other aspects. It shall encourage enterprises to set up or jointly set up research and development institutions, encourage enterprises to cooperate with universities, scientific research institutes and medical institutions to carry out research and innovation of medical devices, strengthen the protection of intellectual property rights of medical devices, and improve the independent innovation ability of medical devices.

Article 10 The State shall strengthen the informatization–based construction of the supervision and administration of medical devices, improve the level of online government services, and provides convenience for the administrative licensing and filing of medical devices.

Article 11 Medical device industry organizations shall enhance self–discipline, promote the construction of credit system, supervise and urge enterprises to conduct manufacturing and operating activities in accordance with law and guide the honesty and trustworthiness of enterprises.

Article 12 Units and individuals that have made outstanding contributions to the research and innovation of medical devices should be commended and rewarded in accordance with relevant national regulations.

Chapter II Medical Device Registration and Filing

Article 13 Class I medical devices shall be administrated through filing. Class II and Class III medical devices shall be administrated through registration.

Registrants and filing applicants of medical devices shall strengthen quality management for the whole life cycle of medical devices and assume the responsibility for the safety and effectiveness of medical devices throughout the whole process of research and development, manufacturing, operation and use in accordance with the law.

Article 14 The following documentation shall be submitted for the filing of Class I medical devices and the registration of Class II and Class III medical devices:

(1) Product risk analysis report;

(2) Product technical requirements;

(3) Product testing report;

(4) Clinical evaluation materials;

(5) Draft label and instructions for use;

(6) Quality Management System documents related to product research and development and manufacturing;

(7) Other materials for proving the safety and effectiveness of the product.

Product testing report (which shall comply with the requirements specified by NMPA), may be the self-test report generated by the registration applicant/filing applicant of medical device, or the testing report issued by the qualified medical device testing institution entrusted thereby.

For the exemption from clinical evaluation in accordance with Article 24 of the Regulations, the submission of evaluation materials can be exempted.

Medical device registration applicants and filing applicants shall ensure the legality, authenticity, accuracy, completeness, and traceability of the materials submitted.

Article 15 For domestic Class I medical devices, the filing applicant shall submit filing materials to the municipal (with districts) medical product administration.

For the foreign filing applicants who exports Class I medical devices to

China, the domestic enterprise legal person designated by it shall submit the filing materials to the NMPA and the certification documents of the competent authority of the country (region) where the filing applicant is located to allow the medical devices for marketing. For innovative medical devices not sold abroad, the certification document that the competent authority of the country (region) where the filing applicant is located allows the medical device to be marketed is not required.

The filling shall be completed upon submission of filing materials complying with the provisions of the Regulations to the department in charge of drug supervision and administration. The department in charge of drug supervision and administration shall, within 5 working days from the date of receiving the filing materials, publish the filing information to the public through the online government affairs service platform of NMPA.

As for the recorded medical device, when the contents specified in the filing materials have changed, the filing applicant shall apply to the original filing authority for the modification of filing information.

Article 16 For Class Ⅱ medical devices, the registration applicant shall submit registration dossiers to the medical product administrations at the level of provinces, autonomous regions and municipalities. For domestic Class Ⅲ medical devices, the registration applicant shall submit registration dossiers to NMPA.

The overseas registration applicant who intends to export Class Ⅱ and Class Ⅲ medical Devices to China shall entrust its enterprise legal person within the territory of the People's Republic of China to submit the registration dossiers and the documentary evidences certifying this medical device has been approved to be marketed in the country (or region) where the registration applicant is located to NMPA. For innovative medical devices not sold overseas, the documentary evidences certifying this medical device has been approved to be marketed in the country (or region) where the registration applicant is located is not required.

NMPA shall make provisions on the procedures and requirements for medical device registration review, and strengthen the supervision and guidance of the medical product administration of the people's government of provinces, autonomous regions, and municipalities directly under the Central Government.

Article 17 The medical product administration who accepts the registration application shall review the safety and effectiveness of medical devices and the capabilities of registration applicants such as the quality control to ensure that safety and effectiveness of the medical devices.

The medical product administration who accepts the registration application shall forward the registration dossiers to the Technical Review Center within three working days upon the date of acceptance. After completing the technical review, the Technical Review Center shall submit the review opinions to the medical product administration who accepts the registration application as the basis for review and approval.

When the medical product administration who accepts the registration application considers that it is necessary to audit the quality management system (QMS) during technical review on medical devices, it shall organize to conduct the QMS audit.

Article 18 The medical product administration who accepts the registration application shall make the decision within 20 working days after receiving the review opinions. The medical device complying with the requirements shall be approved to be registered and the Medical Device Registration Certificate shall be issued accordingly. As for the medical devices which cannot comply with relevant requirements, the application shall not be approved, and reasons shall be provided in written form.

The medical product administration who accepts the registration application shall, within 5 working days from the date of approving the registration application, release the registration related information to the public through the online government affairs service platform of NMPA.

Article 19 The medical product administration accepting the registration application may conditionally approve the registration of medical devices for treating rare diseases and diseases that severely endanger life and have not been effectively treated, and those under urgent need for dealing with public health emergencies, and should specify the relevant matters in the Medical Device Registration Certificate.

In case of particularly major public health emergencies or other emergencies that seriously threaten public health, the competent health authority under the State Council shall put forward suggestions for emergency use of medical devices in accordance with the prevention and control of the event. After demonstration and approval, the medical product administration may permit that medical devices can be used for emergencies within a certain range and time limit.

Article 20 Registrants, filing applicant for medical devices shall fulfill the following obligations:

(1) Establish a quality management system suitable for the products and maintain its effective operation;

(2) Formulate a post-marketing study and risk control plan and ensure its effective implementation;

(3) Conduct adverse event monitoring and re-evaluation in accordance with the law;

(4) Establish and implement product traceability and recall system;

(5) Other obligations stipulated by the NMPA.

The domestic enterprise legal person designated by the overseas medical device registrants and filing applicant shall assist the registrants and filing applicant in fulfilling the obligations specified in the preceding paragraph.

Article 21 If substantial changes in the design, raw materials, production process, scope of application, methods of application and other factors have happened to the registered Class II and Class III medical devices, so that the safety and effectiveness of the medical devices may be affected, the registrant shall apply to the original registration authority for registration modification. If other changes have happened, the changes shall be filed or reported as required by NMPA.

Article 22 The Medical Device Registration Certificate is valid for five years. In the case of the expiration of the Medical Device Registration Certificate which needs to be renewed, the registrant shall apply to the original registration department for registration renewal within 6 months before the expiration of the validity period.

With the exception of the circumstances specified in the paragraph 3 of this Article, the medical product administration who receives the application of registration renewal shall make the decision on whether to approve the renewal or not before the expiration of the Medical Device Registration Certificate. If the decision is not made within the specified time limit, it is deemed that the registration renewal is approved.

In the case of any of the following circumstances, the registration renewal shall not be approved:

(1) The registrant fails to apply for registration renewal within the stipulated time;

(2) The mandatory standards of medical devices have been revised, while this medical device applied for registration renewal fails to comply with new requirements;

(3) For the medical device with conditional approval, the items specified in the medical device registration certificate are not completed within the specified time limit.

Article 23 As for the newly-developed medical devices which are not listed in the Classification Catalogue for Medical Devices, the applicant may apply for product registration in accordance with relevant requirements for Class III medical devices set forth in the Regulations, or apply for product registration or filing after determining the product classification based on the classification rules and applying to NMPA for the classification confirmation accordingly.

As for the registration directly applied for as a Class III medical device, NMPA will confirm the classification in accordance with the risk level of the device, and the medical device approved for registration shall be timely included into Classification Catalogue of Medical Devices. As for the application of classification confirmation, NMPA shall determine the classification within 20 working days upon the date of acceptance and inform the applicant of the classification result.

Article 24 Clinical evaluation shall be conducted for the registration and filing of medical devices; however, clinical evaluation may be exempted under any of the following circumstances:

(1) The medical device to be registered has clear working mechanism, finalized design and mature production process; the predicate medical devices which have been marketed have been in clinical use for many years and no severe adverse events have been associated with these devices and the medical

device to be registered doesn't change the conventional uses;

(2) The safety and effectiveness of the medical device to be registered can be proved through non-clinical evaluation.

NMPA shall formulate guidelines for clinical evaluation of medical devices.

Article 25 The clinical evaluation of medical devices can be conducted on the basis of product characteristics, clinical risks and available clinical data. It can be proved that medical devices are safe and effective by conducting clinical trials, or by analyzing and evaluating clinical literatures and clinical data of the predicate medical device.

In accordance with the regulations of NMPA, when conducting clinical evaluation of medical devices, if the existing clinical literature and clinical data are insufficient to confirm the safety and effectiveness of the products, clinical trials shall be carried out.

Article 26 Medical device clinical trials shall be conducted in the certified clinical trial institutes in accordance with the requirements of Good Clinical Practice for Medical Device Trials, and shall be recorded in the medical product administrations at the level of provinces, autonomous regions and municipalities where the clinical trial applicant is located. The medical product administration who accepts the clinical trial filing shall report the filing to the medical product administration and the competent health authority at the same level where the clinical trial institution is located.

The medical device clinical trial institutions shall be recorded. The Qualification Authentication Conditions for Medical Device Clinical Trial Institutions and Good Clinical Practice for Medical Device Trials shall be formulated and promulgated by NMPA jointly with the competent health authority under the State Council.

The state government shall encourage medical institutions to carry out clinical trials, include the evaluation of clinical trial conditions and capabilities into the level review of medical institutions, and encourage medical institutions to carry out innovative clinical trials of medical devices.

Article 27 Clinical trials for Class III high-risk medical devices to humans shall be approved by NMPA before the initiation. During the review and approval for clinical trials, NMPA shall conduct the systematic evaluation on the equipment, professionals and other conditions of the clinical trial institutions, on the risk level, clinical trial protocols, and clinical benefit-risk comparative analysis report of the medical devices to be initiated clinical trials. CFDA shall make a decision and inform the sponsor of the decision within 60 working days from the date of receiving the application. Failure to notify within the time limit shall be deemed as approval. As for the clinical trials which are approved for initiation, NMPA shall inform the medical product administrations and the competent Departments of Health at the level of provinces, autonomous regions and municipalities where the clinical trial institutions are located.

The clinical trials for Catalogue of Class III High-risk Medical Devices to Humans shall be formulated, adjusted and promulgated by NMPA.

Article 28 For clinical trials of medical devices, ethical review shall be carried out in accordance with the provisions, and detailed information such as the purpose, use and possible risks of the trials shall be communicated to the subjects, and written informed consent of the subjects shall be obtained; if the subjects are persons without or with limited civil capacity, written informed consent of their guardians shall be obtained in accordance with the law.

No fees related to clinical trials shall be charged to the subjects in any form.

Article 29 For medical devices under clinical trials, which are intended for treating diseases that severely endanger life and have not been effectively treated yet, and are deemed to benefit the patient through medical observations, they may be used for free on other patients with similar diseases in the institution carrying out the medical device clinical trial after ethical review and obtaining the informed consent, and the safety data may be used for medical device registration application.

Chapter III Medical Device Manufacturing

Article 30 For medical device manufacturing, the following conditions should be complied with:

(1) Manufacturing sites, environmental conditions, manufacturing facilities and technical professionals appropriate to the medical devices to be produced shall be equipped;

(2)Inspection institutions or full-time inspection personnel, as well as inspection equipment for quality inspection of the medical devices to be produced shall be equipped;

(3) A management system that can guarantee the quality of medical devices shall be established;

(4) After-sales service capacity appropriate to the medical devices to be produced shall be possessed;

(5) The medical device manufacturing shall accord with the requirements stipulated in the files concerning product development and production processes.

Article 31 In order to manufacture Class I medical devices, the manufacturer shall apply to the municipal (with districts) medical product administration for manufacturing filing, and complete the filing after submitting the relevant materials set forth in Article 30 of the Regulations.

If the medical device filing applicant is engaged in production of Class I medical devices by themselves, it can complete the production filing by submitting the relevant materials in accordance with the conditions specified in Article 30 of the Regulations at the time of product filing in accordance with Article 15 of the Regulations.

Article 32 In order to manufacture Class II and Class III medical devices, the manufacturer shall apply to the medical product administration at the level of provinces, autonomous regions and municipalities for manufacturing licensing, and submit the relevant materials set forth in Article 30 of the Regulations and the registration certificate of the medical device to be manufactured.

The medical product administration who accepts the application of manufacturing licensing shall review the application materials, and conduct the audit in accordance with Good Manufacturing Practice for Medical Devices formulated by NMPA, and make a decision within 20 working days from the date of receiving the application. If the application complies with the prescribed requirements, the Medical Device Manufacturing License shall be issued. If the application fails to comply with the prescribed requirements, the decision of non-approval shall be made and reasons shall be provided in written form.

The Medical Device Manufacturing License is valid for 5 years. In the case of the expiration of the Medical Device Manufacturing License which needs to be renewed, the licensing renewal shall be conducted in accordance with the laws and regulations related to administrative licensing.

Article 33 Good Manufacturing Practice for Medical Devices shall clarify the specific requirements for those items which will affect the safety and effectiveness of medical device, such as design and development, production equipment, raw material procurement, production process control and release of medical devices, organization structuring and personnel allocation of the enterprise and so on.

Article 34 The registrants and filing applicant for medical devices can produce medical devices by themselves, or they may entrust enterprises that comply with the requirements of the Regulations and have the corresponding conditions to produce medical devices.

Where medical devices are entrusted to be manufactured, the registrants and filing applicant for the medical devices shall be responsible for the quality of the medical devices entrusted to them, and shall strengthen the management of the production behavior of the entrusted manufacturer to ensure that the medical devices are produced in accordance with the statutory requirements. The medical device registrant or filing applicant shall sign the entrustment agreement with the entrusted manufacturer to specify the rights, obligations and responsibilities of both parties. The entrusted manufacturer shall organize production in accordance with laws and regulations, Good Manufacturing Practice for Medical Devices, mandatory standards, product technical requirements and commissioned agreement, be responsible for the production behaviors, and accept the supervision of the entrusting party.

The entrusted production for high-risk implantable medical devices is not allowed. The specific catalogue shall be formulated, adjusted and promulgated by NMPA.

Article 35 Registrants, filing applicant and entrusted manufacturer for medical devices shall establish and maintain the Quality Management System (QMS) suitable for its medical devices based on the requirements of Good Manufacturing Practice for Medical Devices and shall keep the effective operation of the System. The production activities shall be performed in strict accordance with the registered or recorded product technical requirements, and ensure that all ex–factory devices comply with the mandatory standards and the registered or recorded product technical requirements.

Registrants, filing applicant and entrusted manufacturer for medical devices shall conduct self–inspection concerning the QMS periodically, and submit a self–inspection report in accordance with the provisions of NMPA.

Article 36 If the production conditions of the medical device change and do not comply with the requirements of the medical device QMS any more, the registrants, filing applicant and entrusted manufacturer for medical devices shall take rectification measures immediately. If the changes may affect the safety and effectiveness of medical devices, the production activity shall be stopped immediately. Besides, it is required to report this situation to the original production license or production filing department..

Article 37 The product name of medical devices shall use the common name. which shall comply with the nomenclature specified by NMPA.

Article 38 The state shall, in accordance with the categories of medical devices, implement the unique device identification system step by step so as to realize the traceability of medical devices. The specific measures shall be formulated by NMPA jointly with the relevant authorities under the State Council.

Article 39 Medical devices shall be accompanied with instructions for use and labels. The contents of instructions for use and labels shall be consistent with relevant contents involved in the registration or filing, so as to ensure the authenticity and accuracy.

The instructions for use and labels of medical devices shall indicate the following items:

(1) The common name, models and specifications;

(2) The name, residence, and contact information of the registrants, filing applicant and entrusted manufacturer;

(3) Production date, service life or expiry date;

(4) Product performance, main structure, scope of application;

(5) Contraindications, precautions, warnings and other information should be noticed;

(6) Instructions or graphic guidance for installation and use;

(7) Product maintenance methods, special storage and transportation conditions and methods;

(8) Other information which shall be indicated based on the product technical requirements.

As for the Class II and Class III medical devices, Medical Device Registration Certificate number shall also be indicated.

For those devices used by the customers themselves, special instructions for safe use shall also be indicated.

Chapter IV The Operation and Use of Medical Devices

Article 40 For the operation of medical devices, the enterprise shall possess business places and storage conditions appropriate to its operation scale and scope, as well as the quality management system and the quality management organization or personnel appropriate to the medical devices to be operated.

Article 41 In order to operate Class II medical devices, the operation enterprise shall apply to the municipal (with districts) medical product administration for operation filing, and submit the relevant materials set forth in Article 40 of the Regulations.

According to the provisions of NMPA, the Class II medical devices whose product safety and effectiveness are not affected by the circulation process may be exempted from operation filing.

Article 42 In order to operate Class III medical devices, the operation enterprise shall apply to the municipal (with districts) medical product administration for operation licensing, and submit the relevant materials set forth in Article 40 of the Regulations.

The medical product administration who accepts the application of operation licensing shall review the application materials, conduct the audit when necessary and make a decision within 20 working days from the date of receiving the application. If the application complies with the prescribed requirements, the Medical Device Business Certificate shall be issued. If the application fails to comply with the prescribed requirements, the decision of non-approval shall be made and reasons shall be provided in written form.

The Medical Device Business Certificate is valid for 5 years. In the case of the expiration of the Medical Device Manufacturing License which needs to be renewed, the licensing renewal shall be conducted in accordance with the laws and regulations related to administrative licensing.

Article 43 Where the registrants and filing applicant for medical devices operates the medical device they registered or filed, they do not need to handle the business license or file the medical devices, but they shall comply with the business conditions stipulated in the Regulations.

Article 44 To engage in operation of medical devices, enterprises shall establish a quality management system suitable for the medical devices being operated in accordance with the requirements of the quality management standards for the operation of medical devices formulated by NMPA, and ensure the effective operation of the system.

Article 45 Medical device operating enterprise and organization using medical devices shall purchase medical devices from medical device registrant, filing applicant, medical device manufacturing enterprises and the medical device operating enterprises with legal qualifications. When purchasing medical devices, the operating enterprise or the organization using medical devices shall check the qualification of the supplier and the qualified certificates of the medical devices, and establish a filing system for the incoming inspection. The sales filing system shall also be established if the operating enterprises wholesale Class Ⅱ / Ⅲ medical devices or retail Class Ⅲ medical devices.

The following items shall be recorded:

(1) The name, model, specifications and quantity of the medical device;

(2) The lot number, shelf-life or expiry date and sales date of the medical device;

(3) The name of the medical device registrant, filing applicant and entrusted manufacturer;

(4) The name, address and contact information of the supplier or purchaser of the medical device;

(5) The document number of the related certificates.

The incoming inspection records and sales records shall be authentic, accurate, complete and traceable, and shall be kept until the deadline stipulated by NMPA. The State shall encourage the adoption of advanced technology to establish the above-mentioned filing systems.

Article 46 Only the registrant, filing applicant and operating enterprises of medical devices can engage in online sale of medical devices. Operators engaged in online sales of medical devices shall inform the relevant information about online sales of medical devices to the municipal (with districts) medical product administration of the place where they are located, except for those dealing in the Class I Medical Devices and Class II Medical Devices as stipulated in the second paragraph of Article 41 of the Regulations.

The operator of an e-commerce platform providing services for online transaction of medical devices shall implement real-name registration of networked medical device operators, check their operation license and filing status as well as the registration and filing status of the medical devices operated by them, and administer their operation behaviors. If an operator of an e-commerce platform discovers that a networked medical device operator has violated the provisions of the Regulations, it shall instruct the operator to stop the violation in time and immediately report to the local municipal (with districts) medical product administration where the operator is located. If serious illegal acts are found, it shall immediately stop providing online transaction platform services.

Article 47 The transportation and storage of medical devices shall comply with the requirements specified in the instructions for use and labels. If there are some special requirements for temperature, humidity and other environmental conditions, the appropriate measures shall be taken to ensure the safety and effectiveness of the medical device.

Article 48 The organization using medical devices shall possess storage sites and conditions appropriate to the type and quantity of the medical devices in use. The organization using medical devices shall strengthen the technical training of the staff and make sure that the medical device is used under the requirements of instructions for use, standard operation procedure, and so on.

The organization using medical devices shall have large medical equipment in accordance with the large medical equipment allocation plan made by the competent health authority under the State Council, meeting the functional level and clinic service needs. Such organizations shall also have relevant technical conditions, supporting facilities and professional technicians with necessary qualifications and capabilities, and have been approved by the competent health authority of the people's governments at above provincial level, and have obtained large medical equipment allocation license.

Rules on Allocation and Management of Large Medical Equipment shall be jointly formulated by the competent health authority and other relevant authority under the State Council. The catalogue of large medical equipment shall be proposed by the competent health authority and other relevant authority under the State Council, and be submitted to the State Council for approval before its official implementation.

Article 49 When using medical devices which can be repeatedly used with safety and effectiveness, the organization shall follow the instructions about sterilization and administration stipulated by the competent health authority under the State Council.

The single-use medical devices are not allowed to be used repeatedly. The single-use medical devices which have been used shall be destroyed and recorded in accordance with relevant regulations. Catalogue of Single-Use Medical Devices shall be formulated, adjusted and promulgated by NMPA jointly with the competent health authority under the State Council. For medical devices included in the Catalogue of Single-Use Medical Devices, sufficient evidence and reasons why they cannot be reused shall be given. Medical devices which can be repeatedly used on the premise of ensuring safety and effectiveness shall not be listed in the Catalogue of Single-Use Medical Devices. The Catalogue of Single-Use Medical Devices shall be adjusted if some single-use medical devices can be repeatedly used on the premise of ensuring safety and effectiveness after the design, production and sterile techniques are improved. And repeat use is allowed.

Article 50 As for the medical devices need to be checked, inspected, calibrated and maintained periodically, the organization using these medical devices shall check, inspect, calibrate and maintain these medical devices periodically and make records accordingly in accordance with the requirements of instructions for use, as well as timely perform analysis and evaluation to ensure that medical devices are in good condition and to guarantee the good performance of the medical devices. As for the large medical equipment which can be used for a long term, the logbook shall be created for them one by one to keep the records concerning use, maintenance, transfer and the actual duration, etc. The logbook shall be preserved for at least five years after the expiration date of the medical device.

Article 51 The organization using medical devices shall properly keep the source materials of the purchased Class III medical devices and also ensure the traceability of these materials.

When using large medical devices and implantable or interventional medical devices, the organization shall record the name, key technical parameters and other necessary information closely related to the safety of use of the medical device in the medical records.

Article 52 When the potential safety hazards of medical devices in use are discovered, the organization using these medical devices shall stop using these medical devices immediately and inform the registrants and filing applicant of medical devices or other organizations responsible for the product quality to perform the maintenance. The medical device shall not be used any more if it fails to comply with the safety criteria for use after the maintenance.

Article 53 For in vitro diagnostic reagents which have no predicate products available in the market of China, qualified medical institutions may, according to the clinical needs of the organization, develop the reagents on its own and use them within the institution under the guidance of certified physicians. Specific provisions shall be formulated by the medical product administration directly together with competent health authority under the State Council.

Article 54 The medical product administrations and the competent Departments of Health shall supervise and administrate the quality of medical device during the use process and the use behavior of medical devices respectively in accordance with their own duties.

Article 55 The medical device operating enterprises and organizations using medical devices are not allowed to operate and use those medical devices which are not legally registered, which have no qualified certificates as well as those which are expired, ineffective and disused.

Article 56 When the transfer of medical devices in use occurs among those organizations using medical devices, the transferor shall ensure the medical device transferred is safe and effective. It is not allowed to transfer expired, ineffective, disused and unqualified medical devices.

Article 57 The imported medical devices shall be those which have been registered or recorded in accordance with the requirements set forth in Chapter II of the Regulations.

The imported medical devices shall be accompanied with instructions for use and labels in Chinese. The instructions for use and labels shall comply with the requirements of the Regulations and the relevant mandatory standards. The country (region) of origin of medical devices, and the name, address and contact information of the domestic enterprise legal person designated by the overseas registrant and filing applicant of medical device shall be indicated in the instructions for use. Those medical devices which have no instructions for use and labels in Chinese or those whose instructions for use and labels fails to comply with the requirements set forth in this Article are not allowed to be imported.

If a medical institution needs to import small quantity of Class II and Class III medical devices for clinical emergencies, it may import such devices with the approval from the medical product administration directly under the State Council or the people's government of the province, autonomous region or municipality directly under the Central Government authorized by the State Council. Imported medical devices shall be used for specific medical purposes in designated medical institutions.

It is forbidden to import expired, ineffective, disused and other used medical devices.

Article 58 China Inspection and Quarantine authorities (CIQ) shall inspect the imported medical devices in accordance with law. Those disqualified devices upon inspection are not allowed to be imported.

NMPA shall timely report the registration and filing status of the imported medical devices to CIQ. The CIQ where the import port is located shall timely report the customs clearance status of the imported medical devices to the local municipal (with districts) medical product administration of the people's government.

Article 59 The enterprise who exports medical devices shall ensure that the exported medical devices comply with the requirements of the importing country (region).

Article 60 The advertisements of medical devices shall be authentic and legal, and shall be consistent with the instructions for use of medical devices registered or filed with the department in charge of drug supervision and administration, and shall not include false, exaggerated and misleading contents.

Before being released, advertisements of medical devices shall be reviewed by advertising censorship authorities determined by the people's government of provinces, autonomous regions or municipalities directly under the central government and the approval number for advertisements of medical devices shall be obtained. No advertisement shall be issued without being reviewed.

As for the medical device which has been ordered to suspend the manufacturing, importing, operation and use by the medical product administration under the People's Government at or above the provincial level, it is not allowed to publish any advertisements related to this medical device during such suspension.

Provisions on Review of Medical Device Advertisements shall be formulated by NMPA.

Chapter V Adverse Event Handling and Medical Device Recalls

Article 61 The State shall establish the monitoring system for adverse events of medical device, and shall timely collect, analyze, evaluate and control the adverse events of medical device.

Article 62 Registrant and filing applicant of medical device shall establish an adverse event monitoring system of medical devices, equip relevant organization and personnel appropriate for actively monitoring the adverse events related to its product, and report investigation, analysis and evaluation and product risk control to the Technology Institutions for Medical Device Adverse Event Monitoring in accordance with the provisions specified by NMPA.

Medical device manufacturing and operating enterprises and the organization using medical devices should assist the medical device registrant and filing applicant to conduct adverse event monitoring on the medical devices manufactured, operated or used; if adverse event or suspected adverse event of medical device is found, they shall report to the Technology Institutions for Medical Device Adverse Event Monitoring according to the provisions of NMPA.

Other units and individuals discovering an adverse event or suspected adverse event of medical device has the right to report to the medical product administration or the Technology Institutions for Medical Device Adverse Event Monitoring.

Article 63 NMPA shall strengthen the information network construction of medical device adverse event monitoring.

The Technology Institutions for Medical Device Adverse Event Monitoring shall strengthen the information monitoring of medical device adverse events and actively collect information about adverse events. When discovering adverse events or receiving adverse event reports, the Technology Institutions for Medical Device Adverse Event Monitoring shall timely verify and investigate, analyze and evaluate the adverse events as necessary, and make suggestions concerning the adverse event handling to the medical product administrations and the competent Departments of Health.

The Technology Institutions for Medical Device Adverse Event Monitoring shall publish their contact information so that the medical device registrant, filing applicant, manufacturing enterprises, operating enterprises and organization using medical devices can report medical device adverse events more conveniently.

Article 64 The medical product administrations shall timely take such control measures as publishing warning information and ordering enterprises to suspend the manufacturing, import, operation and use of the related medical devices in accordance with the evaluation results of medical device adverse events.

The medical product administrations at or above the provincial level shall organize investigation and deal with those medical device adverse events which have caused unexpected or a mass of serious injuries or deaths jointly with the competent health authority and relevant authorities at the same level, and strengthen monitoring on of similar medical devices.

The medical product administrations shall timely inform competent health authority at the same level of the adverse event monitoring of organization using medical devices.

Article 65 The medical device registrant, filing applicant, the medical device manufacturing enterprises, the medical device operating enterprises and the organizations using medical devices shall coordinate with the Technology Institutions for Medical Device Adverse Event Monitoring, the medical product administration and health competent department to investigate the medical device adverse events.

Article 66 In the case of any of the following circumstances, the medical device registrant and filing applicant shall take the initiative to reevaluate the marketed medical device:

(1) When some cognitional changes concerning the safety and effectiveness of the medical device occur in accordance with the development of scientific research;

(2) The monitoring and evaluation results of adverse events indicate that the medical device may have defects;

(3) Other situations in which the medical device shall be reevaluated

based on the requirements of NMPA.

In accordance with the re-evaluation results, the registrant and filing applicant of medical device shall take corresponding control measures and improve the marketed medical devices, and make change registration or change filing according to the regulations. In case the re-evaluation results indicate that the safety and effectiveness of the marketed medical device cannot be guaranteed, the medical device registrant or filing applicant should apply for cancellation of the Medical Device Registration Certificate or cancellation of filing; in case the medical device registrant or filing applicant fails to do so, the Medical Device Registration Certificate and filing should be revoked by the medical product administration.

The medical product administration of the people's government at or above the provincial level shall re-evaluate the marketed medical devices according to the monitoring and evaluation of adverse events of medical devices. Where the reevaluation results indicate that the marketed medical device fails to ensure its safety and effectiveness, the Medical Device Registration Certificate and filing should be revoked.

The medical product administration shall timely release the information related to the Registration Certificate for Medical Device or filing that has been revoked to the public. After the Registration Certificate has been revoked, the corresponding medical device is not allowed to be manufactured, imported, operated and used any more.

Article 67 When discovering that the manufactured medical devices cannot comply with the requirements of mandatory standards and the registered or recorded product technical requirements, or the medical devices have other defects, the medical device registrant and filing applicant shall ① immediately stop production activities, ② inform relevant medical device operating enterprises, organizations using medical devices and consumers to stop operating activities and stop using these devices, ③ recall relevant medical devices which have been marketed, ④ take remedial measures or destroy these devices, ⑤ record and publish relevant information, and ⑥ report the recall and handling situations of these devices to the medical product administrations and the competent Departments of Health.

When discovering that the manufactured and operated medical devices exist circumstances prescribed in the preceding paragraph, the entrusted medical device manufacturer and operating enterprise shall ① immediately stop production and operation activities, ② inform relevant medical device registrant and filing applicant, and ③ record actual situations of discontinuing production and operation activities and informing other related entities. When considering that some medical devices need to be recalled in accordance with the requirements set forth in the preceding paragraph, the medical device registrant and filing applicant shall immediately recall these medical devices.

Where the medical device registrant, filing applicant, entrusted manufacturer or operating enterprise fail to recall devices or fail to stop production and operation activities in accordance with the stipulations of this Article, the medical product administrations have the right to order them to recall relevant devices or stop production and operation activities.

Chapter VI Supervision and Inspection

Article 68 The state shall establish a system of professional and specialized inspectors and strengthen supervision and inspection of medical devices.

Article 69 The medical product administration shall strengthen supervision and inspection on the development, production and operation of medical devices as well as the quality of medical devices during their use, and shall focus on the supervision and inspection of the following items:

(1) Whether the medical device manufacturing enterprise performs the production activities in accordance with the registered or recorded product technical requirements or not;

(2) Whether the medical device manufacturing enterprise keeps the effective operation of its Quality Management System (QMS) or not;

(3) Whether the production and operation conditions of the medical device comply with the statutory requirements or not.

If necessary, the medical product administration may conduct extended inspection over other relevant units and individuals that provide products or services for the R&D, manufacturing, operation, use and other activities of medical devices.

Article 70 The medical product administrations have the following rights during supervision and inspection:

(1) Conduct on-site inspection and field sampling;

(2) Review, copy, seal up and detain relevant contracts, bills, books of accounts, and other related materials;

(3) Seal up and detain ① those medical devices which fail to comply with the statutory requirements, ② illegally-used parts and accessories, and raw materials, and ③ the tools or facilities illegally used for medical device production and operation activities;

(4) Seal up the sites used for medical device production and operation activities which are against the provisions set forth in the Regulations.

When conducting supervision and inspection, the medical product administrations shall show their law-enforcement credentials and keep the confidentiality of commercial secrets of the enterprises or organizations being inspected.

The relevant organizations and individuals shall coordinate with the supervision and inspection and provide relevant documents and materials, and shall not conceal, refuse or obstruct.

Article 71 The competent health authorities shall strengthen supervision and inspection over the use of medical devices by medical institutions. During supervision and inspection, they may enter medical institutions to consult and copy relevant files, records and other relevant materials.

Article 72 If hidden dangers of product quality and safety exist in the manufacturing and operation of medical devices while measures are not taken to eliminate them in time, the medical product administration can take such measures as warning, appointment for interview, and ordering rectification within a time limit.

The medical product administration may take emergency control measures ordering the suspension of production, import, operation and use, and issue safety warning information for medical devices that cause harm to human bodies or are proved to be potentially harmful to human health.

Article 73 The medical product administration shall strengthen the random inspection on the medical devices manufactured, operated and used by the medical device registrant, filing applicant, manufacturing enterprises, operating enterprises and organizations using medical devices. Inspection fees and any other fees are not allowed to be charged for the random inspection, the costs needed for the random inspection shall be included in the government budget at the corresponding level. The medical product administrations at or above the provincial level shall timely publish medical device quality announcements in accordance with the random inspection results.

The competent health authority shall supervise and assess the usage status of large medical equipment, and timely correct and offer punishments in accordance with the law once any violations against rules, or excessive inspection and treatment concerning such large medical equipment are found.

Article 74 In the event that a medical product administration fails to timely discover safety and systematic risks of medical device, or fails to timely eliminate potential safety hazards of medical device in the region, the medical product administration of the people's government at the same level or above may make inquiries with the responsible person.

In the event that a local people's government fails to assume its duties on medical device safety or fails to eliminate major potential safety hazards of medical devices in the region in a timely manner, the people's government at the higher level or its medical product administration may make inquiries with the responsible person.

The interviewed department and local people's government shall immediately take measures to rectify the problems in supervision and administration of medical devices.

Article 75 The qualification authentication for medical device testing institutes shall be implemented under the unified management in accordance with relevant provisions of the State. Only the testing institutes officially identified by the Certification and Accreditation Administration Department of the State Council and NMPA can conduct tests for medical devices.

When needing to test some medical devices during the law enforcement, the medical product administration shall entrust the qualified medical device testing institutions and pay relevant testing fees accordingly.

If the parties have any objection to the testing conclusion, they may, within 7 working days from the date of receiving the testing conclusion, submit an application for re-testing to the department implementing the sampling testing or the medical product administration at the next higher level, and the department receiving the application for re-testing shall choose an agency randomly from the list of re-testing agencies to carry out the re-testing. The testing institution performing the retest shall issue the retest results within the time limit stipulated by NMPA. The retest results shall be the final test results. A re-testing institution shall not be the same one conducting the preliminary test; where there is one qualified testing institution for relevant test items, the department or personnel undertaking the test shall be changed for the re-test. The list of re-testing institutions shall be published by NMPA.

Article 76 As for the medical devices which may contain hazardous substances or the devices which have potential hazards due to some unauthorized modifications in the design, raw materials and the manufacturing process, the medical device testing institutes can conduct the tests by supplementing extra test items and test methods approved by NMPA if these above-mentioned devices cannot be tested based on the test items and test methods stipulated in relevant national standards and industry standards. Those corresponding test results obtained by supplementing extra test items and test methods could be considered as the basis of medical device quality identification by the medical product administrations.

Article 77 The market supervision authority shall conduct supervision and inspection on medical device advertisements, and investigate and handle the illegal activities in accordance with the laws and regulations related to the advertisement management.

Article 78 The medical product administrations shall timely publish such daily supervision and administration information as medical device licensing, filing, random inspection, and investigation and handling situations concerning illegal activities via the online government affairs service platform of NMPA. However, it is not allowed to reveal the commercial secrets of the parties involved.

The medical product administration shall establish credit filing systems for the medical device registrants and filing applicants, manufacturers, manufacturing enterprises, operating enterprises, and organization using medical devices, and increase the supervision and inspection frequency on units with poor credit record, and intensify the punishment for dishonest conduct according to law.

Article 79 The medical product administrations shall publish their contact information, and accept consultations, complaints and reports. The medical product administrations and relevant authorities shall timely reply the consultations related to medical device supervision and administration, and shall timely verily, deal with and reply the complaints and reports. The situations about the consultations, complaints and reports, as well as the corresponding response, verification and handling status shall be recorded and preserved.

Where the reports related to medical device research and development, manufacturing, operation and use are verified to be true through investigation, the medical product administrations and other related authorities shall reward those informants accordingly. The relevant departments shall not disclose the information of any informant.

Article 80 When formulating, adjusting and modifying the catalogues involved in the Regulations and the provisions related to medical device supervision and administration, NMPA shall solicit public opinions, and listen to the suggestions from experts, medical device registrant, filing applicant, manufacturing enterprises, operating enterprises, organization using medical devices, consumers, industry associations and other related organizations by holding hearings or discussion meetings.

Chapter VII Legal Liability

Article 81 In the case of any of the following circumstances, the medical product administration shall confiscate the illegal incomes, the medical devices manufactured or operated illegally, and the tools, facilities, raw materials and other possessions used for illegal manufacturing and operation activities. If the value of the medical devices manufactured or operated illegally is less than RMB 10,000 Yuan, the enterprises involved shall be imposed a fine of no less than RMB 50,000 Yuan and no more than RMB 150,000 Yuan. If the value of the medical devices manufactured or operated illegally is more than RMB 10,000 Yuan, the enterprises involved shall be imposed a fine of no less than 15 times of the value and no more than 30 times of the value. In serious cases, the party involved shall be ordered to suspend production or business operation, and any medical device licensing application made by the relevant responsible person and unit shall not be accepted within 10 years. The income from the organization during the occurrence of the legal representative, principal responsible person, person(s) in charge and other directly responsible personnel of the illegal organization shall be confiscated, and a fine of more than 30% and less than 3 times of the income shall be imposed. They shall be prohibited from engaging in the production and operation of medical devices for a lifetime:

(1) Manufacture or operate Class II / III medical devices, which have no Medical Device Registration Certificates;

(2) Manufacture Class II / III medical devices without permission;

(3) Operate Class III medical devices without permission.

When discovering serious circumstances prescribed in Subparagraph (1) in the preceding paragraph, the original certificate–issuing authority shall revoke the Medical Device Manufacturing License or the Medical Device Operating License.

Article 82 Those randomly equipped with the large medical equipment without approval shall be ordered to stop the use by the competent health authority of the people's government at or above county level, which will give a warning and confiscate all illegal income; if such illegal revenue is less than RMB 10,000 Yuan, the fine between RMB 50,000 Yuan and RMB 100,000 Yuan shall be imposed; if such income is over RMB 10,000 Yuan, the fine equal to 10~30 times the illegal income shall be imposed; under serious cases, the application of relevant responsible persons and units for using large medical equipment shall not be accepted within five years. The legal representative, principal responsible person, person(s) in charge and other directly responsible personnel of the unit shall be confiscated of the income earned from the unit during the period when the violation occurs, and shall be fined not less than 30% but not more than 3 times the income obtained, and punishment shall be given according to law.

Article 83 Where any party applies for administrative licenses of medical devices by providing false materials or other deceptive means, such licenses shall not be issued; the administrative license of medical device which have obtained by any party shall be revoked by the original certificate–issuing authorities, confiscate the illegal revenue, the medical devices illegally manufactured, operated and used, and any medical device licensing application made by the relevant responsible person and unit shall not be accepted within 10 years; if the value of the medical devices illegally manufactured, operated and used is less than RMB 10,000 Yuan, a fine above RMB 50,000 Yuan but less than RMB 150,000 Yuan shall be imposed; if the value of the medical devices is above RMB 10,000 Yuan, a fine more than 15 times but no more than 30 times of the value of the goods shall be imposed. In serious cases, the enterprise shall be ordered to suspend production and business. The income from the organization during the occurrence of the illegal act of legal representative, principal responsible person, person(s) in charge and other directly responsible personnel of the illegal organization shall be confiscated, and a fine of more than 30% and less than 3 times of the income shall be imposed. They shall be prohibited from engaging in the production and operation of medical devices for a lifetime.

The Medical Device License is not allowed to be forged, altered, transacted, leased and lent, in case of any violation, the License shall be seized or revoked by the original certificate–issuing authority and illegal incomes shall be confiscated. If the illegal incomes are less than RMB 10,000 Yuan, the enterprise involved shall be imposed a fine of no less than RMB 50,000 Yuan and no more than RMB 100,000 Yuan. If the illegal incomes are more than RMB 10,000 Yuan, the enterprise involved shall be imposed a fine of no less than 10 times of the illegal incomes and no more than 20 times of the illegal incomes. Any activity against the public security administration shall be given public security punishment by the Public Security Organs.

Article 84 Under any of the following circumstances, the medical product administration shall publish the information of the enterprise and the names of medical devices involved to the public and order it to make rectifications within a time limit; if it fails to make rectifications within the time limit, the illegal income and the medical devices illegally produced and operated shall be confiscated; if the value of the medical devices illegally produced and operated is less than RMB 10,000 Yuan, it shall also be fined not less than RMB 10,000 Yuan but not more than RMB 50,000 Yuan; if the value of the medical devices is more than RMB 10,000 Yuan, it shall also be fined more than 5 times and less than 20 times of the value of the medical devices. In serious cases, the income obtained from the organization during the occurrence of the illegal act of the legal representative, principal responsible person, person(s) in charge and other directly responsible personnel of the illegal organization shall be confiscated, and a fine of not less than 30% but not more than 2 times of the income shall be imposed. In addition, they shall be prohibited from engaging in the production and operation of medical devices within five years:

(1) Manufacturing and operating Class I medical devices without filing;

(2) Engaging in the manufacturing of Class I medical devices without filing;

(3) Operating of Class II medical devices that shall be filed but have not been filed;

(4) The materials that have been filed do not meet the requirements.

Article 85 In case that the applicant provides false materials when applying for the filing, the medical product administration shall publish the information of the enterprise who applies for the filing and the names of medical devices involved to the public, confiscate the illegal revenue and the medical devices illegally manufactured and operated; if the value of the medical devices illegally manufactured and operated is less than RMB 10,000 Yuan, a fine above RMB 20,000 Yuan but less than RMB 50,000 Yuan shall be imposed; if the value of the medical devices is above RMB 10,000 Yuan, a fine more than 5 times but no more than 20 times of the value of the goods shall be imposed. In serious cases, the party involved shall be ordered to suspend production or business operation. The income from the organization during the occurrence of the illegal act of legal representative, principal responsible person, person(s) in charge and other directly responsible personnel of the illegal organization shall be confiscated, and a fine of more than 30% and less than 3 times of the income shall be imposed. They shall be prohibited from engaging in the production and operation of medical devices for a lifetime.

Article 86 In the case of any of the following circumstances, the medical product administrations shall order the party involved to make corrections, confiscate the medical devices manufactured, operated or used illegally. If the value of the medical devices manufactured, operated or used illegally is less than RMB 10,000 Yuan, the party involved shall be imposed a fine of no less than RMB 20,000 Yuan and no more than RMB 50,000 Yuan. If the value of the medical devices manufactured, operated or used illegally is more than RMB 10,000 Yuan, the party involved shall be imposed a fine of no less than 5 times of the value and no more than 20 times of the value. In serious cases, the party involved shall be ordered to suspend production or business operation until the relevant Medical Device Registration Certificate, Medical Device Manufacturing License or Medical Device Operating License is revoked by the original certificate-issuing authority. The income from the organization during the occurrence of the illegal act of legal representative, principal responsible person, person(s) in charge and other directly responsible personnel of the illegal organization shall be confiscated, and a fine of more than 30% and less than 3 times of the income shall be imposed. They shall be prohibited from engaging in the production and operation of medical devices for 10 years:

(1) Manufacture, operate or use those medical devices, which cannot comply with the requirements of relevant mandatory standards or the registered or recorded product technical requirements;

(2) The medical device manufacturing enterprise fails to conduct the production activities in accordance with the registered or recorded product

technical requirements, or the medical device manufacturing enterprise fails to establish Quality Management System (QMS) and keep the effective operation in accordance with the stipulations of the Regulations, thus affecting the safety and effectiveness of the products;

(3) Operate or use those medical devices, which have no qualified certificates as well as those which are expired, ineffective and disused, or use those medical devices which are not legally registered;

(4) The party involved refuses to recall devices or stop manufacturing, importing and operating activities after being ordered by medical product administration to recall relevant devices or stop manufacturing, importing and operating activities;

(5) Entrust those enterprises which do not possess those conditions stipulated in the Regulations to produce medical devices, or fail to manage the production activities of the Entrusted Party;

(6) The party involved imports expired, ineffective, disused and other used medical devices.

Article 87 If the medical device operating enterprises and organization using medical devices have conducted checking of incoming goods and other obligations prescribed in the Regulations, and can provide sufficient evidences to prove that they are not aware that the medical devices they have operated and used comply with the conditions stated in Item 1 of Paragraph 1 of Article 81, Item 1 of Article 84, Item 1 and Item 3 of Article 86 of the Regulations, and can provide the actual source of those goods, they can be exempted from relevant administrative punishments, but the illegal medical devices they have operated and used shall be confiscated.

Article 88 In the case of any of the following circumstances, the medical product administration shall order the party involved to make corrections and the party involved shall be imposed a fine of no less than RMB 10,000 Yuan and no more than RMB 50,000 Yuan. If the party involved refuses to make corrections, the party involved shall be imposed a fine of no less than RMB 50,000 Yuan and no more than RMB 100,000 Yuan. In serious cases, the party involved shall be ordered to suspend production or business operation until the relevant Medical Device Manufacturing License or Medical Device Operating License is revoked by the original certificate–issuing authority. The income from the organization during the occurrence of the illegal act of legal representative, principal responsible person, person(s) in charge and other directly responsible personnel of the illegal organization shall be confiscated, and a fine of more than 30% and less than 2 times of the income shall be imposed. They shall be prohibited from engaging in the production and operation of medical devices for 5 years:

(1) Fail to make corrections, stop the production activities or report the situation in accordance with the requirements set forth in the Regulations when the production conditions change and do not comply with the requirements of the medical device QMS anymore;

(2) The production, instructions for use and labels of medical devices cannot comply with the requirements of the Regulations;

(3) Fail to transport and store medical devices in accordance with the requirements indicated in the instructions for use and labels of medical devices;

(4) Transfer expired, ineffective, disused and unqualified medical devices.

Article 89 In the case of any of the following circumstances, the medical product administration and the competent health authority shall order the party involved to make corrections and give a warning accordingly. If the party involved refuses to make corrections, the party involved shall be imposed a fine of no less than RMB 10,000 Yuan and no more than RMB 100,000 Yuan. In serious cases, the party involved shall be ordered to suspend production or business operation until the relevant Medical Device Registration Certificate, Medical Device Manufacturing License or Medical Device Operating License is revoked by the original certificate-issuing authority. The legal representative, principal responsible person, person(s) in charge and other directly responsible personnel of the illegal organization shall be fined not less than RMB 10,000 Yuan but not more than RMB 30,000 Yuan:

(1) Fail to submit the QMS self-inspection report in accordance with relevant requirements;

(2) Purchase medical devices from suppliers without legal qualification;

(3) The medical device operating enterprise or the organization using medical devices fails to establish and conduct the filing system for the incoming inspection in accordance with the stipulations of the Regulations;

(4) The operating enterprise wholesaling Class Ⅱ / Ⅲ medical devices or retailing Class Ⅲ medical devices fails to establish and conduct the sales filing system in accordance with the stipulations of the Regulations;

(5) The medical device registrants, filing applicant, or manufacturing or operating enterprise or organization using medical devices fails to conduct adverse event monitoring according to the provisions of the Regulations, fails to report adverse events as required, or fails to coordinate with the Technology Institutions for Medical Device Adverse Event Monitoring, the medical product administration, or the competent health department to investigate the medical device adverse events;

(6) The medical device registrants and filing applicants fail to formulate post-market research and risk control plans and ensure their effective implementation in accordance with relevant provisions;

(7) The medical device registrants and filing applicant fail to establish and implement the product traceability system in accordance with the provisions;

(8) The medical device registrants, filing applicant and operating enterprises fail to notify the medical product administration in accordance with the provisions when engaging in network sales of medical devices;

(9) As for the medical devices needing to be checked, inspected, calibrated and maintained periodically, the organization using these medical devices fails to check, inspect, calibrate and maintain these medical devices periodically, make records accordingly in accordance with the requirements of instructions for use, and timely perform analysis and evaluation to ensure that medical devices are in good condition;

(10) The organization using medical devices fails to properly keep the source materials of the purchased Class III medical devices.

Article 90 In the case of any of the following circumstances, the competent health authority under the people's government at or above the county level shall order the party involved to make corrections and give a warning accordingly. If the party involved refuses to make corrections, the party involved shall be imposed a fine of no less than RMB 50,000 Yuan and no more than RMB 100,000 Yuan. In serious cases, it shall be fined not less than RMB 100,000 but not more than RMB 300,000, and it shall be ordered to suspend the use of relevant medical devices until the relevant Practicing License is revoked by the original certificate-issuing authority. The income from the organization during the occurrence of the illegal act of legal representative, principal responsible person, person(s) in charge and other directly responsible personnel of the illegal organization shall be confiscated, and a fine of more than 30% and less than 3 times of the income shall be imposed. And punishment shall be given according to law:

(1) The organization using medical devices which can be repeatedly used fails to follow the stipulated instructions about sterilization and administration;

(2) The organization using medical device repeatedly uses single-use medical devices, or the organization fails to destroy the single-use medical devices which have been used in accordance with relevant regulations;

(3) The organization using medical devices fails to record the information of large medical equipment and implantable or interventional medical devices in the medical records and other related records;

(4) When the potential safety hazards of medical devices in use are discovered, the organization using these medical devices fails to stop using these medical devices immediately and inform the parties involved to perform the maintenance, or the organization continues using these medical devices which cannot comply with the safety criteria for use after the maintenance;

(5) The organization using medical devices that use large medical equipment against the regulation and cannot ensure medical quality and safety.

Article 91 Those who import medical devices in violation of the relevant laws and administrative regulations on import and export commodity inspection shall be dealt with by CIQ according to law.

Article 92 Where the operator of an e-commerce platform providing services for online transaction of medical devices violates the Regulations and fails to implement real-name registration, to review the license, registration and filing status, to stop and report violations, to suspend providing online transaction platform services, etc., relevant punishment shall be imposed by the medical product administration according to the *E-commerce Law of the People's Republic of China*.

Article 93 If a clinical trial is carried out without the filing of a medical device clinical trial institution, the medical product administration shall order it to stop the clinical trial and make rectifications; if it refuses to make rectifications, the clinical trial data shall not be used for product registration and filing, and the organization shall be fined not less than RMB 50,000 Yuan but not more than RMB 100,000 Yuan, and the case shall be announced to the public; if serious consequences are caused, it shall be prohibited from carrying out relevant professional clinical trials of medical devices within five years and shall be fined not less than RMB 100,000 but no more than RMB 300,000. The competent health department shall confiscate the income obtained from the organization during the period of the illegal act by the legal representative, principal responsible person, person(s) in charge and other directly responsible personnel of the illegal organization and impose a fine of more than 30% and less than 3 times of the income, and punishment shall be given according to law.

Where a clinical trial sponsor carries out a clinical trial without filing, the medical product administration shall instruct the sponsor to stop the clinical trial, impose a fine above RMB 50,000 Yuan but less than RMB 100,000 Yuan on the sponsor, and announce to the public; where serious consequences are caused, a fine above RMB 100,000 Yuan but less than RMB 300,000 Yuan shall be imposed. The clinical trial data shall not be used for product registration and filing, and the medical device registration applications submitted by relevant responsible persons and the organization will not be accepted within 5 years.

Where a clinical trial sponsor carries out a clinical trial of Class III medical devices with higher risks to human beings without approval, the medical product administration shall instruct the sponsor to stop the clinical trial immediately, impose a penalty above RMB 100,000 Yuan but less than RMB 300,000 Yuan on the sponsor and announce to the public; where serious consequences are caused, a penalty above RMB 300,000 Yuan but less than RMB 1,000,000 Yuan shall be imposed. The clinical trial data shall not be used for product registration; the application for medical device clinical trials and medical device registration submitted by relevant responsible persons and units shall not be accepted within 10 years; and confiscate the illegal revenue obtained by the legal representative, principal responsible person, person(s) in charge and other directly responsible personnel during the occurrence of the illegal activities from their units, a penalty between 30% of and 3 times the illegal revenue shall be given.

Article 94 If a medical device clinical trial institution fails to comply with the clinical trial quality management standards, the medical product administration shall order it to make rectifications or immediately stop the clinical trial, and impose a fine of not less than RMB 50,000 Yuan but not more than RMB 100,000 Yuan; if serious consequences are caused, it shall be prohibited from carrying out clinical trials of relevant professional medical devices within five years, and the competent health department shall confiscate the income obtained from their organization during the period of the illegal act by the legal representative, principal responsible person, person(s) in charge and other directly responsible personnel, and impose a fine of more than 30% and less than 3 times of the income they have obtained, and punishment shall be given according to law.

Article 95 The clinical trial testing institutions of medical devices offering false reports shall be imposed the fine of no less than RMB 100,000 Yuan and no more than RMB 300,000 Yuan by the medical product administration; all illegal incomes, if any, shall be confiscated; the organization shall be prohibited from carrying out relevant professional medical device clinical trials within 10 years; the competent health department shall confiscate the income from the organization made by the legal representative, principal responsible person, person(s) in charge and other directly responsible personnel of the illegal organization during the period of illegal act. In addition, they shall be fined more than 30% and less than 3 times of their income and punishment shall be given according to law.

Article 96 If the medical device testing institution issues false test reports, the corresponding qualification–awarding authority shall revoke the Qualification Certificate for Medical Device Testing and shall not accept the qualification authentication application submitted by the relevant person in charge and the organization within 10 years. The institute involved shall be imposed a fine of no less than RMB 100,000 Yuan and no more than RMB 300,000 Yuan; all illegal incomes, if any, shall be confiscated. The income from the organization during the occurrence of the illegal act of legal representative, principal responsible person, person(s) in charge and other directly responsible personnel of the illegal organization shall be confiscated, and a fine of more than 30% and less than 3 times of the income shall be imposed; the person who has been fired is not allowed to be engaged in works related to medical device testing within 10 years since the penalty decision of being fired has been made.

Article 97 Whoever violates the provisions of the Regulations on advertising administration of medical devices shall be punished in accordance with the provisions of the *Advertising Law of the People's Republic of China*.

Article 98 If a domestic enterprise legal person designated by an overseas medical device registrants or filing applicant fails to perform relevant obligations in accordance with the Regulations, the medical product administration of the people's government of the province, autonomous region or municipality directly under the central government shall order it to make rectifications, give a warning and impose a fine of not less than RMB 50,000 Yuan but not more than RMB 100,000 Yuan; in serious cases, it shall be fined not less than RMB 100,000 Yuan but not more than RMB 500,000 Yuan, and its legal representative, principal responsible person, person(s) in charge and other directly responsible personnel shall be prohibited from being engaged in the production and operation of medical devices within 5 years.

If the foreign medical device registrants and filing applicant refuse to execute the administrative penalty decisions made in accordance with the Regulations, they shall be prohibited from importing medical devices within 10 years.

Article 99 Where any institution engaged in research, development, manufacture, operation and testing of medical device employs the personnel prohibited from conducting manufacture, operation and testing of medical device in violation of the Regulations, the medical product administration shall order it to make corrections and give a warning to it; in case the concerned institution refuses to make correction, the party involved shall be ordered to suspend production or business operation until the relevant license is revoked.

Article 100 The Medical Device Technical Review Center or the Technology Institutions for Medical Device Adverse Event Monitoring who fail to perform duties in accordance with the stipulation of the Regulations and result in serious mistakes on the technical review and monitoring shall be ordered by the medical product administration to make corrections, circulate a notice of criticism and give a warning accordingly. If the consequences are serious, the legal representative, principal responsible person, person(s) in charge and other directly responsible personnel shall be punished in accordance with the law.

Article 101 Any staff member of the medical product administration or other relevant departments who, in violation of the provisions of the Regulations, abuses his/her power, neglects his/her duty or engages in malpractice for personal gain, shall be punished according to law.

Article 102 If some activities against the Regulations constitute a crime, the party involved shall be subject to criminal liabilities in accordance with law. If personal injuries, property damages or other damages are caused, the party involved shall undertake compensation liabilities in accordance with law.

Chapter VIII Supplementary Provisions

Article 103 The definition of the following terms in the Regulations:

"Medical device" means any instrument, apparatus, implement, in vitro reagent, calibrator, material or other similar or related article, including software needed, intended to be used for human beings directly or indirectly, which does not achieve its primary intended action by pharmacological, immunological or metabolic means, but which may be assisted in its intended function by such means, for one or more of the specific purpose(s) of:

(1) Diagnosis, prevention, monitoring, treatment or alleviation of disease;

(2) Diagnosis, monitoring, treatment, alleviation of or functional compensation for an injury;

(3) Investigation, replacement, modification, or support of the anatomy or of a physiological process;

(4) Supporting or sustaining life;

(5) Control of pregnancy;

(6) Providing information for medical or diagnostic purposes by means of in vitro examination of specimens derived from the human body.

A registrant or filing applicant of medical device refers to an enterprise or R&D institution that has obtained a Registration Certificate for Medical

Device or completed the filing of medical device.

"Organizations using medical devices" refer to those organizations that provide other people with medical services or other technical services by sing medical devices, including medical institutions, technical service institutions for family planning, as well as blood stations, blood plasma stations and adaptive organizations for rehabilitative and assistive devices.

Large medical equipment refers to the large medical devices based on complex technology, requiring large investment, high operating cost, huge impact on the medical fee and shall be incorporated into the catalogue management.

Article 104 Fees can be charged for the registration of medical devices. The specific charging items and charging standards shall be stipulated in accordance with relevant provisions of the finance and pricing departments under the State Council.

Article 105 Provisions on the Medical Devices Developed by Medical Institutions for Dealing with Public Health Emergencies shall be formulated by NMPA jointly with the competent health authority under the State Council.

The storage, allocation and supply of non-profit contraceptive devices shall comply with the provisions formulated by the competent health authority under the State Council together with the medical product administration.

The technical guidelines on TCM Medical Devices shall be formulated by medical product administration in conjunction with State Administration of Traditional Chinese Medicine under the State Council.

Article 106 The supervision and administration of medical devices used for armed forces shall be carried out in accordance with the Regulations and the relevant provisions of the military.

Article 107 The Regulations shall come into force from June 1, 2021.

Measures for the Administration of Registration and Filing of Medical Devices

(Decree No.47 of the State Administration for Market Regulation)

CHAPTER I General

Article 1 This Measures is formulated according to the Regulations for the Supervision and Administration of Medical Devices, aiming to regulate the registration and filing of medical devices and ensure their safety, effectiveness and controllable quality.

Article 2 These Measures shall apply to the registration, filing and supervision and administration of medical devices within the territory of the People's Republic of China.

Article 3 Medical device registration is the process of medical device registration applicant (hereinafter referred to as the Applicant) submitting an application for medical device registration according to legal procedures and requirements, and the medical products administration conducting review on their safety, effectiveness and quality controllability etc. based on scientific cognition in accordance with laws and regulations, then deciding if the application can be allowed.

Medical device filing is the process of medical device filing applicants (hereinafter referred to as filing applicants) submitting filing materials to the medical products administration in accordance with legal procedures and requirements, and the medical products administration filing the submitted filing materials for future reference.

Article 4 The National Medical Products Administration (NMPA) shall take charge of the national medical device registration and filling management, establish the medical device registration and filling management system, organize the evaluation, review and approval of the domestic Class III and imported Class II and Class III medical devices, filing of the imported Class I medical devices, as well as related supervision and management work according to law; supervise and guide the registration and filing of local medical devices.

Article 5 The Center for Medical Device Evaluation of NMPA (hereinafter referred to as CMDE) is responsible for the clinical trial application of medical devices requiring clinical trial approval, and other technical evaluation such as the application for registration, change registration, renewal registration of domestic Class III and imported Class II and Class III medical devices.

The Center for Medical Device Standardization Administration of NMPA, National Institutes for Food and Drug Control, Center for Food and Drug Inspection of NMPA (hereinafter referred to as Inspection Center), Center for Drug Re-evaluation of NMPA, Administrative Affairs Acceptance Service and Complaint Reporting Center of NMPA, Information Center of NMPA and other professional technical institutions undertake the management, classification, definition, inspection, audit, monitoring and evaluation, certification preparation and delivery of medical device standards required for the implementation of medical device supervision and management as well as corresponding information construction, management and related work.

Article 6 The medical products administration of the provinces, autonomous regions and municipalities directly under the Central Government shall be responsible for the registration of the following medical devices within their respective administrative areas:

(1) Evaluation, review and approval of the registration of domestic class II medical device;

(2) Verification of the quality management systems of domestic class II and class III medical devices;

(3) Organization of the supervision and administration of medical device clinical trial institutions and clinical trials according to law;

(4) Supervision and guidance on the filing of domestic class I medical devices by the medical products administration at the municipal level divided into districts.

The professional technical institutions for medical devices set or designated by the medical products administration of the provinces, autonomous regions and municipalities directly under the Central Government shall take charge of the technical evaluation, inspection, validation, monitoring and evaluation required for the implementation of medical device supervision and administration according to law.

The medical products administration at the municipal level divided into districts shall be responsible for the filing management of domestic class I medical devices.

Article 7 The registration and filing management of medical devices shall follow the principles of legality, science, openness, fairness and impartiality.

Article 8 Class I medical devices shall be subject to product filing management. Class II and Class III medical devices shall be subject to product registration management.

The domestic Class I medical devices shall be filed, and the filing applicant shall submit the filing materials to the medical products administration at the municipal level divided into districts.

The domestic Class II medical devices shall be reviewed by the medical products administration of the provinces, autonomous regions and municipalities directly under the Central Government, and the Medical Device Registration Certificate shall be issued after approval.

The domestic Class III medical devices shall be reviewed and approved by the NMPA, and then a Medical Device Registration Certificate shall be issued.

The imported Class I medical devices shall be filed, the filing applicants shall submit the filing materials to the NMPA.

The imported Class II and Class III medical devices shall be reviewed and approved by the NMPA, and then a Medical Device Registration Certificate shall be issued.

Article 9 It is emphasized that the registrants and filing applicants of medical devices should strengthen the whole life cycle management of medical devices, and take responsibility for the safety, effectiveness and quality controllability of medical devices in the whole process of development, manufacturing, operation and use according to law.

Article 10 The NMPA shall give priority to the review and approval of clinically urgent-needed medical devices, implement special review and approval for innovative medical devices, encourage the research and innovation of medical devices, and promote the high-quality development of medical device industry.

Article 11 The NMPA shall establish and improve systems such as medical device standards and technical guidelines in accordance with the law, standardize medical device technical evaluation and approval as well as quality management system audit, and guide and serve medical device R&D and registration applications.

Article 12 The medical products administration shall timely disclose the relevant information of medical device registration and filing according to law. The applicant can query the review and approval progress and results, and the public can consult the review and approval results.

Without the consent of the applicant, the medical products administration, professional technical institutions and their staff, experts participating in the review and other personnel shall not disclose the trade secrets, undisclosed information or confidential business information submitted by the applicant or the filing applicant, except as otherwise specified by law or involving national security and major social and public interests.

CHAPTER II Basic Requirements

Article 13 Medical device registration and filing shall comply with relevant laws, regulations, rules, and mandatory standards, follow the essential principles of medical device safety and performance, and refer to relevant technical guidelines to prove that the registered and filed medical devices are safe, effective, and controllable in quality, and ensure that the information in the whole process is true, accurate, complete and traceable.

Article 14 Applicants and filing applicants shall be enterprises or research institutions that can bear corresponding legal responsibilities.

Overseas applicants and filing applicants shall designate enterprise legal persons in China as agents to handle the registration and filing of relevant medical devices. The agent shall assist the registrants and filing applicants to fulfill the obligations specified in paragraph 1 of Article 20 of the *Regulations for the Supervision and Administration of Medical Devices*, and assist the overseas registrants and filing applicants to implement the corresponding legal responsibilities.

Article 15 The applicants and filing applicants shall establish a quality management system suitable for the product and maintain its effective operation.

Article 16 The personnel handling registration and filing matters of medical devices shall have corresponding professional knowledge and be familiar with the laws, regulations, rules and related regulations of registration management of medical device registration and filing administration.

Article 17 When applying for registration or filing, the applicant or filing applicant shall submit relevant materials in accordance with the requirements for registration and filing of the NMPA, and shall be responsible for the authenticity of the materials.

The registration and filing materials shall be in Chinese language. Source text shall also be provided for translations from foreign language materials. For references of unpublished literatures, proof of permission by copyright owner of the materials shall be provided.

Article 18 When applying for registration of imported medical devices and filing imported medical devices, it shall submit the certification documents that the competent authorities of the country (region) where the applicants and the filing applicant are registered or where the production address is located approve the medical devices to be marketed and sold.

If the country (region) where the registered place or production address of the applicants and filing applicants does not manage this product as medical device, the applicants and filing applicants need to provide relevant documents, including certificates issued by the said country (region) approving the marketing of this product.

For innovative medical devices that are not marketed in the country (region) where the applicants or the filing applicants is registered or where the place of production is located, relevant documents need not be submitted.

Article 19 Medical devices shall comply with applicable mandatory standards. If the structural features, intended uses and use methods of the products are inconsistent with the scope of application of mandatory standards, the applicants and filing applicants shall explain that the mandatory standards are not applicable, and provide relevant materials.

If there are no mandatory standards, the applicants and filing applicants are encouraged to adopt recommended standards.

Article 20 The registration and filing of medical devices shall comply with the relevant requirements of the classification rules and classification catalogue of medical devices.

Article 21 The medical products administration shall continuously promote the reform of the evaluation, review and approval system, strengthen scientific research on medical device supervision and administration, establish a medical device registration management system led by technical evaluation and supported by audit, inspection, monitoring and evaluation, optimize the evaluation, review and approval process, improve the ability, quality and efficiency of evaluation, review and approval of medical devices.

Article 22 The professional technical institutions of medical devices shall establish and improve the communication system, clarify the form and content of communication, and organize communication with the applicant according to work needs.

Article 23 Professional technical institutions of medical devices shall establish an expert consultation system according to work needs, listen to expert opinions on major issues in the process of review, audit and inspection, and give full play to the technical support role of experts.

CHAPTER III Medical Devices Registration

Section I Product research and development

Article 24 The research and development of medical devices should follow the risk management principles and consider the existing recognized technical level, so as to ensure that all known and foreseeable risks and unexpected impacts of products are minimized and acceptable, and ensure that the benefits of products outweigh the risks in normal use.

Article 25 The engagement in the research and development of medical device products shall conform to the requirements of relevant laws, regulations and mandatory standards in China.

Article 26 The applicant or filing applicant shall prepare the product technical requirements for medical device to be registered or filed.

The product technical requirements mainly include the functional and safety indicators and test methods that can be objectively judged for the finished medical devices.

Medical devices shall meet the product technical requirements registered or filed.

Article 27 The applicants and filing applicants shall prepare the IFU and labels of the medical devices applying for registration or filing.

The IFU and labels shall comply with the requirements of Article 39 of the *Regulations for the Supervision and Administration of Medical Devices* and relevant provisions.

Article 28 In the research and development of medical devices, non-clinical study on medical devices shall be carried out according to the scope of application and technical characteristics of the products.

Non-clinical study includes product chemical and physical performance study, electrical safety study, radiation safety study, software study, biological characteristics study, biological materials safety study, disinfection and sterilization process study, animal test study, stability study, etc..

When applying for registration or filing, the non-clinical evidence generated in the research and development activities shall be submitted, including the overview of non-clinical study reports, study protocols and study reports.

Article 29 The functional and safety indicators and methods determined during the non-clinical study of medical devices shall be compatible with the intended use conditions and purposes of the products, and the study samples shall be representative and typical. If necessary, methodological verification and statistical analysis shall be carried out.

Article 30 When applying for registration or filing, test shall be carried out in accordance with the product technical requirements and a test report shall be submitted. Only those who pass the test can conduct clinical trials or apply for registration and filing.

Article 31 The products for test shall be able to represent the safety and effectiveness of the products applied for registration or filing, and their production shall meet the relevant requirements of the production quality management specifications of medical devices.

Article 32 The test report of medical device products submitted for registration or filing may be the self-test report issued by the applicants and filing applicants or the test report issued by a qualified medical device test institution entrusted.

Section II Clinical evaluation

Article 33 In addition to the circumstances specified in Article 34 of the Measures, clinical evaluation shall be conducted for the registration and filing of medical devices.

Clinical evaluation of medical devices refers to the activity of analyzing and evaluating clinical data by scientific and reasonable methods to confirm the safety and effectiveness of medical devices within their scope of application.

When applying for medical device registration, clinical evaluation data shall be submitted.

Article 34 Under any of the following circumstances, clinical evaluation may be exempted:

(1) With definite operating mechanism, established design, mature manufacturing process, have no serious adverse event record for predicate devices which have been marketed and clinically applied for years; and without changing the conventional purpose of use;

(2) Other circumstances that can prove the safety and effectiveness of the medical device through non-clinical evaluation.

For medical devices exempted from clinical evaluation, clinical evaluation data can be exempted from submission.

The catalogue of medical devices exempted from clinical evaluation shall be formulated, adjusted and published by the NMPA.

Article 35 The clinical evaluation of medical devices can be conducted on the basis of product characteristics, clinical risks and available clinical data. The safety and effectiveness of medical devices can be proved by conducting clinical trials, or by analyzing and evaluating clinical literature and clinical data of the predicate devices.

In accordance with the regulations of NMPA, when conducting clinical evaluation of medical devices, if the existing clinical literature and clinical data are insufficient to confirm the safety and effectiveness of the products, clinical trials shall be carried out.

The NMPA has formulated guidance for clinical evaluation of medical devices, specifying the requirements for clinical evaluation through the clinical literature and clinical data of predicate devices, the situations in which clinical trials need to be carried out, and the writing requirements for clinical evaluation reports.

Article 36 If the clinical evaluation is conducted through the clinical literature and clinical data of the predicate devices, the clinical evaluation data include the comparison between the registered products and the predicate devices, the analysis and evaluation of the clinical data of predicate devices, the scientific evidence and evaluation conclusion when there are differences between the registered products and the products of the same variety.

If clinical evaluation is carried out through clinical trials, the clinical evaluation data include clinical trial protocol, opinions of ethics committee, informed consent form, clinical trial report, etc..

Article 37 The clinical trials of medical devices shall be carried out in medical device clinical trial institutions that have the corresponding conditions and are filed in accordance with the regulations in accordance with the requirements of the Good Clinical Practice for Medical Devices. Before the commencement of the clinical trial, the clinical trial sponsor shall file the clinical trial with the medical products administration of the provinces, autonomous regions and municipalities directly under the Central Government. The production of clinical trial medical devices shall meet the relevant requirements of the Good Manufacturing Practice for Medical Devices.

Article 38 The clinical trial of Class III medical devices with higher risk to human body shall be approved by NMPA.

The review and approval of clinical trials is a process that the NMPA conducts a comprehensive analysis over medical devices to be carried out with a clinical trial according to the application of the applicant, including risk level, clinical trial protocol, analysis report of comparison between clinical benefits and risks, and determines whether to approve the conduct of the clinical trial.

The catalogue of Class Ⅲ medical devices that need to be reviewed and approved for clinical trials shall be formulated, adjusted and published by the NMPA. Clinical trials of Class Ⅲ medical devices that need to be reviewed and approved shall be carried out in qualified medical institutions at Grade III Class A level.

Article 39 If review and approval of clinical trials of medical devices are required, the applicants shall submit application dossiers such as overview materials, study materials, clinical materials, IFU and labels drafts according to relevant requirements.

Article 40 The CMDE shall evaluation the accepted clinical trial application. For the clinical trial application, a decision on whether to approve the application or not shall be made within 60 days from the date of acceptance, and the applicant shall be notified through the website of the CMDE. Failure to notify within the time limit shall be deemed as consent.

Article 41 If supplementary materials are required during the evaluation process, the applicant shall be informed once of all the contents that needs to be supplemented and corrected by the CMDE. The applicant shall provide the supplementary materials for one time according to the requirement of Deficiency Letter within one year. After receiving the supplementary materials, the CMDE shall complete the technical evaluation within the specified time limit.

If the applicant has objections to the content of Deficiency Letter, it may give its opinion in writing to the CMDE, along with rationales and corresponding technical supporting data.

If the applicant fails to submit supplementary materials within the time limit, the CMDE shall terminate the technical evaluation and make a decision of disapproval.

Article 42 For serious adverse events related to clinical trial medical devices or other serious safety risk information during the clinical trial of medical devices, the clinical trial sponsor shall report to the medical products administration of the provinces, autonomous regions and municipalities directly under the Central Government where the clinical trial institution is located and take risk control measures in accordance with relevant requirements. If no risk control measures are taken, the medical products administration of the provinces, autonomous regions and municipalities directly under the Central Government shall order the sponsor to take corresponding risk control measures according to law.

Article 43 In case of the occurrence of large–scale serious adverse events in clinical trial of medical devices or other major safety problems, the sponsor shall suspend or terminate the clinical trial of medical devices and report to the medical products administration of the provinces, autonomous regions and municipalities directly under the Central Government where the sponsor is located and where the clinical trial institution is located. If it has not been suspended or terminated, the medical products administration of the provinces, autonomous regions and municipalities directly under the Central Government shall order the sponsor to take corresponding risk control measures according to law.

Article 44 Clinical trial that has been carried out, in case of any of the following circumstances, the NMPA shall order the applicant to terminate the clinical trial of medical devices:

(1) The clinical trial application dossiers are false;

(2) The latest study confirmed the existence of problems in the ethicality and scientificity of previously approved clinical trials;

(3) Other circumstances that should be terminated.

Article 45 Clinical trials of medical devices shall be implemented within 3 years after approval. If no informed consent form is signed by the subject within 3 years from the date of approval of the application for clinical trial of medical devices, the license for clinical trial of medical devices will automatically become invalid. If clinical trials are still needed, a new application shall be made.

Article 46 If a medical device used to treat a serious life–threatening disease with no effective treatment means is under clinical trial and may benefit patients after medical observation, it can be used free of charge for other patients with the same condition in the institution where the clinical trial of the medical device is being carried out after ethical review and informed consent, and their safety data can be used for application for medical devices registration.

Section III Verification of Registration System

Article 47 The applicant shall submit relevant materials related to the quality management system related to product research and development and production when applying for registration. If the medical products administration that accepts the application for registration considers it is necessary to verify the quality management system during the product technical evaluation, it shall organize the quality management system audit and access the original data when necessary.

Article 48 The audit of the quality management system of domestic

Class III medical device is carried out by the medical products administration of the provinces, autonomous regions and municipalities directly under the Central Government where the applicant is located after notified by the CMDE.

The audit of the quality management system of domestic Class II medical device is carried out by the medical products administration of the provinces, autonomous regions and municipalities directly under the Central Government where the applicant is located.

Article 49 The medical products administration of the provinces, autonomous regions and municipalities directly under the Central Government shall carry out quality management systems audit in accordance with the requirements of the Good Manufacturing Practice for Medical Devices, focusing on whether the applicant has established a quality management system suitable for the product in accordance with the requirements of the Good Manufacturing Practice for Medical Devices, and the design and development, production management and quality control related to product research and development and production.

During the process of audit, the authenticity of products for test and clinical trial products shall also be verified at the same time, focusing on checking the relevant records of the design and development process, as well as the relevant records of the production process of tested products and clinical trial products.

Where a self-test report is submitted, key audit shall be carried out on the test capability and test results of the applicants and filing applicants or the entrusted institution in the process of research and development.

Article 50 The medical products administration of the provinces, autonomous regions and municipalities directly under the Central Government may carry out quality management systems audit by means of data review or on-site inspection. According to the specific situation of the applicant, the supervision and inspection situation, and the comparison results between the products applied for registration this time and the products that have passed audit on the production conditions and processes, determining whether site inspection and inspection contents shall be carried out, so as to avoid repeated inspection.

Article 51 When conducting technical evaluation on imported class II and class III medical devices, if the CMDE considers it is necessary to verify the quality management systems, it shall notify the Audit and Inspection Center of the NMPA to carry out audit according to relevant requirements.

Section IV Product Registration

Article 52 After completing the research on the safety and effectiveness of medical devices supporting the registration, and making preparations for the audit by the quality management system, the applicant shall apply for the medical device registration, and submit the following application dossiers to the medical products administration through online registration and other application paths according to relevant requirements:

(1) Data for product risk analysis;

(2) Product technical requirements;

(3) Product test report;

(4) Clinical evaluation data;

(5) IFU and Label Draft of Product;

(6) Quality management system documents related to product research and development and production;

(7) Other necessary documents to demonstrate the safety and effectiveness of the products.

Article 53 The medical products administration shall conduct review on application dossiers after accepting an application, and handle respectively according to the following circumstances:

(1) The application items are within the scope of the administrative authority with complete application dossiers and in conformity with the formal review, the application shall be accepted;

(2) If there are errors in the application dossiers that can be corrected on the spot, the applicant is allowed to make rectification on the spot;

(3) If the application dossiers are incomplete or do not comply with the legal form, the applicant shall be informed of all contents to be supplemented or corrected in one time on site or within 5 working days; if failing to inform the applicant within the specified time, the application materials shall be accepted from the receipt date;

(4) If the application items don't fail within the scope of the administrative authority, the decision of not to accept the application shall be made immediately, and the applicant shall be notified to apply to the relevant administrative authority.

For acceptance or rejection of an application for medical device registration, the medical products administration shall issue a notice of acceptance or rejection with the special seal of the department and dated.

If the applicant needs to pay fees after the acceptance of the application for medical device registration, the applicant shall pay the fees in accordance with the provisions. If the applicant fails to pay the fee within the specified time limit, it shall be deemed that the applicant voluntarily withdraws the application, and the medical products administration shall terminate its registration procedure.

Article 54 If supplementary and correction materials are required during technical evaluation, the technical evaluation institution shall notify all the contents that need to be supplemented and corrected at one time. The applicant shall, within one year after receiving the Deficiency Letter, provide supplementary materials once in accordance with the requirements of the Deficiency Letter, and the technical evaluation institution shall complete the technical evaluation within the prescribed time limit after receiving the supplementary materials.

If the applicant has objections to the content of Deficiency Letter, it may give its opinion in writing to the corresponding technical evaluation institution, along with rationales and corresponding technical supporting data.

If the applicant fails to submit supplementary materials within the time limit, the technical evaluation shall be terminated, and the medical products administration shall make a decision of not registering.

Article 55 For an accepted registration application, the applicant may, before making the decision on administrative license, apply to the medical products administration that accepted the application for withdrawal of the registration application and relevant materials, and explain the reasons. If it agrees to withdraw the application, the medical products administration shall terminate its registration procedure.

If any illegal act such as concealing the true situation or providing false information is found in the process of evaluation, audit, review and approval, it shall be handled according to law, and the applicant shall not withdraw the application for registration of medical devices.

Article 56 For an accepted registration application, if there is evidence that the registration application dossiers may be false, the medical products administration may suspend the evaluation, review and approval. It will be decided whether it shall be further reviewed or the registration application shall be denied after audit.

Article 57 During the evaluation of medical device registration application, if the review conclusion is not passed, the technical evaluation institution shall inform the applicant of the reasons for the failure, and the applicant may raise an objection to the technical evaluation institution within 15 days, and the content of the objection is limited to the original application items and the original application dossiers. The technical evaluation institution shall conduct comprehensive evaluation and feedback to the applicant based on the applicant's objections. The objection processing time is not included in the evaluation time limit.

Article 58 The medical products administration accepting the registration application shall make a decision on whether to approve it after the technical evaluation is completed. Medical devices meeting the requirements of safety, effectiveness and controllable in quality shall be approved for registration and issued with Medical Device Registration Certificate, and the approved product technical requirements will be distributed to the applicant in the form of attachment. For the products that are not approved for registration, the reasons shall be given in writing, and the applicant shall be informed of its right of applying for administrative reconsideration or appealing to administrative proceeding by law.

The validity period of the Medical Device Registration Certificate is five years.

Article 59 For accepted registration application, in case of any of the following circumstances, the medical products administration shall make a decision not to register and inform the applicant:

(1) The applicant's study on the safety, effectiveness and quality controllability of the medical devices to be marketed and the results cannot

prove that the products are safe, effective and controllable in quality;

(2) The quality management systems fail to pass the audit, and the applicant refuses to accept the on-site inspection of the quality management systems;

(3) The registration application dossiers are false;

(4) The contents of the registration application dossiers are confusing, contradictory, or obviously inconsistent with the application items, and the product can not be proved to be safe, effective and controllable in quality;

(5) Other circumstances under which the registration application shall not be approved.

Article 60 The medical products administration shall announce to the public and hold a hearing on the matters that shall be heard for the implementation of administrative license according to laws, regulations and rules, or other major administrative license matters involving public interests that the medical products administration deems necessary. If the application for medical devices registration directly involves a significant interest relationship between the applicant and others, the medical products administration shall inform the applicant and interested parties that they have the right to request a hearing before making an administrative license decision.

Article 61 For urgent-needed medical devices for treatment of rare diseases, diseases which are seriously life-threatening and have no effective treatment means, and those used for coping with public health emergencies, the medical products administration may make a conditional approval decision, specify the validity period, the study work that needs to be completed after marketing, the completion time limit and other related matters in the Medical Device Registration Certificate.

Article 62 For conditionally approved medical devices, the registrant shall collect the data related to the benefits and risks of the medical devices after marketing, continuously monitor and assess the benefits and risks of the products, take effective measures to actively control risks, and complete study and submit relevant materials within the prescribed time limit as required.

Article 63 For conditionally approved medical devices, if the registrant fails to complete the studies or cannot prove that the benefits outweigh the risks, the registrant shall timely apply for the cancellation of the Medical Device Registration Certificate, and the medical products administration may cancel the Medical Device Registration Certificate according to law.

Article 64 For medical devices newly researched and developed that not listed in the classification catalogue, the applicant can directly apply for Class Ⅲ medical device registration or determine the device classification according to the classification principles and apply for classification validation to NMPA so as to apply for product registration or conduct filing for the product.

For medical devices that application is made directly for the registration of Class Ⅲ medical devices, the NMPA shall determine their classification in accordance with the risk level. For the domestic medical devices identified as Class Ⅱ or Class I, the applicant shall be informed to apply for registration or file with the corresponding medical products administration.

Article 65 For registered medical devices of which the management category is adjusted from high class to low class, the medical devices registration certificate shall continue to be valid within the period of validity. If renewal is needed upon expiration of its validity period, application for renewal or filling shall be submitted to the medical products administration in accordance with the adjusted classification 6 months before the expiration of the validity period of the Medical Device Registration Certificate.

If the medical device management category is adjusted from low to high, the registrant shall apply to the corresponding medical products administration for registration according to the changed category. The NMPA shall stipulate the time limit for completing the adjustment in the notice of adjustment of the management category.

Article 66 If the Medical Device Registration Certificate and its attachments are lost or damaged, the registrant shall apply to the original license issuing authority for reissuing, and the original license issuing authority shall verify and reissue the certificate.

Article 67 Where a patent dispute arises during the registration review or after approval, it shall be dealt with according to relevant laws and regulations.

CHAPTER IV Special Registration Procedures

Section I Registration procedures for innovative products

Article 68 For medical devices that meet the following requirements, the applicant may apply for applicable innovative product registration procedures:

(1) The applicant legally owns the patent for invention of core technology of the product through its dominant technical innovation activities in China, or obtains the patent for innovation in China or the right of use through legal transfer; and the time for applying for the registration procedure of innovative products shall be within 5 years from the date of patent authorization announcement; or the application of the patent for invention of the core technology has been made public by the patent administrative authority of the State Council. The Patent Searching and Consulting Center of the China National Intellectual Property Administration shall issue a search report indicating that the core technical scheme of the product has novelty and creativity;

(2) The applicant has completed the preliminary study on the product and the product is basically finalized, the study process is true and controlled, and the study data is complete and traceable;

(3) The main working principle/mechanism of action of a product is the first of its kind in China, the product performance or safety has radical improvement compared with similar products, the product is in the international leading level technically, and has significant value in clinical application.

Article 69 When apply for applicable innovative product registration procedures, the applicant shall submit an application for reviewing of innovative medical devices to the NMPA after the product is basically finalized. The NMPA shall organize experts to review, and those that meet the requirements shall be included in the registration procedure of innovative products.

Article 70 For the application of medical devices registration applicable to the registration procedure of innovative products, the NMPA and the institutions undertaking relevant technical work shall appoint special personnel to be responsible according to their respective responsibilities, communicate in time and provide guidance.

For the medical devices included in the registration procedure of innovative products, the CMDE can communicate with the applicant on major technical problems, major safety problems, clinical trial protocol, summary and evaluation of phased clinical trial results in product research and development before the acceptance of registration application and during technical evaluation.

Article 71 If the applicant voluntarily requests to terminate the medical devices included in the innovative product registration procedure, or the

NMPA finds that they no longer meet the requirements of the innovative product registration procedure, the NMPA shall terminate the innovative product registration procedure of relevant products and inform the applicant.

Article 72 Medical devices included in the innovative product registration procedure are not applicable to the innovative product registration procedure if the applicant fails to apply for registration within the prescribed time limit.

Section II Priority Registration Procedures

Article 73 Medical devices that meet one of the following conditions may apply for priority registration procedures:

(1) Diagnosis or treatment of rare diseases and malignant tumors with obvious clinical advantages; diagnosis or treatment of unique and multiple diseases of the elderly and there is no effective diagnosis or treatment method at present; used for children with obvious clinical advantages; or there is a clinical urgent-need and there is no medical device approved for registration of the same product in China;

(2) Medical devices that have been listed in the National Science and Technology Major Project or National Key Research and Development Project;

(3) Other medical devices subject to priority registration procedures as stipulated by the NMPA.

Article 74 When applicable to priority registration procedure, the applicant should submit an application for priority registration of medical devices to the medical products administration when applying for the registration of medical devices. In the case of Paragraph 1 of Article 73, the NMPA shall organize experts to conduct a review. If it meets the requirements, it shall be included in the priority registration procedure; if it falls under Paragraph 2 of Article 73, the CMDE shall review it. If it meets the requirements, it shall be included in the priority registration procedure; if it falls under Paragraph 3 of Article 73, the NMPA shall listen to opinions widely and organize experts to demonstrate to determine whether it shall be included in the priority registration procedure.

Article 75 For the medical device registration application included in the priority registration procedure, the NMPA shall give priority to the review and approval, and the medical products administration of the provinces, autonomous regions and municipalities directly under the Central Government shall give priority to the audit of the medical device registration quality management systems.

During the technical evaluation of medical device products included in the priority registration procedure, the CMDE shall actively communicate with the applicant in accordance with relevant regulations, and may arrange special exchanges when necessary.

Section III Emergency Registration Procedures

Article 76 The NMPA may, in accordance with the law, implement emergency registration for medical devices that are required for public health emergencies and have no similar products marketed in China, or that have similar products but whose supply cannot meet the needs for emergency treatment of public health emergencies.

Article 77 When applying for applicable emergency registration procedures, the applicant shall apply to the NMPA for emergency registration application. Those meeting the conditions shall be included into the emergency registration procedures.

Article 78 The NMPA shall immediately handle the application for registration of medical devices subject to emergency registration in accordance with the requirements of unified command, early intervention, on-call review and scientific review and approval, and carry out medical device product test, system audit and technical evaluation in parallel.

CHAPTER V Change Registration and Renewal of Registration

Section I Change Registration

Article 79 The registrant should take the initiative to carry out post-market study on medical devices, and further validate the safety, effectiveness and quality controllability of medical devices, and strengthen the continuous management of marketed medical devices.

In case of any substantial changes of the designs, raw materials, production process, scopes of application or use methods, etc., of the registered medical device products of Class II or Class III, which may affect the safety and effectiveness of such medical devices, registrants shall apply to the original registration departments for change registration. In case of any other change thereof, they should be filed with the original registration department within 30 days from the date of the change.

Product name, model, specification, structure and composition, scope of application, product technical requirements, and production address of imported medical devices, etc. stated in the Medical Device Registration Certificate, are matters specified in the preceding paragraph that need to be registered for change. The name and domicile of the registrant and the name and domicile of the agent belong to the matters that need to be filed as specified in the preceding paragraph. For change of domestic medical device production address, the registrant shall file a record when applying for change corresponding to production license.

In case of other changes, the registrant shall do the relevant work in accordance with the requirements of the quality management systems and report to the medical products administration in accordance with the regulations.

Article 80 For change of registration application, the technical evaluation institution shall focus on the changed part, and evaluate the safety, effectiveness and controllability in quality of the products after change to form a review opinion.

Where the medical products administration deems that it is necessary to inspect the quality management system during the technical evaluation of the application for change registration, it shall organize an inspection on the quality management system.

Article 81 Medical device registration change document shall be used together with the original Medical Device Registration Certificate, and the expiration date of the validity period is the same as the original Medical Device Registration Certificate.

Section II Renewal Registration

Article 82 If the Medical Device Registration Certificate is for renewal upon validity period, the registrant shall apply for renewal registration to the original registration department 6 months before the validity period of the Medical Device Registration Certificate, together with the application dossiers in accordance with the relevant requirements.

Except the situation stipulated in Article 83 in the Measures, the medical products administration, upon receipt the application for renewal registration, shall make decision on renewal registration prior to the validity period of the Medical Device Registration Certificate. If no decision is available after the due time, the renewal application shall be deemed having been approved.

Article 83 The renewal registration shall not be approved in any of the following circumstances:

(1) The applicant fails to apply for renewal registration within the specified time limit;

(2) The new mandatory standards for medical devices have been issued and implemented and the medical devices applying for renewal of application cannot comply with the new requirements;

(3) For the medical device with conditional approval, the items specified in the Medical Device Registration Certificate are not completed within the specified time limit.

Article 84 If the approval time of renewal registration is within the validity period of the original Medical Device Registration Certificate, the starting date of the validity period of the renewal registration certificate shall be the next day after the expiration date of the original Medical Device Registration Certificate; If the approval time is not within the validity period of the original Medical Device Registration Certificate, the starting date of the validity period of the Medical Device Registration Certificate for renewal registration shall be the date of approval of renewal registration.

Article 85 Where there is no provision in this chapter for the acceptance and approval procedures of the application for change registration application and renewal registration application of medical device, the relevant provisions of Chapter 3 of the Measures shall apply.

CHAPTER VI Medical Device Filing

Article 86 Filing for Class I medical devices shall be conducted prior to manufacturing.

Article 87 Filing of medical devices, the filing applicant shall submit the filing materials to the medical products administration in accordance with the

Regulations for the Supervision and Administration of Medical Devices and obtain the filing number.

Article 88 For a filed medical device, where the contents set forth in the filing information form and the filed product technical requirements are changed, and the filing applicant shall apply for change of filing information to the original filing authority and submit a description of the changes and related documents. The medical products administration shall publish the changes in the filing information.

Article 89 If the management category of the filed medical devices is adjusted to Class II or Class III medical devices, the filing applicant shall apply for registration in accordance with the relevant provisions of the Measures.

CHAPTER VII Working Time Limit

Article 90 The time limit stipulated in the Measures is the longest time for the acceptance, technical evaluation, audit and review and approval of medical device registration. The working time limit related to the special registration procedures shall be implemented according to the relevant provisions of the special registration procedures.

The CMDE and other professional technical institutions shall specify and publish their respective working procedures and time limit to the public.

Article 91 After receiving the medical device registration application and clinical trial application, the medical products administration should put forward the registration application dossiers to the technical evaluation institution within 3 working days after the date of acceptance. The acceptance requirements of clinical trial applications shall apply to the provisions of Article 53 of the Measures.

Article 92 The time limit for technical evaluation of medical device registration shall be implemented in accordance with the following provisions:

(1) The time limit for technical evaluation of medical device clinical trial application is 60 days, and the time limit for technical evaluation after supplementation and correction of application dossiers is 40 days;

(2) The time limit for technical evaluation of class II medical device registration application, change registration application and renewal registration application is 60 days, and the time limit for technical evaluation after supplementation and correction of application dossiers is 60 days;

(3) The technical evaluation time limit for the application for registration of Class Ⅲ medical devices, change registration application and renewal registration application is 90 days, and the technical evaluation time limit after supplementation and correction of application dossiers is 60 days.

Article 93 The time limit for audit of the quality management systems of Class Ⅲ medical devices in China shall be implemented in accordance with the following provisions:

(1) The CMDE shall notify the medical products administration of the provinces, autonomous regions and municipalities directly under the Central Government to start the audit within 10 days after accepting the application for medical device registration;

(2) The medical products administration of the provinces, autonomous regions and municipalities directly under the Central Government shall, in principle, complete the audit within 30 days after receiving the audit notice, and feed back the audit information, audit results and other related materials to the CMDE.

Article 94 The medical products administration accepting the application for registration shall make decisions within 20 working days from the dates when the review opinions are received.

Article 95 The medical products administration shall issue and serve the relevant administrative license documents within 10 days from the date of making the decision on review and approval of medical device registration.

Article 96 If it is necessary to extend the time limit due to special circumstances such as product characteristics and technical evaluation and audit, the extended time limit shall not exceed 1/2 of the original time limit. After being approved by the person in charge of relevant technical institutions such as medical device technical evaluation and audit, the technical institution that extended the time limit shall inform the applicant in writing and inform other relevant technical institutions.

Article 97 The original license issuing authority shall reissue the Medical Device Registration Certificate within 20 days after receiving the application for re-issuance.

Article 98 The following time is not included in the relevant working time limit:

(1) The time taken by the applicant for supplementary materials and rectification after audit;

(2) Time for delaying the audit due to the applicant;

(3) The time when external expert consultation is needed, the expert consultation meeting is held, and the drug-device combination products need to be jointly evaluation with the drug evaluation agency;

(4) If the evaluation, review and approval procedures are suspended in accordance with regulations, the time taken during the suspension of the evaluation, review and approval procedures;

(5) The time taken for quality management systems audit.

Article 99 The time limit stipulated in the Measures shall be calculated on working days.

CHAPTER VIII Supervision and administration

Article 100 The medical products administration shall strengthen the supervision and inspection of the research and development of medical devices, when necessary, conduct extended inspections on the units and individuals that provide products or services for the research and development of medical devices, and the relevant units and individuals shall cooperate with them, provide relevant documents and materials, and shall not refuse, conceal or obstruct.

Article 101 The NMPA shall establish a step–by–step implementation system for the unique device identifier (UDI), applicants and filing applicants shall submit UDI related information in accordance with relevant regulations, so as to ensure that the data is true, accurate and traceable.

Article 102 The NMPA shall timely inform the medical products administration of the provinces, autonomous regions and municipalities directly under the Central Government of the agent's information. The medical products administration of the provinces, autonomous regions and municipalities directly under the Central Government shall organize daily supervision and management of agents in their respective administrative regions.

Article 103 The medical products administration of the provinces, autonomous regions and municipalities directly under the Central Government shall, according to the filing situation of medical device clinical trial institutions, organize the supervision and inspection of clinical trial institutions that have been filed within their respective administrative regions. For newly filed medical device clinical trial institutions, the supervision and inspection shall be carried out within 60 days after filing.

The medical products administration of the provinces, autonomous regions and municipalities directly under the Central Government shall organize daily supervision and inspection on medical device clinical trial institutions in this administrative region in compliance with Good Clinical Practice for Medical Practice, and supervise them to continuously meet the prescribed requirements. The NMPA shall supervise and inspect the clinical trial institutions of medical devices as required.

Article 104 If the medical products administration deems it necessary, the authenticity, accuracy, integrity, standardization and traceability of clinical trials can be checked on site.

Article 105 If the medical products administration undertaking the filing of Class I medical devices finds that the filing information are not standardized during the post-filing supervision, it shall order the filing applicant to make corrections within a time limit.

Article 106 If the medical products administration fails to discover the systemic and regional risks in the registration management of medical devices within its administrative area in time, or fails to eliminate the systemic and regional hidden dangers in the registration management of medical devices within its administrative area in time, the medical products administration at a higher level may conduct questioning to the principal responsible persons of the medical products administration at a lower level.

CHAPTER IX Legal Liabilities

Article 107 Any institution or individual that violates the provisions under Article 79 and fails to file the changes as required shall be ordered to make corrections within a time limit; if it fails to make corrections within the time limit, it shall be fined RMB 10,000 – 30,000.

Article 108 Those who carry out clinical trials of medical devices without complying with the Good Clinical Practice shall be punished in accordance with Article 94 of the *Regulations for the Supervision and Administration of Medical Devices.*

Article 109 Where a technical evaluation institution for medical devices fails to perform its duties in accordance with the Measures, resulting in major errors or serious consequences in the evaluation, the medical products administration shall order it to make corrections, report criticisms and give warnings; where serious consequences are caused, the legal representative, principal responsible person, direct responsible person in charge and other responsible persons of the illegal institution shall be given sanctions according to law.

Article 110 Any staff member of the medical products administration who, in violation of regulations, abuses his power, neglects his duty or engages in malpractices for personal gain shall be punished according to law.

CHAPTER X Supplementary Provisions

Article 111 In principle, medical device registration or filing units shall be based on the technical principle, structure and composition, performance indicator and scope of application of products.

Article 112 The medical devices approved for registration refer to those consistent with the content limited in Medical Device Registration Certificate and attachments thereof and are manufactured within the validity period of Medical Device Registration Certificate.

Article 113 If the combined parts listed in the column of "Structure and Composition" in the Medical Device Registration Certificate are used for replacement of consumables, after–sales service and maintenance, they can be sold separately.

Article 114 In applying for medical device product registration, change registration and clinical trial approval, the applicant may quote the registered medical device master file with the authorization of the owner of the medical device master file. The work procedures related to the registration of master documents of medical devices shall be stipulated separately.

Article 115 The format of Medical Device Registration Certificate shall be normalized by NMPA uniformly.

Registration numbers shall be arranged in the following form:

× 1 XZ × 2 × × × × 3 × 4 × × 5 × × × × 6, wherein:

× 1 shall mean the abbreviation of the place where the registration review and approval authority is located:

"G" (Guo) shall be adopted for domestic Class Ⅲ medical devices, imported Class Ⅱ and Class Ⅲ medical devices;

The domestic Class Ⅱ medical devices adopt the abbreviation of the province, autonomous region and municipality directly under the Central Government where the registration review and approval department is located;

× 2 shall indicate the form of registration:

"Z" (Zhun) is applicable to domestic medical devices;

"J" (Jin) is applicable to imported medical devices;

"X" (Xu) is applicable to medical devices in Hong Kong, Macau and Taiwan;

× × × × 3 shall indicate the year of initial registration;

× 4 shall the product management category;

× × 5 shall indicate the product classification code;

× × × × 6 shall indicate the serial number of initial registration.

For the renewal registration, × × × × 3 and × × × × 6 shall remain the same. If the product management category is adjusted, a new number shall be assigned.

Article 116 The filing number for Class I Medical Device shall be arranged in the following form:

×1 XB × × × ×2× × × ×3, wherein:

×1 shall mean the abbreviation of the place where the filing authority is located:

"G" (Guo) shall be adopted for imported Class I medical devices;

The domestic Class I medical devices should be marked with the abbreviation of the province, autonomous region or municipality directly under the Central Government where the filing department is located plus the abbreviation of the municipal administrative region where the district is located (if there is no municipal administrative region with corresponding district, it is only the abbreviation of the province, autonomous region or municipality directly under the Central Government);

× × × ×2 shall indicate the year of filing;

× × × ×3 shall indicate the serial number of filing.

Article 117 Electronic documents of Medical Device Registration Certificate, change registration document produced by medical products administration have the same legal effect as paper documents.

Article 118 The NMPA, may, according to work necessity, authorize the medical products administration of the provinces, autonomous regions and municipalities directly under the Central Government and relevant social organizations to conduct the specific work in accordance with law.

Article 119 The medical products administration of the provinces, autonomous regions and municipalities directly under the Central Government may formulate special registration procedures for class II medical devices within their administrative regions with reference to the provisions of Chapter

IV of the Measures, and report them to the NMPA for filing.

Article 120 The items and standards of registration fees for medical device products shall be implemented in accordance with the relevant provisions of the competent department of finance and price under the State Council.

Article 121 The registration and filing of in vitro diagnosis reagents administered as medical devices are applicable to the *Administrative measures for IVD Registration and filing.*

Article 122 Relevant provisions on the supervision and administration of customized medical devices shall be separately formulated by the NMPA.

The relevant provisions on the registration administration of drug–device combination products shall be formulated separately by the NMPA.

Relevant provisions on the emergency use of medical devices shall be separately formulated by the NMPA together with relevant departments.

Article 123 The medical devices from Hong Kong, Macao and Taiwan shall be registered and filed by reference to the import medical devices.

Article 124 The Measures shall come into force as of October 1, 2021. On July 30, 2014, the Decree No.4 *Provisions for Medical Device Registration* promulgated by former CFDA shall be abolished at the same time.

Measures for the Administration of Registration and Filing of In Vitro Diagnostic Reagents

(Decree No. 48 of the State Administration for Market Regulation)

CHAPTER I General

Article 1 This Measures is formulated according to the *Regulations for the Supervision and Administration of Medical Devices*, aiming to regulate the registration and filing of in vitro diagnostic reagents (IVD reagents) and ensure their safety, effectiveness and controllable quality.

Article 2 This Measures shall apply to the registration, filing and supervision and administration of IVD reagents within the territory of the People's Republic of China.

Article 3 The IVD reagents mentioned herein refer to IVD reagents administered as medical devices, including reagents, kits, calibrators, quality controls, etc. for in vitro examination of specimens derived from human body in the course of disease prediction, prevention, diagnosis, treatment and monitoring, prognosis observation, and health status evaluation, which can be used independently or in combination with instruments, apparatus, equipment or systems.

IVD reagents for blood screening and IVD reagents with radionuclide labeling, both administered as drugs, shall not be under the regulation scope of this Measures.

Article 4 IVD reagents registration is the process of IVD reagents registrant (hereinafter referred to as the Applicant) submitting an application for IVD reagents registration according to legal procedures and requirements, and the medical products administration, in accordance with laws and regulations and based on scientific cognition, carrying out review on the safety, effectiveness and quality controllability of IVD reagents to decide whether to approve such application.

IVD reagents filing is the process of IVD reagents filing applicant (hereinafter referred to as filing applicant) submitting filing materials to the medical products administration, in accordance with legal procedures and requirements, and the medical products administration filing the submitted filing materials for future reference.

Article 5 National Medical Products Administration (NMPA) is in charge of the registration and filing management of IVD reagents nationwide, and is responsible for establishing the registration and filing management system of IVD reagents, organizing the review and approval of domestic Class Ⅲ and imported Class Ⅱ and Class Ⅲ IVD reagents, the filing of imported Class Ⅰ IVD reagents and related supervision and administration work according to law, and supervising and guiding the registration and filing of local IVD reagents.

Article 6 The Center for Medical Device Evaluation of NMPA (hereinafter referred to as the CMDE of NMPA) is responsible for the technical evaluation of the application for registration, change registration and renewal registration of domestic Class Ⅲ and imported Class Ⅱ and Class Ⅲ IVD reagent products.

Center for Medical Device Standards Administration NMPA, National Institutes for Food and Drug Control, Center for Food and Drug Inspection of NMPA (hereinafter referred to as Inspection Center of NMPA), Center for Drug Re-evaluation of NMPA, Administrative Matters Acceptance Service and Complaint Reporting Center of NMPA, Information Center of NMPA and other professional technical institutions undertake the management, classification, definition, inspection, audit, monitoring and evaluation, certification preparation and delivery of IVD reagents standards required for the implementation of IVD reagents supervision and administration as well as corresponding information construction, management and related work.

Article 7 The medical products administration of the provinces, autonomous regions and municipalities directly under the Central Government shall be responsible for the administration of the registration of the following IVD reagents within their respective administrative areas:

(1) Review and approval of registration of Class II IVD reagents in China;

(2) Audit of Quality Management System of Class II and Class III IVD reagents in China;

(3) Organization of the supervision and administration of medical device clinical trial institutions and clinical trials according to law;

(4) Supervision and guidance on the filing of Class I IVD reagents within the territory of the departments responsible for drug supervision and administration at the municipal level divided into districts.

The professional technical institutions for medical devices set or designated by the medical products administration at provincial level, autonomous regions and municipality level directly under the Central Government shall take charge of the technical evaluation, inspection, validation, monitoring and evaluation required for the implementation of IVD reagents supervision and administration according to law.

The medical products administration at the municipal level divided into districts are responsible for the filing management of Class I IVD reagent products in China.

Article 8 The IVD reagents registration and filing shall be conducted under the principles of legality, science, openness, fairness and justice.

Article 9 The Class I IVD reagents shall be subject to product filing management. The Class II and Class III IVD reagents shall be subject to product registration management.

When filing the domestic Class I IVD reagents, the filing applicant shall submit filing documents to the medical products administration at the municipal level divided into districts.

Domestic Class II IVD reagents shall be subject to review by medical products administration of provinces, autonomous regions and municipalities directly under the Central Government, and Medical Device Registration Certificates will be issued after approval by such departments.

Domestic Class III IVD reagents shall be subject to review by the NMPA, and Medical Device Registration Certificates will be issued after approval by the NMPA.

When filing the imported Class I IVD reagents, the filing applicant shall submit filing documents to the NMPA.

Imported Class II and Class III IVD reagents shall be subject to review by the NMPA, and Medical Device Registration Certificates will be issued after approval by the NMPA.

Article 10 IVD reagents registrants or filing applicants shall strengthen the life cycle quality management of IVD reagents, and shall be legally responsible for the safety, effectiveness and quality controllability of IVD reagents in the whole process of research and development, production, operation and use.

Article 11 The NMPA implements priority review and approval for clinically urgent-needed IVD reagents, and conducts special review and approval for innovative IVD reagents. Research and innovation of IVD reagents shall be encouraged, so as to promote the high-quality development of medical device industry.

Article 12 The NMPA shall establish and improve systems such as IVD reagents standards and technical guidelines, regulate the technical evaluation of IVD reagents and audit of quality management systems, and guide and serve the research and development and registration of IVD reagents.

Article 13 The medical products administration shall disclose the relevant information on the registration and filing of IVD reagents in a timely manner according to law. Applicants can inquire about the progress and results of review and approval, and the public can consult the review and approval results.

Without the consent of the applicant, the medical products administration, professional technical institutions and their staff, experts participating in the review and other personnel shall not disclose the trade secrets, undisclosed information or confidential business information submitted by the applicant or the filing applicant, except as otherwise specified by law or involving national security and major social and public interests.

CHAPTER II Basic Requirements

Article 14 The registration and filing of IVD reagents shall comply with relevant laws, regulations, rules and mandatory standards, follow the essential principles of safety and performance of IVD reagents, and refer to relevant technical guidelines to prove that the registered and filed IVD reagents are safe, effective and controllable in quality, so as to ensure the truthfulness, accuracy, completeness and traceability of information.

Article 15 Applicants and filing applicants shall be enterprises or research institutions that can bear corresponding legal responsibilities.

Overseas applicants and filing applicants shall designate enterprise legal persons in China as agents to handle the registration and filing of relevant IVD reagents. The agent shall assist the registrants and filing applicants to fulfill the obligations specified in paragraph 1 of Article 20 of the *Regulations for the Supervision and Administration of Medical Devices*, and assist the overseas registrants and filing applicants to implement the corresponding legal responsibilities.

Article 16 The applicant and filing applicant shall establish the quality management system related to product research and development and manufacture, and shall keep its effective operation.

Article 17 Personnel in charge of IVD reagents registration or filing affairs shall have relevant expertise and be familiar with laws, regulations, rules and registration administration concerning IVD reagents registration and filing management.

Article 18 When applying for registration or filing, the applicant or filing applicant shall submit relevant materials in accordance with the requirements for registration and filing of the NMPA, and shall be responsible for the authenticity of the materials.

The registration and filing materials shall be in Chinese language. Source text shall also be provided for translations from foreign language materials. For references of unpublished literatures, proof of permission by copyright owner of the materials shall be provided.

Article 19 When applying for registration of imported IVD reagents and the filing of imported IVD reagents, the supporting documents for the marketing approval issued by the competent authorities of the country (region) where the applicant and the filing applicant are registered or where the production address is located shall be submitted.

If the country (region) where the registered place or production address of the applicant or filing applicant does not manage this product as medical device, the applicants and filing applicants need to provide relevant documents, including certificates issued by the said country (region) permitting the marketing of this product.

For IVD reagents reviewed and approved in accordance with the innovative product registration procedures that are not marketed in the country (region) where the applicant or filing applicant is registered or where the place of production is located, relevant documents are not required to be submitted.

Article 20 IVD reagents shall meet the applicable mandatory standards. If the product structural features, technical principles, intended use and use methods are inconsistent with the scope of application of mandatory standards, the applicant and the filling registrant shall put forward an explanation of the non-application of mandatory standards and provide relevant information.

If there are no mandatory standards, the applicants and filing applicants are encouraged to adopt recommended standards.

Article 21 The registration and filing of IVD reagents shall follow the relevant requirements of the classification rules and classification catalogue of IVD reagents.

Article 22 The medical products administration has continuously promoted the reform of the review and approval system, strengthened scientific research on IVD reagents supervision and administration, established a IVD reagents registration management system led by technical evaluation and supported by audit, inspection, monitoring and evaluation, optimized the review and approval process, improved the ability, quality and efficiency of review and approval.

Article 23 The professional technical institutions of medical devices shall establish and improve the communication system, clarify the form and content of communication, and organize communication with the applicant according to work needs.

Article 24 Professional technical institutions of medical devices shall establish an expert consultation system according to work needs, listen to expert opinions on major issues in the process of evaluation, audit and inspection, and give full play to the technical support role of experts.

CHAPTER III Registration of IVD Reagents

Section I Product research and development

Article 25 The research and development of IVD reagents should follow the risk management principles and consider the existing recognized technical level, so as to ensure that all known and foreseeable risks and unexpected impacts of products are minimized and acceptable, and ensure that the benefits of products outweigh the risks in normal use.

Article 26 The research and development and experimental activities of IVD reagent products shall meet the requirements of relevant laws, regulations and mandatory standards in China.

Article 27 The applicant and the filing applicant shall prepare the product technical requirements for applying for registration or IVD reagents.

The product technical requirements mainly include the functionality, safety indicator and test method of the finished product of IVD reagents which can be objectively judged.

Product technical requirements for Class III IVD reagents shall clearly specify requirements for main raw materials, production process in the form of appendices.

IVD reagents shall meet the product technical requirements of registered or filed products.

Article 28 The applicant and the filing applicant shall prepare the IFU and labels of IVD reagents for registration or filing.

The IFU and labels shall comply with the requirements of Article 39 of the *Regulations for the Supervision and Administration of Medical Devices* and relevant provisions.

Article 29 In the research and development of IVD reagents, non-clinical study of IVD reagents should be carried out according to the intended use and technical features of products.

Non-clinical study refers to the test or evaluation of IVD reagents under laboratory conditions, including the selection and preparation of main raw materials, product production process, product analysis performance, cut-off value or reference interval, product stability, etc..

To apply for registration or filing, non-clinical evidence generated in research and development activities shall be submitted.

Article 30 The functional and safety indicators and methods determined during the non-clinical study of IVD reagents shall be compatible with the intended use conditions and purposes of the products, and the study samples shall be representative and typical. If necessary, methodological verification and statistical analysis shall be carried out.

Article 31 When applying for registration or filing, inspection shall be carried out in accordance with the product technical requirements and a test report shall be submitted. Only those who pass the test can conduct clinical trials or apply for registration and filing.

Article 32 If the same registration involves products in different packaging specifications, registration inspection may be done only with products in one packaging specifications. The products for test shall represent the safety and effectiveness of the products to be registered or filed, and their production shall meet the relevant requirements of the Good Manufacturing Practice for Medical Devices.

Article 33 The test report submitted for the registration or filling can be the self–test report of the applicant or the filing applicant, or the test report issued by a qualified medical device test institution entrusted.

For Class Ⅲ IVD reagents, test reports of three different production batches of products shall be provided.

Article 34 Where there are applicable national standard materials, the reagents shall be tested with the national standard materials. The National Institutes for Food and Drug Control should be responsible for the preparation and calibration of national standard materials.

Section II Clinical evaluation

Article 35 Clinical evaluation of IVD reagents refers to the process of analyzing and evaluating clinical data by scientific and reasonable methods, and confirming whether the products meet the use requirements or intended uses, so as to prove the safety and effectiveness of IVD reagents.

Article 36 Clinical trials of IVD reagents refer to the systematic study on the clinical performance of IVD reagents in the corresponding clinical environment.

The NMPA has formulated guidelines for clinical trials of IVD reagents, specifying the requirements for conducting clinical trials and formulating clinical trial reports.

Article 37 To carry out clinical evaluation of IVD reagents, clinical trials should be conducted to prove the safety and effectiveness of IVD reagents.

Clinical trials may be exempted in the following conditions:

(1) With clear reaction mechanism, standardized design and mature manufacturing technique; the marketed IVD reagents of the same variety have been put in clinical application for years and there is no record of serious adverse events. In addition, the regulated use will not be changed;

(2) It can be proved that the IVD reagent is safe and effective by comparing the methodologies of the same variety.

The catalogue of Class II and Class III IVD reagents exempted from clinical trials shall be formulated, adjusted and issued by the NMPA.

Article 38 For IVD reagents exempted from clinical trials, the applicant shall prove the safety and effectiveness of the products by comparing the clinical samples that meet the intended use with the methodology of the same variety.

NMPA formulates relevant guidelines for clinical evaluation of IVD reagents exempted from clinical trials.

Article 39 Clinical evaluation data of IVD reagents refers to the documents formed by the applicant's clinical evaluation.

IVD reagents for clinical trials, clinical trial data include clinical trial protocol, opinions of ethics committee, informed consent form, clinical trial report and relevant data, etc..

For IVD reagents listed in the catalogue of exemption from clinical trials, clinical evaluation data include comparative analysis with similar products on the market, methodological comparison data, relevant literature data analysis and empirical data analysis, etc..

Article 40 When the same registration includes different packing specifications, products with one packing specification can be used for clinical evaluation, and the products for clinical evaluation should represent the safety and effectiveness of the products applied for registration or filed.

There is no need to submit clinical evaluation data when calibrators and quality controls are applied separately.

Article 41 The clinical trials of IVD reagents shall be carried out in the medical device clinical trial institutions with required conditions and filed in accordance with the regulations in accordance with the requirements of Good Clinical Practice for Medical Devices. Before the commencement of the clinical trial, the clinical trial sponsor shall file the clinical trial with the medical products administration of the provinces, autonomous regions and municipalities directly under the Central Government. The production of IVD reagents for clinical trials should meet the relevant requirements of the Good Manufacturing Practice for Medical Devices.

Article 42 For serious adverse events related to IVD reagents in clinical trials during clinical trials of IVD reagents, or other serious safety risk information, the clinical trial sponsor shall, in accordance with relevant requirements, report to the medical products administration of the provinces, autonomous regions and municipalities directly under the Central Government where the clinical trial institutions are located, and take risk control measures. If no risk control measures are taken, the medical products administration of the provinces, autonomous regions and municipalities directly under the Central Government shall order the sponsor to take corresponding risk control measures according to law.

Article 43 In case of large-scale serious adverse events related to IVD reagents clinical trials during clinical trials of IVD reagents, or other major security issues, the sponsor shall suspend or terminate the clinical trials of IVD reagents, and report to the medical products administration of the provinces, autonomous regions and municipalities directly under the Central Government where the clinical trial institutions are located. If it has not been suspended or terminated, the medical products administration of the provinces, autonomous regions and municipalities directly under the Central Government shall order the sponsor to take corresponding risk control measures according to law.

Article 44 When carrying out clinical evaluation of IVD reagents expected to be used by consumers themselves, the applicant should also evaluate the cognitive ability of consumers without medical background to IFU.

Article 45 If an IVD reagent used to diagnosis of a serious life-threatening disease with no effective diagnosis means is under clinical trial and may benefit patients after medical observation, it can be used free of charge for other patients with the same condition in the institution where the clinical trial of the IVD reagent is being carried out after ethical review and informed consent, and their safety data can be used for application for IVD reagent registration.

Section III Verification of Registration System

Article 46 The applicant shall submit relevant materials related to the quality management system related to product research and development and production when applying for registration. If the medical products administration that accepts the application for registration considers it is necessary to verify the quality management system during the product technical evaluation, it shall organize the QMS audit and access the original data when necessary.

Article 47 The audit of the quality management system of Class III IVD reagents in China shall be carried out by the medical products administration of the provinces, autonomous regions and municipalities directly under the Central Government where the applicant is located notified by the CMDE of

NMPA.

The audit of the quality management system of Class Ⅱ IVD reagents in China shall be carried out by the medical products administration of the provinces, autonomous regions and municipalities directly under the Central Government where the applicant is located.

Article 48 The medical products administration of the provinces, autonomous regions and municipalities directly under the Central Government shall carry out quality management systems audit in accordance with the requirements of the Good Manufacturing Practice for Medical Devices, focusing on whether the applicant has established a quality management system suitable for the product in accordance with the requirements of the Good Manufacturing Practice for Medical Devices, and the design and development, production management and quality control related to product research and development and production.

During the process of audit, the authenticity of products for test and clinical trial products shall also be verified at the same time, focusing on checking the relevant records of the design and development process, as well as the relevant records of the production process of test products and clinical trial products.

Where a self-test report is submitted, key audit shall be carried out on the test capability and test results of the applicants and filing applicants or the entrusted institution in the process of research and development.

Article 49 The medical products administration of the provinces, autonomous regions and municipalities directly under the Central Government may carry out quality management systems audit by means of data review or on-site inspection. According to the specific situation of the applicant, the supervision and inspection situation, and the comparison results between the products applied for registration this time and the products that have passed audit on the production conditions and processes, determining whether on-site inspection and inspection contents shall be carried out, so as to avoid repeated inspection.

Article 50 When the CMDE of NMPA conducts technical evaluation on imported Class II and Class III IVD reagents, if it considers it is necessary to carry out QMS audit, it shall notify the Inspection Center of NMPA to carry out audit according to relevant requirements.

Section IV Product Registration

Article 51 After completing the study on the safety and effectiveness of IVD reagents supporting the registration, and making preparations for the audit of the quality management system, the applicant shall apply for the registration of IVD reagents, and submit the registration dossiers to the medical products administration through online registration application paths according to relevant requirements:

(1) Data for product risk analysis;

(2) Product technical requirements;

(3) Product test report;

(4) Clinical evaluation data;

(5) Draft Instruction for Use and Label;

(6) Quality management system documents related to product research and development and production;

(7) Other necessary dossiers to demonstrate the safety and effectiveness of the products.

Article 52 The medical products administration shall conduct review on registration dossiers after accepting an application, and handle respectively according to the following circumstances:

(1) The application items are within the scope of the administrative authority with complete registration dossiers and in conformity with the formal review, the application shall be accepted;

(2) If there are errors in the registration dossiers that can be corrected on the spot, the applicant is allowed to make rectification on the spot;

(3) If the registration dossiers are incomplete or do not comply with the legal form, the applicant shall be informed of all contents to be supplemented or corrected in one time on site or within 5 working days; if failing to inform the applicant within the specified time, the registration dossiers shall be accepted from the receipt date;

(4) If the application items don't fail within the scope of the administrative authority, the decision of not to accept the application shall be made immediately, and the applicant shall be notified to apply to the relevant administrative authority.

The medical products administration shall issue a notice of acceptance or a notice of denial with special stamp of the administrative authority and dated, depending on whether the IVD reagents registration application is accepted or not.

After the application for registration of IVD reagents is accepted, if the applicant needs to pay the fees, the applicant shall pay the fees according to the regulations. If the applicant fails to pay the fee within the specified time limit, it shall be deemed that the applicant voluntarily withdraws the application, and the medical products administration shall terminate its registration procedure.

Article 53 If supplementary and correction materials are required during technical evaluation, the technical evaluation institution shall notify all the contents that need to be supplemented and corrected at one time. The applicant shall, within one year after receiving the Deficiency Letter, provide supplementary materials once in accordance with the requirements of the Deficiency Letter, and the technical evaluation institution shall complete the technical evaluation within the prescribed time limit after receiving the supplementary materials.

If the applicant has objections to the content of Deficiency Letter, it may give its opinion in writing to the corresponding technical evaluation institution, along with rationales and corresponding technical supporting data.

If the applicant fails to submit supplementary materials within the time limit, the technical evaluation shall be terminated, and the medical products administration shall make a decision of not registering.

Article 54 For an accepted registration application, the applicant may, before making the decision on administrative license, apply to the medical products administration that accepted the application for withdrawal of the registration application and relevant materials, and explain the reasons. If it agrees to withdraw the application, the medical products administration shall terminate its registration procedure.

If, in the process of evaluation, audit and review and approval, it is found that there are suspected illegal acts such as concealing the true situation or providing false information, they shall be dealt with according to law, and the applicant shall not withdraw the application for registration.

Article 55 For an accepted registration application, if there is evidence that the registration dossiers may be false, the medical products administration may suspend the review and approval. It will be decided whether it shall be further reviewed or the registration shall be denied after audit.

Article 56 During the evaluation of the application for registration of IVD reagents, if an evaluation conclusion is proposed to be made that does not pass, the technical evaluation institution shall inform the applicant of the reasons for rejection, and the applicant may raise objections to the technical evaluation institution within 15 days, and the contents of objections are limited to the original application items and original registration dossiers. The technical evaluation institution shall conduct comprehensive assessment and feedback to the applicant based on the applicant's objections. The objection processing time is not included in the evaluation time limit.

Article 57 The medical products administration accepting the registration application shall make a decision on whether to approve it after the technical evaluation is completed. IVD reagents that meet the requirements of safety, effectiveness and controllability in quality shall be approved for registration and issued with the Medical Device Registration Certificate, and the approved product technical requirements and IFU will be distributed to the applicant in the form of attachment. For the products that are not approved for registration, the reasons shall be given in writing, and the applicant shall be informed of its right of applying for administrative reconsideration or appealing to administrative proceeding by law.

The validity period of the Medical Device Registration Certificate is five years.

Article 58 For accepted registration application, in case of any of the following circumstances, the medical products administration shall make a decision not to register and inform the applicant:

(1) The applicant cannot, through study and its findings, prove the safety, effectiveness and controllability in quality of the IVD reagent proposed for marketing;

(2) The quality management system fails to pass the audit, and the applicant refuses to accept the on-site inspection of the quality management

systems;

(3) The registration dossiers are false;

(4) The contents of the registration dossiers are confusing, contradictory, or obviously inconsistent with the application items, and the product can not be proved to be safe, effective and controllable in quality;

(5) Other circumstances under which the registration application shall not be approved.

Article 59 The medical products administration shall announce to the public and hold a hearing on the matters that shall be heard for the implementation of administrative license according to laws, regulations and rules, or other major administrative license matters involving public interests that the medical products administration deems necessary. If the application for medical devices registration directly involves a significant interest relationship between the applicant and others, the medical products administration shall inform the applicant and interested parties that they have the right to request a hearing before making an administrative license decision.

Article 60 For urgent-needed IVD reagents for treatment of rare diseases, diseases which are seriously life-threatening and have no effective treatment means, and those used for coping with public health emergencies, the medical products administration may make a conditional approval decision, specifying the validity period, the study that needs to be completed after marketing, the completion time limit and other related matters in the Medical Device Registration Certificate.

Article 61 For conditionally approved IVD reagents, the registrant shall collect data on benefits and risks after the IVD reagents are marketed, continuously monitor and assess the benefits and risks of the applied products, take effective measures to actively control risks, and complete study and submit relevant materials within the prescribed time limit as required.

Article 62 For conditionally approved IVD reagents, if the registrant fails to complete the study as required within the time limit or cannot prove that the benefits outweigh the risks, the registrant shall apply for cancellation of the Medical Device Registration Certificate in time, and the medical products administration may cancel the Medical Device Registration Certificate according to law.

Article 63 For a newly researched and developed IVD reagent not yet listed in the classification catalogue of IVD reagents, the applicant may directly apply for a Class III IVD reagent registration, determine the product category in accordance with the Classification Rules and apply to the NMPA for product registration or filing after category confirmation.

Where a Class III IVD reagent registration is directly applied for, the NMPA shall determine the class based on its risk degree. For the domestic IVD reagents identified as Class II or Class I, the applicant shall be informed to apply for registration or filing with the corresponding medical products administration.

Article 64 Where, for a registered IVD reagent, whose management category is adjusted from a higher category to a lower category, the Medical Device Registration Certificate within its period of validity shall remain valid. If renewal is needed, the registrants shall apply for registration renewal or filing to the corresponding medical products administration six months before the expiration of the Medical Device Registration Certificate in accordance with the adjusted category.

For registered IVD reagents adjusted from a lower management category to a higher category, the registrant shall submit registration application to the corresponding medical products administration in accordance with the adjusted category. The NMPA shall stipulate the time limit for completing the adjustment in the notice of adjustment of the management category.

Article 65 If the Medical Device Registration Certificate and its attachments are lost or damaged, the registrant shall apply to the original license issuing authority for reissuing, and the original license issuing authority shall verify and reissue the certificate.

Article 66 Where a patent dispute arises during the registration review or after approval, it shall be dealt with according to relevant laws and regulations.

CHAPTER IV Special Registration Procedures

Section I Registration procedures for innovative products

Article 67 For IVD reagents that meet the following requirements, the applicant may apply for the application of innovative product registration procedures:

(1) The applicant legally owns the patent for invention of core technology of the product through its dominant technical innovation activities in China, or obtains the patent for innovation in China or the right of use through legal transfer; and the time for applying for the registration procedure of innovative products shall be within 5 years from the date of patent authorization announcement; or the application of the patent for invention of the core technology has been made public by the patent administrative authority of the State Council. The Patent Searching and Consulting Center of the China National Intellectual Property Administration shall issue a search report indicating that the core technical scheme of the product has novelty and creativity;

(2) The applicant has completed the preliminary study on the product and the product is basically finalized, the study process is true and controlled, and

the study data is complete and traceable;

(3) The main working principle/mechanism of action of a product is the first of its kind in China, the product performance or safety has radical improvement compared with similar products, the product is in the international leading level technically, and has significant value in clinical application.

Article 68 When apply for applicable innovative product registration procedures, the applicant shall submit an application for reviewing of innovative medical devices to the NMPA after the product is basically finalized. The NMPA shall organize experts to review, and those that meet the requirements shall be included in the registration procedure of innovative products.

Article 69 For the application for registration of IVD reagents applicable to innovative product registration procedures, the NMPA and the institutions undertaking relevant technical work shall designate special personnel to be responsible for timely communication and provide guidance according to their respective duties.

For IVD reagents included in the innovative product registration procedures, the CMDE of NMPA can communicate with the applicant on major technical issues, major security issues, clinical trial protocols, summary and evaluation of staged clinical trial results before accepting the application for registration and during the technical evaluation process.

Article 70 If the IVD reagents included in the innovative product registration procedures are voluntarily requested to be terminated by the applicant or the NMPA finds that they no longer meet the requirements of the innovative product registration procedure, the NMPA may terminate the innovative product registration procedure of related products and inform the applicant.

Article 71 IVD reagents included in the innovative product registration procedure are not applicable to the innovative product registration procedure if the applicant fails to apply for registration within the prescribed time limit.

Section II Priority Registration Procedures

Article 72 For IVD reagents that meet one of the following conditions, priority registration procedures may be applied for:

(1) Diagnose rare diseases and malignant tumors with obvious clinical advantages, diagnose unique and multiple diseases of the elderly and there is no effective diagnostic means at present, which is specially used for children and has obvious clinical advantages, or urgent-needed clinically and there is no medical device approved for registration of the same variety of products in China;

(2) Medical devices that have been listed in the National Science and Technology Major Project or National Key Research and Development Project;

(3) Other medical devices subject to priority registration procedures as stipulated by the NMPA.

Article 73 To apply for the priority registration procedure, the applicant shall, when applying for the registration of IVD reagents, submit an application for the priority registration procedure to the NMPA. Under the circumstances of Paragraph 1 of Article 72, the NMPA shall organize experts to conduct examination, and those that meet the requirements shall be included in the priority registration procedure; under the circumstances of Paragraph 2 of Article 72, it shall be reviewed by the CMDE of NMPA, and those that meet the requirements shall be included in the priority registration procedure; under the circumstances of Paragraph 3 of Article 72, the NMPA shall listen to opinions extensively and organize experts to demonstrate whether to include them in the priority registration procedure.

Article 74 The NMPA shall give priority to the review and approval of the application for registration of IVD reagents included in the priority registration procedure, and the medical products administration of the provinces, autonomous regions and municipalities directly under the Central Government shall give priority to the audit of the registration quality management system.

During the technical evaluation of medical device products included in the priority registration procedure, the CMDE shall actively communicate with the applicant in accordance with relevant regulations, and may arrange special exchanges when necessary.

Section III Emergency Registration Procedures

Article 75 The NMPA may, in accordance with the law, implement emergency registration for IVD reagents that are required for public health emergencies and have no similar products marketed in China, or that similar products have been marketed but whose supply cannot meet the needs for emergency treatment of public health emergencies.

Article 76 When applying for applicable emergency registration procedures, the applicant shall apply to the NMPA for emergency registration application. Those meeting the conditions shall be included into the emergency registration procedures.

Article 77 The NMPA shall immediately handle the application for registration of IVD reagents for emergency registration in accordance with the principles of unified command, early intervention, on-call review and scientific review and approval, and carry out IVD reagents product test, system audit and technical evaluation in parallel.

CHAPTER V Change Registration and Renewal Registration

Section I Change Registration

Article 78 The registrant shall take the initiative to carry out post-marketing research on IVD reagents, further confirm the safety, effectiveness and quality controllability of IVD reagents, and strengthen the continuous management of marketed IVD reagents.

For substantive changes in the design, raw materials, production process, scope of application and use method of the registered Class II and Class III IVD reagents that may affect the safety and effectiveness of the IVD reagents, the registrant shall apply to the original registration department for change registration. Other changes shall be filed to the original registration department within 30 days after the changes.

The product name, packing specifications, main components, intended use, product technical requirements, IFU, production address of imported IVD reagents, etc. stated in the Medical Device Registration Certificate belong to the matters that subject to change registration as specified in the preceding paragraph. The name and domicile of the registrant and the name and domicile of the agent belong to the matters that need to be filed as specified in the preceding paragraph. If the production address of IVD reagents in China is changed, the registrant shall handle the filing procedures after handling the corresponding production license change.

In case of other changes, the registrant shall do the relevant work in accordance with the requirements of the quality management systems and report to the medical products administration in accordance with the regulations.

Article 79 Substantial changes in the core technical principles of registered Class Ⅱ and Class Ⅲ IVD reagents, or other major changes that have a significant impact on the safety and effectiveness of products and essentially constitute new products, are not belong to the change application items stipulated in this Chapter, and shall be handled in accordance with the provisions of the registration application.

Article 80 For change registration application, the technical evaluation institution shall focus on the changed part, and evaluate the safety, effectiveness and controllability in quality of the products after change to form an evaluation opinion.

Where the medical products administration deems that it is necessary to verify the quality management system during the technical evaluation of the application for change registration, it shall organize an audit on the quality management system.

Article 81 Medical device change registration document shall be used together with the original Medical Device Registration Certificate, and the expiration date of the validity period is the same as the original Medical Device Registration Certificate.

Section II Renewal Registration

Article 82 If the Medical Device Registration Certificate is for renewal upon validity period, the registrant shall apply for renewal registration to the original registration department 6 months before the validity period of the Medical Device Registration Certificate, together with the registration dossiers in accordance with the relevant requirements.

Except the situation stipulated in Article 83 in this Measures, the medical products administration, upon receipt the application for renewal registration, shall make decision on renewal registration prior to the validity period of the

Medical Device Registration Certificate. If no decision is available after the due time, the renewal application shall be deemed having been approved.

Article 83 The renewal registration shall not be approved in any of the following circumstances:

(1) The applicant fails to apply for renewal registration within the specified time limit;

(2) The new mandatory standards for IVD reagents or national standard materials are issued and implemented, and the IVD reagents applied for renewal registration cannot meet the new requirements;

(3) For the IVD reagents with conditional approval, the items specified in the Medical Device Registration Certificate are not completed within the specified time limit.

Article 84 If the approval time of renewal registration is within the validity period of the original Medical Device Registration Certificate, the starting date of the validity period of the Medical Device Registration Certificate for renewal registration shall be the next day after the expiration date of the original Medical Device Registration Certificate; If the approval time is not within the validity period of the original Medical Device Registration Certificate, the starting date of the validity period of the Medical Device Registration Certificate for renewal registration shall be the date of approval of renewal registration.

Article 85 If the acceptance, review and approval procedures of application for change or renewal of IVD reagents registration are not stipulated in this chapter, it shall be referred to relevant provisions in Chapter III of this Measures.

CHAPTER VI Filing of IVD Reagents

Article 86 Filing for a Class I IVD reagent shall be conducted prior to production.

Article 87 For the filing of IVD reagents, the filing applicant shall submit the filing information to the medical products administration in accordance with the *Regulations for the Supervision and Administration of Medical Devices* and obtain the filing number.

Article 88 For a filed IVD reagent, where the contents set forth in the filing information form and the filed product technical requirements changed, the filing applicant shall submit a description of the change and related documents to the original filing department and apply for change of filing. The medical products administration shall publish the changes in the filing information.

Article 89 If the management category of the filed IVD reagents is adjusted to the Class II or Class III IVD reagents, it shall apply for registration in accordance with the provisions of this Measures.

CHAPTER VII Working Time Limit

Article 90 The time limit stipulated in this Measures is the longest time for the acceptance, technical evaluation, audit and review and approval of IVD reagents registration. The working time limit related to the special registration procedures shall be implemented according to the relevant provisions of the special registration procedures.

The CMDE and other professional technical institutions shall specify and publish their respective working procedures and time limit to the public.

Article 91 After receiving the application for registration of IVD reagents, the medical products administration shall transmit the registration dossiers to the technical evaluation institution within 3 days from the date of acceptance.

Article 92 The time limit for technical evaluation of IVD reagent registration shall be implemented in accordance with the following provisions:

(1) The time limit for technical evaluation of the application for registration, change registration and renewal registration of Class II IVD reagents is 60 days, and the time limit for technical evaluation after supplementation and correction of registration dossiers is 60 days;

(2) The time limit for technical evaluation of the application for registration, change registration and renewal registration of Class III IVD reagents is 90 days, and the time limit for technical evaluation after supplementation and correction of registration dossiers is 60 days.

Article 93 The time limit for audit of the quality management system of Class III IVD reagents in China shall be implemented in accordance with the following provisions:

(1) The CMDE of NMPA shall notify the medical products administration of the provinces, autonomous regions and municipalities directly under the Central Government to start the audit within 10 days after accepting the application for IVD reagents registration;

(2) The medical products administration of the provinces, autonomous regions and municipalities directly under the Central Government shall, in principle, complete the audit within 30 days after receiving the audit notice, and feed back the audit information, audit results and other related materials to the CMDE.

Article 94 The medical products administration accepting the application for registration shall make decisions within 20 working days from the dates when the evaluation opinions are received.

Article 95 The medical products administration shall issue and serve the relevant administrative license documents within 10 days from the date of making the decision on review and approval of IVD reagents registration.

Article 96 If it is necessary to extend the time limit due to special circumstances such as product characteristics and technical evaluation and audit, the extended time limit shall not exceed 1/2 of the original time limit. After being approved by the person in charge of relevant technical institutions such as medical device technical evaluation and audit, the technical institution that extended the time limit shall inform the applicant in writing and inform other relevant technical institutions.

Article 97 The original license issuing authority shall reissue the Medical Device Registration Certificate within 20 days after receiving the application for re-issuance.

Article 98 The following time is not included in the relevant working time limit:

(1) The time taken by the applicant for supplementary materials and rectification after audit;

(2) Time for delaying the audit due to the applicant;

(3) The time when external expert consultation is needed, the expert consultation meeting is held, and joint evaluation with the drug evaluation institution;

(4) If the evaluation, review and approval procedures are suspended in accordance with regulations, the time taken during the suspension of the evaluation, review and approval procedures;

(5) The time taken for quality management systems audit.

Article 99 The time limit stipulated in this Measures shall be calculated on working days.

CHAPTER VIII Supervision and administration

Article 100 The medical products administration shall strengthen the supervision and inspection of the research and development activities of IVD reagents, and when necessary, it may conduct extended inspections on units and individuals that provide products or services for the research and development of IVD reagents. Relevant units and individuals shall cooperate and provide relevant documents and materials, and shall not refuse, conceal or obstruct them.

Article 101 The NMPA shall establish a step–by–step implementation system for the unique device identifier (UDI), applicants and filing applicants shall submit UDI related information in accordance with relevant regulations, so as to ensure that the data is true, accurate and traceable.

Article 102 The NMPA shall timely inform the medical products administration of the provinces, autonomous regions and municipalities directly under the Central Government of the agent's information. The medical products administration of the provinces, autonomous regions and municipalities directly under the Central Government shall organize daily supervision and management of agents in their respective administrative regions.

Article 103 The medical products administration of the provinces, autonomous regions and municipalities directly under the Central Government shall, according to the filing situation of medical device clinical trial institutions, organize the supervision and inspection of clinical trial institutions that have been filed within their respective administrative regions. For newly filed medical device clinical trial institutions, the supervision and inspection shall be carried out within 60 days after filing.

The medical products administration of the provinces, autonomous regions and municipalities directly under the Central Government shall organize daily supervision and inspection on medical device clinical trial institutions in this administrative region in compliance with Good Clinical Practice for Medical Practice, and supervise them to continuously meet the prescribed requirements. The NMPA shall supervise and inspect the clinical trial institutions of medical devices as required.

Article 104 If the medical products administration deems it necessary, the authenticity, accuracy, integrity, standardization and traceability of clinical trials can be checked on site.

Article 105 If the medical products administration undertaking the filing of Class I IVD reagent products finds that the filing information are not standardized during the post–filing supervision, it shall order the filing applicant to make corrections within a time limit.

Article 106 If the medical products administration fails to discover the systemic and regional risks in the registration management of IVD reagents within its administrative area in time, or fails to eliminate the systemic and regional hidden dangers in the registration management of IVD reagents within its administrative area in time, the medical products administration at a higher level may conduct questioning to the principal responsible persons of the medical products administration at a lower level.

CHAPTER IX Legal Liabilities

Article 107 Those who violate the provisions of Article 78 of this Measures and fail to file the changes in accordance with the requirements shall be ordered to make corrections within a time limit; those who fail to make corrections within the time limit shall be subject to a fine of RMB 10,000 to 30,000.

Article 108 Those who fail to comply with the Good Clinical Practice when carrying out clinical trials of IVD reagents shall be punished in accordance with Article 94 of the *Regulations for the Supervision and Administration of Medical Devices.*

Article 109 Where a technical evaluation institution for medical devices fails to perform its duties in accordance with this Measures, resulting in major errors or serious consequences in the evaluation, the medical products administration shall order it to make corrections, report criticisms and give warnings; where serious consequences are caused, the legal representative, principal responsible person, direct responsible person in charge and other responsible persons of the illegal institution shall be given sanctions according to law.

Article 110 Any staff member of the medical products administration who, in violation of regulations, abuses his power, neglects his duty or engages in malpractices for personal gain shall be punished according to law.

CHAPTER X Supplementary Provisions

Article 111 Naming for IVD reagents shall comply with the following principles:

IVD reagent product name may generally consist of three parts. Part one, name of the tested substance; Part two, purpose, such as assay kits, quality controls and etc.; Part three, method or principle, such as magnetic particle chemiluminescence immunoassay, fluorescence PCR, fluorescence in situ hybridization, etc., and this part shall be listed in parentheses.

If the tested substance has too many components or in case of other special circumstances, name of indications related to the product or other alternative name may be used.

Class I products, calibrators and quality controls shall be named according to their intended use.

Article 112 The registration or filing unit of IVD reagent shall be a single reagent or a single kit. One registration or filing unit may include different packaging specifications.

Calibrators and quality controls may apply for registration separately or in conjunction with matching IVD reagents in conjunct use.

Article 113 The IVD reagents approved for registration refer to those consistent with the content limited in the Medical Device Registration Certificate and attachments thereof and are manufactured within the validity period of the Medical Device Registration Certificate.

Article 114 The independent reagent components specified in the column of "main components" in the Medical Device Registration Certificate can be sold separately if they are used in the original registered product.

Article 115 The applicant can refer to the master file of registered medical device with the authorization of the owner of the master file of medical device when applying for the registration and change registration of IVD reagent products. The master files of medical devices shall be registered by their owners or agencies, and relevant working procedures shall be stipulated separately.

Article 116 The format of Medical Device Registration Certificate shall be normalized by NMPA uniformly.

Medical Device Registration Certificate numbers shall be arranged in the following form:

$\times 1$ XZ $\times 2 \times \times \times \times 3 \times 4 \times \times 5 \times \times \times \times 6$, wherein:

× 1 shall mean the abbreviation of the place where the registration review and approval authority is located:

"G" (Guo) shall be adopted for domestic Class Ⅲ IVD reagents, imported Class Ⅱ and Class Ⅲ IVD reagents;

The domestic Class Ⅱ of IVD regents is the abbreviation of the province, autonomous region and municipality directly under the Central Government where the registration review and approval department is located;

× 2 shall indicate the form of registration:

"Z" (Zhun) is applicable to domestic IVD reagents;

"J" (Jin) is applicable to import IVD reagents;

"X" (Xu) is applicable to IVD reagents from Hong Kong, Macao and Taiwan;

× × × × 3 shall indicate the year of initial registration;

× 4 shall the product management category;

× × 5 shall indicate the product classification code;

× × × × 6 shall indicate the serial number of initial registration.

For the renewal registration, × × × × 3 and × × × × 6 shall remain the same. If the product management category is adjusted, a new number shall be assigned.

Article 117 The filing number for Class Ⅰ Medical Device shall be arranged in the following form:

× 1 XB × × × × 2 × × × × 3.

Wherein:

× 1 shall mean the abbreviation of the place where the filing authority is located:

"G" (Guo) shall be adopted for imported Class Ⅰ IVD reagents;

The abbreviation of the province, autonomous region, or municipality directly under the Central Government where the filing authority is located plus the abbreviation of the administrative area at the level of municipal government with districts shall be adopted for domestic Class I IVD reagents (if there is no corresponding administrative area at the level of municipal government with districts, it shall only be the abbreviation of the province, autonomous region, or municipality directly under the Central Government);

 $\times \times \times \times 2$ shall indicate the year of filing;

 $\times \times \times \times 3$ shall indicate the serial number of filing.

Article 118 Electronic documents of Medical Device Registration Certificate, change registration document produced by medical products administration have the same legal effect as paper documents.

Article 119 The NMPA, may, according to work necessity, authorize the medical products administration or technical organizations of provinces, autonomous regions and municipalities directly under the Central Government and relevant social organizations to conduct the specific work in accordance with law.

Article 120 The medical products administration of the provinces, autonomous regions and municipalities directly under the Central Government may formulate special registration procedures for Class II IVD reagents within their respective administrative areas with reference to the provisions of Chapter IV of this Measures, and report them to the NMPA for filing.

Article 121 The charging items and charging criteria applicable for the IVD reagents registration shall follow the applicable provisions stipulated by the finance and pricing departments of the State Council.

Article 122 The relevant provisions on emergency use of IVD reagents shall be separately formulated by the NMPA in conjunction with relevant departments.

Article 123 If there is no product of the same variety on the market in China, the medical institution will research and develop IVD reagents according to the clinical needs of the institution and use the IVD reagents in the institution under the guidance of practicing physicians. The relevant management regulations shall be separately formulated by the NMPA in conjunction with relevant departments.

Article 124 The IVD reagents from Hong Kong, Macao and Taiwan shall be registered and filed by reference to the import IVD reagents.

Article 125 The Measures shall come into force as of October 1, 2021. On July 30, 2014, the Decree No.5 *Provisions for In Vitro Diagnostic Reagent Registration* promulgated by former CFDA shall be abolished at the same time.